THE COMPLETE MONEY-SAVING BOOK OF

APPLIANCE REPAIRS

THE COMPLETE MONEY-SAVING BOOK OF
APPLIANCE REPAIRS

by Harvey Morgan with Peter Jones

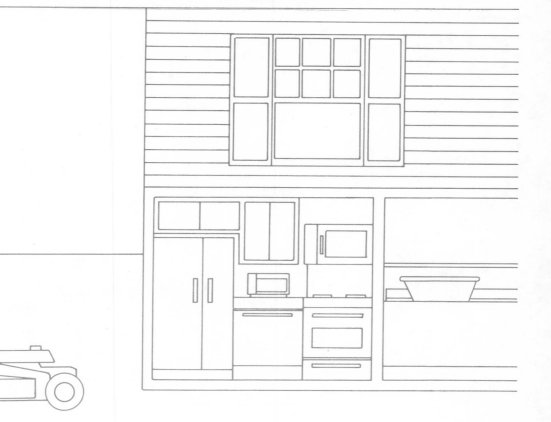

SERVICE COMMUNICATIONS, LTD.

CHARLES SCRIBNERS SONS
New York

Staff

Andrew Bromberg
Editor-in-Chief

Barbara Tannenbaum
Editor

Mary Kornblum
Art Director

Editorial

Martin Clifford
Len Buckwalter
Hal Lindquist
Ron Jones
Jessica Miller
Rochelle Benvenuto
Doreen Kushel

Art

Carl De Groote
Kenneth Rice
Ray Skibinski
Gary Tong
Arline Rogers
Mark Richards
Joseph Lubrano
Jane Dell
Harry Chester, Inc.

Editorial Consultants

Gerald Gould, Ph.D.
Mort Waters

Technical Consultants

Joseph Murphy
Robert Brightman
Leonard Klein

Contents

OUTDOOR EQUIPMENT

Safety

This symbol precedes warnings which appear throughout the book. These warnings help safeguard both you and the appliance you are repairing. In most repair situations, you are dealing with electricity, mechanical parts that can move and tools, all of which can be dangerous if proper precautions are not taken and common sense not used. If you are uncertain about the proper safety procedures to use, *do not* undertake the repair.

In general, when working on appliances they should be unplugged and removed from the source of power. When working on the electrical system of your home, be sure the power is shut off on the particular circuit on which you are making the repair or replacement by removing the fuse or throwing the circuit breaker.

Several appliances found in the home including televisions and air conditioners have the ability to store electrical charges so that even after the plug has been removed the potential hazard of a shock remains. Be sure you follow the procedures to discharge this stored electricity before proceeding with any troubleshooting and repairs.

When repairing gasoline powered outdoor equipment the ignition system must be disconnected to avoid accidental starting of the equipment while holding moving parts. Removal of the spark plug will prevent the accidental ignition of the equipment.

When repairing any pieces of equipment it is wise to look for warnings found either directly on the appliance or in the owner's manual.

Home repair charges run high in dollars and high on the list of consumer complaints. The purpose of this book is to educate the reader in the mechanics and possible breakdowns common to household appliances and to translate this knowledge into sane money-saving repair decisions.

The Complete Money-Saving Book of Appliance Repairs is specifically designed for both the avid handyman who welcomes the challenge of complicated repairs and the average homeowner who must decide whether to do it himself or call the repairman.

Designed to bring repair problems and their solutions into sharp focus, the book clearly shows:

- how household appliances work
- the cause of the problem
- how to make the repair
- the difficulty in making the repair
- the cost of a repairman's charges in parts and labor.

How to use the book

When a problem occurs with a particular appliance, turn to the chapter dealing with that appliance and first read the sections on principle of operation and maintenance and repair. These two sections provide general information on how the machine works and a discussion of the major components, general problem areas and maintenance procedures.

Simple, obvious but often overlooked causes for the malfunctions of an appliance are often brought to light after a review of this information. If you are unable to determine the cause of the problem after reviewing the general information found in these sections, proceed to the troubleshooting charts. You will find that the background provided by these sections will maximize your ability to troubleshoot.

Troubleshooting Charts

Troubleshooting Charts are organized by problem. For instance, if the drum of your clothes dryer is unnecessarily noisy, locate the particular symptom on the chart listed on the problem line. Then review the possible causes under this category. Follow the procedure suggested to examine each of the possible causes until the actual cause is found. Then follow the instructions listed under remedy to make the appropriate repair.

The instructions listed on the chart for a particular remedy are stated in the most simple and concise terms. Refer to the detailed illustrations, their cap-

tions and accompanying text to show you how to disassemble the appliance, reach the particular problem component and repair or replace it.

Many repair procedures and appliance components are common to a number of appliances. These common problems and procedures are treated in chapters one through four and are cross referenced in the text and trouble shooting charts of each appliance. For instance, a mechanism such as a timer may be found in many appliances such as dishwashers, washing machines and dryers.

If while troubleshooting you determine the timer of your dishwasher may be at fault, the troubleshooting chart will refer you to chapter four where information on the timer, how it works, how to check it for a malfunction and how to repair or replace it will be found.

·All repairs are rated for difficulty and the costs for parts and labor are listed. The cost of parts are rounded off to the nearest dollar and are based upon the most current pricing information available. The recommended retail price, suggested by the manufacturer, remains constant nationwide. However, your repairman can often obtain discounts on parts.

The cost of labor is based upon charges by repairmen in major metropolitan areas across the nation. Labor charges will vary (usually lower) in outlying and rural areas.

The difficulty of a repair procedure is rated as follows:

■ Requires few or no tools and little or no experience.

■ ■ Requires minimum tools and only basic experience.

■ ■ ■ Requires a full complement of tools, a working knowledge of the procedures involved, and a reasonable amount of practical experience.

■ ■ ■ ■ Requires the use of specialty tools and a thorough understanding of procedures, as well as considerable prior experience.

■ ■ ■ ■ ■ Requires highly specialized equipment and training. The repair should not be attempted by any layman.

The rating cost information is valuable to the homeowner in helping him decide whether to make the repair himself, in showing him how much money he will save if he performs the repair himself, or in dealing with the repairman if he should decide to call for professional help.

ELECTRICITY

Using Electrical Equipment

Fundamentals of Electricity

Electrical Maintenance and Repair

Fundamentals of Electricity

1

The flow of electricity through a wire can be compared to the flow of water through a pipe. The most common unit for measuring water is the gallon; the comparable unit in electricity is the coulomb. Water flow through a pipe is measured in gallons per minute; electrical flow through a wire is measured in coulombs per second—and 1 coulomb per second equals 1 ampere.

The speed at which water flows depends on the pressure (pounds per square inch), or "push," on the water and on the diameter and smoothness of the water pipe. The speed at which electricity flows also depends on the pressure (volts) and to a large extent on the diameter of the wire conductor. The wire's diameter limits the amount of electricity that can pass through it, much as the diameter of a pipe limits water flow. The smaller the pipe's diameter, the smaller the volume of water. The smaller the wire's diameter, the smaller the amount of electric current that can flow through it and the greater the resistance of the wire to electrical flow. The resistance of a wire is also determined by its length and by how well the particular material it's made of conducts electricity. The flow rate of water (gallons per minute) multiplied by its pressure (pounds per square inch) equals water power. In electricity, the flow rate (amperes) multiplied by the electrical pressure (volts) equals electrical power (watts).

The electrical system in a home is analogous to the plumbing system. Both water and electricity enter the house from an outside source and are divided for use. Water is divided into narrower branch pipes that distribute it throughout the house to service fixtures and appliances. Electricity is divided into wired circuits to service outlets and switches.

Electric Current and Its Path

Ampere (amp). *Amperage* designates the rate of the flow of electricity. One amp is the volume of electricity flowing, for 1 second with a pressure of 1 volt, past a point in a conductor with a resistance of 1 ohm. *Ampacity* is a wire's rated capacity to carry a given number of amps.

Volt. *Voltage* designates the pressure of electricity through a wire. One volt is the amount of pressure which in 1 second moves 1 amp through a wire having a resistance of 1 ohm.

Ohm. *Ohmage* designates a wire's resistance to electrical flow. Ohmage is calculated differently for alternating and direct currents, but generally it can be said that, if 1 volt can push 1 amp through a wire in 1 second, the wire has a resistance of 1 ohm. A wire's resistance depends primarily on the material it is composed of, its length, and its cross-sectional area (or, in practical terms, its diameter).

Watt. *Wattage* measures the amount of power, or work being done, at a given moment. (One watt is approximately 0.0013 horsepower.)

The relationship of volts, amperes, and ohms to one another is expressed by Ohm's Law:

$$Resistance = pressure \div volume$$

or

$$Ohms = volts \div amperes$$

The relationship of volts and amperes to watts is expressed by another mathematical formula:

$$Power = pressure \times volume$$

or

$$Watts = volts \times amperes$$

One thousand watts equals a *kilowatt*. Power companies measure their customers' use of electricity in kilowatts per hour, or kilowatt-hours (kWh).

Electric current must complete a *closed circuit*—a continuous, uninterrupted path—in order to flow. Electricity comes into the house through one wire of the power company's feeder cable. Passing through a kilowatt-hour meter, it then flows to a fuse or circuit-breaker box. Here the electricity is divided into separate branch circuits, each one with a fuse or circuit breaker mounted in it. Each branch circuit serves a separate area or room of the house. To power an appliance, current passes through the appropriate fuse or circuit breaker, along a branch-circuit wire to an outlet, then to the appliance. From the appliance the electricity returns along the circuit to the fuse box and then to the power company, through wires running parallel to the wires by which it was delivered.

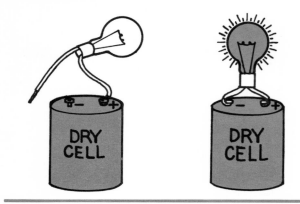

Open circuit (*left*) and closed circuit (*right*). When both wires are connected to the terminals of a dry-cell battery, current can flow continuously and heat the filament, producing light.

Electrical Wire

Wire Composition

Most metals are good conductors. (The minerals in ordinary water make it a good conductor also, and therefore dangerous in combination with electricity. Distilled water does not conduct electricity.) Copper is among the best conductors. Although aluminum is also efficient, it is not recommended for wiring because even a slight buildup of heat, which is inevitable in any circuit, can loosen its electrical connections and present a fire hazard from electrical sparks. Throughout these chapters the use of copper wire for household and appliance circuitry is assumed.

Wires are covered with highly resistant insulation, now usually plastic, to keep electric current confined within the circuit.

Wire Gauge

Gauge numbers rank wire according to diameter. The higher the gauge number, the thinner the wire and the less current it is able to carry. The more current a wire has to carry, the thicker it should be.

No. 20 wire might be used for the speaker connections in a stereo system. Considerably thicker, No. 12 or No. 14 wire would be run in the walls from outlet to outlet for permanent general-purpose circuits. The wire used to service an electric range would be thicker still—typically, No. 6. To deliver electricity to a home,

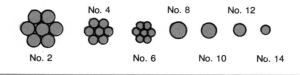

Stranded and solid wires

a utility company might use No. 0 wire. Wires thicker than No. 0—Nos. 1/0, 2/0, and so on—are not used in household circuits.

The proper wire gauge for a circuit depends on the maximum amperage required and the distance from power source to point of delivery. The longer the wire is, the greater the resistance and the more power that is lost as heat in the wire. The loss of voltage as electricity travels along a wire is called *voltage drop*. A 5-percent drop in voltage reduces the amount of light given off by a lamp not by a corresponding 5 percent, but by 17 percent; a 10-percent drop in voltage reduces the amount of light by 32 percent. When voltage drop occurs, paid-for electricity is lost, appliances work less efficiently, and overheating can burn out parts. The following chart indicates how to select the correct wire gauge for a particular project in a house serviced by single-phase alternating current.

When planning to install an outlet for an air conditioner, for example, first read the air conditioner's data plate to learn its wattage requirements. Assuming this to be 1,200 watts, the chart shows that at the 1,200-watt level, No. 14 wire is adequate for a run of up to 45 feet. If the distribution box (*see page 15*) is more than 45 feet away from the proposed outlet, but less than 72 feet away, then No. 12 wire is the correct choice.

	Circuit wattage			
Wire gauge	2400	1800	1200	600
No. 14	——	30	45	90
No. 12	36	47	71	142
No. 10	57	75	113	226
No. 8	90	120	180	360
No. 6	143	191	280	573
Maximum circuit length (in feet)				

Saving pennies by using wiring that is just barely adequate is dangerous false economy. Always use a wire heavy enough to deliver sufficient current to meet the *draw* (maximum power requirements) of the *load* (power-consuming devices such as appliances) on the circuit. When in doubt, it is safer to use a wire slightly too large than one too small.

Stranded and Solid Wire

Solid wire, more durable and reliable but less flexible than stranded wire, is used for the permanent wiring of homes. The only exceptions occur where flexibility is needed to maneuver very thick permanent wires (No. 6 or larger) into position. Thinner stranded wire is used only in light-fixture cords, extension cords (which should never be used as permanent wiring), and small-appliance cords.

WARNING: Never use stranded wire thinner than No. 6 gauge for permanent home wiring.

Color Coding

AC wiring insulation is generally but not invariably color-coded. White should always be used only for the *primary grounded wire,* also called the *neutral wire (see page 29)*; black is usually used for the *delivery wire,* or *hot wire,* the wire carrying current to the load. The following are the most common combinations.

- Two-wire circuit: white and black
- Three-wire circuit: white, black, and red
- Four-wire circuit: white, black, red, and blue

Generally, hot wires are connected to yellow equipment terminals composed of copper or brass; neutral wires to nickel-, tin-, or zinc-plated white terminals; *secondary grounding* (normally, non-current-carrying) *wires* to green terminals.

DC wiring is also color-coded, black for the positive (delivery) wire and red for the negative (return) wire.

WARNING: Never assume that a wire carries or does not carry current on the basis of its color. Always check it with a multimeter (see page 26) to determine whether it is live with current.

From Utility Company to Distribution Box

The transmission of thousands of kilowatts over great distances is made practical by the use of transformers, which change one voltage to another voltage, stepping it up or down as needed. Because transformers operate only on alternating current, most electricity in the United States is AC.

AC and DC

Direct current (DC) is a steady flow of electricity in one direction. A bolt of lightning is DC, as is the electricity delivered by a car battery or a flashlight battery.

By definition, *alternating current* (AC) is a current of regularly fluctuating voltage that regularly reverses its polarity: It goes in one direction for a specific period of time, then turns around and goes in the opposite direction. The standard AC used in the United States does this sixty times per second; hence, it is known as *60-cycle AC,* or *60-hertz (HZ) AC.* If it had a frequency of 1 Hz, a lamp's light would flicker, but at 60 Hz the lamp filament does not get a chance to cool off and, thus, gives off steady illumination.

Electric clocks keep such good time because their motors are synchronized with the 60-Hz AC frequency.

Stepping Down for Delivery

To serve house wiring, which is usually rated at 30 to 200 amps, utility-company transformers reduce voltage several times before the *feeder cable* enters the house.

(The actual voltage provided on a 120-volt AC circuit may range from 104 volts in some localities to 120 volts in others; 240-volt AC service ranges from about 208 volts to 240 volts. Thus, either the number 110 or 120 and the number 220 or 240 may be used as approximate or shorthand indicators of voltage. The numbers 120 and 240 are used here.)

A typical dial meter

Read the dial faces from left to right. On each, the relevant number is the one the pointer has just passed, not the one it is approaching. (Note that on the first and third dials, from left to right, the pointer moves counterclockwise; it moves clockwise on the second and fourth dials.) Thus, the meter reading shown here is 9352 kilowatt-hours. To figure the kWh used in a given period, subtract the earlier reading from the later one.

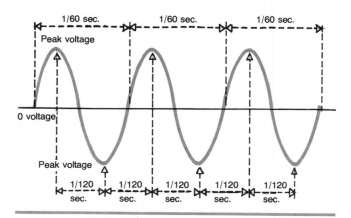

Three cycles of 60-Hz AC

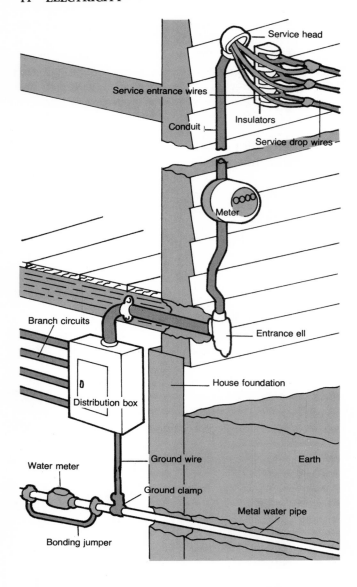

How electricity enters the house. Note the bonding jumper, which is required if equipment, such as a water softener, is connected to the water pipe on the house side of the water meter.

Only an all-electric home, which uses electricity for heating or central air conditioning, would require 200 amps; 150 amps is considered adequate service for other homes. At 240 volts, 150-amp service provides a potential 36,000 watts to the home. Voltage is usually 120 for ordinary house lighting, 240 for electric ranges and water heaters.

The feeder cable can be either the two-wire or three-wire type. With the ever-increasing demand for electricity, the three-wire cable is commonly used today in homes wired for 60 amps or more. In a two-wire feeding system, one wire is positive and the other is neutral. In a three-wire system, two wires are positive, each carrying 120 volts, and the third is a neutral wire serving both of them. Thus, in a three-

wire, 120/240-volt service, two separate 120-volt circuits serve the house. These circuits are kept separate, with *branch circuits* divided between them, but both can be fed together to a load requiring 240 volts (such as an electric range).

Three-phase Current

Ordinary household appliances run on single-phase AC, which is the kind of electricity supplied to most American homes. But some commercial areas and many industrial locations take advantage of three-phase current to improve the efficiency of motors. With single-phase AC, a motor receives a "push" 120 times per second—every time AC reverses direction. Three-phase AC utilizes three separate sources of single-phase current—delivery is timed so that the peak voltage of each phase is staggered. A motor designed for it thus receives three evenly spaced pushes during each cycle, for a total of 360 pushes per second.

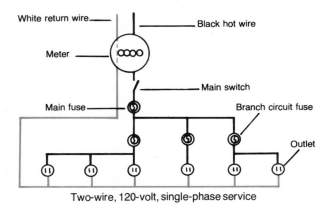

Two-wire, 120-volt, single-phase service

Three-wire, 120/240-volt, single-phase service. In both illustrations, circuit breakers may be used instead of fuses.

Three-phase current is delivered via three positive wires plus a common grounded neutral wire. The voltage between any one of the hot lines and the neutral wire is always 120 volts, but, because the phases are staggered and there is a time lag in the phasing, the voltage between any two of the hot lines is 208 volts, not 120 or 240.

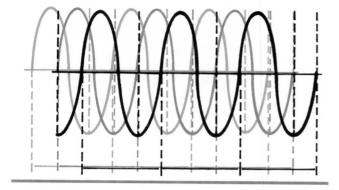

From Distribution Box to Branch Circuit

Electric current in modern homes is usually 100 or 150 amps. At the distribution box it is divided into branch circuits of 15, 20, 30, or more amps each. Each branch circuit is protected from electrical overload by a *current interrupter* (fuse or circuit breaker) mounted in the circuit's hot wire.

The wiring for a typical general-purpose branch circuit consists of a black hot wire, a white return wire, and often an additional ground wire enclosed in a single cable that leads to outlets and light switches.

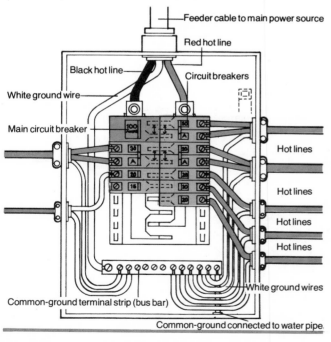

Older distribution boxes may contain fuses; more modern units have circuit breakers. Wires leading from the box serve household circuits of 120 or 240 volts AC. The 240-volt lines carry heavier currents than the 120-volt wires for operating current-hungry appliances such as ranges and central air conditioners.

The return wire for each branch circuit is connected to the return wire of the utility company's feeder cable and to a *ground bar*. The ground bar in turn is connected to a copper grounding cable. The purpose of the ground bar and cable is to transmit any excess current to the earth in the event of a short circuit (*see page 16*)—hence the term *ground*. The copper grounding cable is connected to a water pipe (*not a gas pipe*) that runs into the earth or to a grounding rod that is driven directly into the earth.

Series and Parallel Circuits

A *series circuit* is a basic continuous circuit. Regardless of how many components are wired into this type of circuit, the current must flow through each of them in turn. If the circuit is opened at any point, none of the loads on the circuit can draw current. An

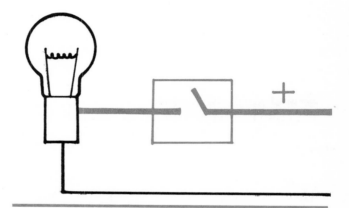

A switch in series with a lamp. Current must flow through the switch before reaching the lamp. The amount of current that will flow to the lamp will be determined by its power requirements. Since the switch shown here is open, no current will flow.

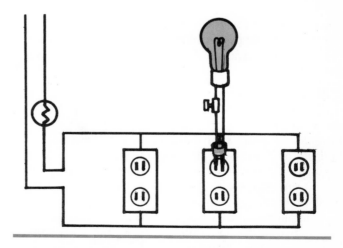

Two outlets connected in a parallel circuit. (The electric wiring joining the outlets is also called a *shunt*.) In this parallel circuit, current may pass through either or both outlets and thus deliver power to one or two *loads*, devices such as appliances which consume power. One load can receive a different amount of current than the other. Removal of one load from a parallel circuit will not affect the operation of the other.

example familiar to many is the old-style Christmas-tree lights—when one light stopped working, the whole circuit was dead.

In a *parallel circuit,* the wiring is divided into subcircuits, so that what happens along one subcircuit does not affect the others. An example is an outlet with two lamps plugged into it—one can be turned on or off without affecting the other.

Both series and parallel circuits are found, individually and in combination, in the home. Safety requires that the current interrupter be wired in series with the branch circuit or circuits it serves, though further beyond it, the circuit may contain parallel wiring.

House Circuits

There are three types of circuits in the home: general-purpose, special-appliance, and major-appliance circuits. The National Electrical Code (NEC) (*see page 21*) specifies requirements for each. The number and type of outlets and switches in a house, together with the total draw, have a great deal to do with how many separate circuits are needed.

General-purpose circuits

In houses built today, general-purpose circuits are normally wired with No. 12 cable and rated at 20 amps. Older houses may have No. 14 cable with a maximum rating of 15 amps. As a rule, there should be one general-purpose circuit for every 400 square feet of floor area, to be used for lamps, light fixtures, and small appliances.

Special-appliance circuits

Special-appliance circuits are wired with No. 12 cable and rated for 20 amps. The NEC requires that at least two of these circuits, each capable of supplying 2,400 watts, be assigned to the kitchen area. A third circuit of 20 amps is usually recommended for any room in which washing machines and electric irons will be used.

Major-appliance circuits

The NEC specifies that high-wattage appliances (such as dishwashers, ranges, oil burners, water pumps and heaters, air conditioners, electric heaters and clothes dryers, and workshop equipment) have exclusive circuits of either 120 or 240 volts. Depending on the load, the circuit may be fused at 15, 20, 25, or 30 amps. A major appliance such as a clothes dryer may be permanently wired directly into the house circuit instead of being connected by a plug and outlet. No other load should be connected to this circuit.

Sometimes a major-appliance circuit can serve more than one appliance. In such a case, a limited number of outlets are wired into the circuit, insuring sufficient power while simultaneously preventing potential overloading of the circuit. For example, two

medium-sized air conditioners might share the same circuit. Individual major-appliance circuits may be either 120- or 240-volt lines.

Grounding

A *ground* (also termed *earth*) is an electrical conductor connected between a circuit and the soil. The return wire for each branch circuit is connected to the return wire of the utility company's feeder cable and ultimately to a copper wire attached to a *grounding electrode.* The grounding electrode is a cold-water pipe or grounding rod connected with the earth. This primary grounding is called *system grounding.* Safety requires that one or more additional *ground wires* be incorporated into an electrical circuit to protect against a possible short circuit.

In a *short circuit,* electricity takes a shorter, more convenient path to the earth than the route provided by the original wiring. If, for example, the insulation wears off the wires inside an appliance and they come

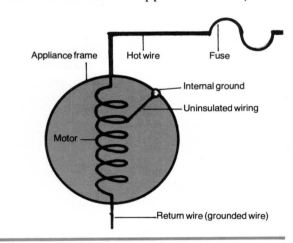

A short circuit inside the metal case makes the case "hot," or live, with current without necessarily blowing the fuse. A person touching the metal case could receive a severe electric shock.

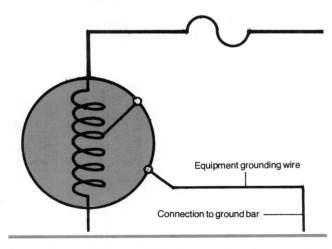

If the metal case is grounded, the hazard of an electric shock is diminished.

in contact with the metal frame, current flows into the frame. Someone touching the frame could become a conductor for the current—and receive a severe electric shock. But if the circuit is provided with a second ground wire (*secondary ground*), the current, taking the path of least resistance, travels through that wire instead of the human body (because copper wire is a better conductor than the human body).

 WARNING: All recently installed wiring should contain secondary grounding circuits.

Another secondary ground path is provided by an uninsulated *equipment grounding wire*. This is not wired into the circuit; instead, it is attached to a part of the installation that normally does not carry current, such as a washing-machine frame or a metal outlet box. In the event of a short circuit, the current—again choosing the path of least resistance—flows through the frame or box, greatly lessening the severity of electric shock to someone touching the appliance. If a cable has a metallic sheathing or is enclosed in conduit pipe, the metal skin should provide another secondary ground.

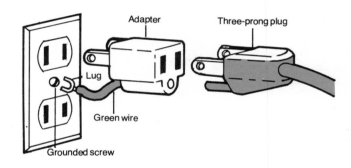

Some appliances are made with three-pronged plugs. The plug's third prong is a safety feature because it grounds the housing of the appliance. The appliance is not automatically grounded by plugging it into a three-hole, grounded receptacle, however. There must be a ground wire in the outlet box that is actually grounded; this is a green or uninsulated wire that is connected to the green screw in the outlet box. When an adapter is used to fit a three-pronged plug into a two-hole outlet, the pigtail wire of the adapter must be attached to the faceplate screw.

The plugs of such appliances as shop tools and refrigerators may have three prongs. The third prong, which is round, is a secondary ground wire. If the outlet does not have three matching holes but the outlet box is grounded (has a secondary grounding circuit), secondary grounding protection can be provided by an adapter plug. The plug of the appliance is plugged into the two-pronged adapter plug, which has a wire that attaches to the screw on the faceplate of the outlet.

 WARNING: Make certain to attach the small wire of the adapter plug to the outlet screw. If this is not done, the grounded circuit will be incomplete and ineffective.

Current Interrupters

Current flowing through a wire inevitably creates heat. As the amperage increases, so does the temperature of the wire. The metal may become hot enough to damage the insulation and even start a fire. Thus, it is essential that the current in the circuit be limited to no more amps than the number the wire is capable of carrying without risk. Maintaining this limit in each circuit is the job of the *current interrupter*, most commonly a fuse or circuit breaker. Current interrupters are always wired into the hot wire, never into the ground wire. The current interrupter opens the circuit to stop any flow of electricity at the instant the wires become overloaded with more power than they are rated to handle safely. The *main fuse* (or *main current breaker*) cuts off all the power coming from the feeder cable.

NOTE: When a fuse blows or a circuit breaker is tripped, find and fix the cause of the failure before replacing the fuse or resetting the circuit breaker.

Fuses

A fuse contains a short strip of metal alloy (usually a combination of tin and lead) that has a low melting point. This strip is called a *fusible link*. Too much current causes the fusible link to melt, thereby opening the circuit. The size of the fusible link determines how much current the fuse allows to pass through the circuit.

Fuses come in two basic shapes: the plug or screw-in type and the cartridge type. Plug fuses are rated for circuits of 15, 20, 25, and 30 amps; cartridge fuses are usually used in circuits of 30 amps and more, although they are available in smaller sizes.

Plug fuse

The basic plug fuse has a threaded base and a flat top marked with its amperage rating. The fusible link is visible through a glass window in the top. When the fuse blows because of an overload, the window usually remains clear. When it blows because of a short circuit, the window usually is blackened. (This does not apply to resettable plug fuses.)

Time-delay (slow-blow) fuse. The time-delay fuse allows extra current to pass for the second or two it takes a motor to start. However, if a machine is overloaded (for example, a washing machine containing too many clothes) and its motor does not reach normal speed quickly, it continues to draw more than its

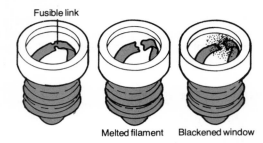

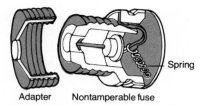

The plug fuse *(left)* has a screw-in base and transparent window at the top. The fuse element, or fusible link, can be seen through the window. The smudge on the blown fuse *(right)* indicates a short circuit; the open fusible link *(center)* indicates an overload.

rated current and causes the fuse to blow. The time-delay fuse looks just like a basic plug fuse, except that a stretched spring is visible through the window. The fusible link is soldered to the bottom of the fuse and attached to the spring. When the time-delay fuse blows because of an overload, the solder softens, allowing the spring to recoil and pull the metal strip away from its contact at the base of the fuse. This breaks the circuit.

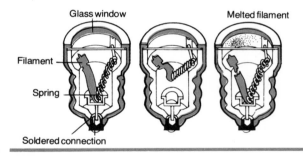

A time-delay fuse absorbs a temporary overload without blowing. Prolonged overload *(center)* melts the solder in the pot (in the base of the fuse), and the spring then breaks contact. A short circuit *(right)* leaves a smudged window, as in a standard fuse.

Stationary power tools, air conditioners, and washing machines all require an extra surge of power to start.

Nontamperable fuse. One drawback to fuses is that they can be misused. When fuses begin blowing frequently, some people replace them with a higher-amperage fuse (or, more dangerously yet, a copper penny) instead of reducing the load on the circuit. The higher-rated fuse allows more current into the circuit than the wires can handle, and thus creates a fire hazard. Nontamperable fuses were developed to prevent people from inappropriately using higher-amperage fuses: The 15-amp adapter accommodates only the 15-amp nontamp fuse. Likewise, adapters for 20, 25, and 30 amps accept fuses of the same rating only. Nontamps look like regular plug fuses, but their bases are slightly smaller and the diameters of their bodies vary according to their amperage ratings.

An adapter is screwed into the fuse socket to convert the fuse holder into one that will hold only the correctly rated nontamperable fuse. Once installed, the adapter becomes permanently locked in place and thus prevents the use of a fuse designed to carry a bigger load than the circuit can properly handle.

A nontamp fuse is screwed into an adapter installed in the fuse socket. This becomes a permanent installation—once the adapter is in place, it cannot be taken out without damaging the socket. When installing a nontamp, screw it in place as tightly as possible. The spring in the bottom of the fuse must make full contact with the adapter to close the circuit.

Resettable fuse. Another type of plug fuse is actually a circuit breaker internally. It has a screw base, but on top there is a button rather than a glass window. A switch inside trips if the circuit is overloaded. Pushing the button resets the fuse and closes the cir-

A resettable fuse—a circuit breaker contained in a fuse housing—can replace an ordinary plug fuse. When a circuit is overloaded or shorts out, the button on top of the fuse pops out. To reset the fuse, push the button back in.

cuit. The advantage of this type of fuse is that theoretically it must be purchased only once, unlike fuses equipped with a fusible link.

Cartridge fuse

A circuit with an amperage rating over 30 must have a cartridge fuse. There are two types of cartridge fuses, both tubular in shape. Ferrule-contact

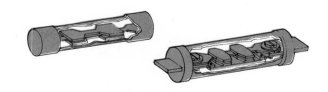

Cartridge fuses are designed to handle a broad range of amperages. A common rating for a ferrule-contact cartridge fuse is 30 amps, but it can also be rated as low as 15 amps. The knife-blade-contact cartridge fuse handles currents of 60 amps or more. A cartridge fuse must be replaced by one of identical size and type. Some cartridge fuses are manufactured with replaceable links.

cartridge fuses have flat ends and are manufactured in ratings of up to 60 amps. Knife-blade-contact cartridge fuses are used only in circuits rated at 60 amps or more. Both types come in regular and time-delay versions.

A fusible link in the cylinder melts when the circuit is overloaded or shorts out, but visual inspection does not reveal whether or not a cartridge fuse has blown. The most reliable way to check its condition is to test it (*see page 26*).

Circuit Breakers

A circuit breaker looks much like an ordinary toggle-type light switch—it consists of a manual switch and a bimetal strip. As long as the heat from electric current flowing through the strip does not exceed the rating of the circuit, the switch remains in place. An overload causes the strip to bend enough to trip the switch. Many breakers also include a magnetic device that opens the breaker the moment there is any heavy current flow due to a short circuit.

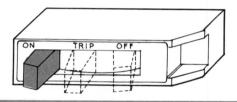

A circuit breaker resembles an ordinary toggle switch. To reset a circuit breaker that has tripped, push the switch toward the Off position and then back to On.

Breakers for 120-volt circuits have a single On/Off handle. For a 240-volt line, two breakers are paired with a joined handle: No matter which half of the circuit has the overload, both sides flip open together. When a breaker opens, its handle jumps toward the Off position. Most circuit breakers are reset by pushing the handle toward the Off position (as far as it will go) and then back to On.

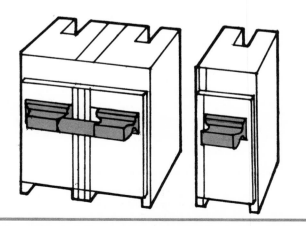

Single circuit breakers are wired into 120-volt circuits. Double circuit breakers are used for 240-volt appliance circuits.

Ground-Fault Interrupters

Dangerous leakage of electricity from an appliance is always a possibility when interior-wiring insulation ages, is wet, or is worn because of vibration. If an appliance has secondary grounding (*see page 17*), the leaking current passes directly to the ground. Also, the leakage will probably cause the fuse to blow—a warning that should not be ignored. However, many home appliances—fans, toasters, television sets, and hair dryers—do not have three-prong grounding plugs for secondary grounding. They may operate properly despite an internal short or current leakage, but in the presence of water become potentially lethal.

 WARNING: Water and any electrical appliance are a dangerous combination. Touching an appliance with wet hands, while standing on a wet floor or wet earth, or while seated or standing on any electrical conductor (such as a metal ladder) can result in electrocution.

The three-wire grounding system has saved many lives, but recently an even better device has come into use. The *ground-fault circuit interrupter* (CFCI or GFI) is designed to interrupt the current in a circuit any time there is as little as 5 milliamperes leaking to the ground by some path other than the return wire. In a properly installed two-wire, 120-volt circuit, the same amount of current flows through the return wire as through the delivery wire. If there is a short circuit in an appliance, part of the current finds its way into either the secondary grounding wire or the user, making the amount of current in the return wire less than that in the delivery wire. However, since the GFCI senses a differential as small as 5 milliamperes and reacts before the differential can increase—breaking the circuit within one-fortieth of a second—this tiny amount of current will barely jolt the user.

NOTE: Even a device protected by a grounding wire could present electric shock hazard. If the wire were to break, the broken wire would not prevent the device from operating, and there would be no indication of the lack of grounding.

The GFCI is highly recommended for use with any electrical equipment operated outdoors, near water, in gardens, in driveways, or on metal ladders. Toasters, hair dryers, radios, record players, hedge trimmers, electric lawn mowers, and snow blowers are often used near water; electric saws and drills are liable to present problems when the operator is on an aluminum ladder. The National Electrical Code specifies that GFCIs be used in circuits to laundry rooms, bathrooms, and swimming pools.

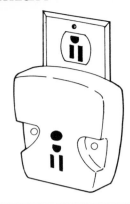 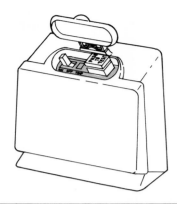 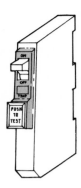

The ground-fault circuit interrupter can detect very minute current leaks, caused when a bare wire touches either another wire or something metal that acts as a conductor.

The GFCI is available in two types: an adapter that is plugged into the receptacle of a grounded wall outlet and can be used with any appliance; and a type that is permanently installation in a receptacle box and replaces a circuit breaker. The adapter comes in indoor and outdoor models.

Household Electrical Needs

The idea that a house is adequately wired is often taken for granted by the homeowner. That is, he or she assumes the wiring is capable of carrying all the current needed by appliances and that it is adequately and evenly distributed throughout the house. But this is not necessarily true. The average home's demand for electrical power has increased substantially in recent years, so that the electrical-service capacity of an older home is often insufficient for the demands of today's family. It is not uncommon for the living patterns of families to change within a home. The addition of kitchen appliances and equipment, the expansion of a den or recreation room, or the installation of air conditioners in a few bedrooms can easily create demands for electricity that were not originally envisioned, and for which the home's electrical service was not designed. It is therefore essential to know the current capacity of a home's electrical service in order to determine its actual electrical-service requirements.

The maximum potential capacity of a home's electrical service is usually stated on the door of the fuse or distribution box. The actual total capacity can be determined by reading the current rating on the main fuse or circuit breaker. When a number of fuses or circuit breakers are used instead of a single one, their total amperage represents the actual capacity.

It is highly unlikely that all household appliances would be used simultaneously, so a home's service is not necessarily inadequate if the requirements are a bit more than its maximum capacity. However, if requirements exceed the maximum potential of the electrical system by more than 20 percent, the electrical service is inadequate.

Wiring List

Before upgrading of a home's electrical capacity is planned, it is essential to know the present electrical capacity of the house, the extent to which branch circuits are overloaded, and what future household electrical installations are anticipated. A wiring list enables the homeowner to analyze the present wiring; it enumerates what appliances each circuit in the house serves and the draw made on the circuit.

Using a wiring list

Compare the wattage of each circuit with the total wattage of the lights and appliances it serves—that is, the amount of wattage the circuit can deliver without blowing a fuse (or activating a circuit breaker) *versus* the potential peak demand made on it if all the lights and appliances served by the circuit draw power at the same time. A 120-volt circuit is operating at its capacity when the power usage approaches 1,800 watts on a 15-amp line; 2,400 watts on a 20-amp line; and 3,600 watts on a 30-amp line. Although it is unlikely that at any particular time all the loads will be drawing power from a circuit, the total load on any circuit should not exceed 80 percent of the circuit's capacity if any of the loads has a motor, because motors require an extra surge of electricity to start.

If the amperage printed on the switch of the main fuse or circuit breaker is 30 (as in many older houses with a two-wire system) or 60 (still common, probably with a three-wire system), the house needs considerably more electrical service and several new branch lines before it can accommodate a normal complement of modern appliances. The ideal, by present-day standards, is a three-wire 120/240-volt system with 150-amp service. A house heated or centrally air-conditioned by electricity requires 200-amp service.

Most distribution boxes have space inside the door for listing the location of each circuit. This is a good place to post the wiring list for future reference. The list must be considered not only a compilation of what appliances are in the house at present but also a guide to how many appliances the electrical system will be able to serve in the future.

How to add circuits to an existing wiring system is discussed in Chapter 3.

Safety First

UL listing

In the United States, The Underwriters' Laboratories, Inc., abbreviated UL, tests all electrical materials and equipment submitted to it by manufacturers. Items that pass UL's rigorous testing are described as *UL listed* and bear notification of the listing either directly on them or on an attached label. For safety's sake, only items that are UL listed should be used in electrical work, and only for their listed purpose. (For example, a 20-amp fuse is listed for use in a 20-amp circuit only, and not as a replacement for a 15-amp fuse.) In many localities inspectors will automatically refuse to approve work done with unlisted materials.

National Electrical Code

The requirements of the National Electrical Code, known as the NEC, are intended for safety first and foremost. The Code covers the proper methods for performing electrical work—"proper" meaning safe, not necessarily most efficient. The Code is updated every three years. For the latest edition, send $5.50 to: National Fire Protection Association, 470 Atlantic Avenue, Boston, Massachusetts 02210. An abridged version costs $2.00. The National Fire Protection Association (NFPA) is the parent body of the committee that updates and revises the Code.

Local restrictions

Some localities require that any electrical work in the home be done by a licensed electrician; others permit some do-it-yourself wiring with approved materials, followed by inspection. Check the local codes and homeowner's insurance policy before planning any electrical work. When in doubt, consult an electrician. Electricity must be handled knowledgeably to ensure absolute safety.

Preparing a wiring list

1. Turn on all the lights in the house. Then remove any one branch-line fuse (or trip one circuit breaker to Off). Note the amperage of the fuse (or circuit breaker).

2. Calling this circuit No. 1, go through the house, making a list of which lights and appliances are not on. Check all electrical fixtures in the garage, on the exterior of the house, and in the yard as well. Also check each outlet by plugging a night light or test light into it. (*See page 26*) Be sure to examine such out-of-the-way places as closets, attic, and basement.

3. When circuit No. 1 has been completely listed, replace the fuse (or reset the circuit breaker) and proceed to the next circuit, which will be No. 2. Continue through the entire array of fuses (or circuit breakers), making a list of what outlets, lights, and appliances each controls.

4. Add to the appropriate circuit list any appliance that is frequently plugged into that circuit but was not at the time the list was written: electric frying pan, hair dryer, electric toothbrush, electric typewriter, and so on.

5. Now determine the wattage for each light and appliance on the list. The wattage of light bulbs is printed on the bulb (for example, 100 watts). Wattages of appliances are stamped on them, often on a small metal data plate. If the wattage is not indicated, amperage will be. To determine the wattage, use the formula *amps* × *volts* = *watts*. Voltage is probably 120 volts for all circuits except those servicing electric ranges or central air conditioning, which are 240 volts.

6. Add up the wattages of the appliances and lights on each circuit, then compare the total to the wattage the circuit was designed to deliver. (To find this total, multiply the amperage shown on the fuse or the circuit-breaker handle by the circuit's voltage.)

2

Using Electrical Equipment

All minor jobs of maintenance and repair on household electrical circuits and appliances require an understanding of and ability to perform certain electrical procedures and tests. For example, before an appliance can be repaired, the house circuit or internal circuit of the appliance must be examined to trace the source of the malfunction. A homeowner familiar with testing procedures can use a hot-line tester, continuity checker, or multimeter to pinpoint the problem in the wiring or electrical component. Then, armed with the knowledge of some common repair methods, such as splicing wires, soldering, and fastening wires to terminals, he or she can proceed to repair or replace an electrical part, install a new fixture, or rewire an outlet or switch. This chapter outlines and explains the fundamental step-by-step procedures, electrical tools, and test equipment involved in larger electrical projects.

Tools for Electrical Repairs

Many of the tools needed to perform home electrical repairs can be found in the average homeowner's tool kit. These include: a *brace and bit* or an *electric drill* with a full complement of bits and bit extensions, for drilling deep into walls; *slip-joint pliers* for twisting heavy wires; *round-* and *long-nose pliers* for making wire loops; *side cutters* for cutting wires; *screwdrivers* in various blade sizes, for both slotted and Phillips-head screws; a *hacksaw* for cutting flexible armored cable; a *keyhole saw* for cutting wall openings for outlet and switch boxes; steel *fish wire (snake)* for pulling cables through walls; and *hammers, tape measure, chisel,* and *wrenches.*

A *jackknife* can scrape insulation from wires, but many electricians prefer to use a *wire stripper,* which can be adjusted to the varying wire diameters and can cut through insulation without nicking the wire. A *crimping tool,* which looks like a pair of flattened pliers, cuts wires, crimps connectors, measures wire diameters, and strips insulation. A set of *nut drivers* is handy for reaching hard-to-get-at nuts and bolts. A *soldering iron* or *soldering gun* of 50 to 150 watts can handle most of the repair jobs encountered; both are used with solder and *sandpaper* or *emery cloth.* Plastic *electrician's tape* is used for wrapping wire connections.

In buying tools, look for those with plastic insulation covering the handles. Uninsulated tools already

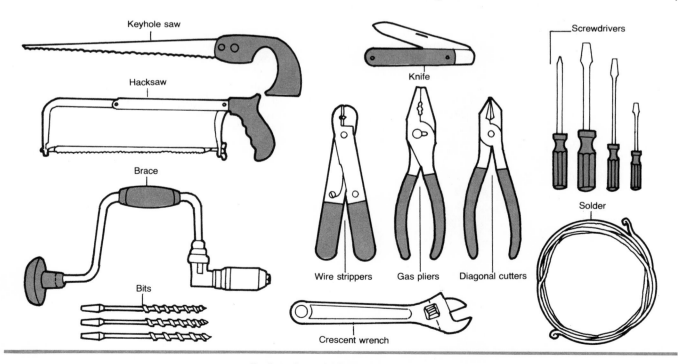

Keyhole saw

Hacksaw

Brace

Bits

Knife

Wire strippers

Gas pliers

Diagonal cutters

Crescent wrench

Screwdrivers

Solder

Basic tools useful for electrical repairs

in the tool kit can be made safer by wrapping electrician's tape around their handles. And always check for the UL listing before buying any electrical apparatus.

Making Circuit Connections

Soldering

The National Electrical Code prohibits the use of soldering for making many kinds of connections in household wiring. Accordingly, soldering is seldom used in household wiring, but it is very useful in making electrical connections in appliances.

Soldering insures a solid joint where wires must be electrically connected, so long as the joint is not subjected to mechanical stress (such as pulling) or heat sufficient to melt it. The tip of a soldering iron or gun heats the twisted wires, and their heat in turn melts the solder. The soldering gun is more popular than the soldering iron, because it heats up in seconds; the iron takes several minutes. (Actually, the word *iron* means tool, so in the discussion below *soldering iron* will mean either type.)

Solder is a metal alloy—usually 60 percent lead and 40 percent tin. The solder used for electrical work comes in the form of a hollow wire filled with rosin flux. The flux absorbs the oxides formed on the wires as they are heated and promotes fusion. The convenience of rosin-flux solder does away with the messiness of having to apply a separate solder to a joint.

> **WARNING: Never use acid-core solder—it will eventually corrode and destroy the joint. It is used to join metals structurally, not for electrical connections. Solder packages clearly indicate the type they contain, so acid-core solder can be easily avoided.**

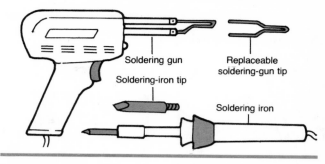

Soldering gun and soldering iron. The soldering gun heats very rapidly.

The secret of good soldering is threefold: cleanliness, adequate heat, and proper application of the solder itself. Try to avoid direct contact between fingers and a wire that has been stripped of insulation, as natural body oils may prevent solder from adhering properly.

The wires to be joined must be shiny bright and free of any insulation. Clean them thoroughly: Strip carefully with a jackknife or wire stripper; buff lightly with fine sandpaper if the wire ends are corroded or dull; then wipe them with a rag.

The tip of the soldering iron must also be clean and shiny. Preparing an iron for use is called *tinning*; it improves the efficiency of heat transfer from the iron's tip to the joint. To tin, plug the iron in. When it has heated up, touch its tip to the rosin-flux solder and let a drop or two of solder melt onto it. There will be smoke for a few seconds as the flux is "cooked out." When the smoking stops, wipe the tip of the iron clean with quick dabs of a rag or a slightly dampened sponge. If the tip still is not clean, unplug the iron and let it cool down. Polish the cool tip with a file or an emery cloth; then plug the iron back in and melt a

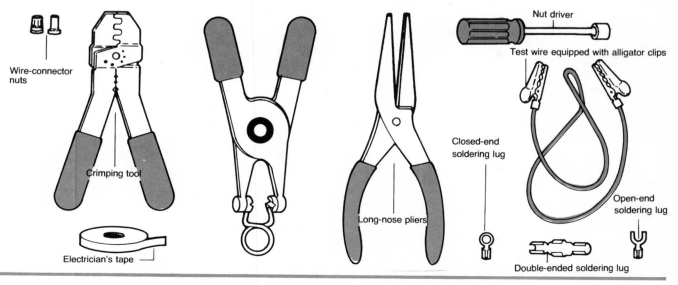

Additional tools and supplies that will be helpful for in-home electrical work

Procedure: Soldering

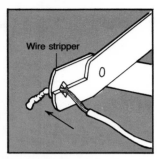

1. Strip the insulation from the ends of the wires with a wire stripper or knife. Make sure all the insulation is removed.

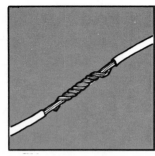

2. Clean the wires with fine steel wool, sandpaper, or emery cloth. Twist the wires together securely with pliers or clean fingers.

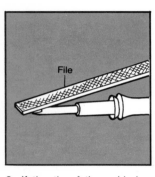

3. If the tip of the soldering iron is obviously dirty, clean it with a fine file, steel wool, sandpaper, or emery cloth. The tip should be shiny.

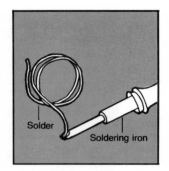

4. Plug in the soldering iron and allow it to reach operating temperature—this takes about 3 to 5 minutes for a soldering iron, 3 to 5 seconds for a soldering gun. Then, tin the tip: Apply some solder and wipe clean.

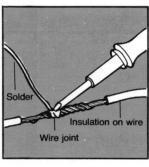

5. Heat the joint with the tip of the iron and touch the solder wire to the hot joint. The solder will melt onto the joint. Apply only enough solder to cover the joint readily. Remove the tip of the iron immediately.

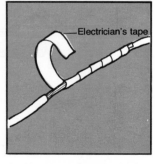

6. After the soldered joint has cooled, pull gently on it to make sure the connection is firm. Wrap the joint with electrician's tape, extending it to cover the edge of the insulation. The wrapping should not be too bulky; the wrapped wire should have about the same-size diameter as the insulated wire.

fresh coat of solder over the tip. Clean the tip again with the rag or sponge.

To secure an electrical connection, apply the iron to the joint until the wires are hot enough to melt the solder. Always apply the solder to the wires, not to the tip of the soldering iron. The heated wires will make the solder flow smoothly into and around the joint. Use the minimum amount of solder necessary—it will be a surprisingly small amount. Remember that a *coating* of solder will effect the best joint; a blob is excess. As soon as the solder has flowed into the joint, withdraw the iron. Do not move the joint until it has cooled.

The surface of the cooled, solidified solder should be smooth and shiny. If it is dull with a crystalline, grainy look, reheat the joint and let it cool again.

> **WARNING:** Do not touch the newly soldered joint until it has cooled off.

Using Wire Nuts

Although soldering is easy and fast, using wire nuts to make circuit connections is even simpler. Wire nuts are an acceptable substitute when soldering is prohibited by the NEC, so long as the joint will not be visible and will not be subjected to any mechanical stress.

The wire nut (a brand name that is used as a generic term) is a hollow, cone-shaped, insulated screw-on connector. Some have a coiled wire spring inside. Wire nuts come in sizes suitable for the gauge and number of wires to be connected. Small wire nuts are made for stranded wire used in lamps and lighting fixtures.

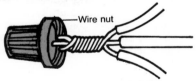

To use a wire nut, strip the wires, twist them together, and then force the wire nut onto the wires. Turn the wire nut in a clockwise direction to secure it firmly.

Always use a wire nut that is appropriately sized for the wires it is connecting. The wires are stripped, then twisted together with pliers and inserted in the nut. The nut is then screwed down over them until it covers the twisted ends. Electrician's tape should be wrapped over the gap between the base of the wire nut and the insulated wires. Wire nuts are easily removed by unscrewing; they should not be pulled off.

Simple Splicing

The simplest way to connect two wire ends is to strip about an inch of insulation from each, twist the bare ends together, and then cover the joint with electrician's tape. For neatness, bend back the pigtail

Another method of splicing wires is to strip them, twist the exposed ends together, and then cover with electrician's tape.

that results from twisting the ends together until it is against one of the wires; then tape it flat to the wire.

For an elegant splice in two-wire cords, such as lamp cords, cut the ends of each cord's wires separately. Make one wire in the cord about 1½ inches longer than the other, so that each cord has a long and a short wire. Strip about ½ inch of insulation from each of the wires. Twist together the long wire of one cord with the short wire of the other, and repeat the procedure with the remaining pair of wires. Tape over the exposed wires. A relatively slim splice results, because the cut ends are staggered.

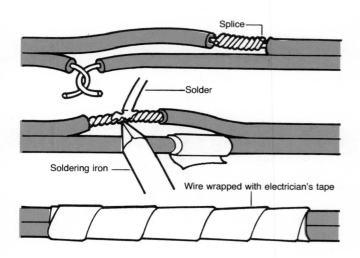

Splice

Solder

Soldering iron

Wire wrapped with electrician's tape

Join insulated wires, such as lamp cords, by following the method shown here. Separating the spliced wires minimizes the possibility of a short circuit. Tape each joint after soldering the connections. Then, as a final step, cover both joints with a layer of electrician's tape.

Using Screw Terminals

To connect a wire to a screw terminal, strip about an inch of insulation from the wire. With long-nose pliers, form the wire into a loop. Place the loop around the screw in a clockwise direction, so that tightening the screw does not drive the wire away from the screw. The loop should go about three-fourths of the way around the screw; trim off any excess. The insulation should go up to the screw but not under it. Stranded wires under screws will not separate if they are first soldered to form a solid wire.

Using Lugs

In many appliances a small lug connects the end of a wire to a screw terminal. The wire is inserted in the lug's tubular sleeve and crimped or soldered to it. (Crimp only stranded, not solid, wires.) The other end of the lug is then attached to the screw terminal. Other wire lugs merely slip tightly onto a terminal and are held in place by friction or spring action. The latter are often used in dishwashers, washing machines, and clothes dryers.

Troubleshooting Appliances

Trouble in an electrical circuit is often invisible—an appliance does not work, but there is no apparent cause for its failure. The first step in troubleshooting is to make sure the appliance is getting current. Plug it into a receptacle on another circuit. Then examine the line cord and plug for possible breaks, and perform a continuity test on them (*see page 28*).

WARNING: Before working on an electrical device that is normally attached to a power line, disconnect it. Shutting off the power to an appliance is not enough. Pull out the plug from the wall outlet or disconnect the fuse or circuit breaker for the branch circuit. Violations of this rule could result in fire, severe injury, or death.

If the source of trouble has not been found, inspect the internal wiring after removing the housing. Examine all wires and the parts to which they are attached. Look and feel for evidence of excessive heat: discolored or crumbling insulation, signs of charring nearby. Make a "sniff test" to detect any residual burned smell. Try to avoid disturbing wiring and electrical components during this examination.

If the cause for appliance failure cannot be traced, clear the vicinity of flammable materials, plug the appliance into the wall outlet, turn it on briefly, and then turn it off. Listen for crackling sounds; watch for smoke, sparks, and other signs of trouble. If none of these is evident, turn the appliance on again for about ten seconds, then unplug it and quickly feel for heat around the wires and components. Be prepared to pull away quickly from sudden excessive heat in one of the parts.

The next step is testing the internal circuit of the appliance to determine where the break in its continuity has occurred. Use a continuity checker or a multimeter (*see page 26*).

Testing Devices

Hot-line Tester

Testing for continuity

A hot-line tester is a simple, inexpensive device consisting of a neon light and two probes that can be used to test circuits for continuity over a wide range of voltages. The tester shows whether or not a circuit is continuous by lighting up when current passes through it.

To test for a closed circuit, simply put one probe into each slot of the receptacle. If the circuit is continuous, the light will go on.

 WARNING: Never touch the end of a probe while the hot-line tester is in operation.

Testing for grounding

Older outlets were ordinarily made with two equally sized slots. The advent of newer, specialized appliances has given rise to other, more specialized types: the pole-for-pole type which uses two differently shaped slots to make sure an appliance plug corresponds to the wires in the circuit, and the three-pronged grounded outlet. In modern receptacles where one slot is longer than the other, this is called the wider slot, because when the receptacle is installed, the slots are horizontal. This wider slot is supposed to be connected to the grounded return wire of the circuit. Some manufacturers insure that an appliance will be properly grounded by making one prong of the appliance's plug wider than the other, so it cannot be plugged into the receptacle in the wrong way.

To test the receptacle's grounding, insert one probe in the narrow slot and touch the screw terminal or metal faceplate with the other. (Remove a painted-over faceplate and touch the second probe to the side of the outlet box.) If the light goes on, the circuit is grounded. If it does not go on, the grounded wire is broken or improperly connected.

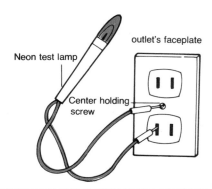

To test an outlet for continuity, insert both prongs of the tester into the outlet. To test the grounding of an outlet, insert one probe in the narrow slot while touching the faceplate screw with the other probe.

Testing a cartridge fuse

The hot-line tester can also be used to check the condition of cartridge fuses, which give no visual indication when they blow.

Touch one probe of the hot-line tester to the white return wire and the other probe to the black wire on the incoming side of the fuse. If the light goes on, power is entering the fuse. Now touch one probe to the white line and the other to the exit side of the fuse. If the light goes on, power is leaving the fuse; if it does not go on, the fuse has blown.

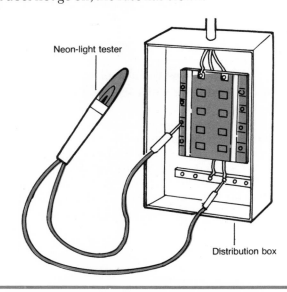

How to test fuses in the distribution box

Continuity Checker

A continuity checker looks much like a hot-line tester, but it does not use electricity from household circuits. Power in the circuit being tested should be turned off before the checker is put into operation. The continuity checker has its own power source, one or two small flashlight batteries. It checks continuity in circuit components such as fuses, switches, and wires, pinpointing the source of a short circuit. Like the neon tester, the continuity checker's lamp lights when the circuit is closed and does not light when the circuit is open.

 WARNING: Never use a continuity checker on a live circuit or anything connected to it.

The use of a continuity checker is limited to testing components with a resistance of no more than 50 ohms. With greater resistance, the lamp lights dimly or not at all.

Multimeter

A multimeter provides an accurate and informative check on just about any electrical device. More versatile than the hot-line tester or continuity checker, it

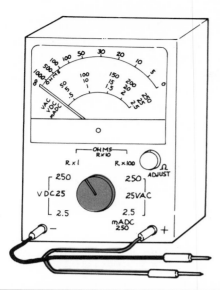

The multimeter—also known as a multitester or volt-ohm-milliammeter (VOM)—is a versatile test instrument. Use it to test AC or DC voltages, DC current, and resistance.

is a multipurpose tool—a combination of ohmmeter, voltmeter, and ammeter (ampere meter). The multimeter can be used to check continuity and to measure resistance, voltage, and DC amperage.

 WARNING: The multimeter's ohmmeter function operates on a battery and must not be used to measure resistance or check continuity in a live circuit. Disconnect power before testing resistance.

Multimeters range in cost from a few dollars to over a hundred dollars. Even the least expensive models adequately detect electrical problems, but the more costly ones are designed to provide more information more accurately, and may be wired with some kind of overload-protection device.

A multimeter can be operated easily. With the selector switch set for the desired reading, the probes are firmly attached to or held in contact with the test points on the appliance part, heating element, or fuse or circuit breaker. When the ohmmeter function is used, the battery in the meter sends a very slight electrical current through the part being tested and the meter indicates the amount of resistance.

Parts of a multimeter

Selector switch. Each multimeter has a rotary switch that clicks through as many as twenty or more settings in one rotation. This switch is usually the largest knob on the meter and is clearly labeled as to function and range. A typical multimeter might have four voltage ranges for both AC and DC—0–1, 0–10, 0–100, and 0–1,000—and be capable of measuring resistance as high as several million ohms and DC current up to 10 amperes.

Meters are most accurate at the upper end of their scales. Set the range switch to the highest position for the first reading, then readjust it downward one range at a time until the pointer is approximately in the middle of the scale.

Pointer. The pointer should indicate zero when the meter is at rest. If it does not, turn the zero-adjustment screw below the meter's face until the pointer reads zero. The ohmmeter function is adjusted by means of a knob.

Ohms-adjustment knob. Each time the selector is turned to the ohms scale from another function's mode, the pointer must be zero-adjusted on the ohms scale. To do this, insert the test leads in their jacks; holding them together at the tips, rotate the adjustment knob till the pointer reads zero. If the pointer cannot be adjusted to zero, the meter's battery is faulty and must be replaced.

Test leads and jacks. The black lead and probe are usually seated in the minus (common) jack. The red lead connects to the positive jack.

Test probes. Both probes must firmly touch the appropriate points of the unit being tested. Needle probes can often reach hard-to-get-at parts of an appliance, but alligator-clip probes grip firmly, leaving hands free to manipulate the meter. Meter leads with insulated alligator-clip probes already attached can be purchased.

Functions of a multimeter

Ohms scale. On the voltage and amperage scales of the multimeter, low amounts of volts and amps are indicated by small movements of the meter needle. On the ohms scale, however, the lower the resistance being measured, the farther the needle swings up the scale, to the right.

In determining resistance, a full-scale reading—0 ohms—indicates continuity. A reading of zero across the terminals of a cartridge fuse means the fuse is sound. If the needle points to zero when the probes are placed at the ends of a piece of wire, the reading indicates the wire is unbroken. No movement of the meter needle, on the other hand, would indicate infinite resistance—a blown fuse or a break in the wire concealed by the insulation.

As an experiment, take a piece of ordinary two-wire lamp cord. Strip the two wires at one end and keep them apart. Make sure the other ends are not touching each other or anything else. Touch the stripped ends with the probes and check the meter reading. The pointer will not have moved at all, indicating infinite resistance. Now strip and twist together the far ends of the wires and again touch the probes to the near ends. This time the meter will register full-scale resistance—0 ohms.

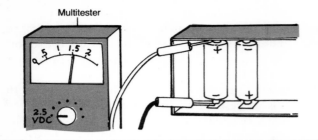

Multitester

Testing batteries with a multitester

Voltage scale. To test a D-cell flashlight battery with a multimeter, set the selector for a scale in the range of 2.5–10 volts DC. Place the black probe (−) against the negative pole of the battery, and the red probe (+) against the positive pole. If the meter indicates less than 1.3 volts, replace the flashlight battery. Lantern batteries generally deliver 6 volts; the voltages of fully charged automobile batteries range from 11.5 to 13 volts.

Amperage scale. The amperage settings on the multimeter are of limited use for the do-it-yourselfer. Most units can read current only when there is DC voltage, and thus are not suitable for common house-powered electrical devices.

NOTE: If properly maintained, the multimeter will last for years. Remove the battery before storing the multimeter for extended periods of time.

Testing for continuity with a multimeter

Preliminary steps. In testing an electrical component for continuity, the objective is simply to ascertain whether or not electricity can flow through it. This calls for the use of the ohms mode. Before testing an appliance, follow these steps:

1. Disconnect the appliance from its source of power.

2. Set the multimeter selector switch to the proper ohms position. If resistance is being measured, use the lowest scale, since most high-voltage appliances have relatively low resistance. If testing for a short circuit, again use the lowest scale. To test for current leakage between the appliance wiring and the metal frame, use a higher range.

3. Hold the probes together and zero-adjust the ohms scale.

NOTE: Always unplug any appliance being tested for electrical continuity—turning it off is not sufficient. Power from a live circuit feeding into the multimeter's battery will destroy the tester.

Testing. The multimeter test is simple, informative, and easy to perform on any plug-in appliance.

1. First, with the appliance unplugged, turn the On/Off switch to On. Naturally, since the appliance is unplugged, it will remain dormant. (Some appliances do not have a specific On/Off control. Pop-up toasters, for example, are turned on by a lever that activates the heating element as it lowers the toast carriage.)

2. Set the multimeter to its lowest resistance range. Then, while watching the meter, touch one probe to each prong of the plug. The pointer should move up the scale. If it does not, advance the meter switch to the next higher range and try again. When the pointer moves up the scale, it indicates that there is a path into the appliance along which current can flow. This probably eliminates both the cord and the On/Off switch as the source of the appliance failure.

3. Let the internal wiring of the appliance serve as a guide from one part to another. Test each wire and part in turn. Sometimes vibrations loosen connections or a sharp metal edge cuts the insulation and causes a short circuit. Keep in mind that there is little or no current flow where resistance is very high or infinite. Conversely, little or no resistance means heavy current flow or a short circuit.

4. If, despite resetting the meter switch to higher and higher ranges, the pointer still does not move, power cannot flow to the appliance. A systematic approach is the best way to track down the defective element. The line cord is the first conductor in the current path—check it for continuity. If it is sound, move on to the next unit, probably the On/Off switch. Test probes on the switch wires will quickly reveal the condition of the switch. Turn the switch on and off a few times. If the pointer does not move, the switch is probably broken. Replacing it restores the appliance to working order.

Electrical Materials and Their Use

Cable

Cable refers to two or more wires carried together in a sheath. Both *armored cable* (AC) and *nonmetallic-sheathed cable* (NMC) are used extensively in homes throughout the United States. They are flexible, fairly easy to maneuver, and are manufactured with different numbers of internal wires. The wires within the outer sheath are color-coded. The cable unit as a whole is identified by the wire size, or gauge, of the internal wires and the number of them, typically either two or three, within the sheath. Thus, a three-wire cable using No. 10 wire is labeled 10–3; a two-wire cable with No. 14 wire is labeled 14–2. Cable can be purchased in rolls of 25, 50, 100, and 250 feet.

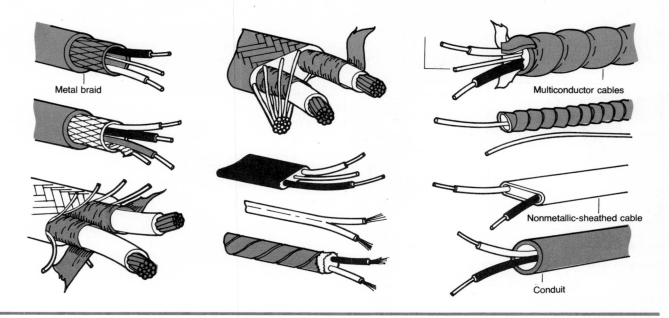

Various types of cables used in electrical work

Two-wire cables carry alternating current in 120-volt circuits. The black wire should always be used as the hot wire, the white as the neutral wire. The neutral wire is connected to the ground bar in the distribution box and provides a continuous ground to all outlets and sockets throughout the house. Cable usually contains an additional wire either with no insulation or colored green. This secondary grounding wire attaches to the outlet box or *junction box* (a box that houses wire splices) at one end and is grounded within the distribution box at the other end. Under normal operating conditions, this green (or bare) wire carries no current; its purpose is to protect the person using the equipment, in case of an equipment malfunction, by diverting the current to a ground. The metallic sheath of armored cable provides an additional secondary ground.

Three-wire cables carry current for circuits of *240* volts. The first hot wire is black, the second hot wire is red, and the neutral wire is white or gray.

Before purchasing cable, check the local electrical code for possible restrictions on the type being considered. In addition, there may be requirements for insulation and installation. Some community codes allow armored cable to be run exposed in walls and ceilings where conditions are dry. Often codes still require either thin-wall tubing or a lead sheath for insulation; all codes require a lead sheath where cable is run in a damp location or through any kind of masonry. Lead sheath is manufactured in flexible and rigid types.

Both armored and nonmetallic-sheathed cable are approved by the NEC for wiring in dry places, but the wires they carry must be Type T (thermoplastic) or Type R (rubber). The NEC defines cable locations as follows:

Dry. Dry areas are not normally subject to dampness but may be damp or wet temporarily, as in a building under construction.

Damp. A damp area is a partially protected location (under a canopy or marquee, or a roofed open porch) or interior place subject to moderate moisture, such as a basement, barn, or cold-storage warehouse.

Wet. This is either an underground area, concrete slab, or masonry in contact with the earth; a place subjected to saturation with water or other liquids, such as a vehicle-washing area; or any unprotected area exposed to weather.

Armored cable

Armored cable (often called BX cable) may have two or three color-coded wires plus a bare copper wire used as a grounding conductor. The color-coded wires are individually insulated, then wrapped together in paper and encased in a spiral-grooved, galvanized-steel sheath.

BX cable is more difficult to work with than nonmetallic-sheathed cable. Care must be taken not to nick the internal wires when cutting the sheathing with a hacksaw. When trying to pass BX around obstacles, the cable must be maneuvered so that its grooves do not catch on corners and edges. BX cannot be bent in sharp curves without damaging the armor; it is also somewhat difficult to cut and to prepare for connection to a junction box. But for all its drawbacks, BX is more fire-resistant and less prone to deterioration and breaks than nonarmored cable. BX is approved for use in exposed or open installations in dry locations.

The NEC requires that the cut ends of armored cable be covered by fiber bushing to protect the wires.

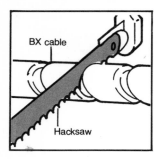 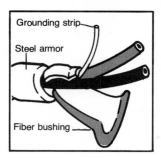

To saw BX cable (*left*), hold the hacksaw blade at a diagonal angle to the spirals of the armor. After sawing, twist the cut end of the armor and pull it off. After BX cable is cut, insert a fiber bushing (*right*) around the wires inside the armor to prevent the sharp, newly cut edge from damaging the wires' insulation.

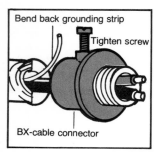 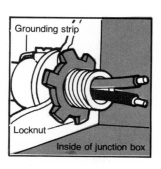

To install a connector onto BX cable (*left*), bend the grounding strip (or wire) back over the outside of the armor and insert the fiber bushing around the wires. Then, slip the connector over the armor and bent-back grounding strip. Push the connector onto the cable as far as it will go; tighten the screw to anchor it to the cable. To secure the cable inside the junction box (*right*), remove the locknut of the connector and slip the connector into the knockout of the box. Then, drive the locknut down tightly so that its teeth bite into the metal of the box.

Nonmetallic-sheathed cable

This cable is available in two forms—NM (nonmetallic) and NMC (nonmetallic, corrosion-resistant)—and is the least expensive and easiest cable to work with. These cables are easily stripped with a knife or with a wire stripper especially made for them. NM, often referred to as Romex (a brand name), is covered with a fibrous or plastic jacket; its use is restricted to dry locations. NMC may be used in dry, damp, and wet locations, because its wires are individually insulated and embedded in plastic. Type UF (underground feeder) cable is similar to NMC and may be used to replace it in circuit wiring inside the house.

All nonmetallic-sheathed cables now contain a secondary grounding wire.

Conduit

Conduit is metal pipe used to enclose wiring. It is manufactured in two types: thin-walled conduit, which is rigid but can be bent around corners with a special curved tool called a *hickey*; and thicker, rigid conduit (made of a heavier-gauge metal), which, like a water pipe, requires couplings and fittings to lead and position it in the desired directions. Conduit used in the home is ½ inch or ¾ inch in diameter.

Steel conduit is usually galvanized; aluminum conduit is coated with enamel or plastic for protection against corrosion. Both galvanized-steel and aluminum conduit are designed for use in wet locations.

The smooth finish inside conduit allows electrical wires to be pulled through it easily without damage to their insulation. The number of wires that the metal tube can receive depends on the wire size and the conduit diameter. A ½-inch-diameter conduit can hold a maximum of four No. 14 wires or three No. 12 wires. A ¾-inch-diameter pipe can hold a maximum of six No. 14 wires or five No. 12 wires.

The NEC prohibits wire splices inside conduit as a safeguard against short-circuiting or other failures. Wires must be continuous within the pipe; all splices must be made in switch, outlet, or junction boxes. The NEC also limits the number of bends permitted in conduit, to insure that wires can be threaded through it safely.

Electrical wires are threaded through conduit after it is in position. A snake is used to pull the wires through long runs, which should be supported every 6 feet or so with hangers. Conduit is fitted and secured to junction boxes with threaded connectors; threaded collars lock the conduit and boxes in place.

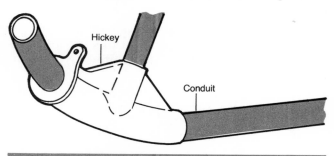

Making a bend in conduit with a hickey. Bend the conduit by pulling the handle back in the direction of the bend.

Electrical Boxes

Every circuit in a house has one or more metal electrical boxes that contain receptacles or switches. A box may be rectangular, square, octagonal, or round. A number of tabs, called *knockouts,* are partially punched out on each side of the box. The knockouts can be removed as needed by tapping with a screwdriver and hammer, leaving a hole large enough to allow cable to enter the unit. Some boxes have two

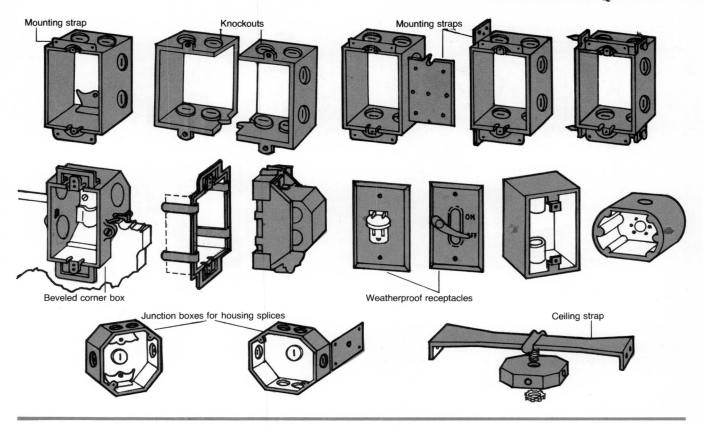

Mounting strap

Knockouts

Mounting straps

Beveled corner box

Weatherproof receptacles

Junction boxes for housing splices

Ceiling strap

Wall boxes, ceiling boxes, boxes for damp locations, and accessories

knockout sizes: The larger size fits a BX or Romex connector; the smaller size allows only the cable to enter the box, to be held in place by built-in clamps.

New-work boxes are used in new construction, when wall studs and ceiling joists are exposed and readily accessible. They are attached directly to structural supports with nails or screws. *Old-work* boxes are used in remodeling and new installations made in already completed houses. They are attached to the surfaces of walls or ceilings.

Wall-mounted switch boxes have detachable sides to facilitate the joining of two or more to form larger assemblies for rows of switches. Spanners are available to hold ceiling boxes between ceiling joists, and electrical boxes come in a wide variety to meet every kind of construction and remodeling need.

Built-in clamps. There are two kinds of built-in clamps found in electrical boxes. One has a flat metal strap that holds only Romex cable. To adapt it for BX cable, remove the strap and use external connectors. The second kind of clamps can hold either BX or Romex cable. It has an L-shaped extension to hold the BX bushing in place. When Romex cable is used, the extension is bent off with pliers and the strap that remains is tightened against the Romex cable.

When using external connectors with an electrical box, remove the built-in clamps—either type—to provide more room for cables inside the box.

Receptacles

A wall receptacle, or outlet, which is installed in the metal electrical box, can be one of several models. Old-style outlets have two equal-sized slots to receive a plug's prongs. Newer outlets have two different-length slots to make sure the plug's prongs correspond to the polarity of the wires in the circuit. They may also be grounded outlets, with a third hole for a three-pronged plug. The round hole receives the plug's grounding prong, to which the line cord's neutral wire connects.

The black wire is attached to the dark or yellowish terminal of the receptacle. The white wire is attached to the white, nickel-plated terminal, forming a con-

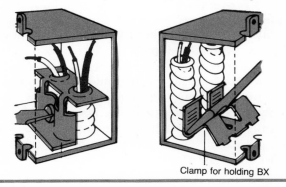

Clamp for holding BX

Clamps are used in boxes to hold the cable firmly in position and, thus, eliminate stress on the connected wires.

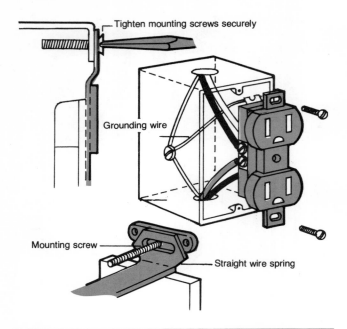

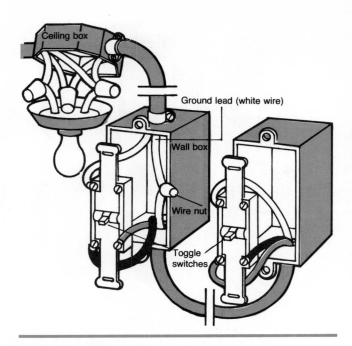

The grounded receptacle has two parallel slots plus an extra hole to receive a three-pronged plug. The third hole in the receptacle is the contact point between the grounding wire in the receptacle box and the grounding wire of the appliance cord (which is connected to the plug's third prong).

tinuous ground back to the distribution box. If there is a third, red wire—as in 240-volt circuits—it attaches to a dark or yellowish terminal. The green or uninsulated wire in the cable is an additional grounding conductor and attaches to a secondary ground terminal (usually a screw painted green) at the back of the receptacle.

Switches

The purpose of a switch is to interrupt the flow of current by opening the circuit into which the switch is wired. Switches come in the form of buttons, levers, and dials.

Conventional switches are completely mechanical in action. *Mercury switches* are a little different. Moving the handle of a mercury switch changes the position of a tiny vial of mercury hidden inside the housing of the switch. When the switch is moved to On, the vial is tilted enough to let a drop of mercury fall into place between two normally open contacts. The mercury completes the circuit, allowing power to flow. Mercury switches are better than mechanical switches because they have a much simpler action that is less prone to wear. They are also silent—there is no audible click when the switch is turned on or off. Another noiseless switch, the *AC-only switch,* is in wide use. Note that it may not be used to control incandescent lights at more than 120 volts.

Lamp outlet controlled by two toggle switches

Types of switches

The nomenclature used to describe types of switches is easy to understand with the help of a few key terms.

Pole. Think of a *pole* as a lever that either bridges a gap or creates one, depending upon its position. A single-pole switch opens or closes a single circuit. A double-pole switch opens or closes two circuits at once.

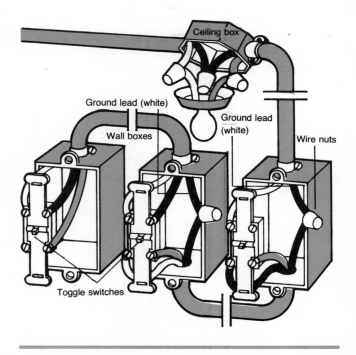

Lamp outlet controlled by three toggle switches

Throw. Think of *throw* as the action of the pole. A single-throw switch can be either open or closed. A double-throw switch can be turned to a third terminal. For example, the switch of a two-speed fan is a double-throw switch (commonly called a three-way switch).

Single-pole toggle switch. This is the most widely used wall switch. It is designed to fit in an electrical box and has two terminal screws; the words *Off* and *On* are printed on opposite sides of its handle. Before installing this switch, cut the hot wire and disconnect the fuse or circuit breaker.

Double-pole switch. It is often desirable, and sometimes required, to interrupt both wires leading to an appliance. In particular, the NEC requires that 240-volt motors or appliances be serviced by switches in this manner. To accomplish this, a double-pole, single-throw switch is used. The double-pole switch has four terminals for the black (or red) and white wires. Toasters often employ double-pole switches.

Three-way switch. It is convenient to be able to turn a light on or off from two different places, such as from the garage and the house or from both ends of a stairway, hall, or large room. This is made possible by the *three-way switch*. This switch derives its name from the fact that it has three terminals. When two of these switches are wired to a light fixture, the hot wire is connected to the common terminal on one of the switches. On the other switch, the hot wire runs from the marked terminal to the fixture. Two wires called *travelers* connect the remaining terminals between the switches. The white neutral wire runs from the fixture back to the power source. If the switches are properly wired, the light will be on when both switch handles are either up or down; it is turned off by setting one switch handle up and the other one down.

Four-way switch. When a light is to be controlled from three different locations, the wiring becomes somewhat more complicated. One of the three switches must be a *four-way switch*. The other switches are a pair of three-way switches connected in the usual manner to the power source and the light; the four-way switch is connected between them. The four-way switch has four terminals.

Other switches. Some switches can be turned on and off only with a special key. Others have a spring-loaded handle: As soon as the lever is released by the user, the switch returns to its original position. A *dimmer* can replace a toggle switch in any switch box. Dimmers can also be used in place of three-way switches. Different dimmers are made for incandescent and fluorescent lights; they are not interchangeable.

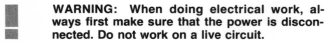

Electrical Maintenance and Repair

3

Household electrical circuits often require work—to install, maintain, or repair. This chapter offers guidance in several of the most common types of electrical tasks found in the home. Even a homeowner who prefers to hire someone else to correct a problem or wire a new installation can understand the nature and amount of electrical work required, identify the part or component that needs to be replaced or repaired, and make plans to accommodate a new appliance within older circuitry.

WARNING: When doing electrical work, always first make sure that the power is disconnected. Do not work on a live circuit.

Electric Cord and Plug

Replacing the Cord

A damaged cord should be replaced or repaired as soon as possible to prevent appliance damage and fire. The cord requires replacing when it is frayed, its outer cover has partially disintegrated, it has one or more breaks, or it heats up after a few minutes of use. Factory-made cords tagged "replacement" are available for many appliances, or a new cord can be made from parts. Take a piece of the old cord to the hardware or electrical supply store to make sure the replacement parts are similar.

Rubber or braid-covered *parallel cord,* available in gauges No. 18 and No. 16, is used for small, nonheating household appliances such as radios, fans, and lamps. *Twisted lamp cord*—two separately insulated wires twisted together—is used primarily as an extension for drop lights or as a general-purpose extension cord, and is available in gauges ranging from No. 18 to No. 10. *Heating cord,* for use with heat-producing appliances, is available in No. 18 to No. 12 gauge and has a woven fabric covering. Each wire within the cord is covered with asbestos and plastic insulation. *Flexible heavy-duty cord,* covered with thick plastic, is designed for portable outdoor equipment. It is available in No. 18 to No. 10 gauge.

A damaged cord can be salvaged if the undamaged part is long enough to complete the run. Cut off the damaged portion and splice the undamaged wires (*see page 24*). If the break is near the plug, attach a new plug rather than splice the cord.

Replacing the Plug

Male plugs with two or three prongs fit into receptacles or corresponding *female plugs.* Many types of male plugs are available. A simple nondurable hard plastic plug is used primarily for lamps. The semi-heavy-duty *finger-grip plug,* made of durable rubber or synthetic, is intended for small appliances and lamps. A *three-pronged plug* is used on many appliances, hand-operated tools, and motors. Female plugs for appliances such as toasters, coffeemakers, frying pans, and popcorn poppers come in various sizes. Some can be unscrewed and taken apart so that repairs can be made to the wires inside; other female plugs with cases held together by rivets cannot be repaired.

To replace a plug on a parallel cord, cut off the damaged plug with wire cutters. Slip the new plug onto the cord. Strip about ½ inch of insulation from the wires. If the cord is stranded, do not cut any of the small strands. Twist the stranded wires together tightly. Tie an *Underwriters knot* by looping the black wire clockwise, then looping the white wire over the black wire, passing the end through the loop in the black wire, and pulling tight. In a three-wire plug the green grounding wire is not included in the Underwriters knot but is secured to the green terminal.

Pull the cord down into the plug so that the knot is seated firmly in it. Pull each wire end clockwise around its screw terminal, so that tightening the screw secures the connection. If the screw terminals are of different metals, pull the black wire around the yellow screw and the white wire around the white screw. (This is especially important in the case of polarized plugs, in which one prong is wider than the other.) Make sure that the bare wire fits all the way around the screw terminals. Tighten the screw. The insulation should come up to the screw but not under it. Place the insulation cover back over the plug.

Female plugs with cases held together by rivets cannot be repaired, only replaced. If the case is held together by screws, take the screws out and check the two wires to see if they are properly attached to their screw terminals; clean and tighten if necessary. If this does not solve the problem, replace the plug.

When removing a plug or receptable, make a

sketch of the original wiring and follow this when attaching the new plug or receptacle.

Switches and Receptacles

Replacing a Single Switch or Receptacle

When a switch or receptacle fails, replace it immediately. A nonfunctioning electrical component within the walls of a house is a fire hazard.

 WARNING: Before removing the faceplate that covers a defective switch or receptacle, remove the fuse for that circuit or flip the circuit breaker to Off.

Before removing the faceplate, double-check to make sure the power to the box is off. Take the faceplate off. Loosen the screws that hold the switch or receptacle component in place and gently pull the component out of the box. Make a sketch of which wires attach to which screw terminals on the component. Disconnect the wires and remove the component.

Examine the inside of the box and the wires carefully with a flashlight. Look for any sign of frayed or worn insulation, or burning. Make sure the box is in safe condition. Wrap electrician's tape carefully around wiring whose insulation seems frayed or worn. Be sure there is no metal-to-metal contact from wire to wire or from wire to box. When in doubt, consult an electrician.

Take the component to an electrical supply store or hardware store and get a matching replacement.

To attach a wire to a screw terminal of the new component, hook the wire clockwise around the screw and tighten the screw to make a firm connection with the wire. Then gently fold the wires behind the new switch or receptacle and press the component back into place in the box. Attach the switch or receptacle to the electrical box with the screws provided.

Replace the faceplate and restore the fuse or reset the circuit breaker. Then test the component for any sign of malfunctioning, such as a flickering light (if it is a switch, or a receptacle with a lamp plugged into it) or a slight buzzing sound from the electrical box. These are warning signs that poor connections have been made. Immediately remove the fuse or flip the circuit breaker and reexamine the work to find the cause.

 WARNING: If the electrical system gives off danger signals, heed them. Ignoring signs of possible malfunction can result in electrical shock or fire.

Replacing a Multiple Switch or Receptacle

The procedure for replacing multiple switches or receptacles is essentially the same as that for replacing

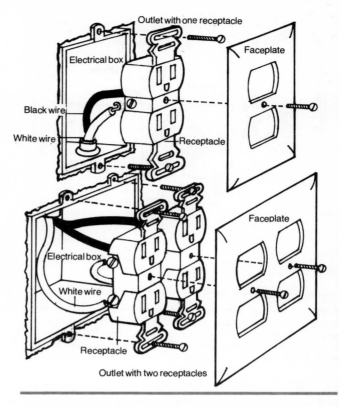

How to replace outlet receptacles. Single receptacle (*top*), double receptacle (*bottom*). Make sure that power has been turned off before replacing a receptacle. Remove the appropriate fuse or circuit breaker. Check for the interruption of power by inserting a lamp into the old outlet before starting the job. No leads should touch the metal box after replacement of the receptacle.

a single unit. Before beginning work, however, check how many branch circuits enter the box. At the distribution box, be certain to turn off all the circuits that enter the electrical box.

When the faceplate is removed, the homeowner may be faced with a tangle of wires that initially appears incomprehensible. The first task is to determine what each wire is—where it comes from, where it goes. Make a sketch of the wires, noting their colors and to what screw terminals they are attached. Then proceed to detach only the wires that go to the component being replaced. Even though a sketch has been made, it is a good idea to label each wire temporarily—for example, with a piece of masking tape. Remove the tag before restoring power to the circuit.

Installing a Dimmer

A dimmer can replace a switch controlling an incandescent light to provide convenience and versatility. With the use of a dimmer, a hall light can become a night light; a reading lamp can provide softer illumination for a party; a dining-room light can complement the candles at a special dinner instead of overwhelming them. To adjust the light level for the

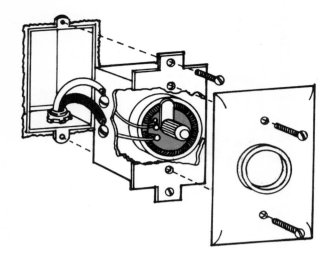

To install a dimmer, connect the existing wires to the two terminal screws on the dimmer and place the dimmer in the electrical box. Mount the faceplate and then fasten the round control knob to the shaft protruding from the dimmer. The central shaft operates as a switch. Push in to turn on and off.

lowest possible illumination, set the dimmer to a high level and then keep turning it down. Dimmers are inexpensive and easily installed. Attach the dimmer following the manufacturer's instructions.

Dimmers are rheostats—they reduce the current to a fixture by increasing electrical resistance (*see page 58*). When purchasing a dimmer, select one rated for a high wattage, to protect it from being damaged when a bulb burns out, but do not exceed 500 watts apiece when installing two dimmers in a two-switch electrical box or 400 watts for three dimmers in a three-switch box.

Various installations are possible. Use a *single-pole dimmer* to control a light fixture from a single switch box. To control a light from two locations, buy a *three-way dimmer* and replace one of the two three-way switches. Dimmers can also be attached directly to a lamp. A *light-socket dimmer* screws into the lamp, and then the bulb is screwed into the socket. An *outlet-switch dimmer* is plugged into a wall receptacle, and then the lamp is plugged into the dimmer receptacle.

Dimmers are made for both fluorescent and incandescent fixtures, but the two types are not interchangeable.

Lamps and Light Fixtures

Repairing an Incandescent Lamp

If a lamp does not work properly, first see if a new light bulb will solve the problem. Then check whether the plug or lamp cord is frayed or worn. If this does not show the source of the trouble, a quick repair may yet be possible without disassembly of the lamp.

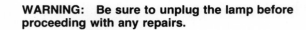

WARNING: Be sure to unplug the lamp before proceeding with any repairs.

Once the lamp is unplugged, examine the flat spring that juts up from the center inside the bulb socket. This is an electrical contact. If it appears corroded, try buffing it lightly with fine sandpaper. Sometimes bending this spring slightly will improve its contact with the base of the light bulb. Also examine the threaded area of the socket; it too is an electrical contact.

If these measures have not solved the problem, the internal wiring may be loose or frayed, or the switch may be broken. Since the lamp must be taken apart, plan to install a new cord, a new plug, and a new socket. Make a sketch of how the lamp comes apart.

To get at the inside of the lamp, approach it from both the base and the top. Remove the covering from the base of the lamp to expose both the metal tube that runs the length of the lamp and the tube's fasteners. (This tube is comparable to conduit in that it encloses and protects the lamp's wiring.) The socket on top of the lamp probably screws onto the top end of this metal tube, or it may be held on with a setscrew. When the fasteners on the bottom of the lamp are loosened, the metal tube and socket should lift out. Cutting the cord inside the lamp (since this cord will be replaced anyway) may make the job easier.

When the repair has been completed, follow the sketch to reassemble the lamp.

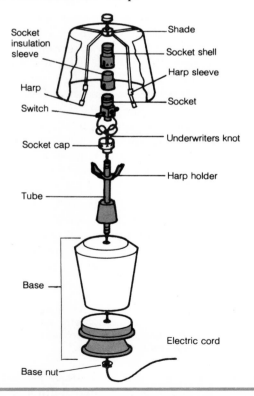

Anatomy of an incandescent lamp

Replacing a Light Fixture

Replacing a light fixture is similar in several respects to replacing a switch or receptacle. The wiring for the light fixture, like that for a switch or receptacle, is contained in an electrical box mounted in the wall or ceiling. After making sure no current flows to the box, replacing the fixture is theoretically a simple

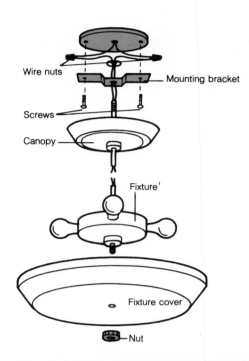

Exploded view of a ceiling-fixture installation

matter of attaching the wires of the new lighting fixture with wire nuts or solder just as the old lighting fixture was attached.

WARNING: When replacing a light fixture, observe all the safety precautions indicated for changing a switch or receptacle. Before removing the old fixture, be sure to remove the applicable fuse or flip the circuit breaker to Off. Also check the condition of the wires in the box.

The problems come not in the wiring process itself, usually, but in the process of securing the fixture to the wall or ceiling. Overhead fixtures can be especially difficult. Professional electricians hang them from the electrical box with a variety of ingenious hardware. When a fixture is bought, it usually comes with one or more pieces of hardware for attaching it, but frequently different accessories are needed to suit a particular installation.

When confronted with a fixture that cannot be attached to an electrical box with the hardware supplied, take the fixture (or the part of it that will fit over the box), together with a sketch of the electrical

box that includes point-to-point measurements, to an electrical supply store or a well-stocked hardware store. The appropriate hardware should cost less than two dollars.

Fluorescent Fixtures

Fluorescent light fixtures set up a current within themselves to produce light; they do not use house current directly. In a fluorescent tube, an electric arc generated by internal terminals (called cathodes) passes through a mixture of argon gas and mercury vapor. This electrified mixture releases invisible ultraviolet energy. The ultraviolet rays radiate against the inside of the tube, which is coated with phosphors that glow in their presence. Different phosphor mixes yield different colors of visible light such as "cool white," "warm violet," and "daylight."

A fluorescent fixture consists of a ballast in the lamp base, lamp holders (sockets), and a starter (if needed). Essentially, there are two types of fluorescent fixtures found in the home. The older, *preheat* type requires a starter to heat the electrodes (cathodes) in the tube so they can begin to produce light. The newer *rapid-start* and *instant-start* types get heat directly from the ballast. The rapid-start light comes on gradually over a period of several seconds and the instant-start turns on almost immediately; neither flickers or flashes as the starter-type lamp initially does.

Parts of a fluorescent fixture

Glass tube. The basic fluorescent light is a glass tube with a maximum diameter of 1½ inches and a maximum length of 8 feet. The older, preheat tubes differ from the newer starterless ones primarily in their cathode terminals: Rapid-start and instant-start cathodes are designed to warm almost instantly without the extra boost provided by a starter.

Fluorescent lights come in different shapes: straight, circular and U-shaped. A significant feature of any fluorescent light is its relatively low operating temperature. The bulb never feels more than warm to the touch. Temperatures below 65 degrees Fahrenheit around a fluorescent lamp could cause the light to malfunction. Also, turning the lamp on and off frequently will reduce the life of a fluorescent tube considerably.

Lamp holder. The lamp holders on a straight-tube fixture extend from each end of the metal housing, and are made to receive the double pins on each end of the tube. The pins are placed in the slots of the sockets, and the tube is rotated 90 degrees until it fits snugly in place.

Ballast. Essentially, this small black box is a simple kind of transformer. It performs two functions: When the lamp is turned on, it increases the line voltage to help establish the electrical arc in the tube;

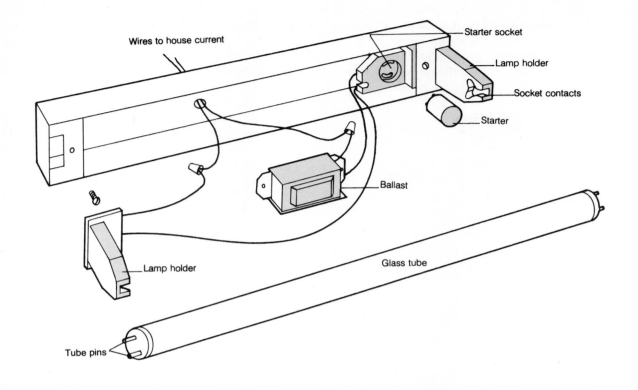

Wires to house current

Starter socket

Lamp holder

Socket contacts

Starter

Ballast

Lamp holder

Glass tube

Tube pins

Parts of a fluorescent fixture

after the lamp is lit, the ballast limits the flow of current so that the tube will not burn out due to excessive current flow. A color-coded wiring diagram is usually pasted on the top of the ballast. Also printed on it is the capacity of the individual fixture, its type, and all the information necessary to choose replacement parts.

Starter. The starter is a small metal canister about 1¼ inches long, with two small terminals protruding from one end. It starts an old-style fluorescent light by warming its cathode terminals so that an arc can pass between them. To install it, push the starter into its socket and give it a clockwise twist until it locks into place. The starter socket is wired directly to the ballast and is located in a recess just above one tube in a straight-tube unit. On a circular lamp, the starter socket is found in the face of the lamp housing, within the ring of the circular tube.

Repairing a fluorescent fixture

Glass tube. Nearly all malfunctions of fluorescent light fixtures are failures of the tube. If the light does not start or is slow to start, the tube is probably damaged. Either an electrode inside has broken or there is a loss of vacuum in the tube. A blinking or dim light is often an indication that the tube is aging and about to burn out.

When buying a fluorescent tube, be sure to replace it with the type specified on the ballast housing. A new tube should be the same wattage and type (rapid-start, instant-start, or starter-type) as the one being replaced. If the fixture holds two tubes, replace both at once. They are wired in series, and an old tube in a fixture with a new one will decrease the efficiency of the entire unit.

WARNING: Handle fluorescent tubes with extreme caution—they shatter very easily. Call a physician if cut by phosphor-coated glass particles.

To replace a tube, twist it out of the socket and twist in the new one. To replace a circular tube, look for a hooklike clamp in the middle of the bulb. Swing the hook to one side and pull it down (or just pull the glass tube out from under the hook). The plastic part of the lamp contains a plug; pull it down gently and install the new tube.

Lamp holder. A lamp holder (socket) that is misadjusted will prevent the pins from making firm contact and cause a fluorescent light to blink on and off. When replacing the tube does not cure a blinking light, check the lamp holder. Adjust it so that it fits snugly against the end of the tube. A broken lamp holder can break the internal circuit and prevent the fixture from starting. Before removing it from the fixture, be sure current is shut off in the circuit. Removal of the holder can usually be accomplished by loosening one screw and disconnecting two wires. Replace it with an identical type; use the broken holder as a guide when buying a replacement.

Ballast. When a fluorescent light gives off a loud hum, this indicates that something is loose in the ballast. It is not unsafe so long as the ballast does not overheat. If the hum is loud enough to be annoying, replace the ballast or the fixture.

When replacing the tube or starter does not remedy a blinking light, a new lamp that repeatedly fails, a tube that lights only at the ends, or a light that will not start, the problem may be in the ballast. Perhaps the fixture was repaired with the wrong ballast—an improperly rated one that does not match the wattage of the tube or tubes. Or the ballast may have been poorly connected or installed.

Rarely does a ballast need replacing, but if it does, buying a new fixture is often simpler and no more expensive.

Starter. Starters burn out and need replacement. Sometimes the ends of the tube light but the middle remains dark, or the ends stay on all the time. Either of these conditions indicates a defective starter. When the lamp lights only once in a while, the source of trouble is also probably the starter.

To replace a starter, twist out the old one and take it to the hardware store to get a matching substitute. A starter must be replaced with one of identical rating.

FLUORESCENT LAMP TROUBLESHOOTING

PROBLEM: Fluorescent lamp does not light or begins to light slowly.

Possible Cause	Procedure	Remedy	Rating	Parts	Labor
No power at source.	Find cause.	Repair			
	Check fuse or circuit breaker.	Replace fuse or reset circuit breaker.			
Tube burned out.	Install new tube to see if fixture is working.	Replace old tube.	■	$3-6	$20
Tube dirty.	Remove.	Clean with damp cloth. Dry thoroughly before returning tube to fixture.	■		$20
Tube and ballast incompatible.	Check label on ballast.	Replace tube.	■	$3-10	$10
Temperature in room too low.	Warm room to minimum of 60°F.	Restart lamp.	■		
Tube incorrectly seated in socket.	Check for dust or corrosion on pins.	Clean, reseat tube.	■		
Starter faulty.		Replace.	■	$2	$20
Ballast burned out.		Replace.	■ ■ ■	$10-20	$25

PROBLEM: Fluorescent lamp blows fuse or trips circuit breaker.

Possible Cause	Procedure	Remedy	Rating	Parts	Labor
Circuit overloaded.	Reduce number of appliances on circuit.	Replace fuse or reset circuit breaker.	■		$20
Switch short-circuited.	Check circuit continuity.	Repair or replace.	■	$3	$20

(Continued on next page)

PROBLEM: Fluorescent lamp shocks user. *(Continued from preceding page)* ▬▬▬▬

Possible Cause	Procedure	Remedy	Rating	Parts	Labor
Case short-circuited.	Test circuit continuity.	Repair.	■		$20
Wiring defective.	Inspect for bare wires.	Insulate.	■		$20

PROBLEM: Fluorescent tube is discolored or only partially lights. ▬▬▬

Possible Cause	Procedure	Remedy	Rating	Parts	Labor
Tube practically burned out.	Check ends of tube for blackening.	Replace tube.	■	$3-10	$20
Ballast connection poor.	Check tube for blackening at one end.	Tighten connections or replace ballast.	■ ■ ■	$10-20	$25
Wiring faulty.	Test circuit continuity.	Repair.	■ ■		$20
Starter or ballast defective.	Check tube for light at ends, not center.	Replace starter.	■	$1.50	$20

PROBLEM: Fluorescent lamp fixture hums. ▬▬▬▬▬

Possible Cause	Procedure	Remedy	Rating	Parts	Labor
Ballast overheated.	Check wiring and capacitor.	Repair or replace.	■ ■ ■	$10-20	$25
Ballast incorrect for fixture.	Check label.	Replace ballast.	■ ■ ■	$10-20	$25
Ballast incorrectly installed.	Check all connections.	Tighten.	■		$20
Ballast connections loose.	Check all connections.	Tighten.	■		$20
Ballast old or noisy.	Feel for vibrations.	Tighten connections or replace.	■ ■ ■	$10-20	$25

PROBLEM: Fluorescent lamp flickers, blinks on and off, or light swirls inside tube. ▬▬▬

Possible Cause	Procedure	Remedy	Rating	Parts	Labor
Tube is new.	Keep using fixture.	Problem should disappear after a few hours' use.			
Tube pins not making adequate contact.	Rotate tube, check pins for corrosion.	Clean pins and tighten tube in socket, or replace.	■		$20
Tube burning out.	Check ends of tube for blackening.	Replace.	■	$10-20	$20
Temperature in room too low.	Warm room to minimum of 60°.	Restart lamp or replace with low-temperature unit.			

PROBLEM: Fluorescent lamp flickers, blinks on and off, or light swirls inside tube. *(Continued)* ▬

Possible Cause	Procedure	Remedy	Rating	Parts	Labor
Voltage inadequate.	Check house current.	Wait for full supply.			
Starter defective.	Check socket.	Replace.	■	$1.50	$20
Ballast defective.	Check connections.	Tighten connections or replace.	■ ■ ■	$10-20	$25
Socket loose.	Check.	Tighten.	■		$20

PROBLEM: Fluorescent tube burns out too fast. ▬▬▬

Possible Cause	Procedure	Remedy	Rating	Parts	Labor
Light turned on and off too frequently.	Try to avoid frequent use of switch.	Replace tube or entire fixture with rapid-start or instant-start type.	■ ■	$10-50	$20
Starter faulty.	Check.	Replace.	■	$1.50	$20
Ballast faulty.	Check.	Replace.	■ ■ ■	$10-20	$25
Wiring faulty.	Check.	Repair.	■		$20

House Signaling System—Doorbells, Buzzers, or Chimes

A house signaling system operates either doorbells, buzzers, or chimes. The system consists of four components:

- Push button (or buttons)
- Signaling unit—bell, buzzer, or chime
- Transformer
- Wiring—light-gauge (typically No. 18), insulated wire connecting the components.

Although there are dozens of different kinds of bells, buzzers and chimes on the market, they all operate in about the same way. Electricity flowing through a fine coil of wire energizes an electromagnet to pull a clapper. An interrupting contact in bell and buzzer systems causes the clapper to vibrate. In a chimes system, the electromagnet attracts rods that then strike the musical tubes. When the push button is depressed, it completes the circuit between the transformer and the signaling unit.

Transformer

Most home-signaling-system transformers have a capacity of about 5 to 15 volts. They consist of a primary winding coil, which is connected to a 120-volt circuit, and a secondary or low-voltage winding, well insulated from the primary winding.

In a transformer, electricity is transferred from one coil to the other to increase or decrease voltage. Home signaling systems employ step-down transformers: They transform 120 volts into a much lower voltage appropriate for the signaling system. A door-

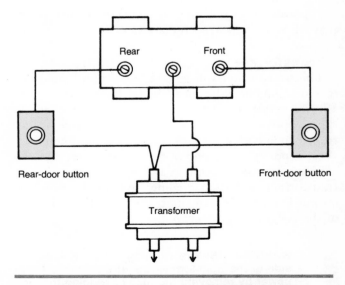

Wiring diagram of a house signaling system

bell or buzzer system requires a 6- to 10-volt transformer. Chimes typically have a transformer of between 15 and 20 volts.

Modern transformers are supplied with a threaded device by which they attach to the knockout opening of a fuse cabinet or junction box. The primary-coil leads (wires) are connected to the house circuit. The secondary-coil leads on the front of the unit connect to the unit's interior wiring.

Repairing a House Signaling System
Push buttons

Trouble in a house signaling system is usually caused by push-button failure. The internal parts of the button, usually made of iron, corrode easily. The metal contacts can be cleaned with fine sandpaper, but generally it is better to install a new button. Make a sketch of how the button is connected to the rest of the system for use in installing the replacement button.

To check whether a button is faulty, disconnect its two terminal wires and touch them together. If this causes the bell to sound, the button is defective and should be replaced. If the bell does not sound, check for a loose connection at the bell. Make sure wires and terminal points are not corroded.

Signaling unit

If the problem has not been corrected, the next step is to see if power is reaching the signaling unit. Use a multimeter (*see page 27*) or hot-line tester (*see page 26*) to check for continuity.

If there is power going to the bell, then the problem is probably mechanical—one or more moving parts are jammed. Try cleaning the unit; if that does not work, it must be replaced.

If power is not reaching the unit, the transformer may be faulty and need replacement.

Transformer

The transformer will generally be found attached to a junction box either near the push button or at the 120-volt service-entry point. First, determine whether there is power at the low-voltage (output) side of the transformer with a continuity tester or multimeter. If there is power at this end of the transformer, there is a break or short circuit in the wiring between the transformer and the signaling unit. (If there is no output from the transformer, then the 120-volt side of the system must be examined.)

WARNING: Before working with the 120-volt side of the transformer, be sure to turn off the power by removing the fuse or tripping the circuit breaker to Off.

Assuming there is power at the transformer, there must be an interruption in the wiring to the signaling unit. Examine all accessible wiring for breaks or worn insulation—if there are any splices, they should be checked very carefully. If no obvious break in the accessible portion of the wiring can be discovered, replace the entire length: Simply disconnect the old wire from the signaling unit and transformer; then tie the new wire to one end and pull it into place with the old one. Be sure that the new wire is the right gauge for the particular system.

NOTE: A bell that will not stop ringing is caused by one of two things: a shorted or faulty push button; or a short in the wiring, between the button and the bell. If the button is not physically stuck, disconnect it from the wiring. If this stops the ringing, the fault is in the push button. If the ringing does not stop, then the wiring must be replaced.

Replacing a Bell or Buzzer with Chimes

If chimes replace a bell or buzzer system, the same wires can be used as long as they are in good condition. However, the transformer must be replaced with one that delivers 15 to 20 volts.

Procedure: Installing a New Signaling System

1. Drill a hole through the door frame for the push button. The hole size will depend on the size of the button.

2. Drill a second hole from the cellar ceiling, and fish the button wires through the two holes. Either separate wires or twin-wire cable may be used, provided all connections are made carefully. If a new system is being installed to replace an old system, use the old wires to pull the new wires through the house.

3. Connect the wire to the two terminals on the back of the button and screw the button to the door frame. Connect the remaining wires.

4. In the cellar, tack the wires to floor or ceiling supports (the places they are usually run) with insulated staples.

NOTE: When setting up a double signaling system, connect the signaling devices to their buttons in series with the transformer.

DOORBELL, BUZZER, OR CHIMES TROUBLESHOOTING

PROBLEM: Doorbell, buzzer, or chimes do not work.

Possible Cause	Procedure	Remedy	Rating	Parts	Labor
No power at source.	Find cause.	Repair.			
	Check fuse or circuit breaker.	Replace fuse or reset circuit breaker.	■	$5	$20
Push button dirty or broken.	Remove from door frame and inspect.	Clean or replace.	■	$1.50	$20
Push button faulty.	Short-circuit terminals by bridging them with screwdriver.	If bell rings, replace push button.	■	$1.50	$20
Wiring loose or faulty.	Check at button, signaling unit, and transformer.	Clean contacts, tighten connections, repair breaks.	■ ■		$25
Sounding mechanism faulty.	Check all connections.	Clean and tighten entire mechanism, or replace.	■ ■		$25
Transformer faulty.	Check for proper voltage rating to handle equipment. (Bells and buzzers require 6-10 volts; chimes need 15-20 volts.)	Replace with properly rated transformer.	■	$6	$20
Interrupter contacts faulty.	Check for corrosion or binding.	Clean with fine sandpaper or bend contact arms to open position.	■		$20
Solenoid core jammed.	Check coil.	Clean and lubricate with silicone spray.	■		$20

PROBLEM: Doorbell, buzzer, or chimes do not stop ringing.

Possible Cause	Procedure	Remedy	Rating	Parts	Labor
Push button short-circuited.	Remove push button from door frame.	Clean contacts or rewire.	■	$1.50	$20
Push button stuck.	Pry button free.	Repair or replace.	■	$1.50	$20

Upgrading Electrical Service

Before upgrading an electrical system, ask the utility company if it can supply more service to the house. The company wants to sell more electricity, but it may not be able to immediately supply more power to the house.

If the utility company can accommodate the house, the next step is to check with the local building administration for the codes and regulations concerning materials that must be used and techniques that must be followed, and to obtain a permit to do the wiring. Many communities allow homeowners to install new wiring up to the distribution box but stipulate that the distribution-box fuses or circuit breakers must be wired by a licensed electrician; others demand that all work be inspected by an authorized expert, such as an insurance underwriter. The only way to learn the local regulations is to ask local authorities. Whether the community requires an inspection or not, having one is a good idea and typically costs only a few dollars.

Planning New Circuits

The ideal arrangement on each floor of a house is to have all of the outlets and light fixtures evenly distributed among 15- or 20-amp circuits, with each circuit serving no more than 400 to 600 square feet of

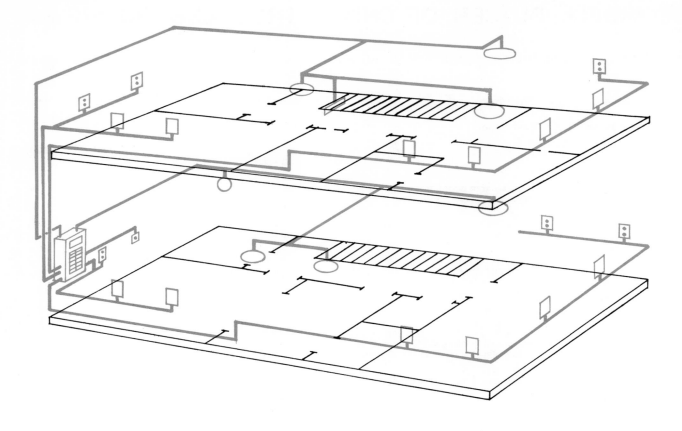

Skeletal view of outlets and light fixtures. The lines represent branch circuits leading back to the distribution box. Each branch circuit is protected by a fuse or circuit breaker in the box.

floor space. When adding new circuits, keep the wall outlets on a separate circuit from the overhead lights. Outlets should be spaced between 7 and 12 feet apart, with no more than seven on one circuit, and each wall should have at least one outlet.

Along with the 15- or 20-amp general-purpose circuits, there should be at least two 20-amp special-appliance circuits in the kitchen for smaller appliances. Rarely will more than two appliances be used simultaneously on the same circuit, so two 20-amp lines should be enough. For safety reasons, these outlets should be located at least 1½ feet away from the sink or other water source. The house will also require separate 20-amp circuits for major appliances and workshop power tools. There should be separate 240-volt circuits for an electric range, air conditioners drawing more than 1,500 watts, a water heater, and other large power users.

If a wiring list (*see page 20*) shows that one or two new circuits (usually for appliances in the kitchen or basement) and a few more outlets throughout the house would be sufficient to meet present needs, it is possible that the house wiring can be upgraded merely by adding a few more circuits to the system.

Installing a New Branch Circuit

When planning any changes, first examine existing equipment. Provided the electrical service entering the house is adequate, an add-on fuse or circuit breaker box can be connected to the system via an unused socket in the distribution box.

Measuring the cable run

Measure carefully from the distribution box to the farthest proposed outlet to determine how much cable will be needed for the new circuit. Figure generously. Local codes and a knowledgeable electrical-supply-store owner can help in deciding the size of cable to use; the variables are the length of the run and the wattage the new circuit will have to carry. The table on page 12 illustrates how to determine the wire gauge needed.

Preparing the cable route

Once the length of the cable run and the wire gauge have been determined, the next step is to cut the hole for the electrical box or boxes.

Tap the wall lightly with a mallet. A solid sound means there is a stud behind; a hollow sound indicates the space between the studs. A good place for an outlet is right next to a stud, for then the electrical box can be attached to it. About 15 inches from the floor is a convenient height for an outlet.

If the box will be placed between studs in a lath-and-plaster wall, chip away the plaster until one complete lath is uncovered. Center the electrical box over the lath and mark the outline of the box on the wall. Chip away the plaster inside the outline with a chisel. The center lath should be cut away; leave the top and bottom laths intact. Be careful not to break these laths, as they will be needed to anchor the box to the wall. If the wall is wallboard, mark the electrical-box outline and cut it out, making sure the hole is no more than ⅛ inch larger than the box. If the box will be fitted against a stud, cut into the wall close to the stud. After exposing the side of the stud, cut the rest of the hole as described above.

Next, determine where the cable will emerge in the basement near the distribution box, and drill a hole for it. If the cable is running from the first floor into the basement, drill at an angle up through the basement ceiling into the inside of the first-floor wall. Often the location of the hole can be measured from a radiator pipe or other fixture.

Running the cable

The next step is to run the cable. If the cable must travel from an upper floor to the basement, it is often easier to start at the outlet or fixture hole rather than at the distribution box, because then gravity helps rather than hinders. Use a snake to fish for the cable. Openings may have to be made in walls to bring the

cable around studs and spacers. These holes will have to be replastered after the cable is in place.

Do not cut the cable from the spool until it has been fished through the walls, in case more cable is needed

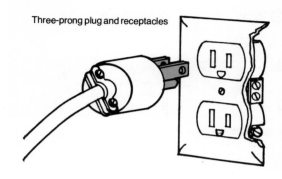

Three-prong plug and receptacles

If an appliance has a three-pronged plug, no adapter is needed. The grounding prong on the plug automatically connects with the grounding terminal of the outlet, if the outlet box is already grounded.

for the run than was originally estimated. If, for some reason, the cable length is insufficient to complete the run, there are two solutions. Either withdraw the cable and start over with a new, longer spool; or cut into the wall and mount a junction box in the cable route to accommodate a splice.

NOTE: All splices must be made inside junction boxes, and all junction boxes should be readily accessible—not hidden behind walls.

Attaching the cable

Once the cable as been run, and before the electrical box is secured to the wall, attach the cable to the box with a clamp. Some boxes come equipped with clamps; clamps can also be purchased separately. Different clamps are required for Romex and BX cable. Be sure to use the proper type. *(See pages 28 - 30.)*

Grounding the circuit

Either at this time or after the electrical box is secured to the wall, the secondary grounding conductor (a green or uninsulated wire) should be attached to the box. Its purpose is to drain off any excess current in the event of a short circuit. Secondary grounding is a critical part of proper electrical installations. *(See page 16.)* There are various techniques for attaching the secondary grounding wire, and particular methods may be dictated by local electrical codes.

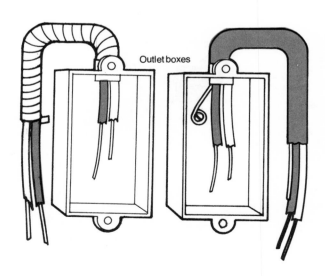

Outlet boxes

Insert BX or nonmetallic-sheathed cable securely into the box before mounting it in place. Be sure to connect the grounding wire.

Procedure: Four Ways to Attach the Secondary Grounding Wire

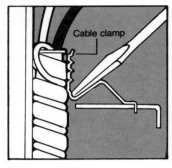

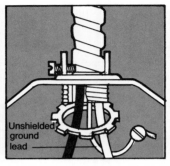

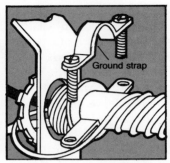

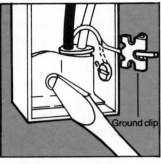

1. Several turns of the secondary grounding wire in a Romex cable can be wrapped around the end of the nonmetallic-sheathed cable so that the wire will fit under the cable clamp in the electrical box. This procedure can also be followed with BX cable, although the metallic sheath of a BX cable itself provides a secondary grounding circuit when it is clamped to the electrical box (as long as the cable is also grounded at the distribution box).

2. The secondary grounding wire can be wrapped around a grounding screw (painted green) in the back of the electrical box. If the box does not have a specific grounding screw, attaching the wire to another unused screw on the electrical box serves the same function.

3. If several cables enter the box, all the secondary ground wires can be twisted and held together by a grounding lug (a metal strap) that is then attached to the back of the box.

4. The secondary grounding wire can be placed in a grounding clip, which is forced over the edge of the box by tapping it lightly with pliers or the handle of a screwdriver. This kind of connection is more easily loosened than the others, and is generally considered the least reliable method of those listed here.

 WARNING: The secondary grounding wire is not designed to carry a circuit load. Make sure it is not attached to and does not touch any circuit terminals.

Installing the electrical box

It is important to attach the box securely so that there will be no movement, which could disturb the internal wiring and possibly lead to a short circuit. A very good arrangement is to mount the box on the side or front of a stud. Use a box with a metal flange, and attach it with nails or sturdy wood screws. If the box is mounted in lath, lighter wood screws can be used to attach it. Check with an electrical supply store for various pieces of hardware to hold an electrical box in a wallboard opening. A common device is a mounting clamp that squeezes the edge of the wallboard as a screw is tightened. Another is a metal strip with tabs that bend over the front edge of the box.

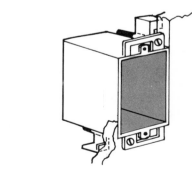

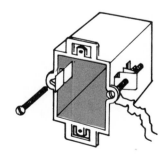

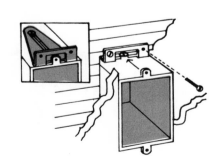

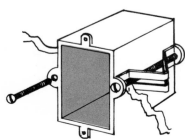

Electrical boxes have screw or nail holes punched out in the back; attachment plates are available for mounting the boxes in all positions. Mount the box by cutting out a suitable space in the wall. Punch out the holes of the electrical box and make all cable connections before mounting it. If the box cannot be supported, use an offset hanger equipped with a mounting stud. Deep or shallow offset hangers can be purchased. The box must be supported rigidly—fasten it to a stud if possible. If too much plaster is accidentally knocked out to make a hole for the box, patch with fresh plaster flush to the sides of the box.

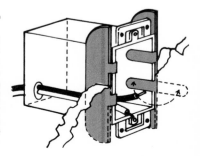

Installing the receptacle

Strip the cable wires. Attach the black wire to the brass-coated terminal and the white wire to the nickel-plated terminal. If it has not already been done, attach the secondary ground wire by one of the methods already described. *(See page 46.)*

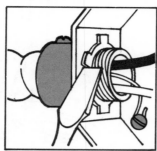

A side screw (*left*) or flanged nut (*right*) can hold BX cable securely. When using the flanged nut, put the screwdriver blade against the flange and then tap the screwdriver with a hammer to force the nut to make a tight fit.

Fold the wires inside the box and push the receptacle component back until it is in place. Attach the component to the front of the box with the two screws provided.

Install the faceplate. If the plate appears crooked, remove it and loosen the screws holding the receptacle to the box. The component must be absolutely vertical for a proper installation. Shift the component as needed, retighten the screws, and replace the faceplate.

Attaching the wires at the distribution box

Before attaching the wires at the distribution box, pull the main switch to Off. When the front panel of the box is removed, the feeder-cable terminals and the various branch circuits are all exposed.

Procedure: Readying Nonmetallic-sheathed Cable for the Receptacle

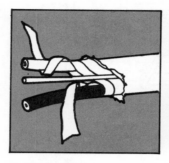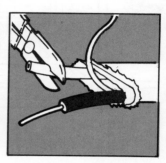

1. Slit the sheath about 6 to 8 inches along the length of the cable by inserting the knife point between the wires. Be careful not to cut into the inner insulation of the wires. Fold back the two halves of the sheath and cut them off.

2. Remove the paper and filler from around the wires. The bare wire is the secondary grounding wire and should not be cut off.

3. Strip about 1 inch of insulation from the ends of the wires. The cable is now ready to be connected.

Procedure: Readying BX Cable for the Receptacle

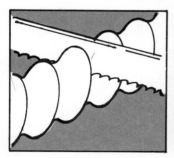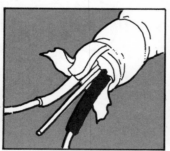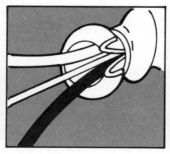

1. Approximately 8 inches from the end of the cable, make a diagonal cut (not parallel with the grooves) on the armor with a fine-toothed hacksaw blade. Rotate the cable while cutting until the armor is completely severed, being careful not to slice into the insulation or wire inside. Twist the armor until it breaks and pull it free.

2. Inside the cable are a bare or green grounding wire, a white wire, a black wire (and, in the case of a three-wire cable, a red wire), all wrapped in brown paper. Unwind the paper and tear it off.

3. Straighten any ragged edges in the armor with pliers. Then place a red fiber bushing around the wires to protect them from the sharp edges of the armor, and jam it inside the end of the armor.

4. Measure off the length of wire needed to make the connection, allowing extra for a generous loop that can be bent around the inside of the box. Strip about ¾ inch of insulation from the end of each wire, without nicking the wire. The cable is now ready to be connected to the receptacle or switch.

NOTE: If an inspector does not find bushing on all cable ends, the job will not be approved.

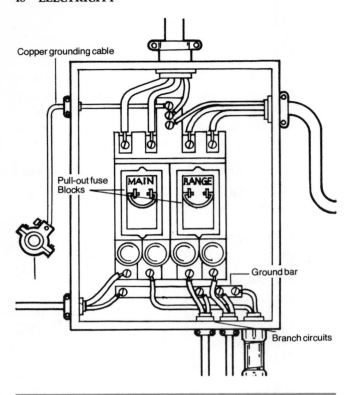

Copper grounding cable

Pull-out fuse Blocks

MAIN

RANGE

Ground bar

Branch circuits

How wires are connected in the distribution box

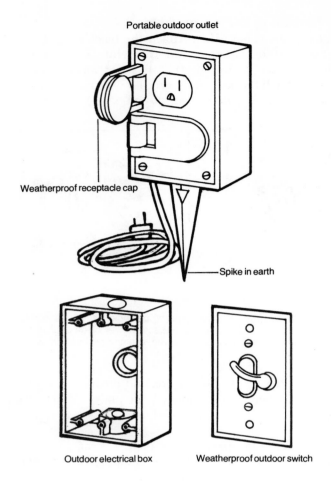

Portable outdoor outlet

Weatherproof receptacle cap

Spike in earth

Outdoor electrical box

Weatherproof outdoor switch

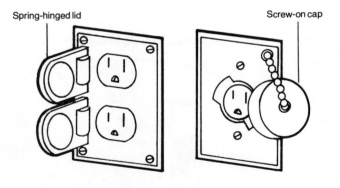

Spring-hinged lid

Screw-on cap

NOTE: This is the only dangerous part of the procedure described for installing a new circuit. It is strongly recommended that the homeowner ask a licensed, experienced electrician to perform the task. The electrician should also be requested to examine the rest of the new wiring job.

Attach the black and white wires to an empty fuse or circuit-breaker terminal set (black to positive, white to neutral). Attach the ground wire to an unused terminal of the ground bar. Then replace the front panel of the distribution box. Turn the main switch on, but before turning on the new circuit, check it carefully with a continuity tester or multimeter. *(See page 26 .)*

WARNING: Even though the main switch is pulled to Off, the feeder wires and the terminals above the switch are live with current. The full electrical service to the house is present in them and represents a potentially deadly shock.

Installing Outdoor Lighting

For outdoor lighting or outlets, the National Electrical Code requires completely different equipment from that used inside the house. For example, it is

Accessories for outdoor electrical installations: an outdoor electrical box; a weatherproof outdoor switch; a receptacle with a spring-hinged lid; a weatherproof outlet with a screw-on cap; and a portable outdoor outlet, which is grounded by a third wire leading to a spike forced into the earth.

dangerous (and illegal in most communities) to use BX cable outside. Cable used outdoors should be no lighter than No. 12 gauge and approved for outdoor use by the NEC. Special weatherproof receptacles and switches must be used outdoors. The receptacles have screw-on caps or spring-loaded covers to protect them from exposure to weather conditions. The switches

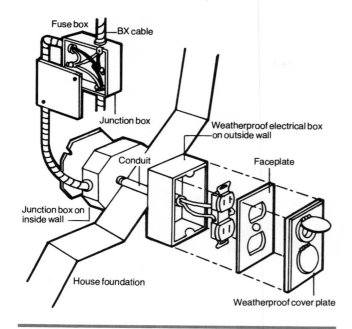

Installing an outdoor receptacle

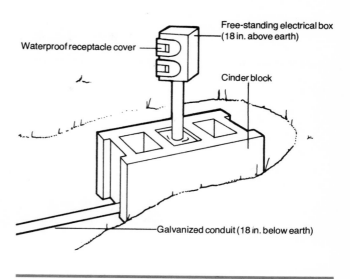

A freestanding, waterproof outdoor receptacle. The receptacle is attached to a vertical piece of conduit. The conduit is positioned in the opening of a cinder block, which is then filled with concrete.

are encased in soft rubber. Outlet boxes are watertight and must be installed with a rubber gasket or caulking to prevent water from touching the wires. The NEC requires the use of a ground-fault current interrupter for outdoor wiring (*see page 19*).

NOTE: Any tools or appliances plugged into an outdoor receptacle should be the grounded or double-insulated type. (The latter uses the equipment's plastic housing as an insulator; it has two prongs.)

Running the cable

Running cable outside is easier than snaking it through a wall, but it still requires some hard work. The cable can be buried as shallowly as 6 inches, but only if it is protected by a heavy cover so that a garden tool churning the earth could not damage it. Otherwise, cable should be buried a minimum of 18 inches below the surface of the earth. The cable should be routed through galvanized conduit.

All boxes and fixtures should be at least 18 inches above the earth. One way to secure freestanding

boxes is to route the conduit to which they are attached through a concrete foundation buried 18 inches below the earth. A cinder block filled with mortar will serve as the foundation.

WARNING: Before connecting the outdoor wiring to the inside distribution box, be absolutely certain that all the wiring is complete and all connections have been properly made and tested.

Connecting outdoor fixtures

When the outdoor receptacles, switches, and lights have been planned and installed, their wires should be brought to the house distribution box on a separate circuit. The outdoor wires should come together in an exterior weatherproof junction box attached to the house at least 18 inches above the earth; from there they should be run through the outside wall via a conduit that enters a junction box on the inside of the house. The inside junction box must be controlled by a switch inside the house. A cable from the distribution box supplies the power.

APPLIANCES

Essentials of Home Appliances

Small Appliances

Television

Large Appliances

Essentials of Home Appliances

4

Appliances have much in common. The basic design of a particular appliance is similar from model to model, and from manufacturer to manufacturer. For example, most have an On/Off switch; many have a motor, a solenoid, a timer, a heating element, or a thermostat. Thus, a homeowner repairing an appliance encounters problems common to appliance repair in general: where to buy parts, how to disassemble the unit, and how to check it for electrical and mechanical malfunctions.

Using Manuals, Warranties, and Parts Lists

When an appliance is purchased, a warranty and an owner's manual are included. The warranty spells out to what extent the manufacturer is responsible for the product. A typical warranty includes a promise to replace defective materials and to correct poor workmanship for one year from purchase. Certain parts may be guaranteed for a longer time. For example, an air conditioner may have a ninety-day general warranty, but its compressor system may be guaranteed for five years. To put the warranty into effect, the purchaser must answer some questions on the card and mail it to the manufacturer.

The owner's manual tells how to have the appliance repaired while under warranty. The manual may also have a parts list, which is useful if the appliance needs repair after the warranty has expired. Even more useful is a service manual, which usually can be purchased from the manufacturer; it spells out in great detail how to troubleshoot the appliance.

Buying Parts

When an appliance breaks down and a hard-to-get part is needed, contact the manufacturer. The manufacturer should be able to mail the part or tell you where it can be purchased. Identify the appliance by model number and serial number.

Disassembly and Reassembly— General Remarks

Don't start by taking the appliance apart. Non-operation does not always mean repair is needed. Check first: Did a fuse blow? If the appliance relies on water, are the faucets to the supply line open? Is the power cord seated and undamaged?

If these steps do not help, it may be necessary to investigate further. Allow plenty of time, and do not expect to do the work as quickly as a professional. If special tools will ease the job, buy them. Most home appliances are not difficult to repair with the right tools and parts, but they will certainly *seem* complicated when first opened up.

WARNING: Before beginning a disassembly, disconnect the appliance from its power source. If the appliance has a capacitor (as on a capacitor-start motor in an air conditioner), discharge the capacitor by shorting the terminals with a screwdriver blade or a resistor *(see page 62)*. If the appliance has a heating element, be sure it has cooled.

Disassemble as little of the appliance as possible; every part removed means more work. Note how the parts fit. If a particular assembly looks complicated, make a sketch to show the relationship of one part to another. Label the parts with masking tape. For parts that must align or fit together just so, mark them directly with a pencil to show their position for reassembly. Keep screws, nuts, and washers in a small container, or in separate, labeled containers.

Excessive force should not be used. Make sure that a hidden fastener, which might be the reason parts do not separate, has not escaped notice. If metal parts seem to be "frozen," apply penetrating oil and wait ten minutes before trying again.

To avoid marring finished surfaces, apply tape to pliers and wrenches. If metal and plastic parts have been force-fitted, heat applied judiciously is sometimes helpful. With a soldering iron, warm the metal just enough to make it expand slightly and to soften the plastic a bit. Apply only a little heat at a time. Loosen the two pieces while they are warm.

After a repair has been completed, and before reassembly, check other parts of the appliance. Vacuum the inside carefully. Clean electrical contacts and examine switches. Oil motor bearings and examine motor shafts for looseness and other signs of wear *(see page 63)*. Lubricate other moving parts. Examine wires to make sure insulation is not damaged or frayed; if it is, wrap electrical tape around it. Make sure that wires at terminals are attached firmly. Perform a continuity test on the appliance *(see page 26)*.

Put parts back in reverse order. Do not overtighten screws or nuts. Do not force parts to fit. When replacing a component that moves in normal operation, test it by hand to be sure it is not binding.

After reassembly, turn the appliance on. Be alert for unusual noise, heat, or odor.

Common Parts

Appliance Cords and Plugs

Cords and plugs are a common source of trouble. Inspect them and replace or repair them if they are worn or frayed. Make sure their terminals are tight.

It may be possible to buy a replacement that exactly

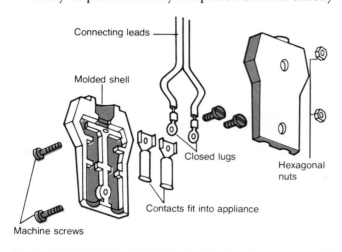

An electric female plug is held together by a pair of machine screws and hex nuts. Wires from the line cord end in closed lugs which are fastened to a pair of contacts that fit into the appliance. This type of female plug is used only in older appliances.

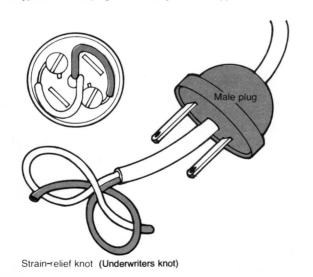

Strain-relief knot (Underwriters knot)

Top view (*left*) and side view (*right*) of a two-prong male plug. Wrap each wire around the holding screw in a clockwise direction. Before making connections, tie the line cord into a strain-relief knot. Always remove the plug from the outlet by pulling on the plastic housing of the plug, not on the connecting wires.

matches the original cord set, although one made up from materials purchased in an electrical supply store will serve just as well. When replacing a cord set, be sure to get wires of the same gauge as the original and with a secondary ground wire if called for. (Replacement and repair of cords and plugs are discussed on page 34 .)

The original equipment cord may have a strain-relief device to protect it from loosening. An Underwriters knot *(see page 34)* is an effective strain relief in a homemade cord set.

Leveling Legs

These are found on many large appliances. The legs are adjustable to compensate for an uneven floor. They are usually threaded shafts with flat heads, about an inch or more in diameter. Many appliances will not operate at their best unless level. A washing machine that is not level will wobble and become noisy during its spin-dry cycle.

To set up an appliance correctly, place a carpenter's level on the top of the cabinet, front to back, then side to side, adjusting the legs as needed. To level an oven, place the level on the racks, not on top of the oven. To level an air conditioner, use the carpenter's level side to side and front to back, then give the machine a ¼-inch pitch to the rear; the front should be slightly higher than the back so that condensation drains off outside, not into the room. A refrigerator should also have a slight backward tilt so that the door will swing shut by itself.

Hidden Fasteners

Concealed screws, bolts, or clips often hold the outer shell of an appliance in place. Such fasteners may be hidden under decorative trim, which must be carefully pried up. The service manual will show where they are located. Plastic parts of some appliance housings use a *tab-and-notch* arrangement that can be separated with a screwdriver, but be careful not to use excessive force. *Spring clamps* hold the sheet metal tops of many large appliances, such as washing machines. To release, slide a putty knife under the top and push it against the spring.

Knobs

When an appliance is disassembled, knobs may first have to be removed. There are several ways of fastening knobs to shafts. A common method has a flat section of the shaft matching an opening in the knob. The knob opening may have a small *leaf spring*. When the knob is pushed onto the shaft, the spring retains the knob. Remove the knob by pulling straight off the end of the shaft.

A similar design uses a flat shaft but with a *spring clip* inside the knob. The knob can be removed if the spring clip is depressed with a screwdriver blade.

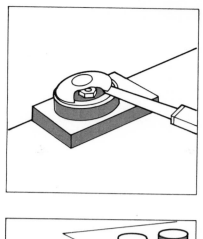
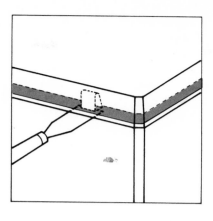
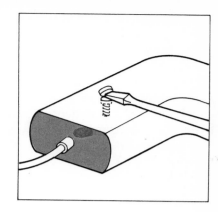
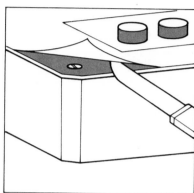
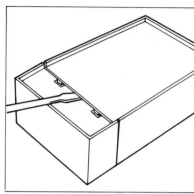
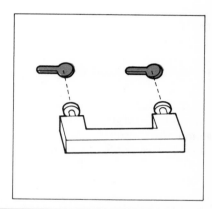

Appliances can have a variety of hidden fasteners which must be located before repair work can be started. An instruction manual, sometimes offered with the appliance, details the location. Here, six pictures show a few of the ways hidden fasteners can be removed. Fasteners are usually force-fit types.

Another type uses a *setscrew.* The hub of the knob has a threaded hole to receive the screw, which may have a slotted head or a recessed hexagonal head requiring an Allen wrench to turn it. The shaft may be flat or have a recess to receive the tip of the screw.

Another system uses a small steel pin—called a *drift pin*—that passes through matching holes in the knob and the shaft, locking knob to shaft. Drift pins can be tapped out with a nail or awl.

If a control turns only clockwise, the knob may be screwed to the shaft. It is removed by turning the knob counterclockwise.

If there is no apparent fastener, but the center of the knob is covered by a metal cap, a retainer may be hidden beneath the cover. Pry the cover off or unscrew it to reveal the fastener.

Wiring Harness

When an appliance has a great many functions to perform during its cycle, each function is served by a separate electrical circuit. In a dishwasher, for example, there are separate circuits for Rinse, Hold, Normal Wash, Pot Wash, Light Wash, Dry, etc. To expedite wiring, the manufacturer uses different colored wires for each circuit and encases them all in a water-proof sleeve. The wires and the sleeve are called a *wiring harness.* The wires leave the harness at various points in order to connect to the parts that perform the functions called for during the operation of the appliance.

If many wires have been badly damaged, the best bet is to replace the entire harness rather than try to replace individual wires. When rewiring, make absolutely certain that each color-coded wire goes to its proper terminal. Work with one wire at a time: Remove one old wire from its terminal and then attach the corresponding wire from the new harness. Quite often the appliance will have a wiring diagram pasted somewhere on the machine (check the back) indicating where wires go and their colors.

Wire Terminals

The wires in an appliance may be fastened by several methods, including the following:

Screw terminal. When the screw is loosened, the wire comes free. A screw terminal may receive either a bare wire or one to which a lug is attached (*see page 25*).

Quick-connect terminal. This is a flat or round metal prong that receives a mating female lug, to which the wire is soldered or crimped. To remove the lug from the terminal, grasp it with pliers and pull gently. Avoid movements that would bend the terminal, because it might break. If a quick-connect terminal breaks on an expensive piece of equipment, such as a compressor, it may be necessary to replace the entire piece of equipment. Therefore, if the lug is frozen on the terminal, cut the wire and splice the new wire to it rather than risk breaking either part. (*See page 24*.)

Self-locking terminal. This accepts a solid wire that is held by a flat spring within the device. Next to the hole that receives the wire is a slot. The blade of a small screwdriver or a straightened paper clip pushes the spring back, releasing the wire so that it can be pulled free. Or there may be a push-button release.

Heating Elements

In heat-producing appliances such as toasters, irons, and broilers, the heating element is a flexible resistance wire or a rigid unit called a Calrod. (Calrod is actually a brand name.) Heating elements have high electrical resistance, which translates into heat when current flows through them.

Resistance wire. This is flat or coiled springlike metal alloy. If a resistance-wire heating element burns out, a temporary repair can be made by crimping a mending sleeve over the two loose ends where the break occurred. As soon as possible, however, the entire element should be replaced, as it will deteriorate rapidly.

It may be possible to get an exact replacement heating element. If not, new resistance wire can be installed. Jot down the wattage and voltage of the appliance (*see page 21*), the length of resistance wire needed, and, with coiled wire, the number of coils per inch, and take a piece of the old wire to the electrical supply store.

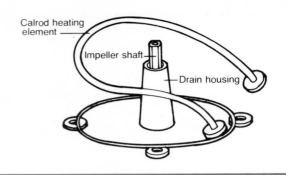

Calrod heating element

Rigid heating element (Calrod). Rigid heating elements are found in ovens, frying pans, dishwashers, and other appliances. The heating element may be an open wire formed into a coil and held in place by porcelain insulators, or it can be enclosed in a metal sheath. (This sheath functions as the heating surface of a burner unit in an electric range.)

Deterioration is more likely to occur at the connecting terminals than in the heating element itself. Calrods rarely burn out, but are easily replaced if they do; they usually have screw-in or plug-in terminals.

Transformers

Transformers increase or decrease the voltage supplied to them and can be used only with alternating current. A step-down transformer is used to lower 120-volt alternating current to about 12 volts to operate chimes or bells. A step-up transformer increases 120 volts to 20,000 volts to power the picture tube in a color TV set.

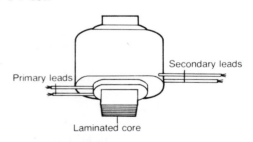

A transformer is a device for stepping voltage up or down. It has no moving parts. Primary wires (leads) connect to the power cord via a switch. Some transformers are encased in metal shells; others are open types. Primary leads are usually color-coded black.

Internally, a transformer consists of two coils of wire wound on iron cores. The *primary* and *secondary windings* are not connected to each other. House current passing through the primary winding creates an electromagnetic field. The secondary winding absorbs the current from the primary winding through induction (*see page 61*).

The ratio of the turns in the secondary winding to the number in the primary winding determines the

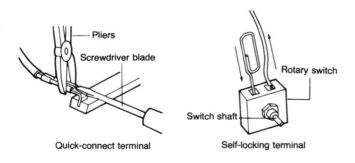

A quick-connect terminal can be removed by tapping with a screwdriver. Do not try to disengage the terminal by pulling on the connecting wire. Instead, grip the terminal with pliers and pull gently; tapping gently with the screwdriver can help *(left)*. Wires are held in position by the spring action in the self-locking terminal. To release the wire, insert the screwdriver blade or opened end of a paper clip *(right)*.

output voltage. If, for example, the wire in the secondary coil is wound around the core twice as many times as in the primary coil, the output voltage will be twice the input voltage.

Damage to a transformer may occur if the current exceeds the amount the transformer is designed to handle. This could happen because of a short circuit in the transformer or in the device it supplies. The heat generated by the excess current can destroy the transformer unless it is protected with a fuse. Damaged transformers should be replaced.

Switches

All switches open and close contacts to complete a circuit. A switch consists of mechanical and electrical elements. Mechanical failure can be determined only by manually working the switch and noting whether the unit makes and breaks its contacts. If the trouble cannot be repaired by bending its contacts, cleaning them, or tightening a terminal screw, replace the switch. If the mechanical parts of a switch prove to be in working order, the switch can be tested for continuity (*see page 26*).

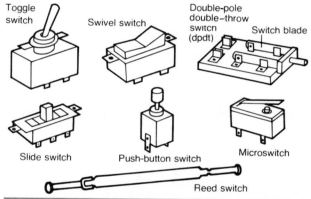

A wide variety of switches is available. Some are built into appliances; others are mounted on the surface panels of equipment.

Centrifugal. The centrifugal switch found in open, air-cooled, split-phase motors consists of a stationary housing and a rotating mechanism. The stationary component is normally attached to an end plate of the motor and has two contacts. When the motor is not running, the contacts are held together by a spring in the rotating (or centrifugal) part of the switch.

To start the split-phase motor, the centrifugal switch makes the connection (or contact) between the starting winding and the power. Then, current flowing through the starting and main windings creates a rotating magnetic field inside the stator. The stator magnetic field passes into the rotor and activates its spinning action. Once the motor has been started, the starting winding is no longer needed. The centrifugal switch, therefore, automatically disconnects it from the circuit: As the motor approaches running speed, the rotating part of the switch is pulled away

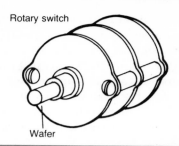

Rotary switch

Wafer

A rotary switch is used to control a number of circuits. The switch may consist of two or more wafers holding the switching elements. Dirty or worn contacts lead to intermittent operation or circuit failure.

from its contacts by centrifugal force, breaking the connection between the starting winding and the power. (*See also pages 62, 64, and 65.*)

Rotary. A rotary switch consists of a shaft, a cam, and flexible metal strips that the cam depresses and releases. Each strip is an electrical contact for a separate circuit. As the shaft is rotated, the cam depresses each strip in turn, closing one contact after another. The number of metal strips in the switch determines the number of circuits the switch can control. Rotary switches are used in dishwashers and clothes washers.

Push button. When the button is depressed, a flexible metal strip is forced against a contact, closing a circuit. Doorbells and chimes are operated by push buttons.

Infinite control (stepless). These are rotary switches without individual stops. The switch can be stopped at any point in its rotation to provide an "infinite" number of control positions.

This kind of switch is often used with a thermostat—for example, to control the oven temperature in an electric range.

Infinite heat control. This form of rotary switch is often used in toasters. The control device is manually pressed against a strip of bimetal, which must then expand to open or close a contact. Alternatively, there can be a resistance coil wrapped around the bimetal that accomplishes the same expanding action. When the control knob is turned, it moves a cam or screw, which bears down on the bimetal strip. Current in the resistance coil makes the bimetal bend to open or close the circuit. The harder the screw presses against the bimetal, the more heat is required to open or close the switch.

Slide control. A slide control is a flat version of the rotary infinite control switch. Like the rotary version, a slide switch often governs a thermostat or rheostat.

Solid state. A solid-state switch is a complicated electronic device that cannot be repaired and must be replaced if it fails. To check, set the voltmeter at its 150−200 AC scale and place the probes on either side of the switch. When the switch is closed, the meter should read between 1 and 2½ volts. If it does not, replace the switch.

Microswitch. A microswitch is a small plastic box containing switches; its shape is often dictated by the design of the apparatus in which it is used. It requires very little pressure to activate it, and almost always is engineered to meet a specific purpose—for example, to stop the spinning action when the lid of a washing machine is opened.

On the face of a microswitch there is an indication of its normal position: NO (normally open) or NC (normally closed).

One or more small buttons with insulated studs protrude from the switch. Each button bends an internal strip of spring metal to open or close a circuit. The button is actuated by levers or rollers on the outside of the switch box. The metal strip has a silver contact at its free end opposite a corresponding silver contact that is in a fixed position. When the button is depressed, it bends the spring until it abruptly snaps to a second position, causing the silver contacts to meet and complete the circuit. If the microswitch controls multiple circuits, there are two terminals for each circuit, and a flexible metal blade that can close or open all contacts at the same time.

Heat from a loose connection will cause the switch to carbonize and short-circuit. This situation usually is accompanied by an odor. When the button is depressed manually, the switch responds with a click as the spring bends. No click means the switch is faulty and must be replaced.

When testing a microswitch for continuity, place the probes on any two of the terminals and depress the button manually.

Microswitches cost between $2 and $6 and can be purchased at appliance and electrical supply stores, but it is best to get an exact replacement from the manufacturer. If that is impossible, take along the old one. Be sure to get a switch that operates the same as the old one (NO or NC) and bears the same markings.

Timers

The timer is the heart of any appliance that cycles, such as a washing machine, clothes dryer, or dishwasher. It is responsible for timing each operation, then shutting itself off when the cycle is completed.

A timer is powered by a small motor which turns a series of cams on a shaft. Each cam is next to a flexible metal contact that faces a stationary contact; as the cams rotate, they apply or remove pressure on the contact arms to open or close the circuits. Some timers have a flat plate on the shaft; notched concentric circles in the face of the plate open and close circuits. All timers have a cam for each function as the appliance goes through its cycle. Cams may have an extra notch to operate two functions at the same time—for example, in a dishwasher, to add fresh water *and* turn on the heating element.

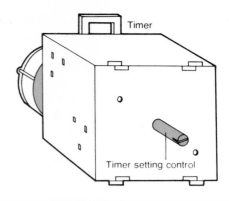

Various types of timers are used. If a timer is defective, it is preferable to replace it rather than open it to make a repair. Timers are often completely sealed; some are equipped with adjustment shafts.

The movement of the timer mechanism is not continuous; the cams rotate in jumps of a few degrees every few seconds. The amount of rotation and the time interval depend upon the timer's design. Rotation is accomplished as the timer motor winds a spring fastened to a trip arm. When the spring is wound, the motor arm trips and releases the spring, which causes the cam to jump forward. This avoids slow opening or closing of contacts that would result in arcing. The final step of the cycle breaks the circuit to the timer motor, and the timer stops.

See timer troubleshooting chart at end of chapter.

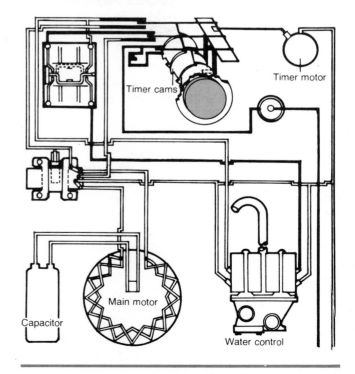

Timer arrangement in a washing machine

Dishwashers may have special cycles built into the timer—for example, Pots and Pans or Rinse and Hold. These can be selected by pushing a button or rotating the dial to the required function. This type of timer has a clutch or ratchet for manual rotation.

Some appliances have a line switch that is controlled by a push/pull dial-and-knob assembly on the appliance control panel. Pushing the dial opens the AC line; pulling the dial closes it. Dishwashers may have the AC line controlled by the lever that locks the door. Opening the door lever turns off the power.

Faulty timers are a common problem, but they can be checked with a multimeter. It is not necessary to remove the timer, but all wires must be removed from the timer terminals (make a sketch and note wire colors or label them before removing them).

To check for continuity, place one probe on the common terminal and touch the other probe to each timer terminal in turn; rotate the timer manually to each succeeding part of the cycle in order to test all terminals, noting when contacts are open and closed. If the contacts are open, the meter will read infinite ohms (needle all the way to the left); if they are closed, the reading should be zero ohms (needle to far right).

Timer cycling charts are usually pasted to the back of the kick plate at the base of the machine, under a lid, or on the back of the appliance.

If a timer is faulty, replace it.

Thermostats

A thermostat is a switch that controls the temperature of a heat-producing or cooling device. There are three types: bimetal-strip, thermodisc, and gas-containing.

Bimetal-strip and gas-containing thermostats usually adjust with a dial. Some can be recalibrated if at fault. The calibration screw is in the center of the dial, probably hidden under a removable cap.

Bimetal-strip thermostats. This switch is made of two strips of different metal alloys bonded together. The two metals have different rates of expansion when heated, and so the bimetal bends as the temperature changes. The bimetal strip is one contact of a switch, and as it bends it opens or closes with another contact.

When this thermostat is governed by an infinite control switch, rotating a knob makes a cam or screw move the strip farther from or closer to the other switch contact, thus requiring more or less heat to close the contacts. These thermostats are used in space heaters, toasters, and air conditioners.

Thermodiscs. These are concave or convex pieces of bimetal, about an inch in diameter, that open or close a contact by "popping" when affected by a change in temperature. Every thermodisc has a critical rating—the temperature at which it snaps on or off. Unlike a bimetal strip, it is not adjustable. Thermodiscs are found in washing machines, dishwashers, and other heat-producing appliances. They are often used as safety switches on motors.

Thermodiscs may be tested for continuity with a multimeter. If they fail, replace them; they cannot be repaired.

A thermodisc may lose its calibration and react to a temperature different from its original rating. The only way to test for this is by observation. Put a ther-

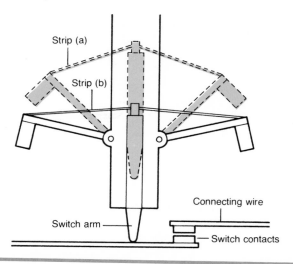

When the strip is cool, it contracts (a), pulling the switch arm up into the containing cylinder. This permits the switch contacts to close, completing a circuit. When the strip becomes hot, it expands and permits the switch arm to move down (b). Pressure of the switch arm pushes against the part holding the switch contact. The switch contacts separate, opening the circuit.

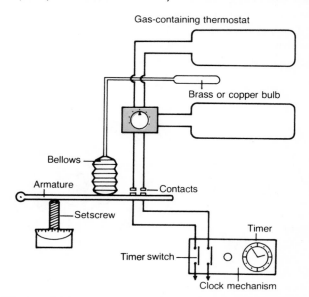

A gas-containing thermostat in a sealed expandable chamber consists of bellows to which a thin tube is attached. The tube ends in a brass or copper bulb. The bulb is filled with gas or liquid. Heat causes expansion of the gas or liquid, pushing the bellows against the armature, separating the switch contacts. The timer switch is controlled by a clock mechanism.

mometer in the same environment and see if the disc responds at the correct temperature. (If the appliance is a dryer, place the thermometer in the exhaust; for a hot-water heater, put it in the stream of water coming from a nearby faucet; for an oven, place the thermometer inside the oven.) If the thermostat does not react when the temperature is within a few degrees of its rating, it is defective and should be replaced.

Gas-containing thermostats. These have a sealed expandable chamber, usually in the form of a bellows, which is fitted with an inert gas. A thin capillary tube is attached to the bellows and has a brass or copper bulb at its other end. The bulb is also filled with gas or with a liquid, such as silicone oil. The contents of the bulb expand and contract in response to heat and cold. This causes a movement of the bellows. The bellows motion then opens or closes electrical contacts.

When the thermostat dial is turned to change the temperature setting, it alters the distance the contacts must move before they can touch.

A leak in the bellows or capillary tube is not a home repair. Remove the unit and take it to a repair shop that specializes in such work. An old thermostat can be rebuilt for about half the price of a new one.

Rheostats

Rheostats control the amount of electricity used by an appliance or a light fixture. They are made of a solid, insulated core wound with coils of uninsulated resistance wires.

Because a rheostat controls the amount of current going to a lamp or motor, it causes a lamp to dim as the knob is turned from high to low, or a motor to slow down. A sliding contact moves along the resistance coil and picks up the flow of electricity at what-

ever point the contact touches the coil. Some rheostats have buttons that are depressed at different points along the coil to make contact and transmit the selected power to the appliance. If the contact is made near the beginning of the rheostat the electricity flows around one or two coils, meeting relatively little resistance. However, if a button at the far end of the rheostat is depressed, the current must flow through more coils and will meet more resistance.

While a rheostat limits the current to an appliance, it does not affect the amount of current used. The extra current is used up in the form of heat.

Each rheostat has a rating stamped on it. The number of turns in the coil and the wire size determine the resistance of the rheostat. When testing for resistance with a multimeter, set the ohms selector at the stated rating. The meter should show increasing

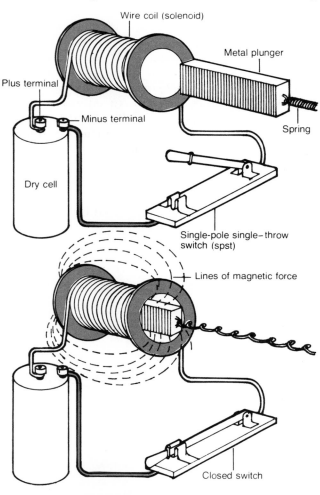

Basic operation of a solenoid. The metal plunger shown here is positioned near the open end of the coil. When the switch is closed, current flows through the coil turns, producing invisible lines of magnetic force around the coil. The coil becomes an electromagnet, pulling the metal plunger into the core of the coil. The plunger will remain in position until the switch is opened. When this is done, the magnetic lines of force disappear, and the spring pulls the metal plunger out of the coil.

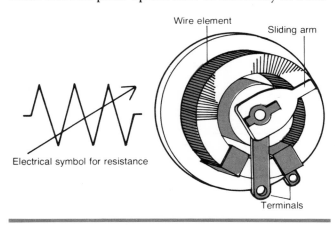

The electrical symbol for fixed resistance and variable resistance *(left)*. A rheostat *(right)* is a variable resistor using a wire element. It is normal for rheostats to become warm while operating. Wires are connected to the terminals and usually soldered into position. The sliding arm is controlled by the knob in front of the rheostat. Misadjustment of the rheostat can cause an appliance to work poorly or not at all.

ohmage as the dial or slide is moved. When the rheostat is at its limit, the meter should read approximately the same number of ohms as the rheostat is rated for. A continuity test can be performed on a rheostat by putting one probe against the middle of the coil and touching the other probe first to one and then to the other contact. The ohmmeter should in each case read about half the resistance of the rating. If there is an incorrect reading or the coil looks burned, replace the rheostat.

Rheostats have now been replaced by solid-state switches in food blenders and electric drills. Some electric mixers are equipped with a mechanical speed governor rather than a rheostat. Both devices produce little heat and are therefore more efficient then a rheostat.

Solenoids

Solenoids are used to operate switches, levers, and valves automatically. A solenoid is a coil of wire wound around a hollow, insulated tube. When an electric current passes through the coil it creates a magnetic field that pulls or repels a plunger—the core—that operates a switch, lever, or valve.

Solenoids can be tested with a continuity checker or a multimeter. Their terminals may corrode—especially on washing machines—and must be

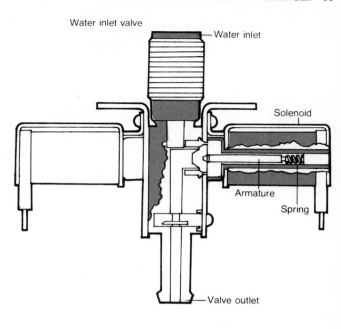

Use of a solenoid in a washing machine

cleaned. If a solenoid gives off a burning odor, it is drawing too much current or is shorted and should be replaced. Excessive moisture can cause it to short.

A loud hum or vibration usually means the plunger is misaligned or the return spring is broken or jammed. The plunger can also become jammed with dirt.

Relays

Relays, like solenoids, are electromagnetic switches. Wire wound around an iron core creates a magnetic field when current passes through it. The magnetic field attracts a steel plate—the laminated armature—carrying contacts that are then pulled open or closed against a fixed contact. Contacts may be of the normally open (NO) or the normally closed (NC) type. Relays are used to switch from one circuit to another (unlike solenoids, which usually open or close single circuits). Relays are commonly used to control motors, although they may be put to other uses.

When testing a relay for continuity, place one probe on the common contact and touch each of the other contacts in turn. Resistance of a closed contact should be zero ohms or barely above. If anything goes wrong with a relay, such as a burned-out coil or burned contacts, replace it. Relays are also subject to mechanical problems, such as misaligned contact plates or a jammed or broken return spring. A misaligned contact plate may be corrected by merely loosening one or two screws and repositioning the plate. Take a broken spring to a hardware store for a replacement.

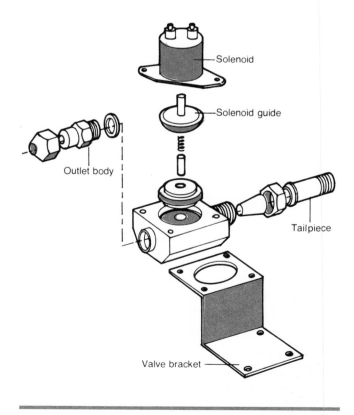

Solenoid used in an appliance. This arrangement shows an exploded view of an inlet valve.

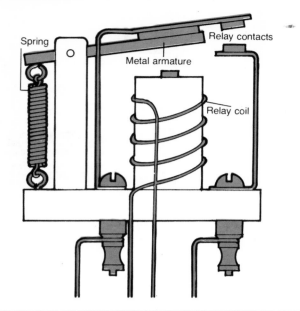

Basic parts of a relay. When current flows through the relay coil, it becomes an electromagnet, attracting the metal armature. This action closes the relay contacts, turning the connected circuit on. With no current moving through the relay coil, the pulling action of the coil stops. The spring pulls on the metal armature, causing the relay contacts to open. This type of relay is known as an NO (normally open) type. Other relays are NC (normally closed). In NC relays, current flowing through the relay separates the relay contacts. The action is opposite that of a NO relay.

Sensors and Responders

A *sensor* is a small disc or tube containing a pair of tiny electrodes. A *responder* is a block of plastic with several terminals that connect it to the switch it governs. Sensors and responders are used in pairs. They operate on self-generated low-voltage current. The sensor reacts to heat and transmits it as electricity to the responder, which in turn opens or closes electrical circuits that control the source of heat. Sensors and responders are used in ovens and clothes dryers to switch off heat when it rises above a preset temperature.

If a sensor fails, the appliance will not work. If the responder fails, the temperature will be too high or the heat will come on very slowly or not at all. Both sensors and responders can be tested for continuity (*see page 26*). The ohmmeter should read zero resistance or barely above with both when they are closed.

Motors

An electric motor converts the electrical energy it receives from a power source into the mechanical energy of its own rotating shaft. The motor does this by taking advantage of the fact that when two magnets are placed near one another they move so that the north pole of one aligns with the south pole of the other.

Every motor contains two magnets, one stationary and one rotating. The stationary magnet is called the *stator;* the rotating magnet is called the *rotor.* If the rotor and the stator were simple electromagnets, they would align with each other and the motor shaft would fix in one position rather than rotate. For the motor to work, the magnetic field or the polar position of one of these magnets has to shift rapidly. *Windings* are the coils of wire wound around the stator or the rotor to electromagnetize it. The winding system, complex in most motors, is what shifts the magnetic field so that the rotor turns.

Basic motor terms

Stator. A stationary magnet, usually an electromagnetic.

Rotor. A rotating magnet.

Armature. A rotor electromagnetized by its own winding circuit. Found in brush motors.

Winding, or coil. The wire wound around the metal core of the rotor or stator to electromagnetize it.

Field winding. The winding of a stator. It provides the electromagnetic field in which the rotor rotates.

Brushes. Electrical contacts, found only in brush motors. Usually they are blocks of carbon held in place by spring clips. Current passes from them to the commutator of a brush motor and then to the armature's windings.

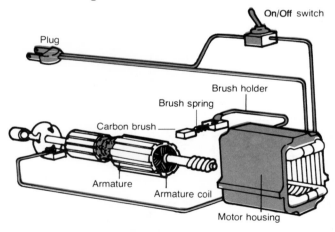

Basic parts of a universal motor

Commutator. A rotating metal cylinder mounted on the armature's shaft; found only in brush motors. It has longitudinal stripes of conductive and nonconductive materials. Mounted in series between the brushes and the armature windings, it switches the windings on and off rapidly.

Shaft. The protruding rotating part of the motor. It is an extension of the rotor.

End plates. The removable part of the motor housing, at either end.

Bearings. Fittings between the shaft and the end plates to reduce friction.

How the brush (universal) motor works

The universal motor is used in many appliances and is one of the easiest to understand. However, it has more parts than do other motors. Its rotor has its own winding circuit and is therefore called an *armature*. Rotating on the same shaft with the armature is a striped cylinder called a *commutator*. Pressing against the commutator on either side are two stationary electrical contacts called *brushes;* these are usually blocks of carbon in spring-loaded holders. House current enters and leaves the motor through wires connected to the brushes.

The commutator is actually a switch. Its longitudinal stripes are alternating bands of conductive and nonconductive materials. There are several windings on the armature, and each conductive stripe of the commutator is wired to one end of a winding. When house current enters through the brush in contact with one stripe of the commutator, it flows through the winding and out through a stripe on the opposite side, which is in contact with the other brush. The armature is momentarily electromagnetized and rotates to align with the stator's electromagnet. But this rotation also causes the commutator to rotate. The first winding is switched off and another winding is activated. This new winding is located a few degrees away from the first on the rotation circle, so that the armature's polar alignment is again different from the stator's, and the rotation continues.

Universal motors are medium-sized, relatively powerful, and versatile. They can run on either AC or DC, and they can reverse direction. Universal motors are found primarily in appliances with medium power needs, such as sewing machines, mixers, vacuum cleaners, and drills.

For maintenance and repair of universal motors and induction motors (below), see page 63 and the troubleshooting charts at the end of the chapter.

How the brushless (induction) motor works

The induction motor, though it operates on much the same principle of one magnet attempting to catch up and align with another, is of much simpler construction than the universal motor. There are no armature, commutator, and brushes in an induction motor. The rotor is a solid core spinning inside the hollow stator. There are windings only on the stator; however, in most types of induction motors the stator's windings are made up of a number of coils distributed around the cylindrical circumference (somewhat like the coils in the armature of a brush motor). When current enters the winding, it passes from one coil to another and so creates a magnetic field that, in effect, rotates inside the stator.

How does the rotor become magnetized? Merely by its close proximity to the stator. This process is called *induction:* electrical current in the form of magnetism

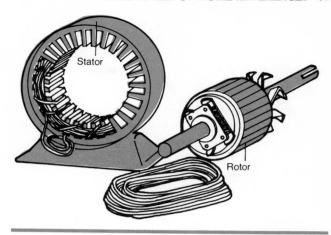

In an induction motor, the rotor fits inside the stator. Magnetic fields surrounding the rotor and stator produce the turning motion of the rotor.

passes from one conductor into another, even though they are not wired together. Transformers also operate by induction, to step up or step down voltage (*see page 54*).

Although the rotor becomes magnetized, there is a momentary time lag that prevents its magnetic field from ever being quite in alignment with the stator's, and so it rotates in an attempt to catch up.

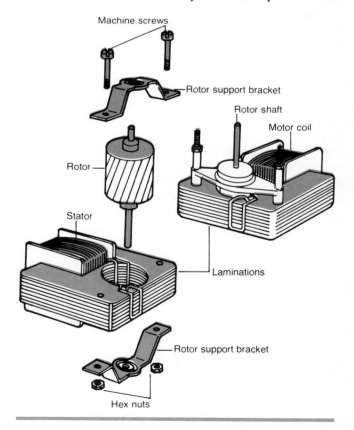

A shaded-pole motor. The rotor is held in position by a pair of rotor support brackets and a pair of machine screws. The shading coil is a single turn of heavy copper wire.

There are many variations upon the basic induction motor design. The principal types of induction motors in the home are the *split-phase, capacitor-start,* and *shaded-pole.* A *repulsion-induction* motor is a combination of a brush and induction motor.

Shaded-pole motor

The shaded-pole motor is the simplest form of induction motor. Rather than having several windings all around the stator, there is only one winding, along one side of the stator. The shading poles are two sets of thick copper wires looped at opposite points on the stator. Through induction (*see page 61*) they pick up current from the coil and create supplementary magnetic fields that simulate the rotating magnetic field effect in more elaborate induction motors.

Shaded-pole motors are very small, have low torque, and can be used only in small, low-power appliances, such as small fans, movie projectors, and electric toothbrushes. The shaded-pole motor is inexpensive to manufacture and runs trouble-free for the most part. If it malfunctions, it should be replaced.

Synchronous motor

A synchronous motor is one that keeps perfect or near-perfect rotation speed because the speed is synchronized with the cycles of alternating current. The term refers primarily to shaded-pole motors found in electric clocks, timers, tape recorders, and other devices requiring constant perfect motor speed.

Split-phase motor

The split-phase motor is the type of induction motor most commonly found in home appliances that require a fairly powerful motor, such as washing machines, compressors, clothes dryers, and table saws. Around the stator there are two sets of windings (two circuits). When the motor is first started, both the *main running winding* and the *starting winding* are activated, but after the motor reaches approximately 75 percent of its running speed, the supplementary starting winding is switched off and the motor runs with only its main winding.

If a split-phase motor hums but does not turn over,

switch off the motor immediately or the main winding may burn out.

Capacitor-start motor

The capacitor-start motor is a split-phase motor with a capacitor wired into the starting winding circuit. The capacitor builds up a high charge of voltage and then releases it in sudden spurts. This provides extra power to the starting windings and gives the split-phase motor higher starting torque (turning force).

As in other split-phase motors, the starting windings are turned off when the motor reaches about three-quarters of its running speed.

Testing a capacitor. If the capacitor has malfunctioned, the motor may hum but not start up, or it may start up very gradually. Immediately turn the motor off to avoid damage to the windings.

In testing a capacitor, handle it with extreme care, as it continues to hold an electrical charge long after the appliance is turned off. To discharge a capacitor, place the blade of a large screwdriver across its two terminals.

Capacitors can be tested with an ohmmeter. The ohmmeter should be set at a range where the highest ohmage is greater than the resistance rating printed on the capacitor. Place one probe on each terminal of the capacitor. The needle should move to a low ohmage reading and then *gradually* move up the scale toward the rating of the capacitor. It may take several minutes for the ohmmeter needle to climb the scale. A reading of *steady* high ohms indicates an open circuit. If the needle stays at the far end of the scale (low ohmage), the capacitor is short-circuited.

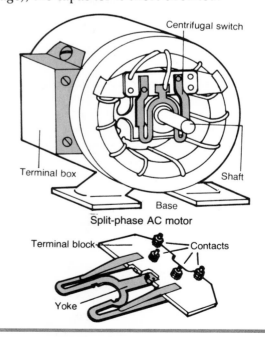

Split-phase AC motor

Detail of a centrifugal switch in an AC motor

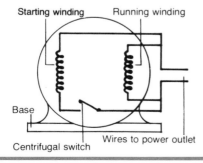

Electrical circuit diagram of a centrifugal switch

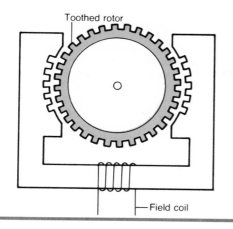

The toothed type of rotor for a synchronous self-starting motor. When current flows through the field coil (stator), it becomes an electromagnet.

To troubleshoot electric motors found in appliances, use the charts at the end of the chapter.

Maintenance and Repair of Motors

Similar procedures keep the components of different electric motors in safe, optimal working condition. To prevent overheating, never overload a motor or operate it while it is wet. Vacuum the ventilation slits in the frame to keep them free from obstruction. Lubricate bearings with two or three drops of light oil; too much oil causes grime and lint buildup inside.

If a motor labors, check the horsepower rating on the data plate to see if the motor can deliver the power required for the job. After disconnecting the motor from its power source, check the end plates to see if they are cracked, loose, or out of alignment. Examine the motor shaft. Is it bent? Is the rotor obstructed by anything? If the shaft has play, the bearings are worn and need replacing. Turn the shaft by hand. If it will not move, it may be fused at one or both ends to the bearing socket. If it turns with difficulty, the bearings probably need lubrication.

If the motor gives no response when switched on, turn off the power, then perform continuity checks on the power cord, the plug, the On/Off switch, and the power supply. Check the windings. Any loose wires or breaks? Examine the insulation—if part of a winding is blackened, it is burned out. To test for a short in a winding, perform a continuity test between one end of each winding and the core around which it is coiled, and between the end of the winding and the motor case. If there is no short the ohms reading should be infinity or close to it (needle at far left). If a short circuit exists, replace the motor. It pays to rewind only large motors—above 3 horsepower.

Universal motor. Normal maintenance is occasional *light* oiling (a drop or two) on the bearings and replacement of brushes when they have worn down.

The brushes—small, rectangular blocks of carbon—are easy to check. Each brush should move freely in its holder; the spring should push it firmly against the commutator. When a brush wears to less than a half inch in length, or if it barely touches the commutator, it will cause excessive sparking and must be replaced. To clean or replace a brush, unscrew the brass or plastic insulating cap that fastens it to the holder.

Excessive sparking can wear away the surface of the commutator. If the surface is rough or dirty, sand it down with a fine sandpaper. An old toothbrush dipped in solvent will remove the dirt between the segments. If mica strips separate the segments, see if the mica projects above the segments. If it does, pare it down with a knife.

A continuity test with an ohmmeter can be performed on the brushes to make sure they are making good contact. To test the commutator with an ohmmeter, set the meter at Rx1 and hold the probes to adjacent bars on the commutator. Each adjacent pair of bars should be tested, and each set should show approximately the same reading.

Motor Protection

Because motors can be overloaded—too much of a load in the clothes washer, for example—motor-protection devices are often incorporated as part of the motor. There are two types in use—those that operate on a temperature rise and those that work on a magnetic principle.

Thermal relay. One kind consists of a bimetallic strip. When the motor runs too hot, the strip bends and opens the circuit, preventing damage to the motor. The motor must be given a chance to cool down before restarting; two or three minutes is generally enough.

Fusible-alloy relay. This type of motor-protecting device is often part of a motor starting switch. It depends on the melting of a low-temperature alloy. When the temperature reaches a certain point, a trigger is tripped which mechanically trips the switch to the motor. To reset the tripping mechanism, pull the handle of the switch down. This resets the switch. Then push the handle up to restart the motor.

Motor-mounted relay. This type of thermal-overload relay is mounted on or inside the motor and is actuated by the heat generated within the motor. It uses a small disc, concave in shape, which snaps to convex when subjected to excessive heat and opens the electrical contacts to the motor.

Magnetic relay. This type of motor-protecting device is similar to a circuit breaker. When too much current passes to the motor—due to an overload—the magnetic pull is enough to trip the relay and open the circuit. Its chief advantage is that it acts instantaneously—there is no waiting for the motor to overheat.

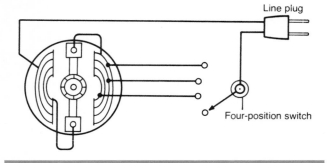

The tapped type of motor speed control. The speed is adjusted when the switch is moved from one position to another.

Motor Speed Control

Most speed-control devices work by varying the magnetism produced by the motor's windings.

Tapped-field. The tapped-field control is found in blenders, mixers, and variable-speed drills. Turning the speed-control knob of the motor "taps" the stator's winding at different points to include more or less of it in the winding circuit. The more wire that is used, the greater its resistance and the slower the motor will turn.

Rheostat. Rheostats can be used to reduce the current to a motor, thus reducing the magnetism in the coils (see page 58).

Rectifier (diode). Rectifiers permit current to pass in only one direction. Since alternating current changes direction 120 times per second, placing a diode in the circuit reduces the voltage by half as it passes current only one way.

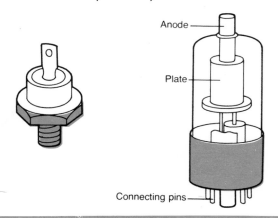

Types of rectifiers. Solid state (left) and tube (right). The solid-state type is replacing the tube because it is more efficient, dependable, and requires less room.

The switch in a rectifier speed control can be easily checked. Set the ohmmeter at Rx100. Place the probes across the diode and note the meter reading. Then reverse the probes for a second reading; one should be under 100 ohms and the other over 1,000. If both readings are about the same, the diode is defective.

NOTE: Diodes are extremely delicate. When testing a diode, disconnect one end from the circuit so that other components will not produce a false reading. To disconnect a diode, heat the soldered connection with a soldering iron for a few seconds, just enough to melt the solder and free the diode.

Because of their directional quality, diodes must be properly placed in the circuit. Be sure to note the position of the old diode before disconnecting it.

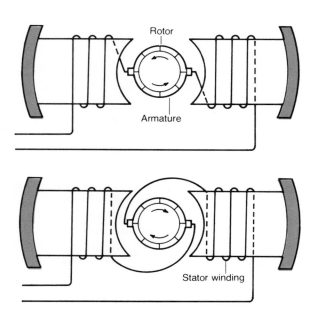

When the leads to the brushes of a universal motor are reversed, the rotor turns in the opposite direction. In this motor, the current that flows through the field windings also passes through the rotor coil. This can be done by a reversing switch on the motor or on the appliance.

Centrifugal governor. Some appliances use a centrifugal governor, which is similar to a centrifugal switch (see page 55) but mounted on the motor shaft. As the hinged part of the switch moves, it drives a pin into a variable resistor circuit. The farther the pin is driven, the more resistor in the circuit and the slower the motor will run.

If the centrifugal governor is not working, examine the electrical contacts for pitting or fusing.

If a centrifugal switch functions intermittently, the switch contacts may be dirty. Another possibility is a loose motor shaft that does not allow contact to be made. Jiggle the shaft. If it is loose, insert a washer over the motor shaft so that it presses against the end plate.

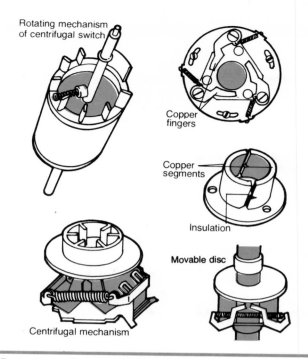

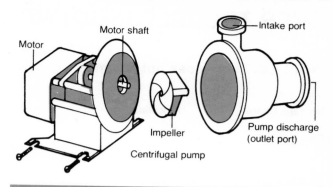

Parts of a pump. Water is pulled in by the impeller and then forced out of the outlet port.

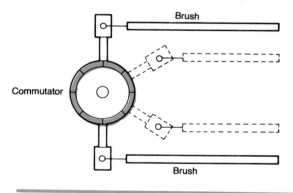

Parts of a centrifugal switch. A centrifugal switch is often used to start a split-phase AC motor. As the motor speed increases, weights move down on the motor shaft, taking the movable disc with them. This action opens the switch contacts.

Movable brushes. On some appliances equipped with universal motors, speed is controlled by mechanically moving the brushes that contact the commutator. As the brushes lift away from the commutator, electrical contact diminishes, and the motor slows down.

Movable brush control. To decrease the speed, the brushes are moved away from the center position on the commutator. This type of motor speed control is used on older appliances.

Pumps

The body of a centrifugal pump has an intake and an outlet port. Inside the housing is an impeller, or fan, connected to a shaft. The shaft, supported by bearings, passes through a seal in the casing of the pump and connects to a motor, either directly or by a belt and pulley driven by the motor. When water enters the intake port, the rotation of the impeller (dri-

ven by the motor) pushes it to the outlet port. Hoses are clamped to the ports to carry the liquid to and from the pump. Hose clamps may loosen; retighten them to prevent leaks. The pump impeller may break or become clogged. The bearings on the impeller drive shaft must be lubricated. If neglected to the point where they seize, they will have to be replaced. Gaskets and seals can dry out, crack, and allow leaks to start; if this happens, replace them. If corrosion has affected the housing itself badly enough, the entire pump will have to be replaced.

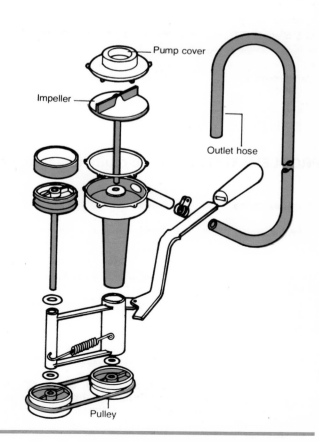

Pump used in a washing machine

TIMER TROUBLESHOOTING

PROBLEM: Timer does not advance.

Possible Cause	Procedure	Remedy	Rating	Parts	Labor
Camshaft bound.	Remove timer assembly.	Lubricate axis points at front and back of shaft. If badly worn, replace.	■ ■ ■	$8	$25
Cam gear loose or stripped.	Tighten peened end. If necessary, place gear in vise and repeen.	If teeth are broken, replace timer.	■ ■ ■	$40+	$25
Gear box jammed.	Clean and lubricate.	If teeth are missing on any gears, replace box.	■ ■ ■	$15	$25
Timer motor faulty.	Test circuit continuity of motor.	If no continuity, replace motor.	■	$12	$25
Timer motor control faulty.	Test circuit continuity of switch.	If no continuity, replace switch.	■	$6	$25

PROBLEM: Timer skips cycles.

Possible Cause	Procedure	Remedy	Rating	Parts	Labor
Contacts burned or worn.	Clean and adjust contacts. Check that burning is not caused by any component connected to timer.	Replace timer if necessary	■ ■ ■	$40+	$25
Cam broken or chipped.	Remove timer assembly and inspect.	Replace camshaft if necessary.	■ ■ ■	$8	$25

PROBLEM: Timer causes circuits to act intermittently.

Possible Cause	Procedure	Remedy	Rating	Parts	Labor
Contacts dirty.	Remove timer assembly and inspect.	Clean and tighten contacts. Replace timer if contacts are broken.	■ ■ ■	$40+	$25
Contact bar rivets faulty.	Remove timer assembly and inspect.	If loose, tighten contact bar.	■ ■ ■		$25

NOTE: Timers can be rebuilt. Check the local telephone directory or authorized service center for timer rebuilding shops. The cost of rebuilding depends on the malfunction and complexity of the timer.

To troubleshoot cordless appliance motors, see Chapter 8, *Introduction to Outdoor Equipment.*

CAPACITOR-START MOTOR TROUBLESHOOTING

PROBLEM: Motor does not start.

Possible Cause	Procedure	Remedy	Rating	Parts	Labor
No power reaching unit.	Check for power at outlet. Check fuse or circuit breaker.	Replace fuse or reset circuit breaker.	■	$8	$20
	Check motor overload device.	Reset; replace if defective.	■	$6	$20
	Check for loose motor terminals.	Tighten loose terminals. Replace burned terminals.	■	$2-10	$25
Plug disconnected.	Check.	Reseat plug in outlet.			
Cord set faulty.	Check cord and plug for continuity. Check for broken or worn wires and loose terminals. Check cord connection at motor.	Repair or replace cord set.	■	$5-8	$25
Bearings bound.	Rotate armature to see if bearings are dry or bound.	Lubricate bound bearings. Replace worn bearings.	■ ■	$5-10	$25
Cut-out switch faulty.	Check for proper contact between parts. Stationary and moving parts must meet when motor is not running for it to be able to start.	Adjust moving part of switch for firmer contact. Clean dirty or sticking contacts. Replace switch if contacts are stripped, pitted, broken, or burned.	■ ■ ■	$3-10	$25
Open circuit in main windings.	Test circuit continuity of windings.	If no continuity, replace windings.	■ ■ ■	$5-20	$30
Open circuit in starting windings.	Connect test lamp to black lead in capacitor and other capacitor lead. Close starting switch. If lamp lights, starting windings are all right.	If starting windings are open, locate opening and repair break. If windings are burned, replace.	■ ■ ■	$5-20	$25
Capacitor faulty.	Discharge and check capacitor (see page 62).	If resistance is low, replace capacitor.	■ ■ ■	$5-10	$25

PROBLEM: Motor hums but does not operate.

Possible Cause	Procedure	Remedy	Rating	Parts	Labor
Capacitor faulty.	Test circuit resistance.	If resisitance is low, replace capacitor.	■ ■ ■	$5-10	$25
Open circuit in starting windings.	Connect test lamp to black lead in capacitor and other capacitor lead. Close starting switch. If lamp lights, starting windings are all right.	If starting windings are open, locate opening and repair break. If windings are burned, replace.	■ ■ ■	$5-20	$25
External overload.	Disconnect belt and see if motor runs.	If motor runs, reduce load and restart motor.			

(Continued on next page)

PROBLEM: Motor smokes. *(Continued from preceding page)*

Possible Cause	Procedure	Remedy	Rating	Parts	Labor
Short circuit in windings.	Open the motor and check continuity of windings.	If no continuity, replace both windings.	■ ■ ■	$5-20	$30
Cut-out switch faulty.	Check for proper contact between stationary and moving parts. Parts must meet when motor is not running for it to be able to start.	Adjust moving part of switch for firmer contact. Clean dirty or sticking contacts. Replace switch if contacts are stripped, pitted, broken, or burned.	■ ■ ■	$3-10	$25
Bearings bound.	Rotate rotor by hand to see if bearings are bound.	Lubricate bound bearings. Replace worn bearings.	■ ■ ■	$5-10	$25
Excessive moisture causing short circuit.	Unplug appliance.	Let motor dry or apply heat. Reinsulate if necessary.	■	$3	$25

FOR OTHER PROBLEMS, REFER TO SPLIT-PHASE MOTOR TROUBLESHOOTING CHART.

SHADED-POLE MOTOR TROUBLESHOOTING

PROBLEM: Motor does not start.

Possible Cause	Procedure	Remedy	Rating	Parts	Labor
No power reaching unit.	Check for power at outlet. Check motor and house fuse or circuit breaker.	Replace fuse or reset circuit breaker.	■	$8	$20
	Check for loose motor terminals.	Tighten loose terminals. Replace burned terminals.	■ ■	$5	$25
Plug disconnected.	Check.	Reseat plug in outlet.			
Cord set defective.	Check cord and plug for continuity. Check for loose terminals or broken or worn wires. Check cord connection at motor.	Repair or replace cord set.	■	$5-8	$25
On/Off switch faulty.	Test switch for circuit continuity.	Repair or replace switch.	■ ■ ■	$5	$10
Bearings bound or worn.	Open up motor and rotate rotor shaft to check bearings.	Lubricate bound bearings. Replace if worn.	■ ■ ■	$5-10	$25
Rotor shaft does not turn.	Open up motor and rotate shaft.	Clean shaft; replace if badly worn.	■ ■ ■	$15	$25
Opening in field coil.	Test circuit continuity of coil.	If no continuity, replace coil.	■ ■ ■	$5-10	$25

PROBLEM: Motor overheats.

Possible Cause	Procedure	Remedy	Rating	Parts	Labor
External overload.	Check the unit being driven.	Reduce load and restart motor.	■		
Bearings bound.	Open up motor and rotate rotor shaft.	Lubricate bound bearings. Replace worn bearings.	■ ■ ■	$5-10	$25
Field coil short-circuited.	Test circuit continuity of coil.	If no continuity, replace coil.	■ ■ ■	$5-10	$25

PROBLEM: Motor has poor torque.

Possible Cause	Procedure	Remedy	Rating	Parts	Labor
Power supply poor.	Test with multimeter.	If current supply insufficient, replace line cord.	■ ■ ■	$5-8	$25
Field coil short-circuited.	Check for smoking. Test circuit continuity of coil.	If smoking is evident or test shows no continuity, replace coil.	■ ■ ■	$5-10	$25
Bearings bound.	Open up motor and rotate rotor shaft.	Lubricate bound bearings. Replace if worn.	■ ■ ■	$5-10	$25
Rotor shaft worn.	Open up motor and examine shaft.	Clean shaft; replace if badly worn.	■ ■ ■	$15	$25

PROBLEM: Motor vibrates too much or is excessively noisy.

Possible Cause	Procedure	Remedy	Rating	Parts	Labor
Bearings worn.	Open up motor and rotate rotor shaft to check bearings.	Lubricate bound bearings. Replace worn bearings.	■ ■ ■	$5-10	$25
Rotor shaft worn.	Open up motor and examine shaft.	Clean shaft if necessary. Replace if badly worn.	■ ■ ■	$15	$25
Parts loose.	Check for loose mounting bolts, end plates, screws, cooling fan, etc.	Tighten all loose parts and connections. Replace worn or broken parts. Clean entire motor.	■ ■ ■	$5-20	$35

PROBLEM: Motor smokes.

Possible Cause	Procedure	Remedy	Rating	Parts	Labor
Field coil short-circuited.	Test circuit continuity of coil.	If no continuity, replace coil.	■ ■ ■	$5-10	$25
Bearings bound.	Open up motor and rotate shaft.	Lubricate bound bearings. Replace worn bearings.	■ ■ ■	$5-10	$25
Excessive moisture causing short circuit.	Unplug appliance.	Let dry or apply heat. Reinsulate if necessary.	■	$3	$25

SPLIT-PHASE MOTOR TROUBLESHOOTING

PROBLEM: Motor does not start.

Possible Cause	Procedure	Remedy	Rating	Parts	Labor
No power reaching unit.	Check for power at outlet. Check motor and house fuse or circuit breaker.	Replace fuse or reset circuit breaker.	■	$8	$20
	Check motor overload device.	Reset. Replace if defective.	■ ■	$8	$25
	Check for loose motor terminals.	Tighten loose terminals. Replace burned terminals.	■ ■	$5	$25
Plug disconnected.	Check.	Reseat plug in outlet.	■		
Cord set faulty.	Check cord and plug for continuity. Check for loose terminals or broken or worn wires. Check cord connection at motor.	Repair or replace cord set.	■	$5-8	$25
Cut-out switch faulty.	Check for proper contact between parts. Stationary and moving parts must meet when motor is not running for it to be able to start.	Adjust moving part of switch for firmer contact. Clean dirty or sticking contacts. Replace switch if contacts are stripped, broken, pitted, or burned.	■ ■ ■	$8-12	$25
Bearings bound.	Turn rotor by hand to check bearings.	Lubricate bound bearings. Replace worn bearings.	■ ■ ■	$5-10	$25
Field short-circuited	With continuity tester, check for short circuit between windings and motor frame.	If shorted, replace field windings.	■ ■ ■	$10-35	$25
Short circuit in windings.	Check to see if motor draws excessive power, lacks torque, overheats, or hums.	If any of these symptoms is present, there is probably a short circuit in the windings. Replace windings.	■ ■ ■	$10-35	$25
Open circuit in windings	Test both starting and main windings for circuit continuity.	If no continuity, replace windings.	■ ■ ■	$10-35	$25
	Check for loose terminals.	Tighten loose terminals. Replace if burned.	■ ■	$5	$25
Rotor shaft does not turn.	Open up motor. Check to see if motor is dirty.	Use brush or vacuum cleaner to clean motor thoroughly.	■		$10
	Check to see if shaft is worn or bent.	If shaft is worn or bent, replace.	■ ■ ■	$5-15	$25
	Inspect for burrs on rotor or stator.	If burrs are present, remove with a file.	■ ■		$25
	Check for worn bearings.	Replace worn bearings.	■ ■ ■	$5-10	$25

PROBLEM: Motor overheats or does not reach running speed.

Possible Cause	Procedure	Remedy	Rating	Parts	Labor
External overload.	Disconnect belt and see if motor runs.	If motor runs, reduce load and restart motor.	■		

Possible Cause	Procedure	Remedy	Rating	Parts	Labor
Field short-circuited.	With continuity tester, check for short circuit between windings and motor frame.	If shorted, replace field windings.	■ ■ ■	$10-35	$25
Windings short-circuited.	Test both windings for circuit continuity.	If no continuity, replace windings.	■ ■ ■	$10-35	$25
Bearings bound.	Turn rotor by hand to check bearings.	If bearings dry or bound, lubricate. Replace worn bearings.	■ ■ ■	$5-10	$25
Cut-out switch faulty.	Check for proper contact between parts.	Adjust moving part of switch for firmer contact with stationary part. Clean dirty contacts. If parts are stripped, pitted, broken, or burned, replace switch.	■ ■ ■	$8-12	$25

PROBLEM: Motor vibrates too much or is excessively noisy.

Possible Cause	Procedure	Remedy	Rating	Parts	Labor
Bearings worn.	Examine bearings.	If bearings are dry or bound, lubricate. Replace worn bearings.	■ ■ ■	$5-10	$25
Parts loose.	Check for loose mounting bolts, pullys, screws, etc. Check cooling fan (if there is one) and tighten all connections.	Tighten loose parts; replace worn parts. Clean entire motor.	■ ■	$3-12	$25
Pulleys misaligned.	Check.	Realign or replace pulleys.	■ ■	$5-12	$25
Belt worn.	Inspect.	Replace.	■	$3-10	$25
Rotor shaft does not turn.	Open up motor. Check shaft to see if it is bent, worn or unbalanced.	If shaft is damaged, replace.	■ ■ ■	$5-15	$25
	Examine rotor shaft for burrs.	Remove burrs with a file.	■ ■		$25

PROBLEM: Bearings wear excessively.

Possible Cause	Procedure	Remedy	Rating	Parts	Labor
Belt too tight.	Check tension.	Adjust to tension recommended by owner's manual.	■	$3-10	$25
Pulleys out of alignment.	Use straightedge to view alignment.	Realign or replace pulleys.	■ ■	$5-12	$25
Oil dirty or inefficient.	Check bearings for wear. Wash with motor-cleaning solvent.	Use type of oil recommended in owner's manual.	■	$1	$25
Bearings dirty.	Clean thoroughly.	If bearings are worn, replace.	■ ■ ■	$5-10	$25

(Continued on next page)

PROBLEM: Motor smokes. *(Continued from preceeding page)* ▬▬▬▬▬

Possible Cause	Procedure	Remedy	Rating	Parts	Labor
Short circuit in windings.	Open the motor and test circuit continuity of windings.	If no continuity, replace both windings.	■ ■ ■	$10-35	$25
Cut-out switch faulty.	Check for proper contact between stationary and moving parts. Parts must meet when motor is not running for it to be able to start.	Adjust moving part of switch for firmer contact. Clean dirty or sticking contacts. Replace switch if contacts are stripped, pitted, broken, or burned.	■ ■ ■	$8-12	$25
Bearings bound.	Rotate rotor by hand to see if bearings are bound.	Lubricate bound bearings. Replace worn bearings.	■ ■ ■	$5-10	$25
Excessive moisture causing short circuit.	Unplug appliance.	Let motor dry or apply heat. Reinsulate if necessary.	■	$3	$25

UNIVERSAL MOTOR TROUBLESHOOTING ▬▬▬▬

PROBLEM: Motor does not start. ▬▬▬▬▬▬▬

Possible Cause	Procedure	Remedy	Rating	Parts	Labor
No power reaching unit.	Check for power at outlet. Check motor and house fuse or circuit breaker.	Replace fuse or reset circuit breaker.	■	$8	$20
	Check for loose motor terminals.	Tighten loose terminals. Replace burned terminals.	■ ■	$5	$25
Plug disconnected.	Check.	Reseat plug in outlet.	■		
Cord set defective.	Check cord and plug for continuity. Check for loose terminals or broken or worn wires. Check cord connection at motor.	Repair or replace cord set.	■	$5-8	$25
On/Off switch faulty.	Test switch for circuit continuity.	Repair or replace switch.	■ ■ ■	$5	$10
Brushes worn.	Visually check to see if brushes are touching commutator. Check for excessive arcing.	If brushes are worn or there is excessive arcing, replace brushes.	■ ■	$5-10	$15
	If it cannot be ascertained visually if brushes are making proper contact, continuity-test with an ohmmeter.	If resistance is greater than the motor's rating, there is not enough current flowing through the motor. Replace brushes.	■ ■	$5-10	$15
Brushes sticking.	Check brushes and spring tension.	Clean brushes. If worn, replace.	■ ■	$5-10	$15
Bearings bound.	Rotate armature to see if bearings are dry or bound.	Lubricate bound bearings. Replace worn bearings.	■ ■	$5-10	$25
Armature shaft does not turn.	Open up motor and examine armature shaft.	Clean armature shaft. Replace if badly worn.	■ ■ ■	$15	$25
Speed control faulty.	Inspect control for burned, broken, or pitted contacts. Turn control to see if there is speed difference between settings.	Repair or replace if necessary.	■ ■ ■	$5-10	$25

Possible Cause	Procedure	Remedy	Rating	Parts	Labor
Armature windings open or short-circuited.	Open up motor and bar-to-bar-test commutator for defects in armature windings.	Replace armature if windings are faulty.	■ ■ ■	$5-20	$25

PROBLEM: Motor vibrates too much or is excessively noisy.

Possible Cause	Procedure	Remedy	Rating	Parts	Labor
Bearings worn.	Rotate armature shaft to check bearings.	Lubricate bound bearings. Replace worn bearings.	■ ■	$5-10	$25
Armature shaft does not turn.	Open up motor to examine shaft.	Clean shaft if necessary. Replace if badly worn.	■ ■ ■	$15	$25
Parts loose.	Check for loose mounting bolts, screws, etc. Check cooling fan (if there is one) and all connections.	Tighten all loose parts; replace worn or broken parts. Clean entire motor.	■ ■ ■	$5-20	$35

PROBLEM: Motor overheats or smokes.

Possible Cause	Procedure	Remedy	Rating	Parts	Labor
Armature coils short-circuited.	Run motor to see if there is excessive arcing.	If arcing is excessive, replace armature.	■ ■ ■	$5-20	$25
	Open up motor and bar-to-bar-test commutator for defects in armature coils.	If coils are defective, replace armature.	■ ■ ■	$5-20	$25
Field coils (within stator) short-circuited.	Examine field coils.	If coils are black, field is burned. Replace coils.	■ ■ ■	$5-20	$25
Bearings bound.	Rotate armature shaft to see if bearings are bound.	Lubricate bound bearings. Replace bearings if worn.	■ ■	$5-10	$25
External overload.	Check the unit being driven.	Reduce load and restart motor.			
Excessive moisture causing short circuit.	Unplug appliance.	Let motor dry or apply heat. Reinsulate if necessary.	■	$3	$25

PROBLEM: Motor sparks or causes excessive interference to TV set.

Possible Cause	Procedure	Remedy	Rating	Parts	Labor
Armature coils short-circuited.	Run motor to see if there is excessive arcing.	If there is excessive arcing, replace armature.	■ ■ ■	$5-20	$25
	Check for debris or metal particles on commutator bar. Bar-to-bar-test commutator for defects in coils.	Clean commutator bar. Replace armature if coils are defective.	■ ■ ■	$5-20	$25
Field coils short-circuited.	Examine field coils.	If coils are black, field is burned. Replace coils.	■ ■ ■	$5-20	$25
Brushes out of position or worn.	Check condition and position of brushes.	Realign brushes if necessary. Replace if worn.	■ ■ ■	$1-5	$25
Commutator rough.	Examine armature for high mica, pitting, or discoloration of brass bars.	File down mica. Polish commutator bars if pitted. Replace commutator if necessary. Replace armature if bars are loose.	■ ■ ■ ■	Commutators $10-15 Armature $10-15	$25

NOTE: The cost of replacing a motor depends on its size and model. The price of a new motor can vary from $5 to $100.

5

Small Appliances

Blankets/
Heating Pads

Blenders

Can Openers/
Knife Sharpeners

Coffee Makers

Dental Irrigators

Fans

Food Processors

Food Waste Disposers

Frying Pans

Hair Blower/
Stylers

Hair Curling
Wands

Hair Dryers

Heaters

Humidifiers

Irons

Knives

Mixers

Shavers

Slow Cookers

Toasters

Toaster/Broilers

Toothbrushes

Vacuum
Cleaners

Waffle Iron/
Griddles

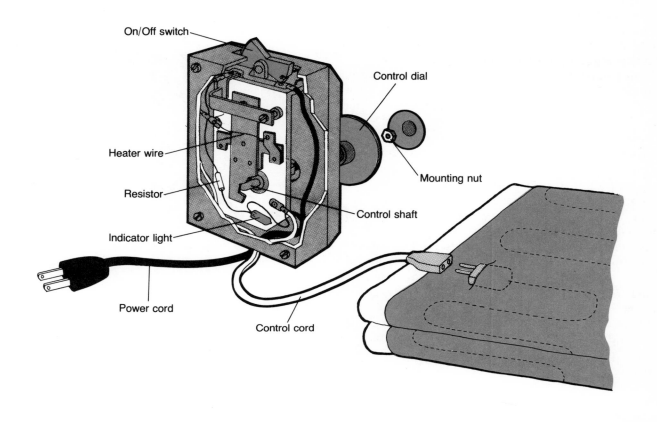

On/Off switch

Control dial

Heater wire

Mounting nut

Resistor

Control shaft

Indicator light

Power cord

Control cord

Electric blanket

Principle of Operation

All electric blankets contain a flexible heating element sewn into the fabric in the form of a grid to distribute heat throughout the blanket. The insulated resistance wires terminate at a male plug that is inserted into the receptacles of a cord leading from the control unit. The control unit contains an adjustable thermostat with an indicator light. It is attached to a cord that is plugged into an outlet.

Current flows into the thermostat control unit when the On/Off switch is closed. The neon lamp lights and the current continues from the thermostat control unit into the heating element. When the heating element attains its preset temperature, contacts in the thermostat open; as cold air in the room cools the blanket, the thermostat contacts close until the heating element again reaches the desired setting.

The thermostat in most electric blankets contains a heater wire that simulates the temperature in the blanket heating element. When the temperature reaches the selected setting, the bimetal strip in the thermostat opens the contacts to both the heating element and the heater wire. Since it is smaller, the heater wire cools faster than the blanket element so the contacts in the thermostat close before there is any appreciable drop in the blanket temperature. There are also one or two small magnets attached to the arm of the thermostat to slow down the return action of the bimetal strip, keeping the heater wire and heating element pretty much in synchronization.

Heating pads function exactly as small electric blankets. Each one contains a simple heating circuit embedded in a fabric pad, a heating element, a safety thermostat, a cord set, a control box with a thermostat, and usually an indicator lamp assembly as well as heat control switches.

Differences in Electric Blankets and Heating Pads

All electric blankets have the same basic design; their differences are in the thermostats controlling them. A blanket for a double, queen-size, or king-size bed may have dual controls. The blanket therefore has two heating systems, each controlled by a separate thermostat. The controls, which are interconnected, contain a thermostat and indicator lamp. Some blankets also incorporate a series of tiny thermostats attached to the heating wires that open their contacts and keep the blanket from overheating if the control malfunctions. These can be felt as small lumps in the fabric.

Several deluxe models, as a safety feature, have an additional temperature-sensitive circuit sewn into the fabric that also controls the heating element. The sensor circuit is made up of two wires separated by a plastic coating that decreases impedance as the temperature in the blanket increases, a double bimetal thermal switch, and two resistors connected in series, one at either end of the thermal switch. When current passes through the sensor wires, unequal amounts of heat are developed in the resistors, forcing a bimetal switch to close the thermal switch contacts. As the bimetal cools, it opens the switch again.

Some older heating pads use a dual heating element with a three-pole switch instead of a control box. One of the elements uses 20 watts of power and the other uses 40 watts. The three-pole selector switch that connects the elements allows the use of either one, or both, elements to provide a low 20 watt, a medium 40 watt, or a high 60 watt temperature.

Disassembly
Electric Blanket

Little can be done to repair a broken heating element in an electric blanket, but repairs on the control unit can be made safely. To disassemble a blanket control unit, unplug the cords from both the blanket and outlet. In most models, the back cover is held in

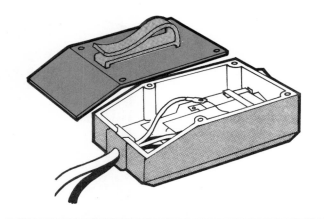

Undo all screws in the bottom of the control unit and separate the housings.

place with setscrews. If the thermostat must be taken out of its housing, lift the control dial off of its shaft. A mounting nut may be hidden under a decal; pry up the decal with a knife blade. Unscrew the mounting screws holding the thermostat in place and pull it from the housing. After the unit is reassembled and the mounting nut is in place, use a drop of any household cement to reglue the decal.

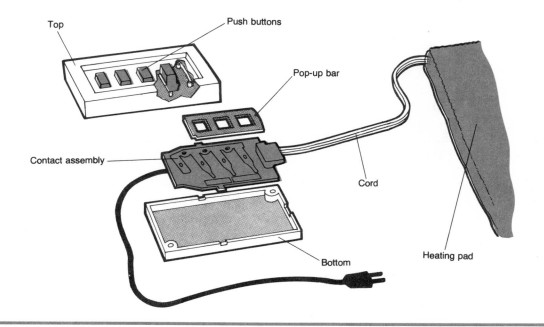

A heating pad and its control unit.

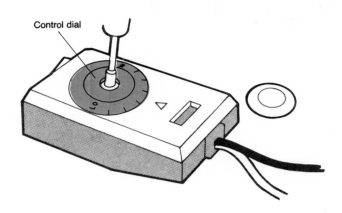

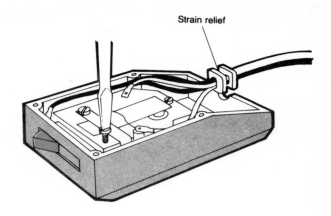

Remove the mounting nut in the center of the control dial. The nut may be hidden under a decal that must be pried up.

The control unit and power cord can be removed once their retaining screws are freed.

The control unit attached to heating pads is taken apart by removing the screws that hold the two halves of the unit together. As the housing is taken apart the contact assembly may spring loose if it is not held in place with the blade of a screwdriver; before removing the contact assembly, carefully note the position of each push button and the pop-up bar.

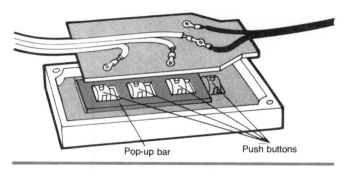

Pop-up bar   Push buttons

Note the exact location of the pop-up bar and the push buttons before removing them from the unit.

Maintenance and Repair

Thermostat Controls. Whenever a control unit is taken apart, examine all of its contacts for defective welds, loose connections, or breaks in any of the wires. For complete information concerning the repair and maintenance of thermostats, *see page 57*.

Whenever a safety thermostat is used in a heating pad, it is normally closed unless there is an excessive current flow into the pad. If the safety thermostat does break the circuit, examine the control unit and the cord set for problems (*see pages 28*).

Heating Elements. To test a blanket for broken wires in the heating element, check for continuity at the blanket plug prongs (*see page 26*). If there is no continuity, replace the blanket; it is nearly impossible to buy blanket repair parts. A replacement blanket can be purchased without buying the controls.

If the blanket shows continuity, the problem is in the thermostat control unit.

Use an ordinary meat thermometer to test a heating pad for correct heat. Fold the pad over the probe of the thermometer, and turn it to its highest setting for twenty minutes. Pads made before 1971 should read about 180°F. All models manufactured after June 1971 should read approximately 155°F. If the temperature is below 155°F., replace the entire unit.

Cord and Plug. The control-cord plug is designed to be inserted in the blanket in only one way, to insure that the unit will always operate properly. For repair and replacement of cords and plugs, *see page 34*.

To guard against shock, protect the blanket or pad from pins and wetness unless the unit is specifically constructed to withstand moisture. Replace a heating pad if its waterproof lining or the seal at the cord entry is damaged.

BLANKET AND HEATING PAD TROUBLESHOOTING

PROBLEM: Blanket or heating pad does not heat.

Possible Cause	Procedure	Remedy	Rating	Parts	Labor
No power at outlet.	Check fuse or circuit breaker.	Replace fuse or reset circuit breaker.			
Plugs disconnected.		Reseat plugs in outlet and in blanket's sockets.			
Cords defective.	Inspect for breaks.	Repair or replace.	■	$8	$25
Heating element defective.	Check circuit continuity with ohmmeter.	Replace blanket.	■	$30	
Switch or thermostat contacts dirty or defective.	Take apart control unit.	Clean all contacts. Replace broken parts.	■ ■ ■ ■ ■	$20	$25

PROBLEM: Blanket or heating pad blows fuse or trips circuit breaker.

Possible Cause	Procedure	Remedy	Rating	Parts	Labor
Circuit overloaded.	Reduce number of appliances on circuit.	Replace fuse or reset circuit breaker.			
Cord, plug, control unit, or blanket short-circuited.	Inspect for breaks. Test control unit for resistance. (If ohm reading is high, unit is not shorted.)	Repair or replace.	■ ■ ■	$15	$20

PROBLEM: Blanket or heating pad shocks user.

Possible Cause	Procedure	Remedy	Rating	Parts	Labor
Cord frayed.	Take apart control unit to remove cord.	Replace.	■ ■ ■	$8	$25
Metal object stuck in blanket.	Inspect for pin, clip, or other metal object.	Remove	■		$10
Plugs in wrong sockets.	Reverse plugs in sockets of dual-control blanket.				

PROBLEM: Blanket or heating pad does not stay at selected temperature.

Possible Cause	Procedure	Remedy	Rating	Parts	Labor
Thermostat faulty.	Test for continuity. (Ohmmeter should jump from high to near zero when control dial is rotated from low to high.)	Repair or replace control unit or thermostat.	■ ■ ■	$20	$10

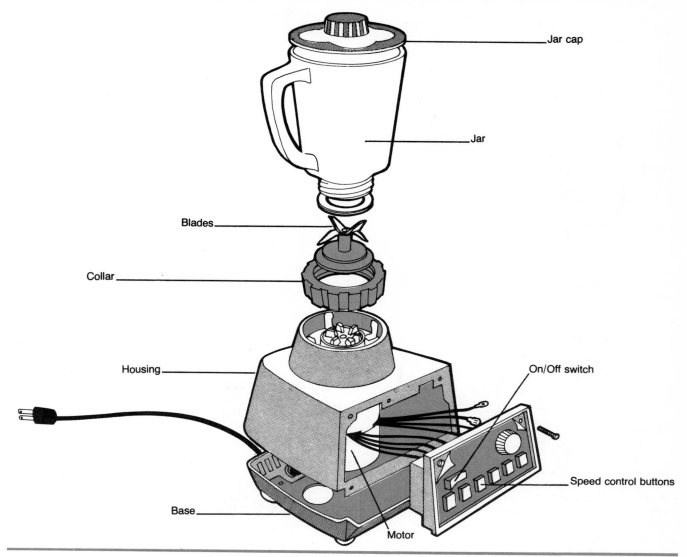

Blenders

Jar cap

Jar

Blades

Collar

Housing

On/Off switch

Speed control buttons

Base

Motor

Multi-speed blender

Principle of Operation

Blenders consist of numerous sharp blades rotating rapidly in the base of a plastic or glass jar. Ingredients are placed in the blender jar from the top, the cover is fitted firmly into place, and the jar is then locked into a recess in the top of the base by rotating about half a turn. The high speed of the blade rotation causes the food to circulate, bringing all of it into contact with the knives.

The base of the blender houses the motor with a speed-selector control on its front panel. The control may be a dial or a series of buttons; some models also have a separate On/Off switch and/or timer. The speed-control switches are positioned directly in front of a rheostat inside the base, which controls the motor speed. The shaft of the universal motor (3200 rpm) protrudes through the top of the base in the center of the recess designed to hold the blender jar. It is notched to lock into a hole in the base of the jar thus linking the motor with the blades. When the blender is turned on, electricity from the cord passes through the speed-selector switch and energizes the motor, which rotates the cutting blades. The blender continues running until either the timer breaks its electrical circuit or the motor is shut off.

Differences in Blenders

The blender jar may be a one-piece unit with the cutting blades sealed in the bottom of its base; or it can be a multiple-piece unit with removable blades assembled inside a plastic housing that screws to the bottom of the jar with a rubber seal keeping it water-tight.

Some models include a 60-second timer that can be set prior to operation to shut off the blender automatically at a specific time. Models without timers run only as long as the speed-control button is depressed manually. Most manufacturers offer accessories for special operations such as chopping fruits and vegetables or crushing ice.

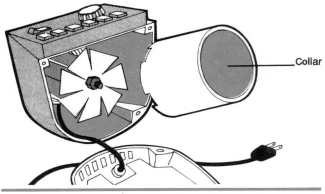

Remove the mounting screws in the base of the machine, and pull out the motor collar.

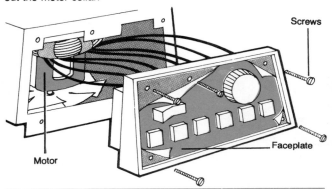

The control faceplate may have set screws hidden under its decorative panel or be held in place by screws reached from inside the base.

Disassembly

Disconnect the blender from its outlet, remove the jar, and turn the base upside down. Remove the setscrews in its bottom and pull off the base plate. There is a protective plastic collar inserted in the base around the motor that can be pulled from the housing by hand or with pliers. In some models, the control plate must also be removed. The faceplate screws are usually hidden at each corner under a thin decorative facing, that can be pried away from the plate with a screwdriver blade. There may also be screws driven into the back of the control plate from inside the housing.

To remove the motor, first disconnect all leads from the control switches. Grip the motor shaft with an adjustable wrench applied to the drive stud at the back of the motor, and unscrew the drive stud by rotating it counterclockwise. Remove the dirt shield, washers, and fan. The motor can now be withdrawn from the housing.

Maintenance and Repair

Blender Jar. The glass or plastic jar is the most easily broken part of a blender. It should be firmly attached to the base before the machine is turned on. The shape of the jar makes it easy to overturn. To eliminate this problem, it is a good idea to hold the jar firmly in place during use.

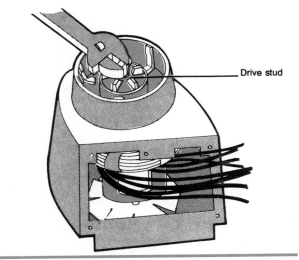

In some models the drive stud may have to be freed with a wrench.

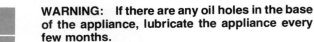

WARNING: If there are any oil holes in the base of the appliance, lubricate the appliance every few months.

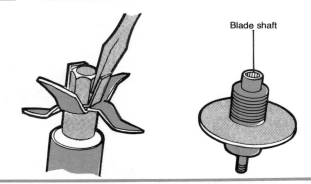

To unjam a jammed blade it may be necessary to put back the metal tabs that hide the assembly nut.

Blade Assembly. Usually when something goes wrong with a blender it is because the blades are not able to turn freely. Always check them first to be sure they are not bent or bound, or in need of sharpening. The blade assembly can be removed for cleaning by unscrewing the nut at the top of the blade shaft. The nut may be covered by metal tabs that must be pried open with the blade of a screwdriver. If the shaft cannot be removed from the plate around it, tap it against a flat surface.

Cord and Plug. The cord must be traced to the brush housings on the motor. The housings are typically held against the motor by a clip that must be pried open to remove the brushes. The motor lead is inserted through slots in the brush housing. See page 28 for testing and repair of cords and plugs.

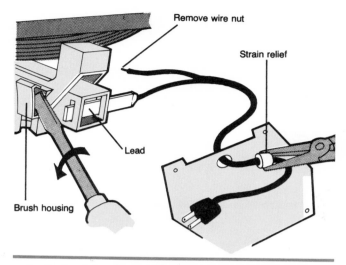

Pry the brush housing retaining clip to face the motor brushes.

Motor. Blenders incorporate universal motors, which means their brushes may have to be replaced from time to time. They usually have a governor attached to them to maintain constant speed at the motor's different settings (*see page 61 and 64*).

Speed Controls. Many of the newer blenders employ solid state rectifiers (diodes) behind each speed-control switch. The diodes rarely cause a problem, but if they malfunction, they must be replaced. If the blender fails to operate at one of its speeds, the trouble could be either the switch or the resistor. With a multimeter set at the Rx1 scale, test the switch for continuity (*see page 26*). If the meter reads zero ohms, the switch is functioning and the resistor can be assumed to be defective. If the switch is faulty, replace it. Resistors are usually soldered in position; break the connections and solder a resistor identical in value in its place. See page 59 for further information concerning switches.

If the switches all operate properly, the problem is an open field winding in the motor. Rheostats and tapped field arrangements are used on older models to control motor speeds. Rheostats are discussed on page 58. Tapped field switching is covered on page 64.

The On/Off and pulse switches used in blenders can be tested by touching a meter probe to each of their leads. Set the meter at Rx1 and push the switch to its "On" position (*see page 26*). The meter should read zero ohms if the switch is functioning. Replace the switch if it is defective.

Timer. Though blender timers are small, they function and are repaired in the same way as larger timers. Because of size, it may be simpler to replace a faulty blender timer than try to repair it (*see page 56*).

WARNING: Always disassemble the blender jar and its components after using, and wash them thoroughly so that no food particles build up (particularly around the blades) and cause the machine to jam. Blender knives are extremely sharp. Handle them with care.

BLENDER TROUBLESHOOTING

Problem: Blender does not start.

Possible Cause	Procedure	Remedy	Rating	Parts	Labor
No power at outlet.	Check fuse or circuit breaker.	Replace fuse or reset circuit breaker.			
Plug disconnected.		Reseat plug in outlet.			
Cord defective.	Check for breaks.	Repair or replace.	■	$3	$10
Controls faulty.	Check circuit continuity with multimeter for each control component.	Replace if defective.	■ ■ ■	$10	$10
	Contacts dirty.	Clean and realign contacts.			
	Check for broken wires.	Repair or replace.	■ ■ ■		$10
Motor shaft bent, bearings bound.	Remove base plate and motor end plates.	Lubricate bearings, replace shaft.	■ ■ ■		$10
Brushes worn.	Check for wear.	Replace.	■	$2	$7.50
Armature worn.	Check for broken or burned windings.	Replace.	■	$15	$7.50
Motor housing cracked.	Take apart, inspect.	Replace.	■ ■ ■ ■ ■	$15	$15

(Continued on next page)

PROBLEM: Blender blows fuse or trips circuit breaker. *(Continued from preceding page)*

Possible Cause	Procedure	Remedy	Rating	Parts	Labor
Circuit overloaded.	Reduce number of appliances on circuit.	Replace fuse or reset circuit breaker.			
Cord or plug short-circuited.	Inspect for breaks.	Repair or replace.	■	$3	$10
Switch or motor short-circuited.	Test circuit continuity.	Repair or replace.	■ ■ ■	$3	$7.50
Speed control short-circuited.	Test for resistance.	Repair or replace.	■ ■	$10	$10

PROBLEM: Blender shocks user.

Possible Cause	Procedure	Remedy	Rating	Parts	Labor
Cord frayed.	Inspect for breaks.	Replace.	■	$3	$5

PROBLEM: Motor operates but blades do not turn.

Possible Cause	Procedure	Remedy	Rating	Parts	Labor
Universal motor defective.	Check.	Repair or replace.	■ ■ ■	$10	$10
Container improperly seated.		Reseat container.			

PROBLEM: Blender does not operate at all speeds.

Possible Cause	Procedure	Remedy	Rating	Parts	Labor
Wiring faulty.	Check circuit continuity with ohmmeter.	Repair	■	$5	$7.50

PROBLEM: Blender is excessively noisy.

Possible Cause	Procedure	Remedy	Rating	Parts	Labor
Fan blades in motor bent or broken.	Check.	Realign blades or replace fan.	■	$2	$7.50
Armature bent or dirty.	Remove from housing to clean.	Replace if bent.	■ ■ ■	$15	$7.50
Loose parts rattling in housing.	Check.	Remove. Repair if necessary.	■		$7.50
Blade and seal assembly faulty.	Examine blade and seal assembly for worn, bent, or broken parts.	Realign or replace blades. If seal is loose replace.	■ ■ ■	$5	$10

Can Openers/Knife Sharpeners

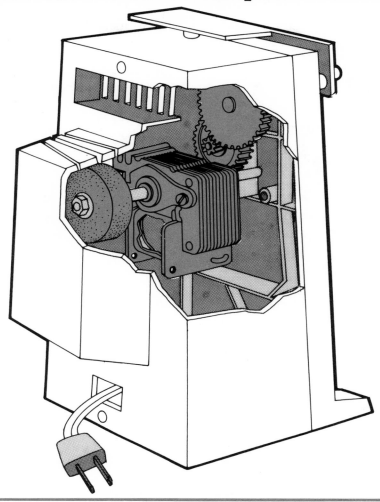

Combination can opener and knife sharpener

Principle of Operation

An unopened can is placed against the feed gear on an electric can opener and pushed upward so that either a cutting blade, or a cutter wheel, is inside the folded lip of the can. The operating level is then depressed to lock the can in place, puncture its top, and activate the motor. The lever pushes against a switch button, which closes the power circuit to the shaded-pole (a brushless, slow-speed motor) or universal motor (*see page 61*) that has a governor-type control gear and drive shaft assembly. The motor activates a pinion gear which turns the main gear and drive shaft assembly that rotates the cutting wheel. Gears are used in the can opener since the shaded-pole motor doesn't supply enough torque, that is, turning power. The arrangement is a reduction gear assembly. This reduces the turning speed of the cutter wheel, but increases its torque. In some openers a belt and chain drive is used instead of gears.

As soon as the lid is completely cut out, it is lifted off the can by a magnet suspended from the operating lever. The lever can then be raised, opening the starter switch and freeing the can. With automatic models, the weight of the can is drawn slightly away from the cutting wheel as the lid is removed, so that a spring-loaded switch can automatically open the circuit to the motor and shut off the appliance.

Differences in Can Openers

Most newer can openers have a grinding wheel for sharpening knives. The sharpener consists of an abrasive wheel driven by the motor. This wheel is accessible through an aperture in the can opener housing. The combination of the shape of the wheel and the angle of the opening in the housing make it easy to apply a knife blade at the proper angle to obtain the best results.

Manual-type openers have an operating lever

To change the belt, first remove the motor and drive wheel.

which is depressed when the can is positioned under the cutting blade. A spring holds the lip of the can against the toothed drive wheel; by applying slightly more pressure on the lever, contacts in the motor switch are closed, allowing the motor to run until the level is manually raised.

Automatic openers operate in the same fashion except that the pressure of the can, when it is pushed sideways against the cutter, locks the can in place and activates the motor until the can is opened. Once the lid is removed the pressure eases, allowing a spring to open the switch contact and shut off the motor. All can openers have a magnet suspended over the lid to lift it free of the can once it has been cut.

Some cans are equipped with aluminum lids and so the magnet will not be able to hold them. To keep

Manual-type can opener.

such lids from falling back into the can after the cutting action is finished, do not open the cover completely. After removing the can bend the cover back and forth a few times and it will separate from the can.

Disassembly

Unplug the can opener and lift the release knob on the front end of the unit; then pull off the cutter assembly. Remove all screws holding the front plate and housing together and pry the front plate away from the housing. Hold the open end of the rotor shaft and remove the feed gear, using pliers. If the

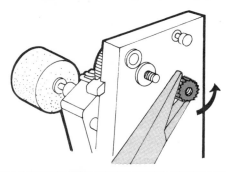

If the unit has a grinding wheel, use it to hold the motor shaft when loosening gear.

appliance is a knife sharpener/can opener combination unit, the grindstone is attached to the open end of the rotor shaft with a C-clamp and makes an easy handle to grip while freeing the gears. Remove all mounting screws or bolts from the motor and lift the motor out of the housing. The gears can be released by freeing the clamps that hold them to their shaft.

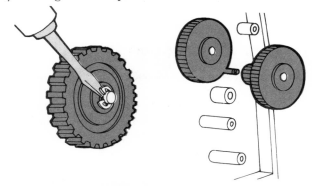

Gears are usually held on their shaft with C-clamps that can be pried open.

Maintenance and Repair

Motors. The universal and shaded-pole motors used in electric can openers usually do not malfunction. However, if the grindstone is used for an extended period of time, the motor may overheat; simply wait 10 or 15 minutes for the motor to cool. If the sharpener is used frequently, open the housing and

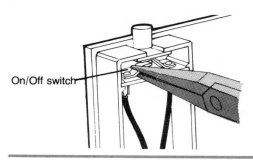

Bend the contact slightly with pliers to make them close properly.

use a vacuum cleaner to remove any metal filings that may have accumulated inside. Filings can build up around the gears and cause a short circuit or damage the motor bearings. For repair of motors, see page 63.

Switches. Can openers use momentary On/Off switches which close to On only as long as the handle is depressed or the weight of the can (on automatic models) is against them. For tests and repair of switches, see page 92.

Gears. Typically, the gears are made of tough nylon but they can still wear down and begin slipping. If one of the gears can be hand held while the other is rotated, the gear teeth are not meshing properly and the gear should be replaced. If the cutting wheel turns unevenly or not at all, the belt is probably worn or broken and must be replaced. To replace the belt it is necessary to open the unit's housing and remove the motor. Then dismantle the drive wheel and pull off the old belt.

The feed gear on the outside of the appliance should be sharp enough to bite into the rim of any can. When the teeth behind the blade become worn, replace the gear, making certain that the teeth slant in the direction that the gear rotates.

Grindstone. The grindstone is attached to the op- posite end of the motor shaft from the opener so that it can rotate at the motor's normal high speed, and is aligned with a slot in the housing through which a knife blade can be pulled. If the stone does not pro- duce clean, sharp edges, it is either dirty and should be cleaned, or it has developed a wobble and must be replaced. Remove the back of the unit and pull off the clamp holding the stone to the motor shaft. Install a new grindstone in its place.

Cutters. There are two types of cutters: wheels and blades. The cutter wheel rotates as it cuts through the top of the can, while the blade (sometimes called a plough) slices its way through the lid. The straight blade is held tightly in place by a bolt; the wheel has a spring behind it wrapped around a bolt. When either a blade or wheel becomes too dull to cut properly, replace it. The cutter assembly is removed simply by undoing the bolt that holds it in place. Be careful to install a new cutter wheel so that its bevelled side faces the opener.

Dirt on the cutter wheel is a common cause of trou- ble. Some of the contents of opened cans spill onto the wheel and form a greasy deposit. It is almost impossible to avoid this.

When the cutting blade becomes greasy, it may slide rather than cut, with the result that only part of the can is opened. If possible, take off the cutter and soak it in a hot detergent solution. Remove the dirt with a small, hard bristle brush, such as a toothbrush. If the dirt has become hard and caked, scrape it away with a knife.

If removing the cutter wheel is difficult, unplug the appliance and apply a detergent solution to the cutter wheel with a toothbrush, scraping it with a knife or a screwdriver blade if necessary.

After cleaning the cutter wheel assembly, lubricate it with a few drops of mineral oil, or lightweight household oil.

CAN OPENER TIPS

Can openers are designed to open cans hav- ing rims. Some cans, such as those used for evaporated or condensed milk, are rimless and cannot be opened by an electric can opener.

If the rim of the can is uneven, or if the can has been made with a heavy vertical seam which ex- tends up into the rim, the can opener may stall. When this happens, help the cutting action by turning the can gently in its direction or rotation.

Cans which have been stored in a freezer should be opened at once. This also applies to cans that have cardboard bodies.

Before using an electric can opener, examine both ends of the can. Open the end that is smooth, round and has no bumps or dents in it. If the can is too tall to fit between the counter and the cutter wheel, move the can opener over to the edge of the counter. Hold the can while it is being opened.

KNIFE SHARPENER TIPS

Make sure the knife is clean and dry before sharpening. A wet or greasy blade can prevent sharpening. Grease transferred to the sharp- ening wheel will reduce friction between knife blade and wheel, hindering sharpening action.

Do not try to sharpen scissors or knife blades that have serrated or wavy edges.

If knife is curved near the end of the blade, tilt the handle of the knife slightly for this portion of the blade.

If the knife grinder stalls, the knife blade is being pressed too hard against the grinder.

If the motor is used for more than five min- utes, it may overheat. Let the motor cool for fif- teen minutes before using grinder again.

WARNINGS: Never immerse an electric can opener in water.

Clean the cutter wheel or blade assembly regularly with hot, soapy water; do not scour with abrasives.

Never open aerosol cans.

Do not allow children to use such appliances except under close, personal supervision.

When not using the can opener, unplug it.

Also remove plug when cleaning or disassembling.

Keep fingers away from cutting wheel or any other moving parts.

Do not remove cord by pulling on the cord. Instead, remove by pulling on the male plug. If either cord or plug is damaged, replace.

Do not use opener to open cans of liquids which are flammable.

CAN OPENER/KNIFE SHARPENER TROUBLESHOOTING

PROBLEM: Can opener/knife sharpener does not start.

Possible Cause	Procedure	Remedy	Rating	Parts	Labor
No power at outlet.	Check fuse or circuit breaker.	Replace fuse or reset circuit breaker.			
Plug disconnected.		Reseat plug in outlet.			
Cord defective.	Check for breaks.	Repair or replace.	■	$3	$5
Switch contacts faulty.	Open appliance and check switch contacts for dirt or corrosion.	Clean or replace.	■ ■	$5	$7.50
Overheat protector tripped.	Turn off appliance.	Wait 10 minutes. and start.			
Brushes worn.	Check for wear.	Replace.	■	$3	$7.50
Gear train or grinding wheel bound.	Inspect grinding wheel and all gears for binding and wear.	Release bound parts. Replace worn gears.	■ ■ ■	$10	$7.50
Motor faulty.	SEE ELECTRIC MOTOR TROUBLESHOOTING CHARTS—CHAPTER 4				

PROBLEM: Can opener blows fuse or trips circuit breaker.

Possible Cause	Procedure	Remedy	Rating	Parts	Labor
Circuit overloaded.	Reduce number of appliances on circuit.	Replace fuse or reset circuit breaker.	■		
Cord, plug or motor short-circuited.	Check for breaks and test circuit continuity.	Repair or replace.	■	$3	$5
Wiring short-circuited.	Inspect visually.	Mend any bare wires with electrical tape.	■		$7.50

PROBLEM: Can opener shocks user.

Possible Cause	Procedure	Remedy	Rating	Parts	Labor
Cord frayed.	Inspect for breaks.	Replace.	■	$3	$5
Case short-circuited.	Test circuit continuity.	Tape or replace all bare wires. Tape terminals.	■		$7.50

PROBLEM: Motor runs continuously.

Possible Cause	Procedure	Remedy	Rating	Parts	Labor
Return spring in switch faulty.	Check for wear or breaks.	Replace.	■	$3	$7.50
Switch contacts not opening.	Check.	Repair or replace.	■	$3	$7.50
Switch short-circuited.	Test circuit continuity.	Replace.	■	$3	$7.50

(Continued on next page)

CAN OPENER/KNIFE SHARPENER *(Continued from preceding page)*

PROBLEM: Motor runs but has no power.

Possible Cause	Procedure	Remedy	Rating	Parts	Labor
Cutter dull or damaged.	Check.	Replace.	■	$2	$5
Drive gear bound.	Inspect. Check alignment of teeth.	Clean and lubricate.	■		$7.50
Brushes worn or windings defective.	Check.	Replace.	■	$2	$7.50

PROBLEM: Cutter does not pierce can lid.

Possible Cause	Procedure	Remedy	Rating	Parts	Labor
Cutter bent or dull.	Check.	Replace.	■	$2	$5
Cutter assembly bound.	Inspect.	Clean and lubricate or replace.	■	$2	$5
Cutter spring faulty or misaligned.	Check for wear and proper alignment.	Repair or replace.			
Clearance between driver and cutter improper.	See owner's manual for proper clearance (between .005 and .012 for wheels and .015 and .030 for blades.)	Clean assembly. Remove feed gear. Add space washers, one at a time to feed gear shaft. Reassemble and test after each addition.	■		$5
Feed gears worn or dirty.	Operate. If feed gear rotates but does not turn can, teeth are either worn or clogged.	Clean or replace.	■	$2	$7.50
Gears stripped.	Inspect.	Replace.	■	$2	$7.50

PROBLEM: Can stalls or does not turn.

Possible Cause	Procedure	Remedy	Rating	Parts	Labor
Cutter assembly clogged.		Clean.	■		$5
Drive wheel bound.	Inspect for damage or wear.	Clean and lubricate or replace.	■	$2	$7.50
Cutter assembly loose.	Check.	Tighten.	■		$5

PROBLEM: Motor runs too fast or too slow.

Possible Cause	Procedure	Remedy	Rating	Parts	Labor
Governor worn.	Check actuator for wear.	Replace or adjust actuator.	■	$3	$7.50
Governor arms misaligned.	Check.	Realign arms or replace.	■	$3	$7.50
Brushes worn.	Check.	Replace.			

PROBLEM: Motor excessively noisy.

Possible Cause	Procedure	Remedy	Rating	Parts	Labor
Field armature misaligned.	SEE ELECTRIC MOTOR TROUBLESHOOTING CHARTS—CHAPTER 4				
Motor needs lubrication.	Check bearings.	Lubricate.	■		$7.50

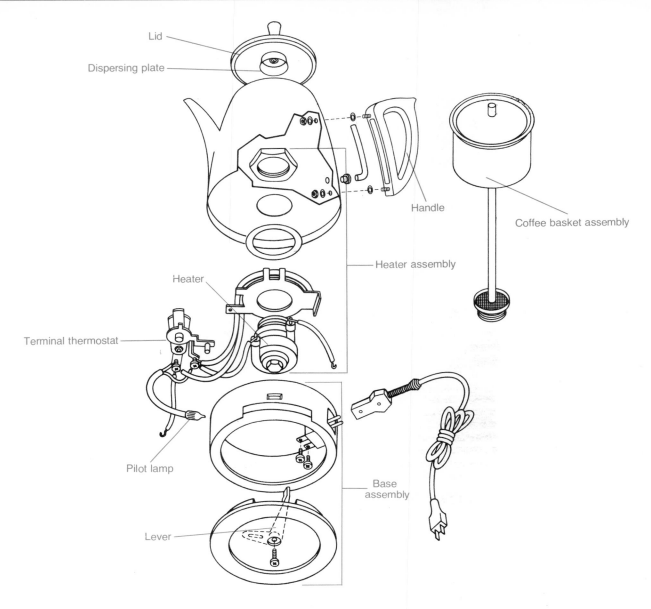

Lid

Dispersing plate

Handle

Coffee basket assembly

Heater assembly

Heater

Terminal thermostat

Pilot lamp

Base
assembly

Lever

Percolator

Principle of Operation

Percolator

Cold water is poured into the pot to a premeasured level, somewhere below the bottom of the basket containing the coffee grounds. A hollow percolating tube supports the coffee basket over the water level. Its base fits into a center recess in the bottom of the pot. The heating chamber is in this recess. When the control level or dial is set for the desired brewing strength, and the percolator is plugged into a wall outlet, a tiny amount of water immediately enters the heating chamber through a small valve. The valve is simply an easily movable flat ring that moves freely in the base of the percolating tube. In appearance it resembles a flat, ring type of washer. Directly above the valve are a pair of plates with holes. Since the chamber is surrounded by the main heating element in the base of the unit, the water boils almost immediately. This pushes the ring valve up, effectively covering the holes in the plate, so that for the moment no more water can enter the well.

With the valve closed, the heated water escapes through the percolator tube to the coffee basket.

Here it seeps through the coffee grounds, then flows back into the water in the pot. As soon as the heated water leaves the heating chamber, the valve opens and more cold water enters the chamber to be boiled.

The liquid in the pot is cycled through the heating chamber several times, until it is hot enough to open the unit's thermostat contacts. Current then ceases to pass into the heating element and the perking cycle ends. Most modern percolators have a dual-temperature-control switch consisting of a bimetal switch and contacts, all of which are wired in parallel to the main heater and a warming element. When the coffee reaches the correct temperature, the bimetal strip opens the heater contact, diverting the current to the warming element. If the percolator has a neon indicator light, it is hooked in series with the warming element and goes on at the same time, indicating the coffee has finished perking. When used it works only as an indicator for the warming circuit, not the main heater. As the coffee cools, the bimetal switch closes its contact to the heater element and the coffee repercolates. However, the thermostat-closing temperature is usually set much lower than the keep-warm temperature, so the coffee must stand for a considerable time before it cools enough to reactivate the heater.

Automatic Drip

Drip coffee makers have a plastic housing containing a metal water chamber connected to the heater chamber via small hoses. A basket containing a paper filter and the coffee grounds is poised over the top of

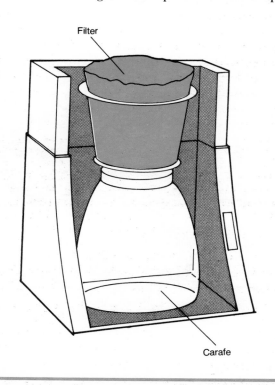

Filter

Carafe

Drip coffee maker (gravity)

a glass carafe, which is placed on a warming plate in the base of the unit. When the appliance is switched on, water feeds down a hose to the heater chamber where it is brought to a boil and immediately forced up a second tube to the spout over the coffee filter. It then drips through the coffee grounds and filter and into the carafe. Once all the water has passed through the heater chamber, a bimetal switch on the thermostat breaks the contact to the main heating element; the warming plate continues to keep the coffee in the carafe warm until the unit is shut off.

Vacuum

To start the brewing cycle, water is placed in the lower bowl and coffee is put in the basket in the top bowl. When the pot is plugged in, current goes into both the main and the keep-warm heater elements positioned in the base of the bottom bowl. With both elements working, the water comes to a boil quickly, and a rubber seal around the spout at the bottom of the top bowl contains the pressure building up in the lower bowl. As the water reaches about 200°F., pressure forces almost all of it up the spout to mix with the coffee grounds in the top bowl. The small amount of water left in the bottom bowl continues boiling, creating steam which agitates the coffee in the upper bowl. When the water has boiled away, the thermostat shuts off the high-heat element and the lower bowl begins to cool, producing a partial vacuum in the lower bowl. This draws the coffee down through the filter and into the lower bowl, where the low-heat element keeps it between 165°F. and 180°F.

Differences in Coffee Makers

There are two basic types of coffee makers in wide use today: percolator and automatic drip. Some vacuum coffee makers are still in use though they are no longer manufactured for domestic use.

Although coffee makers (or brewers) exist in a great variety of external designs, the basic electrical circuitry always includes a heating element and a cord. Most newer coffee makers also include an adjustable thermostatic switch. The thermostat shuts off the heating element when the coffee is fully brewed. Coffee makers may have additional features such as an indicator light and a separate warming element.

Percolator

Percolators are tall metal pots, often urns. The heating element is contained within its own housing in the base of the pot. When small amounts of heated water reach the coffee basket through the tube, they soak into the coffee grounds, become flavored, and then drip through the basket's porous bottom back into the pot. The cycle repeats itself until the desired brew strength is reached. If the percolator is thermostatically controlled, the main heating element shuts

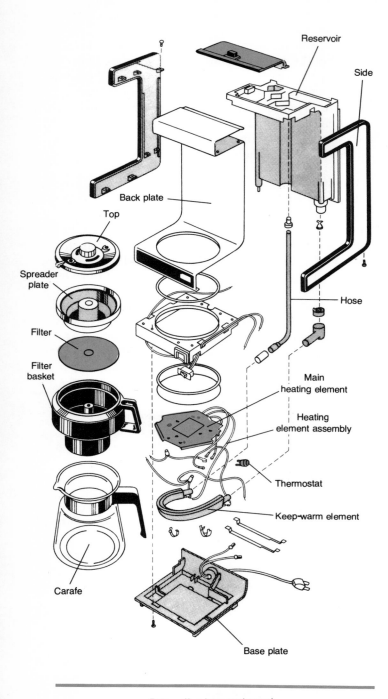

Drip coffee brewer (pump)

Automatic Drip

Automatic drip coffee makers are of two sorts: the percolator type and the flow-through type. Both types have a carafe and a separate plastic housing containing a metal reservoir for the cold water, a heating element, and a thermostat. In the percolator type, the cold water container and heating chamber are both located in the base of the plastic housing. As in an electric percolator, small amounts of water are heated in a heating chamber and then pumped up a percolator tube. The heated water bubbles onto the ground coffee in the filter basket and drips into the carafe below. This system differs from that of an electric percolator in that the water is cycled through the heating system only once.

In the flow-through (drip) model, the water reservoir is in the housing above the filter basket. A heating element may sit beneath the reservoir or the cold water may be fed by gravity through a tube and over a

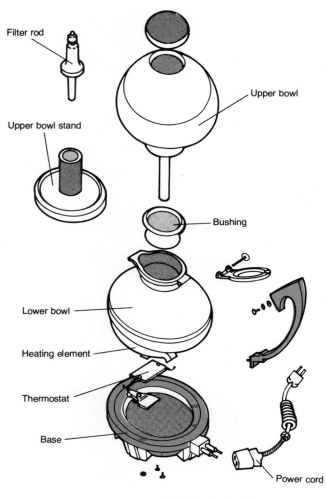

Vacuum coffee maker

off when all the water in the pot has reached the proper temperature. (Thus, strong coffee will be slightly hotter than weak coffee produced by the same pot.)

In the non-automatic percolator, the user must judge when the brewing is completed and unplug the cord from the wall outlet and remove the basket and tube from the pot. To keep the coffee warm, the cord must be plugged back into the outlet.

separate heating element. In either case, the heated water drains over the ground coffee in the filter basket and then into the carafe.

In both the percolator and flow-through types, the carafe sits on a warming element. This may be controlled by the thermostat that governs the main heating element, or it may be controlled by a separate switch.

Vacuum

Vacuum coffee makers consist of two separable glass or metal containers that fit one on top of the other. The top bowl has a spout and rubber bushing extending down from the bottom, and holds the coffee grounds in a basket. The lower bowl has a handle; the heating elements are contained in a separate chamber at its base.

Disassembly

Percolator

All of the electrical elements in percolator-type coffee makers are found in the base of the unit. Turn the appliance upside down and loosen the screw or screws that hold the bottom plate to the housing. The heat-

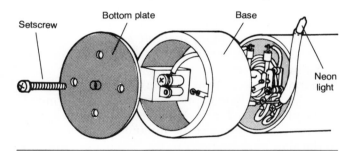

Undo both lead wires attached to the base and disengage the neon bulb from its retaining slot.

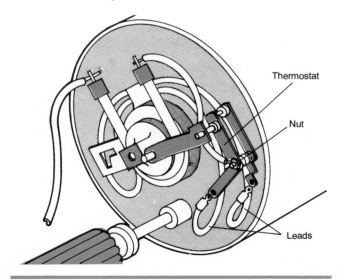

Free all leads from the thermostat terminals and undo the nut holding the thermostat in position. Remove the thermostat.

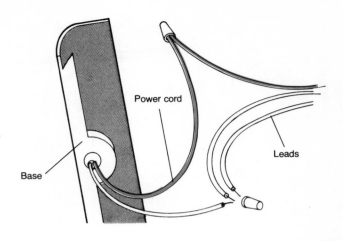

Remove all screws in the base plate and disconnect all wires attached to the power cord.

ing elements, thermostat, indicator lamp, and cord set are attached to the housing or each other in various ways; disassembling them almost always simply requires loosening a screw or small bolt.

Automatic Drip

Pump Type. To disassemble a pump-type coffeemaker, remove all screws in the base plate and lift it off the housing. Undo the wire units holding the leads to the cord so that the base plate can be set aside. The entire heating unit is held in place with spring clips that can be pried open with a screwdriver to free the element. Undo any screws holding the thermostat mount bracket. The heating unit is normally under the thermostat. Disconnect the cord, unplug the elbows, and pull out the tube encasing the element.

Gravity-Feed Type. Unscrew the retaining screws at the bottom of the unit. Remove the center nut holding the bottom plate over the keep-warm element;

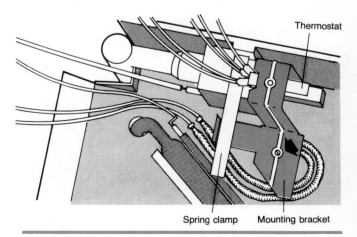

Pry the spring clamp(s) out of their slots to free the heating unit.

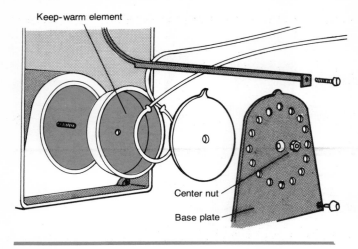

The center nut in the base of the bottom plate holds both the plate and the keep-warm element in place.

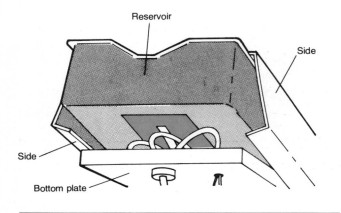

Bend the sides of the top unit outward so that the support plate drops enough to slide the reservoir free.

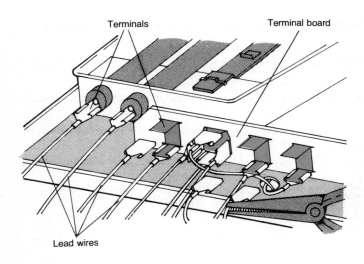

Remove each of the lead wires by gripping the terminal clips with pliers. Label each wire and its corresponding terminal.

take out the screws holding the base to the stand and pry the sides of the stand apart to remove the reservoir. Note where each of the wires connected to the rear terminal board is attached, then remove them. The main heating element and its supporting plate can now be slid up through the top of the stand.

Vacuum Coffeemaker

Detach the two units from one another. Access to the heating element and thermostat is very easy. Simply unscrew the base from the lower container to expose these components.

Maintenance and Repair

Cord and Plug. The easiest way to check the cord and plug is to substitute one from another appliance. Sometimes the defect is visible, so examine the plug and cord carefully. The plug may be cracked or the wire may have separated from it. Or, set a multimeter to read high resistance. Touch the metal tips of the probes against each other and you will see the multimeter pointer swing from the right side of the scale to zero on the left. This indicates that the resistance testing portion of the multimeter is functioning. With the plug inserted in the percolator but not in an outlet, touch the test probes to the terminals of the male plug. No meter reading at all means either the resistance element in the percolator is open or the cord and plug are defective.

Remove the cord from the percolator and connect a small length of bare copper wire across the terminals of the male plug. This is shorting one terminal against the other. Now connect the multimeter metal probes to the plug that connects to the percolator. An indication on the meter means the cord is good and the fault is in the percolator.

Switches. The on-off switch must be replaced by a manufacturer's part if it is faulty. Some drip makers have a two-way switch which can be set for brewing or "warm." Others do not have the "warm" capability. If the switch has three leads, turn it to "on" and clip the multimeter probes to all three wires, letting one probe hold two of the leads at the same time. Set the meter to the Rx1 scale; if it reads zero ohms, the switch is functioning. If the switch must be replaced, squeeze the back of its sides and push it through the hole where it is mounted in the housing. If there is a separate keep-warm switch, disconnect all three of its leads and touch the meter probes to any two of the leads. Set the meter to the Rx1 scale; if it reads higher than zero ohms, the switch is faulty and must be replaced.

Heating Elements. To test the main heating element, the meter is set to the Rx1 scale. Touch the probes to the heating element terminals; also test the terminals on the thermostat. The meter should read between 7 and 15 ohms if the unit is working. If it is broken, replace the entire heating element with a manufacturer's replacement part. The keep-warm element is also tested with the meter set at the Rx1 scale. Remove one lead from the element terminal, then touch the meter probes to the terminals. If the element is working, it will read between 100 and 300 ohms.

Thermostat. This is likely to be in any number of designs. Its function is to control how long the coffee percolates (not more than 20 minutes) and to shut the appropriate heating elements off at the proper time. If the water heats, but the coffee does not percolate, or the coffee is too strong, the thermostat is probably defective. Test the thermostat by unplugging the coffee maker and setting it to "strong." Set a multimeter to the Rx1 scale, and touch the meter probes to the thermostat terminals; if the thermostat is broken, the meter will read more than 50 ohms (*see page 26*).

Neon Bulb. The indicator light is designed to go on when the coffee has finished percolating. If it fails to light, the coffee maker can continue to function properly and replacement of the light is only a matter of user convenience. To replace the bulb, undo its connections to the thermostat. The replacement bulb will be attached to a wire that is connected to the thermostat terminals.

Heating Elements. Set the multimeter to the Rx1 scale and touch its probes to the terminals of the heating element. The main heating element will have a higher resistance reading than the warming element.

WARNINGS: Most percolator pots should not be immersed in water—the base containing the heating element is not encased in a watertight chamber.

Plastic housings can easily be cleaned with a mild solution of baking soda and warm water. See the owner's manual for cleaning instructions; thorough cleaning should be done every month or two.

Coffee stains and mineral deposits from tap water can build up on the inside of the pot. See the owner's manual for proper cleaning procedures.

To properly maintain a percolator, it should be washed and dried thoroughly after each use.

PERCOLATOR TROUBLESHOOTING

PROBLEM: Percolator does not start.

Possible Cause	Procedure	Remedy	Rating	Parts	Labor
No power at outlet.	Check fuse or circuit breaker.	Replace fuse or reset circuit breaker.			
Plug disconnected.		Reseat plug in outlet.			
Cord faulty.	Check for breaks.	Repair or replace.	■	$5	$7.50
Heating element faulty.	Check circuit continuity with ohmmeter.	Replace.	■ ■	$5	$10
Thermostat contacts dirty.	Take apart, inspect.	Clean or replace.	■	$2.50	$7.50

PROBLEM: Percolator blows fuse or trips circuit breaker.

Possible Cause	Procedure	Remedy	Rating	Parts	Labor
Circuit overloaded.	Reduce number of appliances on circuit.	Replace fuse or reset circuit breaker.			
Cord short-circuited.	Inspect for breaks.	Repair or replace.	■	$3	$7.50
Heating element short-circuited.	Check circuit continuity.	Repair or replace.	■ ■	$5	$10

PROBLEM: Percolator shocks user. ━━━━━━━━━━━━━━━━

Possible Cause	Procedure	Remedy	Rating	Parts	Labor
Cord frayed.	Inspect for breaks.	Replace.	■	$3	$7.50
Case short-circuited.	Test circuit continuity.	Repair.	■		$7.50

PROBLEM: Percolator heats but does not percolate. ━━━━━━━━━

Possible Cause	Procedure	Remedy	Rating	Parts	Labor
Thermostat out of calibration.	Test and adjust.	Reset to operate at 175°F.-190°F.	■		$7.50
Thermostat stuck in open position.	Inspect.	Replace.	■	$2.50	$7.50
Valve clogged, bent, or broken.	Check.	Clean, repair, or replace.	■		$7.50

PROBLEM: Coffee boils after it is perked. ━━━━━━━━━━━━

Possible Cause	Procedure	Remedy	Rating	Parts	Labor
Thermostat stuck in closed position.	Inspect.	Replace.	■	$2.50	$7.50

PROBLEM: Coffee does not remain hot. ━━━━━━━━━━━━

Possible Cause	Procedure	Remedy	Rating	Parts	Labor
Warming element defective.	Inspect.	Replace.	■ ■	$5	$10

COFFEE BREWER TROUBLESHOOTING

PROBLEM: Coffee brewer does not start. ━━━━━━━━━━━━

Possible Cause	Procedure	Remedy	Rating	Parts	Labor
No power at outlet.	Check fuse or circuit breaker.	Replace fuse or reset circuit breaker.			
Plug disconnected.		Reseat plug in outlet.			
Cord defective.	Check for breaks.	Repair or replace.	■	$8	$25
Brewing element defective.	Check circuit continuity with ohmmeter.	Replace.	■ ■	$5	$10

(Continued on next page)

COFFEE BREWER TROUBLESHOOTING *(Continued from preceding page)*

PROBLEM: Coffee brewer blows fuse or trips circuit breaker.

Possible Cause	Procedure	Remedy	Rating	Parts	Labor
Circuit overloaded.	Reduce number of appliances on circuit.	Replace fuse or reset circuit breaker.			
Cord or plug short-circuited.	Inspect for breaks.	Repair or replace.	■	$3	$7.50
Heating element short-circuited.	Check circuit continuity.	Repair or replace.	■ ■	$5	$10

PROBLEM: Coffee brewer shocks user.

Possible Cause	Procedure	Remedy	Rating	Parts	Labor
Cord frayed.	Inspect for breaks.	Repair or replace.	■	$3	$7.50
Case short-circuited.	Test circuit continuity.	Repair.	■		$7.50

PROBLEM: Coffee does not return to lower bowl, or it cycles between bowls.

Possible Cause	Procedure	Remedy	Rating	Parts	Labor
Thermostat out of adjustment.	Check.	Readjust or replace.	■		$7.50
Bowls do not fit together properly.	Inspect top bowl and gasket. Flex seat ring for cracks or breaks.	Replace			

PROBLEM: Coffee boils over.

Possible Cause	Procedure	Remedy	Rating	Parts	Labor
Seat ring or gasket faulty.	Inspect.	Replace.	■	$1	$7.50
Thermostat defective.	Check for excessive heat at specific settings.	Repair or replace.	■	$2.50	$7.50
Filter cloth faulty.	Inspect for holes.	Replace.	■	$.50	$7.50
Vacuum leak.	Check for loose handle.	Repair or replace.	■		$7.50

PROBLEM: Coffee drains out of upper bowl too soon.

Possible Cause	Procedure	Remedy	Rating	Parts	Labor
Thermostat out of adjustment.	Check owner's manual for length of time coffee should remain in upper bowl. Adjust thermostat.	Replace if necessary.	■	$2.50	$7.50

Dental Irrigators

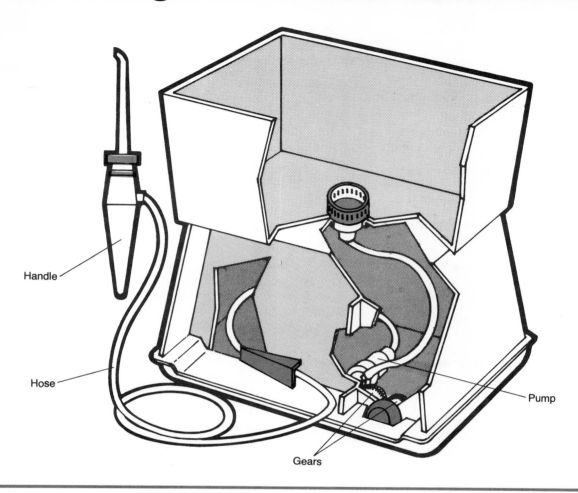

Handle

Hose

Pump

Gears

Dental irrigator

Principle of Operation

A dental irrigator contains a pulsator pump motor, an adjustable valve, a water reservoir, and tubing. The reservoir must first be filled to operate this appliance. Gravity feeds the water through the base of the reservoir to the pulsator pump. The pump forces water through the tubing and the pressure-adjustment valve. This valve may be located in the housing or in the handle.

Differences in Dental Irrigators

Except for the location of the adjustment valve, there are no significant differences in dental irrigators; all of them function in the same manner.

Maintenance and Repair

These are sealed units, and very few repairs can be made on them.

Cord Set. See page 52.

Handle. If the handle breaks, replace it in the following manner.

First, slide the hose fitting out of the handle and down the hose; pull the hose out of the handle. Then slide the hose all the way down into the new handle, and push its fitting over the hose connection.

Finally, run the unit to test the connection.

Tubing. New tubing can be installed in the same manner as the handle is installed. Disconnect the tubing from the appliance handle and from the main housing. Buy replacement tubing of the same interior dimensions as the original tubing from a hardware store. It may be necessary to stretch the end of the tubing with a wedge-shaped tool, such as a ballpoint pen, before fitting it.

WARNING: Do not attempt to disassemble a dental irrigator or any other sealed unit. Do not immerse the unit, even if it is supposed to be waterproof.

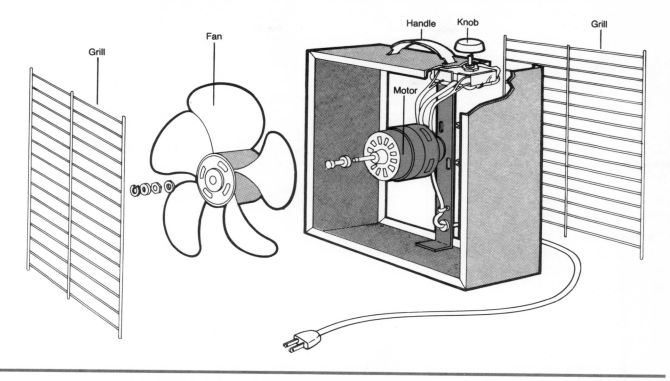

Portable fan

Principle of Operation

When a fan is switched on, current flows into the motor and rotates its shaft. The fan blades, which are either directly attached to the motor shaft or connected to it by a drive belt, immediately begin rotating and will continue turning until the motor is manually shut off. All fans consist of a propeller assembly with two to five blades, a motor, and a selector control switch. But there may also be an oscillating assembly attached to the motor housing that can be engaged to turn the entire assembly back and forth as the blades rotate.

Differences in Fans

Portable fans

Portable fans can be either oscillating or stationary and are mounted on heavy metal bases. They normally have two or three blades connected directly to a shaded-pole motor. The blades are always contained within a protective wire guard, and they are controlled by an On/Off switch, which may offer either a two- or three-speed control.

Floor fans

Floor fans stand on the floor and are movable. Designed for either vertical or horizontal operation, they may have oscillating capabilities.

Window fans

Whether portable or permanently installed, window fans have a reversible feature that allows air to be drawn into, or expelled from, the room they service.

Exhaust fans

Exhaust fans are usually built into the ceilings of kitchens, bathrooms, or laundries, and carry exhaust either directly or through a duct system to the outside. Each consists of a shaded-pole motor and four

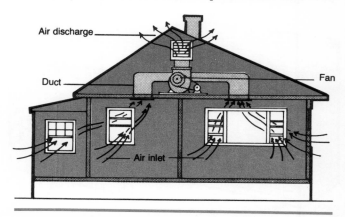

How air flows through a house using an attic fan

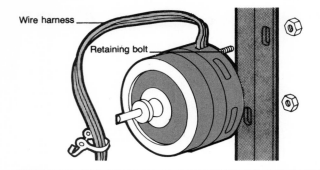

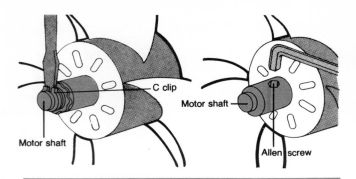

The motor is bolted to the frame. Before removing the motor itself, release the strain-relief brackets holding the wiring harness leading from the motor.

Disengage the C-clip or loosen the Allen screw holding the fan blades to the motor shaft.

deeply pitched blades. The blade pitch allows them to draw large quantities of air out of a room.

Attic fans

Attic fans function specifically as exhaust fans and consequently have more powerful split-phase or capacitor-start motors. The blades are often installed away from the motor and are belt driven.

Disassembly

Unplug the fan and remove the front and back grills by undoing their setscrews or by freeing a set of clips. Remove the C-clip, or loosen the allen screw that holds the blade assembly to the motor shaft, and pull the blades from the shaft. Pull off the switch knob, and loosen the locknut that holds the switch in position. Lift the switch out of the frame. There are usually retaining loops, which hold the wiring harness (*see page 53*) to the sides of the frame, that must be removed to free the wires; they may be attached with a screw or merely inserted in an expansion plug that can be pried away from the frame with the blade of a screwdriver. If there is an oscillating device, it may be necessary to unscrew and lift out the oscillator control switch before the housing can be totally detached from the motor. To expose the switches to view, unfasten the screws holding together the casing around them and then take the casing apart.

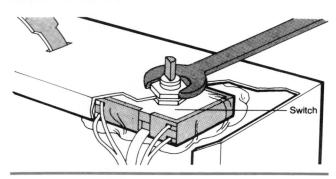

Remove the switch from the fan housing.

Maintenance and Repair

Cord Set. If a fan does not start, first check the cord set. Fan cords, particularly the ones on portable units, are bent and pulled constantly, causing the wires to break, usually near the plug. See page 52 for repair of cord sets and plugs.

Blades. Fan blades, particularly in kitchen exhaust fans, can accumulate so much grime and grease that the blades are thrown off balance, wearing the bearings down unevenly. Regularly clean the accumulation of dirt or grease on fan blades and around their hub with a solvent.

The blades of a fan are usually riveted to a hub that is locked on the motor shaft with setscrews. Each blade is assembled at exactly the same pitch as its

Window fan (portable)   Ventilation fan   Oscillating fan   Stationary window fan

mates; if any blade becomes bent, loose, or unaligned, the fan will rotate off balance, causing considerable vibration and noise. If the rivets that hold a blade to the hub loosen, they can sometimes be tightened by tapping them with a ball peen hammer, provided the blade is metal. If that fails, the blade must be re-riveted. Plastic blades may crack if the fan is dropped, or they may warp if it is exposed to high temperatures. Do not try to repair plastic blades; replace them.

The easiest way to check blade alignment is to place the hub of the assembly on a flat board. The bottoms of the blades should touch the board; the high side of each blade should measure exactly the same distance above the surface. If a metal blade is out of alignment, bend it carefully back into position.

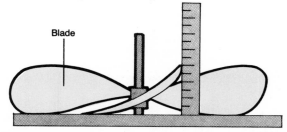

The blades of a fan should measure the same length when laid on a flat surface.

Motors. Many fans are driven by shaded-pole motors, which have low starting torques; because of this the blades will stop more easily when any foreign object is caught in the fan blades.

Attic and exhaust fans normally employ a split-phase or capacitor-start motor (*see pages 60-62*). Check the owner's manual for instructions on oiling a particular fan motor. Most fans should be oiled periodically by putting two or three drops of light machine oil in each oil hole.

Selector Control Switch. In nearly every instance, three-speed fans will have a tapped-field control (*see page 64*), while two-speed fans normally use a device called a reactance choke. If a fan fails to operate at one speed but does work on the other speeds, the problem is most likely in the field windings. However, first check for dirty contacts, loose wires, and dirt in the switch. Replace a switch that cannot be restored.

Oscillating Assembly. Most oscillating mechanisms consist of a worm gear attached to the motor shaft that engages a short rotor gear shaft. The rotor shaft has a worm on one end that meshes with a spur gear on a vertical shaft. The gears, turning at right angles to each other, permit the fan to move back and forth as the motor shaft rotates.

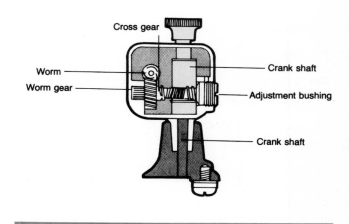

Anatomy of a typical oscillating assembly.

An oscillator that fails to operate properly can be disassembled, and each of its components can be inspected closely for wear. Worn parts can be replaced, but it is often easiest, and less time consuming, to replace the entire assembly.

OSCILLATING FAN TROUBLESHOOTING

PROBLEM: Fan does not start.

Possible Cause	Procedure	Remedy	Rating	Parts	Labor
No power at outlet.	Check fuse or circuit breaker.	Replace fuse or reset circuit breaker.			
Plug disconnected.		Reseat plug in outlet.			
Cord defective.	Check for breaks.	Repair or replace.	■	$3	$5
Switch defective.	Test circuit continuity.	Replace.	■	$1.50	$7.50
Motor faulty.	Check for loose contacts or binding rotor.	Repair or replace.	■	$10-35	$10

(Continued on next page)

PROBLEM: Fan blows fuse or trips circuit breaker. *(Continued from preceding page)*

Possible Cause	Procedure	Remedy	Rating	Parts	Labor
Circuit overloaded.	Reduce number of appliances on circuit.	Replace fuse or reset circuit breaker.			
Cord or plug short-circuited.	Inspect cord and plug for breaks.	Repair or replace.	■	$3	$5
Switch or motor short-circuited.	Test circuit continuity.	Repair or replace.	■	Switch $1.50 Motor $10-35	Switch $7.50 Motor $10

PROBLEM: Fan shocks user.

Possible Cause	Procedure	Remedy	Rating	Parts	Labor
Cord frayed.	Inspect for breaks.	Repair or replace.	■	$3	$5
Case short-circuited.	Test circuit continuity.	Repair.	■		$7.50

PROBLEM: Fan does not oscillate.

Possible Cause	Procedure	Remedy	Rating	Parts	Labor
Parts in oscillating assembly worn.	Check for worn gear, pinion, and compression stud.	Replace.	■	$15	$15
Spur gear broken or worn.	Check for worn or broken teeth.	Replace	■	$5	$15
Rotor shaft bent.	Check.	Repair or replace.	■	$10	$15
Spur gear pin loose or improperly set.	Check.	Knurl pin end and tap in place. Repair or replace.	■		$7.50

PROBLEM: Fan oscillates sluggishly.

Possible Cause	Procedure	Remedy	Rating	Parts	Labor
Arm gummy or in need of lubrication.	Examine oscillating mechanism.	Clean and oil.	■		$7.50

PROBLEM: Oscillating assembly rattles.

Possible Cause	Procedure	Remedy	Rating	Parts	Labor
Bearings worn.	Check.	Replace.	■	$6	$10
Rotor worn.	Check.	Replace.	■	$10	$15
Gear case improperly greased or in need of lubrication.	Check.	Clean and replace lubrication with type recommended by manufacturer.	■	$2	$10

(Continued on next page)

PROBLEM: Fan has magnetic hum. *(Continued from preceding page)*

Possible Cause	Procedure	Remedy	Rating	Parts	Labor
Bearings loose.	Check for wear.	Replace.	■	$6	$10
Air gap uneven.	Check.	Loosen field screws, and realign field coils.	■		$7.50
Rotor off balance.		Replace rotor or entire motor.	■	$10-35	$10

NON-OSCILLATING FAN TROUBLESHOOTING

PROBLEM: Fan does not start.

Possible Cause	Procedure	Remedy	Rating	Parts	Labor
No power at outlet.	Check fuse or circuit breaker.	Replace fuse or reset circuit breaker.			
Plug disconnected.	Check plug at wall outlet.	Reseat plug in outlet.			
Cord defective.	Check for breaks.	Repair or replace.	■	$3	$5
Switch defective.	Test circuit continuity.	Replace.	■	$1.50	$7.50
Motor faulty.	Check for loose contacts or binding rotor.	Repair or replace.	■	$10-35	$10

PROBLEM: Fan blows fuse or trips circuit breaker.

Possible Cause	Procedure	Remedy	Rating	Parts	Labor
Circuit overloaded.	Reduce number or appliances on circuit.	Replace fuse or reset circuit breaker.			
Cord or plug short-circuited.	Inspect cord and plug for breaks.	Repair or replace.	■	$3	$5
Switch or motor short-circuited.	Test circuit continuity.	Repair or replace.	■ ■	Switch $1.50 Motor $10-35	Switch $7.50 Motor $10

PROBLEM: Fan shocks user.

Possible Cause	Procedure	Remedy	Rating	Parts	Labor
Cord frayed.	Inspect for breaks.	Repair or replace.	■	$3	$5
Case short-circuited.	Test circuit continuity.	Repair.	■		$7.50

(Continued on next page)

PROBLEM: Motor does not change speeds properly. *(Continued from preceding page)*

Possible Cause	Procedure	Remedy	Rating	Parts	Labor
Speed control faulty.	Check for broken contacts.	Repair or replace.	■	$5	$10
Bearings dirty, dry or misaligned.	Visually inspect.	Clean, lubricate, and realign or replace	■	$6	$15

PROBLEM: Reverse does not operate.

Possible Cause	Procedure	Remedy	Rating	Parts	Labor
Switch faulty.	Inspect for loose or broken contacts.	Repair or replace.	■	$1.50	$7.50
Field windings faulty.	Test circuit continuity.	Replace motor.	■	$10-35	$10

PROBLEM: Motor runs hot or stops and starts.

Possible Cause	Procedure	Remedy	Rating	Parts	Labor
Lubrication needed.		Oil bearings at front and rear.	■		$7.50
Motor faulty.	SEE ELECTRIC MOTOR TROUBLESHOOTING CHARTS—CHAPTER 4				

PROBLEM: Fan has magnetic hum.

Possible Cause	Procedure	Remedy	Rating	Parts	Labor
Air gap uneven.	Check.	Loosen field screws and realign field coils.	■		$10
Rotor off balance.		Replace rotor or entire motor.	■	$10-35	$10

PROBLEM: Fan vibrates or is excessively noisy.

Possible Cause	Procedure	Remedy	Rating	Parts	Labor
Blades defective.	Check for distortions or broken parts, balance and alignment, or loose hub.	Repair or replace.	■	$10	$10
Bearings dirty.		Clean and lubricate.	■		$7.50
Rotor shaft bent.	Check.	Replace.	■	$12	$15
Fan guards loose.	Check.	Tighten or replace.	■		$7.50
Screws or bolts loose or missing.	Visually inspect.	Tighten or replace.	■		$7.50
Blades strike frame.	Inspect.	Straighten.	■		$7.50
Window or table vibrates.		Place cushion between fan and table or window ledge.			

Food Processors

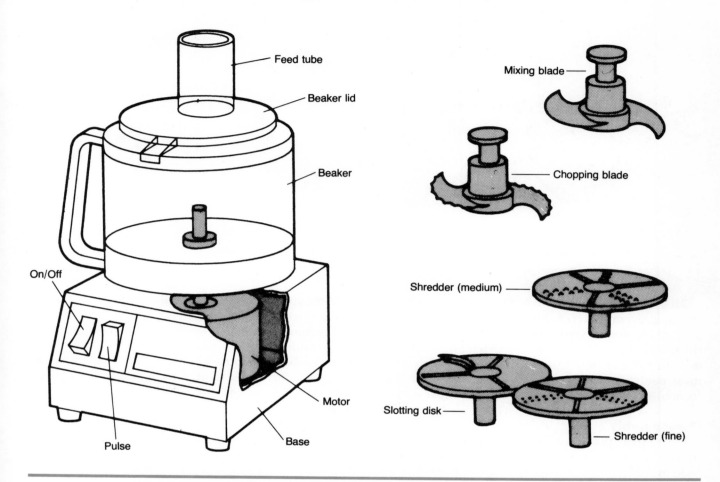

Feed tube

Beaker lid

Beaker

On/Off

Motor

Pulse

Base

Mixing blade

Chopping blade

Shredder (medium)

Slotting disk

Shredder (fine)

A typical food processor.

Principle of Operation

All processors have a heavy, compact base which contains a heavy duty high torque motor protected by a thermodisc relay and controlled by an On/Off switch. The motor is normally mounted vertically so that all the cutting disk fit directly onto the motor shaft protruding through the bottom of a removable plastic bowl or beaker. A food pusher (usually made of plastic) fits into a channel at the top of the beaker. In some units the pusher is also a measuring cup.

The beaker (or bowl) may have to be twisted or depressed to start the machine. On some models there is a pulse switch. A spring-loaded switch is depressed to complete contact between the unit's relay and motor. The motor rotates all cutting blades at the same high speed. It continues running only as long as the switch is depressed. As soon as the switch is released, the motor stops.

Differences in Food Processors

Processors use either direct drive or belt drive motors. The direct drive is the model in which the motor is vertically mounted. Motors in belt drive models are mounted with the shaft downward. A small pulley is attached to the shaft in the front of the base of the machine. The pulleys are connected by a drive-belt. There are also a few belt drive models with motors in a cabinet behind the beaker. The cutting blades rotate via a drive belt and pulley system.

There are also differences in the On/Off mechanisms. With some models, a cam extends from the edge of the beaker lid. When the lid is rotated, the cam depresses a spring-loaded rod attached to the side of the beaker which engages the motor switch. Other switching arrangements include pushing down on the entire beaker, which also activates a spring-loaded rod and a simple pulse switch that maintains contact with the motor for as long as it is manually depressed.

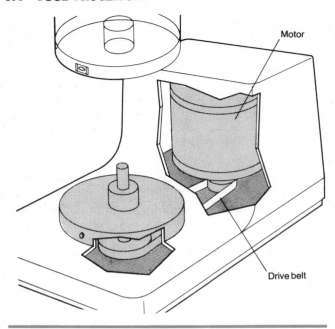

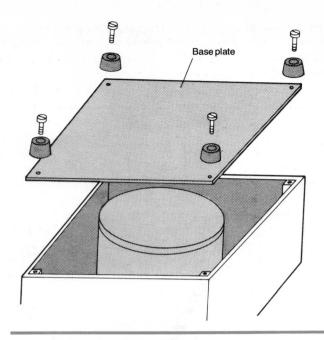

Some processors are belt driven rather than direct driven.

To open a food processor, remove the screws in the base.

All food processors perform a wide range of chores by using several different kinds of cutters including: a steel blade for mixing, chopping and pureeing; a thick-shredder; a thick-slicer; a sharp plastic blade for mixing doughs and sauces. Additional blades for most models such as a ripple-cutter, thin-slicer and french-fry cutter can also be purchased separately.

Disassembly

Every food processor now on the market can be disassembled by loosening the screws (sometimes hidden under caps) in the base of the machine and taking off the bottom plate. The motor and switch can then be removed by undoing the setscrews that hold them in the base.

> **WARNINGS: Any processor on the market should always be disconnected from its power source when it is not in use, during cleaning, and especially when its cutting blades are being inserted or removed. Cutting blades (including the plastic ones) are extremely sharp; treat them with the same caution as any carving knife.**
>
> **Never put fingers in the feed tube; use the food pusher.**
>
> **Always wait until the cutter comes to a complete stop before removing the beaker lid.**

Maintenance and Repair

Capacitor-Start Motor. Processors have heavy-duty, capacitor-start motors that run at only one speed. With models in which the cutters are mounted directly on the motor shaft, the motor is positioned vertically with its shaft protruding up through the top of the unit's base. For details on capacitor-start motors, see page 62.

Thermostatic Relay Switch. Not all models include a thermostatic relay switch, which is designed to automatically break contact between the cord and motor whenever too much food is pushed into the cutters and the motor overheats. The operator must then wait from fifteen to thirty minutes for the motor to cool before turning on the appliance again. In some models, the relay is reactivated by a reset button. A few food processors have no relay at all. See page 59 for repair of thermostatic relay switches.

On/Off Switch. The On/Off switches on processors can be either a lid-cam-switch-rod assembly or a standard toggle switch.

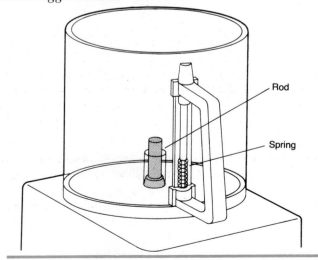

The spring-loaded cam switch rod is depressed to complete the motor contact when the beaker switch is closed.

Typically, the switch has three leads: one to the motor, one to the cord and one to the capacitor. In those models using a toggle On/Off switch, there is either a "pulse" position or a separate "pulse" switch that activates the motor for as long as the button is depressed. See page 55 for troubleshooting and repair of switches.

Spring-Loaded Switch Rod Assembly. If the On/Off switch is not a pulse type that operates directly, there is a spring-loaded rod that connects the switch to the motor contacts. The rod fits inside a spring that forces it to break the contact whenever it is not manually held in its depressed position. The as-

sembly on some models is inside the base of the machine, or, it stands within a tube molded to the side of the bowl. Both the rod and spring can be removed for cleaning; if the spring becomes too compressed to repair, replace it.

Beakers, Lids, Blades. Beakers (bowls) and beaker lids are made from an extremely strong plastic. Should they become worn, cracked, or broken, they cannot be repaired, but must be replaced by a manufacturer's part. All of the blades and cutters, with the exception of the plastic dough blades, are made of steel. The knives can be sharpened; manufacturers offer replacement blades and cutters.

FOOD PROCESSOR TROUBLESHOOTING

PROBLEM: Food processor does not start.

Possible Cause	Procedure	Remedy	Rating	Parts	Labor
No power at outlet.	Check fuse or circuit breaker.	Replace fuse or reset circuit breaker.			
Plug disconnected.		Reseat plug in outlet.			
Cord defective.	Check for breaks.	Repair or replace.	■	$3	$5
Capacitor defective.	Check.	See page 62.	■	$5	$7.50
Relay defective.	Check circuit continuity.	Repair or replace.	■	$5	$7.50
Motor defective.	Check.	See page 62.	■	$10	$10
Switch defective.	Test circuit continuity.	Repair or replace.	■	$2.50	$7.50
	Examine for dirt or loose contacts.	Clean and tighten.	■		$7.50
Cover not set firmly on bowl.	Check.	Reseat cover.			
Beakers or blades not locked firmly into position.	Check.	Reseat beaker and blades.			

PROBLEM: Food processor blows fuse or trips circuit breaker.

Possible Cause	Procedure	Remedy	Rating	Parts	Labor
Circuit overloaded.	Reduce number of appliances on circuit.	Replace fuse or reset circuit breaker.			
Cord or plug short-circuited.	Inspect for breaks.	Repair or replace.	■	$3	$5
Switch or motor short-circuited.	Test circuit continuity.	Repair or replace.	■	Switch $2.50 Motor $10	Switch $7.50 Motor $10

PROBLEM: Food processor shocks user.

Possible Cause	Procedure	Remedy	Rating	Parts	Labor
Cord frayed.	Inspect for breaks.	Repair or replace.	■	$3	$5
Case short-circuited.	Test circuit continuity.	Repair.	■ ■ ■		$10

PROBLEM: Motor does not stop. ▬▬▬▬▬▬▬

Possible Cause	Procedure	Remedy	Rating	Parts	Labor
Switch rod spring worn or dirty.	Check for foreign matter clogging spring or jamming switch rod.	Clean, repair, or replace.	■	$2.50	$7.50
Switch defective.	Test circuit continuity. Check contacts.	Repair or replace.	■	$2.50	$7.50

PROBLEM: Processor does not cut properly. ▬▬▬▬▬▬

Possible Cause	Procedure	Remedy	Rating	Parts	Labor
Cutting blades dull.	Check for dull or bent cutting edges.	Sharpen or replace.	■	$3	$7.50
Drive belt worn. (In appropriate models)	Check.	Replace.	■	$2	$7.50
Cams or slots for cutting blade worn.	Check motor shaft and blade hubs for wear.	Replace blades.	■ ■ ■	$5	$10

PROBLEM: Processor shuts off during operation. ▬▬▬▬▬▬

Possible Cause	Procedure	Remedy	Rating	Parts	Labor
Relay switch defective.	Test circuit continuity.	Replace.	■	$5	$7.50
	Check for dirt on contacts.	Clean.	■		$7.50
Overheating caused by too thick or too hard a mixture.	Turn off appliance, wait 15 to 30 minutes.				
Overheating due to processor in use too steadily.	Turn off appliance, wait 15 to 30 minutes.				

PROBLEM: Processor leaks. ▬▬▬▬▬▬

Possible Cause	Procedure	Remedy	Rating	Parts	Labor
Bowl cracked or broken.	Check.	Replace.	■	$5	
Blade not completely set in socket.	Check.	Reseat firmly.			$5

PROBLEM: Pulsator does not work. (In appropriate models.)

Possible Cause	Procedure	Remedy	Rating	Parts	Labor
Switch contacts dirty or corroded.	Check.	Clean or replace.	■	$2.50	$7.50
Switch defective.	Check circuit continuity.	Repair or replace.	■	$2.50	$7.50

PROBLEM: Processor moves on counter. ▬▬▬▬▬▬

Possible Cause	Procedure	Remedy	Rating	Parts	Labor
Large chunk lodged under blade when hard ingredient is processed.	Hold machine until movement stops.				

Food Waste Disposers

Principle of Operation

All food waste disposers are canisters mounted under the drain opening of a sink and are usually wired directly into their own 15-amp branch circuit. Current drain is about 7.5 amperes using a delay action fuse. When food waste is deposited in the disposer, cold water is flushed through it, and the unit is turned on. The motor is energized, and its shaft rotates a flywheel inside the disposer at approximately 1725 to 1750 rpm. Flyweights attached to the flywheel throw the food waste against the cutting blades on the shredder ring (located around the walls of the grind chamber). The metal shredder ring fits around the inside of the grind chamber and is perforated by a series of sharp-edged holes. The flywheel is a round plate located inside the ring and threaded to the motor shaft. Either two or four flyweights are loosely bolted to the top surface of the flywheel so that they can swing freely as the flywheel rotates. The food is shredded until it is small enough to be washed between the teeth in the shredder ring and into a drain. When the food particles are completely ground up and have drained away, the unit becomes noticeably quieter. Water should run through the disposer for at least twenty seconds after the appliance has been shut off.

Differences in Food Waste Disposers

There are two basic types of food waste disposers: the continuous feed and batch feed. The continuous feed type shreds food waste continuously for as long as any waste is pushed into it and motor is operating. Batch feed units require that only a given amount of food waste be put into the grind chamber of the machine at one time.

All disposers have an overload switch to protect the motor in case the unit jams; some models have an automatic reversing switch on the motor so that if the unit jams, the motor will automatically reverse itself. Many deluxe disposers come with an insulating shell that wraps around the canister and deadens its sound. Most modern units not only have a one-and-one-half inch drain hole in one side, but also provide an additional half-inch opening that may be used to connect a dishwasher drainpipe.

Disassembly

Disconnect water inlet and drain pipe connections. However, in some units the grinding section of the disposer can be removed without disturbing the plumbing or tying up the sink.

Loosen the mounting screws in the support flange

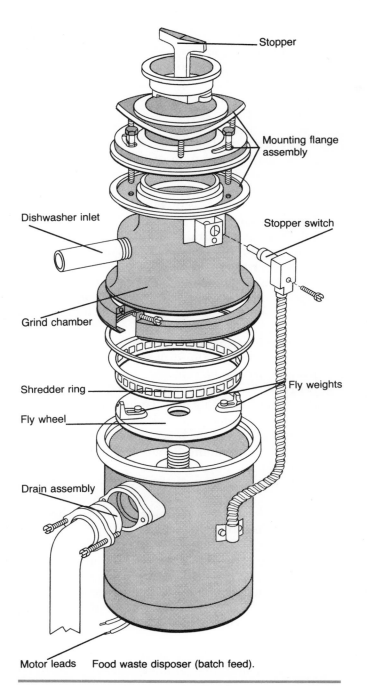

Stopper

Mounting flange assembly

Dishwasher inlet

Stopper switch

Grind chamber

Shredder ring

Fly weights

Fly wheel

Drain assembly

Motor leads   Food waste disposer (batch feed).

under the sink drain; rotate the disposer until it drops free of the flange. If there is a clip holding an insulation shell around the appliance, pry it open and remove the shell. If the appliance is a batch feed model, next remove the switch mounting screws, and pull the stopper switch away from the unit. Undo the retaining screws in the bottom of the canister and remove the bottom plate from the canister to gain access to the motor. The lid on the top half of the canister must be unbolted before the shredder ring and flywheel can be repaired. The shredder ring merely lifts out of its housing. The flywheel is threaded on the motor shaft and is rotated counter-clockwise for removal.

Maintenance and Repair

Motor. Motor sizes in disposers range from one-third to one-half hp and may be either capacitor-start or split-phase. See pages *63–73* for troubleshooting and repair of motors.

The capacitor-start motor has substantial torque or turning power and can handle about two quarts of waste. The split-phase motor can handle only about one quart. In the capacitor-start motor, a centrifugal switch opens the connection to the capacitor after the motor has reached operating speed.

Start Switch. Usually a toggle switch is installed somewhere near the disposer, connected to the unit's 15-amp circuit, and wired to leads coming from the motor *(see page 55)*.

The disposer may have its start switch mounted on the wall near the kitchen sink. This switch is an ordinary On/Off toggle type—the same as those used throughout the rest of the home. This switch is used with the continuous feed waste disposer. In batch feed models, the disposer turns on when the control cover of the disposer is set to its grind position. When the waste has been disposed of, the lid is twisted in the opposite direction to shut off the motor. See page 55 for switch repair.

Reverse Switches. Several types are used by different manufacturers. All of them are designed to reverse the rotation of the flywheel each time the unit is used, so that one time it rotates clockwise, and the next time counter-clockwise, to increase the life of the cutting elements. The switch also automatically reverses the motor if it jams.

Overload Protector Switch. This usually located at the bottom of the disposer and shows as a red button. If the unit jams, the motor will hum for about thirty seconds and then shut off. The motor overload protector switch opens at a certain temperature caused by excessive current flow when the motor is jammed. Manual reset is always used on continuous feed models; automatic reset on batch feed models. After the obstruction is removed from the unit, the protector

switch button is depressed to start the motor again.

Stopper Switches (batch feed units only). All batch feed units are energized by a switch located at the top of the disposer, directly under the sink. To start the appliance, a cam on the bottom of the drain stopper is rotated against the switch, closing contact to the motor. The cam may become worn and either not start the switch or stop the unit as soon as the user lets go of the stopper. When this happens, remove the cam from the stopper by unscrewing its mounting screw, and replace it with a new cam.

The more recent disposal units contain a magnetic switch that is mounted on the neck of the disposal. It is activated by a permanent magnet mounted in the removable cover. If the magnetic switch malfunctions, replace it.

If the switch appears to be defective, remove its mounting screw and pull the switch out of the disposer. Take off the bottom of the disposer and disconnect the two leads coming to the motor from the switch. Test the switch with a multimeter *(see page 28)* set at Rx1. Replace the switch with a manufacturer's replacement part.

Sink Strainer and Drain Mounting Assembly. The assembly consists of an outlet drain, gasket, mounting bolts, and a clamp that holds the disposer housing to the sink drain. The gasket may become worn and need to be replaced; occasionally vibrations from the unit will loosen the mounting bolts which must then be retightened.

Shredder Ring and Flywheel. After prolonged use, the cutting edges on the shredder ring may become dulled and need to be replaced. The flyweights may, on occasion, break. When this occurs, a replacement flywheel and flyweights must be installed.

To replace either the shredder ring or the flyweights, shut off the power and remove the disposer from its mounting flange. Undo the lid of the canister and lift the shredder ring out of its casing. If the flywheel resists easy removal, hold a block of wood against one of the flyweights and tap it counter-clockwise with a hammer until the wheel can be unthreaded from the motor shaft.

Seals. There are four seals in a disposer. One is a gasket between the sink drain and the unit's mounting flange. The second is between the drainpipe at the side of the unit and the housing. The third gasket fits into the rim of the shredder housing. The fourth is between the grind chamber and the motor housing. Anytime it is necessary to loosen the grind chamber clamping ring and disengage the chamber, the seal should be replaced to guarantee a watertight connection.

Any of the gaskets may become worn and allow water to leak out of the disposer. Should this happen, replace the seal.

WARNINGS: Food waste disposers are made to handle relatively small amounts of food. Do not put metal, china, glass, cloth, or any material that cannot readily be shredded into a disposer.

When attempting to free a jammed disposer, use a wooden stick (broom handle, wooden spoon, etc.); never bare hands.

Cold water is recommended by most manufacturers because it congeals grease and washes away more thoroughly than hot.

Several American cities have ordinances requiring disposers be a part of all new kitchen construction, though the units are prohibited in some communities because the extra bulk in the sewage system would tend to cause blockages.

FOOD WASTE DISPOSER TROUBLESHOOTING

PROBLEM: Waste disposer does not start.

Possible Cause	Procedure	Remedy	Rating	Parts	Labor
No power at outlet.	Check fuse or circuit breaker.	Replace fuse or reset circuit breaker.			
Plug disconnected.		Reseat plug in outlet.			
Cord defective.	Check for breaks.	Repair or replace.	■	$3	$20
Overload protector tripped or defective.	Remove overload. Push overload button. If protector is automatic, wait.	If protector is defective, replace.	■	$8	$20
Continuous feed wall switch defective.	Test circuit continuity.	Replace.	■	$3.50	$20
Batch feed stopper switch defective.	Test circuit continuity.	Replace.	■	$6	$20
Motor defective.	Test circuit continuity.	Replace motor or entire appliance.	■ ■ ■	$45	$35
Inoperative capacitor.	Test circuit continuity.	Replace.			

PROBLEM: Waste disposer blows fuse or trips circuit breaker.

Possible Cause	Procedure	Remedy	Rating	Parts	Labor
Circuit overlodaded.	Reduce number of appliances on circuit.	Replace fuse or reset circuit breaker.			
Cord or plug short-circuited.	Inspect for breaks.	Repair or replace.	■	$3	$20
Switch or motor short-circuited.	Test circuit continuity.	Repair of replace.	■ ■ ■	Switch $8 Motor $45	$35

PROBLEM: Waste disposer shocks user.

Possible Cause	Procedure	Remedy	Rating	Parts	Labor
Cord frayed.	Inspect for breaks.	Repair or replace.	■	$3	$20
Case short-circuited.	Test circuit continuity.	Repair.	■		$30

PROBLEM: Motor does not stop.

Possible Cause	Procedure	Remedy	Rating	Parts	Labor
Switch defective or stuck.	Check mechanical action. Test circuit continuity.	Repair or replace.	■	$8	$25
Wiring short-circuited.	Test circuit continuity and inspect terminals for dirt and too much play.	Repair broken or exposed wires and defective connections.	■		$25
Flow interlock stuck or out of adjustment.	Check plunger.	Adjust or replace.	■	$10	$35

PROBLEM: Waste disposer does not start but motor hums.

Possible Cause	Procedure	Remedy	Rating	Parts	Labor
Fly wheel jammed.	Check for foreign objects.	Use stick, wooden spoon, or broom handle to free obstruction.			
Motor defective.	Check circuit continuity.	Replace motor or entire appliance.	■	$45	$35

PROBLEM: Waste disposer runs for short time, then stops.

Possible Cause	Procedure	Remedy	Rating	Parts	Labor
Relay defective.	Test circuit continuity.	Replace.	■	$12	$25
Stator winding short-circuited.	SEE ELECTRIC MOTOR TROUBLESHOOTING CHARTS—CHAPTER 4				

PROBLEM: Waste disposer overheats, smokes, continuously shuts off.

Possible Cause	Procedure	Remedy	Rating	Parts	Labor
Motor faulty.	SEE ELECTRIC MOTOR TROUBLESHOOTING CHARTS—CHAPTER 4		■ ■ ■	$45	$35
Overload protector switch defective.	Test circuit continuity. Check loose connections.	Repair or replace.	■	$8	$20
Fly wheel partially jammed.	Check grind chamber for foreign connections.	Remove			

PROBLEM: Water drains slowly when motor is shut off.

Possible Cause	Procedure	Remedy	Rating	Parts	Labor
Disposer drain partially clogged.	Run appliance for 15 or 20 seconds.				
Drain line clogged.	Fill sink with water. Turn on disposer and drain sink.	If water rises in adjacent sink, hold stopper over drain. Clean out			

(Continued on next page)

(Continued from preceeding page)

Possible Cause	Procedure	Remedy	Rating	Parts	Labor
		clogged line with plumber's snake or plunger. Do not use chemical cleaner.			
Cutting elements worn.	Remove unit from mounting flange. Check cutting holes for wear.	Replace shredder ring if worn.	■ ■ ■	$25	$35

PROBLEM: Water drains and backs up when disposer stops.

Possible Cause	Procedure	Remedy	Rating	Parts	Labor
Drain blocked or water going into vent.	Check.	Unclog.	■		$25

PROBLEM: Disposer drains improperly.

Possible Cause	Procedure	Remedy	Rating	Parts	Labor
Water flow insufficient.		Increase flow of cold water during operation.			
Drain clogged.		Clean out with plumber's snake or plunger.	■	$25	
Flywheel or shredder defective.	Check.	Replace.	■ ■ ■	$25	$35
Grease trap blocked.	Inspect.	Clean.			

PROBLEM: Disposer stops when stopper is released. (In batch feed models)

Possible Cause	Procedure	Remedy	Rating	Parts	Labor
Stopper swtich defective.	Inspect for worn cam.	Replace.			

PROBLEM: Disposer has offensive odor.

Possible Cause	Procedure	Remedy	Rating	Parts	Labor
Food particles stuck.	Flush with ice cubes, wait 1 minute, then run with 2 lemons. Flush thoroughly.				

PROBLEM: Disposer grinds too slowly.

Possible Cause	Procedure	Remedy	Rating	Parts	Labor
Water supply insufficient.		Increase flow of cold water during operation.			

Possible Cause	Procedure	Remedy	Rating	Parts	Labor
Foreign objects in machine.	Check.	Remove.	■		$20
Flywheel or shredder ring worn or defective.	Check.	Replace.	■ ■ ■	$25	$35

PROBLEM: Disposer leaks.

Possible Cause	Procedure	Remedy	Rating	Parts	Labor
Drain gasket loose.	Check.	Tighten screws.			
Drain seal faulty.	Check.	Apply plumber's putty or replace.	■		$25
Seal between hopper and shredder faulty.	Check.	Replace gasket.	■	$3	$25

PROBLEM: Disposer is excessively noisy.

Possible Cause	Procedure	Remedy	Rating	Parts	Labor
Foreign object in unit.	Check.	Remove.			
Mounting screws loose.	Check flange under sink.	Tighten.	■		$20
Broken parts in flywheel assembly.	Check for broken flyweights.	Replace.	■ ■ ■	$25	$35
Motor faulty.	Check.	See page 00.			

PROBLEM: Disposer vibrates excessively.

Possible Cause	Procedure	Remedy	Rating	Parts	Labor
Mounting bolts loose.	Check.	Tighten.	■		$20
Metal object in grind chamber.	Check.	Remove.	■		$20
Shredder or flyweight broken.	Check.	Replace.	■ ■ ■	$25	$35
Motor bearings worn.	Remove motor from bottom of disposer to check.	See page 00.			

PROBLEM: Disposer does not grind.

Possible Cause	Procedure	Remedy	Rating	Parts	Labor
Blades or hammers stuck or worn.	Inspect.	Relase. Replace if necessary.	■ ■ ■	$25	$35
Shredder worn or defective.	Inspect.	Replace.	■ ■ ■	$25	$35

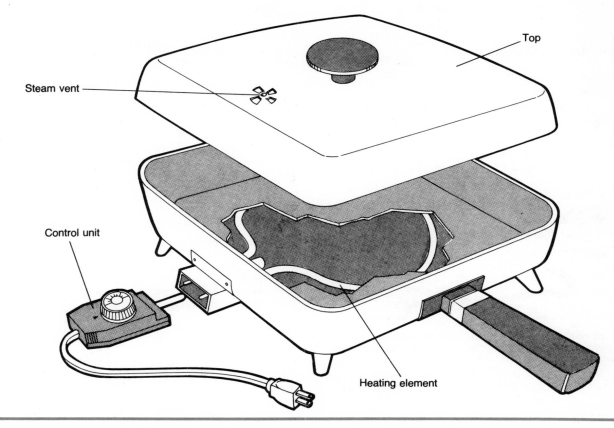

Steam vent

Top

Control unit

Heating element

Frying Pan and control unit

Principle of Operation

An electric frying pan contains a heating element welded or molded into the bottom of the skillet and ending at terminal pins encased in a watertight terminal box. In most models, a detachable control unit contains the line cord and a thermostatic switch. When the control unit is plugged into the terminal prongs and the desired temperature is set, electricity flows through the thermostat to the heating element. When the desired temperature is reached, the thermostat opens.

Differences in Frying Pans

Most electric frying pans are square; some are round. Some models are coated with a nonstick compound, and many have a movable steam vent in their lids. Other common features include lids that can be kept partially open, handles for safe carrying, and a neon light in the thermostat control to signal when the unit has reached the preset temperature. In some frying pans, the thermostat is built into the skillet rather than being part of the detachable control unit.

Disassembly

Since the heating element is welded or molded into the pan, it cannot be disassembled. The legs and handles on the skillet are removable with a screwdriver, and the thermostat control and cord can be disen-

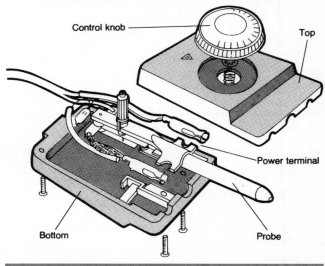

Control knob

Top

Power terminal

Bottom

Probe

Anatomy of a probe control unit

gaged from the pan. Some models have control units that cannot be taken apart. Those control units that can be disassembled are made in halves which are held together by setscrews. To disassemble, remove the screws and pull the two covers apart.

Maintenance and Repair

Skillet. Nothing can be done to repair a skillet. The heating element is an integral part of the bottom of the pan and cannot be removed. The heating element can be tested, however, by setting a multimeter to the Rx1 scale and touching its probes to the terminal pins. If the meter reads well above 10 to 15 ohms, the element is not functioning and the entire skillet must be replaced.

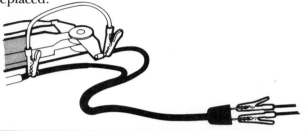

Test the power cord by attaching a jumper cable between one terminal of the thermostat and the power-cord leads. The meter probes are attached to the prongs on the cord.

The legs and handles attached to the skillet are held in place by screws. Replace broken legs and handles with identical parts from the manufacturer.

Cord Set. If possible, disengage the cord from its terminals when testing for continuity (*see page 26*). When replacing a cord that cannot be removed from its terminals, cut it off, leaving about three-

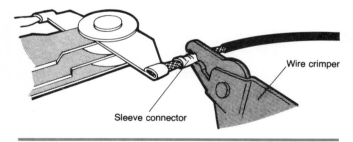

Sleeve connector   Wire crimper

If a cord must be replaced, cut the lead wires ¾ inch from the terminals; connect the new wire with sleeve connectors.

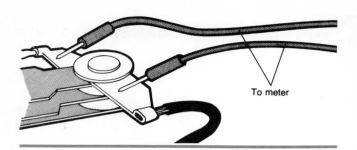

To test a thermostat, touch the meter probes to each terminal.

quarters of an inch of line on the terminals. Attach the replacement cord with crimped-sleeve connectors, wire nuts, or solder splices.

Thermostatic Switch. If the thermostat is pitted or corroded, it probably needs to be replaced (*see page 57*). If the frying pan does not attain the temperatures the control is set for, the thermostat may be adjustable (*see page 57*).

WARNING: Never submerge a control unit in water. Clean a control unit with a damp cloth after it is unplugged.

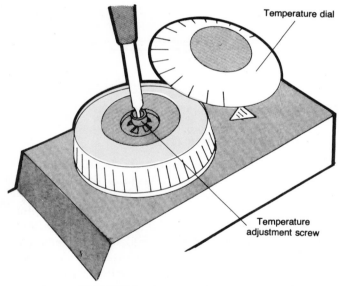

Temperature dial

Temperature adjustment screw

The adjustment screw may be hidden under a plastic plug or under the decorative dial cap. In either case, pry off the covering to reach the screw.

PROCEDURE FOR MAKING TEMPERATURE-CONTROL ADJUSTMENT

1) Turn control knob off, loosen setscrew and remove control from its shaft.

2) Turn control shaft until indicator light goes on.

3) Replace control unit on its shaft with pointer at lowest temperature setting.

4) Place an oven thermometer in appliance and close lid.

5) Turn control knob to its highest setting.

6) Wait for light to go out, then read thermometer. Temperature at which the control cuts out should be 20°F. higher than temperature indicated on control.

7) If thermometer reads 20° F. less than indicated heat, reset knob on shaft so that it will read 20°F. less than thermometer. Then turn control to its highest temperature.

8) Let appliance cool until light goes on again (which means thermostat has closed) and read thermometer again. It should read approximately the same as control unit indicator. If not, reset knob on its shaft so the two temperatures agree.

9) Recycle appliance several times and test against thermometer each time current goes on or off. The cut-out temperature should average 20°F. higher than indicator on control unit.

FRYING PAN TROUBLESHOOTING

PROBLEM: Frying pan does not heat.

Possible Cause	Procedure	Remedy	Rating	Parts	Labor
No power at outlet.	Check fuse or circuit breaker.	Replace fuse or reset circuit breaker.			
Plug disconnected.		Reseat plug in appliance and outlet.			
Cord defective.	Check for breaks.	Repair or replace.	■	$3	$7.50
Heating element defective.	Check circuit continuity with ohmmeter.	Replace	■ ■ ■	$5	$10
Thermostat control faulty.	Check circuit continuity. See if bimetal is warped. Look for burned contacts. Inspect female receptacles for dirt.	Adjust parts or replace.	■ ■ ■	$9	$7.50
Male prongs faulty.	Test circuit continuity. Inspect for dirt.	Clean or replace.	■	$3	$7.50

PROBLEM: Frying pan blows fuse or trips circuit breaker.

Possible Cause	Procedure	Remedy	Rating	Parts	Labor
Circuit overloaded.	Reduce number of appliances on circuit.	Replace fuse or reset circuit breaker.			
Cord or plug short-circuited.	Inspect for breaks.	Repair or replace.	■	$3	$10
Switch short-circuited.	Test circuit continuity.	Repair or replace.	■	Switch $10	Switch $10

PROBLEM: Frying pan shocks user.

Possible Cause	Procedure	Remedy	Rating	Parts	Labor
Cord frayed.	Inspect for breaks.	Repair or replace.	■	$3	$7.50
Case short-circuited.	Test circuit continuity.	Repair.	■		$7.50
Grounded unit.	Check.	Replace defective part.	■		$7.50

PROBLEM: Food sticks to frying pan.

Possible Cause	Procedure	Remedy	Rating	Parts	Labor
Thermostat too high.	Lower temperature.				

PROBLEM: Frying pan heats, but indicator light does not go on.

Possible Cause	Procedure	Remedy	Rating	Parts	Labor
Bulb burned out.		Replace.	■	$1	$7.50
Resistor shorted.	Test circuit continuity with ohmmeter.	Replace. First coat resistor with waterproof varnish.	■	$3	$7.50

Hair Blower/Stylers

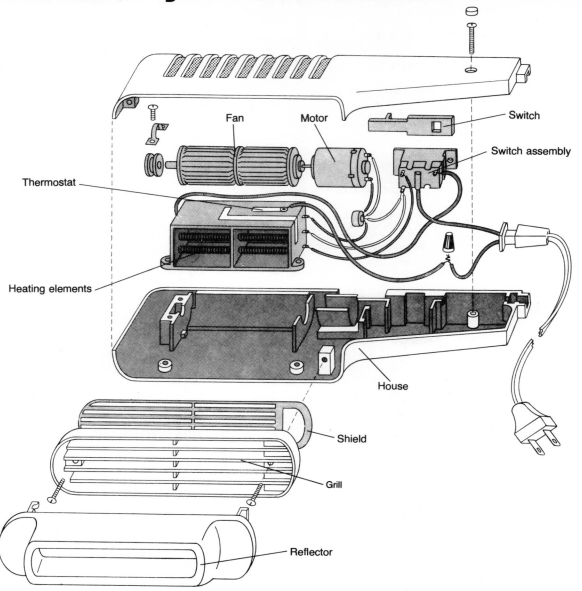

Fan
Motor
Switch
Switch assembly
Thermostat
Heating elements
House
Shield
Grill
Reflector

Principle of Operation

Blower-stylers consist of a plastic housing containing a small shaded-pole or universal motor, a fan, one or more heating elements, On/Off switch, cord set, and an overheat protector. The desired heat is selected by setting the On/Off switch. Electricity from the cord energizes both the motor to run the fan and the heating elements which are made of resistance coils. As the heating elements warm the air in the appliance, it is blown through a grill in front of the unit by the fan. Most blower-stylers offer three levels of heat (low, medium, high) from two heating elements which can

be used singly or together. One of the elements produces a low wattage and the other a higher wattage. When the blower-styler is set at "low," only the low watt element is turned on. The "medium" setting uses only the high watt element. Both elements operate when the setting is "high." As a safety feature, the heaters are wired in series to the motor so they cannot function without the motor blowing the heated air out of the appliance.

Differences in Hair Blower-Stylers

The many versions of blower-stylers range from a simple unit consisting of a heat element, fan and motor, to ones that incorporating a reservoir for misting, and others having reciprocating brush and comb attachments. All blower-stylers, however, consist of the same basic elements and are repaired in the same manner. In most instances, repair of a blower-styler means replacement of parts from the manufacturers.

Disassembly

Remove the blower grill screws and pry off the grill shield, then undo the screws holding the housing halves together. The screws may be hidden under plastic plugs which must first be pried out of their

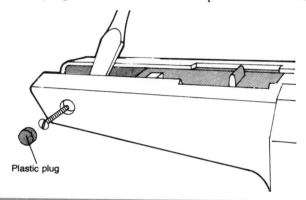

Plastic plug

Pry out the plastic plugs hiding the retaining screws in the housing. Undo all screws.

sockets with a screwdriver blade or awl. Free the retaining screws holding the heater assembly to the housing. Note where each of the leads from the cord is connected before disconnecting them. Remove the screws holding the motor shaft retainer, and pry off the bearing from the motor shaft. The motor can now be lifted out of its retaining clamps so that the fan, motor, switch, and cord can be removed. The wires connecting the motor, switch, and heater may be soldered, which means the solder must be broken or melted if the wires must be disconnected. The fan can be pried away from the motor with a screwdriver.

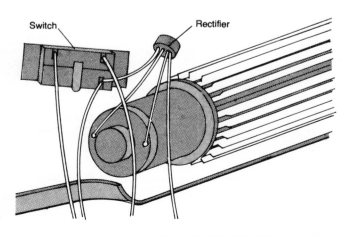

Switch
Rectifier

The switch, fan, motor and rectifier can be pried out of their positions.

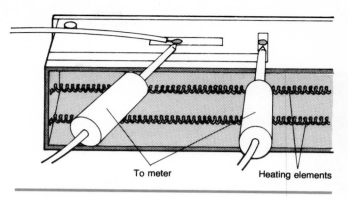

To meter
Heating elements

To test the heating elements, touch the meter probes to the heating element terminals.

Maintenance and Repair

Motors. Of necessity, the shaded-pole or universal motors (*see page 61*) used in hand-held blower-stylers are small and easier to replace than to repair. Because their only function is to drive a small fan, few problems develop with them.

Some models use a small DC motor with a rectifier, which converts AC power to 12 volts DC power. To test the motor, unsolder either of the leads to the rectifier and set the meter to Rx1. If the motor is functional, the meter will read 5-50 ohms. Any higher reading means the motor should be replaced.

Heating Element. Units offering a range of heat selection incorporate two heating elements, both made of resistance coils. The heating assembly can be tested for resistance by turning it to Off and placing the meter probes against each of the terminals with the scale set at Rx1. If either of the elements is working, the meter will read no higher than 15-50 ohms. If one element is faulty, the entire assembly must be replaced.

Overheat Protector. The overheat protector is located on the top of the heater. Test it by setting the multimeter to Rx1 and placing the meter probes

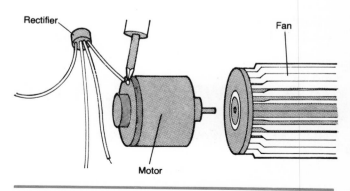

Rectifier
Fan

Motor

The rectifier is soldered to the motor. Melt its connections with a soldering iron.

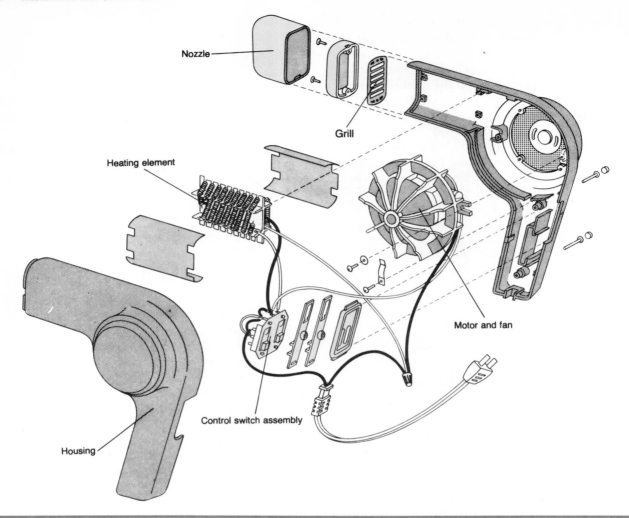

Nozzle

Grill

Heating element

Motor and fan

Control switch assembly

Housing

against the protector's terminals. If the meter reads above zero ohms, the overheat protector is faulty and must be replaced.

Switch. If the switch contacts become dirty, clean them with electrical contact cleaner. Otherwise, the switch can be tested for continuity using the Rx1 ohms scale; if it is faulty, replace it with a manufacturer's component.

Cord and Plug. To test the cord, disconnect it completely and clip the meter probes to the prongs of the plug. Use the Rx100 scale; if the cord is not damaged, the needle will read above zero ohms. If the needle jumps or reads zero ohms, replace it!

WARNINGS: Never use a blower-styler while taking a bath or shower, or anywhere near water.

Never immerse hair dryers in water or operate near any aerosol products.

Keep the air intake grill free of hair and lint; be sure to unplug the unit before cleaning the grill.

HAIR BLOWER-STYLER TROUBLESHOOTING

PROBLEM: Hair blower-styler does not work.

Possible Cause	Procedure	Remedy	Rating	Parts	Labor
No power at outlet.	Check fuse or circuit breaker.	Replace fuse or reset circuit breaker.			

(Continued on next page)

PROBLEM: Hair blower-styler does not work. *(Continued from preceding page)*

Possible Cause	Procedure	Remedy	Rating	Parts	Labor
Plug disconnected.		Reseat plug in outlet.			
Cord defective.	Check for breaks.	Repair or replace.	■	$3	$7.50
Heating element defective.	Check circuit continuity with ohmmeter.	Replace.	■	$5	$7.50
Overheat protector faulty.	Retrip protector. Test for continuity.	Replace.	■	$2	$7.50

PROBLEM: Hair blower-styler blows fuse or trips circuit breaker.

Possible Cause	Procedure	Remedy	Rating	Parts	Labor
Circuit overloaded.	Reduce number of appliances on circuit.	Replace fuse or reset circuit breaker.			
Cord or plug short-circuited.	Inspect for breaks.	Repair or replace.			
Switch or motor short-circuited.	Test circuit continuity.	Repair or replace.	■	Switch $2.50 Motor $8	$7.50

PROBLEM: Hair blower-styler shocks user.

Possible Cause	Procedure	Remedy	Rating	Parts	Labor
Cord frayed.	Inspect for breaks.	Repair or replace.	■	$3	$7.50
Case short-circuited.	Test circuit continuity.	Repair.	■		$7.50

PROBLEM: Unit heats but blower does not work.

Possible Cause	Procedure	Remedy	Rating	Parts	Labor
Fan faulty.	Check for dirt and bent, broken or jammed blades.	Clean. Realign parts if possible. If parts are broken, replace fan.	■	$3	$7.50
Motor faulty.	Test circuit continuity.	Replace.	■	$8	$7.50
Rectifier faulty.	Test circuit continuity.	Replace.	■	$2	$7.50

PROBLEM: Blower works but unit heats improperly or not at all.

Possible Cause	Procedure	Remedy	Rating	Parts	Labor
Switch faulty.	Check contacts for dirt and misaligned or broken parts.	Clean. If parts are broken replace switch.	■	$2.50	$7.50
Heating element defective.	Test circuit continuity.	Replace.	■	$5	$7.50

Hair Curling Wands

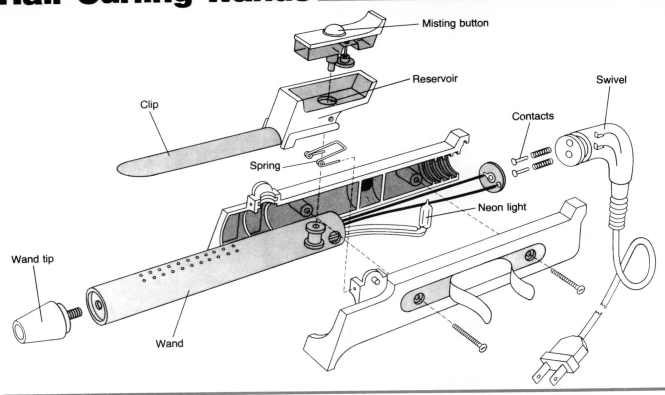

Misting button

Reservoir

Swivel

Clip

Contacts

Spring

Neon light

Wand tip

Wand

Hair curling wand

Principle of Operation

A reservoir is filled with water and screwed into the tip at the end of the barrel of the wand before the appliance is plugged in. Power enters the heating element directly from the cord set and, within five to ten minutes, a dot of heat-sensitive paint on the clip changes color (from red to black), or a neon light goes on indicating the heating element has reached operating temperature. The heating element is housed with a thermostat and safety fuse. Since most models have no On/Off switch, the appliance must be unplugged in order to be turned off. A spring-operated clip on the barrel holds the strand of hair being curled. When the button on the tip is pushed, it brings the wick, which is saturated with water from the reservoir, into contact with the end of the heating element, causing steam. Steam escaping through holes in the barrel curls the hair. Some older wand-type hair curlers do not incorporate a steam spray reservoir.

 WARNING: Always unplug the curler before filling its spray reservoir.

Disassembly

The reservoir screws out of the plastic tip. The tip comes out by depressing the small plastic tab that locks it into place at the end of the barrel, while pulling on the tip at the same time. To disassemble the rest of the wand, unscrew the two screws located on the underside of the handle (sometimes hidden under the manufacturer's label). The two-piece handle will readily separate. The clip and its spring then lift out, as does the cord set's swiveling, single-tip contact prong. In the inside of the bottom of the handle are the wires running into the barrel where they connect to the heating element. (In some early models there is a lamp that glows when the wand is plugged in. The wires that supply its power run into a plastic housing right below the lower end of the barrel. To disassemble the lamp for replacement, remove the screws that hold the top of the housing in place and lift the top off.) The heating element, safety fuse, and thermostat sit inside a cylindrical metal tube inside the barrel. The tube can be removed from the barrel by placing a screwdriver blade into the front of the barrel (after first removing the reservoir and tip), and slowly and firmly applying pressure against the end of the heating element.

Maintenance and Repair

Curling wands are made so that most of the parts cannot be easily repaired and usually must be replaced when they malfunction.

Heating Element. Test the heating element with a multimeter set to 1 ohm mode (*see page 28*). When the heating element in a hair curler fails to operate correctly, it must be replaced by a new unit, which will include the element, wiring, neon bulb, and swivel unit contacts.

Thermostat and Safety Fuse. If it is a separate part of the heating element, check it for proper functioning (*see page 57*).

Cord and Plug. See page 34. If the cord is functioning, examine the contact pins at the end of the swivel for dirt or corrosion. Remove the pins and their springs and spray their sockets with contact cleaner.

Spring. If the curler heats up but does not steam, spring that operates the reservoir tip needs replacing.

Wick Assembly. If the wick assembly leaks, the unit must be replaced.

Clip Assembly. If the ready dot does not change color, the clip assembly needs replacing. In models with an indicator lamp, if it fails to light, replace the lamp assembly.

HAIR CURLING WAND TROUBLESHOOTING

PROBLEM: Hair curler does not heat.

Possible Cause	Procedure	Remedy	Rating	Parts	Labor
No power at outlet.	Check fuse or circuit breaker.	Replace fuse or reset circuit breaker.	■		
Plug disconnected.		Reseat plug in outlet.	■		
Cord defective.	Check for breaks.	Repair or replace.	■	$3	$5
Heating element defective.	Check circuit continuity.	Replace.	■	$4.50	$7.50
Contacts at swivel faulty.	Check for dirt. Examine pins for worn springs.	Clean. Repair or replace.	■		$7.50

PROBLEM: Hair curler blows fuse or trips circuit breaker.

Possible Cause	Procedure	Remedy	Rating	Parts	Labor
Circuit overloaded.	Reduce number of appliances on circuit.	Replace fuse, or reset circuit breaker.	■		
Cord or plug short-circuited.	Inspect for breaks.	Repair or replace.	■	$3	$5
Switch, motor, or heating element short-circuited.	Test circuit continuity.	Repair or replace.	■	Switch $2.50 Motor $2.50	Switch $7.50 Motor $7.50
Moisture in wiring.	If unit has gotten wet, wait 24 hours before turning on.				

PROBLEM: Hair curler shocks user.

Possible Cause	Procedure	Remedy	Rating	Parts	Labor
Cord frayed.	Inspect for breaks.	Repair or replace.	■	$8	$25
Case short-circuited.	Test circuit continuity.	Repair.	■		$7.50

PROBLEM: Curler does not reach desired temperature and does not steam.

Possible Cause	Procedure	Remedy	Rating	Parts	Labor
Heating element faulty.	Test circuit continuity. Check contacts at swivel for dirt.	Clean contacts. Replace element.	■	$5	$7.50
Steam vents clogged (Unit sputters)	Clean vents with toothpick. Fill reservoir with half white vinegar and half water.	Run until empty.	■		$7.50
Contacts at swivel dirty. (Temperature low)	Inspect.	Polish pins, swivel contacts with steel wool or contact cleaner.			$7.50

Hair Dryers

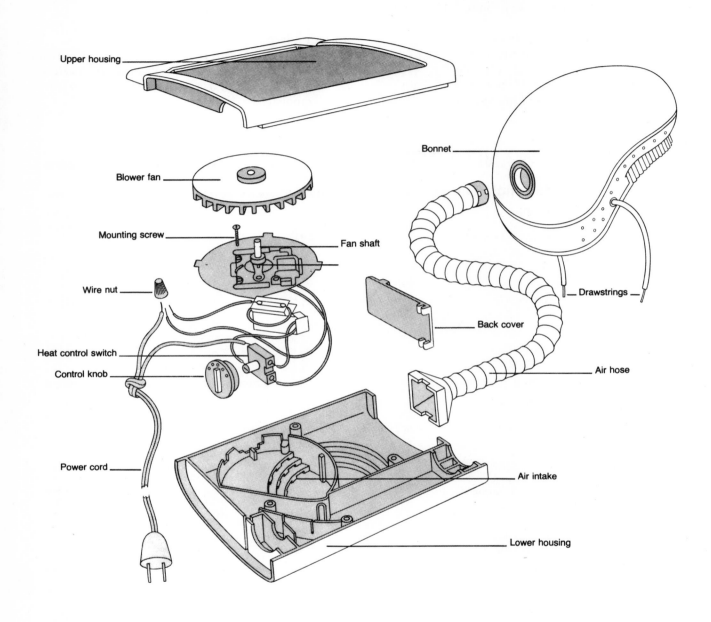

Upper housing

Blower fan

Mounting screw

Wire nut

Heat control switch

Control knob

Power cord

Fan shaft

Bonnet

Drawstrings

Back cover

Air hose

Air intake

Lower housing

Hair dryer

Principle of Operation

Hair dryers come in various forms—large, standing salon-type models; portable bonnet types; hand-held styling guns—but all have the same basic parts: heating element, fan, switches, overheating protector, and cord set. In all models, the fan blows air over the heating element and then through a vent onto the user's hair. Most dryers provide three levels of heat (low, medium, and high) with two heating elements that can be used singly or together.

Differences in Hair Dryers

Heating elements are usually made of coiled resistance wire and may be insulated or bare. The motor in a hair dryer is usually either a shaded-pole or universal type, although a few dryers use a DC motor with a rectifier.

Switching arrangements vary widely. In basic models one switch controls both motor and heating element, which are wired in series. On models with a separate heating element switch, this switch is governed by the motor switch so that the unit cannot heat up unless the motor is on.

Some salon models include a steam or moisture attachment positioned in the support arm between the base and the hood. The assembly consists of a water tank and a heater, which is connected in series to the air-heating element. When the steam unit is turned on, water boils in the tank, and the steam travels through a duct into the hot air stream. When the water in the tank has boiled away, a bimetal thermostat on the bottom of the tank shuts off the unit. A fuse in the water-heating circuit opens in case of malfunction.

Disassembly

Styling guns

The housing of a pistol-type dryer consists of two nearly identical halves. The screws or clips that hold it together may be hidden under plastic caps or decorative decals. The blower grill, mounted at the end of the pistol barrel, may also have to be removed.

Bonnet- and salon-type dryers

In most bonnet- and salon-type dryers, retaining screws are accessible from the bottom of the unit, and they hold the lid of the housing to the base.

Inside the housing, retaining screws hold the heating elements, switches, and motor in place. The fan blades may be attached to the motor shaft by a setscrew or they may simply be pressed on. Be careful to

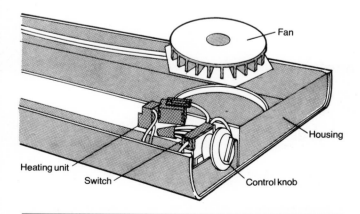

Remove all retaining screws and separate the housing halves

record which leads go to each terminal of the motor, heating unit, and switches before disconnecting them.

Maintenance and Repair

Motor. Shaded-pole motors are discussed on page 62. See pages 60 and 61 for universal motors.

Fan Blades. The fans in hair dryers are either molded plastic or metal. If the plastic breaks or melts, the entire fan unit must be replaced. Metal fans can sometimes be gently bent back into place.

Heating Element. If a heating element is not functioning, test it with a multimeter in the Rx1 mode. A data plate in the unit may indicate the rated resistance of the heating element. The element should measure approximately the rated resistance. If the rating is now known, the element can still be tested. The pointer should be in the middle of the scale, at neither zero nor infinity. Replace a failed element with a manufacturer's part rather than trying to mend the resistance wire. See page 54 for additional information on heating elements.

Switches. After cleaning the contacts of a switch that is suspected of malfunctioning, check it with a

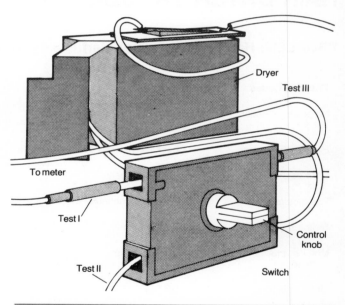

Switch leads must be tested separately. Rotate the control knob during each test.

continuity tester (*see page 26*) or a multimeter in the ohms mode (*see page 27*). If the switch has failed, replace it with a similar unit from the manufacturer.

Overheat protector. Standing models may use a fuse, while hand-held appliances may use a tiny thermostat or a thermal cutout to provide protection against overheating. If these devices are blown or malfunctioning, the dryer does not turn on. Check them for continuity (*see page 27*). Replace them if they are faulty.

Cord Set. See page 52.

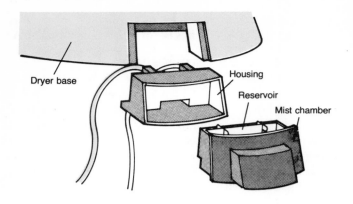

The mist chamber is removable; its housing is connected to the heating elements and the control switch.

Misting Assembly. To maintain a misting unit, clean it periodically by filling with warm vinegar, then flushing the tank with water after fifteen or twenty minutes. Most manufacturers recommend the use of distilled water in misting assemblies. If a misting assembly does not work, check its fuse or circuit breaker and the heating element for continuity *(see page 123).*

Plastic Bonnet and Hose. Plastic bonnets and hoses are found only in bonnet-style dryers. They are made of thin, flexible plastic. Temporary repairs can be made with duct tape, available in a heating supply store.

WARNING: Never use a blower-styler while taking a bath or shower or anywhere near water. Keep the air-intake grill free of hair and lint and be sure to unplug the unit before cleaning the grill.

HAIR DRYER TROUBLESHOOTING

PROBLEM: Hair dryer does not start.

Possible Cause	Procedure	Remedy	Rating	Parts	Labor
No power at outlet.	Check fuse or circuit breaker.	Replace fuse or reset circuit breaker.			
Plug disconnected.	Check plug at wall outlet.	Reseat plug in outlet.			
Cord defective.	Check for breaks.	Repair or replace.	■	$3	$5
Thermostat faulty.	Test circuit continuity with ohmmeter.	Replace.	■	$2.50	$7.50
Switch faulty.	Check manually.	Replace.	■	$2.50	$7.50
Motor or blower jammed.	Visually inspect.	Vacuum case and blower.	■		$7.50
Motor defective.	SEE ELECTRIC MOTOR TROUBLESHOOTING CHARTS—CHAPTER 4				

PROBLEM: Hair dryer blows fuse or trips circuit breaker.

Possible Cause	Procedure	Remedy	Rating	Parts	Labor
Circuit overloaded.	Reduce number of appliances on circuit.	Replace fuse or reset circuit breaker.			
Cord or plug short-circuited.	Inspect for breaks.	Repair or replace.	■	$3	$5
Switch or motor short-circuited.	Test circuit continuity.	Repair or replace.	■	Switch $2.50 Motor $8	$7.50

PROBLEM: Hair dryer shocks user.

Possible Cause	Procedure	Remedy	Rating	Parts	Labor
Cord frayed.	Inspect for breaks.	Repair or replace.	■	$3	$5
Case short-circuited.	Test circuit continuity.	Repair.	■		$7.50

PROBLEM: Motor operates but dryer gives no heat.

Possible Cause	Procedure	Remedy	Rating	Parts	Labor
Connections at heating element loose.	Check heating elements leads at thermostat.	Tighten.	■		$7.50
Fuse link to heating element faulty.	Test circuit continuity.	Replace.	■	$1	$7.50
Thermostat faulty.	Test circuit continuity.	Replace.	■	$2.50	$7.50

PROBLEM: Dryer heats but motor does not operate.

Possible Cause	Procedure	Remedy	Rating	Parts	Labor
Contacts loose.	Inspect throughout unit.	Repair.	■		$7.50
Switch faulty.	Check for loose contacts or dirty terminals. Test circuit continuity.	Clean and tighten. Replace if necessary.	■	$2.50	$7.50
Thermostat faulty.	Check for proper cutoff. Test circuit continuity.	Replace.	■	$2.50	$7.50
Motor defective.	Check circuit continuity. Inspect bearings and impeller for binding.	Replace.	■	$8	$7.50
Fan shaft stuck or dirty.	Inspect for hair wound around ends.	Remove.	■		$7.50

PROBLEM: Dryer does not stay at desired setting or only heats at one setting.

Possible Cause	Procedure	Remedy	Rating	Parts	Labor
Thermostat or heating element defective.	Test circuit continuity.	Replace.	■	Thermostat $2.50 Element $4.50	$7.50
Temperature control switch dirty or defective.	Check for dirty contacts; then test circuit continuity.	Clean or replace.	■	$2.50	$7.50
Connections loose.	Inspect.	Tighten throughout unit.	■		$7.50
Fuse faulty.	Check insertion and amperage.	Reset or replace.	■		
Overheat protector broken or tripped (unit overheats).	Let unit cool for 30 minutes. Start unit.	Replace.	■	$2.50	$7.50
Air flow blocked.	Check fan, hose, and bonnet for foreign object.	Remove	■		$7.50

(Continued on next page)

PROBLEM: Dryer does not shut off. *(Continued from preceding page)*

Possible Cause	Procedure	Remedy	Rating	Parts	Labor
Switch short-circuited.	Test circuit continuity.	Repair or replace.	■	$2.50	$7.50

PROBLEM: Dryer is excessively noisy.

Possible Cause	Procedure	Remedy	Rating	Parts	Labor
Foreign object in blower.	Detach hose; check.	Remove			
Impeller or fan blade loose or bent.	Check.	Repair or replace.	■	$3	$7.50
Motor loose.	Check mounting bolts.	Tighten.	■		$7.50

PROBLEM: Unit does not switch to drying from steam phase.

Possible Cause	Procedure	Remedy	Rating	Parts	Labor
Thermostat faulty.	Check for continuity.	If no continuity, replace	■ ■ ■	$2.50	$10
Attachment cord faulty.	Check for continuity.	If no continuity, replace.	■ ■ ■	$1-5	$10
Switch connections loose.	Check.	Repair connections.	■ ■ ■		$10

PROBLEM: Steamer leaks.

Possible Cause	Procedure	Remedy	Rating	Parts	Labor
Housing cracked.	Check.	If housing is cracked, replace dryer.			
Gasket defective.	Check for wear or breaks.	Replace if worn or broken.	■	$2-5	$7.50

PROBLEM: Unit does not steam.

Possible Cause	Procedure	Remedy	Rating	Parts	Labor
Steamer attachment and cord faulty.	Test for continuity.	If no continuity, replace parts.	■ ■ ■	Steamer $5-10 Cord $1-5	$15
Steamer temperature-control faulty.	Test for continuity.	If no continuity, replace.	■ ■ ■	$3-7	$15
Steamer fuse defective.	Check fuse for proper amperage.	Insert new fuse of right size.	■ ■ ■	.50-$1	$10
	Test fuse for continuity.	If no continuity, replace.		.50-$1	$10

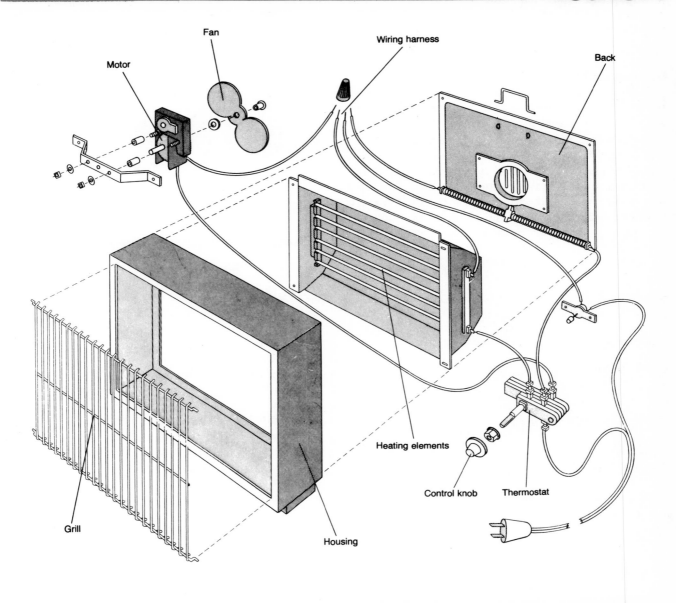

Fan

Motor

Wiring harness

Back

Heating elements

Control knob

Thermostat

Grill

Housing

Electric heater

Principle of Operation

With both natural- and forced-draft heaters the principle of operation is essentially the same. When a natural-draft heater is switched on, power from the cord set heats a resistance wire and warmed air around the wire is reflected off of a shiny metal plate and into the room beyond the heater. Forced-air heaters assist the movement of their warmed air by use of a small fan positioned near the heating element. The amount of heat generated by the unit is controlled by a small thermostatic switch that allows the user to select a low, medium, or high temperature in the heating element.

Most new heater models also include a tipover switch, which automatically shuts off the unit should it fall over while the heater is in operation.

Differences in Heaters

Heaters are manufactured in a range of sizes and shapes, but they all divide into one of two groups: natural-draft and forced-draft heaters. The natural-draft units allow air to rise naturally past a heating element; the forced-draft units employ a fan to distribute the heated air. Most heaters use either a coiled or a flat wire heating element, although occasionally a compound rod is employed. Some heaters use more than one heating element to provide a range of heat settings, and some use multiple-speed fans. The switching arrangements that govern such design differences are similar to those in hair dryers (*see page 122*).

Disassembly

Remove all screws in the unit's housing and pull off the panels they hold in place. Normally, this will be a back or end panel through which the cord enters the appliance. Remove the cord strain relief device and control knob, then pull the thermostat out of the unit. The cord is almost always connected with quick connect terminals in newer models. Undo the motor mounting screws and withdraw the motor if there is one. The heating element and reflector assembly can be taken out by removing their mounting screws.

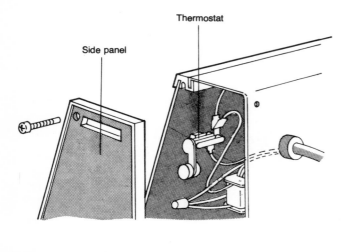

Remove the retaining screws holding the side panels, and pull the panels off the unit.

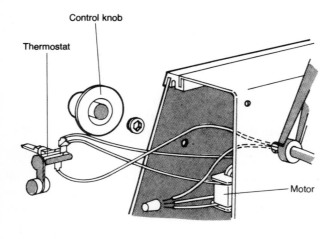

Release the cord strain relief device and control knob to free the thermostat.

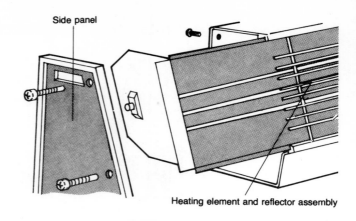

Slide the heating element and reflector out of their slots

Maintenance and Repair

Reflector Assembly. A reflector is made of a polished metal that should be cleaned occasionally with a soft cloth.

Heater. Typically, a heater is a resistance wire held in place with insulated spacers; rods are connected to the cord and held in place with bolts. The element can be checked for an open circuit by prying the lead off of one terminal and touching the multimeter probes to both terminals. Set the meter at Rx1; if it reads between 5 and 30 ohms, the element is functional. If the element is bad it should be replaced.

Thermostat. The thermostats attached to heaters may develop dirty contacts that can be polished with fine sandpaper. See page 57 for repair and replacement of thermostats.

Switches. See pages 54-55.

Tipover Switch. A tipover switch is wired in series to the motor, thermostat, and heater and is spring-loaded so that any weight applied to the switch (such as the unit tipping over on the knob) will break contact to the operational units and shut off the appliance. The switch's main component may be a rod that emerges from the bottom of the heater below the thermostat. As long as the heater is standing upright it will work properly, but as soon as it is tipped over, the spring holding the rod releases it from pressing against a bimetal switch, which then breaks the contact and shuts off the heating element. No matter what configuration the tipover switch has, its mechanism should operate freely. It should be kept clean and replaced if faulty.

Motor and Fan. The motor is normally a small shaded-pole type (*see page 62*). To test the motor, set a multimeter to the Rx1 scale and touch its probes to the motor leads. (Isolate the motor by disconnecting its leads from the other wires in the appliance.) The meter will read between 5 and 25 ohms if the motor is functional.

HEATER TROUBLESHOOTING

PROBLEM: Heater does not heat.

Possible Cause	Procedure	Remedy	Rating	Parts	Labor
No power at outlet.	Check fuse or circuit.	Replace fuse, or reset circuit breaker.	■		
Plug disconnected.		Reseat plug in outlet.	■		
Cord defective.	Check for breaks.	Repair or replace.	■	$3	$5
Heating element defective.	Test circuit continuity with ohmmeter.	Replace.	■	$8-15	$10
Thermostat contacts dirty or unit defective.	Inspect, check for continuity.	Polish contacts with fine sandpaper or replace unit.	■	$4-12	$10
Tip-over switch faulty.	Check contacts for dirt. Make sure mechanism operates freely.	Clean. Free mechanism or replace unit.	■	$4.50	$7.50
On/Off switch faulty.	Check for continuity.	Clean contacts or replace.	■	$4.50	$7.50
Fan burned out.	Check for continuity.	Replace fan.	■	$10	$10

PROBLEM: Heater blows fuse or trips circuit breaker.

Possible Cause	Procedure	Remedy	Rating	Parts	Labor
Circuit overloaded.	Reduce number of appliances on circuit.	Replace fuse or circuit breaker.	■		
Cord or plug short-circuited.	Inspect for breaks. Check for continuity. Inspect for bare wires touching metal housing.	Repair or replace.	■	$3	$5

PROBLEM: Heater heats, but fan does not operate.

Possible Cause	Procedure	Remedy	Rating	Parts	Labor
Fan motor binding.	Inspect.	Oil shaft or replace.	■	$10	$10
Fan blade hub worn.	Check.	Replace blade assembly.	■	$3	$10
Fan clogged or bound.	Inspect blades and housing.	Clean and realign or replace assembly.	■		$7.50

(Continued on next page)

PROBLEM: Heater heats poorly.

Possible Cause	Procedure	Remedy	Rating	Parts	Labor
Heating element faulty.	Test circuit continuity.	Replace.	■	$8-$15	$10
Thermostat faulty.	Test continuity.	Clean contacts, or replace.	■	$4-12	$10

PROBLEM: Heater is excessively noisy.

Possible Cause	Procedure	Remedy	Rating	Parts	Labor
Fan clogged or bound.	Inspect blades and housing.	Clean and realign or replace assembly.	■		$7.50
Fan motor needs oil.	Inspect.	Clean or lubricate motor shaft.	■		$7.50

PROBLEM: Heater shocks user.

Possible Cause	Procedure	Remedy	Rating	Parts	Labor
Cord frayed inside housing.	Take apart unit to remove cord, and inspect for breaks. Test circuit continuity.	Repair or replace.	■	$3	$5
Wiring defective.	Inspect for bare wires. Test for continuity.	Wrap with insulating tape.	■		$10

PROBLEM: Heater does not shut off when tipped over.

Possible Cause	Procedure	Remedy	Rating	Parts	Labor
Tip-over switch faulty.	Inspect for dirty contacts, bent or broken parts.	Clean. Repair or replace.	■	$4.50	$7.50

PROBLEM: Heater does not shut off.

Possible Cause	Procedure	Remedy	Rating	Parts	Labor
On/Off switch faulty.	Inspect. Check for continuity.	Clean or replace.	■	$4.50	$7.50
Wiring short-circuited.	Inspect bare wires. Test for continuity.	Reinsulate after separating.	■		$10

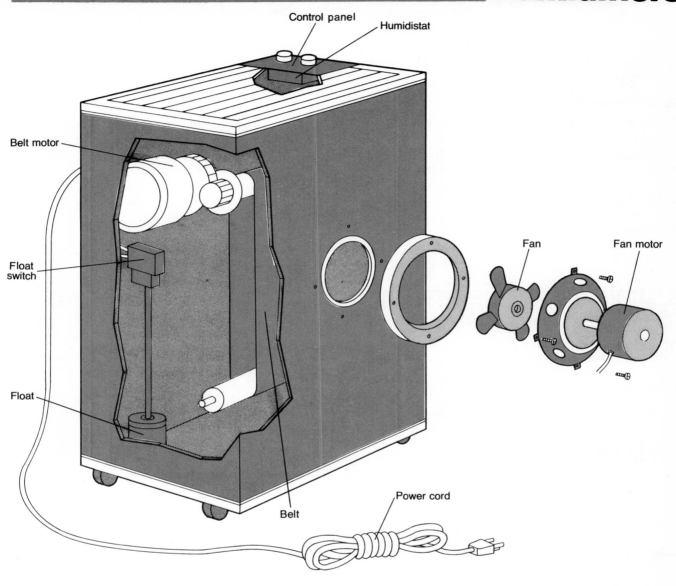

Control panel · Humidistat

Belt motor

Fan · Fan motor

Float switch

Float

Power cord

Belt

Humidifier

Principle of Operation

A portable humidifier consists of a housing with a water reservoir at the bottom. After water is poured into the reservoir, the lid is closed before the humidifier is activated and both the belt and fan motors are energized. Either a motor-driven, fiber-covered drum or continuous belt rotates through the water, bringing moisture up in front of a motor-driven fan that pulls moisture from the belt into the room. There is also a float switch connected to a rod and float, monitoring the water level; this switch turns off the unit whenever the reservoir is empty. The unit is controlled by a humidistat that governs the amount

of moisture brought into the room by the fan.

The belt type humidifier uses a continuous belt suspended between rollers to carry moisture past the fan. The belt is usually rotated by its own small motor. The drum-type may or may not use a separate motor to move the drum. If the fan motor is used, it is conn ed to the drum by pulleys and a drive belt.

Differences in Humidifiers

Some humidifiers have belts that rotate through the water reservoir bringing the moistened material up past the fan, and other models accomplish this function using a fiber-covered drum.

Disassembly

Pull off the selector switch and humidistat knobs, then pry the control panel from the lid. The motor and fan are attached to the housing with either screws or bolts which can be detached from outside the housing. All leads to the motor and float switch can be disconnected by lifting the lid of the unit.

Maintenance and Repair

Belt and Fan Motors. See page 60 for troubleshooting and repair of motors.

Lid Switch. The lid of a humidifier has a switch that closes contacts to the motor(s) only when the lid is properly shut. The switch is tested with the ohmmeter set at Rx1 (*see page 28*).

Float Switch. This switch is attached to a long shaft and a float. When the float falls below a preset level in the reservoir the switch contacts are opened, shutting off the humidifier. To test the switch from the appliance, set the ohmmeter at Rx1. The meter should read zero when the switch is closed and must be replaced if it is faulty (*see page 28*).

Humidistat. Test the humidistat by removing one of its leads and touching the terminals to the meter probes. Turn the humidistat from high to low. The meter should read zero ohms when the humidistat is in the high position and jump to high ohms as the unit is turned to low. If the meter does not jump, the humidistat is faulty and must be replaced.

Tips. The belt or drum can become clogged and should be cleaned from time to time. If the fan becomes noisy but is not loose, the motor bearings probably need lubrication. Put two or three drops of oil in each of the oil holes at both ends of the fan motor.

HUMIDIFIER TROUBLESHOOTING

PROBLEM: Humidifier does not start.

Possible Cause	Procedure	Remedy	Rating	Parts	Labor
No power at outlet.	Check fuse or circuit breaker.	Replace fuse or reset circuit breaker.			
Plug disconnected.	Check.	Reseat plug in outlet.			
Cord defective.	Check for breaks.	Repair or replace.			
Float switch faulty.	Test circuit continuity.	Replace.			
Float misplaced.	Check.	Replace.			
Lid switch faulty.	Test circuit continuity.	Replace.			
Humidistat faulty.	Test circuit continuity.	Replace.			
Fan motor defective.	Test circuit continuity.	Repair or replace.			
	Check for dirty or broken contacts.	Clean or repair.			
Drum misplaced.	Reseat drum on drive and idler wheels.	If wheels are worn or fail to revolve, replace.			

PROBLEM: Humidifier blows fuse or trips circuit breaker.

Possible Cause	Procedure	Remedy	Rating	Parts	Labor
Circuit overloaded.	Reduce number of appliances on circuit.	Replace fuse or reset circuit breaker.			
Cord or plug short-circuited.	Inspect for breaks.	Repair or replace.			

Errata

Due to an error in printing, the *Humidifier Troubleshooting* charts on pages 132 and 133 appear without the listings for *Rating, Parts,* and *Labor*.

These charts are reprinted below and on the reverse side of this sheet with the missing information included.

HUMIDIFIER TROUBLESHOOTING ▬▬▬▬

PROBLEM: Humidifier does not start. ▬▬▬▬▬▬▬▬▬▬

Possible Cause	Procedure	Remedy	Rating	Parts	Labor
No power at outlet.	Check fuse or circuit breaker.	Replace fuse or reset circuit breaker.	■		$25
Plug disconnected.	Check.	Reseat plug in outlet.	■		$25
Cord defective.	Check for breaks.	Repair or replace.	■ ■	$2-5	$25
Float switch faulty.	Test circuit continuity.	Replace.	■ ■	$3-5	$25
Float misplaced.	Check.	Replace.	■ ■	$5	$25
Lid switch faulty.	Test circuit continuity.	Replace.	■ ■ ■	$3-7	$35
Humidistat faulty.	Test circuit continuity.	Replace.	■ ■ ■ ■	$20-50	$35
Fan motor defective.	Test circuit continuity.	Repair or replace.	■ ■ ■ ■	$50-75	$35
	Check for dirty or broken contacts.	Clean or repair.			
Drum misplaced.	Reseat drum on drive and idler wheels.	If wheels are worn or fail to revolve, replace.	■ ■		$25

PROBLEM: Humidifier blows fuse or trips circuit breaker. ▬▬▬▬

Possible Cause	Procedure	Remedy	Rating	Parts	Labor
Circuit overloaded.	Reduce number of appliances on circuit.	Replace fuse or reset circuit breaker.	■		$25
Cord or plug short-circuited.	Inspect for breaks.	Repair or replace.	■ ■		$25

PROBLEM: Humidifier shocks user. ▬▬▬▬▬▬▬▬▬▬▬

Possible Cause	Procedure	Remedy	Rating	Parts	Labor
Cord frayed.	Inspect for breaks.	Repair or replace.	■	$5-10	$25
Case short-circuited.	Test circuit continuity.	Repair.	■ ■	$5-10	$25

PROBLEM: Motor operates but unit does not humidify. ▬▬▬▬▬▬

Possible Cause	Procedure	Remedy	Rating	Parts	Labor
Water in reservoir too low.	Check.	Refill.	■		$25
Belt or drum bound.	Check.	Clean and free mechanism.	■ ■		$25
Motor belt worn, loose or broken.	Check.	Tighten or replace.	■ ■ ■	$3-$0	$25
Fan loose or fan motor defective.	Check.	Tighten, repair or replace.	■ ■ ■ ■	$5-15	$35

PROBLEM: Humidifier has unpleasant odor. ▬▬▬▬▬▬▬▬

Possible Cause	Procedure	Remedy	Rating	Parts	Labor
Drum sleeve dirty.	Remove drum and drain out trapped water.	Remove sleeve and wash with mild detergent.	■		$25

PROBLEM: Water gauge inaccurate. ▬▬▬▬▬▬▬▬▬▬▬

Possible Cause	Procedure	Remedy	Rating	Parts	Labor
Float jammed.	Check.	Free float.	■	$5-10	$25

PROBLEM: Humidifier is excessively noisy. ▬▬▬▬▬▬▬▬

Possible Cause	Procedure	Remedy	Rating	Parts	Labor
Belt or drum mechanism clogged.	Check.	Clean with vinegar and water solution.	■		$25
Fan motor bearings bound.	Check.	Lubricate or replace.	■ ■ ■	$5-15	$35

PROBLEM: Humidifier shocks user.

Possible Cause	Procedure	Remedy	Rating	Parts	Labor
Cord frayed.	Inspect for breaks.	Repair or replace.			
Case short-circuited.	Test circuit continuity.	Repair.			

PROBLEM: Motor operates but unit does not humidify.

Possible Cause	Procedure	Remedy	Rating	Parts	Labor
Water in reservoir too low.	Check.	Refill.			
Belt or drum bound.	Check.	Clean and free mechanism.			
Motor belt worn, loose or broken.	Check.	Tighten or replace.			
Fan loose or fan motor defective.	Check.	Tighten, repair or replace.			

PROBLEM: Humidifier has unpleasant odor.

Possible Cause	Procedure	Remedy	Rating	Parts	Labor
Drum sleeve dirty.	Remove drum and drain out trapped water.	Remove sleeve and wash with mild detergent.			

PROBLEM: Water gauge inaccurate.

Possible Cause	Procedure	Remedy	Rating	Parts	Labor
Float jammed.	Check.	Free float.			

PROBLEM: Humidifier is excessively noisy.

Possible Cause	Procedure	Remedy	Rating	Parts	Labor
Belt or drum mechanism clogged.	Check.	Clean with vinegar and water solution.			
Fan motor bearings bound.	Check.	Lubricate or replace.			

Irons

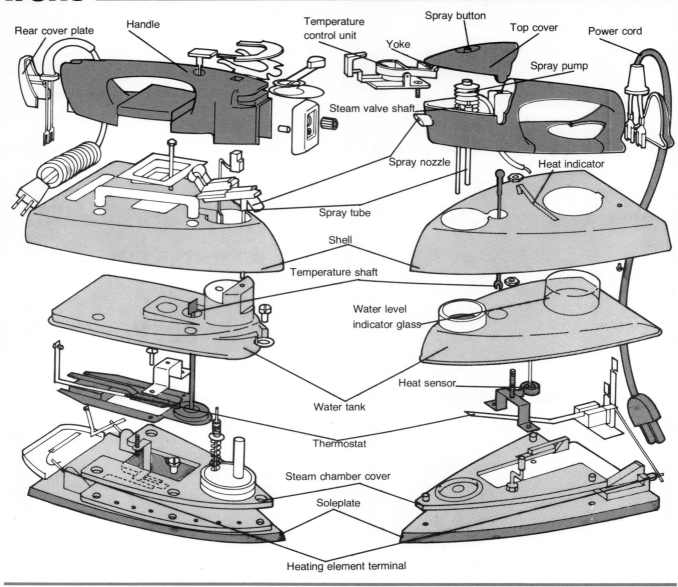

Rear cover plate · **Handle** · **Temperature control unit** · **Spray button** · **Yoke** · **Top cover** · **Power cord** · **Spray pump** · **Steam valve shaft** · **Spray nozzle** · **Heat indicator** · **Spray tube** · **Shell** · **Temperature shaft** · **Water level indicator glass** · **Heat sensor** · **Water tank** · **Thermostat** · **Steam chamber cover** · **Soleplate** · **Heating element terminal**

Steam-spray iron.   "Burst" steam-spray iron

Principle of Operation

Every iron consists of a soleplate, a cover, a thermostat, or other heat control device, a heating element assembly, a cord set, and a handle. When an iron is switched on, electricity flows through its thermostat (to control the heat) to the heating element in the soleplate. Modern irons use a bimetal blade thermostat (*see page 57*).

Differences in Irons

Irons fall into two categories: dry and steam.

Steam irons have the same components found in dry irons, plus a water reservoir and steam chamber.

Steam irons are especially useful for pressing permanent press fabrics, raising the nap of velvets and corduroys, and steaming woolens.

Irons use either the boiler or the flash method, to generate steam in an iron. In the boiler type, a water tank sits directly on the heating element in the soleplate. Steam from the boiling water is forced into a tube and then out through holes in the bottom of the soleplate. In the flash type, the water reservoir is positioned away from direct heat. The steam chamber is part of the soleplate. Water passes through an adjustable valve, strikes the soleplate, vaporizes, and is forced out through holes in the bottom of the soleplate.

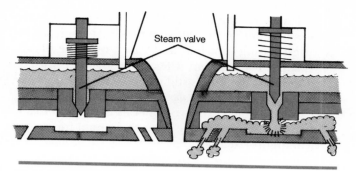

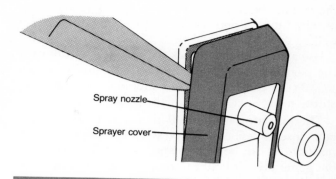

When the steam valve is closed it prevents water from entering the steam chamber. As the valve is opened, water drips into the heated chamber and is boiled, turning it to steam.

Unthread the sprayer nut and pry the sprayer cover free.

In addition to the other components found in a steam iron, a steam/spray iron has a nozzle that sprays a fine mist of water from the front of the iron.

Disassembly

All irons include a great many small parts, which must be reassembled in their exact position. When taking apart any iron, it is wise to make detailed notes on how and where each piece is positioned in the appliance.

While nearly every iron is unique in its construction, the disassembly procedure is generally in this order. Unplug unit. Remove the rear cover plate by loosening its retaining screw. Disconnect the cord

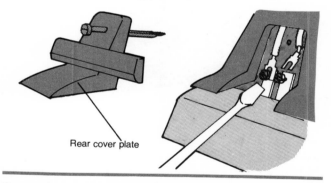

Remove the rear cover plate and disconnect the power cord from its terminals.

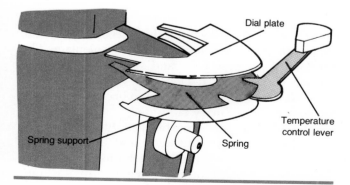

Push down on the dial plate and move the heat control lever to its highest position. The dial plate, control lever, spring and support plate will release from the handle.

from its terminals and pull it from the iron. To remove the dial plate, turn the temperature control lever to its maximum heat position while depressing the dial plate, then pull the dial plate, lever, spring and support, from the appliance. The spray nut can be removed with long-nosed pliers; then pry up the edges of the spray cover and remove it from the front of the handle. Next, pry off the saddle plate and remove the mounting screw and clamp. The spray assembly usually must be tilted while the handle is simultanously lifted to disengage the spray lever. Pull out the spray assembly and water level tube from the shell. The tank hold-down screw can now be undone and the appliance shell removed. All bolts and the heating element lead can now be loosened and the thermostat slid out of position. The steam chamber typically must be pried off its base.

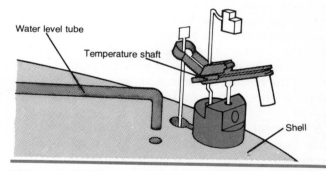

With removal of the tank hold-down screw and then the holddown, the spray assembly and water level tube can be removed to free the shell.

Maintenance and Repair

Cord. The cord is one of the chief causes of troubles in irons due to the constant flexing action when it is in use. Older irons used a male plug inserted into the iron. On newer models, the cord is fastened inside the iron by a pair of spade lugs, held in position by a pair of terminal screws. To remove the cord, simply loosen, but do not remove, the screws.

On other irons the cord terminates at a pair of slide-on fasteners. If the fasteners are corroded, or if the contact between the slide-on fasteners and their terminal lugs is poor or loose, the iron will not heat well.

Use a multitester to check the cord for continuity if the iron works only intermittently or not at all (*see page 28*). A replacement cord should be an exact substitute made specifically for the iron.

Thermostat. The bimetal thermostat can become bent, lose its resilience, or be stuck in an open or shut position. It can be rebent and its terminals cleaned, but generally it is better to replace the entire unit if it is faulty (*see page 57*).

An improperly adjusted thermostat is indicated when the iron steams in uneven spurts.

Test a thermostat by placing the probes of a multimeter to its terminals. Set the meter to the Rx1 scale. Open and close the contacts by turning the cam or depressing its arm (depending on its design). The needle will jump from high to low when the contacts open and close if the thermostat is operational. If the needle does not jump, replace the thermostat. See page 57.

Soleplate and Heating Element. The heating element is made of resistance wire that is either wound around an insulating sheet of mica or wound into a spiral and inserted in a metal tube. The element is either attached to the soleplate or built into it. The soleplate is usually made of aluminum or stainless steel and may be coated with a nonstick substance similar to Teflon. If the heating element should break, do *not* attempt to splice it together; replace the entire element. Test the heating element with a multimeter set to the Rx1 scale. Touch the meter probes to the element terminals; if the needle reads high, the element is broken. If the element is a separable unit, it can be replaced with a manufacturer's part. If the heating element is an integral part of the soleplate, the entire soleplate must be replaced (*see page 54*).

A variety of problems may arise with the soleplate. If the iron sticks to fabrics, first check the appropriate temperature setting in the owner's manual. A dirty soleplate or one coated with excessive starch may also cause sticking.

To clean the soleplate, blend some mild cleanser with a small amount of water to make a paste. Apply the paste with a clean moist cloth. Work on a small area at a time. Wipe thoroughly with a clean cloth.

Do not use steel wool pads on the soleplate since these will scratch the metal. If there are any rough scratches, try removing them with emery or fine sandpaper. If the iron still does not glide easily, warm it on its lowest setting and run it over waxed paper.

Starch often accumulates on the soleplate, making it sticky. Starch caked on the soleplate can also stain clothing. Place a sheet of flat aluminum foil (not the quilted type) on the ironing board and sprinkle with table salt. Dampen the salt slightly. Heat the iron on its lowest setting (not hot) and run it over the damp salt-sprinkled aluminum. Clean the soleplate with a damp cloth. If the iron is still not smooth enough, run it over waxed paper (*see above*).

In a steam iron, excessive minerals in the water can also cause staining. See the owner's manual for proper cleaning instructions.

If the temperature of the soleplate itself is suspect, the only sure way of testing the calibration is to take the iron to an authorized service center and put it on an iron test stand.

Steam Valve. In boiler-type systems, the steam valve is a spring-loaded plunger. When the steam button is depressed, the valve stem closes off the passage of water from the reservoir to the soleplate. The spring can become worn and require replacing.

Pressure Valve. The flash type system uses an adjustable valve that meters water entering the steam chamber. This may become corroded and require cleaning or replacement.

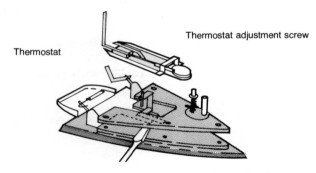

Undo the bolts in the steam chamber cover and pry the cover off the chamber.

Distilled or demineralized water should be used in older steam and steam/spray irons.

Tap water normally contains minerals (such as calcium) that cause hard whitish deposits or corrosion in the aluminum or stainless steel of the soleplate. The interiors of the reservoirs and steam chambers can develop corrosion that clogs the valves and steam holes. Newer models are treated to prevent corrosion and so can use ordinary tap water.

If the steam vents become blocked, fill the tank with distilled white vinegar and water and run the iron at maximum heat. Push the steam button, letting the vinegar pass through the entire system until it is completely gone. One steam tankful of vinegar should be enough to free the unit. Subsequently, use only distilled water.

STEAM OR STEAM/SPRAY IRON TROUBLESHOOTING
(See dry iron troubleshooting charts for mutual problems)

PROBLEM: Iron steams when on dry setting.

Possible Cause	Procedure	Remedy	Rating	Parts	Labor
Steam valve system faulty.	Check for bent or broken steam knob wire connector, or weak valve spring, or corroded valve stem.	Repair or replace parts of entire system.	■ ■ ■	$5	$10

PROBLEM: Iron leaks water.

Possible Cause	Procedure	Remedy	Rating	Parts	Labor
Gaskets at steam chamber or spray body worn out.	Inspect for breaks or improper sealing.	Replace.	■	$3	$7.50
Water reservoir leaking.	Apply soapy water to all seams and blow air into reservoir. Bubbles will apear at site of leak.	Apply silicone adhesive or epoxy to small leaks, or replace unit.	■		$7.50
Overfilled tank.	Pour off excess.				

PROBLEM: Iron sprays inadequately or not at all.

Possible Cause	Procedure	Remedy	Rating	Parts	Labor
Spray cap or connector assembly clogged.	Check steam pressure in boiler and tank by pressing spray knob. If there is pressure, water tube is clogged.	Remove and clean water tube and nozzle opening. If there is no pressure replace valve between boiler and steam passage. Use fine wire to clean hole in cap.	■	$2	$7.50
Gasket worn.	Inspect.	Replace.	■	$2	$7.50
Pump assembly faulty.	Take apart handle to check.	Replace.	■ ■ ■	$3	$10
Bellows faulty.	Some models have bellows behind spray mechanism. Check for cracks or leaks.	Replace.	■ ■ ■	$1	$10

PROBLEM: Iron steams inadequately or not at all.

Possible Cause	Procedure	Remedy	Rating	Parts	Labor
Tank empty.		Fill.			
Thermostat set improperly.		Set heat control higher.			
Steam or water passages clogged.	Fill tank with a mixture of water and white vinegar, turn gauge to highest steam setting and let run till tank is empty.	Vinegar removes hard water deposits in passages. Use distilled water.	■		$7.50
Steam valve faulty.	Observe valve shaft through fill port. When temperature settings are altered valve should turn. If not, take apart and check for worn or clogged parts.	Replace worn or broken parts (along with new gaskets). Clean gummy deposits with paint thinner.	■ ■ ■	$5	$10

(Continued on next page)

PROBLEM: Fill port steams.

Possible Cause	Procedure	Remedy	Rating	Parts	Labor
Fill tube valve malfunctioning.	Check for loose connections or worn valve seat.	Repair or replace.	■	$2	$7.50

PROBLEM: Iron sputters or spits.

Possible Cause	Procedure	Remedy	Rating	Parts	Labor
Overfilled tank.	Poor off excess.				
Steam setting turned on too soon.	Wait two to five minutes for iron to heat.				
Steam valve corroded.	Inspect.	Clean or replace.	■	$3	$7.50
Thermostat faulty.	Consult authorized service center to check calibration.	Adjust according to manufacturer's temperature rating.	■	$3	$7.50

PROBLEM: Iron spots or sticks to clothes.

Possible Cause	Procedure	Remedy	Rating	Parts	Labor
Starch or dirt on soleplate.	Clean.		■		$7.50
Tank or passages dirty or clogged with minerals.	Fill tank with a mixture of water and white vinegar. Turn gauge to highest setting and let steam until tank is empty.	Vinegar should remove deposits. Use distilled water.	■		$10

DRY IRON TROUBLESHOOTING

PROBLEM: Iron does not heat.

Possible Cause	Procedure	Remedy	Rating	Parts	Labor
No power at outlet.	Check fuse or circuit breaker.	Replace fuse or reset circuit breaker.			
Plug disconnected.		Reseat plug in outlet.			
Cord defective.	Check for breaks.	Repair or replace.	■	$3	$5
Heating element defective.	Check circuit continuity.	Replace element or soleplate, depending on model.	■	$7	$5
Thermostat faulty.	Check for loose or dirty contacts, then test circuit continuity.	Clean or replace as needed.	■ ■ ■	$3	$7.50
Travel model set for overseas operation.	Change voltage setting. If failure continues, contacts may be fused.	Replace.	■ ■ ■	$3	$7.50

PROBLEM: Iron blows fuse or trips circuit breaker.

Possible Cause	Procedure	Remedy	Rating	Parts	Labor
Circuit overloaded.	Reduce number of appliances on circuit.	Replace fuse or reset circuit breaker.			
Cord or plug short-circuited.	Inspect for breaks.	Repair or replace.	■	$3	$5

(Continued on next page)

PROBLEM: Iron shocks user.

Possible Cause	Procedure	Remedy	Rating	Parts	Labor
Cord frayed.	Inspect for breaks.	Repair or replace.	■	$3	$5
Case short-circuited.	Test circuit continuity.	Repair.	■		$7.50
Heating element grounded.	Check.	See page 54.	■ ■ ■	$7	$5

PROBLEM: Cord sparks.

Possible Cause	Procedure	Remedy	Rating	Parts	Labor
Connections loose or wires broken in plug.	Visually inspect.	Repair or replace	■	$3	$5

PROBLEM: Iron gets too hot, or not hot enough.

Possible Cause	Procedure	Remedy	Rating	Parts	Labor
Cord defective.	Test circuit continuity.	Repair or replace.	■	$3	$5
House voltage low.	Remove all other appliances from circuit.				
Thermostat faulty.	Test circuit continuity.	Replace.	■ ■ ■	$3	$7.50
	Needs recalibration.	Consult authorized service center.	■ ■		$7.50

PROBLEM: Iron does not shut off.

Possible Cause	Procedure	Remedy	Rating	Parts	Labor
Thermostat defective.	Check circuit continuity.	Replace.	■ ■ ■	$3	$7.50
Contacts welded.	Check thermostat or temperature control.	Separate or replace.	■ ■	$3	$7.50

PROBLEM: Iron tears, spots, or sticks to clothes.

Possible Cause	Procedure	Remedy	Rating	Parts	Labor
Starch or dirt on soleplate.	Clean.		■		$7.50
Soleplate nicked, scratched, or rough.	Inspect.	Remove with fine emery or sandpaper, then buff or polish.	■		$7.50

PROBLEM: Soleplate is blistered.

Possible Cause	Procedure	Remedy	Rating	Parts	Labor
Excessive heat.	Consult authorized service center to check calibration of thermostat.	Adjust or replace. (Soleplate sometimes can be smoothed with emery board or buffing wheel.)	■ ■	$3	$7.50

Knives

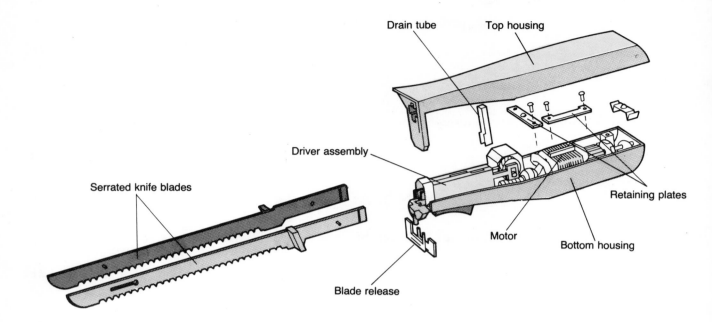

Serrated knife blades

Drain tube · Top housing

Driver assembly

Retaining plates

Blade release

Motor

Bottom housing

Electric knife

Principle of Operation

Electric knives are all pretty much identical in their operation, whether they are powered by a small universal motor or by batteries. When activated by an On/Off switch, the motor or batteries drive a worm gear, which rotates the small reduction (pinion) gear that moves a driver arm on each side. The pinion gear has an eccentric pin on each side of it that holds the blade-driver arms. With each rotation of the pinion gear, one blade moves forward approximately half an inch while the other blade retreats half an inch. The twin serrated blades of the knife are attached to the driver arms so that they can move back and forth. Plastic guides hold the blades close enough to rub against each other. This friction continuously sharpens the blades, as well as giving them an extraordinary ability to slice food.

Differences in Knives

Aside from a range of housing designs, the only real difference among electric knives is their source of power. Some models use a small universal motor; others incorporate batteries. Otherwise, the switches, gears, mountings, and knife blades are practically identical.

Disassembly

Remove all screws visible in the housing and separate the top and bottom halves. Pull the blade release buttons off their latch springs and free the driver assembly mounting screws. The driver assembly and front bearing retainer can now be lifted from the bottom housing. The motor is mounted to the housing with screws; remove them and pry the motor and fan out of position.

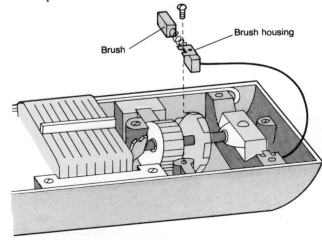

Brush housing

Brush

Remove all mounting screws in the bottom of the handle.

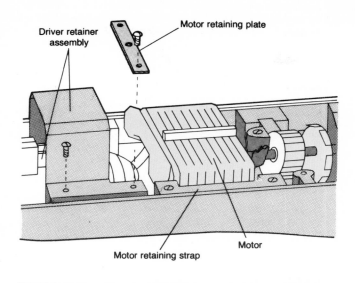

The driver assembly and motor can be lifted out of the handle once their retaining plates are removed.

Maintenance and Repair

Cord Set. If the knife has a cord it can be tested with a multimeter set to the Rx1 scale (*see page 26*).

On/Off Switch. Test the On/Off switch with a multimeter set to the Rx1 scale and its probes touching each of the switch terminals. The meter should read zero ohms when the switch is in its closed position. If the meter gives a high reading, replace the switch.

Motors. Only universal motors are used in electric knives (*see page 61*). Some models have a DC version of the motor that can operate only when it is plugged into an AC outlet, which means the motor is wired to a rectifier. Cordless models incorporate a complement of four or five batteries and are sold with a battery charger. Other models can either use AC power from a wall outlet or operate on batteries.

Charging Unit. Not much can be done to repair a recharger other than to replace it. The unit can be tested by setting a multimeter to the Rx100 scale and touching its probes to the prongs of its cord. The

meter will read between 500 and 1000 ohms if the unit is functioning. If the meter reads zero or higher, either the cord or the transformer is defective.

Power Pack. The batteries in a cordless knife can be tested with a multimeter set to the 2.5 VDC scale. Hold the red meter probe to the plus side of the battery and the black probe to the minus terminal. If the reading is below 1 volt when the knife is turned on, replace the battery.

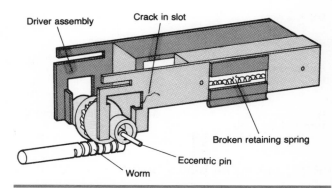

If the slots that hold the knife blades are cracked, replace the entire driver assembly.

Gear Train. Many of the problems that develop in electric knives stem from the gear train. The pinion gear is normally made of plastic or fiber and it eventually wears and has to be replaced. If the motor shaft can be turned manually while the driver arm is held tightly, the gear is worn and should be replaced. The driver-retainer assembly is subject to constant vibration and often develops cracks around the slot used to hold the eccentric pin in the reduction gear and the springs that retain the knife blades. Because all the parts are riveted together, it is necessary to replace the entire drive assembly if any part of it is cracked or broken. The bearings and gears can be given a drop of silicone oil if they stick.

Knife Blades. The blades are serrated and cannot be sharpened. They should be replaced if they become dull or if the height of their teeth is not identical.

KNIFE TROUBLESHOOTING

PROBLEM: Knife does not start.

Possible Cause	Procedure	Remedy	Rating	Parts	Labor
No power at outlet.	Check fuse or circuit breaker.	Replace fuse or reset circuit breaker.	■		
Plug disconnected.		Reseat plug in outlet.	■		

(Continued on next page)

PROBLEM: Knife does not start. *(Continued from preceding page)*

Possible Cause	Procedure	Remedy	Rating	Parts	Labor
Cord defective.	Check for breaks.	Repair or replace.	■		$5
Switch defective.	Test circuit continuity.	Replace.	■	$2	$7.50
Contacts dirty.	Take apart unit.	Replace broken parts. Clean with fine sandpaper.	■		$7.50
Brushes worn.	Inspect.	Replace.	■	$2	$7.50
Rectifier defective.	Test internal diodes.	Replace.	■	$3	$7.50
Battery worn out. (cordless model)	Check with voltmeter.	Replace all batteries, not just weak or worn-out ones.	■	$3	$7.50
Battery worn out. (convertible model)	If knife operates when plugged in, batteries need replacing.	Replace all batteries, not just weak or worn-out ones.	■	$3	$7.50

PROBLEM: Knife blows fuse or trips circuit breaker.

Possible Cause	Procedure	Remedy	Rating	Parts	Labor
Circuit overloaded.	Reduce number of appliances on circuit.	Replace fuse or reset circuit breaker.	■		
Cord short-circuited.	Inspect for breaks.	Repair or replace.	■	$3	$7.50
Switch or motor short-circuited.	Test circuit continuity.	Repair.	■	$2	$7.50

PROBLEM: Knife shocks user.

Possible Cause	Procedure	Remedy	Rating	Parts	Labor
Cord frayed.	Inspect for breaks.	Repair or replace.	■	$3	$5
Case short-circuited.	Test circuit continuity.	Repair.	■		$7.50
Wiring defective.	Inspect for bare wires.	Insulate.	■		$7.50

PROBLEM: Knife operates slowly, with reduced power.

Possible Cause	Procedure	Remedy	Rating	Parts	Labor
Brushes worn.	Inspect.	Replace.	■	$2	$7.50
Gears bound.	Lubricate pinion and worm gears. Be sure to lubricate tiny gear train bearings.		■		$7.50

PROBLEM: Motor operates but blades do not move.

Possible Cause	Procedure	Remedy	Rating	Parts	Labor
Blades improperly inserted.	Check.	Reinsert.	■		$5
Safety switch defective. (where applicable)	Check.	Replace.	■	$2	$7.50
Pinion gear worn or broken.	Check.	Replace.	■	$3	$7.50

Mixers

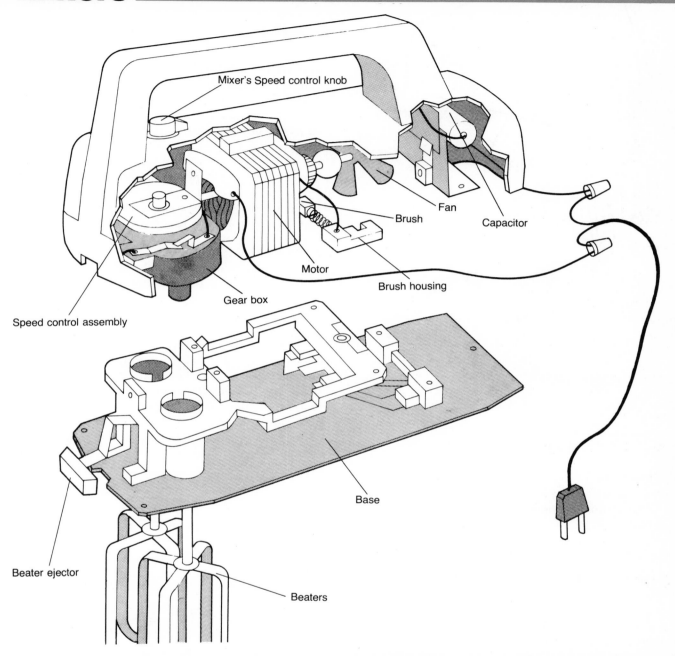

Mixer's Speed control knob

Fan

Brush

Capacitor

Motor

Brush housing

Gear box

Speed control assembly

Base

Beater ejector

Beaters

Hand-held mixer.

Principle of Operation

A mixer rotates beaters at various speeds circulating food in a bowl until it is thoroughly blended. Heavy food such as dough is usually blended slowly, while light foods such as eggs are beaten at high speeds.

The beaters are inserted into the power head and locked in place before the machine is activated. The speed-control switch, which may use a governor, an SCR, a rheostat, or an adjustable-brush system to regulate the universal motor, is then set. When the On/Off switch is engaged, current from the cord passes through the speed-control unit to the motor, which has a direct drive to gears in the power head. The speed at which the beaters are set can be changed while the motor is operating.

Differences in Mixers

There are three types of mixers sold today: stationary, portable, and convertible, all of which resemble

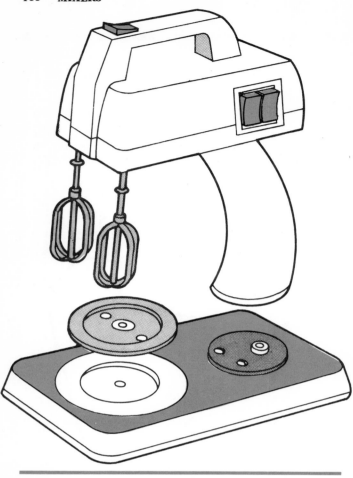

Stationary mixer.

one another and perform similar functions. A basic mixer consists of a plastic or metal housing covering a power head that permits the removable beaters to mesh with a set of gears. Some models have a large handle attached to their tops. The motor speed-control switch is on or near the handle.

Stationary Mixers

One model consists of a speed-controlled motor in a housing fitted with two beaters. The motor case is hinged to the top of a pedestal and positioned over a revolving turntable which holds the mixing bowl. The entire motor assembly can be swung upward to allow easy removal of both the bowl and the beaters. The beaters are usually ejected from their power head by pushing a large handle laterally, down the side of the motor case.

Another type of stationary mixer consists of a bowl in a fixed position with one beater driven by an eccentric cam and shaft. This model keeps the beater turning along the sides of the bowl and moving the contents into the center of the bowl, accomplishing the same mixing function. The eccentric cam rotates in one direction while the beater rotates in the opposite direction.

Portable Mixers

These function like the stationary machines, but they do not have pedestals. Their motors are almost as powerful as larger models and operate in the same manner, but they must be hand-held.

Convertible Mixers

These offer the convenience of both the stationary and portable types. They have a pedestal and turntable, but the mixer housing can be removed and used in the same manner as a portable unit.

At least three speeds are offered on all models, while the larger stationary units provide a wider range of speeds for handling almost any type of mixing operation. There are also several different kinds of mixer blades sold as accessories for special operations such as kneading dough or juicing.

Disassembly

Remove all assembly screws located in the base of the mixer and pull off the housing. Remove the screws that hold the bearing retainer and lift it off the motor. The brushes can now be removed; take them off carefully to prevent them from springing out of their receptacles. The control knob is attached to the speed control unit with a spring metal clip that must be squeezed before the knob can be withdrawn from the control linkage. Disconnect the governor spring and remove the control linkage, cam follower, and speed cam. Disconnect the beater ejector spring and remove all screws and/or nuts holding the gear cover in place. The gears can now be lifted from the gear

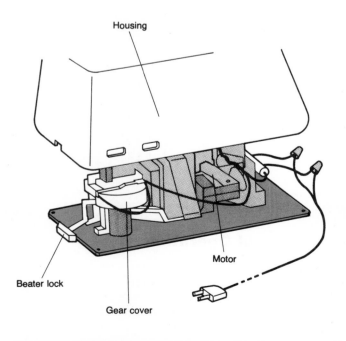

Housing

Beater lock

Gear cover

Motor

Undo all retaining screws in the base plate and lift off the upper housing.

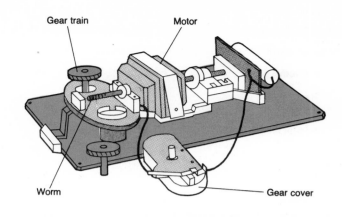

With the gear cover removed, the gears can be lifted out of their positions.

box. Remove the governor switch mounting screws and take off the governor switch. The motor is held to its base with a spring metal strap which requires considerable force to pry free.

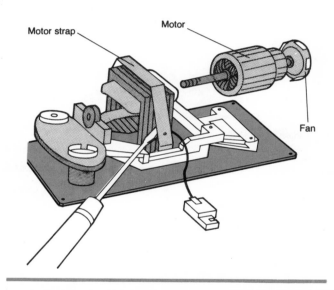

Pry off the motor retaining strap to free the motor field. The rotor and fan are disengaged by pulling.

Maintenance and Repair

Turntables. Some stationary mixers have a turntable that enables the bowl to rotate with the beaters, but at a slower speed. A mechanical level protruding from under the turntable regulates the spin of the bowl by manually changing its position in relation to that of the beaters. The turntable revolves freely on a spindle, and has no electrical connections. The lever can be bent back into alignment if it fails to work properly.

Beater Ejectors. In most models, the beaters are inserted or removed from their sockets by manually pushing or pulling them, sometimes with an accom-

panying twist. On some of the larger stationary models, ejection of the beaters is accomplished by pushing the handle sideways until they pop out of their sockets.

Gear Box. This is a sealed, oil-filled housing containing the gears that engage the beater stems! It is found at the front of the motor shaft, at the point where the beaters are inserted. If the beaters fit firmly in their holes but do not rotate properly when the motor is turned on, the gears are most likely stripped and should be replaced. To get at the gears, remove the screws in the retaining plate that covers and holds the gears in place. Remove the plate along with the ejector mechanism that stands on the retaining plate. The gears can now be pulled from the bottom housing.

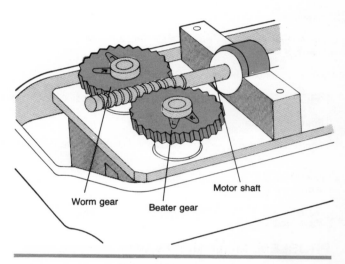

Gear train of a mixer.

Universal Motor. See page 61 for testing and repair information concerning universal motors.

Speed Controls. Mixers may use a governor, tapped field, adjustable brush, or silicon controlled rectifiers (SCR) to alter the speed of their motors. For information concerning the repair of governors, see page 64. Tapped field controls are covered on page 64. Adjustable brush controls are on page 65. SCR information is found on page 64.

Cord and Plug. To test a mixer cord, disconnect the cord from the appliance. Attach the probes of a multimeter to the prongs of the plug; set the meter to the Rx100 scale. If the meter reads zero or jumps, the cord is faulty and should be replaced.

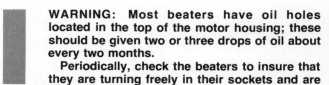

WARNING: Most beaters have oil holes located in the top of the motor housing; these should be given two or three drops of oil about every two months.

Periodically, check the beaters to insure that they are turning freely in their sockets and are not bent.

Be sure to keep the beaters clean at all times.

MIXER TROUBLESHOOTING

PROBLEM: Mixer does not start.

Possible Cause	Procedure	Remedy	Rating	Parts	Labor
No power at outlet.	Check fuse or circuit breaker.	Replace fuse or reset circuit breaker.			
Plug disconnected.		Reseat plug in outlet.			
Cord defective.	Check for breaks.	Repair or replace.	■	$3	
Switch faulty.	Check circuit continuity.	Replace.	■	$2.50	$7.50
Rheostat defective.	Check for burned wires or faulty contacts.	Replace.	■	$3	$7.50
Governor faulty.	Check for pitted contacts.	File smooth or replace.			
Brushes worn or not contacting commutator.	Unscrew brush caps. Check brushes and springs.	Replace.	■	$2	$7.50
Motor shaft bound or bent.	Check armature rotation.	Lubricate or replace.	■		$7.50
Armature winding broken.	Check.	Replace.	■ ■ ■	$8	$12

PROBLEM: Mixer blows fuse or trips circuit breaker.

Possible Cause	Procedure	Remedy	Rating	Parts	Labor
Circuit overloaded.	Reduce number of appliances on circuit.	Replace fuse or reset circuit breaker.			
Cord or plug short-circuited.	Inspect for breaks.	Repair or replace.	■	$3	$7.50
Switch or motor short-circuited.	Test circuit continuity.	Repair or replace.	■	$2.50	$7.50

PROBLEM: Mixer shocks user.

Possible Cause	Procedure	Remedy	Rating	Parts	Labor
Cord frayed.	Inspect for breaks.	Repair or replace.	■	$3	$7.50
Case short-circuited.	Test circuit continuity.	Repair.	■ ■ ■	$10	$10
Wiring defective.	Inspect for bare wires.	Insulate.	■		$7.50

PROBLEM: Mixer sparks, sputters.

Possible Cause	Procedure	Remedy	Rating	Parts	Labor
Brushes worn.	Check.	If less than ⅜ inch long, replace.	■	$2	$7.50
Commutator worn.	Check for excess carbon.	Lightly sand and clean.	■ ■ ■	$10	$10
Power head faulty.	Check for worn gear teeth or oil leak.	Replace.	■ ■ ■	$10	$10

PROBLEM: Mixer hums but beaters do not turn.

Possible Cause	Procedure	Remedy	Rating	Parts	Labor
Bearings bound.	Check.	Lubricate or replace.	■		$7.50
Gears, coupling dirty or defective.	Check.	Clean and lubricate or replace.	■		$7.50
Beater stems not locked into shafts.	Clean shafts, check stems.	If stems are worn, replace beaters.	■	$5	$7.50

(Continued on next page)

PROBLEM: Mixer hums but beaters do not turn. *(Continued from preceding page)*

Possible Cause	Procedure	Remedy	Rating	Parts	Labor
Teeth on beater gears ripped.	Inspect.	Replace.	■	$5	$7.50
Beater blades clash.	Realign beater gears. Lubricate.	Replace.	■	$5	$7.50
Food mixture too thick.	Lift beaters from bowl to see if they can operate.	Thin down mixture or beat by hand.			

PROBLEM: Motor operates hot.

Possible Cause	Procedure	Remedy	Rating	Parts	Labor
Shaft bound.	Check.	Clean and lubricate.	■		$7.50
Winding in armature short-circuited.	Check.	Replace.	■ ■ ■	$8	$12
Field coil short-circuited.	Check.	Replace.	■ ■ ■	$10	$10

PROBLEM: Mixer only operates at one speed.

Possible Cause	Procedure	Remedy	Rating	Parts	Labor
Contacts dirty.	Check circuit continuity. Check all connections.	Clean or replace.	■		$7.50
Control-plate spring loose.	Remove cover and check.	If unhooked, attach to top of control plate. If worn or broken, replace.	■		$10
Control-plate contacts welded.	Turn from low to high speed. Contacts should separate.	If welded, replace.	■		$10
Capacitor defective.	Discharge and check capacitor (see page 62).	Repair or replace.	■	$5	$10
Governor defective.	Turn motor on, then off. Observe governor as it recedes when armature slows.	If it does not move smoothly, replace.	■	$10	$10
Switch faulty.	Check.	Replace.	■	$2.50	$7.50

PROBLEM: Mixer is excessively noisy and vibrates too much.

Possible Cause	Procedure	Remedy	Rating	Parts	Labor
Gears defective.	Check for loose gear-case cover.	Tighten.	■		$10
	Remove cover, check for worn or broken teeth.	Replace entire assembly.	■ ■ ■	$10	$10
Beater hitting bowl.	Check. Beater should just clear bottom of bowl.	Readjust or switch bowls.			
Governor defective.	Turn motor on, then off. Observe governor as it recedes when armature slows.	If it does not move smoothly, replace.	■	$10	$10
Armature shaft worn or bent.	Inspect.	Replace.	■	$10	$10
Cooling fan blade bent.	Check.	Repair or replace.	■	$3	$7.50

PROBLEM: Pedestal mixer bowl does not rotate.

Possible Cause	Procedure	Remedy	Rating	Parts	Labor
Beaters too far from bowl.	Inspect.	Adjust clearance.			

Shavers

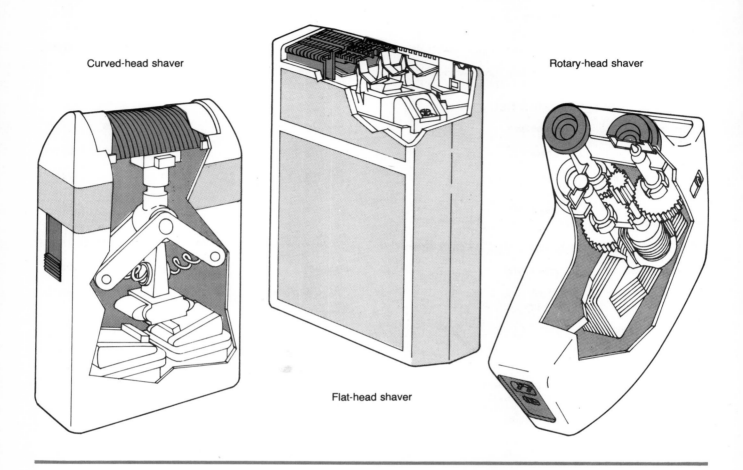

Curved-head shaver

Flat-head shaver

Rotary-head shaver

Principle of Operation

When an electric shaver is turned on, its motor moves a sharp cutter across the underside of the thin metal shield that forms the head of the unit. The shield is perforated with tiny holes so that individual whiskers are drawn inside the machine, where the rapidly moving cutter slices them off.

All types of shavers can be purchased as battery-powered units, which function in precisely the same manner as motor-operated shavers.

Differences in Shavers

Shavers found on the market today offer three basic kinds of shaving heads—curved, flat, and rotary—and are powered by small universal or vibratory motors or by rechargeable batteries.

Curved-head shaver

The curved head is made of an extremely thin, perforated metal that flexes with the contours of the skin

it passes over. Directly behind the head is a single cutter with dozens of tiny blades that travel back and forth on a pivot arm linked to a vibratory motor. The spring-loaded pivot arm, located between the field magnets of the motor, is pulled back and forth at the same 60 cycles per second rate as the house current that energizes it.

Flat-head shaver

The flat-head shaver uses either a universal or a vibratory motor. The head is composed of a series of slots fitted directly over three cutters. The cutters oscillate so that the center cutter is always moving in a direction opposite to that of the two outside cutters.

Rotary-head shaver

The rotary-head shaver employs a universal motor. Directly under each of the shaver's round heads, a reduction gear rotates a sharp cutting wheel. The heads and cutter assembly are mounted on springs so that they can float with the contours of the skin they are shaving.

Disassembly

Shavers, no matter what type, are delicate. All their parts are minuscule and often require jeweler's tools to work on. Manufacturers prefer to have a defective machine returned for repair, so many models cannot be disassembled. Some manufacturers ingeniously hide the screws that hold the housings of their shavers together.

Curved- or Flat-head shaver

Set the control dial to clean, then remove the shaving head, the cutters, and the foam rubber pad under them. Then rotate the control dial to its lowest posi-

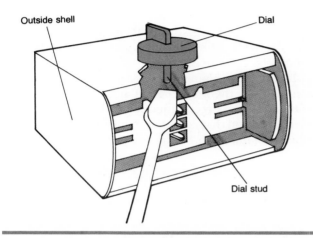

Pry the inner and outer shells apart with a screwdriver. The stud must be disengaged from the inner shell.

tion, and carefully pry the inner and outer housings apart. Slide the body of the shaver out of its housing. Pry the vibrator cover off the top of the inner housing. Be careful not to bend the whisker guards, which extend from either end of the guard. Undo the mounting screws in the inner housing cover. The field magnet and vibrator are a single unit held in place by a screw near the bottom of the housing. The vibrator is attached to the field magnets with screws.

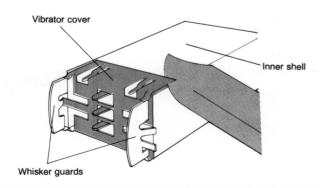

Be careful when prying the vibrator cover off the inner shell not to harm the whisker guards.

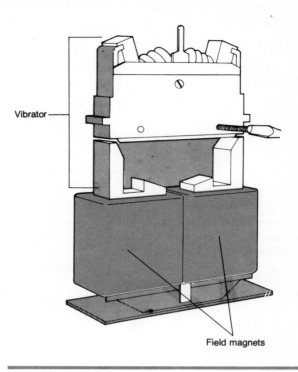

Remove the screws in the vibrator and lift it off the field magnets. Rotors can also be removed by undoing their retaining screws.

Rotary-head Shaver

Remove the shaving heads, undo the retaining screws in the housing, and separate the two halves. If the unit has a trimmer, remove it by pressing down its retaining clip and sliding it out. Remove the screws behind the faceplate and pull off the gear cover. The

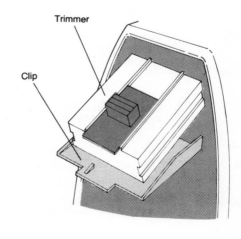

Trimmers can be removed by pressing down on the retaining clip.

satellite gears around the pinion gear can be lifted off of their shafts. Undo the motor mounting screws. Remove the motor, switch, switch arm, and terminal block.

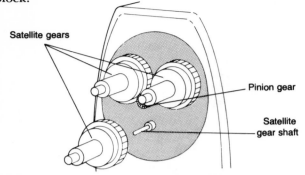

Satellite gears are merely lifted off their pins. The pinion gear is permanently attached to the motor shaft.

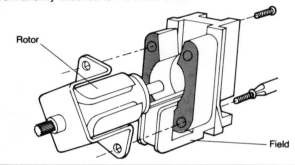

The brush assembly in rotary-head shavers should be replaced regularly.

Maintenance and Repair

Cord Set. See page 52.

On/Off Switch. See pages 54-55.

Universal Motors. Universal motor brushes must be changed periodically. See page 60.

Vibratory Motors. The field coil in a vibratory motor can be checked with a multimeter set to the Rx1 scale. Touch the probes of the meter to the coil terminals. The coil is all right if the meter reads between 100 and 200 ohms. If the meter reads infinity, there is a break in the wiring. If it reads zero, there is a short circuit. In either case, replace the motor.

Gears and Mechanical Parts. The gears and other mechanical parts in most shavers will rarely cause any problems. If they are worn or broken, the part should be replaced. In a few instances, the piece may be bent and can be realigned.

Blades. If the blades break or become dull, replace them or have them sharpened at a repair shop.

Oil a shaver as recommended in its user's manual. Use only the oil that comes with the unit or one specifically recommended by the manufacturer.

NOTE: Manufacturers include a head-cleaning brush with their shavers, which should be used after every shave to get all whiskers and pre-shave powder out of the head.

SHAVER TROUBLESHOOTING

PROBLEM: Motor runs slowly or not at all.

Possible Cause	Procedure	Remedy	Rating	Parts	Labor
No power at outlet.	Check fuse or circuit breaker.	Replace fuse or reset circuit breaker.	■	$8	$20
Defective cord and plug.	Test cord for continuity.	If faulty, replace.	■	$3	$7.50
Faulty switch.	Check for defective contacts, loose wires, dirty terminals. Test for continuity.	Clean terminals, tighten wires, rebend contacts. If no continuity, replace switch.	■	$2	$7.50
Motor bearings seized.	Clean and lubricate bearings.	If lubrication fails, replace bearings.	■	$2	$7.50
Cutters binding against shaving head.	Clean and lubricate cutters and shaving head. Inspect for damage.	If lubrication fails, replace cutters and shaving head.	■	$5	$7.50
Loose wire connection.	Test all wires for proper continuity.	Tighten loose connections.	■	$1	$7.50
Motor defective.	Test for continuity.	If bad, replace motor.	■	$10	$7.50

Slow Cookers

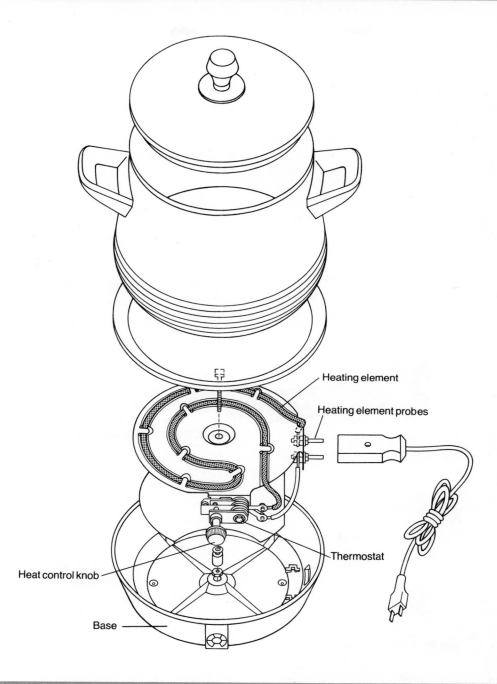

Heating element

Heating element probes

Thermostat

Heat control knob

Base

Slow cooker

Principle of Operation

The electrical circuit in a slow cooker consists of a single or double heating element made of resistance wire, a switch controlling the heating element, and a thermostat (which in some models is incorporated in the control switch). Current flows through the switch to the heating element; when the desired tem-

perature is reached, the thermostat opens the circuit. In all models, the heating element and the switch are in the base of the unit.

Slow cookers require only about 70 watts at their low temperatures and 160 watts at high temperature.

Differences in Slow Cookers

The principal variation in slow cookers is the

switching arrangement. Most models have a Lo/Hi switch; turning from Lo to Hi either activates a second heating element wired in series with the first, or it adjusts the thermostat so that additional heat must build up before the circuit turns off.

Some models have an additional setting, an automatic switch from Hi to Lo after the unit has heated up. Here, the two elements are wired in parallel, and this third setting is controlled by a thermostat in the circuit of the second heating element. When the thermostat opens, current can flow only through the first (Lo) heating element.

All food cookers or warmers with their heating elements and thermostats permanently installed inside the appliance (corn poppers, saucepans, egg cookers, potato bakers, fondue pots) function in the same manner as slow cookers. While disassembly may vary slightly, and the electrical components inside

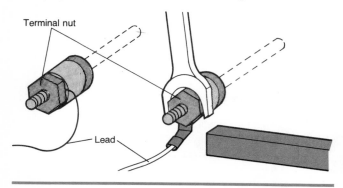

Loosen the retaining nuts holding all terminals and disconnect their wires.

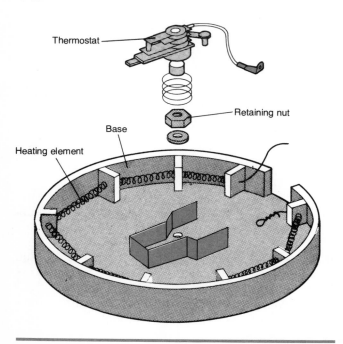

Remove the retaining screw or bolt that holds the thermostat to the base of the appliance. Lift off the thermostat assembly.

may appear somewhat different, their repair can be accomplished by following the repair procedures used for slow cookers.

Disassembly

Unplug the unit, and take off the plastic feet. Remove the screws holding the base to the cooker body. In many models, there is a single center screw. The leads to the terminal pins for the plug must be removed with a set wrench or pliers. The thermostat is held in place with a setscrew in the center of the element tray. The thermostat is usually held tightly against the cooking surface by a spring and washer.

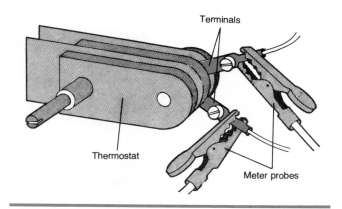

The thermostat can be tested by clipping the probes of a multimeter to its terminals.

Maintenance and Repair

Thermostats. The thermostat may function as either a timer or a temperature control. Its malfunction is usually apparent in a failure to shut off the heat, resulting in overheating. In instances where the thermostat is held against the cooking plate by a spring, the spring should be replaced if it is weak or broken. If the thermostat itself fails to function properly, replace the entire component (*see page 57*).

Cord and Plug. See page 28.

Heating Element. Many slow cookers have a single strand heating element integral with their base, which means that if the element fails, the appliance must be replaced. To test a slow cooker heating element, unplug the appliance and allow it to cool. Set a multimeter to the Rx1 scale and touch its probes to both leads of the element. The meter will read between 50 and 200 ohms if the element on a slow cooker is good. A good reading on corn poppers is between 20 and 40 ohms. If the reading is high, the element is faulty and must be replaced. If the element is an integral part of the appliance, replace the appliance.

 WARNING: No part of the appliance should be immersed in water. Clean all surfaces with a sponge dipped in soapy water; do not use scouring pads or abrasive cleaners.

SLOW COOKER TROUBLESHOOTING

PROBLEM: Cooker does not heat.

Possible Cause	Procedure	Remedy	Rating	Parts	Labor
No power at outlet.	Check fuse or circuit breaker.	Replace fuse or reset circuit breaker.			
Plug disconnected.		Reseat plug in outlet.			
Cord defective.	Check for breaks.	Repair or replace.	■	$3	$5
Heating element defective.	Check circuit continuity.	Replace element.	■ ■ ■	$10	$10
Thermostat defective.	Test circuit continuity.	Replace thermostat.	■	$2.50	$7.50
Wiring defective.	Inspect for bare wires and corrosion on terminals.	Insulate, clean corroded terminals.	■		$7.50

PROBLEM: Cooker blows fuse or trips circuit breaker.

Possible Cause	Procedure	Remedy	Rating	Parts	Labor
Circuit overloaded.	Reduce number of appliances on circuit.	Replace fuse or reset circuit breaker.			
Cord or plug short-circuited.	Inspect for breaks.	Repair or replace.	■	$3	$5
Switch or motor short-circuited.	Test circuit continuity.	Repair or replace.	■	$2.50	$7.50

PROBLEM: Cooker shocks user.

Possible Cause	Procedure	Remedy	Rating	Parts	Labor
Cord frayed.	Inspect for breaks.	Repair or replace.	■	$3	$5
Case short-circuited.	Test circuit continuity.	Repair.	■		$7.50

PROBLEM: Cooker does not maintain proper temperature.

Possible Cause	Procedure	Remedy	Rating	Parts	Labor
Thermostat defective.	Test to see if contacts open and close.	Repair or replace. Calibrate.	■	$2.50	$7.50

PROBLEM: Indicator lamp does not light.

Possible Cause	Procedure	Remedy	Rating	Parts	Labor
Lamp or resistor defective.	Test.	Replace.	■	$1	$7.50

Toasters

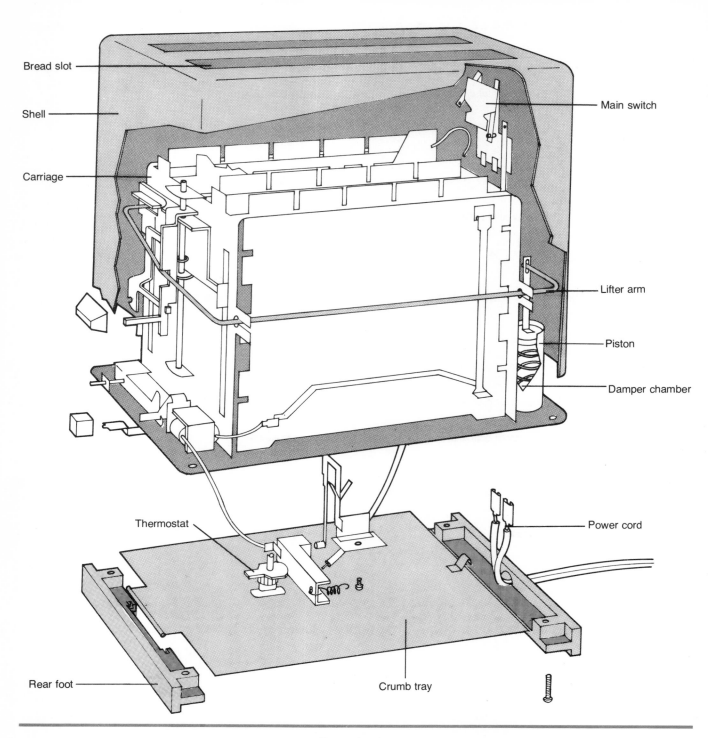

Bread slot

Shell

Carriage

Main switch

Lifter arm

Piston

Damper chamber

Thermostat

Power cord

Rear foot

Crumb tray

Pop-up toaster

Principle of Operation

Pop-up toasters operate by means of heating elements that are wound around mica boards, a bi-metal thermostat control, and a latch-catch and spring mechanism. Bread is placed in a rack through slots in the top of the metal frame; then a lever is depressed, lowering the bread and rack. This action pushes two contact points together. The circuit is then completed and the current flows into the thermostat and heating elements. The rack latches into a catch when the bread is all the way down, keeping the bread in place between the glowing heating elements. The bread absorbs and reflects heat built up in the cavity until the bimetal releases the carriage, and the toast pops up. This action automatically puts the toaster into its "Off" position.

Adjustments are made with a dial that increases or decreases the distance, and therefore the time that the bimetal blade must travel to trip the trigger arm that pops up the rack. Another kind of pop-up timing mechanism is a wound spring clockwork timer. In this design, pushing the rack down winds a spring timer, which is connected to the trigger arm. When the spring unwinds, it activates the trigger arm and releases the latch, breaks the circuit, and the return spring pops the rack up.

The spring that makes the rack pop up is compressed or stretched when the rack is lowered. Some designs use a spring contained in a pistonlike assembly, attached to the rack by an extension of the rod. This type of spring return is compressed by the rod when the rack is lowered. Other toasters use a spring made fast to two points, one of which is fastened onto a stationary part of the frame, while the other end of the spring is attached to a point on the rack itself, so that when the rack is lowered the spring is pulled into tension.

Differences in Pop-Up Toasters

Older pop-up toasters use a standard clock timer run by a spring-operated motor. Depressing the carrier lever winds the clock spring, lowers the carriage, latches it, and closes the circuit to the heating elements. The clock ticks off a specific amount of time, then releases the carriage and opens the circuit. The clock-timer may also have a bimetallic blade that bends as the temperature in the toasting cavity increases, until it releases a spring-loaded lever on the clock.

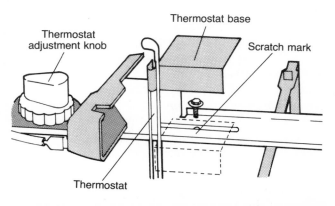

Before freeing the thermostat, mark the exact position of its setscrew so that it can be reassembled in its correct position.

The single-cycle control system uses a bimetal blade that touches the bread. The bimetal is bent by heat toward a switch, which it opens when the bread is toasted. When the switch opens, the carrier latch releases the rack and the toast pops up.

The double-cycle control consists of a small resistance coil wrapped around a bimetal blade and connected in series to the main heating elements. The mechanism actually has two switches, one that controls the main heating elements, and the other that turns the auxiliary heater on and off. When the carriage is depressed, the main switch is closed, but the heater switch is left open, allowing its coil to heat along with the main heating elements. The bimetal blade bends away from the main switch and eventually breaks the main heating element circuit; at the same time, it closes the heater circuit. The bimetal blade then cools and bends back toward the main switch. During its return to the main switch, it trips the carriage latch, releasing the carriage from the bottom of the toaster.

All toasters have a dial controlling the degree of browning from light to dark. Some models have a selector knob that can be set at either "keep warm" or "pop-up". If the keep-warm setting is used, the toast will not rise when the current shuts off; the latch must be tripped by lifting the carrier lever.

There are two basic mechanical designs that allow the bread carrier to sink automatically to the bottom of the unit and complete the circuit to the heating elements. In some models, the weight of the bread is enough to push the carrier downward. The carriage depresses a lever that turns on a switch connected to the thermostat. With the current on, the hot wires expand, forcing the carrier to descend. When the thermostat opens the circuit to the heating elements, the wire cools and contracts, allowing the carriage to rise again. When the toast is removed from the slots, the starting lever in the carriage returns to its upper position and the toaster is ready for the next browning cycle.

In some models a small motor is used to depress and raise the carrier; this is usually employed in units having a two-cycle control thermostat.

There can be one or as many as eight slots in the toaster housing, each large enough to toast at least one slice of bread. The bottom of every toaster is vented to keep the unit from becoming too hot; there is also a crumb tray at the bottom of the unit that either slides out or is a hinged door.

Disassembly

Remove the retaining screws in all of the feet and partially lift the front feet and crumb tray. Pry the cord leads off their terminals beneath the rear feet, then remove the bottom of the appliance. Release the strain relief mechanism and pull the cord set out of the rear foot assembly. Pull the knobs off the temperature control and undo the screw(s) holding the control in place. The shell can now be removed from the body.

Mark the position of the thermostat, then remove its mounting screw and pull it out of the body. Remove all leads from their terminals on the thermostat and free the keeper release switch.

Pull the end of the lifter arm out of its retaining slot. The lifter is attached to a carriage release piston and spring that reside in the damper chamber. Pry the piston from the end of the lifter arm. In some models the lifter is a coiled, flat spring that must be bent slightly so that the hole in its end can be disengaged from its mounting tab.

Maintenance and Repair

Heating Elements. Toaster heating elements usually are connected in parallel so that if one element fails, the others will continue to operate. One element is attached to insulated bushings on a mica board

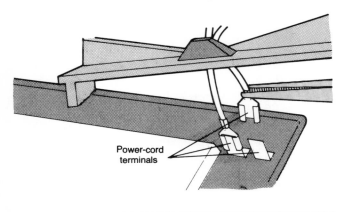

Power-cord terminals

Remove the retaining screws in the unit's feet and lift the shell enough to disconnect the power cord terminals.

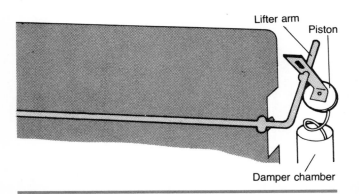

Lifter arm
Piston

Damper chamber

Pull the lifter arm from its slot and rotate it to remove the piston and spring from the damper chamber.

against the outside of the unit. The wall between oven chambers is also a mica board, which supports a heating element on both its sides. Any of the heating elements in a toaster can be replaced by removing the guard wires above the element and disconnecting the terminal screws or nuts.

Note that heating elements are not interchangeable; when ordering a replacement, be sure to list the proper part name and number. To check a heating element, look down the slot of the unit. If any of the heating elements are not red when the toaster is turned on, they are broken and should be replaced. But, if none of the elements are glowing, check the cord and thermostat before changing the elements.

Cord and Plug. Since the cord and its connecting male plug remain in fixed position in toasters, they should theoretically never wear out. If the toaster fails to operate completely, check the outlet by plugging in a lamp known to be in good working order. It is possible that the fuse controlling the outlet may have opened.

To test the cord, remove the male plug from its outlet. Put a jumper, a short length of copper wire, across the cord's terminals inside the toaster. Connect a multitester set to its Rx1 position across the terminals of the male plug (see page 28).

Thermostat. The heating cycle is controlled by the warping and straightening properties of a bimetal thermostat blade (see page 57). To test the thermostat and keeper release switch, disconnect the switch lead and clip the probes of a multimeter to the lead and the switch terminal. Set the meter to the Rx100 scale; if the meter reads zero ohms or below, the switch is faulty (see page 27).

Controls. While their assembly varies from model to model, all connections, wires, mechanical parts, springs and bimetal strips found in toasters can become worn and need to be replaced.

The repair of individual parts is a matter of observing the mechanical action closely and then either repairing specific parts that are malfunctioning or replacing them. Sometimes a part can be repaired by bending it slightly. In instances where the part is worn, it is best to replace it with a manfacturer's replacement part.

Latching and Pop-Up Mechanisms. All parts of the latching mechanism must be kept clean of crumbs or foreign objects that can prevent the parts from moving freely. In addition, springs can wear out or break and must be replaced.

 WARNING: Clean the crumbs from the crumb tray regularly so they do not build up and touch any part of the toaster.

WARNING: Never put a toaster in water. The outside of the toaster can be cleaned by any commercial product made for that purpose. Toasters are equipped with trays, either removable or hinged, for disposing of bread crumbs. If bread gets caught or breaks while in the toaster, unplug the unit. Turn the toaster upside down and shake gently. Poking around inside the toaster with a knife or fork can break the heating elements.

There are variations in automatic carriage and in latching and pop-up mechanisms. In some toasters there is a combination consisting of a spring and cylinder, known as a dashpot, that pushes the carriage up when toasting is finished. In some toasters the spring that makes the rack pop up is compressed or stretched when the rack is lowered.

Whatever the arrangement may be, the mechanisms are not held in position by screws but are kept in place by spot welding or rivets and so cannot be removed.

See pages 54-57 for repair information on bimetal switches, timers, resistance wires, and thermostats.

POP-UP TOASTER TROUBLESHOOTING

PROBLEM: Toaster does not heat.

Possible Cause	Procedure	Remedy	Rating	Parts	Labor
No power at outlet.	Check fuse or circuit breaker.	Replace fuse or reset circuit breaker.			
Plug disconnected.		Reseat plug in outlet.			
Cord defective.	Check for breaks.	Repair or replace.	■	$3	$7.50
Heating element defective.	Check circuit continuity.	Replace.	■ ■ ■	$10	$10

PROBLEM: Toaster blows fuse or trips circuit breaker.

Possible Cause	Procedure	Remedy	Rating	Parts	Labor
Circuit overloaded.	Reduce number of appliances on circuit.	Replace fuse, or reset circuit breaker.			
Cord or plug short-circuited.	Inspect for breaks.	Repair or replace.	■	$3	$7.50

PROBLEM: Toaster shocks user.

Possible Cause	Procedure	Remedy	Rating	Parts	Labor
Cord frayed.	Inspect for breaks.	Repair or replace.	■	$3	$7.50
Case short-circuited.	Test circuit continuity.	Repair.	■		$7.50

(Continued on next page)

PROBLEM: Toaster over- or undertoasts.

Possible Cause	Procedure	Remedy	Rating	Parts	Labor
Interior of shell stained.	Check.	Clean with bicarbonate of soda, or mild detergent on damp cloth.	■		$10
Selector control faulty.	Bend blade nearer or farther away from tension bar.	Replace if broken.	■		$7.50
Bimetal switch defective.	Test circuit continuity.	Replace.	■	$2.50	$7.50
Release mechanism jammed.	Inspect.	Adjust tabs and clean. If worn or broken, replace parts.	■	$5	$12

PROBLEM: Toaster smokes.

Possible Cause	Procedure	Remedy	Rating	Parts	Labor
Crumbs in mechanism.	Clean entire toaster.	Empty crumb tray, shake toaster upside down.			
Release mechanism jammed.	Inspect.	Adjust taps and clean. If worn or broken, replace parts.	■ ■ ■	$5	$12
Bimetal switch faulty.	Check circuit continuity.	Replace.	■	$2.50	$7.50

PROBLEM: Toaster does not shut off.

Possible Cause	Procedure	Remedy	Rating	Parts	Labor
Contacts welded.	Separate and clean with emery board.	Replace if necessary.	■		$7.50

PROBLEM: Toaster toasts only one side of bread or toasts unevenly.

Possible Cause	Procedure	Remedy	Rating	Parts	Labor
Heating element or connections faulty.	Check entire machine for circuit continuity.	Repair breaks, replace broken parts.	■ ■ ■	$6	$7-12
Reflecting surfaces dirty.	Check.	Clean with mild detergent on damp cloth.	■ ■ ■		$12

PROBLEM: Bread does not stay down.

Possible Cause	Procedure	Remedy	Rating	Parts	Labor
Hold-down latch bent or broken.	Inspect. Check for binding.	Straighten to permit clearance or replace.	■		$7.50
Carriage binding.	Inspect.	Repair.	■	$7.50	

PROBLEM: Toast does not pop up.

Possible Cause	Procedure	Remedy	Rating	Parts	Labor
Carriage bent or jammed.	Clean crumbs from entire machine. Inspect alignment.	Replace if necessary.	■		$7.50
Release switch or spring faulty.	Realign switch, inspect spring.	Replace worn parts.	■	$3	$7.50
Thermostat or bimetal heater faulty.	Test circuit continuity.	Replace.	■	$2.50	$7.50

PROBLEM: Toast pops out of toaster.

Possible Cause	Procedure	Remedy	Rating	Parts	Labor
Dashpot defective.	Tamp down asbestos packing around edge to seal air leaks.		▫		$7.50
Flywheel assembly faulty.	Inspect.	Repair or replace bent or broken parts.	■	$5	$10

PROBLEM: Toast rises too slowly.

Possible Cause	Procedure	Remedy	Rating	Parts	Labor
Dashpot faulty.	Add pinhole to asbestos packing.				
Flywheel assembly faulty.	Inspect.	Repair, or replace bent or broken parts.	■	$5	$10
Spring too weak.	Inspect.	Replace.	■	$1	$7.50

Toaster/Broilers

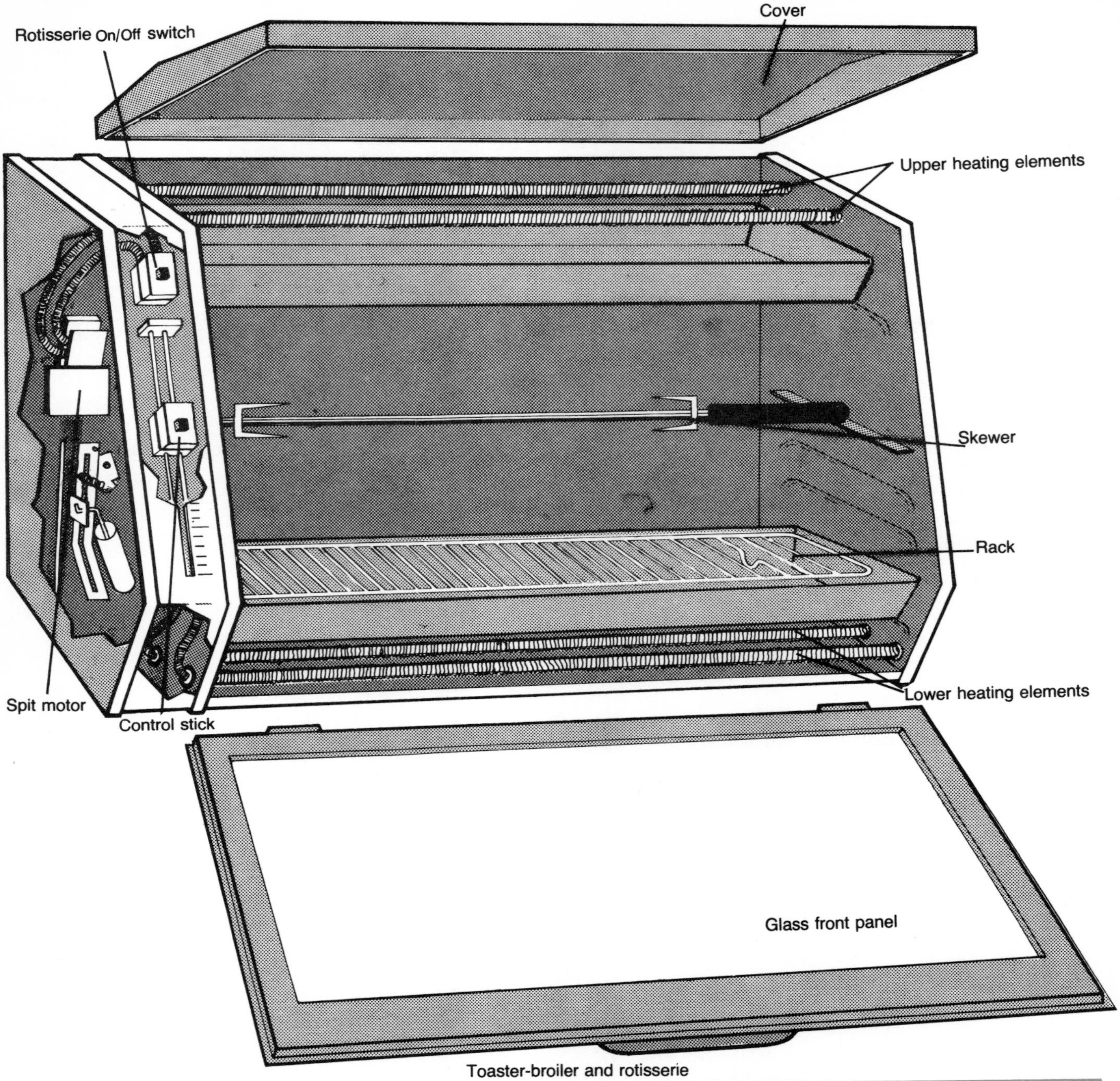

Rotisserie On/Off switch

Cover

Upper heating elements

Skewer

Rack

Lower heating elements

Spit motor

Control stick

Glass front panel

Toaster-broiler and rotisserie

Principles of Operation

A toaster/broiler (also called a counter top broiler, electric toaster oven, or table broiler) functions as either a broiler or a toaster, depending on the setting selected. The metal cabinet contains an exposed heating element that is usually wound around a ceramic core positioned on the back of the unit in line with the food rack, or across the top of the cabinet. The toaster/broiler may also have two or more heating ele-ments—one in the base and the other near the top. Metal reflectors behind the elements direct the heat to both the top and bottom of the food rack at the same time. There is an operating lever assembly in the front of the unit connected to a timer with the control level situated between the arms of a double-pole switch.

The toaster/broiler oven has a glass front door, usually hinged for upward movement. Opening this door turns the unit off automatically. Inside the oven is a metal tray with openings to permit heat to rise from the straight wire heating elements located beneath it. This shelf slides forward when the door is opened.

The oven is equipped with an On/Off switch and a light which signals when the power is on.

The unit may be equipped with two printed scales: One for oven temperature; the other for light to dark toast. The same temperature control slide arm can be used for the oven and toaster sections in some models.

The operating lever is designed to depress and release a push button which opens and closes contacts with the main switch, and also pushes on a bell crank so that its tab can clear the arm of a bimetal temperature control assembly and depress the spring contact on a shunting switch. The bell crank holds the shunting switch open while the main switch is closed, with the result that the heating element and bimetal heater are energized in series. The right end of the bimetal assembly is held in place by the heat-up adjustment screw; the left side is mounted on a pivot pin. As the bimetal heats, its center arches, but since both its ends are held in place, the bimetal arm is forced to rotate in a counterclockwise direction across the tab on the bell crank. When it clears the tab the bell crank is free to rotate, and the force of the spring contact closes the shunting switch. Current is now diverted around the bimetal heater; the bimetal begins to cool and straighten. At the same time the bimetal arm is trapped by the tab on the bell crank. As it cools it is forced against the point of a cool-down adjustment screw which in turn strikes a compensator. The opposite end of the bimetal also pushes against the tab on the bell crank, causing the latch to free the pin on the operating lever assembly. The operating lever springs up, opening the main switch contacts and ending the heating cycle.

Differences in Toaster Broilers

Toaster/broilers are sold under many different names and designs but all of them are portable, electrically powered, and capable of baking or broiling, making toast, thawing and heating frozen foods, and a host of other cooking chores.

Sophisticated modern models have an electric clock timer connected to the thermostat.

Some toaster/broilers include a rotisserie attachment; using a small split-phase motor. This part consists of a spit which is inserted through an opening in one end of the appliance so that its pointed end can fit into a gear box mounted on the opposite side of the appliance.

The toaster/broiler is also equipped with a metal tray, removable from the rear, for disposing of bread crumbs and other food particles. Some toaster/broil-

ers have slots, just like regular toasters; others use trays located inside the unit.

Disassembly

Unplug the unit and remove the retaining screws that hold both sides of the unit to the housing. The back can now be lifted free, along with the oven door. The control cover cannot be removed until the control knob(s) is pried off its stem. In many models the cover on the control slides off when it is pushed to one side or the other, or the corners of its decorative decal may have to be pried loose to locate hidden retaining screws.

The heating element, thermostat, clockwork, On/Off switch, and motor are now exposed and may be unscrewed or unplugged from their connections to the circuit and removed.

NOTE: Many toaster/broilers are constructed with welded or riveted parts, or with high temperature solder that makes their repair difficult without the use of special tools.

Maintenance and Repair

Should anything go wrong with a toaster/broiler, first clean all of the mechanical parts, then examine each part closely for wear or breakage.

Heating Element. The heating element may be in the form of a resistance wire or a solid bar(s), or both. To test the element, disconnect both ends and touch probes of a multimeter to its terminals. The meter is set at the Rx1 scale and should read between 10 and 20 ohms (*see page 28*). If it reads higher, replace the element.

Temperature Control. Control of the temperature consists of several mechanical devices positioned behind the control cover, including the main switch assembly, bell crank, push button, shunting switch, and bimetal assembly. All of these assemblies should be cleaned and lubricated if the appliance does not heat properly. Any worn or broken parts should be replaced with manufacturer's replacement parts. If the mechanical parts all appear to be in working order and the temperature is still not correct, the bimetal may not be functioning properly. The entire bimetal assembly should be replaced by a manufacturer's replacement.

Thermostats. Some models have a thermostat behind the control knob. To test it, unplug the unit and touch the probes of a multimeter set the Rx1 scale to each of its terminals. The meter should read zero ohms; any higher reading means the thermostat is faulty and should be replaced with a similar unit (*see page 28*).

Control Switches. The control switch may be one

or more buttons, or a knob protruding from a switch box. One of the terminals to the box connects the cord. To test the switch, clip one probe of the multimeter to the cord terminal and the other probe to each of the other terminals in turn (*see page 28*). The meter should read zero ohms in each instance. If the switch has a control knob rather than buttons, rotate the knob to each of its settings. At least one of the settings will read zero ohms. If the switch is faulty it must be replaced.

Rotisserie. Should the spit fail to rotate when the motor is activated, either the gears are jammed or the motor has failed. Try rotating the large gear nearest the motor by hand. If the gear will not turn, the gears may be jammed or stripped. In this case the gear box assembly must be replaced. In some cases the gear box can be removed from the motor by undoing its

mounting screws. In other instances the gears and motor are not separable and the entire assembly must be replaced.

If the gears appear to be in working order but the spit will not turn, test the motor. Disconnect the motor leads and touch them to the probes of a multimeter set to the Rx1 scale (*see page 28*). The motor is operational if the meter reads between 40 and 100 ohms. A higher reading means the motor is defective and must be replaced.

Timer. See page 56 for repair.

Oven Door. The door of the oven may be a problem if it does not latch properly, or form a tight seal when closed. If necessary, the latch can be replaced and the hinges of the door tightened or replaced. If the glass of the door cracks or breaks, replace it with one constructed of the same type of heat resistant glass.

TOASTER/BROILER TROUBLESHOOTING

PROBLEM: Toaster/broiler does not heat.

Possible Cause	Procedure	Remedy	Rating	Parts	Labor
No power at outlet.	Check fuse or circuit breaker.	Replace fuse or reset circuit breaker.			
Plug disconnected.	Check.	Reseat plug in outlet.			
Cord defective.	Check for breaks.	Repair or replace.	■	$3	$5
Heating elements faulty.	Check circuit continuity.	Replace.	■	$6	$7.50
Switch defective.	Inspect mechanical action, test circuit continuity.	Replace defective parts or entire unit.	■	$3	$7.50
Connection loose or defective.	Check all connections for dirty contacts or lose wires.	Clean and repair.	■		$7.50

PROBLEM: Toaster/broiler blows fuse or trips circuit breaker.

Possible Cause	Procedure	Remedy	Rating	Parts	Labor
Circuit overloaded.	Reduce number of appliances on circuit.	Replace fuse or reset circuit breaker.			
Cord or plug short-circuited.	Inspect for breaks.	Repair or replace.	■	$3	$5
Switch short-circuited.	Test circuit continuity.	Repair or replace.	■	$3	$7.50

PROBLEM: Toaster/broiler shocks user.

Possible Cause	Procedure	Remedy	Rating	Parts	Labor
Cord frayed.	Inspect for breaks.	Repair or replace.	■	$3	$5
Case short-circuited.	Test circuit continuity.	Repair.	■		$7.50

PROBLEM: Broiler does not heat.

Possible Cause	Procedure	Remedy	Rating	Parts	Labor
Heating element faulty.	Examine, then test circuit continuity.	Replace.	■	$6	$7.50
Temperature control faulty.	Examine all mechanical workings, then test circuit continuity.	Replace.	■	$4	$7.50

PROBLEM: Indicator light goes on but toaster/broiler does not heat.

Possible Cause	Procedure	Remedy	Rating	Parts	Labor
Contacts dirty or welded.	Check.	Clean with fine sandpaper.	■		$7.50
Heating elements faulty.	Test circuit continuity, inspect for breaks.	Replace.	■	$6	$7.50

PROBLEM: Toaster/broiler gets too hot or not hot enough.

Possible Cause	Procedure	Remedy	Rating	Parts	Labor
Heat control or thermostat out of adjustment.	Consult owner's manual for adjustment procedure.	Adjust or replace.	■	$4	$7.50
Timer defective.	Check leads and contacts.				

PROBLEM: Toaster/broiler door does not latch or stay latched.

Possible Cause	Procedure	Remedy	Rating	Parts	Labor
Latch spring faulty.	Observe mechanical action.	Repair or replace.	■		$7.50
Detector switch faulty. (on certain models)	Check contacts, screw on bimetal blade.	Replace faulty parts or entire switch.	■	$2.50	$7.50

PROBLEM: Rotisserie does not turn.

Possible Cause	Procedure	Remedy	Rating	Parts	Labor
Motor defective.	Check gear box, then circuit continuity.	Replace either if faulty.	■	$10	$10

PROBLEM: Rotisserie only operates on one setting.

Possible Cause	Procedure	Remedy	Rating	Parts	Labor
Switch faulty.	Check.	Replace.	■	$2.50	$7.50

Toothbrushes

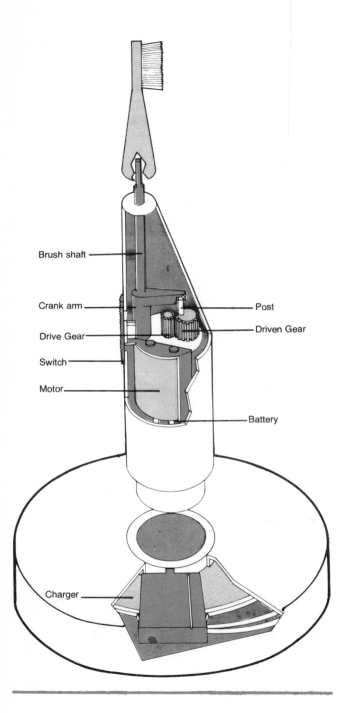

Brush shaft

Crank arm

Drive Gear

Switch

Motor

Post

Driven Gear

Battery

Charger

Principle of Operation

In an electric toothbrush, a small DC motor drives a set of gears, which moves the brush. In order to convert AC line voltage to low-voltage DC, the circuit requires a transformer and a rectifier, which are con-tained in the handle of a cord model and in the storage base of a cordless model.

Differences in Toothbrushes

Cordless toothbrushes have somewhat more complicated circuitry than cord models. The cord leads to a storage base, which is a recharging unit. In the storage base, low-voltage DC, produced by the transformer and rectifier, charges a nickel-cadmium battery and then powers the motor when the toothbrush is in use.

In either cord or cordless models, the main switch may be a pressure-sensitive device attached to the brush stem or a conventional toggle switch in the handle.

Disassembly

Most units are hermetically sealed and no disassembly is possible. In some cordless models it is possible to remove the bottom cover of the storage base for access to the transformer and rectifier. This cover is held in place with screws or spring clamps.

Maintenance and Repair

Little maintenance is necessary other than cleaning. Repair of internal parts is not possible in most units, and if it is, it is usually uneconomical.

Switch. See page 55.

Cord Set. See page 52.

Charging Unit. If access to the transformer coils or induction coils is possible, they can be checked with a multimeter. Resistance should read about 2500 ohms. Substantially less resistance (under 50 ohms) means that a large part of the coil has been short-circuited. A resistance reading of infinity means a break in the internal wiring. Replace the unit.

Battery (Cordless Models). Restore a nickel-cadmium battery that does not hold a charge by putting it through a number of discharge-recharge cycles. Discharge the battery fully until the motor comes to a dead stop. Then store the handle for at least twenty-four hours to allow it to charge fully. Repeat this cycle six or eight times or more. This technique is good for any nickel-cadmium-battery-powered device.

Gears. The gears inside the toothbrush handle may become worn or stripped. To check them, place a brush on the handle and turn on the appliance. Grip the handle with one hand, the brush with the other. If the motor slows down noticeably, the gears are all right. If the brush can be held still while the motor is running, the gears are stripped and the handle should be replaced.

Vacuum Cleaners

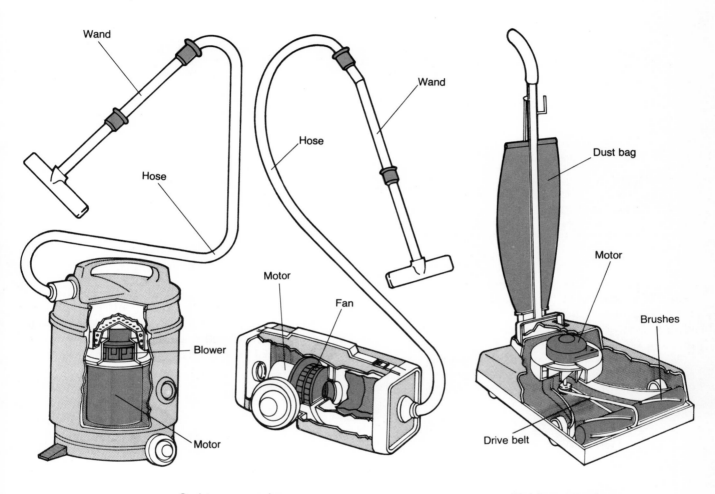

Canister vacuum cleaners.

Upright vacuum cleaner.

Principle of Operation

All vacuum cleaners operate according to the same general principle. The housing contains two systems, one electrical and one pneumatic. The electrical system is a fan motor (typically a universal motor) controlled by an On/Off switch. The pneumatic system is the movement of air: Suction created by the fan draws a mixture of air and dirt through a duct into a filter bag. The dirt remains in the bag while the air passes through the porous walls of the bag and is vented into the room.

Upright vacuum cleaners are somewhat different in internal design from canister or tank vacuums in that the motor may drive not only the fan blades attached to one shaft but also a belt attached to the opposite end. The belt runs a revolving beater bar in the head of the vacuum cleaner.

Differences in Vacuum Cleaners

Manufacturers provide a wide array of attachments for different chores, such as cleaning dusty surfaces, upholstery, draperies, walls, etc. Attachments for spraying paint, insecticides, or floor wax and for filtering the air can also be purchased.

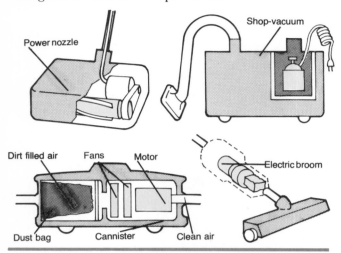

An option available on some canister models is a beater-bar attachment. The beater bar operates from a supplementary motor in the suction head. It is plugged into an auxiliary circuit that connects through the unit's housing.

Many upright units have a high-low switch that regulates motor speed and mechanically lifts the brushes from the floor when in the high position.

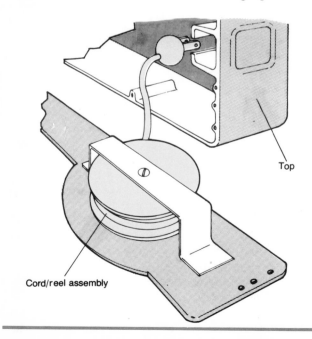

Remove all screws in the top cover to free the cord/reel assembly.

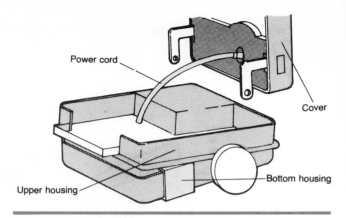

Remove all retaining screws and pry apart.   upper and lower housings

Disassembly

In most canister models, opening the lid to replace the dirt bag also exposes the motor housing. The motor may be covered by a paper filter and a protective metal grill, which is attached with screws. When the housing is opened, the switch is also accessible. Leads may be soldered or attached with lugs. Make note of where wires are attached before disconnecting them.

Access to the working parts of an upright model is usually through the bottom plate, held on with spring clamps. After the bottom plate is removed, unhook the drive belt and pull out the brush or beater bag. Any additional housing screws are now accessible.

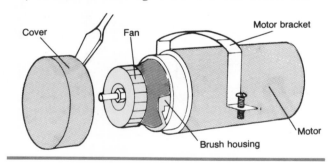

Unscrew the motor retaining bracket and pry off the motor to reach the brush housings.

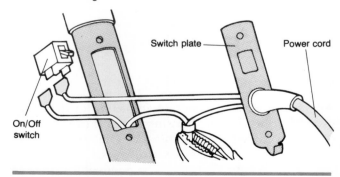

Remove the switch plate and disconnect all terminals or wire nuts to free the power cord.

Maintenance and Repair

Change dirt bags and filters regularly, and keep the inside of the housing clean.

Suction hose and connections. The most common complaint with canister or tank vacuum cleaners is that they lose their suction. In most cases, this is caused by an obstruction in the hose that can be cleared by disassembling the wand pipes, nozzle, and hose, and then probing for the blockage. An alternative method is to disconnect the hose from the air-intake port, and then insert it into the exhaust port at the rear of the canister. The obstruction should be blown free.

Typically, a vacuum hose is made of plastic and is therefore subject to tears and small punctures. It is generally best to replace a damaged hose rather than to try to patch it. Make an emergency repair with duct tape from a heating supply store. The hose connections between the pipe sections, as well as between the hose and the intake port, can also become worn or loose, permitting a loss of suction. In many cases, it is because the connections were glued, and the glue has dried and cracked. Disassemble the connection and clean off the old glue, then apply a liberal coating of epoxy cement to the fitting before reassembly.

There is only one likely point of leakage in the air system of an upright cleaner: the point where the bag attaches to the housing. Such a leak may cause some of the dirt to blow back into the room. Listen carefully at this junction and observe the machine while it is running. See the owner's manual for installation of the dust bag and for defective coupling.

Motor. Keep the motor clean and oil the bearings regularly. Universal motors are discussed on page 60.

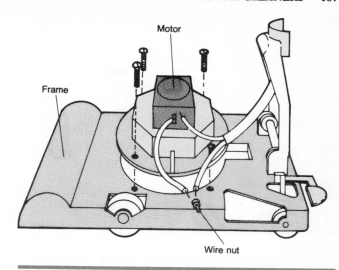

To remove the motor on an upright undo all wire connections and free the mounting bolts.

Switch. Check for continuity (*see page 54*), and replace with a manufacturer's part if faulty.

Cord Set. See page 52.

Drive belt. A tight belt on the beater bar or rotary brush can impede functioning (applies to upright models or beater-bar accessory on canister model). Adjust as necessary. If the drive belt is worn or broken, replace it.

Rotary brushes or beater bar. The bristles can wear away and no longer reach the carpet. On some models brush height is adjustable, and moving the brush closer to the floor may improve performance. On an upright vacuum cleaner bristles should be flush with the casing lip. If the bristles are completely worn, replace the brush.

VACUUM CLEANER TROUBLESHOOTING

PROBLEM: Vacuum cleaner does not start.

Possible Cause	Procedure	Remedy	Rating	Parts	Labor
No power at outlet.	Check fuse or circuit breaker.	Replace fuse or reset circuit breaker.			
Plug disconnected.		Reseat plug in outlet.			
Cord defective.	Check for breaks.	Repair or replace.	■	$3	$7.50
Switch defective.	Test circuit continuity.	Replace.	■	$2	$7.50

(Continued on next page)

PROBLEM: Vacuum cleaner does not start. *(Continued from preceding page)*

Possible Cause	Procedure	Remedy	Rating	Parts	Labor
Connections loose.	Check for loose connections or dirty terminals.	Repair or clean.	■		$7.50
Fan jammed.	Inspect.	Repair or replace.	■		$7.50
Bearings bound or faulty.	Inspect.	Clean and lubricate. Replace if worn.	■ ■ ■	$4	$10
Motor brushes worn.	Inspect.	Replace.	■	$2	$7.50
Motor defective.	SEE ELECTRIC MOTOR TROUBLESHOOTING CHARTS—CHAPTER 4				

PROBLEM: Vacuum cleaner blows fuse or trips circuit breaker.

Possible Cause	Procedure	Remedy	Rating	Parts	Labor
Circuit overloaded.	Reduce number of appliances on circuit.	Replace fuse or reset circuit breaker.			
Cord or plug short-circuited.	Inspect for breaks.	Repair or replace.	■	$3	$7.50
Switch or motor short-circuited.	Test circuit continuity.	Repair or replace.	■	Switch $2 Motor $15	Switch $7.50 Motor $15

PROBLEM: Vacuum cleaner shocks user.

Possible Cause	Procedure	Remedy	Rating	Parts	Labor
Cord frayed.	Inspect for breaks.	Repair or replace.	■	$3	$7.50
Case short-circuited.	Test circuit continuity.	Repair.	■		$7.50

PROBLEM: Motor sparks.

Possible Cause	Procedure	Remedy	Rating	Parts	Labor
Commutator dirty.	Check.	Lightly sand.	■ ■ ■		$10
Brushes worn or incorrectly set.	Inspect.	Repair or replace.	■	$2	$7.50

PROBLEM: Motor operates hot.

Possible Cause	Procedure	Remedy	Rating	Parts	Labor
Hose, bag, cleaning tools, or vents clogged.	Inspect.	Clean.			
Motor defective.	SEE ELECTRIC MOTOR TROUBLESHOOTING CHARTS—CHAPTER 4				

PROBLEM: Motor starts and stops.

Possible Cause	Procedure	Remedy	Rating	Parts	Labor
Cord defective.	Test circuit continuity.	Repair or replace.	■	$3	$7.50
Switch faulty.	Test circuit continuity and mechanical action.	Replace.	■	$2	$7.50
Wiring harness short-circuited.	Test circuit continuity.	Repair or replace.	■	$3	$10
Connections loose.	Check all connections.	Tighten.	■		$10

PROBLEM: Motor operates too fast.

Possible Cause	Procedure	Remedy	Rating	Parts	Labor
Dust bag too full.	Check.	Empty or replace.			
Fan loose.	Check.	Tighten to motor shaft.	■		$7.50
Motor defective.	SEE ELECTRIC MOTOR TROUBLESHOOTING CHARTS—CHAPTER 4				

PROBLEM: Vacuum cleaner has little or no suction.
(See special problems of upright cleaners next)

Possible Cause	Procedure	Remedy	Rating	Parts	Labor
Hose or tools clogged.	Inspect.	Remove clog.			
Dust bag clogged or too full.	Inspect.	Empty or replace.			
Motor filter or exhaust screen clogged or dirty.	Inspect.	Clean. If damaged, replace.			
Cleaner clogged.	Inspect interior of unit.	Clean			
Swivel cap leaking.	Check washer and assembly for worn or or broken parts.	Replace worn or broken parts.	■	$3	$7.50
Housing, attachments, or hose leaking, cracked or broken.	Check for loose connections, leaking gaskets, missing screens, or breaks in hoses.	Repair or replace.	■	$10	$7.50
Fan loose.	Check connection to shaft.	Tighten.	■		$7.50
Drive belt loose or worn.	Inspect.	Tighten or replace.	■		$7.50
Seals at motor base or unit lid faulty.	Inspect.	Replace.	■	$3	$7.50
Suction control improperly set.	Check.	Reset.			
Attachments improperly connected.	Check.	Readjust.			

(Continued on next page)

PROBLEM: Vacuum cleaner has little or no suction. *(Continued from preceding page)* ▰▰▰▰▰▰
(See special problems of upright cleaners next)

Possible Cause	Procedure	Remedy	Rating	Parts	Labor
Foreign object in fan or armature.	Check.	Remove.			
Brush contact poor.	Check.	Repair or replace.			
Motor defective.	SEE ELECTRIC MOTOR TROUBLESHOOTING CHARTS—CHAPTER 4				

PROBLEM: Upright vacuum cleaner has little or no suction. (See previous entry for more.) ▰▰▰

Possible Cause	Procedure	Remedy	Rating	Parts	Labor
Nozzle adjustment incorrect.	Check.	Adjust for carpet height.			
Nozzle adjustment assembly faulty.	Check mechanism and handle tension spring. Look for worn or broken parts.	Repair or replace.	■	$5	$7.50
Brushes worn or out of adjustment.	Check. Bristles should be flush with casing lip.	Adjust.	■	$2	$7.50
Belt worn or broken.	Check.	Replace.	■	$2	$7.50
Casters worn.	Check. Wheels on rear caster mechanism should swing freely.	If worn, replace.	■	$2	$7.50
Agitator brush jammed.	Check for dirty bearings.	Clean and lubricate bearings.	■		$7.50

PROBLEM: Upright vacuum cleaner motor operates but brush does not rotate. ▰▰▰▰▰▰

Possible Cause	Procedure	Remedy	Rating	Parts	Labor
Belt loose or broken.	Check.	Replace.	■	$2	$7.50
Bearings bound.	Check.	Lubricate or replace.	■	$4	$10
Brush jammed.	Check.	Clean out foreign objects.			

PROBLEM: Upright vacuum cleaner is hard to push. ▰▰▰▰▰▰

Possible Cause	Procedure	Remedy	Rating	Parts	Labor
Carpet height adjustment set too low.	Reset higher.				
Brushes worn.	Check.	Replace.	■	$5	$7.50
Brush spindles bound.	Check.	Lubricate.	■		$7.50

PROBLEM: Dust bags bursting.

Possible Cause	Procedure	Remedy	Rating	Parts	Labor
Excess use on fine dirt.		Change bags often when picking up fine dirt.			

PROBLEM: Dust leaks from vacuum cleaner.

Possible Cause	Procedure	Remedy	Rating	Parts	Labor
Dust bag punctured.	Check for tiny holes.	Patch or replace.			
Old dust bag.		Replace.			
Dust bag improperly installed.	Consult owner's manual.				
Sealing gasket worn or broken.	Inspect.	Replace.	■	$2	$7.50

PROBLEM: Motor on two speed vacuum cleaner operates on only one speed.

Possible Cause	Procedure	Remedy	Rating	Parts	Labor
Speed selector switch defective.	Test circuit continuity and proper mechanical action.	Replace.	■	$3	$7.50
Motor defective.	SEE ELECTRIC MOTOR TROUBLESHOOTING CHARTS—CHAPTER 4				

PROBLEM: Cord reel does not rewind.

Possible Cause	Procedure	Remedy	Rating	Parts	Labor
Cord jammed.	Inspect.	Straighten.	■		$7.50
Cord reel spring broken.		Replace.	■	$6	$10
Parts in cord reel assembly loose.	Check.	Tighten or replace reel.			

PROBLEM: Vacuum cleaner is excessively noisy.

Possible Cause	Procedure	Remedy	Rating	Parts	Labor
Foreign objects in unit.	Check.	Remove.			
Fan or armature loose or striking stator.	Check.	Realign or replace parts.	■ ■ ■	$8	$10
Parts loose.	Check entire machine.	Tighten, repair, or replace loose parts.	■ ■ ■	$25	$35
Fan belt worn or broken.	Inspect.	Replace.	■	$2	$7.50
Bearings defective.	Check.	Lubricate or replace.	■	$4	$10

Waffle Iron/Griddles

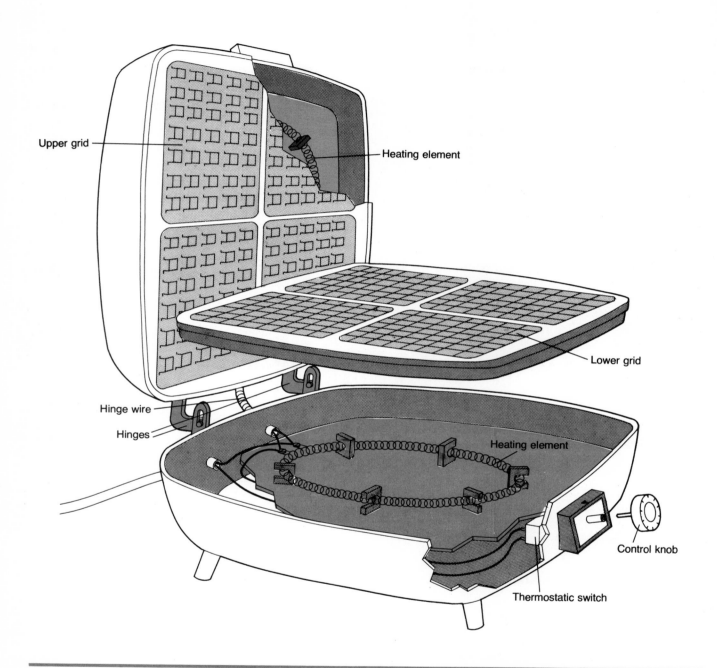

Upper grid

Heating element

Hinge wire

Hinges

Lower grid

Heating element

Control knob

Thermostatic switch

Waffle iron

Principle of Operation

Heating elements are concealed behind both the upper and lower grids of a waffle iron. When the unit is plugged in, current passes through a light-dark thermostatic control switch to the heating elements. When the appliance reaches operating temperature, the thermostat opens the circuit and, in most models, an indicator light signals that the batter can be poured in. The rear hinge, connecting top and bottom halves of the iron, expands to accommodate the rising batter. Most waffle irons shut off automatically when the waffle is baked.

Differences in Waffle Irons

The waffle grids in some models are reversible so that the unit can also be used as a grill. Other models provide separate grill plates.

Disassembly

Access to both the heating elements and the thermostatic switch is by removal of the waffle grids. These grids may be held in place by spring clips or screws. It may be necessary to pull off the thermostat knob and tilt the thermostat.

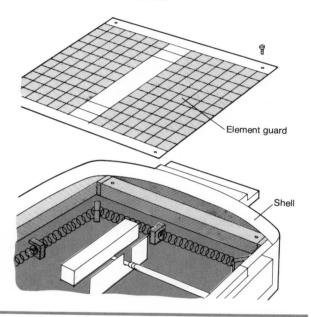

Undo the set screws holding the upper and lower element guards.

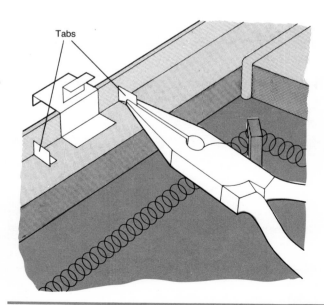

The element trays are held in place by tabs which must be straightened with pliers before the trays can be lifted from their shells.

Maintenance and Repair

Cord Set. See page 52.
Thermostat. See page 57.
Grids. The first time a waffle iron is used, it should be preheated to a medium temperature and then conditioned with a thin coat of cooking oil applied to the grids. One waffle should then be cooked and discarded (it will soak up most of the oil). The grids should not require any more conditioning.

Do not wash the grids after normal usage. If it becomes necessary to remove burned-on batter by washing the grids in soapy water, do not use abrasives. Recondition the grids with oil before using the waffle iron again.

If a grid becomes warped or breaks, replace it with a manufacturer's part.

Heating element. The heating elements are wired in series to the thermostatic control and the indicator light. Some waffle irons employ an open-coil resistance wire; other units use a sheathed resistance wire. In either case, it is stretched around insulated bushings directly beneath the grids.

The heating element should measure approximately 20 to 40 ohms when measured with the multimeter. If there is a break in a resistance wire, it is best to replace it rather than attempting a repair with a mending sleeve (see page 28).

Wires in Leveling Hinges. The upper grid assembly is attached to the bottom of the unit with a pair of expandable hinges. The hinges may be hollow and may contain the wires that connect the upper and

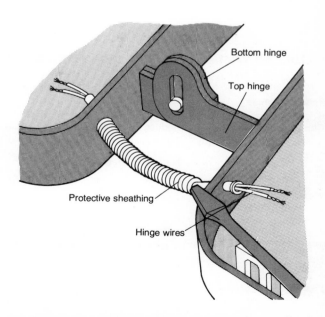

The hinge wires may be protected by a sheathing that must be pried away from the shells.

lower heating elements. These wires are often given further protection by armored sheathing, and wires that are connected outside of the hinges are nearly always sheathed in a springlike coil of steel wire. If it is necessary to replace these wires, be sure the new wires are the same gauge as the old ones, and attach them carefully so that they will not be pinched or kinked when the appliance is opened and closed.

WAFFLE IRON TROUBLESHOOTING

PROBLEM: Waffle iron does not heat.

Possible Cause	Procedure	Remedy	Rating	Parts	Labor
No power at outlet.	Check fuse or circuit breaker.	Replace fuse or reset circuit breaker.			
Plug disconnected.		Reseat plug in outlet.			
Cord defective.	Check for breaks.	Repair or replace.	■	$3	$7.50
Heating element defective.	Check circuit continuity with ohmmeter.	Replace.	■	$10	$10
Hinge wire faulty.	Check.	Replace.	■		$7.50
Thermostat faulty.	Check circuit continuity.	Replace.	■	$2.50	$7.50
Temperature control unit faulty.	Check for worn or broken parts.	Replace worn parts or whole unit.	■	$8	$7.50
Indicator bulb burned out.	Check light connections. In some models bulb is connected in series with heating circuit. If bulb is out, entire circuit is open.	Replace bulb, repair connections.	■	$1	$7.50

PROBLEM: Waffle iron blows fuse or trips circuit breaker.

Possible Cause	Procedure	Remedy	Rating	Parts	Labor
Circuit overloaded.	Reduce number of appliances on circuit.	Replace fuse or reset circuit breaker.			
Cord or plug short-circuited.	Inspect for breaks.	Repair or replace.	■	$3	$7.50

PROBLEM: Waffle iron shocks user.

Possible Cause	Procedure	Remedy	Rating	Parts	Labor
Cord frayed.	Inspect for breaks.	Repair or replace.	■	$3	$7.50
Case short-circuited.	Test circuit continuity.	Repair.	■		$7.50

PROBLEM: Indicator light does not go on.

Possible Cause	Procedure	Remedy	Rating	Parts	Labor
Bulb burned out.	Check.	Replace.	■	$1	$7.50
Circuit open.	If bulb is wired in series with heating circuit, check all connections.	Repair breaks.	■		$7.50

PROBLEM: Feet or handles of waffle iron become excessively hot.

Possible Cause	Procedure	Remedy	Rating	Parts	Labor
Parts improperly mounted.	Check for firm mounting and spacers offsetting parts from unit.	Tighten, repair, or replace.	■		$10

PROBLEM: Waffle iron heats too slowly or not enough.

Possible Cause	Procedure	Remedy	Rating	Parts	Labor
Terminals or connections loose.	Check.	Repair or replace.	■		$7.50
House voltage insufficient.	Reduce appliance load on circuit.	Plug waffle iron into another circuit. Eliminate extension cord.	■		$7.50
Thermostat faulty.	Check.	See page 57			
Heating elements faulty.	Check.	See page 54			

PROBLEM: Waffle iron overheats.

Possible Cause	Procedure	Remedy	Rating	Parts	Labor
Thermostat faulty.	Check for welded or dirty contacts.	Repair or replace.	■	$3	$10

PROBLEM: Only one of two heating elements heats.

Possible Cause	Procedure	Remedy	Rating	Parts	Labor
Wires in coil spring faulty.	Check circuit continuity.	Replace both wires even if only one is broken. Allow about 5″ of slack.	■ ■ ■	$10	$10

PROBLEM: Waffles brown unevenly or stick to grids.

Possible Cause	Procedure	Remedy	Rating	Parts	Labor
Grids dirty.	Inspect.	Scrub thoroughly.			
Grids not seasoned.	Preheat unit on medium setting. Coat grids with cooking oil. Discard first waffle, which will have soaked up excess oil.	Reseason.			

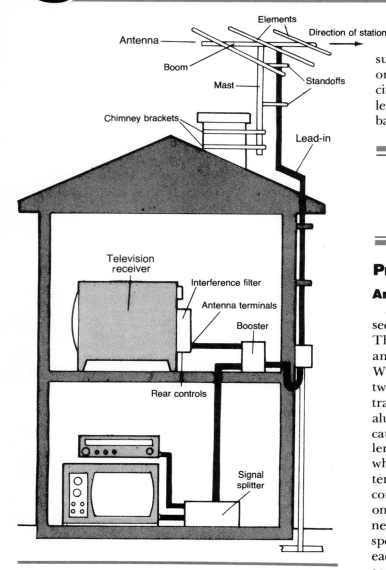

Receiving system

A color television receiver is the most complex instrument ever introduced into the home, but it is also one of the most reliable. By the middle 1970s, television manufacturers had replaced nearly two dozen vacuum tubes with solid-state devices, thereby reducing the number of troubles by about 80 percent. *Solid state* refers to transistors and even smaller integrated circuits which crowd up to 30,000 transistors into the area of a fingertip. These components almost never burn out because of age.

Yet, the picture on any TV set will someday flicker and fade. Fortunately, though, a remarkable number of repairs can be done by a handy person with neither special tools nor electronic skill. This is possible because many TV troubles originate outside the chassis,

such as a defect in the antenna, a misadjustment in one of the tuning controls, or interference from a citizens' band (CB) radio or other source. These problems can be remedied without removing the TV's back cover.

NOTE: Reaching into a set's interior may cause personal injury or void the manufacturer's warranty. Keep the back cover on the TV set at all times. Repairs inside the chassis should be handled by a professional repairperson only.

Principle of Operation

Antenna

A television set is part of a system divided into three sections: the antenna, the lead-in, and the receiver. The TV *signal,* the radio wave which carries picture and sound, enters the set through the antenna. Whether a simple pair of rods or a structure of nearly two-dozen elements, the antenna is designed to extract the most TV signal in the viewers' vicinity. Its aluminum rods and elements vary in dimension because each channel arrives on a wave of different length, and most signals are picked out of the air when antenna and TV wavelength agree in size. Antenna elements *resonate,* or tune, the TV signal according to wavelength. Channel 2, for example, rides on a wave which is over 200 inches long, while channel 83 at the top of the UHF (ultra-high frequency) spectrum is barely over 12 inches. For this reason, each of the eighty-two channels seeks out elements according to its length. All television antennas, however, don't require dozens of elements because many people live less than 25 or 30 miles from the transmitting station, where strong signals enable them to enjoy good reception on antennas of few elements.

UHF, VHF, and FM

It is convenient to describe a radio wave, the invisible force which carries TV, radio, and other services, according to its *frequency.* This is the number of times the wave vibrates each second and is described by the term *megahertz.* The prefix *mega* means 1 million and *hertz* is the number of cycles, or vibrations, per second. Thus, a radio wave with a frequency of 55 megahertz (MHz) vibrates 55 million times each second. The advantage of knowing frequency is that is affects how the wave travels. As frequency grows lower, the radio wave hugs the surface of the earth and easily curves around the horizon or hills. At higher frequencies, waves shun the ground and travel *line-of-sight,* or along the straight path between the transmitting and receiving antennas unobstructed by the horizon. To communicate with a space satellite, for example, a low frequency is impractical because the wave would never leave the earth.

By international agreement, nations of the world group radio frequencies into *bands.* They can be viewed that way because all frequencies within a band behave in much the same manner. As shown in the table, there are five major radio bands, starting at LF (low frequency) and rising toward UHF (ultra-high frequency). The lowest frequencies are useful for navigational beacons (to guide ships and airplanes), while the medium frequency holds the standard AM broadcast for home and car radios. High-frequency stations (HF), which can travel thousands of miles, carry international broadcasts and long-range communications. Notice how the bands always begin and end on multiples of the number 3. This makes it easy to remember the limits of any band if just one is known.

Finally, there are VHF and UHF, the very-high-frequency and ultra-high-frequency bands which carry television and FM. To see more clearly where on the bands TV-station signals are transmitted, consult the table. Between the frequencies of 54 MHz and 88 MHz lie TV channels 2 through 6, followed by a gap which is used for FM broadcasts (88 to 108 MHZ). Then there is an open space (used by police, fire, and aircraft services), followed by another VHF region assigned to television channels 7 through 13.

As television burgeoned during the 1950s, a higher band was opened to accommodate more stations; this is the UHF band, shown in the table. It contains the range of frequencies from 470 MHz to 890 MHz, which carries seventy UHF-TV channels, popularly known as 14 through 83.

In a typical television receiver, there are separate tuning systems for VHF and UHF because no single tuner could, until recently, cope with such a wide range of frequencies. Since the late 1970s, however, new forms of electronic tuning have emerged which can cover the vast television spectrum, and do it with almost no moving parts. These will almost certainly replace the familiar VHF-UHF channel selectors on sets of the last decade.

Lead-in

Once the TV signal is snared by the antenna, it is ducted through a lead-in wire to the television set. In most homes the lead-in is a *twin lead,* a flat, brown ribbon containing two copper conductors. A lead-in must not touch metal surfaces because this would cause the signal to leak away, or short-circuit, and not reach the TV set. To prevent shorting action, *stand-offs,* insulated nails or screws, support the lead-in along its run. TV signals, unlike ordinary electric currents, are fragile and must travel a precise electrical pathway provided by the twin lead.

The lead-in may terminate in various accessories before reaching the television set. Some devices split the signal for VHF (very high frequency), UHF (ultra-high frequency), and FM (frequency-modulation) stereo. Or a booster may be installed in the line to raise the strength of the signal so it can feed several

RADIO FREQUENCIES

Major band	Abbreviation	Range (in megahertz)	Broadcast services
Low frequency	LF	.03 to 3 MHZ	Navigational beacons
Medium frequency	MF	.3 to 3 MHz	Standard AM radio
High frequency	HF	3 to 30 MHz	Shortwave radio Long-range communication
Very high frequency	VHF	30 to 300 MHz	TV channels 2 to 13 FM radio
Ultra-high frequency	UHF	300 to 3000 MHz	TV channels 14 to 83

VHF AND UHF BANDS

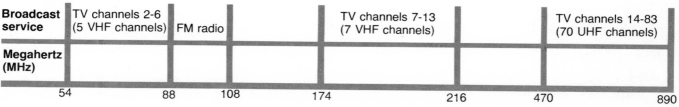

Broadcast service	TV channels 2-6 (5 VHF channels)	FM radio		TV channels 7-13 (7 VHF channels)		TV channels 14-83 (70 UHF channels)
Megahertz (MHz)						

54   88   108   174   216   470   890

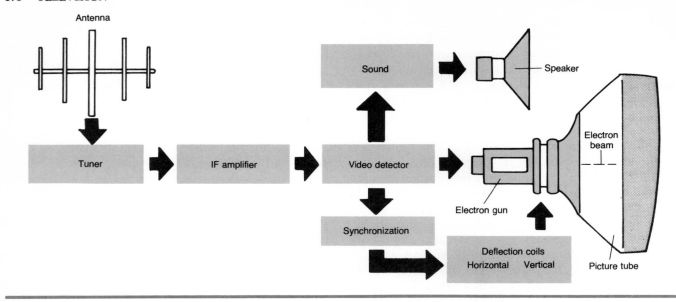

Black-and-white television receiver

receivers (and thus save the cost of an additional antenna). Filters for reducing interference may also be attached to the lead-in.

TV Receiver

The final component is the television set itself. Much of its complexity arises from so many operations happening simultaneously. In much-simplified fashion, the following is what occurs in each major part of the chassis.

Tuner

Because the antenna responds to all channels, the desired program is selected by the tuner. Operated by the channel selector, the tuner contains circuits which are sharply resonant to the wavelengths of the various channels. When a channel is selected, the signal is amplified and then converted down to a frequency of 41 megahertz (MHz). Every selected station is converted to 41 MHz, whether it is on channel 2 (54 MHz) or channel 83 (887 MHz). This step—converting all incoming channels to 41 MHz—was the ingenious concept of Major Edwin Armstrong, a radio pioneer who died in the early 1950s. With this conversion of all signals to one frequency, 41 MHz, the following stages in the TV receiver can work with great efficiency because they are designed to operate on one frequency only, instead of a vast spectrum of eighty-two channels. The process is incorporated in the *superheterodyne* circuit, which now dominates receivers of virtually every type.

IF amplifier

Because the television signal is still weak, it must be raised in strength thousands of times. This boost occurs in the IF, or Intermediate-Frequency, amplifier,

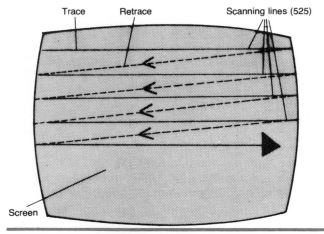

Deflection coils surrounding the neck of the picture tube create the scanning motion (traces and retraces) of the electron beam. The human eye merges the phosphorescent traces into the television picture on the screen.

dubbed *intermediate* because it operates between the channel-frequency selection and the later development of the video and audio signals in the receiver. Only the desired frequency is amplified.

Audio. Before it is amplified, the sound portion of a television program originates in a studio. There are many sources for audio—microphones, disc and tape recordings, sound tracks on film—but the first device for intercepting sound is usually the microphone. As a speaker talks or an instrument plays, the air commences to vibrate exactly in beat with those audio frequencies. The vibrations enter the grillwork opening on the microphone and strike an extremely light metallic element, which responds with sympathetic vibrations. Surrounding the element is a magnet and wire coil, both of which form a miniature electrical generating system. As the element moves, it disturbs the magnetic field and causes tiny electrical currents to move in the turns of the coil. The result is an audio *signal,* an electrical flow which rises and falls in step with the original sound waves emanating from the speaker or other source. After the audio signal is amplified, it is coupled with the video TV signal; together they are transmitted to the home television receiver.

Video detector

Now greatly amplified, the signal is stripped of the program information it carried from the station. The video detector removes the picture and the sound of the original scene: The audio portion is directed to the television receiver's own amplifier and loudspeaker; the video portion, to synchronization circuits and the picture tube.

Picture tube

Scanning. Before a picture can appear, the screen must be *scanned,* or filled with light. The process begins in the electron gun at the narrow end of the picture tube. There a hot filament, an electron-emitting electrode, "boils off" *electrons,* fleeting negative particles of electricity, to be directed toward the screen. Other electrodes accelerate the electrons toward the screen and focus them into a small, compact stream.

At the screen end of the tube, a highly positive electrical charge pulls the negative electrons (opposite charges attract) until they strike the inside of the screen. The inner surface of the screen is coated with a powdery, white phosphor that glows when struck by the electrons. A point of light now glows on the face of the picture tube.

Horizontal and vertical synchronization. To paint the screen with light, the electron beam sweeps horizontally and vertically in the same motion that the eye uses to read a page: from left to right in a straight line, and then from top to bottom. Only the TV sweep is much faster—sixty images every second—so the eye merges the phosphorescent traces into a completely lighted screen. The scanning motion is accomplished by two sets of electromagnetic coils surrounding the neck of the picture tube—one affects vertical movement of the beam, the other operates in the horizontal plane. As electrons move through the tube, the magnetic field produced by these loops of wire—known as *deflection coils*—attracts and repels the beam so it scans the entire screen. In the United States TV system, the standard scanning pattern for the beam of electrons creates 525 horizontal lines per picture (regardless of picture size), which can be seen when the screen is viewed at close range.

Video signal. To create the lights and darks of the original televised image, the electron beam moving through the picture tube is not only deflected but is also *modulated.* This means the intensity of the beam grows stronger or weaker as it passes through electrically charged cylinders in the neck of the tube which comprise the electron gun. When the gun produces a weak beam, little or no light appears on the screen and the viewer sees black area. When the gun strengthens the beam, high brightness is seen. This combination—scanning and modulation—recreates the original picture transmitted by the TV station.

Color. The system just described operates only in black-and-white picture tubes. Color picture tubes differ in several ways. One important difference is that a color picture tube develops not one but *three* electron beams, and divides the screen into thousands of groups of *three* dots. (The black-and-white screen has a uniform coating.) Each dot is a phosphor—similar to the material in a black-and-white screen—only it is capable of glowing light in one of three primary colors when struck by an electron beam. The primary

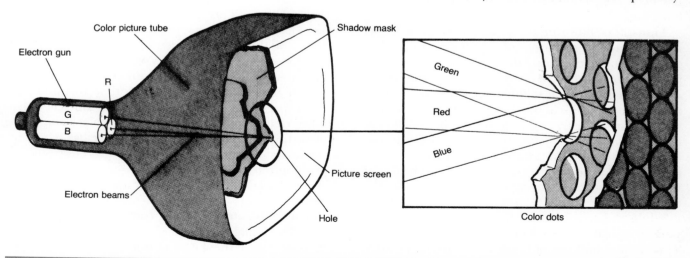

Color picture

colors are: red, blue, and green.

In the color tube, three electron guns create the three separate beams of electrons, thus keeping color signals sent by the station completely apart. (Color must not mix at any point in the system or it will become contaminated; contamination is visible in the picture as random color blotches that remain stationary, incorrect color, or color fringing.) An instant before the beams illuminate their color dots, they pass through a *shadow mask* with over 300,000 holes. There is a hole for each of the phosphor-dot trios. The mask prevents the three beams from sweeping across the screen and indiscriminantly striking every color dot—it does this by shadowing two of the three phosphor dots of each trio. In this way the beams are aligned with their appropriate colors. Like the artist who mixes primary colors for a desired hue, a TV set produces primary colors that glow in different intensities of red, blue, and green to produce thousands of other hues.

Correcting Reception Problems

TV Receiver

 WARNING: Tampering inside the chassis is not for the handy person at home. Not only are the circuits alive with dangerous voltages, but they also take considerable skill, test equipment, and service literature to troubleshoot.

Chassis

Nearly all television sets manufactured after 1975, as mentioned earlier, are solid state. If a set was produced prior to that time, statistics state that approximately 80 percent of the troubles encountered are caused by vacuum-tube failures. A vacuum tube may expire after several years, but the life of a transistor is yet unknown. It was invented in 1948 and no scientist has lived long enough to ascertain if one will ever burn out.

Transistors, however, do develop faults. If a TV set is placed in the tight corner of a shelf or a cloth is laid over its ventilation holes, the life of the television's parts can be cut in half. Anything which blocks the circulation causes heat to build up within the cabinet and shortens the life of the components. Because heat is the greatest enemy of the circuit, be sure to allow at least 2 inches of free space around the cabinet for air to enter at the bottom. There, cool air can enter and, through the process of convection, pick up heat, rise upward, and escape through the openings near the top.

While the television is operating, a faint, high-pitched squeal may emanate from the rear of the set. This is the sound of the horizontal-deflection system inside the set, which vibrates more than 15,000 times per second. Although the noise grows louder as the set ages, it is a normal occurrence and does not signify trouble.

The moment after a TV set is turned on, it may suddenly go dead. This is not strange because the act of turning on the set, in fact, triggers many failures. The reason for this is: Switching on a cold set causes a strong onrush of current, which may deliver the final stroke to a weakened part. Sound and picture may even appear briefly as a transistor, capacitor, resistor, or some other electronic component fails under the surge. A set that expires in this manner, in almost all cases, will need a professional repairperson. The trouble originates in the chassis, not in the antenna system or the electrical outlet.

 WARNING: A smoky or burnt odor emanating from the TV set indicates developing short circuits in the wiring or parts. Any acrid smell should be a warning to turn off the set and call a professional TV serviceperson.

Automatic controls

TV receiver problems also occur because the operating controls have not been adjusted correctly. If the television doesn't work or works improperly, read the manufacturer's instruction booklet. This is especially important today because, increasingly, TV sets are acquiring automatic controls that may be preset by the viewer in the home.

Two TV parts that operate with mechanical movement—the *tuner* (which houses the channel selector) and the *volume control*—are subject to recurring problems due to grease buildup.

Tuner. In older sets, the tuner contains a large drum that rotates with the channel selector, producing a *thunk* sound at each channel position. During this operation, spring contacts move into position to complete connections to a series of tuning coils. Within three or more years of repeated use, the contacts fail to press firmly and airborne grease coats their surfaces. This causes classic symptoms: flashes on the screen or snow on certain channels. When either of these appear, gently tapping the channel selector with a fingertip may restore the picture. If the snow disappears as the channel selector is slowly rocked back and forth, it is also time to call a TV serviceperson. A servicer can clean the contacts with a spray cleaner or, in serious cases, replace the complete tuner. These mechanical problems, however, are less common in new TV sets with electronic or push-button tuning. With fewer contacts, they are not as prone to dirt and grease buildup as the drum-type tuners.

Volume control. Volume controls suffer a similar fate. The telltale symptoms are: The sound changes in level when the knob is not being touched, or scratchy noises can be heard as the volume control is turned. In addition to this dirt interference, sometimes a volume control wears out because of friction and loss of spring tension. If a technician cannot restore the audio with a spray cleaner, the volume control should be replaced.

Power Source

No picture. Sometimes a dead TV is nothing more than a set that has been unplugged from the wall outlet. Before calling a TV repairperson, inspect the electric cord to see that the plug is firmly seated in the outlet. If it is, and the set will not turn on, check the wall outlet to see if it has power. This can be done by plugging in another appliance such as a lamp. If the lamp goes on, the outlet is alive and the problem is in the TV set or its connections. If it does not light, the outlet is faulty and should be replaced (*see page 35*). Before replacing the plug in the outlet, examine it for cracks or loose prongs. If it is damaged, replace it before using the set again (*see page 34*).

If the set still doesn't go on, inspect the rear cover of the TV. One difficulty traced to the power source starts where the TV's electric cord enters the back of the set. Look closely to see that the cord runs through the back cover into a plug-and-socket arrangement. Because some servicers fail to replace all the screws which secure the back cover, the plug may loosen and remove the power. If jiggling the fitting at the back cover makes the set suddenly come to life, be sure the plug is fully seated in its socket and the cover is securely fastened.

> **WARNING: While checking the back of the TV set, do not allow the rear cover to come off completely. Color TV operates with more than 20,000 volts and, although the voltage is not usually lethal because the current is miniscule, it can deliver an electric shock. If a tool is being held while a shock is delivered, it may crack the picture tube and produce an *implosion*, a breakage that causes flying glass. The shards of glass would be launched with such force that they could cause personal injury. (When these tubes are handled in the factory, workers are often suited in protective clothing and eye shields.)**

Picture shrinkage. A typical problem that appears to be a TV fault but can actually arise at the electrical outlet is shrinking pictures. At certain times of the day, black bars appear at the top and/or bottom of the screen as the picture fails to fill the tube. One reason for this could be low voltage—a phenomenon that recurs because of voltage cutbacks, or brownouts, by the electric utility company during times of heavy power demand. Picture shrinkage may also occur as a set's components age. On some sets there may be vertical adjustments (*see page 187*) to offset the problem. Newer televisions, however, are often designed to *overscan,* or reproduce a picture bigger than the screen, to compensate for this.

Lead-in and Connections

Many problems which beset a TV system are not electronic but are caused by mechanical forces which degrade the signal somewhere between the antenna and the terminals where the lead-in attaches to the rear of the receiver. Because these mechanical forces exert greatest effect on the parts of the system exposed to weather, one of the first casualties is the lead-in cable.

Lead-in

In most cases, television owners do not replace a lead-in cable until the picture has nearly disappeared. It is a good idea, however, to be aware that twin lead is not indestructible and is damaged by weather and sunlight. After four or five years, cracks appear in the plastic insulation and allow the cable to absorb moisture, altering the 300-ohm rating. The result can be an increase of ghosting and snow as the signal weakens or reflects in the line.

Since lead-in deterioration usually occurs over a period of years, it is difficult to recall how brightly the picture may have appeared on the screen when the antenna was first installed. Twin lead deserves replacement if it has been outdoors for more than about five years. Replacing it also gives the TV viewer an opportunity to switch to a newer type of lead-in (*see page 191*) and thus gain more quality reception with less interference.

Troubleshooting

The following troubleshooting chart lists only those television malfunctions that originate outside the set's chassis. These problems can be traced to their sources and corrected by the viewer or by a trained technician. For any given reception problem, there may be causes other than those presented here; those, however, are not for the nonprofessional to test out and deal with. Repairs or replacement of components (solid-state devices or tubes) within the TV chassis should be handled by a trained technician.

The problems, possible causes, and remedies in the following chart apply to both black-and-white and color TV sets, except where a color malfunction is the focus point. Remember to consult the television owner's manual for instructions about adjusting the controls on a particular TV model. The ordinary problems encountered in focusing and tuning the set with the various accessible knobs have not all been elaborated here.

TELEVISION TROUBLESHOOTING

	Problem	Possible Cause	Remedy
	Ghosts (duplicate images to the right of the true picture) appear on the screen.	Lead-in disconnected at terminal on antenna or receiver. Signal being picked up by lead-in. Signal being reflected by a building or other obstruction.	Reconnect lead-in at broken connection. Inspect lead-in. Replace with a new wire if cracked or older than 3—5 years (use a shielded lead-in). Re-aim antenna or replace with a more directional type.
	Bright flashes of light streak across picture screen on windy day.	Lead-in wire brushing against antenna terminal on outdoor antenna.	Reconnect broken lead-in at antenna terminal. Install additional standoffs to prevent lead-in from swaying in the wind.
	Hash (short dashes) run across black-and-white or colored picture.	Ignition systems of passing vehicles, outdoor equipment, and the like interfering with TV signal.	Run lead-in wire from the outdoor antenna to the TV receiver on the side of the house away from the street. Replace lead-in with a shielded type.
	Picture shrinks in from the top and/or bottom of screen.	Service voltage low (brownout by utility company). Components in TV chassis aging. Vertical height (size) and/or vertical linearity controls misadjusted.	Check with utility company for source of power shortage. Adjust vertical controls. Readjust controls.
	Images on the picture screen are severely distorted.	TV tuner overloaded.	Readjust AGC (automatic gain control).
	Picture shrinks in from the top, and picture proportions are distorted.	Vertical height (size) and/or vertical linearity controls misadjusted.	Readjust controls for correct proportions.
	Picture shrinks in from the sides.	Horizontal width or horizontal hold controls misadjusted. Components in TV chassis aging.	Readjust controls. Readjust controls.

	Problem	Possible Cause	Remedy
	Fringes of color appear in black-and-white images.	Color convergence poor. Color imbalanced.	Have TV set "converged" by service technician. Readjust drive and screen controls or have them readjusted by a service technician.
	Picture is predominantly one color—red, blue, or green.	Drive and screen controls misadjusted.	Readjust drive and screen controls or have them readjusted by a service technician.
	Random patches of color remain stationary on picture screen.	Picture tube has become magnetized.	Have service technician degauss (demagnetize) TV set.
	Picture is torn; loses synchronization (rolling, slanting); or resembles negative.	Nearby two-way radio blocking reception of TV signal.	Install a high-pass filter at rear of TV receiver.
	Dark, slanting lines in herringbone pattern superimposed on images.	Nearby two-way radio causing harmonic interference to TV signal.	Request amateur-radio or CB operator to install low-pass filter on the radio set. Increase distance on roof between TV antenna and CB antenna.
	Snow (pepper-and-salt speckles) appears in colored or black-and-white picture.	Antenna or lead-in in poor condition. Signal weak. Tuner dirty. Soot buildup on outdoor antenna terminals.	Repair or replace broken antenna elements. Renew damaged lead-in. Install antenna with more elements (higher gain). Avoid splitting and distributing signals to several TV sets. Have tuner cleaned (contacts sprayed, channel selector rotated). Clean terminals on outdoor antenna with a dry rag.

Lead-in–receiver connection

Although not apparent to the eye, the lead-in is a precision product designed to preserve an electrical rating known as impedance. *Impedance* is the amount of electrical opposition the TV signal will encounter when it travels along the lead-in. When the number of ohms is too low, the signal tends to short-circuit and be lost between the two wires of the lead-in. If the number of ohms is too high, the signal will waste energy as it passes through the wire. The number of ohms, or impedance, therefore, must be close to the value for which the TV system is designed.

For a home TV system, the standard impedance is 300 ohms. Any variation from that value can aggravate the two most common ailments in a television system, ghosts and snow.

Ghosts. *Ghosts* are multiple images on the screen that are usually seen to the right of the main picture. Their source is extra signals that reach the antenna slightly after the main signal has arrived. As the TV signal is split up by obstructions (hills, buildings, and so on) which lie between a home and the transmitting station, the additional weaker signals are being picked up. Thus, the desired picture is projected on the screen, followed by several weaker ones. The most powerful signal is the direct one which forms the main picture, and the ghostly images on the screen are the extra signals which arrive a few millionths of a second later.

If ghosts appear suddenly one day—not after a gradual increase over months—chances are high that one of the two wires in the lead-in is disconnected. The break causes the signal to reflect back and forth along the line, creating the multiple, or ghost, image on the screen. To remedy this, begin checking the lead-in behind the TV, at the set's antenna terminals. (In many instances, the set has been moved during housecleaning, causing the wire to break or become unfastened under the strain.) Turn off the set. Unplug the cord from the wall outlet. If the wires are loose, wind them around the posts of the small screws on the back cover of the TV. Then tighten the screws with a small screwdriver. If the lead-in wire is broken, cutting, stripping, and reattaching the wire will restore picture clarity.

Snow. *Snow,* another common problem, is the speckled appearance created on the screen when TV signals are too weak to generate clear, solid pictures. Snow, in fact, is to television viewing what static is to radio reception. The pepper-and-salt appearance of the screen occurs when electrical noise in the atmosphere and inside the television's circuits grows stronger than the TV signal.

Strain relief. Because the lead-in connection to the antenna terminals at the back of the TV is such a problem area, it is a good idea to provide *strain relief*

there. Either loop the lead-in wire through a slot on the back cover of the set, or secure it in a way that prevents stress on the delicate points where the wire is screwed to the set's antenna terminals. Do not form tight loops in the wire because they can disturb the smooth flow of signals, especially in the UHF band.

Lead-in–antenna connection

A common area of lead-in trouble is where the wire attaches to the antenna on the roof. Check the lead-in wire and the connections at the antenna for breaks. A faulty connection there could cause severe ghosting to suddenly appear. A broken or imperfectly connected lead-in brushing against the terminal(s) of the antenna (on a windy day, for instance) could also produce bright flashes of light on the TV screen. Before reattaching the wire to the outdoor antenna (if this is the source of poor reception), consider whether or not the lead-in itself should be replaced (*see page 191*).

 WARNING: Turn off the TV and unplug the cord from the wall outlet before checking and securing the lead-in wire and connections at the outdoor antenna.

Another source of trouble in the antenna-lead-in system is the bands or fasteners that hold the mast, or stem, of the outdoor antenna to the chimney or side of the roof or house. The standoffs supporting the lead-in away from the building can break and allow the wire to graze a rain gutter or other metal areas that disturb the wire's ability to conduct the signal. Broken standoffs permit the line to sway in the wind and strain the connection between the antenna and the lead-in. With a careful inspection by eye alone, the TV viewer can usually spot these problems and determine if the standoffs should be replaced.

Antenna

Outdoor antenna

Because outdoor-antenna elements are sturdier than the lead-in, they usually take longer to manifest trouble, but a careful examination will reveal potential weak points. Look for damaged or missing elements. Each rod acts as a resonant tuning member for the TV signal. One that has been damaged or broken off causes inefficiency, especially if a home is located more than 50 miles from the TV station.

Note the position of the antenna—its mast and elements. The mast should be perfectly vertical, but its mounting may have loosened, allowing it to lean. When the antenna is out of plumb, it picks up less energy. (Leaning antennas also pose a hazard to people and property below).

TV signals are *horizontally polarized*; that is, the signal wave is sent in a horizontal plane from the transmitting station. For an antenna to extract the maximum signal possible, its elements should lie in a horizontal position. The elements are aligned, on the antenna boom, parallel to each other and perpendicular to the boom. The end of the boom with the shorter elements should be pointed in the direction of the transmitting station.

If poor picture or sound is being caused by an antenna that is improperly aimed at the transmitting station, the antenna must be repositioned on the roof. To do this, two people must work together; one must watch the picture on the TV screen, and the other must go to the roof. The person on the roof must move the arms supporting the antenna boom around until good reception shows down below. Then, when the boom is on target, the set must be turned off, and the bolts holding the antenna arms in place must be tightened. The standoffs or fasteners holding the stem of the antenna to the chimney or side of the house must also be tightened. A screwdriver or a wrench will probably be needed.

When an antenna is mounted on a chimney, after several years it accumulates soot. This coating contains carbon, which is an electrical conductor, and exerts a short-circuiting effect across the antenna terminals to which the lead-in is attached. This soot buildup could cause an increase in snow in the picture unless the terminals are wiped clean.

Evaluate the antenna—lead-in system every couple of years. Although the reception may be good, wind and water extract a toll from any outdoor antenna and reduce the pleasure of TV viewing. The cost of replacing these components, if the installation work is done by the homeowner, is a fraction of the cost of a new television set.

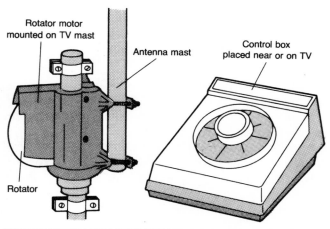

Rotator motor mounted on TV mast

Antenna mast

Control box placed near or on TV

Rotator

Because TV antennas work best only in one direction, they may produce poor reception when stations transmit from different cities. This can be cured by aiming the antenna with a rotator motor mounted on the mast several feet below the TV antenna *(left)*. The motor is activated by a control box *(right)* inside the home, on top of or near the TV. While watching the screen, the viewer rotates the dial on the control box. This causes the motor to swing the outdoor antenna in a circle until the strongest, most ghost-free picture appears. The antenna is turned every time the TV is switched to the station of a different city.

Indoor antenna

About half the population of the United States lives in or near an urban area, which probably explains why nearly half of all residences use some kind of indoor antenna. "Rabbit ears," "bow ties," telescoping whips (collapsible rods), loops, and double loops built into or attached to the television receiver may deliver good results for local reception (when TV signals are strong). Indoor antennas, however, are prone to *multipath,* a condition where TV signals bounce among obstructions and produce ghosts, or double images, on the screen. Furthermore, a simple indoor antenna may not intercept a wide selection of stations without frequent repositioning.

Both single-pole and rabbit-ear antennas are subject to bends. A bent antenna does not affect the picture or sound reception, but does make it difficult to telescope the poles again. If the bent section cannot be straightened by hand, place it between two wooden blocks; squeeze the blocks together while rotating them. This should press out the kink. If the telescoping parts of the antenna still cannot be moved up and down, replace the antenna. To fix a telescoping pole that has separated in the middle, try to reinsert the detached piece and twist it into place. If the pole still comes apart, insert the detached piece into the larger section and crimp with pliers.

Adjusting the Receiver Controls

The trend in television design is to eliminate manual adjustment in favor of automatic control of the set's functions. Automatic controls can now regulate the fine tuning, color (pureness of shades) and color registry, brightness and contrast, vertical and horizontal hold, and other tuning functions. A set may, however, have several manual controls, located at the rear or behind an access door, to make any of the above adjustments or to correct picture size, width, or other quality. These controls should not have to be adjusted more than a slight amount—from one-quarter to one-half turn. If a control needs more changing than that, chances are high that the trouble lies elsewhere. Controls are intended to compensate for normal aging of electronic components and for regular everyday tuning, not for necessary repair or replacement of parts.

NOTE: When a control knob is turned, the original setting should be noted. If adjusting does not improve the picture quality, return the knob to its starting position.

Because of the wide variety of television sets, the features and controls for rendering the picture differ from model to model. Therefore, the instructions for

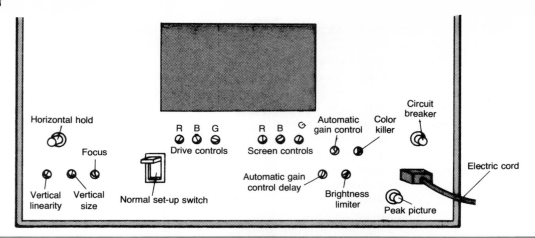

Rear view of a television set

making adjustments described in this section are approximate. Be sure to read and study the television owner's manual to locate and identify each control and other special features before making adjustments. Do not try to adjust any control that is inaccessible from the outside of the set. Controls that are accessible, even though they may be hidden on the back and referred to as service controls, can be adjusted with the aid of the accompanying owner's manual.

 WARNING: Do not tamper with the electrical connections inside the back of the set, even after the TV has been turned off. An electric charge often lingers in the picture tube and can deliver an electric shock.

Automatic gain control (AGC)

The automatic gain control, found at the rear of many sets, determines the overall sensitivity of the receiver. It receives an initial adjustment when the set is first installed and subsequent adjustment whenever there's a change in the antenna system. *Gain* refers to the receiver's ability to amplify, or boost, a signal. Exactly how much gain the receiver requires depends on the incoming signal. First, the receiver samples the strength of the signal and, if that signal is weak, the circuits automatically adjust themselves for higher gain. A strong signal, on the other hand, "tells" the receiver to reduce its gain. The overall effect of AGC, therefore, is to continuously adjust the receiver for the correct amount of amplification over a variety of incoming signals.

The procedure for making the initial adjustment to the AGC is simple. Turn the channel selector to the strongest channel (often the one with the least snow); then slowly move the AGC until the picture distorts or breaks up. At that point, gently reverse the control until the picture returns to normal.

To check for the proper AGC adjustment, rotate the channel selector through its complete range to see if any other channel distorts or breaks up. Do not turn the AGC control too far or the picture will appear dark, even when the contrast control is set for a bright picture. Moving the AGC too far in the opposite direction causes the picture to appear pale and faded. Find a good compromise between the two settings.

Automatic fine tuning (AFT)

Heating and other external influences can cause a TV receiver to drift off a channel (resulting in poor picture quality) and necessitate a readjustment of the fine-tuning knob located on the channel selector. The AFT, a long-standard feature in color TV sets, is designed to fine-tune automatically, even if the manual fine-tuning knob has not been properly adjusted.

Sometimes a picture will develop diagonal lines because of interference from signals on channels adjacent to the one tuned in. Interference can also arise when a set is connected to a cable-TV system that uses all the available channels. A good AFT control will minimize interference from adjacent channels.

Automatic color control (ACC)

This is also sometimes called the automatic chroma control. Aircraft flying overhead can cause a kind of interference called *flutter* that will make the picture's colors fade in and out. The automatic-color-control circuitry is designed to diminish this, and to correct careless fine-tuning, by expanding the range over which color intensity stays constant. There is really no panacea for flutter, however.

Automatic brightness control

This is a built-in light sensor that responds to changes in a room's light and accordingly adjusts the picture brightness. If a set has this automatic control, the screen's image grows brighter when strong daylight is present and dims in the evening when illumination is weaker. Like the AFT, however, it is usually hidden and not normally adjusted by the viewer.

Vertical height and linearity controls

When the picture shrinks down from the top and/or up from the bottom of the screen, it can usually be restored with the *vertical height* (or *size*) and the *vertical linearity* controls. If the picture shrinks down from the top only, the vertical linearity probably needs adjustment. If shrinkage occurs at the top and bottom, the vertical height, and perhaps the vertical linearity, will require some setting changes.

When adjusting the vertical height control, turn only a slight amount each time because it interacts very precisely with the linearity control, which maintains correct proportions between bodies and heads and other objects as movement takes place across the screen. By moving these knobs back and forth ever so slightly, pleasing picture proportion free from geometric distortion can usually be obtained. Place a mirror in front of the screen so that the picture can be viewed while the adjustments are being made at the rear of the set.

Width control

If the set has a picture width control, the amount of horizontal overscan, the portion of the picture which extends beyond the left and right borders, can be adjusted. This control compensates for minor picture shrinkage that may occur as the set's components age.

Convergence controls

In color sets, convergence controls draw the three electron beams into focus until they register correctly at their color dots on the screen. Incorrect convergence shows up as color *fringing*—black-and-white objects are fringed with colors. If there is no black-and-white program on the air, to check for improper color registry, simply turn the color control all the way down until the picture turns black and white. If the images on the screen have colored margins, the convergence needs adjusting.

In older sets, convergence cannot be adjusted by the viewer because the controls are internal—and remedying may require more than a dozen changes in settings. Newer receivers, however, limit convergence adjustment to one or two controls and make them accessible at the rear of the set. The usual procedure is to turn the control knob until the purest color is seen.

Drive and screen controls

The *drive* and *screen* controls balance the three colors—red, green, and blue—that make up a color picture. The drive controls balance the color in the brighter areas, while the screen controls regulate the low brightness, or background, colors. Together they help achieve the brightest color picture possible and at the same time maintain the gray shades that give black-and-white images (on noncolor programs) their realistic three-dimensional appearance.

When the screen develops a cast in predominantly one hue—either red, green, or blue—these controls may require adjustment. (If the controls are really out of kilter, the colored cast will remain evident even when the color control is turned all the way down.) Balancing the color is a bit complicated; first adjust the screen controls, then move on to the drive controls. To coordinate the three colors accurately may require starting over several times.

To adjust the screen controls:

1. Turn the contrast control down, and set the brightness control for a slightly dim picture.
2. Turn the ACC (automatic color control) off (if present), and turn the color down.
3. Turn all three screen controls all the way down.
4. Turn up the red screen control slowly until the picture appears slightly reddish.
5. Turn up the green screen control until a lemon-yellow tinge appears in the picture.
6. Turn up the blue screen control until the picture appears white or gray. (The other screen controls may have to be readjusted a bit to accomplish this.)
7. Now adjust the red, green, and blue drive controls.

To adjust the drive controls:

1. Set the brightness and contrast controls for a normal picture.
2. Turn the color down and tune in a black-and-white program.
3. Turn down all three drive controls.
4. Turn up the red drive control until a slightly pink cast appears in the bright areas of the picture.
5. Turn up the green drive control until there is a slightly orange tinge in the bright areas.
6. Turn up the blue drive control until a bluish green cast appears in the bright areas.
7. Adjust the blue and green drive controls—going back and forth between the two—until the picture's highlights turn white. There should be no trace of color in the black-and-white picture. To check that the drive and screen controls have been set correctly, rotate the brightness control through its entire range. No color should appear in the picture while this is being done.
8. Turn the color control up again, and return the ACC to the On position.

Degaussing circuit

Another affliction to color is caused by the earth's magnetic field. Certain metal parts of the picture tube become magnetized and pull the color beams to the wrong dots, a condition that causes the color to appear contaminated (random color blotches show up) in certain areas of the picture. Modern sets have a built-in automatic *degaussing*, or demagnetizing, *circuit* to remedy the problem; older sets should be manually demagnetized by a TV technician.

Inside the Chassis: Not for the Amateur

Opening the back cover to repair the innards of a TV receiver was once an enticing prospect for the amateur. The chassis within held about two dozen tubes that could be easily removed and replaced. By linking a symptom to a specific tube, the trouble-shooter could yank out a suspicious number, put it in a brown bag, and test it at a local drugstore. A TV picture that rolled continuously, for example, suggested a burned-out tube in the vertical section; the loss of sound usually meant a bad audio tube. When transistors came into use in the 1950s, they improved the TV by replacing many of the tubes that could burn out, but the trouble spots became less accessible to the Saturday mechanic. Transistors have fragile wires and, in most circuits, are permanently soldered in place.

Even if a transistor could be tested at a local store, the trip would rarely reap a reward. The life of a transistor is yet unknown and it almost never burns out spontaneously like the hot filament of a tube. Most troubles in a transistorized set spring from defects in other parts—resistors, capacitors, switches, controls—and they take technical skill to locate.

The solid-state revolution in television began with the "hybrid" set—a TV chassis consisting of a combination of tubes and transistors—that appeared in the 1950s. Because early transistors could cope only with low frequencies, they were restricted to the audio section. Accelerating technology, however, quickly led to the development of the IC, or integrated circuit, where thousands of transistors are crowded onto microminiature "chips"—black rectangles slightly over an inch long with a dozen or more silvery legs that connect into the circuit. These ICs can cheaply handle almost any task in the TV repertoire, and today all chassis are studded with them.

Although TV sets of the 1970s could boast these electronic circuits that improved reliability, the chassis became *more* difficult to service. Much of the circuit is hermetically sealed inside small blocks that can not be repaired by the "tube jockey"—including unskilled persons in the TV service industry. Only sophisticated technicians with expensive test equipment can troubleshoot such circuits, and these people are in short supply. Thus the miracle wrought by solid-state technology also triggered a crisis: where to get reliable TV servicing at reasonable cost. Manufacturers worried about widespread consumer concern over reliable service and took a step the industry had resisted for many years. They tooled up for modularization.

Instead of soldering numerous ICs to one or two large boards, the designers divided the chassis into several zones, each represented by a *module,* a unit containing several ICs and other parts. Because a module is easily plugged in or removed, most servicing can be done by module substitution. This technique was shunned by manufacturers for years because it is expensive to mass-produce reliable plug-in devices (the connectors are notoriously troublesome). Modules, however, have swept through the lines of most manufacturers because they ease the service problem.

For the amateur, however, tinkering with the modules rarely pays off. Because they encompass such large circuit sections, modules are costly and not, as in the case of vacuum tubes, available at a local drugstore. Modules are sold through wholesalers who rarely deal with the consumer. Also, the professional repairer usually carries a set of modules for a particular TV and enjoys the advantages of swapping any number of boards in a chassis until the trouble clears up. The amateur would have to diagnose the problems perfectly every time or pay the heavy cost of purchasing unneeded modules.

Thus, the modern TV has won spectacular gains—more reliability, smaller size, and cost-cutting technology—but these advances also isolate the tinkerer further from the chassis. And that trend can only continue, as manufacturers lump together ICs into even larger blocks known as LSI, or large-scale integration. Television design is approaching the day when everything but the knobs will be hewn from a single electronic block—in a break-through called VSLI, or *very* large-scale integration. As that day dawns, there will be little need (even for a technician) to *ever* remove the back cover of a TV set.

Reducing Outside Interference

There is a raft of problems that have nothing to do with the internal workings of the TV chassis and yet can ruin reception as easily as can a blown resistor or melting capacitor. Often they are troubles that can be cured with an appropriate accessory, which can be installed in the present system with a screwdriver or other hand tool.

The leading types of interference to TV reception are snow and ghosts, caused by problems in the antenna—lead-in system (*see pages 182-4*). Disturbances to sound and picture often spring from other sources as well. Increasingly popular citizens' band (CB) radios can send herringbone patterns across the picture screen or deliver voices through the TV speaker. Other interference is released by the sun during intense periods of solar radiation at certain times of the year. Some varieties of TV static can originate as close by as a passing automobile.

Before tracing the source, there is one principle to know about curing interference: The *stronger* the TV signal, the *less* susceptible is a set to the disturbance. The reason is simple. As the signal from the antenna increases in strength, the AGC (automatic gain control) causes the TV circuit to grow less sensitive. In this fashion, the circuit protects itself against overloading when the set is near a powerful station—or grows more sensitive out in the fringe areas, where it is more than 50 miles from the station. Thus, if a television is furnished with a stronger signal—via an improved antenna—the circuit can grow more immune to outside signals and get rid of stubborn traces of interference.

Several types of interference are caused by two-way (CB, ham, or police) radio services. Because they fall into two main categories—those inside and outside the TV channel band—their symptoms and remedies are different.

Blocking interference

One type of interference is called *blocking*—a two-way radio is operating on a channel far removed from the TV band but is sufficiently strong to blast through the TV band and disturb reception. A classic setup for blocking occurs when the CB and TV antennas share the same roof. Blocking shows up on the screen as pictures that tear; that have lost synchronization (lines roll upward or downward continuously, or slant to the left or right); or even pictures which completely reverse values and resemble negatives. When blocking occurs, there is no distinct number grouping to the channels affected. The interference appears on any or all of the channels in haphazard combinations.

High-pass filter. A device that treats this type of interference is a *high-pass* filter, available where electronic parts or TV accessories are sold. The filter operates by preventing radio signals of 52 MHz or lower from entering the TV receiver. Because the lowest TV channel (channel 2) is on 54 MHz, the filter allows the desired station to pass through without opposition.

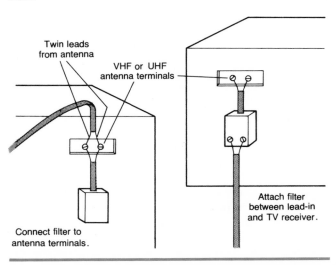

Twin leads from antenna

VHF or UHF antenna terminals

Attach filter between lead-in and TV receiver.

Connect filter to antenna terminals.

A high-pass filter connected at the rear of the TV receiver helps reduce blocking interference from ham, CB, or police radios.

Installing a high-pass filter (or interference trap) is a simple procedure. One type is a little rectangular box with two wire prongs. The prongs slip around the posts of the antenna-terminal screws; the screws are then tightened with a screwdriver. To hang this filter does not require removal of the lead-in, which attaches at the same antenna terminals. The other type of high-pass filter is connected to the TV system between the receiver and the lead-in. The lead-in is removed from the set's antenna terminals; the filter is attached to these at one end, and then connected to the lead-in at the other end. Fittings, or connectors, can be purchased with the filter to match the various types of lead-in.

> **NOTE:** If a high-pass filter is used to reduce blocking interference, the filter must match the lead-in used in the TV system. If the lead-in is ordinary twin lead, the filter should be labeled 300 ohms; if it is coaxial cable, the filter must be marked 75 ohms.

Harmonic interference

Another disturbance to the frequencies used by television signals—caused by CB and other two-way radios—is known as *harmonic* interference. Its symptoms are recognizable because they follow a special pattern. The screen fills with dark, slanting lines that are so close together, they resemble the herringbone design on clothing. Also, the interference worsens on lower channels and decreases on the higher numerals. There is no filter to install on the TV set for this problem, but there is a filter for the offending two-way radio.

Low-pass filter. If the amateur radio-set owner is known (he or she is probably a neighbor if the signals are strong enough to interfere), recommend the installation of a *low-pass* filter on the CB set. Available in electronic and other stores, the filter helps reduce harmonic interference before it reaches a nearby TV.

Electrical interference

In deep fringe areas (over 50 miles from the transmitting station), where TV signals are weak, the receiver can pick up electrical interference through the wall outlet. It appears in the video as *hash*—black-and-white or colored dashes across the screen—and may be audible in the speaker as static. When such interference is obviously produced by an appliance in operation, such as a blender, fluorescent lamp, vacuum cleaner, or hair dryer, it is not worth the expense to eliminate it; simply wait until operation of the appliance or power tool is over.

Line filter. If electric motors outside the home are sparking and causing this problem, a *line*, or *line interference,* filter may be useful. This device plugs into the wall outlet, and the television's electric cord plugs into it. If the electrical interference enters the receiver, it can disrupt the TV's circuits for both sound and picture, so the filter eliminates the interference before it can travel up the line cord to reach the receiver.

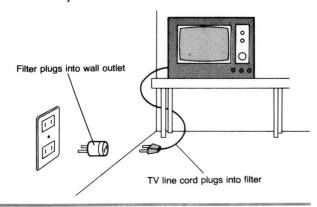

A line interference filter eliminates TV noise caused by household appliances, fluorescent lamps, radios, and other electrical equipment.

Ignition interference

If a viewer's home is near a busy highway and TV reception is already weak, hash in the form of short dashes may appear across the television screen. This is caused by spark plugs in the ignition systems of machinery such as passing vehicles, oil burners, and outdoor equipment that produce sparks and electrical interference. Because the problem cannot be treated at the source, consider these alternatives: If a new TV is being installed, try to run the antenna lead-in on the side of the house *away* from the road. (Any additional distance will enhance reception.) Or change the lead-in to one of the shielded types—this may increase resistance to ignition pickup.

Natural interference

Another source of interference is the sun. During the spring, and sometimes part of the summer, ultraviolet activity of the sun increases and electrifies the earth's upper atmosphere. At other times of the year, TV signals merely pass through the atmosphere, but during these seasons they bounce back because the electrified layers act as a radio mirror. The phenomenon carries TV signals hundreds of miles beyond their usual limits—and causes interference in distant cities. If television programs are being viewed during these periods, which can last several hours each day, one or two dark bars will hover on the screen, and sometimes dim images will be visible behind the main picture. Another symptom of this intense solar activity is a grinding sound in the speaker as the two TV signals, local and distant, mix in the receiver.

The interference is aggravated most during *solar flares,* magnetic storms raging on the face of the sun. As a flare raises electrical activity in the earth's atmo-

sphere, TV signals spill far beyond their usual boundaries and produce annoying but temporary interference.

Keep Watching

The erosion of picture quality is often difficult to perceive because the breakdown occurs over a long period of time. When the TV system—from the tip of the outdoor antenna to the screen of the picture tube—is producing clear, stable images, note carefully how the receiver performs on each channel. Observe the screen, listen to the speaker, manipulate the accessible controls for optimum reception. No system is perfect: Some channels may have a faint flurry of snow across the picture; others might have a slight but acceptable double line caused by ghosting. These are the symptoms to watch, for signs of future trouble.

As mentioned earlier, the first step toward curing interference is establishing a good antenna system that can capture and deliver strong signals to the TV receiver. As follow-up, there are several techniques to strengthen the TV signal—these can be used to rehabilitate an old antenna system or to augment a new one.

The Antenna System

Parts of the Antenna System

Antenna

A good outdoor antenna intercepts selected TV signals and rejects interfering signal waves with three important qualities: gain, directivity, and bandwidth.

Gain. *Gain* describes an antenna's sensitivity in capturing the TV signal. As the signal wave travels, it becomes weaker. Many factors influence this: the distance and type of terrain between the transmitting station and the receiving antenna, the location of the broadcast tower, the condition of the atmosphere, and the frequency on which the program is transmitted. The gain of an antenna is a measure of how well it can intercept the passing signal wave. Engineers calculate gain in decibels but rarely are these figures advertised. To simplify the classification for consumers, manufacturers usually categorize their antenna models according to broadcast area: city, or urban; suburban; and rural, or fringe. Fringe-area antennas must intercept signal waves from the greatest distances, so they have the highest gain. City antennas offer the lowest gain because the distance between the TV sets and the broadcast tower is least.

To raise the gain in an antenna, the number of elements must be increased, and, accordingly, the price. The dimensions of the antenna also grow with gain (to accommodate additional elements), and a solid supporting structure with sufficient space on the roof must be provided. A high-gain antenna can be erected in a city location but will create no noticeable

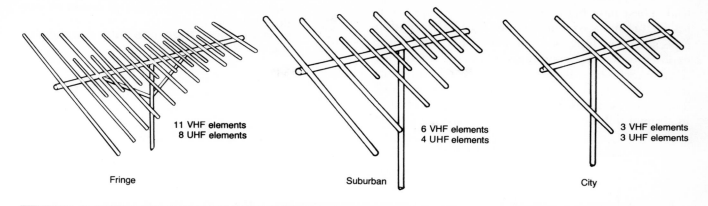

11 VHF elements
8 UHF elements

6 VHF elements
4 UHF elements

3 VHF elements
3 UHF elements

Fringe

Suburban

City

Typical antenna models

improvement on the picture screen because, once an antenna supplies sufficient signal to the set, the receiver cuts back any excess through the AGC (automatic-gain-control) circuit. Therefore, a homeowner is wise to choose an antenna from the appropriate category to get optimum reception without unnecessary expense.

An antenna is providing adequate gain if no snow is visible in the picture.

Directivity. Nearly all TV antennas work best when aimed at the station transmitting the program that the viewer is watching. This is because the antenna elements form an electronic lens which funnels and consequently focuses most energy from one direction only. (That is, the elements are best suited for detecting TV signals in one direction only.) How well the antenna funnels the signal is a measure of its directivity. This quality also includes a measurement known as a *front-to-back ratio*.

During design and testing, the manufacturer aims the antenna at a signal and takes a gain reading (to ascertain the strength of the received signal), then swings the antenna around 180 degrees and takes a second reading. The higher the difference between the two, the better is the front-to-back ratio; in other words, the better is the ability of the antenna to pick up TV signals in one direction and react poorly (reject signals) in the opposite direction. This is a desirable quality, especially when there are numerous obstructions between the TV receiver and the broadcast tower, because it reduces ghosts. The antenna tunes sharply in one direction but tends to react with less sensitivity to the ghost signal, which is arriving from a slightly different direction.

Bandwidth. TV signal waves travel on a band of frequencies rather than on a single frequency. The *bandwidth* of the antenna is the range, or number, of frequencies that it can pick up. The higher the range of frequencies, the more channels that can be intercepted and broadcast. TV programs are transmitted on three frequency bands: VHF (channels 2 to 13),

UHF (channels 14 to 83), and FM stereo (for the audio). There are separate models of antennas for each individual band and various combinations of each. When purchasing a new or replacement antenna, be certain it is designed to receive the TV channels desired.

Choice of an antenna. Before buying a new or replacement antenna, look at the roofs in the neighborhood to see what kinds professional installers have selected. In many instances, the installers, not the homeowners, choose the antenna model, and they choose a model that produces acceptable (if not outstanding) reception. If a particular locality has many three-element antennas and few seventeen-element ones, then the viewers almost certainly live close to the TV station. (Count each element as one pair of rods astride the boom, or center shaft.) After checking the surrounding homes, use the table to choose an appropriate model. These figures are approximate, not rigid, standards, but can serve as a guide.

BASIC ANTENNA MODELS	
Broadcast area	**Distance from TV station (approximate no. of miles)**
City, or urban	0 to 25
Suburban	25 to 50
Fringe, or rural	50 or more

Lead-in

The quality of the lead-in—the cable which brings the TV signal from the outdoor antenna to the set—directly influences what is seen on the screen. There are several grades of lead-in.

Twin lead. The most common cable is twin lead, the ubiquitous flat, brown ribbon with two copper conductors. Some types have thicker strands of wire or a heavier plastic. It is advisable to avoid using the thin, cut-rate variety because it will crack or fail years before a high-quality cable. To get better reception at slightly greater cost, use a tubular or foam-filled twin lead. These have higher immunity to moisture (a critical factor) and are recommended for UHF reception, especially over long outdoor runs where the line is exposed to weather conditions. For areas where electrical interference is heavy (from cars, neon signs, motors, and so on), a shielded twin lead is preferable. This type resembles the regular variety but is encased in a metal foil that helps exclude interfering signals.

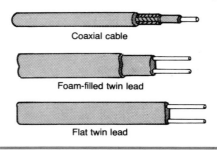

Coaxial cable

Foam-filled twin lead

Flat twin lead

Lead-in wires

Coaxial cable. Another type of lead-in is coaxial cable. Although this is the wire used by cable-TV and other installers in the closed-circuit-TV field, it is also available to the homeowner. Enclosed in a metal shield, it is more durable and weatherproof than regular twin lead. It is also more immune to electrical interference and does not need insulators to run through, as does ordinary (unshielded) twin lead. There are, however, certain disadvantages to coaxial cable. Because its electrical rating is 75 ohms, and the standard for home television is 300 ohms, a pair of matching transformers may be required to hook up the cable to the antenna and TV set. (If a high-pass filter is being installed in a system that uses coaxial cable, it must have an electrical rating of 75 ohms.) To avoid these extra items and expense, choose 300-ohm twin lead unless an elaborate, professional-type setup is being installed.

Installation of the Antenna System

Putting up a new antenna or replacing an old one is within the ken of a handy do-it-yourselfer with ordinary tools. But certain precautions must be followed to avoid the two hazards which lead to injuries—electric shock and falling. Do not attempt the job unless extreme care is taken to prevent electrical hazard while on the roof. Putting up an antenna and fastening the lead-in require surefootedness and alertness. Each year more than a hundred people are electrocuted while holding an antenna (or supporting mast) and allowing it to brush against a nearby electrical wire.

Stand far enough away from other power lines so that the antenna and lead-in can never touch them. The distance should be sufficient for the antenna and lead-in to clear other cables even if they are accidentally dropped.

 WARNING: Do not attempt to install an outdoor antenna if the roof is wet or icy, or if a high wind is blowing. The dangers of falling and electric shock are too great.

Mounting the mast

The accessory industry has designed an abundance of hardware for mounting outdoor TV antennas. There are devices for fastening a mast to nearly any surface: vertical, horizontal, peaked, or slanted. One of the most popular is the chimney mount because a complete antenna array can be attached within minutes. There are wall mounts for vertical surfaces, corner brackets for the edges of a building, towers to loft antennas above the roofline, and vent pipe mounts for attachment to plumbing pipes. In some localities the pipe mount may not be acceptable. Although it is convenient to encircle a plumbing vent pipe with brackets, town ordinances may forbid affixing anything to a plumbing system.

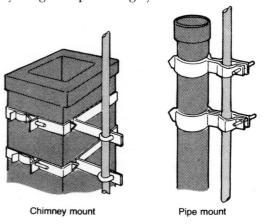

Chimney mount   Pipe mount

Mounts for installation of the antenna mast

All of these mountings are designed to receive the standard TV mast, which is sold in 5- and 10-foot lengths. A 5-foot mast may provide enough clearance for the TV antenna above the roofline, but that height can be increased, if necessary for good reception, with a 10-foot mast. Be sure the mounting brackets are spaced more than a few inches apart to provide ample support. If the mast will rise higher than 10 feet, extra support from guy wires will be needed to prevent lateral swaying. Special fittings and wires for this purpose are sold in local stores.

After the mast is mounted, the antenna—boom and elements—must be positioned for optimum reception. For proper alignment of the outdoor antenna, see page *184–5*.

Fastening the lead-in

When installing a lead-in, keep it from rubbing or touching other surfaces—sides of the house, gutters, pipes, metal frames or objects—by running the cable

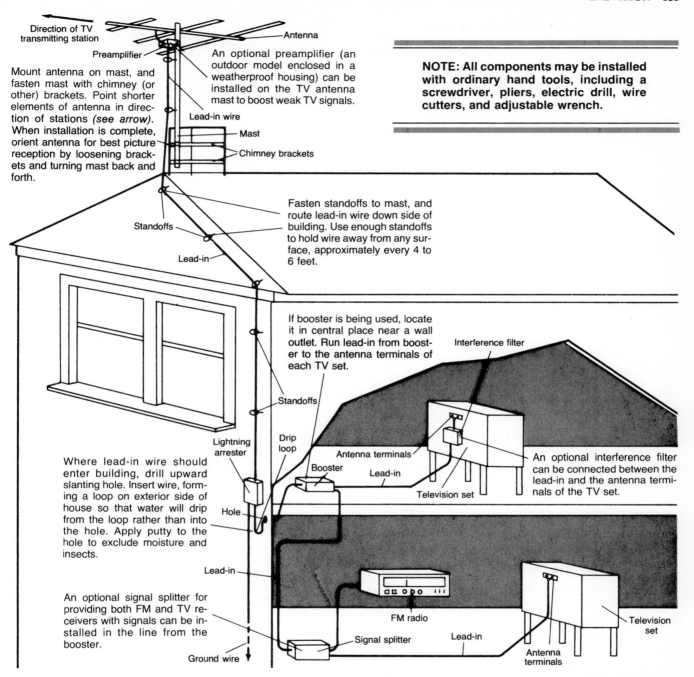

Direction of TV transmitting station

Preamplifier

Antenna

Mount antenna on mast, and fasten mast with chimney (or other) brackets. Point shorter elements of antenna in direction of stations *(see arrow)*. When installation is complete, orient antenna for best picture reception by loosening brackets and turning mast back and forth.

An optional preamplifier (an outdoor model enclosed in a weatherproof housing) can be installed on the TV antenna mast to boost weak TV signals.

Lead-in wire

Mast

Chimney brackets

NOTE: All components may be installed with ordinary hand tools, including a screwdriver, pliers, electric drill, wire cutters, and adjustable wrench.

Standoffs

Lead-in

Fasten standoffs to mast, and route lead-in wire down side of building. Use enough standoffs to hold wire away from any surface, approximately every 4 to 6 feet.

If booster is being used, locate it in central place near a wall outlet. Run lead-in from booster to the antenna terminals of each TV set.

Interference filter

Standoffs

Lightning arrester

Drip loop

Antenna terminals

Booster

Lead-in

Television set

An optional interference filter can be connected between the lead-in and the antenna terminals of the TV set.

Where lead-in wire should enter building, drill upward slanting hole. Insert wire, forming a loop on exterior side of house so that water will drip from the loop rather than into the hole. Apply putty to the hole to exclude moisture and insects.

Hole

Lead-in

An optional signal splitter for providing both FM and TV receivers with signals can be installed in the line from the booster.

FM radio

Signal splitter

Lead-in

Television set

Antenna terminals

Ground wire

Installation of the TV system

through standoffs. Standoffs are made in a variety of styles to cope with any mounting: clip-ons to support the line away from the mast, screw-in or nail types that go into wood or masonry. Besides isolating the line from other surfaces, standoffs spaced every 5 feet or so prevent the wind from swaying the cable into the sides of a building and possibly breaking. The lead-in should not run horizontally for any sizable distance and nowhere along the length of the run should it be formed into tight loops. Looping creates a coil that has an electrical action which interferes

with the TV signal. Form the cable into gentle curves where it changes direction, and allow just enough length behind the TV set to permit the set to be moved 3 or 4 feet from a wall for housecleaning. The lead-in should enter the house through an upward slanting hole drilled into the side of the house, not through a window.

Grounding the antenna

Because a TV antenna is above the roof, it not only intercepts television signals but also attracts lightning.

To reduce this hazard, and the possibility of shock or fire, the antenna should be provided with a good ground. A direct connection that can conduct electricity from the TV mast to the ground will provide this protection.

To ground the outdoor antenna, purchase a heavy bare wire available for the purpose. Fasten it at one end to the bottom of the TV mast, and run the other end of the wire directly (in as straight a line as possible) to a water pipe or ground pipe driven into the earth. All the fixtures necessary for grounding are sold at well-stocked electronic-parts stores or departments.

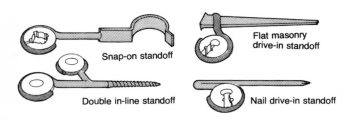

Standoffs and other hardware for guiding the lead-in from the outdoor antenna to the TV receiver while insulating it from other surfaces

Lightning arrester. As an added measure of protection, install a *lightning arrester*. This device is secured to the lead-in just before it enters the house, and also attached to the ground wire mentioned above. A spark-discharge gap inside the arrester may protect a TV set from damage during the strong buildup of static electricity that accompanies a thunderstorm.

Adding more TV sets

Multi-set coupler. Most households have more than one television set, but homeowners usually prefer to drive them all from a single antenna. When a home is located in a strong-signal area—less than 50 miles from the station—it is easy to hook up several sets to the same antenna and split the signal with a *multi-set coupler.* Couplers are manufactured in models that divide the signal into two or more lines for feeding each receiver; a model may be rated for VHF, UHF, FM, or any combination of these frequency bands. But couplers may introduce a problem. In dividing the signal from the single antenna, they also reduce the signal strength flowing to each set. For example, a two-set coupler delivers one-half the antenna power to each set; a four-set model delivers one-quarter the energy. This is not a problem so long as there is sufficient signal in the antenna. Inadequate signal is revealed by snow in the picture. Whether the sets are on or off does not matter—they continuously draw a signal from the antenna.

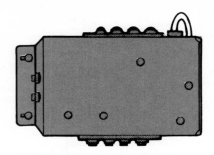

An indoor booster-coupler allows two or more TV receivers to operate from a single antenna and overcomes the loss of TV-signal strength by amplifying the signal delivered to each set.

Booster. The length of the lead-in wire running from the outdoor antenna to the TV receivers is another factor that affects the picture. On runs of less than about 50 feet, there is usually no possible loss of signal which may introduce snow. But lead-in wire running 50 feet or more within a system to feed TV receivers in various parts of the house can sap energy from the original signal. A cure for this problem is an amplifier known as a *booster, preamplifier,* or *distribution amplifier.* As the name implies, it strengthens the signal before splitting it among various sets.

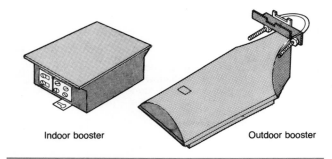

Indoor booster   Outdoor booster

The antenna booster drives two or more TV sets from a single antenna and lead-in wire. The indoor unit boosts and distributes the TV and FM signals; the outdoor booster is enclosed in a weatherproof housing that mounts on the mast.

A convenient location to place the booster is a central point, possibly an attic or basement, from which the lines can branch out to the individual sets. Some boosters are mounted directly on the outdoor antenna, and they offer the additional benefit of amplifying the signal before it even reaches the lead-in. For extremely long lead-in runs, the antenna-mounted preamplifier provides a good solution.

One shortcoming of any booster or amplifier, however, is that it can only make up for losses caused by the lead-in wiring—and not weak reception in a poor antenna system. If an amplifier is used when the picture is snowy, the snow is amplified too, and grows stronger on the screen. Thus, if a booster fails to improve reception, the problem must be solved at the source, the antenna. Either elevate it to a higher location, or replace it with a model that has more gain.

Large Appliances

Air Conditioners

Clothes Dryers

Dehumidifiers

Dishwashers

Microwave Ovens

Electric Ranges

Gas Ranges

Refrigerator/Freezers

Sewing Machines

Trash Compactors

Washing Machines

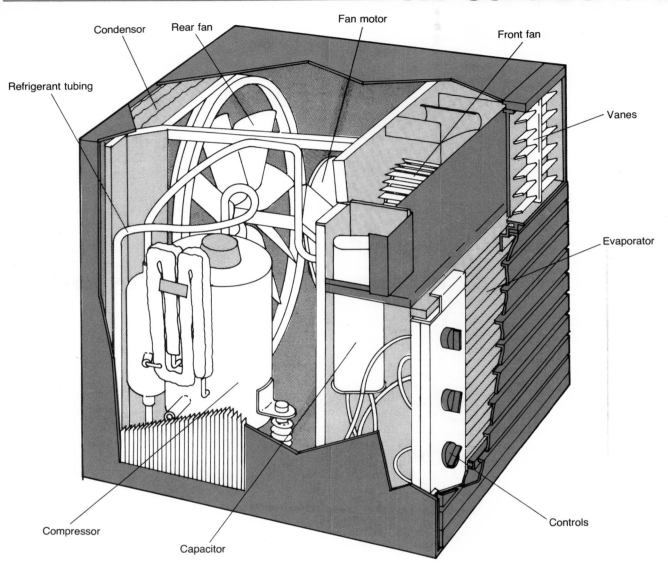

Condensor
Rear fan
Fan motor
Front fan
Refrigerant tubing
Vanes
Evaporator
Compressor
Capacitor
Controls

Principle of Operation

An air conditioner cools a room by transferring room heat to the outdoors. It circulates a refrigerant through a closed plumbing system, and the refrigerant carries the heat from the indoor part of the machine to the outdoor part, where it releases the heat to the outside.

The chassis of an air conditioner consists of a front and rear compartment separated by an insulated wall. The evaporator coil is in the front compartment; the condenser coil and the compressor pump in the rear. When the appliance is installed in a window or a wall, the front compartment remains inside the house, and the rear compartment extends outside. In the front

compartment, a fan circulates warm, moist room air over the cold evaporator, then blows the cooled air back into the room. The refrigerant in the evaporator is gas in its natural state, but here it is compressed to a cold liquid. It absorbs heat through the walls of the evaporator tubing and boils into a gas. This gas is pumped to the rear compartment and through the compressor. When it leaves the compressor, the gas occupies much less space than before—it has been compressed to almost a liquid state, but it is too warm to be a liquid. In order to lose its heat, it passes into the condenser. Another fan blows over the hot condenser coils to help dissipate the heat into the outdoor air. When the refrigerant leaves the condenser, it is once again a cool liquid. It then begins the cycle again.

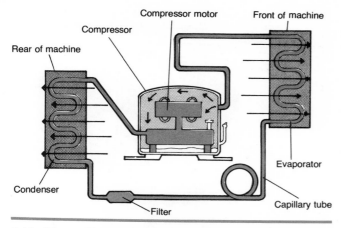

Cold refrigerant circulates through evaporator coil, absorbs room air, passes through compressor. Now warm, it circulates through condenser coil, loses heat, returns to evaporator.

On its way to the evaporator, it passes through a very thin capillary tube. When it emerges into the larger diameter evaporator pipe, it immediately begins to expand, and this expansion helps it to absorb heat.

An air conditioner dehumidifies as well as cools. (The refrigerant-circulating system in an air conditioner is similar to that in a dehumidifier, as well as in a refrigerator or freezer.) As the front fan blows room air on the evaporator coil, moisture condenses from the air. It collects on the coils, drips to a tray in the bottom of the appliance, and drains out the back.

An air conditioner contains two motors. The two fans are driven by one double-shafted motor (one shaft extends through the insulated wall between front and back compartments). The other motor drives the compressor. Both motors are usually capacitor-start types (*see page 62*). They may share a single capacitor or each have its own capacitor wired in series to the motor. The fan motor is often a two- or

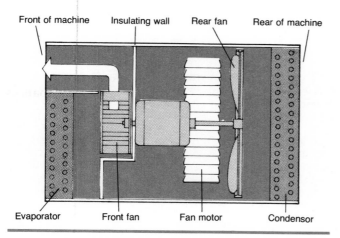

The front fan sucks warm room air through the cold evaporator, then blows it back into room. The rear fan blows outdoor air over the warm condenser, cooling the refrigerant inside. The two fans are powered by one double-shafted motor.

three-speed model, with the higher speeds usually supplied by supplementary windings in the motor.

When electricity enters the appliance, it first passes through the main On/Off switch. Here it divides into two subcircuits—one for the fan motor, the other for the compressor motor. The compressor subcircuit consists of the thermostat, the capacitor-start compressor motor (*see page 62*), a capacitor (*see page 62*), a starting relay (*see page 58*), and a thermal relay (*see page 63*) mounted on the compressor motor. The fan subcircuit is similar except that it lacks a thermostat. The main control of an air conditioner usually has two banks of On terminals—one set for operating the compressor and fan together (the Cool settings), and the other set for operating the fan alone (the Fan settings). Often there are Low, Medium, and High speed options for both the Cool and Fan settings; only the fan speed changes, however, because the compressor is a one-speed motor. When the air conditioner is set at High Cool, the fan is rotating at high speed and the compressor at its normal speed.

The thermostat, a control usually numbered 1 to 10 for selecting room temperature, is a switch in the compressor subcircuit. It is usually a bimetal or gas-containing type (*see pages 57-58*). When the room reaches the correct temperature, the thermostat opens and shuts off the compressor motor. The fan motor continues to run. When the room temperature rises a few degrees, the thermostat closes again, turning on the compressor.

Differences in Air Conditioners

Air conditioners come in various sizes, measured by the amount of heat (British Thermal Units, or BTUs) the appliance can remove per hour. A 12,000 BTU air conditioner is twice as "large" as a 6,000 BTU unit, even though their physical dimensions may be similar.

Another important variation in air conditioners is their Energy Efficiency Ratio (EER). EER is computed by dividing the rated watts of the appliance into the rated BTU. A 5,000 BTU air conditioner that requires 1,000 watts has an EER of only 5, whereas one requiring 500 watts has an EER of 10. The higher the EER, the better. Every new air conditioner is affixed with a label indicating the unit's EER.

Room air conditioners come in two installation designs: the wall unit and the window unit. These are quite similar, except that a wall unit fits through a metal sleeve in the wall.

A heat exchanger or heat pump is an air conditioner that can reverse the direction of the refrigerant-circulating system in order to heat a room instead of cool it. These complete heating and cooling systems are often found in motel rooms in warm climates.

The electrical systems of air conditioners vary little. Central air conditioning systems require 240 volts

AC, as do some older room models, but most wall and window units now available operate on 120 volts AC. Newer air conditioners that are highly efficient may have additional electrical components in the compressor motor circuit, such as a transformer (*see page 41*) to step up voltage.

Switch design varies from model to model. The On/Off switch may be combined with the speed and mode selection switch, or it may be separate. Many air conditioners have a Constant Cool option, which functions either by holding the contacts of the thermostat together mechanically so that it cannot open or by bypassing the thermostat circuit. The effect of either design is the same: the compressor runs constantly. Speed selection possibilities vary from model to model. In the most basic models, only one fan speed is available, but in more expensive models, three or more speeds are possible. Some models allow infinite speed adjustment with a rheostat (*see page 58*).

The vanes on the front panel of the appliance adjust on most models. Adjustment is usually accomplished with a simple lever, but one manufacturer has motorized the vanes to sweep left and right for improved air circulation.

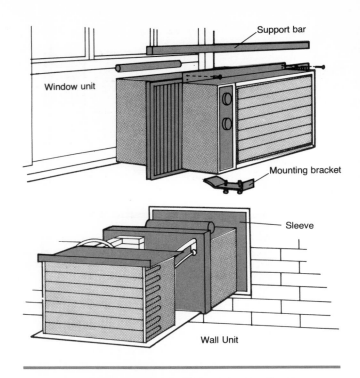

Wall and window units install differently but function the same.

How to Reach Interior Components

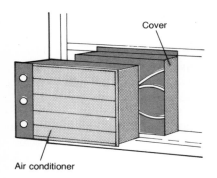

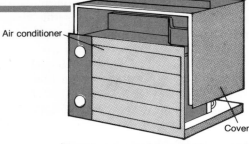

Appliance housing: To reach working parts
The front panel is usually held on with retaining screws or spring clips. Remove these, the front panel, and the air filter behind it. Next, pull the unit out of its metal sleeve or take a window unit out of the window. Then remove the box-like sheet metal cover by unscrewing the sheet metal screws that attach it to the chassis.

Rear compartment: To reach compressor, thermal relay, fan, condenser coils
Both the compressor and fan are housed in the rear compartment of the air conditioner behind the insulated wall. The compressor motor cannot be removed, as the entire compressor-refrigerant system is sealed. Take the appliance to a refrigeration shop for repairs. The fan motor is bolted to the chassis and can be removed. Fan blades are either pressed on or attached with setscrews. Loosen the screws (if any) and pull the blade unit off.

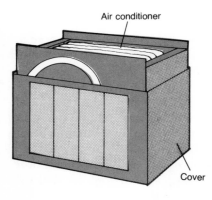

Front compartment: To reach switches, thermostat, capacitor, evaporator coils, exhaust flap, drainage system.
An additional front panel may have to be removed for access to the switches. Switches are sealed and cannot be disassembled. If replacement of a switch is necessary, remove the wire leads and note carefully which terminal each lead attaches to. Make a sketch. Leads may be fastened by solder or with quick-connect terminals (*see page 53*). If soldered, break the connection by melting the old solder with a soldering iron. Be careful when disconnecting wires from the compressor, because if the terminals on the compressor break off, the compressor may have to be replaced. Cut wires rather than pull them from quick-connect terminals if breakage seems possible. Reattach them later with wire nuts.

Maintenance and Repair

Air Filter. The air filter removes dirt from room air before it circulates over the evaporator coils in the front of the machine. Cleaning the air filter regularly is a simple but important task. A buildup of dirt obstructs the air flow over the evaporator coils and may cause the air conditioner to freeze up. The air filter is behind the front panel. Remove it, wash it in a mild soap-and-water solution, and let it dry before replacing it. Vacuum the evaporator coil at the same time.

Compressor. The compressor is part of a sealed refrigeration system. It can neither be removed from the chassis nor worked on by the homeowner. If a leak develops in the refrigeration system, the compressor motor will run, but the air conditioner will not cool. Take the air conditioner to a refrigeration shop for repair.

To test the compressor motor for continuity, attach the leads of a multimeter (*see pages 26-28*) first to the starting winding leads and then to the running winding leads (*see pages 61-62*). Set the multimeter to Rx1. The amount of resistance registered will depend upon the particular motor, but it should not be zero or infinity. If the meter registers at either end of the scale, the motor is faulty.

If the compressor does not run, the problem may not be the compressor motor itself but some other part of the circuit, such as the main switch, speed selection switch, thermostat, capacitor, starting relay, or thermal relay.

Capacitor. The compressor motor and usually the fan motor are capacitor-start types. If the capacitor fails, the motor may hum but not start up. See page 62 for testing of capacitors.

The capacitor is usually soldered to its leads and held in place on the motor housing with a metal strap. Unbolt the strap and reheat the old solder to remove the component.

 WARNING: Capacitors store electricity and can give a dangerous shock. See page 62 for discharing a capacitor.

Starting Relay. The starting relay directs current to the compressor motor's starting winding when the appliance is turned on. If the starting relay fails, the compressor motor may hum but not start up. The starting relay usually has one positive terminal and two negative terminals.

The starting relay is bolted to the motor or to the chassis. Wires are usually attached with screw terminals or quick-connect terminals (*see page 53*). After removing the component, check it for continuity. Set the multimeter to the Rx1 scale. Attach one lead of the multimeter to the positive terminal and the other lead to first one negative terminal, then the other.

The meter should register near zero ohms when the relay is closed, infinity when it is open. If in doubt whether the relay is functioning, replace it.

Control Switches. Most air conditioner breakdowns are switch problems. If a switch is broken, the component it controls may not turn on or off erratically.

Switches have both mechanical and electrical parts. Mechanical breakage is easy to identify—the switch does not move properly. To check for electrical failure, first clean the terminals of the switch with liquid contact cleaner or fine sandpaper, and make sure all wires are firmly attached. Test switch continuity with a multimeter (*see pages 26-28*). The meter should register near zero ohms when the switch is turned on, infinity when it is turned off.

Air conditioner switches are sealed in their housing and so must be replaced if cleaning the terminals does not solve the problem. To replace a switch, remove the screws that hold it to the chassis, and disconnect the leads. Note the color of the wire that attaches to each terminal. Attach each lead to the same terminal of the new switch.

Thermostat. The thermostat in an air conditioner may be a bimetal or a gas-containing type (*see pages 57-58*). The thermostat turns the compressor motor on and off in response to room temperature. If the thermostat fails, the compressor may not turn off or on, or it may turn on and off erratically.

The thermostat is a switch and can be serviced as described in the previous section. The contacts may be accessible; if so, clean them. To recalibrate a thermostat, remove the dial and look in the center of the stalk for a calibration adjustment screw. (Not every thermostat has one.)

If cleaning and recalibration do not improve the thermostat's performance, replace it.

Thermal Relay. The thermal relay is a circuit breaker mounted on the compressor motor (the fan motor may also have one). It may be in the same housing as the starting relay.

If the thermal relay fails, the compressor motor will not start. Test the thermal relay for continuity (*see pages 26-28*). The multimeter should read near zero ohms on the Rx1 scale. Or check the thermal relay by removing it from the circuit and attaching a jumper wire in its place. Make the jumper wire from a short piece of 16 or 18 gauge wire. Solder or clip the wire into the circuit in place of the thermal relay. If the compressor now runs, the thermal relay is faulty. A defective thermal relay cannot be repaired; replace it.

Evaporator and Condenser. Cooling efficiency depends upon air being able to circulate freely around the tubes and fins of the evaporator and condenser coils. Vacuum them regularly, and remove any obstructions such as dirt or twigs. Straighten bent fins with a putty knife or long-nosed pliers. Be careful not to puncture the tubing. These coils and the pipes that connect them to the compressor cannot be repaired by the homeowner. If a refrigerant leak develops, the compressor motor will run but the air conditioner will not cool. Take the appliance to a refrigeration shop for repair.

Fans. By blowing air over the evaporator and condenser coils, the fans help the transfer of heat between the air and the refrigerant in the coils. If the air conditioner ices up, one of the fans may be obstructed or bound. Since the compressor motor is louder than the fan motor, the user may not hear that the fan is not running. A loud rapping or grinding sound means worn bearings or shaft, or a blockage of the fan blade. Check visually, and try turning the motor shaft by hand with the power off. The shaft should turn freely. If it does not, oil the bearings (*see page 63*). If the fan vibrates, make sure the motor is bolted tightly to the chassis.

If the shaft turns but the fan blades do not turn, retighten the setscrews that hold the blade unit in place, or replace the blade unit. Damaged metal fan blades can sometimes be restored to original shape by careful bending and prying.

Exhaust Flap. The exhaust flap covers an opening between the front and rear compartments. Opening the flap allows the air conditioner to exhaust air from the room. (The flap should be opened only when the control is turned to the Fan settings, not the Cool settings.) The exhaust flap is usually operated by a simple lever or a cable.

The cable may rust and prevent operation of the exhaust flap. If the flap is closed, the air conditioner can cool normally, but if the flap is open, the air conditioner's efficiency is decreased. To prevent rusting, oil the cable once or twice a year: Remove the spring clips that hold it in place and take the cable out of the appliance. Holding it vertically, put a few drops of penetrating oil on the metal wire, then slide the cable back and forth in its sleeve to work the oil down into the sleeve. After a few minutes, turn the cable upside down and apply oil to the other end. Then replace the cable.

If the cable rusts, it will not work; buy a replacement, or make a temporary repair by removing the cable from the machine and taping the exhaust flap closed.

If the exhaust flap is controlled by a lever, lubricate moving parts once or twice a season.

Vibration of the exhaust flap may make an annoying clattering sound. Put self-sticking weatherstrip around the exhaust vent to muffle the vibration noise.

Drainage System. Condensed water vapor drips from the evaporator coils in the front of the machine to a collector pan and then out the back of the machine. Drainage holes near the collector pan must be kept clear, or the air conditioner will drip water into the room. Check them regularly, and clean them with a pin or straightened coat hanger.

If water drips into the room and the holes are clear, check the level of the air conditioner. Level it left to right, but pitch it a few degrees backwards so that water drains out of doors.

For additional maintenance and repair, see pages 62-63 and above headings on compressor, capacitor, starting relay, and thermal relay.

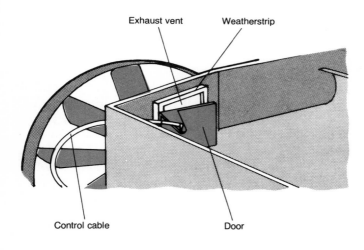

Put self-sticking weatherstrip around exhaust vent if door rattles.

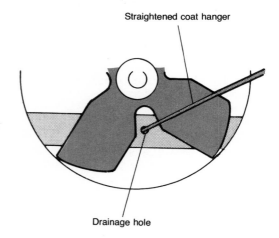

Clear drainage holes in front if air conditioner drips into room. Also check level: air conditioner should pitch slightly toward rear, be level side to side

AIR CONDITIONER TROUBLESHOOTING

PROBLEM: Air conditioner does not start.

Possible Cause	Procedure	Remedy	Rating	Parts	Labor
No power at outlet.	Check fuse or circuit breaker.	Replace fuse or reset circuit breaker.	■		$20
Plug disconnected.		Reseat plug in outlet.	■		$20
Cord defective.	Check for breaks. Test for continuity.	Repair or replace.	■	$5	$20
Switch or thermostat defective.	Check circuit continuity. Check for poor contact at terminals.	Clean terminals. Repair or replace.	■	$5-25	$25
Wires at control panel broken or short-circuited.	Check all wires and contacts.	Repair or replace.	■		$25
Capacitor or start-relay switch faulty.	Check terminals on both.	Clean or repair. (First discharge capacitor.)	■	$10	$25
	Check circuit continuity on both.	Repair or replace.	■	$10	$25
	Check capacitor for oil leak.	Discharge capacitor and replace.	■	$10	$25
Compressor defective.	Check for burned terminals on outside of part.	Clean and repair.	■		$25
	Check motor circuits for continuity.	Consult authorized service personnel.	■ ■ ■ ■	$75-150	$50

PROBLEM: Air conditioner blows fuse or trips circuit breaker.

Possible Cause	Procedure	Remedy	Rating	Parts	Labor
Circuit overloaded.	Reduce number of appliances on circuit.	Replace fuse or reset circuit breaker.	■		$20
Cord or plug short-circuited.	Check continuity. Inspect for breaks.	Repair or replace.	■	$5	$20
Switch or motor short-circuited.	Test circuit continuity.	Repair or replace.			
Unit restarted too soon after use.	Wait five minutes before restarting.		■		$20
Wrong fuse.		Use time-delay fuse of correct rating.	■		$20
Wiring shorted or grounded against frame.	Check for continuity. Examine all connections.	Repair.	■		$25

PROBLEM: Air conditioner shocks user.

Possible Cause	Procedure	Remedy	Rating	Parts	Labor
Cord frayed.	Check continuity. Inspect for breaks.	Repair or replace.	■		$25
Case short-circuited.	Test circuit continuity.	Repair.			

PROBLEM: Air conditioner operates but cools inadequately.

Possible Cause	Procedure	Remedy	Rating	Parts	Labor
Refrigerant leaking from unit.		Consult authorized service center.	■ ■ ■ ■	$35	$35
Outdoor air leaking into room.	Check.	Seal gaps between air conditioner and window.	■		$20
Fan bound or broken.	Use spray lubricant on sticking parts.	Replace, if necessary.	■ ■ ■	$25-60	$35
Unit inadequate for room.	Check BTU ratings against size of room.	Replace unit if necessary.	■		$20
Thermostat faulty.	Check circuit continuity.	Replace.	■ ■	$5-25	$25
Filter clogged.	Check.	Clean or replace.	■	$5	$20

PROBLEM: Air conditioner operates, but does not cool.

Possible Cause	Procedure	Remedy	Rating	Parts	Labor
Fuse blown or circuit breaker tripped.		Replace fuse or reset circuit breaker.	■	◆	$20
Air flow blocked.	Check filter, coils and fins for blockage.	Clean or replace filter. Vacuum coils and fins. Straighten bent fins.	■		$25
Evaporator icing.	Do not operate unit under 70 °F.		■		$20
Filter clogged.	Check.	Replace, or clean if possible.	■	$5	$20
Evaporator clogged.	Remove filter to check.	Clean or replace filter; vacuum evaporator coils.	■ ■ ■ ■	$35	$35
Fan switch faulty.	Check circuit continuity.	Repair or replace.	■	$12	$25
Fan motor capacitor faulty.	Discharge capacitor. Check circuit continuity. Inspect for oil leak.	Replace.	■	$10	$25

(Continued on next page)

PROBLEM: Air conditioner operates, but does not cool. *(Continued from preceding page)*

Possible Cause	Procedure	Remedy	Rating	Parts	Labor
Fan motor contacts or terminals defective.	Check for dirt, breaks or poor contact.	Clean or replace.	■		$25
Fan motor jammed.	Remove foreign objects; check for bent blades.	Replace broken blades or replace motor.	■ ■ ■	$25-60	$35
Motor bearings bound.	Check.	Lubricate bearings or replace bearings or motor.	■ ■ ■	$10	$35
Thermostat improperly set or defective.	Readjust. Check circuit continuity. Check contacts and terminals.	Replace if necessary.	■ ■	$5-25	$25
Temperature control switch defective.	Check circuit continuity, also contacts and terminals.	Clean contacts and terminals or replace switch.	■ ■	$5-25	$25
Compressor capacitor inoperative.	Check.	See page 62.			
Compressor start relay inoperative.	Check.	See page 59.			

PROBLEM: Air conditioner smokes.

Possible Cause	Procedure	Remedy	Rating	Parts	Labor
Fan motor malfunctioning.	Check circuit continuity.	Replace.	■ ■ ■	$25-60	$35
Fan motor bearings bound.	Check.	Lubricate or replace.	■ ■ ■	$10	$35
Electrical switches faulty.	Check contacts and terminals.	Repair or replace.	■ ■	$5-25	$25
Start relay faulty.	Check contacts and terminals.	Repair or replace.	■ ■	$8	$25
Wiring wet.	Unplug machine. Clean drains. Allow machine to dry thoroughly.	Insulate or replace exposed or broken wires.	■		$25

PROBLEM: Air conditioner has bad odor.

Possible Cause	Procedure	Remedy	Rating	Parts	Labor
Drain holes blocked (musty odor).	If necessary slide chassis from cabinet.	Probe hole with stiff wire.	■		$25
Evaporator fins dirty (tobacco or oil smell).	Vacuum. Spray with deodorant.	If problem persists, steam clean fins at automotive shop.	■		$25

PROBLEM: Air conditioner leaks.

Possible Cause	Procedure	Remedy	Rating	Parts	Labor
Drain ports clogged.	If necessary slide chassis from cabinet.	Probe holes or passages with stiff wire.	■		$25
Cabinet seals worn.	Check caulking. Inspect for rust or discoloration.	Clean and recaulk.	■		$25

(Continued on next page)

PROBLEM: Air conditioner leaks. *(Continued from preceding page)*

Possible Cause	Procedure	Remedy	Rating	Parts	Labor
Botton fins on evaporator coil clogged or bent.	Check.	Clean with stiff brush or vacuum cleaner. Straighten bent fins.	■		$25
Installation faulty.		Level machine left to right. Pitch so rear is ½ inch lower than front from drainage.	■		$20
Extremely humid weather conditions.	(Dripping on outside is normal.)	Attach drain pipe to carry water out of the way if necessary.	■		$25

PROBLEM: Compressor turns on and off repeatedly.

Possible Cause	Procedure	Remedy	Rating	Parts	Labor
Thermostat incorrectly set.	Check.	Reset.	■		$20
Overload switch faulty.	Check circuit continuity.	Repair or replace.	■	$8	$25
Condensor air flow blocked.	Check coils.	Vacuum or brush.	■		$25
Thermostat sensor bulb out of position.	Check. Bulb should not touch evaporator coil.	Reposition.	■		$20

PROBLEM: Air conditioner is excessively noisy.

Possible Cause	Procedure	Remedy	Rating	Parts	Labor
Mountings loose or insecure.	Check.	Tighten supports or add additional ones.	■	$5	$20
Loose or blocked fan.	Check.	Tighten loose screws, remove obstructions.	■		$25
Fan motor bearings dry.	Check.	Lubricate.	■ ■		$25
Fan blades bent or dirty.	Check.	Straighten and clean blades or replace.	■ ■	$10-20	$25
Fan belt loose, worn or broken.	Check.	Tighten or replace.	■	$8	$25
Foreign objects in evaporator or compressor coils.	Check.	Remove and clean.	■		$25
Air ducts clogged.	Check.	Clean.	■		$25
Compressor motor mounts old, hardened.	Check.	Replace.	■	$5	$20
Compressor motor worn.	Check.	Consult authorized service center.	■ ■ ■ ■	$75-150	$50
Refrigerant tubing loose.	Check.	Consult authorized service center.	■ ■ ■ ■	$35	$35

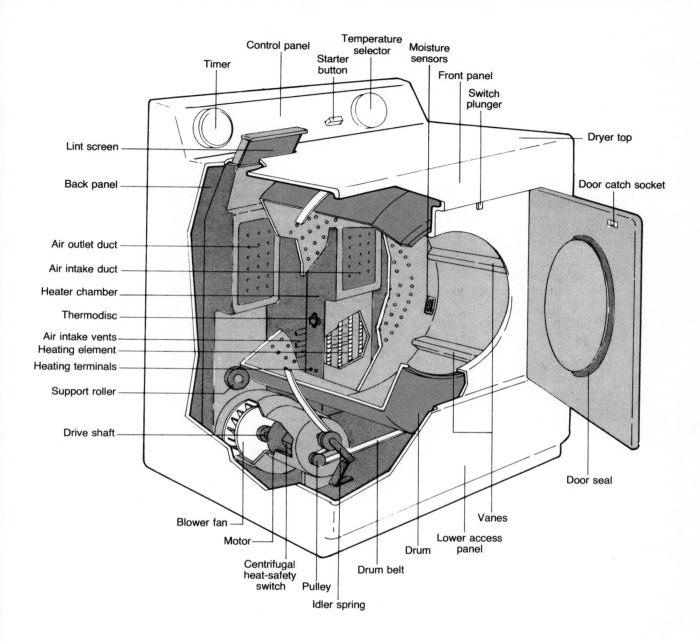

Timer — Control panel — Starter button — Temperature selector — Moisture sensors — Front panel — Switch plunger — Dryer top — Door catch socket — Lint screen — Back panel — Air outlet duct — Air intake duct — Heater chamber — Thermodisc — Air intake vents — Heating element — Heating terminals — Support roller — Drive shaft — Blower fan — Motor — Centrifugal heat-safety switch — Pulley — Idler spring — Drum belt — Drum — Lower access panel — Vanes — Door seal — Door catch socket

Principle of Operation

The clothes dryer is an uncomplicated appliance that dries clothes efficiently in a simple procedure using heat, a steady air flow, and tumbling action. Warm air absorbs moisture more rapidly than cool air. The heat is generated by either an electric or a gas heater. The air flow and tumbling action are provided by a motor; the motor runs a blower fan and supplies the driving force to rotate the dryer's drum. Room air is sucked by the blower fan through the dryer's air-intake vent, past the heater chamber, and through the wet clothing in the drum. The airstream is then exhausted from the dryer unit, usually through a pipe connected to the outside. Most dryers are fitted with a filter to remove lint from the airstream after it has passed through the clothes.

Clothes dryers—whether gas or electric—must have an electric power source to run the motor that drives the drum and blower fan. Electric models operate on a 120/240 volt, 30 amp circuit. Gas dryers use a ⅜-inch or ½-inch gas supply line (check manufacturer's instructions and local plumbing code) and a 120-volt, 15 amp circuit.

The electrical system consists of a timer, a motor to turn the drum and fan, a heating element (in an all-electric dryer), a door switch, a thermostat, a temperature selector switch (in some models), and other switches. The timer and temperature selector must be set and the door must be tightly closed to complete the circuits before the dryer will operate. The timer closes contacts to the single-speed motor. The motor begins turning the drum and blower fan, but not until the drum is rotating at full speed does a centrifugal heat-safety switch on the motor complete the circuit to the machine's ignition system, which heats the heating element in the heater chamber of an electric dryer, or fires a gas jet in a gas dryer. By not activating the heating element until the drum is rotating, the centrifugal heat-safety switch protects clothes from burning in a drum that is heated but has failed to rotate.

The heat inside the dryer is regulated by a thermodisc, which keeps it more or less constant throughout any drying cycle. (Some dryers have a thermostat for each temperature setting.) During a "regular" drying cycle the drum temperature may be as low as 130°F. or as high as 165°F. When it reaches 165°F., the thermodisc shuts off the heater until the temperature drops to 135°F., at which point the heater is turned on again. This cycle is repeated rather quickly, since the evaporation of moisture from the clothes tends to raise the heat level rapidly. About ten minutes before the drying cycle is over, the timer shuts off the heater for the remainder of the cycle; however, the motor, which is also controlled by the timer, continues rotating the drum for another ten minutes, allowing the machine and the clothes to cool.

Differences in Clothes Dryers

One principal distinction between dryers is the source of heat. Gas dryers have a burner assembly and the heat is provided by combustion of fuel gas, usually natural gas. In all-electric dryers, heat is generated by a heating element. In most cases, electric dryers operate on 240 volt electric current. Take special precautions when working with all-electric dryers because of the high voltage.

Some dryers are equipped with automatic moisture sensors in the exhaust vent. From the moisture of the exhausted air, they determine when the proper degree of dryness has been achieved in the clothes and turn the dryer off.

Dryers may be equipped with an alarm, which sounds when the cycle has been completed. Other dryers are equipped with automatic restart switches which restart the drum and fan motor (but not the heater) after a given period of time if the door has not been opened. This feature is to prevent wrinkling of clothes that may sit in the dryer for a long time.

Maintenance and Repair

 WARNING: Unplug the dryer before inspecting and repairing. Do not reconnect the power until the job is completed.

Door Seal. This vinyl or plastic strip helps to make the dryer cabinet airtight. It is mounted either on the inside of the door or around the cabinet door opening, and may be secured with screws or an adhesive. If the door seal is worn or loose, it may prevent the door from closing properly and should be replaced with a similar or identical seal. The seal can be unscrewed easily or, if it is glued on, simply pulled off. In replacing a glued-on seal, use the special nonflammable adhesive recommended by the manufacturer.

Door Catch. Held in place by spring tabs between the inner and outer door panels, the door catch holds the dryer door shut during operation. When the catch fails to secure the door it may require cleaning

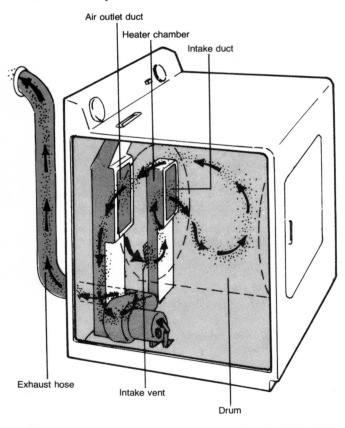

The flow of air through a dryer. Air is drawn through an intake vent into the heater chamber where it is heated, then into the drum. The warm, moist air is expelled from the drum via the air outlet duct and from the dryer by the exhaust hose.

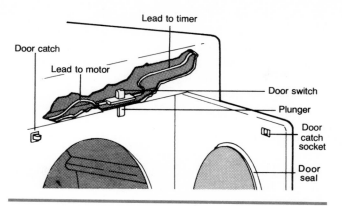

Door assembly. Note cutaway of door switch, with the two switch leads connecting to the timer and motor.

or adjusting. If neither helps, remove the lower access panel and disassemble the door to reach the catch. To remove the catch, depress its spring tabs and push it out through its mounting hole.

Door Switch. A visible plunger or pin protrudes from the dryer's door panel or cabinet door opening, depending on the model. When the dryer door is closed, the door switch is depressed and completes the circuit between the dryer's timer and motor. When the door is opened, the switch opens the electrical circuit to the dryer motor; the motor stops and the heat source is disconnected through the centrifugal switch in the motor.

If the door switch is defective, the dryer will not run. The switch can be tested with a multimeter set at the Rx1 scale (*see pages 26-28*). To reach the switch, remove the dryer top and disconnect the leads; then unscrew the switch mounting screws and remove the unit. Then disconnect the switch leads, and attach a

meter probe to each of the terminals. Close the switch by pushing in the plunger manually; if the meter reads higher than zero ohms, the switch is faulty and must be replaced.

Drum Belt. The drum belt passes around the outside of the drum and is driven by the motor. An idler pulley and spring maintain tension in the belt. If the drum is not rotating properly, test the tension in the belt. The belt should be tight but should give slightly when pulled, indicating that the idler spring is operating properly.

If the drum belt is broken, the drum will not turn at all. If the belt is worn, it will make a thumping noise against the drum. In either case, the belt must be replaced with an identical belt purchased from the manufacturer. Take off the top of the dryer, the lower access panel, and the front panel. Disengage the belt from the pulley on the motor shaft and then lift the drum slightly so the belt can be slid off.

Support Rollers. The drum rests on support rollers that help it rotate smoothly. These rollers make considerable noise if they are worn, and should be replaced. Check the rollers by hand-turning the drum and listening for a single thump with each revolution. If there is more than one thump per revolution, the rollers are worn. The rollers are found directly under the drum and can be inspected only when the drum has been removed from the machine. To remove the drum, unscrew the drum shaft after the rear bearing access plate on the back of the cabinet has been removed, and lift out the drum. If a roller is worn or broken, remove the screw that holds its mounting bracket to the bottom of the cabinet. Pry off the retaining clips and pull the roller off its shaft.

NOTE: Most dryers built within the past few years have sealed-for-life lubrication. If disassembling a dryer, however, be sure that all bearing surfaces are lubricated. Use a manufacturer's recommended lubricant. One important spot to check is around the front edge. The drum of many modern dryers is supported on rollers at the rear, while in front the flange of the door opening serves as a bearing surface. If the surface appears to be dry, lubricate it according to the manufacturer's instructions.

Heaters. The heater unit in both electric and gas dryers is enclosed in a housing attached in the rear of the cabinet, behind the air holes in the back of the drums.

The heating element in an all-electric dryer is a resistance wire that can burn out. To reach the heater, the back panel and, in some cases, the top, remove the retaining screws in the heater housing. Disconnect the leads and attach a multimeter to them. If the meter reads higher than between 8 and 20 ohms, the

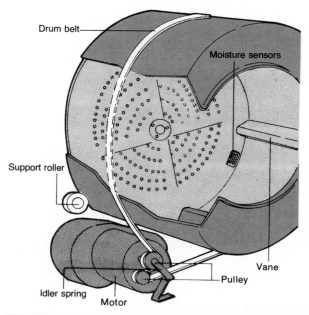

Drum assembly

heater coil is defective and should be replaced. The heater should also be checked for grounding by pulling one of the meter probes from the heater lead and touching it to the air duct. If the meter reads high, the heating element is operating satisfactorily, but if the needle swings toward low, the heater is grounded and should be replaced. To replace the heater, remove the heater duct from the cabinet and unscrew the retaining screws at the base. Then pull the heater out of the cover.

Gas dryers have a pilot light that can be ignited by an electric igniter or a constant pilot light positioned in front of a gas jet. Most newer gas dryers have an activator instead of a constant pilot light. In both cases, the burner is controlled by thermostats and activated by the motor. The burner is usually located at the bottom of the dryer. Reach it by removing the lower access panel in the front. If the dryer is not heating properly, observe the operation of the gas burner. If the dryer is equipped with an igniter, turn it on to see whether the igniter is operating. If not, it should be replaced. If the igniter is operating properly, but the main burner does not ignite, then the gas valve may be defective.

If the main burner makes a loud sound and the flame is predominantly yellow, reduce the gas flow to the burner by adjusting the air-gas mixture: Loosen the thumbscrew that holds the air shutter, which regulates the air flow to the burner, and rotate the shutter until the flame is a light blue color with no yellow tip and makes no sound. Tighten the thumbscrew to lock the shutter in place.

Motor. See pages 60-65.

Timer. See page 56.

Temperature Selector (Thermostat). See pages 57-58.

Fan. The fan is located at one end of the motor. As long as the motor is operating, the fan should likewise be in operation and air should flow through the dryer. If the motor operates but the fan does not, then the drive shaft between the motor and the fan may be broken or the fan may have come loose from the drive shaft. After unplugging the dryer, remove the rear cover and visually inspect the assembly. If the drive shaft is broken, replace the motor and fan assembly. If the blower is detached from the drive shaft, tighten the setscrews or obtain a new coupling device to reattach the fan.

Thermodiscs. Two major thermodiscs (*see page 57*) control the temperature in a dryer; other thermodiscs may be attached to the circuits for each temperature setting.

To test thermodiscs with the multimeter remove

How to Reach Interior Components

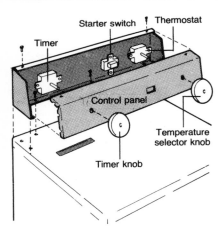

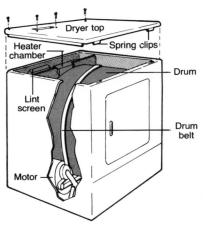

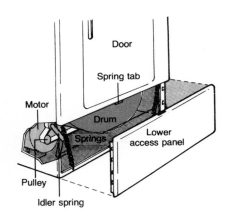

Control panel: To reach timer, thermostats, starter switch

The control panel on most dryers is removed by unscrewing the mounting screws and lifting the panel off the top of the dryer. To remove the timer, thermostats, or starter switch mounted behind the panel, first disconnect the part's leads and pull off its knob; then remove the mounting screws that hold the part to the control panel.

Dryer top: To reach drum, motor, heater chamber

The top of the dryer may be secured with retaining screws located at the corners or, on some models, in the area of the lint screen slot. There may also be spring clips positioned under each corner of the dryer top. To free these, insert screwdriver or the blade of a putty knife under a corner and push against the spring clip; at the same time, pull the top upward. Proceed to each corner until the top is free and can be lifted off the cabinet.

Lower access panel: To reach door, drum, motor

The lower access panel can be pried away from the front of the cabinet by inserting a screwdriver or putty knife blade behind the panel and twisting it slightly. Some models have a spring tab on the cabinet front, over the center of the access panel, which must be depressed before the panel will unlock.

leads from the thermodisc and attach the probes to both terminals.

One of the primary thermodiscs is located near the hot air exhaust duct and turns the heater on and off several times during the course of a drying cycle. How this unit is reached depends on where the duct resides in the individual machine, but usually access will involve removal of the dryer top or the front panel.

The other major thermodisc is attached to the heater as an overheating safety device. Its purpose is to limit the temperature in the heater housing to a safe range in the event that the other control thermodiscs fail or the exhuast system becomes inoperative. Normally, it never has to shut off the heater. This thermodisc is found by removing the back panel.

To test either thermodisc, set the multimeter to Rx1. Remove the leads from the thermodisc and attach the meter probes to both terminals; if the unit has three terminals, use the two outer terminals when testing it. If the meter reads above zero ohms, the thermodisc is faulty and must be replaced.

Lint Filter. The lint filter removes lint from the airstream prior to exhaust from the dryer. Clean the lint filter (or trap) prior to drying every load. Maintenance of the filter is extremely important in assuring satisfactory dryer operation. If the filter becomes completely clogged, some lint can escape and create jamming problems elsewhere in the dryer. Even a partial blockage reduces the dryer's efficiency and limits its capabilities. Most importantly, though, a clogged dryer can be a fire hazard. Lint from many fabrics—particularly synthetics—is highly combustible.

NOTE: Once a year unplug the dryer or turn off the gas supply, remove the service panel, and vacuum away any lint or dust in the vicinity of the motor. Regular cleaning keeps lint away from the bearings, and it helps maintain clean air passageways. It also reduces the possibility of a fire.

Level Legs. A dryer operates satisfactorily only when it is level. Every dryer is equipped with leveling legs which are adjusted by rotating the foot. Level of the dryer can be checked by placing a marble on the upper surface of the cabinet. Adjust the dryer so the marble does not roll.

Exhaust Hose. An exhaust hose vents blower air from the exhaust duct to the outside. If dryer operation is not satisfactory, check the exhaust hose to determine that there is no obstruction or leakage. Remove any obstruction. Patch leaks with duct tape obtained from a heating supply store.

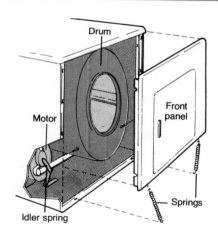

Front panel: To reach drum, motor

First remove the lower access panel. There are large springs located at the bottom corners of the front panel that are hooked to the cabinet frame. Unhook both springs and remove the mounting screws that hold the panel to the cabinet. In those models where the front panel supports the drum, place a block of wood underneath the drum to hold it up once the front panel is removed.

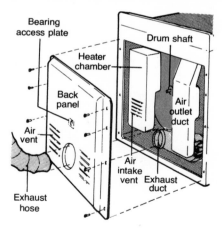

Back panel: To reach heater, intake and outlet ducts, motor, blower fan

First disengage the outlet hose from the back of the machine. Now remove the retaining screws at the corners and lift the panel off the machine.

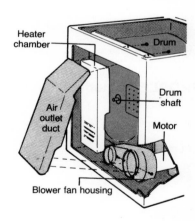

Air outlet duct

With the back panel off, access to the air outlet is now possible. Remove the retaining screws holding the duct in place and pull the duct out. With some models the front panel and drum must be removed first.

CLOTHES DRYER TROUBLESHOOTING ▬▬▬▬▬▬

PROBLEM: Clothes dryer does not start. ▬▬▬▬▬▬

Possible Cause	Procedure	Remedy	Rating	Parts	Labor
No power at outlet.	Check fuse or circuit breaker.	Replace fuse or reset circuit breaker.	■		$20
Plug disconnected.	Check.	Reseat plug in outlet.	■		$20
Cord defective.	Check for breaks.	Repair or replace.	■	$5-10	$20
Door switch faulty.	Check circuit continuity.	Replace.	■	$8	$20
Cycle selector faulty.	Check circuit continuity.	Replace.	■	$10-20	$20
Starter switch faulty.	Check circuit continuity.	Replace.	■	$8	$20
Timer faulty.	Check circuit continuity.	Replace.	■	$10-30	$20
Motor faulty.	Check.	See pages 60-65.	■ ■ ■	$35-65	$30
Overload switch tripped.	Reset.	Replace, if necessary.	■	$10	$20

PROBLEM: Clothes dryer blows fuse or trips circuit breaker. ▬▬▬▬▬▬

Possible Cause	Procedure	Remedy	Rating	Parts	Labor
Circuit overloaded.	Reduce number of appliances on circuit. Put dryer on its own circuit.	Replace fuse or reset circuit breaker.	■		$20
Cord short-circuited.	Inspect for breaks.	Repair or replace.	■	$5-10	$20
Wiring short-circuited.	Check circuit continuity.	Repair.	■		$20

PROBLEM: Clothes dryer shocks user. ▬▬▬▬▬▬

Possible Cause	Procedure	Remedy	Rating	Parts	Labor
Cord frayed.	Inspect for breaks.	Repair or replace.	■	$5-10	$20
Case short-circuited.	Test circuit continuity.	Repair.	■ ■		$25

PROBLEM: Clothes dryer starts but drum does not revolve. ▬▬▬▬▬▬

Possible Cause	Procedure	Remedy	Rating	Parts	Labor
Drum belt loose or broken.	Check.	Tighten or replace.	■	$6-10	$20
Belt pulley assembly loose or broken.	Check pulley and idler spring for wear or breaks.	Replace faulty parts.	■	$15	$20
Drum jammed.	Check vent holes for foreign objects binding drum to case. With machine unplugged, inspect exterior of drum for lint accumulation between drum and case.	Clean.	■ ■		$25
Tension spring defective.	Check spring between motor pulley and blower pulley.	Reattach or replace.	■	$5	$20

PROBLEM: Drum revolves but clothes dryer does not heat.

Possible Cause	Procedure	Remedy	Rating	Parts	Labor
Cycle selector set on "air instead of heat."	Check.	Select proper cycle.	■		$20
Thermostat faulty.	Test circuit continuity.	Replace.	■	$8-35	$25
Timer faulty.	Test circuit continuity; check for loose or dirty contacts.	Repair or replace.	■	$10-30	$20
Centrifugal heat-safety switch in motor faulty.	Check continuity.	Replace.	■ ■ ■	$5-15	$35
Exhaust vent flap malfunctioning.	Check metal flap on outside vent. It should pivot freely.	Repair or replace.	■	$5	$25

PROBLEM: Clothes dryer does not shut off.

Possible Cause	Procedure	Remedy	Rating	Parts	Labor
Thermostat defective.	Check circuit continuity.	Replace.	■	$8-35	$25
Control switch short-circuited.	Check circuit continuity.	Replace.	■	$10-20	$20
Timer motor inoperative or defective.	Check circuit continuity.	Replace.	■	$10	$20

PROBLEM: Clothes dryer smokes.

Possible Cause	Procedure	Remedy	Rating	Parts	Labor
Lint buildup inside case.	Remove front panel to check.	Remove lint.	■		$20
Motor overheating.	Disconnect. Check.	Repair.	■ ■ ■	$20	$35

PROBLEM: Clothes dryer gets too hot.

Possible Cause	Procedure	Remedy	Rating	Parts	Labor
Thermostat faulty.	Check bulb for buildup of lint (acts as insulation).	Clean.	■		$25
	Check circuit continuity.	Replace.	■	$8-35	$25
Electronic control faulty.	Check.	Replace.	■	$20-35	$25

PROBLEM: Clothes dryer operates with door open.

Possible Cause	Procedure	Remedy	Rating	Parts	Labor
Door switch defective.	Test.	Replace.	■	$8	$20
Wiring defective.	Test circuit continuity.	Repair or replace.	■	$5	$25

(Continued on next page)

PROBLEM: Clothes dryer is excessively noisy. *(Continued from preceding page)*

Possible Cause	Procedure	Remedy	Rating	Parts	Labor
Foreign objects in drum.	Check interior with flashlight for small objects.	Remove.	■		$20
Machine not level.	Check with carpenter's level.	Level front to back and side to side.	■		$20
Lint accumulating behind drum.	Remove lint.	Press stiff brush through holes in drum vacuum.	■ ■		$25
Parts of dryer loose.		Tighten loose screws or bolts.	■		$25
Blower fan loose.	Check attachment to shaft.	Tighten.	■ ■		$25
Drum belt loose or worn.	Check.	Tighten or replace.	■	$8	$25
Belt needs lubrication (intermittent squeak).	Check all belts.	Lubricate with thin coating of belt dressing.	■		$20
Support rollers defective or binding.	Revolve drum by hand to check for scraping or binding.	Replace rollers.	■ ■	$15	$25
Idler pulley worn or broken.	Check.	Replace.	■	$15	$20

PROBLEM: Clothes come out of dryer with lint on them.

Possible Cause	Procedure	Remedy	Rating	Parts	Labor
Lint filter clogged.	Clean.	Clean after every load.	■		$20
Vent clogged.	Clean.	Clean once or twice a year.	■		$20

PROBLEM: Clothes dryer rips clothing.

Possible Cause	Procedure	Remedy	Rating	Parts	Labor
Drum surface damaged.	Check by wiping interior with easily snagged fabric.	File or sand down rough spots.	■		$20

PROBLEM: Clothes dryer dries clothes too slowly or inadequately.

Possible Cause	Procedure	Remedy	Rating	Parts	Labor
Load too large for machine.		Remove part of load.	■		$20
Lint filter blocked.	Check.	Clean after each load.	■		$20
Clothes not properly wrung out.	Check washing machine spin dry cycle.	Repair washing machine.	■		$20

(Continued on next page)

PROBLEM: Clothes dryer dries clothes too slowly or inadequately. *(Continued from preceding page)*

Possible Cause	Procedure	Remedy	Rating	Parts	Labor
Drum seals loose.	Check front and rear seals.	Reposition on drum and flange surface, or replace if worn.	■ ■	$12	$25
Vent blocked.	Check.	Clear blockage.	■		$20
Vent leaking.	Check for cracks or holes.	Seal with duct tape or replace.	■		$20
Damper bound (gas dryer).	Check.	Clear.	■		$20
Thermostat faulty.	Check.	Replace.	■	$8-35	$25
Cycle selector switch defective.	Check circuit continuity.	Repair or replace.	■	$10-20	$20
Blower fan loose.	Check attachment to shaft.	If loose, tighten.	■		$20

SPECIFIC GAS DRYER PROBLEMS

PROBLEM: Gas clothes dryer dries too slowly or inadequately.

Possible Cause	Procedure	Remedy	Rating	Parts	Labor
Pilot light won't light or won't stay lit.		Check for draft blowing out light.	■		$20
		Contact power company.	■		$20
	Check pilot line filter.	Remove clog or replace.	■ ■	$1	$20
Glow coil faulty.	Check contacts, circuit continuity in coil, transformer, or line between timer and transformer.	Repair or replace.	■	$12	$25
Main burner faulty.	Check gas ports for blockage.	Clean or replace.	■	$8	$20

SPECIFIC ELECTRIC DRYER PROBLEMS

PROBLEM: Electric clothes dryer dries too slowly or inadequately.

Possible Cause	Procedure	Remedy	Rating	Parts	Labor
Heating element faulty.	Check circuit continuity, condition of contacts.	Replace. If contacts dirty or broken, clean or replace.	■		$20
Electric power inadequate.		Contact power company.	■		$20

Dehumidifiers

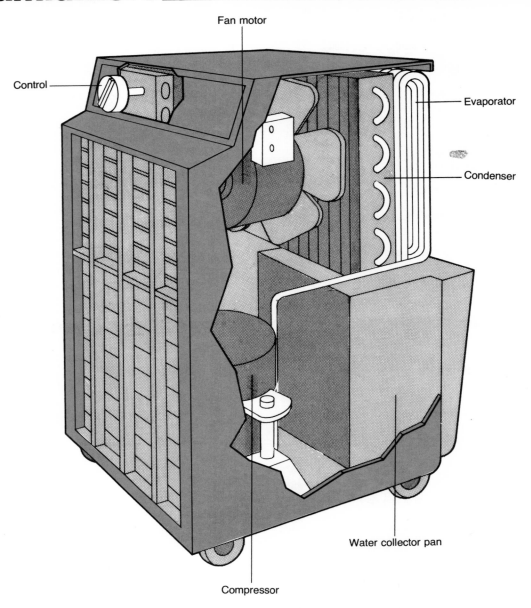

Fan motor

Control

Evaporator

Condenser

Water collector pan

Compressor

Principle of Operation

A dehumidifier operates on the principle of evaporation—when warm, humid air is cooled abruptly, some of its water vapor condenses. This principle is at work, for example, when a car's window fogs up on a cold morning. The warm, moist air exhaled by the driver contacts the cold windows, and tiny droplets precipitate from the exhaled air on the cold window surface.

All dehumidifiers have an electrical circuit in which the basic components are the fan motor, the compressor motor, and an On/Off switch.

The fan blows moist, room-temperature air over a set of cold pipes; moisture from the air precipitates on the pipes, and then drains to a collector pan below.

The set of cold pipes, the evaporator, is part of a refrigerant-circulating system similar to that found in an air conditioner (*see page 196*). In its natural state the refrigerant inside the evaporator is a gas, but here it is compressed to a cold liquid. As this liquid absorbs the heat through the walls of the tubing, it boils into a gaseous state. The gas is then pumped through a compressor, which forces the warm, compressed gas into a second coil of pipes (the condenser) where its

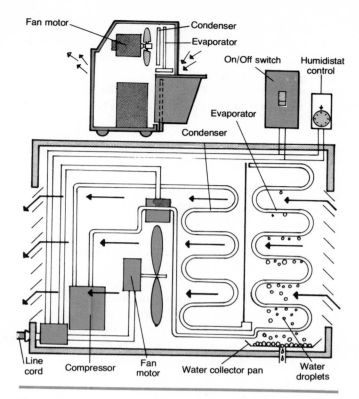

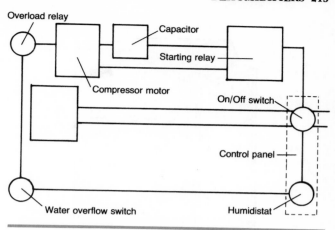

Electrical circuitry of deluxe model.

Moist room air passes over cold evaporator coil, where it drops its moisture. Dried air regains room temperature as it passes over warm condenser coil.

heat dissipates through the walls of the tubing back into the room air. As it loses its heat the gas again becomes a liquid and recirculates.

The stream of air blown by the fan through the dehumidifier first passes over the cold evaporator coil, where it drops its moisture, and then over the warm condenser coil, where it regains its original temperature. A dehumidifier does not change room temperature noticeably.

Differences in Dehumidifiers

The size of a dehumidifer is measured by the amount of water it can remove from the air in twenty-four hours, when air temperature is 80°F. and relative humidity is 60 percent. Room dehumidifiers range in capacity from about ten to about thirty pints.

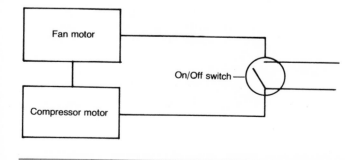

Electrical circuitry of basic dehumidifier.

A variety of switches and controls are available on dehumidifiers. Deluxe models have a variable-speed fan motor, a humidistat control, and an automatic shut-off switch to prevent water overflow from the collector pan.

Compressor motors on large capacity models need an initial boost of current to start up; these models use a capacitor-start motor (*see page 62*) in the compressor. The wiring to the compressor runs through a starting relay (*see page 59*), a switch for the starting circuit of the motor. After the compressor reaches approximately 75 percent of its running speed, the starting relay opens so that the current bypasses the capacitor and the motor's starting winding.

A thermal relay may be mounted on the compressor case (*see page 63*). If the motor overheats, this heat sensor opens and shuts off the compressor.

Disassembly

The box-like sheet metal cover is easily removed by removing the screws that hold it to the chassis. Once the cover and the collector pan—a bucket or drawer—are removed, all components should be readily accessible.

 WARNING: Be sure to unplug the dehumidifier before removing the cover or attempting service.

The main controls and other switches are held in place by screws or bolts. The fan motor is also bolted to the chassis. The fan blades can be removed by loosening the setscrews that hold the blade assembly on the motor shaft. If there are no setscrews, simply pull the blades from the shaft.

Wires to terminals may be soldered or attached with lugs (*see page 25*). Loosen old solder by heating it with a soldering iron (*see pages 23-24*). Pull or unscrew lugs from terminals, but be careful not to damage the terminals—especially on the compressor. Damage to

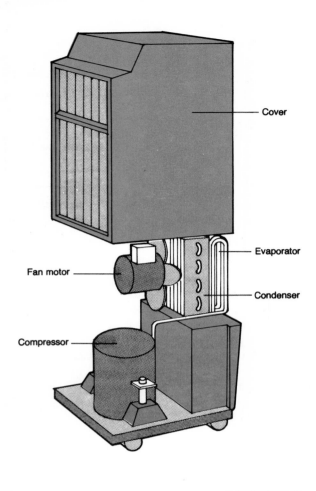

Dehumidifier cover lifts off to provide access to mechanical parts.

these terminals may require repair in a refrigeration shop. If in doubt, cut the wires and reattach them with wire nuts (*see page 24*).

Maintenance and Repair

Compressor. The compressor motor is louder than the fan motor, so if a dehumidifier is producing less than its normal volume of sound, the compressor is probably not operating. Do not assume, however, that the compressor has failed; the problem may be in a variety of other places, particularly the various switches in the circuitry, such as the On/Off switch, the starting relay, or the thermal relay.

Test the parts of the compressor circuit for continuity. Once it is established by elimination that the compressor itself has failed, the dehumidifier will have to be replaced or taken to a refrigeration service shop. The compressor is a sealed unit, and even such minor damage as a broken electrical terminal requires repair shop work and sometimes replacement of the compressor, the most expensive component in the appliance.

Capacitor. The capacitor is part of the starting circuit on a capacitor-start motor. If the compressor or fan is powered by a capacitor-start motor, and if the motor hums but does not start up, this may be the problem. The capacitor is attached to the motor housing. Unbolt it and remove the leads to test it (*see page 62*).

 WARNING: Avoid severe shock by discharging the capacitor (see page 62).

Starting relay. The starting relay is a switch in the compressor motor circuit. It allows current to flow to the motor's starting circuit and, after the motor has built up speed, it switches the starting circuit off and sends current only to the main running circuit of the motor. If the starting relay fails, the motor will hum but not start up. Test it with a multimeter set to the Rx1 scale. The meter should register near zero ohms when the leads are connected from the positive terminal to the first negative terminal (which attaches to the lead from the motor's starting winding circuit), infinity when they are connected from the positive terminal to the second negative terminal. If the starting relay is bolted to the motor housing or to the chassis of the dehumidifier (*see page 59*).

On/Off switch. In most dehumidifiers, the On/Off switch is sealed and cannot be cleaned. Test it for continuity (*see pages 26-28*); if it has failed, replace it with a manufacturer's part.

Evaporator and condenser coils. The evaporator and condenser coils should be washed or vacuumed regularly to remove any dirt or obstructions. If the fins become bent, the refrigerant-circulating system will not work at full efficiency. Straighten the fins with a putty knife or screwdriver. Should a refrig-

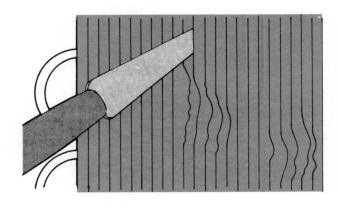

Straighten bent evaporator and condenser fins with a flat blade. Be careful not to puncture tubing.

erant leak develop, the compressor motor will run as usual, but the evaporator coils will not function properly. Do not bother finding the leak and trying to solder it; an experienced technician with special refrigeration tools and equipment will do it when the system is recharged with refrigerant.

Fan. The fan may be at fault if little or no air is coming from the dehumidifier or if the evaporator coils are frosting up. If metal fan blades are bent, try bending them back in place carefully. If a fan blade is broken, replace the blade unit. It is usually held in place with one or two setscrews, or it may simply be pressed on a rubber hub. Turn the fan shaft by hand. If it does not turn easily, apply a drop or two of SAE 10 oil at the oiling points on the fan motor case.

Dehumidifier fans are often split-phase induction types *(see pages 62-63)*.

Thermal relay. If everything else seems in good working order and the dehumidifier will not start up, the thermal relay *(see page 63)* may be jammed in an open position. To check it, bypass its circuitry with a jumper wire. Make a jumper wire from 16 or 18 gauge insulated wire. Strip the ends, and clip or solder the wire into the circuit in place of the heat sensor *(see page 60)*. If the dehumidifier then operates normally, replace the heat sensor, as it cannot be repaired. Or check it with a multimeter set to the Rx1 scale. The meter should read near zero ohms.

Should the thermal relay jam in a closed position, it would no longer act as a safety, and the compressor could burn up. If replacing the compressor, instruct the technician to put a new heat sensor in the circuit.

Speed-selector switch. Many dehumidifiers have a rotary switch *(see page 55)* marked Hi-Lo or Hi-Med-Lo that controls the speed of the fan motor. If the fan is not running properly, the problem may be poor electrical contact in this switch. Clean the contacts with fine sandpaper or liquid contact cleaner, then check for continuity *(see page 26-28)*. Replace the switch if it still does not work properly.

Humidistat. The humidistat is controlled by a dial that allows the user to select room humidity within the range of 30 to 80 percent relative humidity. The sensing device, made of nylon, stretches when moist and contracts when dry. It opens the switch when the desired humidity is reached, shutting off the dehumidifier.

Suspect a faulty humidistat if the dehumidifier removes too much or too little moisture from the air and adjusting the dial has no effect. Clean its contacts, then check the humidistat for continuity with a multimeter *(see pages 26-28)*. Connect the multimeter's probes to the humidistat's terminals. With the multimeter set at Rx1, turn the dial of the humidistat slowly. The meter should read zero for about one-

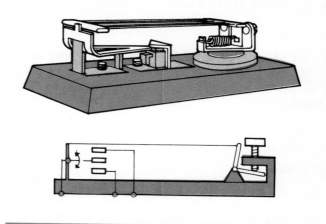

Humidistat measures moisture in air, turns dehumidifier off and on in response to humidity level.

half the rotation, then jump to infinity and stay there.

The nylon humidity-sensing device cannot be serviced. If cleaning the electrical parts does not restore the switch to proper working order, replace it.

Overflow-prevention switch. This switch has failed, obviously, if the collector pan overflows. But if the dehumidifier will not turn on even though the collector pan is empty, the problem could also be here. Like the humidistat, this switch has both electrical and mechanical components. An air pressure capillary tube is the most common switch mechanism. This is a piece of rubber or plastic hose, one end mounted on the electrical switch and the other end hanging in the collector pan. As the water rises in the pan, the air pressure rises in the hose until great enough to open the switch. If the hose ruptures or becomes obstructed, the switch may not operate properly and the pan may overflow.

If this happens, test the switch by removing it from the appliance, and gently lowering the capillary tube end in a bucket of water while the switch is attached to a multimeter set on the Rx1 scale. The meter should read near zero ohms, then jump to infinity as the switch is lowered. To repair the switch, first replace the rubber or plastic hose. If the switch still does not work properly, buy a replacement.

If the dehumidifier will not turn on even though the collector pan is empty or only partly full, the switch may be jamming in the open position; check by using a jumper cable to bypass the switch, as when testing the heat sensor.

Warning Light. Instead of an overflow-prevention switch, some dehumidifiers have a warning light. It operates in the same way except that it does not turn off the dehumidifier. It can be serviced exactly as an overflow-prevention switch. If the bulb burns out, replace it.

DEHUMIDIFIER TROUBLESHOOTING

PROBLEM: Dehumidifier does not operate.

Possible Cause	Procedure	Remedy	Rating	Parts	Labor
No power at outlet.	Check fuse or circuit breaker.	Replace fuse or reset circuit breaker.	■		$20
Plug disconnected.		Reseat plug in outlet.	■		$20
Cord defective.	Check for breaks.	Repair or replace.	■	$3	$20
Overflow switch tripped or defective.	Check for full water container. Check circuit continuity.	Empty water container. Repair or replace switch.	■	$4	$20
Overflow signal light defective.	Check.	Repair or replace.	■	$1.50	$20
On/Off switch defective.	Check for continuity.	Repair or replace.	■	$2	$20
Humidistat incorrectly set or defective.	Check setting, circuit continuity.	Reset or replace.	■	$8	$20
Fan motor defective.	Check circuit continuity.	Repair or replace.	■	$15	$25
Compressor motor defective.	Check circuit for continuity.	Consult authorized service personnel.	■ ■ ■ ■	$85	$35
Starting relay defective (compressor motor).	Check for continuity.	Replace	■ ■	$10	$20

PROBLEM: Dehumidifier blows fuse or trips circuit breaker.

Possible Cause	Procedure	Remedy	Rating	Parts	Labor
Circuit overloaded.	Reduce number of appliances on circuit.	Replace fuse or reset circuit breaker.	■		$20
Cord or plug short-circuited.	Inspect for breaks. Test for continuity.	Repair or replace.	■	$3	$20
Switch or motor short-circuited.	Test circuit continuity.	Repair or replace.	■ ■ ■ ■ ■	Switch $8 Motor $35	Switch $20 Motor $35

PROBLEM: Dehumidifier shocks user.

Possible Cause	Procedure	Remedy	Rating	Parts	Labor
Short-circuited internal wiring.	Test circuit continuity. Inspect for frayed wires touching case and for breaks.	Repair. Wrap wires with insulating tape.	■		$25

PROBLEM: Dehumidifier operates but does not dry air adequately.

Possible Cause	Procedure	Remedy	Rating	Parts	Labor
Unit too small for room.	Check owner's manual for maximum area unit can handle.	Replace with larger unit or add second one.	■		$20
Air circulation obstructed.	Inspect fan, condenser coil, evaporator coil.	Clean. Clear obstructions, reposition.	■		$20
Evaporator or condenser coils dusty.	Check.	Clean with vacuum.	■		$20
Temperature too low.		Operate unit at temperature above 65°F. only.	■		$20
Capacitor defective.		Repair or replace.	■	$8	$20
Humidistat incorrectly positioned or defective.	Inspect, check continuity.	Reposition or replace.	■	$8	$20
Refrigerant leaking.		Consult authorized service personnel.	■	$10	$55
Fan obstructed.	Inspect.	Remove obstruction.	■		$20
Fan blades loose.	Check.	Adjust.	■		$20
Evaporator fins bent.	Straighten.				
Fan motor circuit inoperative.	Check.	Repair or replace.	■	$15	$25

PROBLEM: Dehumidifier excessively noisy.

Possible Cause	Procedure	Remedy	Rating	Parts	Labor
Fan motor needs lubrication.	Check.	Lubricate with SAE 10 motor oil.	■		$20
Fan or fan blades loose.	Inspect.	Tighten screws.	■		$20
Fan binding against case.	Check.	Adjust.	■		$20
Chassis connections loose.	Check.	Tighten.	■		$20
Capacitor defective (humming sound).	Discharge and check capacitor (see page 62).	Replace.	■	$8	$20

PROBLEM: Dehumidifier operates but leaks.

Possible Cause	Procedure	Remedy	Rating	Parts	Labor
Water collection pan ruptured.	Check for cracks or breaks.	Repair or replace.	■	$8	$20
Drain hose cracked.	Check.	Replace.	■	$2	$20
Overflow switch defective.	Check circuit continuity.	Repair or replace.	■	$4	$20
Water collection pan overflowing.	Check for defective overflow switch.	Repair or replace.	■	$4	$20

Dishwashers

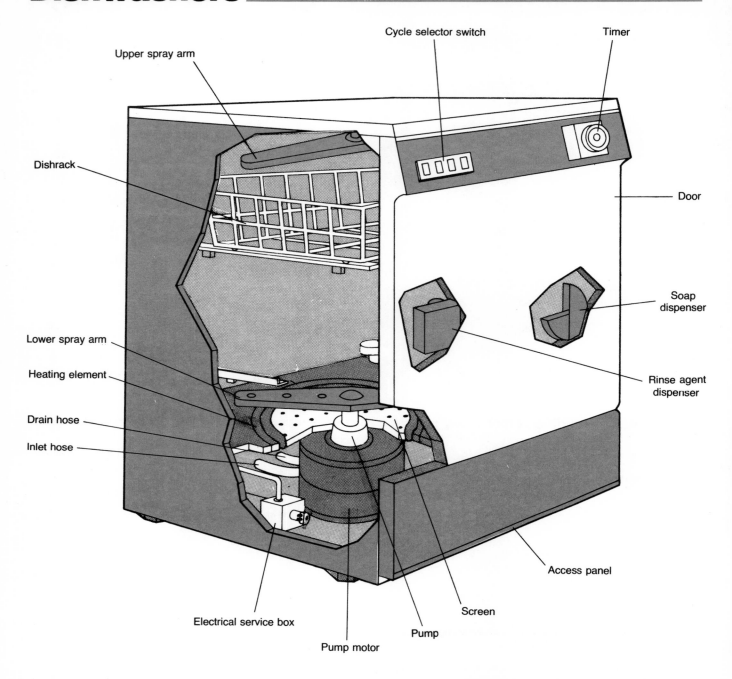

Cycle selector switch

Timer

Upper spray arm

Dishrack

Door

Lower spray arm

Heating element

Drain hose

Inlet hose

Soap dispenser

Rinse agent dispenser

Electrical service box

Pump motor

Pump

Screen

Access panel

Principle of Operation

An automatic dishwasher cleans dishes by spraying them first with a hot detergent solution, then with a hot water rinse. The appliance dries dishes by heating the inside compartment with a heating element.

Hot water (normally about 140°F. to 150°F.) from the home plumbing system enters an inlet valve and is pumped into the sink-like bottom of the dishwasher.

Then the pump forces this water into a spray arm, which rotates from the force of the water and sprays the dishes as it rotates. Detergent is released from a dispenser into the water. Then the pump reverses and pumps the water through an outlet valve and into the house drain system. The rinse cycle is identical except that no detergent is mixed with the water (a rinse agent may be, however).

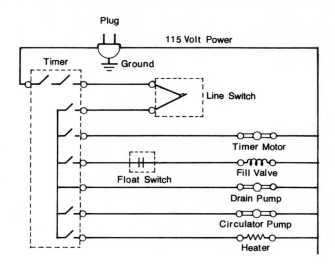

Simplified wiring diagram of a typical dishwasher. Components and wiring may vary.

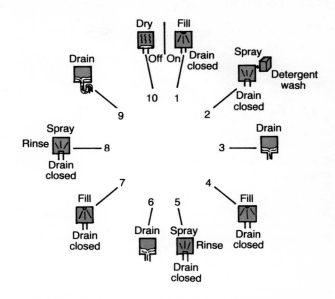

Dishwasher timer cycle. This machine has one wash, two rinses. Each wash and rinse consists of a Fill phase, Spray phase, and Drain phase. A Dry phase follows the last rinse.

The electrical system makes all this happen. The timer is the heart of the system. As it rotates, powered by a synchronous motor (*see page 62*), it first sends current to the solenoid at the inlet valve, so that the inlet valve opens. At about the same time, it turns on the pump so that water is pumped into the dishwasher. Then it closes the inlet valve solenoid and powers the pump to circulate water through the spray arm. It releases the detergent-dispenser latch. Later, it activates the outlet valve solenoid to open this valve, and it reverses the pump motor. This cycle may be repeated several times, and it may include other phases, such as a hot water spray with the drain valve open. To dry the dishes, the timer shuts off the pump and solenoid circuits but powers the heating element. It may also turn on a fan to assist in the drying and open a vent. Finally, it shuts itself off.

Another feature of the electrical system is a safety interlock microswitch in the door latch. It closes the circuit to the On/Off switch or timer. If the door is opened in the middle of a cycle, the switch disconnects and the machine stops abruptly.

Differences In Dishwashers

A cycle selector switch is found on many dishwashers. It modifies the timer cycle so that certain phases are extended or skipped. For example:

Rinse only. Dishes are sprayed with rinse water only. Then the water is pumped out. This cycle is useful when holding a few dishes until a full load accumulates.

Power wash. This option may also be called Pots and

Pans. The wash cycle is extended to insure better cleaning of utensils. Water velocity from the spray arm may be increased.

Mini cycle. A machine with several washes and rinses is adjusted for one short wash and rinse. This phase is useful for a small load of lightly soiled dishes.

Gentle cycle. This phase consists of one or two rinses and a drying. The water velocity from the spray arm may be reduced. The option is useful for fine china and crystal.

Sani cycle. The heating element, normally used for drying, raises the water temperature into the 180°F. range. It is useful for killing bacteria or other microorganisms.

Plate warmer. This is the drying phase only—useful for warming serving dishes.

Also, timer phases may vary considerably from the basic model described under Principle of Operation. Some models take about half an hour for the full wash and dry cycle; others may take twice as long because of multiple wash and rinse phases. The timer housing may list the cycle phases.

In addition to timer variations and a cycle selector switch, convenience features include tilting racks, special rack designs for pots or delicate dishware, and a rinse solution dispenser. Mechanical variations include an air pressure water level switch or a float switch (either functioning as a safety to prevent flooding); reversing and nonreversing pump motors; a single pump or one for inlet and spray, another for outlet; a fan to assist in drying; and an upper spray arm as well as the standard lower spray arm.

How to Reach Interior Components

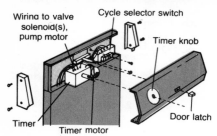

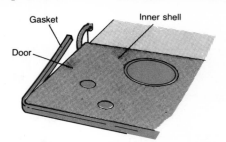

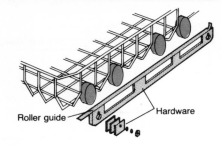

Control Panel: To reach timer, cycle selector switch

The controls are housed in the door or in the chassis above the door. Remove the timer knob and any other knobs, then remove the access panel or the inner shell of the door. Both are held in place with screws. If the controls are in the door, it may be necessary to remove the door gasket.

Door: To reach gaskets and seals

The door gasket may be held in place with screws or clips, or it may be pressed into a channel. Pry up the edge with a screwdriver or putty knife. Be careful not to tear it. Seals around the base of the door may also be pressed in or held with clips or screws. Remove the lower access panel to see them better.

Interior of the Dishwasher: To reach heating element, spray arm, upper pump assembly, upper float switch

Pull out the racks. The lower rack on most models simply lifts out. Unscrew the roller or guides that hold the top rack in place.

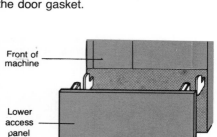

Lower Access Panel: To reach pump and motor

Remove the lower access panel. It is held in place with screws. Dishwashers are designed to be serviced from the front. But if a major repair requires pulling the appliance away from the wall, first remove the fuse or flip the circuit breaker for the dish-

washer circuit, then unhook the hot water supply and the drain hose. Be sure the hot water valve in the line is closed. Place a pan under the plumbing connections as you disconnect them. If the appliance is fitted under a cabinet top, lower the leveling legs before attempting to horse out the dishwasher.

Maintenance and Repair

Timer. The timer (*see page 56*) controls all electrical circuits in the dishwasher. Any malfunction that is not obviously a plumbing breakdown could be the result of a faulty timer. Even some "obvious" plumbing problems, such as flooding, might actually be timer or electrical problems—for example, if the outlet solenoid failed to open the outlet valve.

Inspect the timer terminals for burning, loose wires, or other evidence of wear or poor electrical contact. Clean the terminals with fine sandpaper or liquid contact cleaner. If the housing has a removable cover, examine the contacts and cams inside. Clean the contacts. If the cams are loose or out of place, peen the spacers between them with a punch. If cams or other parts (such as leaf springs) are broken, obtain

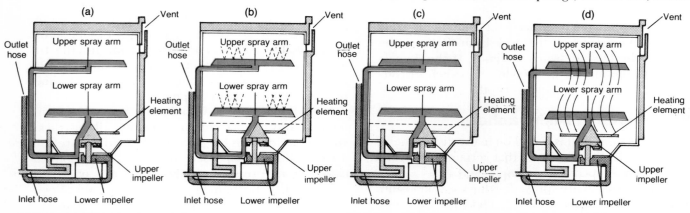

In fill cycle (*a*), water flows into basin-like bottom of dishwasher. In wash cycle (*b*), pump's upper impeller forces water through spray arms; spray arms rotate and spray dishes in racks. In drain cycle (*c*), pump's lower impeller forces water through outlet valve to house's drain-waste-vent system. In dry cycle (*d*), heating element heats air to dry dishes.

replacement parts from a local timer-rebuilding shop; or buy a new timer.

Check the timer for continuity with a multimeter (*see pages 26-28*). Turn the timer through its functions. At each set of terminals, the meter should read approximately zero ohms.

The timer motor is the synchronous type (*see page 62*).

Pump. The pump serves three functions: It forces water into the dishwasher; it then forces this water through the spray arm; and finally it forces the water out of the appliance into the drain system. Poor water supply or flooding could be the result of the pump malfunctioning in the intake or outlet phase. To check whether the pump is forcing water through the spray arm, turn the machine on and listen carefully for the characteristic swishing sound the water makes as it sprays. If this sound is noticeably absent, the pump may not be working properly (or the problem may be in the spray arm). In most machines, the pump's upper impeller is for the spray-arm function, the lower impeller for inlet and outlet. To inspect the pump, remove the intake and outlet hoses and the pump cover. Remove obstructions and replace worn parts.

Motor. See pages 60-65.

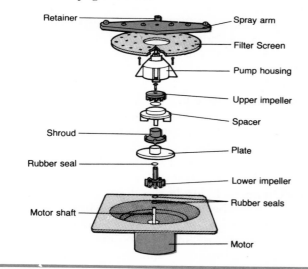

Retainer — **Spray arm**
— **Filter Screen**
Pump housing
Upper impeller
Spacer
Shroud —
Plate
Rubber seal —
Lower impeller
Rubber seals
Motor shaft —
Motor

Pump and pump motor assembly

Cycle Selector Switch. This switch is wired to the timer. It programs the timer to alter its normal cycle. If the machine does not turn on in one cycle, or does not follow the "instructions" given by this switch, the switch may be faulty (or the timer may be the problem). Clean the switch's terminals and examine the wires for looseness or wear. Test the switch for continuity with a multimeter (*see pages 26-28*). The meter should register approximately zero ohms when the cycle selector is turned to a given set of terminals. Replace the switch if defective.

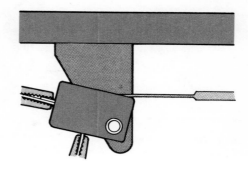

Float switch acts as safety to prevent flooding.

Float Switch. Most but not all dishwashers have a float switch. It is a safety switch that shuts off the inlet solenoid (closing the inlet valve) if the water rises higher than it should. Or the float switch may be used to signal the timer to begin the wash cycle.

If there is flooding, this switch may have malfunctioned. Move it up and down to make sure the mechanical action is not obstructed. Lubricate moving parts and clean the contacts and terminals with fine sandpaper or liquid contact cleaner. Test it for continuity with a continuity tester or multimeter; it should show continuity (zero ohms on a multimeter) when the contacts are closed. If the switch is defective, replace it.

Air Pressure Switch. Dishwashers may use an air pressure switch rather than a float switch to measure water level. Consisting of a capillary tube and a diaphragm, this is the same type of switch as used in a washing machine (*see page 000*). Test by connecting the leads to a continuity tester or multimeter, filling the dishwasher basin with water (use a bucket), and noting whether the switch closes at the appropriate water level. When the switch closes, the continuity tester should show continuity; the multimeter needle should swing to zero. Replace the switch if defective.

Spray Arm. The spray arm is normally trouble-free. If damaged, replace it. If the holes clog and it does not turn or spray properly, clean the holes with a stiff wire.

Shelves and Rollers. If they break or become rusty, replace them with manufacturer's parts.

Gasket and Seals. The door gasket and the apron or seal at the base of the door are vital parts. Water will spray all over the kitchen—and the appliance wiring—if they are not in place. Not only a mess but a severe shock hazard could result. Occasionally, the bottom seal shifts and needs to be repositioned. The door gasket or the seals may crack or deteriorate; replace them. If adjusting the door latch, be sure the gasket fit is snug but not overtight, which could cause gasket wear. Soften a new gasket or seal in hot water before fitting it to the door.

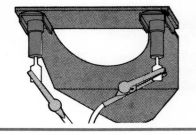

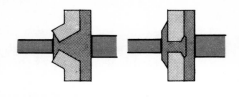

Probe holes in sprayer arm with pin or straightened coat hanger if they are clogged.

Remove lower access panel to find heating element terminals. Test heating element with a multimeter *(see text)*.

Solenoid and inlet valve assembly. Solenoid is an electromagnetic switch controlled by the timer. The solenoid opens and closes the valve.

Heating Element. If the dishes do not properly, the heating element may be faulty. Check the terminals for loose wiring or evidence of burning. Replace the terminals or wires as necessary. Test the heating element with a multimeter; it should register between 10 and 100 ohms. If the meter reads much higher than this, replace the heating element.

Inlet and Outlet Valves. The inlet valve is fitted with a fine-mesh filter to strain out solid impurities. If too little water enters the dishwasher or it enters too slowly, loosen the plumbing inlet connection and remove the filter with long-nosed pliers or fingers. Be careful not to damage the filter. Wash it in tap water.

Internal seals or other parts of these valves may wear and allow some leakage when the valve is closed. Test the valve by removing it, pressing the solenoid to its closed position, and pouring a small amount of water into the inlet port. If water dribbles through, replace the valve-and-solenoid assembly.

Solenoids. The solenoids are the electrical switches that open and close the inlet and outlet valves. If a solenoid fails, flooding will result. Or the dishwasher motor may run but water not enter the machine. Test the sliding action of the solenoid manually to see if it is obstructed. Lubricate it with silicone spray. Clean its terminals and contacts with fine sandpaper or liquid contact cleaner. Test it with a multimeter set to the Rx100 scale. The meter should read 1,000 ohms or less. If the solenoid is defective, replace the valve-and-solenoid assembly.

Hoses and Pipes. The inlet and outlet plumbing connections, which may be either hoses or pipes, can deteriorate and develop leaks. Replace cracked or leaking hoses. If a hose has deteriorated only at the end where it attaches to the appliance or the household plumbing, cut off the bad portion and refit the hose. If a pipe leaks, consult a plumber.

Door. The door latch mechanism, including the safety-interlock microswitch, is a frequent source of malfunction. If the appliance will not turn on even though the door is latched and the other switches have been set properly, the microswitch may have failed. Check it for continuity *(see pages 26-28)*; replace it if defective. If the latch does not close properly, adjust it by loosening the screws that hold the catch in place and shifting the catch. Or build up the catch with a shim under it; obtain longer screws from a hardware store if the old screws no longer hold when the shim is in place. If the door latch mechanism breaks, replace it.

The door springs are another frequent source of trouble. A door spring breaks with a loud bang, and the door then falls or slams open abruptly. The springs may be located inside the door (underneath the inner shell) or below the door (behind the lower access panel). If inside the door, a breaking spring may damage the timer or other switches. Even though only one spring breaks, replace both. Adjust the spring tension, on models equipped with adjusting holes, by lengthening or shortening the spring travel.

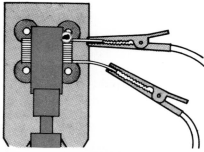

Test solenoid with multimeter on ohms setting *(see text)*.

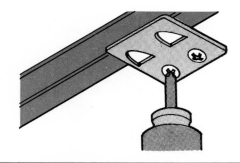

Door latch adjustment.

DISHWASHER TROUBLESHOOTING

PROBLEM: Dishwasher does not start.

Possible Cause	Procedure	Remedy	Rating	Parts	Labor
No power at outlet.	Check fuse or circuit breaker.	Replace fuse or reset circuit breaker.	■		
Plug disconnected (portable model).	Check.	Reseat plug in outlet.	■		
Cord defective.	Check for breaks.	Repair or replace.	■ ■	$5	$20
Door not fully latched or mechanism faulty.	Check for worn parts. Latch must strike door's safety switch. Check circuit continuity in wires.	Replace faulty parts.	■ ■ ■	$6-15	$20
Cycle selector button not fully depressed.	Check.		■		
Cycle selector switch or timer faulty.	Check circuit continuity and contacts.	Replace either part.	■ ■ ■	Switch $15 Timer $35-55	$25
Wires broken.	Check.	Splice, insulate, or replace.	■ ■ ■ ■	$15	$25
Motor defective.	Check circuit continuity. Check for bound bearings.	Replace or repair. Lubricate or replace bearings.	■ ■ ■ ■	$40-60	$35
Safety switch faulty.	Check continuity.	Repair or replace.	■ ■ ■	$6-12	$25
Water inlet valve faulty.	Check solenoid circuit continuity. Check mechanical action.	Replace.	■ ■ ■	$15	$25
Water level control switch faulty.	Check continuity. Check for bound or clogged parts. If applicable, check for jammed float switch.	Replace.	■ ■ ■	$6-12	$25

PROBLEM: Dishwasher blows fuse or trips circuit breaker.

Possible Cause	Procedure	Remedy	Rating	Parts	Labor
Circuit overloaded.	Reduce number of appliances on circuit. Put dishwasher on its own circuit.	Replace fuse or reset circuit breaker.	■		
Cord or plug short-circuited (portable model).	Inspect for breaks.	Repair or replace.	■ ■	$5	$20
Motor short-circuited.	Check circuit continuity.	Repair or replace.	■ ■ ■ ■	$40-60	$35

PROBLEM: Dishwasher shocks user.

Possible Cause	Procedure	Remedy	Rating	Parts	Labor
Cord frayed (portable model).	Inspect for breaks.	Repair or replace.	■ ■	$5	$20
Case short-circuited.	Test circuit continuity.	Repair.	■ ■ ■ ■		$25

(Continued on next page)

DISHWASHER TROUBLESHOOTING *(Continued from preceding page)*

PROBLEM: Dishwasher leaks or floods.

Possible Cause	Procedure	Remedy	Rating	Parts	Labor
Oversudsing (leak from bottom).	Use less detergent.		■		
Door gasket faulty.	Check for deterioration.	Replace.	■ ■	$20	$25
Pump seals defective.	Check.	Replace broken seals. (If sealing face on impeller is worn, replace impeller.	■ ■ ■	$15	$25
External hoses or clamps dislodged or broken.	Check under lower access panel.	Reclamp or replace.	■ ■	$5	$20
Inlet valve defective.	Check for cracks or loose screws.	Replace.	■ ■ ■	$15	$25
Water level switch faulty.	Check function of mechanical parts.	Replace. switch circuit continuity.	■ ■ ■	$6-12	$25
Door misaligned.	Check hinges and springs.	Replace bent or worn parts. Always replace in pairs.	■ ■	$10	$25
External drain hose overlapping in standpipe.	Check for clogging. Check outside drainfield for saturation.	Remove clog. Wait two or three hours for ground to absorb moisture.	■ ■		$20
Heating element fasteners loose.	Check.	Tighten or repair.	■ ■		$20

PROBLEM: Dishwasher fills but does not wash or rinse.

Possible Cause	Procedure	Remedy	Rating	Parts	Labor
Wash arm not turning freely.	Check arm hub bearings. Check arm for bends or twists, hub for clogging.	If damaged, replace.	■ ■ ■	$10	$25
Hub of wash arm faulty.	Check hub for breaks or cracks. Check screen for clogging.	If damaged, replace.	■ ■ ■	$15	$25
Recirculating pump intake or outlet parts clogged.	Remove connections and probe with wire or snake.	Replace rough or corroded parts.	■ ■ ■	$15	$25
Circulating hoses clogged.	Check.	Clean. If interior is rough or cracked, replace.	■ ■	$10	$25
Pump impeller faulty.	Check for broken blades or clogged pump.	Replace entire pump.	■ ■ ■	$15	$25
Motor inoperative.	Check circuit continuity.	Replace or repair.	■ ■ ■ ■	$40-60	$35

PROBLEM: Dishwasher does not drain.

Possible Cause	Procedure	Remedy	Rating	Parts	Labor
Strainer or drain valve clogged.	Check.	Clean.	■ ■		$20
Pump impeller clogged or defective.	Check.	Clean or replace.	■ ■ ■		$25
Drain valve solenoid defective.	Test.	Replace.	■ ■ ■	$8	$20
Timer sticks in "Wash" position.	Check to see if timer advances properly.	Replace if necessary.	■ ■ ■	$35-55	$25

(Continued on next page)

PROBLEM: Water drains from dishwasher during cycles. ▬▬▬▬▬▬▬▬▬

Possible Cause	Procedure	Remedy	Rating	Parts	Labor
Drain hose too low.		Reposition so that hose is higher than highest water level in basket.	■ ■		$20

PROBLEM: Dishwasher is excessively noisy or vibrates too much. ▬▬▬▬▬▬

Possible Cause	Procedure	Remedy	Rating	Parts	Labor
Dishes loaded improperly.	Reload, following owner's manual instructions. Sprayer must be able to turn freely.		■		$20
Water level low in tub.	Reduce use of house water supply while machine is being used. Check inlet valve filter.	Replace or clean filter.	■ ■ ■	$1	$20
Inlet valve defective.	Listen for clatter or knocking sound during fill cycle.	Replace inlet valve.	■ ■ ■	$15	$20
Machine not level.	Check with carpenter's level.	Level machine front to back and side to side.	■ ■		$20
Loose parts in machine.	Check under access panels.	Tighten.	■ ■ ■		$20
Pumping action improper.	Check for worn bearings and parts in motor and pump.	Replace worn parts; tighten loose parts.	■ ■ ■	$10-25	$25
Spray arm worn.	Check bearings and arm.	Replace.	■ ■ ■	$10	$25
Pump impeller worn or loose.	Check.	Tighten impeller lock screw and replace broken parts.	■ ■ ■	$15	$25
Motor bearings worn.	Remove motor end plates, and check bearings.	Replace bearings.	■ ■ ■ ■	$8	$35

PROBLEM: Dishwasher skips cycles. ▬▬▬▬▬▬▬▬▬

Possible Cause	Procedure	Remedy	Rating	Parts	Labor
Cycle selector switch defective.	Check circuit continuity; inspect for burned terminals or wires.	Repair terminals or wires. If no continuity, replace switch.	■ ■ ■	$15	$25

PROBLEM: Dishwasher smokes. ▬▬▬▬▬▬▬▬▬

Possible Cause	Procedure	Remedy	Rating	Parts	Labor
Circulating pump jammed.	Inspect.	Clean and free mechanism.	■ ■		$25
Motor bearings faulty.	Check.	Lubricate or replace.	■ ■ ■ ■	$8	$25
Pump seal leaking.	Check.	Replace.	■ ■ ■	$8	$35
Wires at motor broken.	Check wires and terminals.	Repair or replace.	■ ■		$20

(Continued on next page)

DISHWASHER TROUBLESHOOTING *(Continued from preceding page)*

PROBLEM: Dishwasher smokes.

Possible Cause	Procedure	Remedy	Rating	Parts	Labor
Timer defective.	Check circuit continuity.	Replace.	■ ■ ■	$35-55	$25
Moisture causing short-circuit.	Inspect for charred wire.	Replace.	■ ■ ■		$20
Solenoids burned.	Check circuit continuity.	Replace.	■ ■ ■	$6-12	$25
Foreign objects on heating element.	Check.	Remove foreign object.	■		$25
Heating element not shutting off.	Check circuit continuity of thermostat and timer. Check timer to see if it advances properly.	Replace defective parts.	■ ■	$20	$25

PROBLEM: Dishwasher does not turn itself off.

Possible Cause	Procedure	Remedy	Rating	Parts	Labor
Timer defective.	Check circuit continuity.	Repair or replace.	■ ■ ■	$35-55	$25

PROBLEM: Dishwasher door does not close or seal.

Possible Cause	Procedure	Remedy	Rating	Parts	Labor
Racks binding.	Check.	Realign, repair or replace.	■ ■	$50	$25
Door gasket broken.	Check.	Replace.	■ ■	$20	$25
Latch mechanism faulty.	Check.	Adjust or replace.	■ ■ ■	$10	$25
Hinges worn.	Check.	Replace both hinges.	■ ■	$10	$25
Door return springs worn.	Check.	Replace both springs.	■ ■	$10	$25
Machine not level.	Check with carpenter's level.	Level machine front to back and side to side.	■ ■		$20
Door bent or warped.	Check.	Realign or replace if fault is too severe. All mechanism and wiring must be transferred to new door.	■ ■ ■	$50	$30

PROBLEM: Detergent dispenser does not spring open or does not empty properly.

Possible Cause	Procedure	Remedy	Rating	Parts	Labor
Dish or utensil blocking lid.	Remove obstruction.	Load machine as owner's manual instructs.	■		$20
Detergent put in wet cup or left too long.		Empty cup, dry thoroughly.	■		$20
Hard water deposits blocking lid.	Clean cup and lid with vinegar.	Keep clean.	■		$20
Detergent cup lid solenoid defective.	Test circuit continuity.	Replace.	■ ■ ■	$15	$25

(Continued on next page)

PROBLEM: Dishwasher does not dry dishes adequately.

Possible Cause	Procedure	Remedy	Rating	Parts	Labor
Rinse additive dispenser faulty (where applicable).	Visually inspect.	Repair or replace.	■ ■ ■	$20	$20
Vents clogged.	Check vents behind front panel.	Clean.	■ ■		$20
Sump strainer clogged.	Remove spray arm.	Clean strainer.	■ ■ ■		$20
Drainage system faulty.	Check pump impeller, drainage lines, external drain system.	Clean. Repair or replace.	■ ■ ■	$15	$25
Wiring harness faulty.	Check entire system for breaks and loose connections, especially under door where wires are subject to stain.	Repair or replace.	■ ■ ■ ■	$15	$25
Heating element faulty.	Check continuity of calrod in wash chamber or heater and blower located under wash chamber.	Replace faulty parts.	■ ■ ■	$20	$25

PROBLEM: Racks do not slide.

Possible Cause	Procedure	Remedy	Rating	Parts	Labor
Wire frame bent.	Check alignment.	Twist into shape or replace.	■ ■	$50	$20
Guides bent.	Check.	Realign or replace.	■ ■	$15	$20
Rollers bound or out of line.	Check.	Clean, realign or replace.	■ ■	$10	$25

PROBLEM: Dishwasher does a poor job.

Possible Cause	Procedure	Remedy	Rating	Parts	Labor
Machine improperly loaded or pre-rinsed.	Check owner's manual for instructions.		■		$20
Water supply not hot enough.	Check house water supply. If there is a heating booster check circuit continuity. Check thermostat for broken wires or terminals.	Water temperature should be between 140°F. and 160°F. Replace worn or broken parts.	■ ■		$20
Rinse agent dispenser faulty.	Check mechanism for worn or clogged parts.	Clean. Replace worn parts.	■ ■ ■	$20	$20
Broken impeller in pump.	Check impeller blades under washer arm and hub.	Replace pump if blades are broken.	■ ■ ■	$15	$25
Cycle selector switch or timer faulty.	Check circuit continuity and contacts.	Repair or replace.	■ ■ ■	Switch $15 Timer $35-55	$25
Spray arm jammed.	Check for worn bearings, bent arm.	Repair or replace.	■ ■ ■	$10	$20
Hub clogged or worn.	Clean. Check hub for cracks and wear.	Replace.	■ ■ ■	$15	$20
Spray arm holes clogged.	Check.	Clean.	■ ■		$20
Sump strainer clogged.	Remove screen.	Clean	■ ■		$20

Electric Ranges

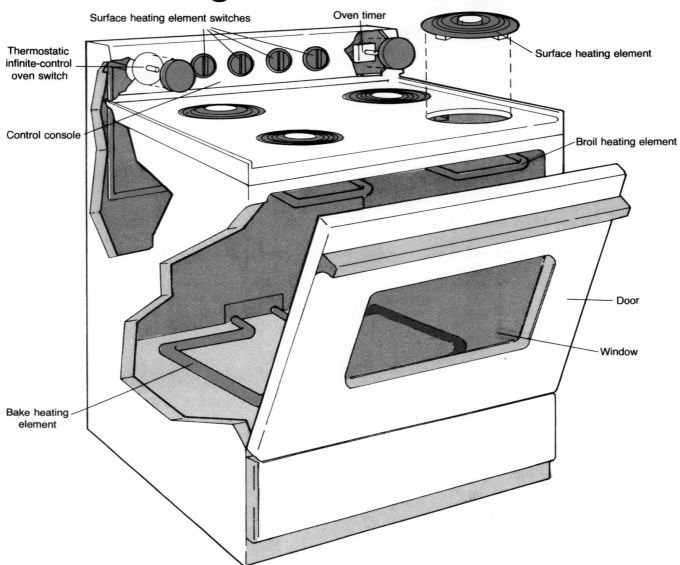

Surface heating element switches

Oven timer

Thermostatic infinite-control oven switch

Surface heating element

Control console

Broil heating element

Door

Window

Bake heating element

Principle of Operation

Heating elements (*see page 54*) in a range transform electrical energy into heat. The metals from which they are made are relatively poor conductors—that is, they have high electrical resistance. Molecular friction results when electricity passes through them, and molecular friction generates heat.

The path of electricity from the outlet box to a stovetop heating element is simple and direct. At a terminal block on the back of the range, the three-wire, 240-volt house circuit (*see page 13*) divides into individual heating element circuits. These are parallel circuits (*see page 15*). Current passes through each circuit to the switch controlling the heating element. When the switch is turned on, current flows into the heating element and also into a neon signal light. Current leaves the heating element and neon light by means of a neutral wire and returns to the ground.

The path to an oven or broiler heating element is identical, except that the circuit includes a thermostat as well as the On/Off switch. The thermostat may be the gas-containing type (*see page 59*) or an electronic sensor (*see page 60*). Nearly every electric oven also has a timer (*see page 56*) for turning the heating element on and off automatically at preset times. The timer may be wired to a surface heating element as well.

Heat is contained within the oven cavity by insulation: Sandwiched within the double walls of the oven is a layer of fiberglass or other insulating material, and a gasket made of asbestos may be mounted around the oven door. Ventilation holes in the top and bottom of the oven cavity allow steam and vapors to escape and promote the circulation of convection currents.

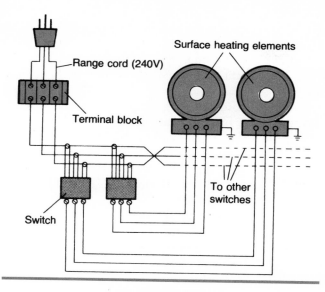

Wiring diagram for cooktop.

Differences in Electric Ranges

Two basic types of switches control the various heating elements. One is the multiple-position switch, available in both rotary and push-button designs. The other is the infinite control switch.

The rotary version of the multiple-position switch contains a cam that depresses contacts to close a different circuit at each stop. In the push-button version, each button depresses a separate circuit's contact.

The infinite control switch contains only one pair of contacts, or points. One point is stationary, and the other is mounted at the end of a piece of bimetal (*see page 57*) around which resistance wire is wound (*see page 54*). When current passes to the heating element, it also passes through the resistance wire to heat the

bimetal. The bimetal bends and, when sufficiently heated, breaks contact with the other point and opens the circuit. An eccentric cam mounted on the control shaft forces the bimetal closer to or further from the other contact, regulating the amount of heat required to separate the points.

Another variation in range design is the self-cleaning option. Self-cleaning ovens are either catalytic or pyrolytic. The catalytic design is the simpler; it consists merely of a grease and dirt resistant compound sealed on the oven walls. To protect the catalytic surface, clean it only with soap and water, *never* with caustic oven cleaning compounds or abrasives.

In a pyrolytic system, a special circuit bypasses the oven thermostat and allows the oven to obtain very high heat—typically 900°F. to 1000°F. The grime that has accumulated on the interior of the oven is burned off. This type of self-cleaning oven has added insulation and an automatic safety lock on the oven door which prevents opening while the oven is hotter than normal cooking temperature.

Abrasives and oven cleaners will not damage the wall surfaces of a pyrolytic oven and may be used as an alternative to the self-cleaning circuit.

Cooktops and ovens can be purchased as separate units and in a wide variety of sizes and capacities. Ranges and cooktops are available with as many as six surface heating elements. Some ranges are equipped with double ovens or broilers. The second oven may be a microwave oven.

Cooktops normally are equipped with four surface heating elements—two 1200 watt units and two 1600 watt units. Cooktop options include a cooking well; a barbecue pit, in which the heating element is embedded in porcelain or lava and food is prepared on a

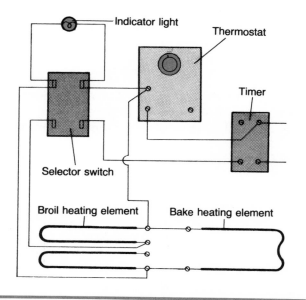

Wiring diagram for oven that contains bake and broil heating elements.

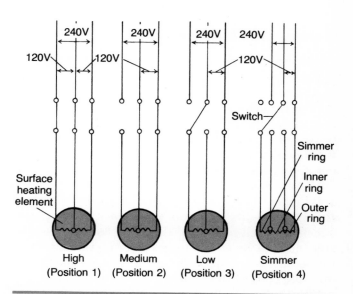

A four-position switch controlling a surface heating element.

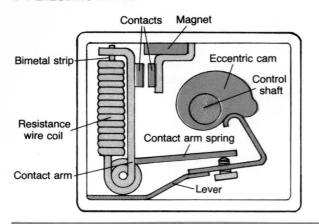

Inside an infinite control switch (shown in the off position). As the control shaft is rotated, the eccentric cam puts greater and greater pressure on the lever, forcing the contacts to close. Resistance wire around the bimetal is connected to oven circuit. When resistance wire heats sufficiently, bimetal bends enough to pull movable contact away from stationary contact, shutting off oven. Force must be great enough to overcome magnet holding contacts together.

grill; and a griddle surface to cover one or more heating elements. A recent innovation in cook top design is a smooth glass cooking surface; hidden beneath are conventional heating elements.

Popular oven options include the rotisserie and the meat probe. The rotisserie is run by a small electric motor in the wall of the oven. The motor is wired into a 120-volt circuit in the appliance. The meat probe is a metal spike wired into the thermostat circuit. When in use, this thermostat overrides the oven thermostat, so that the internal heat of the meat rather than the temperature of the air is measured.

Another oven option is the exhaust duct. A fan sucks grease and smoke through a filter in the oven wall to a vent outside. The filter is removable for cleaning.

Maintenance and Repair

Heating element. The easiest way to test a heating element is by substituting an identical, working element from the same stove.

To test a heating element when no identical substitute is available, remove the heating element from the stove and attach the leads of a multimeter set at the Rx10 mode. If the meter registers infinity, the heating element is bad and must be replaced.

Many surface elements have four terminals. These are double heating elements in a single housing, and they usually are controlled by multiple-position switches. Check each of the two portions separately by attaching the meter first to one pair of terminals, then to the other. Be sure that each pair of terminals are opposite ends of the same wire.

When a heating element does not work, the prob-

lem is more often in the switches or wiring than in the heating element itself.

Switch. A bad switch may not move or turn properly. The circuit may not turn on or off, or it may function intermittently.

When checking a switch, first remove the fuse or flip the circuit breaker that controls the 240-volt circuit to the stove. Then examine the switch terminals. Make sure all terminals are clean and the wires are attached tightly. Clean terminals with fine sandpaper or liquid contact cleaner. If there are signs of burning or deterioration, replace the switch.

If still unsure whether the switch is faulty, test it for continuity with a multimeter or continuity tester (*see pages 26-28*). If the switch is the multiple-position type, attach the leads of the meter or tester to each pair of positive and negative terminals in turn—that is, to the pair of terminals at each switch position. When the switch is turned to that position, the continuity tester should show continuity (zero ohms on the multimeter). When the switch is turned to a different position, the tester should show no continuity (infinity on the multimeter).

An infinite control switch can also be checked with a meter; however, such a test is sometimes inconclusive. The best way to check such a switch is to substitute a good one and see if the circuit then works properly, as was suggested above for heating elements.

Wiring. Poor wiring connections account for a large portion of electric range breakdowns. Arcing, burning, and deterioration of insulation often result from loose connections. The terminals at heating element blocks and at switches are especially prone to such problems.

Symptoms of wiring failure include the smell of burned insulation, one or more circuits that do not operate, and, sometimes, electric shock, a blown fuse, or a tripped circuit breaker.

 WARNING: Before working on the wiring in an electric range, remove the fuse or trip the breaker that controls the 240-volt stove circuit.

First, visually inspect wires for signs of damage (*see page 51*). Then check for continuity with a multimeter or continuity tester (*see pages 26-28*). Replace any damaged wires with insulated wire of the same or slightly larger gauge (*see page 12*). If only a small portion of the wire is damaged, cut off the bad section and attach a short piece of replacement wire with heat-proof ceramic wire nuts (*see page 24*). If damage to the wiring is extensive, especially if wear and crumbling of insulation are present in other areas as well, install a replacement wiring harness (*see page 53*).

Thermostat. See pages 57-58.

Timer. See page 56.

How to Reach Interior Components

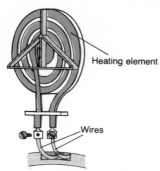

Heating element

Wires

Surface heating elements: To remove cooktop surface
Surface heating elements are attached with plug-in or screw terminals. The heating elements are often hinged. Removing them is simple: twist upwards (if hinged) and pull the element out of its plug, or unscrew the terminals. Access to the terminal block wires is under the cooktop surface.

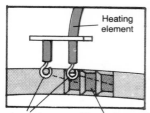

Heating element

Plug-in terminals   Plug-in receptacle

Cooktop surface: To reach switches, quick-connect terminals, fuse or circuit breaker surface:
Lift up the hinged cooktop surface. It may be held with hidden spring clips; insert the blade of a putty knife underneath the hinged surface to release the spring clips. Switches may now be accessible as well, or it may

be necessary to remove a panel held on with retaining screws. To remove a switch, pull off the dial knob to reveal the retaining screws that hold the panel to the chassis. Remove these screws and pull the wires from the quick-connect terminals. Note the colors of the wires—make a sketch marking the terminal each one attaches to. A fuse or circuit breaker, wired into the stove's 120-volt circuit (for the timer, electric clock, and other accessories) is also usually located under the cooktop surface.

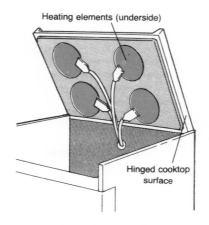

Heating elements (underside)

Hinged cooktop surface

Top rear console: To reach switches, timer, clock
In some models, the switches, timer, clock, and an accessory outlet are located in a console at the top rear of the stove. Front of accessory panel can often be removed after undoing retaining screws. Sometimes access is through a rear panel. Pull the range away from the wall, and unscrew the panel's retaining screws.

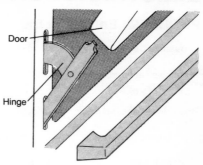

Door

Hinge

Oven door: To reach heating elements
To get at components within the oven cavity, remove the door. In most contemporary models, the door simply lifts off. Open it half way and pull it upwards, away from the bottom hinges. In older models, unscrew the hinges. Baking and broiling heating elements are held to the rear wall with a bracket. Remove the bolts that hold the bracket and unscrew the wire leads. Rotisserie motor, meat probe wiring, and other wiring may be located behind wall panels. Unscrew the sheet metal screws that hold the wall panels in place.

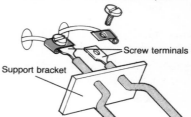

Screw terminals

Support bracket

Back of the range: To reach self-cleaning-oven components, switches, or wiring.
Pull the range away from the wall. Remove the rear access panel held in place with sheet metal screws.

Fuse or circuit breaker. Many electric ranges include a fuse or circuit breaker in the 120-volt circuit for stovetop lights, electric clock, convenience outlets, etc. If this fuse blows or the breaker trips continually, it is an indication of a short circuit in the 120-volt circuit wiring. Proceed as described above, under Wiring.

> **NOTE:** This 120-volt circuit fuse or breaker is not the current interrupter for the main, 240-volt circuit to the stove. That current interrupter is located in the house distribution box (see pages 13-19). Always remove the 240-volt fuse or trip the circuit breaker when working on the 120-volt stove circuit as well as on the 240-volt wiring.

Fan. An electric range may include an exhaust fan or a blower in the pyrolytic self-cleaning system.

Rotisserie. A rotisserie is operated by a small electric motor—usually a universal motor—behind an oven wall panel. If it does not run, the problem may be in the motor itself (*see pages 60-63*), the switch (*see pages 55-56 and above*), or the wiring (*see above*). Check each portion of the circuit for continuity (*see pages 26-28*) to isolate the problem area. Replace defective parts. Lubrication of the gears with a small amount of white grease and the motor bearings with oil often improves the performance of a slow, noisy rotisserie.

Meat probe. Neither the probe nor its wiring have any moving parts to service. If it fails, replace the unit.

ELECTRIC COOKTOP TROUBLESHOOTING

PROBLEM: Entire electric cooktop does not work.

Possible Cause	Procedure	Remedy	Rating	Parts	Labor
No power at source.	Check fuses or circuit breakers.	Replace fuses or reset circuit breakers.	■		$20
Plug disconnected.	Check.	Reseat plug in outlet.	■		$20
Feed cable defective.	Check for breaks.	Repair or replace.	■ ■ ■	$10	$25
Terminal block deteriorated.	Check.	Repair or replace.	■ ■ ■	$5	$20

PROBLEM: Electric cooktop blows fuses or trips circuit breakers.

Possible Cause	Procedure	Remedy	Rating	Parts	Labor
Circuit overloaded.	Put cooktop on its own circuit.	Replace fuses or reset circuit breakers.	■		$20
Feed cable short-circuited.	Inspect for breaks.	Repair or replace.	■ ■ ■	$10	$25

PROBLEM: Electric cooktop shocks user.

Possible Cause	Procedure	Remedy	Rating	Parts	Labor
Feed cable frayed.	Inspect for breaks.	Repair or replace.	■ ■ ■	$10	$20
Case short-circuited.	Test circuit continuity.	Repair.	■ ■ ■		$25

PROBLEM: One or more burners does not heat or heats inadequately.

Possible Cause	Procedure	Remedy	Rating	Parts	Labor
Heating element faulty.	Check circuit continuity.	Replace.	■ ■ ■	$20-30	$25
	Check terminals for burns.	Repair or replace.	■ ■ ■	$5	$25
	Check for loose wires.	Repair or replace.	■ ■ ■		$20
Switch faulty.	Check circuit continuity.	Replace.	■ ■ ■	$10-30	$25

ELECTRIC OVEN TROUBLESHOOTING

PROBLEM: Electric oven does not heat.

Possible Cause	Procedure	Remedy	Rating	Parts	Labor
No power at source.	Check fuse or circuit breaker.	Replace fuse or reset circuit breaker.	■		$20
Plug disconnected.	Check.	Reseat plug in outlet.	■		$20
Heating element not plugged in or defective.	Check connection in unit. Check contact block for burned terminals or wires. Check circuit continuity.	Replace.	■ ■ ■	$15-30	$20
Terminal block deteriorated.	Inspect.	Replace.	■ ■ ■	$5	$20

(Continued on next page)

PROBLEM: Electric oven does not heat. *(Continued from preceding page)*

Possible Cause	Procedure	Remedy	Rating	Parts	Labor
Thermostat faulty.	Check circuit continuity.	Replace.	■ ■ ■	$25-50	$25
Thermostatic heat sensors faulty.	Check.	Replace.	■ ■ ■	$15	$25
Wires loose or shorted.	Check.	Repair.	■ ■ ■ ■		$20
Timer malfunctioning.	Check setting, then circuit continuity.	Reset or replace.	■ ■ ■	$25-50	$25
	Check wiring.	Repair burned wires.	■ ■ ■		$20
Switch faulty.	Check contacts, circuit continuity.	Clean contacts or replace.	■ ■ ■	$15-30	$25

PROBLEM: Electric oven blows fuses or trips circuit breakers.

Possible Cause	Procedure	Remedy	Rating	Parts	Labor
Circuit overloaded.	Put oven on its own circuit.	Replace fuse or reset circuit breaker.	■		$20
Cord of plug short-circuited.	Inspect for breaks.	Repair or replace.	■ ■	$10	$25
Switch short-circuited.	Test circuit continuity.	Repair or replace.	■ ■ ■	$15-30	$25

PROBLEM: Electric oven shocks user.

Possible Cause	Procedure	Remedy	Rating	Parts	Labor
Cord frayed.	Inspect for breaks.	Repair or replace.	■ ■	$10	$25
Wiring defective, case short-circuited.	Inspect. Test circuit continuity.	Repair and insulate wires.	■ ■ ■ ■		$25

PROBLEM: Electric oven does not maintain proper temperature.

Possible Cause	Procedure	Remedy	Rating	Parts	Labor
Heating element not plugged in.	Check.	Reseat in socket.	■		$20
Oven door not completely shut during baking.	Check alignment and gasket.	Realign door. Replace gasket.	■ ■	$10-15	$25
Oven vent blocked.	Check for obstruction.	Clean vent.	■ ■		$20
Thermostat out of calibration.	Check.	Recalibrate or replace.	■ ■ ■	$25-50	$25

PROBLEM: Electric oven does not shut off.

Possible Cause	Procedure	Remedy	Rating	Parts	Labor
Automatic timer defective.	Set on "automatic" and turn clock by hand until timer clicks to "off" position. There should be no current to heating elements.	Repair or replace.	■ ■ ■	$25-50	$25
Thermostat defective.	Check.	Replace.	■ ■ ■	$25-50	$25

(Continued on next page)

ELECTRIC OVEN TROUBLESHOOTING *(Continued from preceding page)*

PROBLEM: Timer does not operate properly.

Possible Cause	Procedure	Remedy	Rating	Parts	Labor
Timer motor defective.	Turn off power. Remove timer motor and post. Check drive gear for mobility.	Replace motor.	■■■	$15	$25
Timer worn, bound or stripped.	Inspect.	Spray with silicone lubricant to free gears, or replace.	■■■	$15	$25

PROBLEM: Oven door does not stay shut.

Possible Cause	Procedure	Remedy	Rating	Parts	Labor
Door out of alignment.	Should line up evenly with sides of unit.	Realign manually.	■■		$20
Hinge or hinge pin faulty.	Check for worn or loose parts.	Replace.	■■	$10	$25
Spring or roller bearings broken.	Inspect.	Replace parts if possible, or entire door.	■■■	$10-50	$30

PROBLEM: Electric oven light or convenience outlet does not operate.

Possible Cause	Procedure	Remedy	Rating	Parts	Labor
15 amp fuse blown.	Inspect.	Replace.	■■		$20
Clock-timer switch incorrectly set or defective.	Reset. Check circuit continuity.	Replace.	■■■	$25-50	$25

PYROLYTIC SELF-CLEANING OVEN TROUBLESHOOTING

PROBLEM: Self-cleaning oven does not clean.

Possible Cause	Procedure	Remedy	Rating	Parts	Labor
No power at source.	Check fuse or circuit breaker.	Replace fuse or reset circuit breaker.	■	$10	$20
Door not latched properly.	Check. Reset controls. Check to be sure latch can operate freely.	Replace if faulty.	■■	$20	$25
Door switch faulty.	Check circuit continuity with latch in "clean" position.	Replace.	■■■	$8	$25
Door gasket defective.	Inspect for wear or breaks.	Replace.	■■	$12	$25
Automatic timer not set.	Check.	Set on manual.	■		$20
Heating element faulty.	Check circuit continuity.	Replace.	■■■	$15-25	$25
Heat shield in door not lifted.	Lift heat shield.	Reset controls.	■	$10	$20
High-limit thermostat defective.	Check circuit continuity. (Circuit should be closed when cool.)	Replace.	■■■	$15	$25
Cycle switch defective.	Check circuit continuity.	Replace.	■■■	$15-25	$25

PROBLEM: Self-cleaning light does not operate properly.

Possible Cause	Procedure	Remedy	Rating	Parts	Labor
Thermostat faulty.	Check.	Repair or replace.	■ ■ ■	$25-50	$25
Timer faulty.	Check.	Repair or replace.	■ ■ ■	$25-50	$25

PROBLEM: Self-cleaning is not complete.

Possible Cause	Procedure	Remedy	Rating	Parts	Labor
Thermostat defective.	Check calibration.	Repair or replace.	■ ■ ■	$25-50	$25
Cycle shut off faulty.	Check timer	Repair or replace.	■ ■ ■	$15	$25

PROBLEM: Oven door does not open after self-cleaning cycle.

Possible Cause	Procedure	Remedy	Rating	Parts	Labor
Cooling period not complete.	Check owner's manual.	Wait prescribed time.	■		$20
Latch control thermodisc faulty.	Examine mechanism.	Replace.	■ ■ ■	$12	$25
Latching mechanism faulty.	Check for binding, electrical malfunction, worn parts.	Repair or replace.	■ ■ ■	$20	$25

PROBLEM: Oven door does not lock for self-cleaning cycle.

Possible Cause	Procedure	Remedy	Rating	Parts	Labor
Lock thermostat bound.	Check.	Replace.	■ ■ ■	$12	$25

PROBLEM: Self-cleaning cycle does not shut off.

Possible Cause	Procedure	Remedy	Rating	Parts	Labor
Clean timer faulty.	Check.	Repair or replace.	■ ■ ■	$25-50	$25
Clean timer switch defective.	Check.	Repair or replace.	■ ■ ■	$12	$25

PROBLEM: Clean cycle shuts off but does not cool properly.

Possible Cause	Procedure	Remedy	Rating	Parts	Labor
Relay contacts sticking.	Check.	Clean contacts or replace relay.	■ ■ ■	$15	$25

Gas Ranges

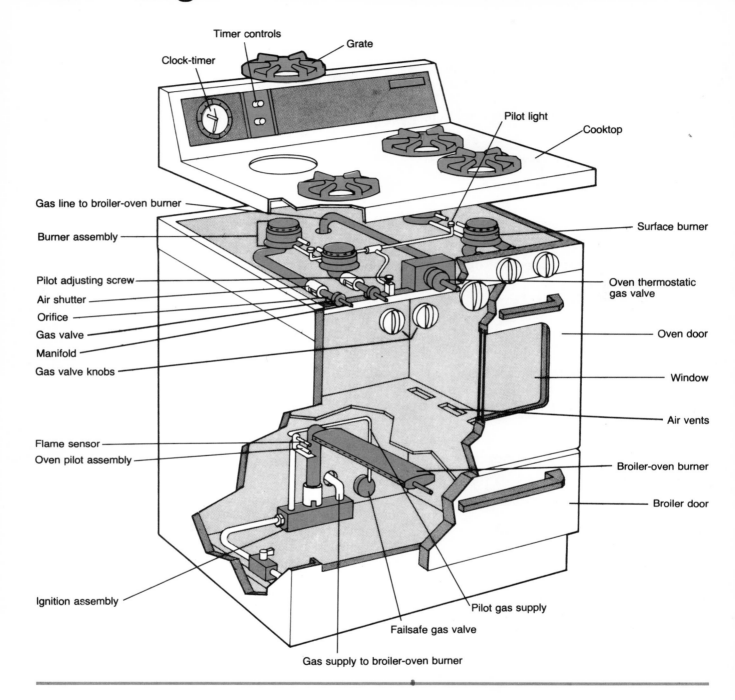

Timer controls

Clock-timer

Grate

Pilot light

Cooktop

Gas line to broiler-oven burner

Burner assembly

Surface burner

Pilot adjusting screw

Air shutter

Orifice

Gas valve

Manifold

Gas valve knobs

Oven thermostatic gas valve

Oven door

Window

Air vents

Flame sensor

Oven pilot assembly

Broiler-oven burner

Broiler door

Ignition assembly

Pilot gas supply

Failsafe gas valve

Gas supply to broiler-oven burner

Principle of Operation

The controlled combustion of natural gas or liquified petroleum (LP) produces the flame in a gas range. Under pressure, gas from the feeder line enters the manifold, a long tube within the front section of the range. The burner control valves connect to the manifold. When one of these valves is opened, gas rushes through it to the burner assembly. At the exit point of the gas valve, an adjustable fitting called an orifice controls the amount of gas entering the burner assembly. Through an air shutter in the burner assembly, air enters the gas stream to create a combustible mixture. The gas-air mixture is ignited by a pilot light or electronic ignition when it reaches the burner.

In most cooktops a burner can be lit directly by a match if the pilot fails to work. But in most ovens, a sensor-responder safety device closes off the gas flow if the pilot fails. The gas valve in an oven, being thermostatically controlled, is somewhat more complicated than the valve in a cooktop. The oven valve cuts back the flow of gas to the burner when the desired oven temperature has been reached, and increases it again when the temperature falls.

Ventilation holes in the floor of the oven allow air to enter and feed the flame. Holes in the oven ceiling allow steam, vapors, and fumes to exhaust. Baffles at the base of the oven cavity help to circulate the warm air evenly through the oven. As in an electric oven, the double wall is insulated.

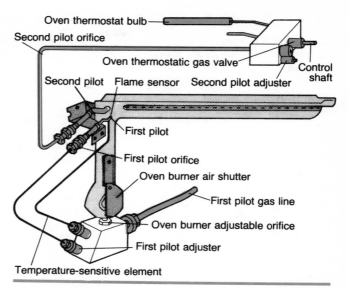

Failsafe two-pilot system. Burner is lit by second pilot. Gas will not flow to burner until second pilot is lit by constant first pilot. If first pilot is unlit, no gas escapes when valve is turned on.

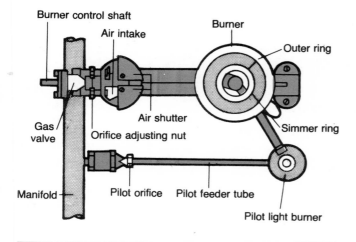

Gas from manifold passes through gas valve on way to burner. Air enters through air intake to make a combustible mixture. Burner shown here, with its inner simmer ring, requires a special dual gas valve and dual tubing system. One tube goes to simmer ring, the other to outer ring.

Differences in Gas Ranges

There are a number of variations in cooktop burner design. One style has two concentric flame rings, the inner for simmer and the outer for higher temperature cooking. This burner requires a special double-outlet gas valve. Another design variation is a temperature-sensitive burner, where the gas valve is thermostatically controlled by a spring-loaded sensor (*see page 60*) mounted in the center of the burner. Cooking wells, barbecue grills, and other options are also available. Cooktops can be purchased without ovens, and ovens without cooktops. Deluxe features for the oven section include a separate burner for broiling, double ovens, and pyrolytic or catalytic self-cleaning capability (*see electric oven pages 235 - 236*).

Various pilot or ignition systems are available for both cooktop and oven. In a constant pilot system, a small pilot flame burns continuously. In a fail-safe two pilot system, two pilot flames are used. The first pilot ignites the second when the gas valve is turned on. The second pilot then heats a sensor. Gas cannot flow to the burner assembly until the sensor, in response to the heat of the second pilot, opens a valve. The second pilot ignites the gas-air mixture.

An electric ignition system is powered by a 120-volt circuit in the stove. Turning the gas valve activates an electric circuit to the sparking device, and the gas-air mixture at the burner is ignited by this spark.

Many gas ranges come equipped with timers. These may be either an electrical device operated by a synchronous motor (*see page 62*), or a spring-wound mechanical timer. An electric timer is wired into the oven control switch to automatically turn the oven on or off at preset times.

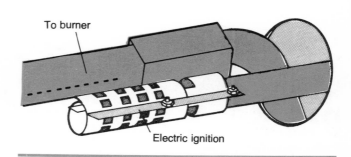

One form of flameless electric ignition. Heating element inside glows red hot.

How to Reach Interior Components

Stove top: To reach burners, gas control valves, gas shut-off valve

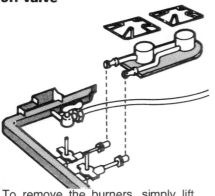

To remove the burners, simply lift out or, in some models, undo the single retainer screw and lift out. Before removing the gas valves, make sure the gas supply is turned off: Turn the gas cock in the feeder line so that it is perpendicular to the gas line. If the feeder is not visible when the burners are removed, pry up the hinged cooktop surface. If there is no shut-off valve in the feeder or behind the stove, turn off the gas at the supply source, where it enters the house. To remove the gas valves, inserted in each burner assembly, pull off the gas knob and unscrew the valve from the manifold.

Oven parts: To reach oven burner assembly, thermostat sensing element, oven pilot ignition

Remove the oven door by simply pulling it off or, in some models, by removing the bolts from its hinges. Take out the oven shelves. One or more panels may cover the burner assembly. Remove the retaining screws, if any, that hold the panels in place and lift them out. The burner assembly itself is held in place at either end with screws or spring clips. Unfasten and pull the burner assembly out. The thermostat sensing bulb is on the back or side wall of the oven, held in place with spring clips or brackets. The pilot ignition is usually beneath the oven cavity. To gain access, remove broiler drawer or remove panel, held in place with retaining screws.

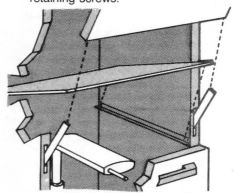

Maintenance and Repair

Cooktop burner assembly. Periodically, soak the cooktop burner assemblies for several hours in a hot soap-and-water solution. Then clean them with a nylon-bristle brush, rinse them, and dry them. Remove any remaining obstructions from the small passages in the burner ring and at its base with a small pin.

Enlarged flame holes indicate deterioration of the burner assembly; replace it.

Oven or Broiler Burner Assembly. Burners in the oven cavity normally require less cleaning than cooktop assemblies, and are not easy to remove. If a portion of the burner does not light, the flame holes are clogged. Clean them with a pin. Enlarged flame holes, as in a cooktop burner, indicate deterioration; replace the assembly.

Gas Valve. To increase or decrease gas flow to the burner, turn the orifice adjusting nut with an open wrench. This adjuster is located on the gas valve where it enters the burner assembly. Opening the orifice increases the gas to the burner, closing it decreases the gas flow.

Adjust air intake by loosening the screw that holds the air shutter in place and moving the shutter. The air shutter is located on the burner assembly near the gas valve orifice.

After long use, gas valves wear and sometimes develop leaks. Some gas valves have an adjusting nut near the orifice to tighten the internal fit of parts. Taking apart a gas valve and greasing it with a compound available for this purpose may also stop leaks. However, for safety's sake replace any gas valve that leaks rather than trying to adjust or repair it.

NOTE: To detect a gas leak, paint the suspected area with a thick solution of soap and water, and watch for bubbles. Gas leaks are more likely to develop in valves or fittings than in tubings.

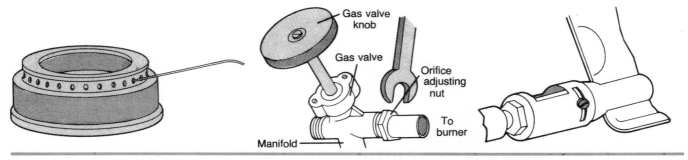

Clean clogged holes in burner with stiff wire.   Adjust gas intake with orifice adjusting nut.   Adjust air supply with air shutter adjusting screw.

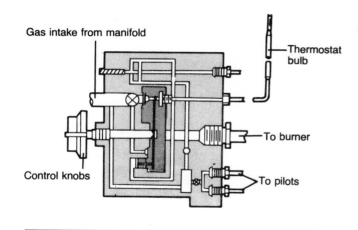

Complex interior of thermostatic gas valve, as used to control oven burner.

If adjustment of the orifice does not improve the flame, remove the orifice by unscrewing it from the valve, and examine it for clogging or wear. Remove obstructions by probing with a pin, and replace the orifice if it is worn.

On burners having an inner simmer ring, the height of the flame can be adjusted. Pull the knob off the valve and examine the valve stem. The adjustment screw is located in its center.

Pilot. The tubing that delivers gas to a pilot light taps the manifold, much as a gas valve taps it. Pilot assemblies include an adjustable orifice but no air shutter (air mixes with the gas as it emerges from the tubing). Adjust the orifice screw if the pilot light frequently goes out or the pilot flame is too high. (The pilot flame should be ½ inch or less in height.) The orifice adjustment screw is located at the start of the tubing near the manifold. If adjusting does not raise the flame sufficiently, the orifice may be clogged. Remove it and clean it with a pin. Also examine the feeder tube for obstructions. If the flame is too high

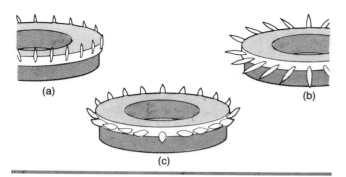

Correctly adjusted flame (a); flame with too little air (b); flame with too much air (c). Gas flame should be cone-shaped, blue without a hint of yellow, and steady. There should be no visible gap between the burner and the base of the flame. Surface burner flame should be about 1½ inches long, oven burner flame about 3 inches long. Too little air produces a weak, yellowish, sooty flame. Too much air causes the flame to roar and lift from the burner.

WARNING: Never use a match to find a gas leak. If a gas leak is suspected, blow out all pilot lights and other open flames. Do not use electrical appliances. Immediately report a gas leak to the utility company or the local fire department.

and adjustment does not lower it, the orifice is worn; replace it.

Pilots equipped with a hood or cover may not get sufficient air. Clean the hood regularly. Drill a small hole in the top of the hood to increase air flow further.

If a top burner lights with a match but not with a pilot, the burner passages are clogged. Clean the burner assembly as described above.

To relight a pilot that has gone out, hold a flame to it. If the pilot assembly includes a red safety button, press the button in for several seconds while holding a lighted match to the pilot area.

If the sensor-responder fails on a two-pilot system, the second pilot will not light and the oven will not work, even though the first pilot is burning.

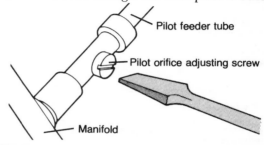

Adjust pilot flame with screwdriver at pilot orifice adjusting screw.

Remove the sensor and responder unit from the pilot area. Connect a multimeter to its leads. Set the multimeter at the Rx1 mode. The meter should read zero ohms. If it reads much higher, replace the unit.

Electric Ignition. If an electric ignition fails, the burner will not light. First, unplug the stove. Then test the wires to and from the ignition assembly for continuity (*see pages 26-28*). Repair or replace any frayed or broken wires. If the ignition contacts are accessible, clean them with fine sandpaper or contact cleaner. Plug the stove in, darken the room, and observe the ignition as it is turned on. If no spark is seen, replace it. If the ignition sparks but the burner still does not light, the problem is in the gas delivery system. Clean the burner assembly (*see above*).

Thermostat. See page 57.

Timer. Home repair of a spring-wound or electrical timer on a gas range is usually not possible. Replace a defective unit.

WARNING: Wear short-sleeved garments when working on a gas range, to avoid a sleeve accidentally catching fire. Keep face away from pilot or burner flames and suspected gas leaks.

GAS COOKTOP TROUBLESHOOTING

PROBLEM: Gas cooktop does not operate.

Possible Cause	Procedure	Remedy	Rating	Parts	Labor
Gas supply to house shut off.	Check other gas appliances.	Contact utility company.	■		$20
Pilot light extinguished.	Check duct for blockage.	Clean with fine wire or toothpick. Relight.	■ ■		$20

PROBLEM: One or more burners do not light evenly.

Possible Cause	Procedure	Remedy	Rating	Parts	Labor
Ducts in burner head blocked.	Remove.	Wash unit and clean holes with fine wire or toothpick.	■ ■		
Flame height improperly adjusted.	Clean burner. Adjust orifice or air shutter.		■ ■		$20
Gas leaks.	Locate by brushing soapy water over all joints. Bubbles indicate leak.	Shut gas supply. Tighten joints and reseal. Call utility company, fire company, or authorized service personnel.	■ ■ ■		$20

PROBLEM: Gas odor is noticeable with all pilot lights lit.

Possible Cause	Procedure	Remedy	Rating	Parts	Labor
Gas leaks.	Locate by brushing soapy water over joints. Bubbles indicate leak.	Call utility company, fire company, or authorized service personnel.	■ ■ ■		$20

(Exercise extreme caution—Do not smoke or light a match. Refrain from using any electrical appliance until gas leak has been repaired.)

PROBLEM: There is a popping sound when burner is lit.

Possible Cause	Procedure	Remedy	Rating	Parts	Labor
Conduction tube between pilot and burner needs repositioning.		Reposition.	■		$20
Pilot light set too low.	Light should be approximately ¼ inch high.	Readjust.	■ ■		$20

PROBLEM: Cooktop heats improperly; flame is wrong color or size.

Possible Cause	Procedure	Remedy	Rating	Parts	Labor
Flame has yellow tip.	Flame needs more air.	Partially open air shutter.	■ ■		$20

(Continued on next page)

PROBLEM: Cooktop heats improperly; flame is wrong color or size. *(Continued from preceding page)* ■

Possible Cause	Procedure	Remedy	Rating	Parts	Labor
Flame is high off burner and makes roaring sound.	Flame is getting too much air.	Partially close air shutter.	■ ■		$20

PROBLEM: Flame is excessively sooty.

Possible Cause	Procedure	Remedy	Rating	Parts	Labor
Air shutter adjustment faulty.	Check adjustment.	Open air shutter slightly.	■ ■		$20
Air passages blocked.	Check for blockage.	Clean with toothpick.	■ ■		$20

GAS OVEN TROUBLESHOOTING

PROBLEM: Gas oven does not operate.

Possible Cause	Procedure	Remedy	Rating	Parts	Labor
Gas supply to house shut off.	Check other gas appliances.	Contact utility company.	■		$20
Pilot light extinguished.	Check duct for blockage.	Clean with fine wire or toothpick. Relight.	■ ■		$20
	If electric, check plug and wires.	Repair.	■ ■ ■		$20

PROBLEM: Moisture condenses in oven or around vent.

Possible Cause	Procedure	Remedy	Rating	Parts	Labor
Door not properly adjusted.	Check.	Realign.	■ ■		$25
Vent blocked.	Check.	Remove obstruction.	■ ■		$20
Vent seal faulty.	Remove trim around vent and inspect.	Repair or replace.	■ ■	$3	$20

PROBLEM: Oven door does not stay shut.

(See same category under electric oven.)

PROBLEM: Gas oven do not turn off on automatic.

Possible Cause	Procedure	Remedy	Rating	Parts	Labor
Timer defective.	Check circuit continuity.	Replace.	■ ■ ■	$35-50	$25

Microwave Ovens

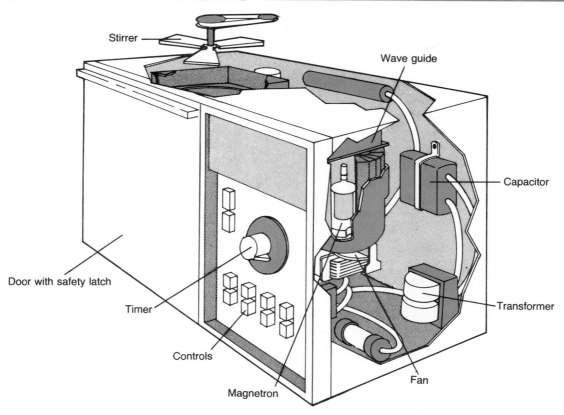

Stirrer

Wave guide

Capacitor

Door with safety latch

Timer

Controls

Magnetron

Fan

Transformer

Principle of Operation

A microwave oven cooks food with ultra-high frequency radio waves (radar). The radar waves oscillate at a rate of nearly five billion times per second. When these waves pass through moist substances, such as uncooked food, the food molecules align with the radar waves and oscillate at the same rate. Friction from the oscillating food molecules generates heat, and the food cooks.

The radar waves in a microwave oven are produced by an electronic component called a magnetron. The waves are tunneled through a wave guide into the oven area. Here they bounce off a slow-turning fan-like device called a stirrer. The stirrer and the inside surfaces of the oven are both made of reflective metal. Radar waves bounce off these reflective surfaces in a random pattern and come into contact with all surface areas of the food.

A small fan located near the magnetron cools the electronic components and also vents some of the steam and vapors produced in the oven.

A timer (*see page 56*) controls the cooking cycle. The oven will not cook, however, unless the safety interlock door latch is closed. There may be one or more additional safety switches to prevent accidental exposure to radiation.

How to Reach Interior Components

Because of the extreme hazard to life and health represented by radiation exposure, it is strongly advised that a microwave oven not be disassembled by the homeowner. The chassis of many models are sealed to prevent tampering.

> **NOTE:** Federal law states specifically that only qualified personnel may work on the microwave generating section of a microwave oven. For a copy of these regulations, write to Department of Health, Education, and Welfare, Rockland, Maryland, 20852.

Maintenance and Repair

Little except routine cleaning can be done to repair or maintain a microwave oven, without removing the housing for access to electrical parts. On some models, however, the door can be adjusted or removed by unscrewing the retaining screws that hold it to its hinges. Adjust the door if it does not close properly. Replace the door if arcing has damaged the door gasket, or if the door is warped or damaged. Be careful when removing the door hinges not to lose small hinge parts.

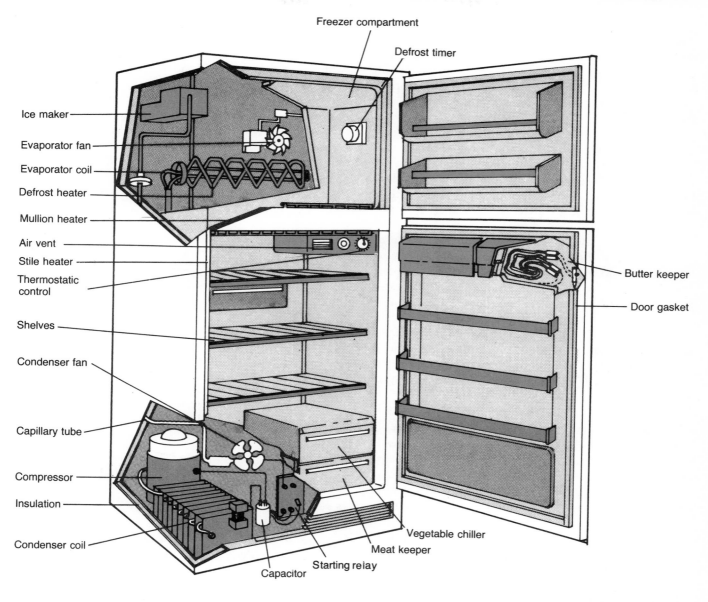

Freezer compartment

Defrost timer

Ice maker

Evaporator fan

Evaporator coil

Defrost heater

Mullion heater

Air vent

Stile heater

Thermostatic control

Shelves

Condenser fan

Capillary tube

Compressor

Insulation

Condenser coil

Capacitor

Starting relay

Meat keeper

Vegetable chiller

Butter keeper

Door gasket

Principle of Operation

A refrigerator or freezer cools much like an air conditioner, using a compressor and a refrigerant-circulating system (*see page 196*). Refrigerant circulates through a coil of tubing (the evaporator) inside the refrigerator or freezer. The refrigerant absorbs heat through the walls of the evaporator and then is pumped to another coil of tubing (the condenser) outside the cold compartment. Heat dissipates through the walls of the condenser coil into the room

air. Having lost its heat, the refrigerant is now cold again and recirculates to the evaporator inside the cold compartment.

The pump that forces the refrigerant through this cycle is called a compressor. The compressor is powered by a capacitor-start motor (*see page 62*). Like all capacitor-start motors, it contains a starting winding and a running winding. It requires a starting relay (*see page 59*) to shut off power to the starting winding once the motor approaches running speed. Refrigerator motors also have a thermal relay or some other overload protector (*see page 63*) wired into their circuit and mounted on the motor case.

The compressor motor is turned on and off by an adjustable gas-containing thermostat (*see page 57*). The thermostat adjustment is the cold control in the refrigerator compartment. The thermostat's capillary tube extends from the cold control into the vicinity of the evaporator coil, which may be located at the top of the compartment, in the back, or in the walls of the freezer section.

Sandwiched between the double walls of the refrigerator or freezer, insulation keeps the cold inside and the warmth outside. A flexible plastic gasket around the door helps to insulate. This gasket may, in addition, function as a door latch: It may be filled either with iron filings that are attracted to a magnet in the door frame or with a magnetized bar.

Refrigerators also contain small heaters to limit condensation in two areas where it is most likely to occur, around the door sill and in the panel between the refrigerator and freezer compartments. These heaters are respectively, called, the stile heater and the mullion heater. The stile heater may be either a loop of the warm condenser coil (containing refrigerant), or a small electric heater made of resistance wire (*see page 54*). The mullion heater is always a resistance-wire electric heater. In the basic refrigerator, these two heaters cannot be turned off.

Differences in Refrigerators and Freezers

Self-defrosting refrigerators require several components not found in other refrigerators. The defrosting device is a heating element made of resistance wire (*see page 54*) located on or near the evaporator coil. At a predetermined frequency (such as every eight or twelve hours), the compressor shuts off and the heating element turns on to melt the frost that has collected on the evaporator coil. A timer (*see page 56*) switches these components off and on. A defrost-limit control—a thermodisc (*see page 57*) mounted near the heating element—switches the heating element off and the compressor back on when the temperature of the evaporator has risen sufficiently to have melted the frost.

Another heating element may be located in the condensate drain below the evaporator coil; it prevents the condensation from freezing in the drain. As the frost melts, it drips to a collector pan and then through a tube or passage way to a collection pan, located beneath the refrigerator near the warm condenser coils and the compressor. A fan may blow over this pan and the condenser coil to hasten the evaporation and to help cool the refrigerant in the condenser.

In addition, self-defrosting refrigerators (and some others) contain a fan and an air-duct system in the cold compartment, near the evaporator coil. The fan circulates cold air through the freezer and refrigerator areas. A microswitch located in the door frame turns this fan off when the door is opened. A small sliding door in the rear of the refrigerator compartment controls the amount of cold air allowed into the refrigerator compartment and assists in temperature control.

Many newer models of refrigerator-freezers are available with a stile and mullion heater switch. This is a small slide or toggle switch (*see page 55*), usually located on the wall of the refrigerator compartment. By turning off the stile and mullion heaters (for example, during periods when the refrigerator door is not opened frequently), the owner can reduce energy use and cost.

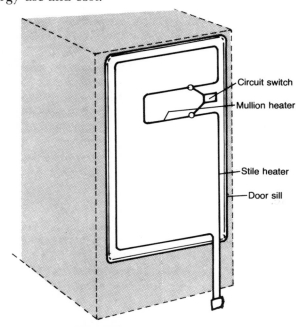

Stile and mullion heater circuit with control switch.

A butter warmer or cheese keeper is a compartment located in a section of the door where insulation is thinner than elsewhere. As a result, the temperature of this compartment tends to be a few degrees higher than that in other parts of the refrigerator. A butter warmer may also include a small heater in the walls of the compartment, with a switch controlling it.

Meat keepers, vegetable chillers, and other drawers in most refrigerators have no special warming or cooling equipment. Some meat keepers, however, have an adjustable air duct for directing cool air from the blower in the evaporator coil area. These meat keepers provide colder temperatures and a drier environment for the storage of meats.

Popular options on refrigerators also include the ice maker, the crushed ice dispenser, and the cold-water dispenser. All require a plumbing hookup from the cold water line in the home. This hookup can be made when the refrigerator is installed, or it can be done later with a kit available from the manufacturer or a plumbing supply house.

For a cold-water dispenser, water enters the refrigerator through a solenoid-controlled valve (*see page 59*) and is held in a storage tank. Pushing a level on the front of the refrigerator door to dispense water also opens the solenoid valve to allow more water to enter the storage tank. When the tank is filled, a float or other type of switch closes the solenoid valve.

An ice maker works in a similar manner. Water enters the freezer compartment through a solenoid valve and fills an ice cube tray. A timer (*see page 56*) measures the period of water flow and closes the solenoid when enough time has elapsed for the tray to have filled. When the ice cubes have frozen, the lowered temperature of the tray activates a thermodisc (*see page 57*), which turns on a heater. The heater loosens the ice cubes, and a motorized release mechanism dumps them into a storage bin. When the storage bin is full, a lever trips a switch to shut off the ice maker. A crushed ice dispenser has an additional motorized crushing device.

Refrigerator-freezer combinations are available in a wide variety of cabinet styles, the most common being top-and-bottom with the freezer on top, and side-by-side. Freezer designs are available in upright and chest models. Regardless of the cabinet style, all electric refrigerators and freezers cool in the same manner.

Maintenance and Repair

Door and Gasket. The door is made of two pieces of molded plastic or sheet metal—an inner and an outer shell. The gasket, which seals the door when it closes, is held in place by screws or clips. Pry up the edge of the gasket to reveal the fasteners.

If excessive condensation forms in the refrigerator or if a puddle of water collects underneath the refrigerator, the door may be warped or the gasket may need replacing. A dollar bill closed in the door should not pull out easily; if it does, there is too much gap. Remove the door from its hinges and lay it on a flat surface. If the door is warped, adjust the tightness of the screws holding the inner shell to the outer shell. If the gasket is worn, buy a manufacturer's replacement. Remove the old gasket a small section at a time and replace it with the same section from the new gasket. If the screws holding the gasket in place are not tightened uniformly, the door may warp.

Insulation. The insulation between the double walls of the door or cooling cabinet rarely needs service. Occasionally, however, condensation seeps into the insulation and freezes. A cold spot, marked by water droplets condensing on the surface during warm weather, may develop on the outside of the appliance. Such a cold spot might also be caused by a hole or thinness in the original insulation.

For access to the door insulation, first unplug the appliance, then take apart the door as described above. To gain access to cabinet insulation, remove the wall panels. Replace bad insulation and fill gaps with styrofoam panels or fiberglass.

Shelves. Shelves and the rollers that hold them occasionally corrode or break. Buy replacement parts from the manufacturer.

Collector Pan. The condensate collector pan is located beneath the appliance. It is a large, shallow container into which melted frost drains from the refrigerator. Clean this pan once a month with a bleach solution to prevent the growth of algae and other organisms that can cause an unpleasant odor and may lead to respiratory disease. Access is through a removable panel at the base of the refrigerator.

Thermostat (Cold Control). The adjustable thermostat turns the compressor on and off in response to changes of temperature in the refrigerator section. The thermostat is usually a capillary tube, gas-containing type (*see page 58*). A refrigerator that stays too warm or too cool may have a faulty thermostat. See if the device can be recalibrated. Remove the dial; the calibration screw (if there is one) is in the center of the control shaft.

The thermostat can be removed for further testing by a refrigeration shop. Screws hold the thermostat to the inner wall of the refrigerator. Be careful of the capillary tube. Damage to the capillary tube or the bellows is an expensive repair that cannot be done at home.

Timer. A timer (*see page 56*) is found in refrigerators having an automatic defrost cycle. The timer is operated by a small synchronous motor (*see page 62*). Its clock-like mechanism turns on the defrost heating element (and turns off the compressor) for a short period every several hours. On most models the timer is easily accessible; it may be located inside the refrigerator compartment, on the back of the refrigerator, or behind a kick panel in front of the machine in the condenser area. It is a sealed unit usually bolted in place; unbolt it and remove the wire plugs from the quick-connect terminals.

Failure of the timer will cause the automatic defrost mechanism to malfunction. The timer may stick in the cooling mode or in the defrost mode. The refrigerator may ice up or not cool properly.

To test the timer, mark a thin line with a felt pen along the shaft and housing. In a few hours, the shaft should have rotated and the line on the shaft moved. If so, the timer is turning properly. Then test each set of terminals for continuity with a multimeter (*see page*

26). Refrigerator timers are generally sealed and cannot be repaired; replace if defective.

Defrost Heater. The defrost heater is a resistance-wire circuit mounted on the evaporator coil. If it fails, the refrigerator will no longer defrost. Remove the wall panels in the freezer or refrigerator compartment for access to the heater and its wire leads. Test the heater for continuity with a multimeter (*see pages 26-28*). It should register between 5 and 20 ohms. Replace if it is defective.

Mullion Heater. The mullion heater is a small electric heater made of resistance wire (*see page 54*) and located behind the panel that separates the refrigerator and freezer compartments. Its purpose is to prevent excessive condensation in this area. Suspect that it has failed if there is unusual frost buildup in this area but the refrigerator otherwise operates normally.

For access to the mullion heater, remove the panel between the refrigerator and freezer compartments. With the refrigerator running and the mullion switch (if any) on, place your hand near the mullion heater to see if it gives off heat. If it does not, replace it. Make sure the refrigerator is unplugged before removing the heater from its circuit. The wires may be attached to screw terminals or quick-connect terminals (*see page 53*).

Stile Heater. The stile heater is located in the door frame. Like the mullion heater, its function is to prevent a buildup of frost. Suspect malfunction if frost or condensation collects in this area.

Electrical stile heaters are serviced exactly as mullion heaters.

Mullion and Stile Switch. Many current refrigerator models include an energy-saving toggle or slide switch (*see page 55*) to turn the mullion and stile heaters off. The switch is usually located on the wall of the refrigerator compartment.

If this switch fails mechanically, it will move with difficulty or not at all. Electrical failure of the switch may not be noticed if it jams in an On position, because the heaters will continue to heat constantly as they do in a basic refrigerator. If it jams in an Off position, excessive frost or condensation may form on the panel between the refrigerator and freezer compartments and around the door.

To test the switch, first clean the terminals with fine sandpaper or liquid contact cleaner. Then check it for continuity (*see pages 26-28*). If it is defective, replace it with a manufacturer's part.

Fans. The small blower in a self-defrosting refrigerator (and some others) distributes cold air evenly. If it fails, the freezer compartment may become colder than necessary and the refrigerator compartment too warm. The evaporator coils may ice up excessively.

This fan is controlled by a microswitch (*see page 56*) in the door frame; when the door is opened, the fan shuts off. To test whether the fan is working, push the microswitch button all the way in. If the refrigerator is not in its defrost cycle, the fan should start up. If it does not start up, wait two hours (the defrost cycle will have ended) and perform the test again.

If the fan has stopped or is not turning normally, lubricate the bearings of the small shaded-pole motor (*see pages 62-63*), and tighten the setscrews, if any, that hold the fan blade unit in place. If the fan still does not work properly after the wire leads are refastened, check the motor and the wiring to it for continuity (*see pages 26-27*). Replace any deteriorated wires. Replace the fan unit if it is defective.

In some refrigerators, a fan blows over the condenser coil and the collector pan. This fan helps to cool the refrigerant in the condenser and also to evaporate the water in the collector pan. It is usually bolted to the chassis and can be removed. Its wires are typically attached to quick-connect terminals. If this fan fails, the refrigerator may not cool as well as it should, and water may spill on the floor beneath the refrigerator. The fan may be a split-phase or capacitor-start type (*see page 62*). Maintenance and repair procedures are the same as for the fan in a dehumidifier (*see page 217*) or an air conditioner (*see page 200*).

Compressor. The compressor circulates refrigerant through the evaporator and condenser coils. If it fails, the refrigerator will not cool properly. The compressor is powered by a capacitor-start motor. Testing procedures are the same as for a compressor in an air conditioner (*see page 199*) or dehumidifier (*see page 216*). If a refrigerant leak develops, or if the

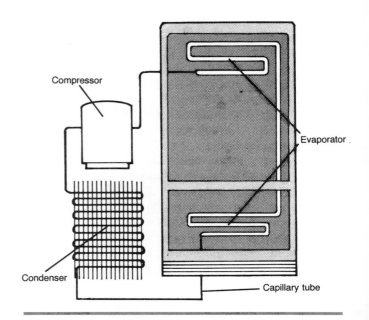

Refrigerant-circulating system

motor fails, the refrigerator will have to be serviced by a refrigeration specialist. However, compressor failure may also be due to the starting relay, overload protector, or capacitor in the motor's starting winding circuit. See the sections on air conditioner and dehumidifier.

Condenser and Evaporator Coils. The evaporator coil (located in the cold compartment) and the condenser coil (located beneath or in back of the refrigerator) are parts of the sealed refrigeration system. If a leak develops, the refrigerator will not cool properly and the coils may ice up. Call a refrigeration specialist.

Butter Keeper. If the butter or cheese keeper fails to warm properly, the problem may be in either the switch or the heating element. Clean the contacts and terminals of the switch with fine sandpaper or liquid contact cleaner, and test it for continuity (*see pages 26-28*) with a multimeter set at the Rx1 mode. The meter should register between 5 and 20 ohms. Also measure the resistance of the heating element; replace whichever component has failed.

Wiring Harness. The wiring harness (*see page 53*) carries the internal wires and is usually attached to frame members. It is not normally a source of malfunction. In some models, however, the harness runs through a door hinge in order to service heating elements, lights, or other electrical components in the door. The frequent flexing of the harness in the hinge may eventually cause the insulation to wear and a wire to short circuit (*see page 16*). Symptoms vary: an electrical component in the refrigerator may not work, the refrigerator may frequently blow a fuse or trip a circuit breaker, or the user may get a shock from the refrigerator.

 WARNING: Short circuits are very dangerous. If there is evidence of one, unplug the appliance immediately and do not use it again until the problem has been found and corrected.

If a short circuit occurs in the wiring harness, gain access to the harness by removing the door panels or wall panels. Check each wire for continuity (*see pages 26-28*) to determine which one has short circuited.

How to Reach Interior Components

Door: To reach wall panels and door panel

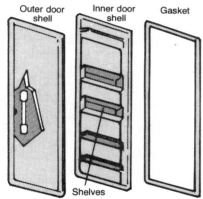

Outer door shell   Inner door shell   Gasket

Shelves

First, unplug the refrigerator or freezer; empty the door shelves. Then remove the door by unbolting the hinges. In some models, only one hinge needs to be removed and the door can be lifted away. Note also that some models have electrical connectors running from cabinet to door through one of the hinges; disconnect.

Wall panels: To reach insulation, wiring harness, fans, heaters

Pull out refrigerator shelves and drawers. (The shelves in a freezer may house the evaporator coil; if so, the pattern of the coil is visible on the surface of the shelves. Do not attempt to remove these shelves.)

Wall panels may be either snap-in devices made of flexible plastic, which can be pried out with a screw-

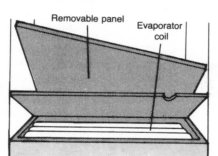

Removable panel   Evaporator coil

driver, or they may be held in place by retaining screws. If a dial switch protrudes from a wall, remove the knob (*see page 52*) before attempting to remove the panel.

Rear access panel: To reach compressor, starting relay, overload protector, capacitor

The compressor and related electrical components are usually located below the cooling compartment. Frequently, access is limited from the front of the appliance. Pull the refrigerator or freezer away from the wall and remove the rear access panel. If there is none, tip the unit on its side to gain access to the compressor area.

The compressor, the evaporator coil, and the condenser coil comprise a sealed, self-enclosed refrig-

eration unit. These parts cannot be removed, so if the cooling system is damaged, the appliance has to be serviced professionally. A starting relay (*see page 59*), an overload protector (*see page 55*), and a capacitor (*see page 62*) are wired into the compressor unit. They are bolted to the compressor or to the chassis and can be unbolted for testing. They may be soldered into the circuit or attached with screw terminals or quick-connect terminals (*see page 53*). To remove soldered connections, heat the old solder with a soldering iron. Screw attachments can simply be unscrewed, but be careful with quick-connect terminals. If the terminals on a compressor are damaged, it is sometimes necessary to replace the entire compressor. Therefore, if there is danger of breaking these terminals, it is better to cut the wires and attach them again later with wire nuts (*see page 24*).

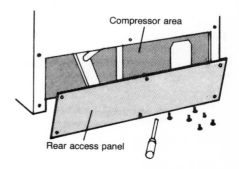

Compressor area

Rear access panel

Repair the wire and reinsulate it by wrapping electrical tape around it, or replace the wire. Test the circuit for continuity again to be certain the problem has been corrected.

Ice Maker or Cold Water Dispenser. If the ice maker or water dispenser fails to work, check the water lines for blockage. Probe with a toothpick or a straightened paper clip, but be careful not to puncture the plastic hosing. These accessories are self-contained units that are factory calibrated. In most models, electrical repairs cannot be made by the homeowner. Remove a defective unit by unscrewing the retaining screws and disconnecting the wires. Take it to a plumbing supply house for an exact replacement.

Interior Light. The interior light, like the fan in a self-defrost model, is controlled by the microswitch in the door frame. The light comes on (and the fan goes off) when the door is opened. If the light fails, replace it with one designed especially for refrigerator use. If the socket becomes damaged, unplug the refrigerator and remove the wall panel for access to the socket. Replace it with a manufacturer's part. Check the wir-

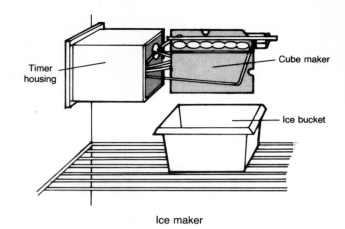

Ice maker

ing to the light and the switch for continuity (*see pages 26-28*).

Door Switch. If both the light and fan do not work, the microswitch located in the door frame should be tested for continuity (*see pages 26-28*). Note, however, that if the light or fan does not work, the problem could be in those components or in the circuit wiring. Replace a defective switch with a manufacturer's part.

REFRIGERATOR/FREEZER TROUBLESHOOTING

PROBLEM: Refrigerator/freezer does not operate.

Possible Cause	Procedure	Remedy	Rating	Parts	Labor
No power at outlet.	Check fuse or circuit breaker.	Replace fuse or reset circuit breaker.	■		$20
Plug disconnected.	Check.	Reseat plug in outlet.	■		$20
Cord defective.	Check for breaks.	Repair or replace.	■ ■	$5	$20
Condenser fan (self-defrost models) blocked or defective.	Inspect for clogging, check circuit continuity of motor.	Clean blockage. Replace faulty motor.	■ ■ ■ ■	$25	$25
Thermostat faulty.	Test circuit continuity.	Replace.	■ ■ ■	$20-35	$25
Compressor relay faulty.	Check contacts, test circuit continuity.	Replace.	■ ■ ■		
Compressor overload switch defective.	Check contacts, test circuit continuity.	Replace.	■ ■ ■		
Timer defective.	Check circuit continuity.	Replace.	■ ■ ■	$20-30	$25

PROBLEM: Refrigerator/freezer blows fuse or trips circuit breaker.

Possible Cause	Procedure	Remedy	Rating	Parts	Labor
Circuit overloaded.	Put refrigerator on its own circuit.	Replace fuse or reset circuit breaker.	■		$20
Cord or plug short-circuited.	Inspect for breaks.	Repair or replace.	■ ■	$5	$20

(Continued on next page)

PROBLEM: Refrigerator/freezer shocks user.

Possible Cause	Procedure	Remedy	Rating	Parts	Labor
Cord frayed.	Inspect for breaks.	Repair or replace.	■ ■	$5	$20
Case short-circuited.	Test circuit continuity.	Repair.	■ ■ ■ ■		$30

PROBLEM: Refrigerator/freezer does not cool properly.

Possible Cause	Procedure	Remedy	Rating	Parts	Labor
Unit on incorrect setting.	Check.	Reset.	■		$20
Excessive frost buildup on evaporator coil.	Defrost manually.	Defrost more frequently.	■		$20
Light bulb stays on after door is closed, heating unit.	Check by depressing button on door frame.	Replace switch.	■ ■ ■	$6	$20
Door needs realignment.	Inspect. Door should line up with cabinet.	Loosen screws in door frame, twist to realign, retighten screws.	■ ■		$20
Door gasket worn.	Close door on sheet of paper. Tugging should be required to remove it.	Replace gasket.	■ ■ ■	$20-35	$30
Condenser coils clogged.	Inspect.	Clean with soft brush or vacuum.	■ ■		$20
Condenser fan blocked or defective.	Inspect for blockage. Check circuit continuity of motor.	Clean. Replace faulty fan motor.	■ ■ ■ ■		
Evaporator fan defective.	Check circuit continuity.	Replace.	■ ■ ■	$15-25	$25
Defrost heater or heater timer (self-defrost models) faulty.	Test circuit continuity.	Replace either part if faulty.	■ ■ ■	$20-30	$25
Freezer overloaded with unfrozen food.	Add no more than 10 percent of freezer capacity at a time.	Give food a chance to freeze before adding more.	■		$20
Refrigerant leaking.		Consult authorized service personnel.	■ ■ ■ ■ ■	$35	$35
Location of unit too near source of heat	Move unit away from radiator, stove or oven.		■ ■		

PROBLEM: Refrigerator/freezer motor cycles on and off too frequently.

Possible Cause	Procedure	Remedy	Rating	Parts	Labor
Air circulation over compressor blocked.	Inspect.	Clean coil and surrounding area with stiff brush or vacuum.	■ ■		$20
Compressor relay defective.	Test circuit continuity.	Replace.	■ ■ ■	$8	$20

PROBLEM: Refrigerator/freezer motor operates continuously or nearly so.

Possible Cause	Procedure	Remedy	Rating	Parts	Labor
Door gasket worn.	Close door on sheet of paper. Tugging should be required to remove it.	Replace if necessary.	■ ■ ■	$20-35	$30

(Continued on next page)

REFRIGERATOR/FREEZER TROUBLESHOOTING *(Continued)*

PROBLEM: Refrigerator/freezer motor operates continuously or nearly so.

Possible Cause	Procedure	Remedy	Rating	Parts	Labor
Thermostat sensor bulb loose or defective.	Check bulb near evaporator coil.	Tighten or replace.	■ ■ ■	$20-35	$25
Condenser coils clogged.	Inspect.	Clean with soft brush or vacuum.	■ ■		$20
Unit on incorrect setting.	Check.	Reset.	■		$20
Refrigerant leaking.		Consult authorized service personnel.	■ ■ ■ ■ ■	$35	$35

PROBLEM: Refrigerator/freezer does not defrost properly.

Possible Cause	Procedure	Remedy	Rating	Parts	Labor
Door faulty.	Inspect both doors. Each one should line up with side of cabinet.	Gently twist to realign or tighten screws in hinges.	■ ■		$20
Door gasket worn.	Close door on sheet of paper. Tugging should be required to remove it.	Replace if necessary.	■ ■ ■	$20-35	$30
Freezer drain blocked.	Probe drain hole with stiff wire.		■ ■		$20
Defrost timer faulty.	Check circuit continuity.	Replace.	■ ■ ■	$20-30	$25
Defrost heater faulty.	Check circuit continuity.	Replace.	■ ■ ■	$20-30	$25

PROBLEM: Moisture condenses on or in refrigerator/freezer.

Possible Cause	Procedure	Remedy	Rating	Parts	Labor
Door gasket worn.	Close door on sheet of paper. Tugging should be required to remove it.	Replace if necessary.	■ ■ ■	$20-35	$30
Thermostat set too cold.	Reset.	Be sure dial does not get bumped accidentally.	■		$20
Doors opened too frequently.		Reduce time doors are open.	■		$20

PROBLEM: Refrigerator/freezer leaks water.

Possible Cause	Procedure	Remedy	Rating	Parts	Labor
Drains clogged.	Probe all drain holes with stiff wire.		■ ■		$20
Drain hose leaking.	Inspect hose for cracks or breaks.	Replace.	■ ■	$3	$20

PROBLEM: Refrigerator/freezer is excessively noisy.

Possible Cause	Procedure	Remedy	Rating	Parts	Labor
Unit not level.	Check with carpenter's level.	Level machine front to back and side to side.	■ ■		$20
Drain pan vibrating.	Check.	Reposition firmly.	■ ■		$20
Condenser or evaporator fan blades binding.	Check for free motion.	Clean and clear.	■ ■ ■		$20

Sewing Machines

Bobbin winder tension bracket and thread guide

Sewing light

Stitch width selector

Spool pin and felt

Bobbin winder spindle

Bobbin winder stop

Pressure regulating dial

Bobbin winder lever

Take-up lever

Stop-motion screw

Hand wheel

Needle thread tension regulator

Stitch length selector

Needle position selector

Electric motor

Feed regulating knob

Plug

Presser foot

Slide plate

Feed dog

Needle clamp

Electrical speed controller

Principle of Operation

Sewing machines have basically the same mechanical components. These include a takeup lever, needle, feed dog and shuttle (hook), and are operated by a step-on or a carbon-controlled foot pedal or knee lever connected to a universal motor.

When the control pedal or lever is depressed, the motor rotates a gear chain which raises and lowers the needle through the material being sewn and activates the bobbin assembly. Every sewing machine forms a lockstitch by using two threads: One comes from a spool on top of the machine via the needle and is wrapped around a second thread coming from a bobbin located under the needle plate.

In actual operation, the free end of the needle thread is held in one hand and the hand wheel is rotated until the takeup lever is in its top position. The lower bobbin thread is now pulled diagonally across the feed and the material to be sewn is positioned under the needle. The hand wheel is again rotated to bring the point of the needle down to the material for the beginning stitch. The presser foot is then lowered to hold the material snugly against the needle plate. As the control pedal is depressed, the needle carries its thread downward to the shuttle assembly. At the same time, the takeup lever measures out the exact amount of needle thread needed to encircle the bobbin case. The measured amount of thread is controlled by tension disks that the thread passes through on its way from the spool to the take-up lever, so that only the proper amount of thread is allowed to come off the spool.

As the gear chain continues to turn, the needle begins its ascent, leaving a loop of thread which a hook or a shuttle point picks up and passes around the bobbin thread. The takeup lever immediately withdraws any excess needle thread used to go around the bobbin case.

As the needle continues upward, the thread takeup spring mounted on the tension unit takes up any slack in the needle thread and tightens it to form the stitch. By this time, the needle is returned to its topmost position and is ready to repeat the stitching cycle.

Differences in Sewing Machines

While modern sewing machines are mechanically the same as older units, the newer models offer numerous attachments that broaden their stitching capabilities. Some machines now incorporate solid state circuitry, which simplifies the operation of changing stitches to pressing a button. The attachments that either come with various machines or can be purchased separately include different sized needles for different types of fabric and a twin needle which permits a double row of parallel stitches. Special presser feet and needle plates can be used for straight or zig-zag stitching, stitching edges, or delicate fabrics. Other special-purpose presser feet include a *darning and embroidery foot* to permit free-motion stitching such as embroidery, darning, and monogramming; a *two-step buttonhole foot* that stitches any length of buttonhole; an *overedge foot* used for edges or stretch fabrics; a *button foot* that holds a button securely while it is being stitched; a *zipper foot* for zippers and corded seams; a *blindstitch hem guide* which positions material for blindstitch hemming; a *chainstitch bobbin case insert* and *chainstitch plate* for chainstitching; and a *seam guide* for keeping seam allowances even.

Aside from the accessories available for different models the only major mechanical differences are in the bobbin assembly. Some models use an oscillating hook which allows the bobbin case to remain stationary while the hook takes the needle thread loop, enlarges it, and passes it around the bobbin case. Alternatively, there may be an oscillating shuttle which has a point on its end that collects the needle thread loop and brings it around the bobbin case by making slightly more than half a turn. It then releases the thread, and the takeup lever draws the thread tight. A third type of mechanism is the rotary hook. With this arrangement, the bobbin remains stationary while the rotating hook carries the thread completely around the case before releasing it. The rotary hook can be positioned either horizontally or vertically.

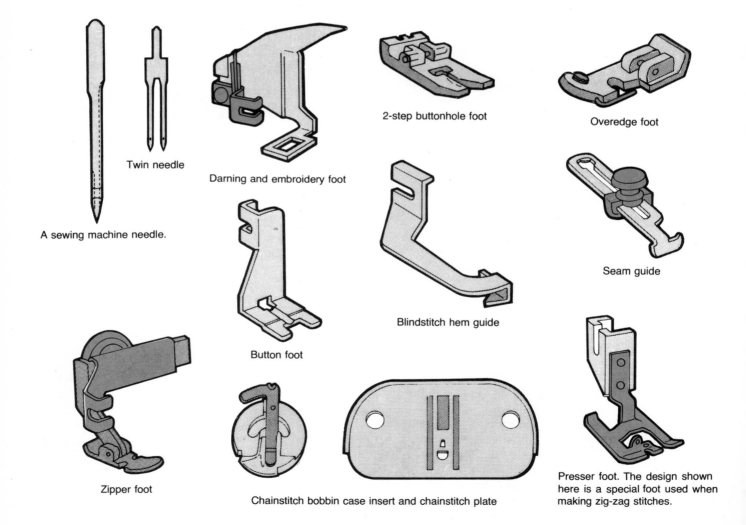

Twin needle

A sewing machine needle.

Darning and embroidery foot

2-step buttonhole foot

Overedge foot

Button foot

Blindstitch hem guide

Seam guide

Zipper foot

Chainstitch bobbin case insert and chainstitch plate

Presser foot. The design shown here is a special foot used when making zig-zag stitches.

Maintenance and Repair

Seventy-five percent of all sewing machine malfunctions are the direct result of owner misuse, since the user must complete as many as ten or fifteen relatively intricate procedures before the machine can be operated properly. When there is a malfunction, the first step is to repeat carefully all of the preparation steps. Only after all the user procedures have been verified should the machine be examined for mechanical failure.

Takeup Lever. The takeup lever raises the thread after a stitch is formed and, in doing so, it locks the upper and bobbin threads into a knot. At the same time it also pulls enough thread from the upper thread spool for the following stitch. The lever is connected to the takeup cam so that its action corresponds precisely with the downward stroke of the needle and the action of the feed dog. If the lever is bent, it will cause thread breakage, skipped and uneven stitching, and possibly needle breakage. Examine the lever's action closely! The lever must be past its lowest position and starting upward at the moment the needle bar reaches its highest position. If the lever is not doing this, it is probably bent forward or backward and is almost impossible to straighten properly; replace the lever. It is possible to straighten a lever that is bent sideways and rubbing against the faceplate, but do this with great caution. The balance and alignment of the part are critical to the entire operation of the machine.

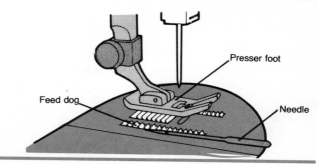

The feed dog and presser foot touch at all points. When the feed dog is in its raised position it should be no higher above the feed cover plate than the thickness of a needle.

Presser Foot. The presser foot holds the material firmly down on the feed dog. In order to do its job, the sides of the foot must be parallel with the slots in the needle plate and resting level against the top of the feed dog. If it is not level, the material will feed past the needle at an angle. To be certain the presser foot is making proper contact with the feed dog, sight along the bottom edge of the foot and observe its alignment with the feed dog. If the two parts do not touch at all points, disassemble the faceplate of the machine to get at the presser foot adjustment screw. Loosen the screw and realign the foot by moving the bar forward or sideways and then retightening the screw.

Feed Dog. The feed dog is a U-shaped part with two rows of saw-toothed edges which rise and fall through slots in the needle plate. The dog on most machines

How to Reach Interior Components

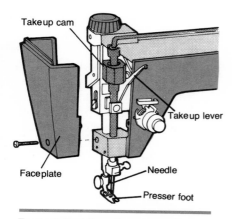

To reach the takeup lever assembly, undo the face plate screw and remove the face plate.

Faceplate: To reach assemblies for pressure dial, takeup lever, presser foot lifter, thread guides, tension disks
Undo the faceplate screw and re-

move the faceplate. Most mechanical failures that can be fixed at home can be done without further disassembling of the upper mechanism. Only occasionally is it necessary to remove the lid or the sides (front plate, back plate) of the machine.

Lid: To reach gears and cams
Remove the retaining screws in the top of the machine and lift the lid off the housing. Some tension disks and stitch selector assemblies may be reached through the top of the machine but most problems with gears and cams should be handled by specialists. If the machine is controlled by solid state circuitry, this system definitely should not be touched.

Slide plate: To reach needle plate, bobbin, bobbin assembly, feed dog
Push or pull the slide plate out of its

position to reveal the bobbin assembly. If necessary, remove presser foot and needle and pry up needle plate to gain clearer access to bobbin assembly and feed dog.

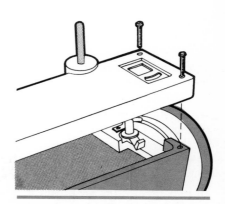

Undo the lid retaining screws and lift the top of the machine.

Oscillating hook

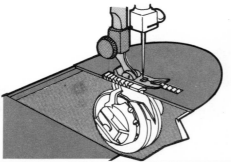

Rotary hook (horizontal)

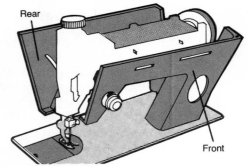

Undo all retaining screws in the sides of the machine and pull the side housings off.

has several raised positions that are manually selected by the user, depending on the thickness of the material being sewn. It must, however, be able to move freely through the slots in the needle plate; if it is bent out of line, it will cause friction and cause the motor to labor. The teeth on a feed dog can become worn and the part must then be replaced. Remove the needle, presser foot, and needle plate, then free the screws holding the feed dog in position. Lift the feed dog out of the machine and put in a new one.

Bobbin Assembly. The bobbin is a small metal spool which resides in a case underneath the needle plate. The case may be positioned either vertically or horizontally and is held in position by a cover which fits over the shuttle, or hook, allowing it to rotate. Exactly how the bobbin assembly is dismantled varies with each model; check the user's manual for specific instructions.

When the machine is making a lockstitch, the upper thread comes from a spool at the top of the machine and is threaded through an eye in the needle point. The lower thread comes from the bobbin. When the needle penetrates the material being sewn, the shuttle hooks the upper thread and wraps it clockwise over the bobbin and around the bobbin thread. As the needle rises out of the fabric, it carries the threads upward and tightens them into a knot against the fabric. Thread can become tangled in the bobbin case if the tension on the upper thread is not enough. If there is too much tension, the threads will break. Tension for the upper thread is controlled by a knob or dial on the front of the machine. On most models, turning the upper thread tension knob clockwise will increase tension on the thread; turning counterclockwise eases tension. The tension on the bobbin is set by the manufacturer and should not have to be changed. The tension can be altered, however, usually by turning a screw on the bobbin case.

Should thread become snarled in or around the bobbin case, remove the needle, presser foot, and slide plate and pry or push the needle plate out of its position. After removing all of the tangled thread, clean the area of any lint or dirt and replace the parts.

When winding thread on the bobbin, be certain that the thread is uniformly wound and does not fill only one side of the spool. If the bobbin is winding poorly, it is probably because the bobbin thread pre-tension guide is not aligned properly. Turn the screw on the pre-tension guide and move it up or down until the thread winds properly.

Motor. Most sewing machines incorporate a universal motor which is controlled by a foot pedal. See page 63 for repair and maintenance information concerning universal motors.

Cord and Plug. As a first check when anything appears to be wrong with the motor, examine the condition of the cord set and its connections at the foot pedal switch and the motor to be sure none of them are loose and no wires are broken. See page 52 for information concerning the testing, repair, and replacement of cords and their plugs.

Foot Pedal. The design of foot pedal or knee lever switches differs with almost every model on the market. Essentially the control unit consists of a switch which is connected to the power cord and also the motor. In many recent models, the switch is solid state circuitry. There is no way of repairing a solid state machine if it fails; the circuitry can only be replaced. Solid state machines are currently sold with a thirty-year plus guarantee and the machine must be returned to its manufacturer for replacement of the control, at no charge to the owner. If the control unit is not solid state, it can be tested and repaired as described on page 56.

Needles. Any needle used in a sewing machine should be absolutely straight and small enough in diameter to prevent the fabric from getting large puncture holes; it must also be heavy enough to pierce the material without bending or being deflected, and its eye should be large enough for the thread to slide freely through it. When changing needles, first raise the needle to its highest position by turning the hand wheel; then loosen the needle clamp screw. Pull the needle out of the clamp. Insert the new needle as far as it will go, with its flat side facing the back of the machine; then tighten the clamp screw.

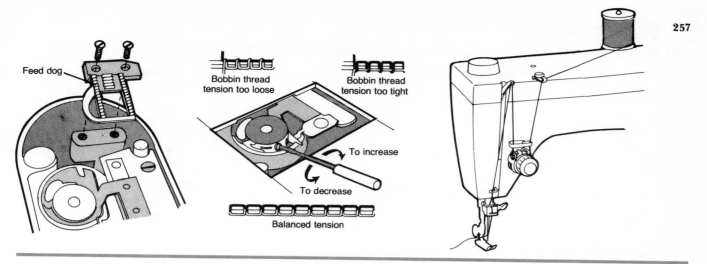

The feed dog is held in position by setscrews.

Tension in the bobbin can be changed by rotating a screw on the outside of its case.

The thread path may vary slightly from machine to machine.

Thread Path. The upper thread must travel from the spool at the top of the machine through thread guides, the presser foot, the needle, and the needle plate. All of these parts must be smooth, with no rough edges or burrs that might sever the thread. If the thread breaks continually, closely examine each of the parts it passes over. Any rough spots may be rubbed smooth with crocus cloth or extra fine emery cloth.

WARNING: Depending on how much a sewing machine is used, it should be periodically cleaned and lubricated. Lint and dust can be removed with a soft cloth or a small brush. Pay particular attention to such tiny areas as tension disks, the takeup lever, thread guides, presser foot, needle bar, and bobbin area.

Use only the lubrication oil recommended by the manufacturer. Place one drop of oil in the hole nearest each moving part and anywhere else designated by the user's manual.

SEWING MACHINE TROUBLESHOOTING

PROBLEM: Sewing machine does not start.

Possible Cause	Procedure	Remedy	Rating	Parts	Labor
No power at outlet.	Check fuse or circuit breaker.	Replace fuse or reset circuit breaker.	■		
Plugs disconnected.	Check.	Reseat plug in outlet and machine.	■		
Cords defective.	Check for breaks.	Replace.	■	$3	$7.50

PROBLEM: Sewing machine blows fuse or trips circuit breaker.

Possible Cause	Procedure	Remedy	Rating	Parts	Labor
Circuit overloaded.	Reduce number of appliances on circuit.	Replace fuse or reset circuit breaker.	■		
Cords or plugs short-circuited.	Inspect for breaks.	Repair or replace.	■ ■	$3	$7.50

PROBLEM: Sewing machine shocks user.

Possible Cause	Procedure	Remedy	Rating	Parts	Labor
Cords frayed.	Inspect for breaks.	Replace.	■ ■	$3	$7.50
Case short-circuited.	Test circuit continuity.	Repair.	■ ■	$1-3	$7.50
Wiring defective.	Inspect for bare wires.	Insulate.	■ ■	$1-3	$7.50

(Continued on next page)

PROBLEM: Sewing machine motor hums but machine does not operate.

Possible Cause	Procedure	Remedy	Rating	Parts	Labor
Hand wheel loose.	Tighten clutch with hand wheel.		■		
Machine set on bobbin winder.	Check.	Reset controls.	■		
Drive belt loose, worn, or broken.	Check.	Replace.	■	$1	$3.75
Lubrication needed.	Check owner's manual for oil points.	Follow instructions.	■ ■		
Brushes worn or stuck.	Unscrew caps in end bells.	Replace.	■ ■ ■		
Motor defective.	SEE ELECTRIC MOTOR TROUBLESHOOTING CHARTS—CHAPTER 4				
Bobbin thread bound.	Check.	Free, reset bobbin in case. Clean out lint.	■		

PROBLEM: Sewing machine operates only at one speed.

Possible Cause	Procedure	Remedy	Rating	Parts	Labor
Speed control short-circuited.	Check circuit continuity. Inspect for broken wires.	Replace unit or repair wires.	■ ■ ■	$3	$7.50

PROBLEM: Sewing machine only operates slowly.

Possible Cause	Procedure	Remedy	Rating	Parts	Labor
Hand wheel loose.	Tighten clutch with hand wheel.		■		
Controls improperly set.	Check all settings, including bobbin winder.	Reset.	■		
Tension disks clogged.	Clean disks regularly.	Switch to cotton-wrapped polyester thread instead of plain polyester, if possible.	■		
Lubrication needed.	Consult owner's manual for oil points.	Follow instructions.	■ ■		

PROBLEM: Needle breaks.

Possible Cause	Procedure	Remedy	Rating	Parts	Labor
Needle bent, loose, or incorrect size for thread or fabric.	Check owner's manual.	Firmly reset. Correct size needle for thread and fabric according to instructions.	■	$.65	
Needle plate faulty.	Check needle hole for rough edges, proper placement under needle, and type of work being done.	Reposition correctly, use proper plate for job or replace.	■ ■	$2-3.50	$4
Bobbin case improperly inserted.	Check.	Reposition.	■		
Operator forcing material through machine too fast.	Machine should feed material at proper speed.	Operator should only guide fabric.	■		
Presser foot loose.	Needle must not touch presser foot opening.	Tighten presser foot thumb screw.	■		
Cushion spring in rocker bent or broken.	Inspect.	Repair or replace.	■ ■	$1	$7.50
Feeder rocker shaft faulty.	Check for proper alignment.	Realign.	■ ■		$7.50

(Continued on next page)

SEWING MACHINE TROUBLESHOOTING (Continued from preceding page)

PROBLEM: Needle thread breaks.

Possible Cause	Procedure	Remedy	Rating	Parts	Labor
Thread faulty.	Check weight of thread for fabric being sewn. Check for correct threading procedure, identical thread in bobbin, proper tension.	Adjust.	■		
Needle defective.	Check for rough hole, bent needle, or loose clamp holding it in place.	Replace or reseat.	■	$.60	
Rough spots along thread guide or presser foot.	Check.	Smooth with fine sandpaper.	■ ■		
Feed dog clogged.	Remove needle plate.	Clean with small brush.	■ ■		

PROBLEM: Bobbin thread breaks.

Possible Cause	Procedure	Remedy	Rating	Parts	Labor
Needle plate faulty.	Check for rough edges.	Smooth edges or replace.	■ ■	$2-3.50	$4
Bobbin wound or inserted improperly.	Consult owner's manual.	Follow instructions.	■		
Bobbin tension too tight.	Ease tension on lower thread.		■		
Bobbin case or tension spring rough.	Check.	Smooth edges with fine sandpaper or replace.	■ ■		
Bobbin case dirty or damaged.	Remove needle plate.	Clean out all lint and broken threads.	■ ■		

PROBLEM: Bobbin cannot be wound, or thread goes on unevenly.

Possible Cause	Procedure	Remedy	Rating	Parts	Labor
Bobbin winder incorrectly threaded.	Check owner's manual.		■		
Bobbin tension spring faulty.	Check.	Replace.	■ ■	$.50	$3.75
Friction wheel worn.	Check.	Replace rubber rim or entire wheel.	■ ■ ■	$1	$7.50
Bobbin tension guide faulty.	Check pre-tension guide alignment.	Realign guide disks.	■ ■	$1	$7.50

PROBLEM: Thread loops or bunches in fabric.

Possible Cause	Procedure	Remedy	Rating	Parts	Labor
Improper thread used.	Check thread used in bobbin to make sure it matches top thread.	Threads must be identical type and weight as well as correctly chosen for fabric.	■		
Thread's path blocked by lint.	Inspect under needle plate.	Clean thoroughly with soft brush.	■ ■		
Bobbin incorrectly wound or seated in machine.	Check.	Rewind and reseat.	■		
Tension uneven or incorrect for fabric.	Adjust needle tension, then bobbin tension.		■		

(Continued on next page)

PROBLEM: Sewing machine skips stitches or does not stitch at all.

Possible Cause	Procedure	Remedy	Rating	Parts	Labor
Machine improperly threaded.	Check owner's manual.	Rethread machine.	■		
Needle defective, wrong for fabric, or improperly inserted in needle bar.	Check for proper size and condition. Check thread size against needle size.	Replace needle, clamp tightly.	■		
Upper tension spring faulty.	Check for wear or breakage.	Repair or replace.	■ ■	$4	$7.50

PROBLEM: Sewing machine produces stitches of uneven length.

Possible Cause	Procedure	Remedy	Rating	Parts	Labor
Operator is forcing fabric through machine	Guide material gently.	Machine should feed fabric at proper speed.	■		
Presser foot needs adjustment.	Consult owner's manual.		■		

PROBLEM: Fabric does not feed through machine or does not feed through evenly.

Possible Cause	Procedure	Remedy	Rating	Parts	Labor
Presser foot needs adjustment	Consult owner's manual for specific adjustments.	Always lower presser foot before adjusting pressure. Check alignment.	■		
Needle of improper size for fabric.	Check owner's manual.	Change needle.	■		
Bobbin thread tension improper.	Check for excess pull.	Loosen tension slightly.	■		
Stitch length adjustment needed.	Check dial.	Reset.	■		
Feed dog damaged, clogged or too high for fabric.	Check owner's manual for proper height for fabric; inspect for ragged teeth and lint clogs.	Adjust, smooth with fine sandpaper or clean.	■ ■	$2.50	$7.50
Needle plate rough.	Check for snagging.	Smooth out rough spots with fine sandpaper.	■ ■		

PROBLEM: Machine produces very loose stitches.

Possible Cause	Procedure	Remedy	Rating	Parts	Labor
Machine improperly threaded.	Rethread machine. Check for worn or broken guides, springs, etc.	Follow instructions in owner's manual. Select proper needle and thread. Replace all worn or broken parts.	■ ■ ■	$1	$7.50
Presser foot needs adjustment.	Check to make sure foot is lowered. Examine lift lever, screw holding foot to bar.	Tighten screw. Replace worn or broken parts.	■ ■ ■	$2.50	$7.50
Feed dog faulty.	Check for worn or broken teeth.	Replace unit.	■ ■		
Tension needs adjustment.	Check.	Adjust.	■	$5	$7.50

(Continued on next page)

SEWING MACHINE TROUBLESHOOTING (Continued from preceding page)

PROBLEM: Sewing machine does not zig-zag.

Possible Cause	Procedure	Remedy	Rating	Parts	Labor
Machine not on proper setting.	See owner's manual.	Follow instructions.	■		
Gear cam worn.	Check for worn or broken parts.	Replace.	■■■	$3	$15
Needle bar drive rod faulty.	Check for loose or broken parts.	Tighten or replace.	■■■	$5	$15
Vertical rock shaft faulty.	Inspect for wear or breakage.	Replace.	■■■	$5	$15

PROBLEM: Sewing machine motor operates hot.

Possible Cause	Procedure	Remedy	Rating	Parts	Labor
Drive belt binding.	Inspect. Consult owner's manual for adjustment.	Follow instructions.	■■		
Zig-zag assembly binding rocker shaft.	Consult owner's manual.	Follow instructions.	■■■	$4.50	$7.50
Main shaft bent.	Inspect.	Replace.	■■■■	$80-150	$45
Motor over-oiled.	Clean motor and re-oil.	Consult owner's manual for proper procedure.	■■		$7.50

PROBLEM: Sewing machine is excessively noisy.

Possible Cause	Procedure	Remedy	Rating	Parts	Labor
Lubrication needed.	Consult owner's manual for oil points.	Follow instructions.	■■		
Feed dog binding.	Check for contact with needle plate.	Adjust.	■■		
Wiring loose.	Check in case or cabinet.	Staple to case or cabinet.	■■		
Armature open or shorted.	Remove drive belt. If noise continues, check circuit continuity.	Replace armature.	■■■■■	$10	$15

PROBLEM: Sewing machine operates stiffly.

Possible Cause	Procedure	Remedy	Rating	Parts	Labor
Lubrication needed.	Consult owner's manual for oil points.	Follow instructions.	■■		
Machine lubricated with wrong oil.	Pour few drops of isopropyl alcohol in every oil hole. Operate for few minutes. Wipe off assemblies.	Clean and lubricate with proper oil.	■■		
Motor belt too tight.	Check.	Readjust at bracket.	■		
Main shaft bent.	Check.	Replace.	■■■■	$80-150	$45
Parts binding.	Check needle plate, feed dog, bobbin case, etc., for binding.	Tighten, repair or replace.	■■■	$5	$7.50

Trash Compactors

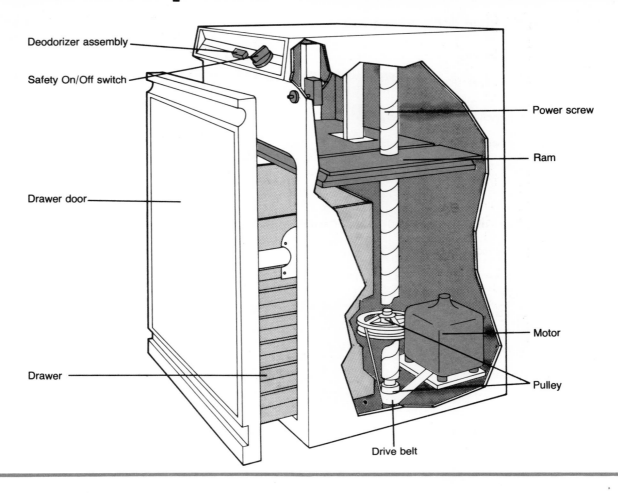

- Deodorizer assembly
- Safety On/Off switch
- Drawer door
- Drawer
- Power screw
- Ram
- Motor
- Pulley
- Drive belt

Principle of Operation

A trash compactor crushes waste paper, bottles, cans, and other dry garbage. Trash emerges from the appliance in a neat, wrapped package occupying about one quarter of its previous volume.

Inside the trash compactor, a ram rides up and down on two power screws. The ram is powered by a drive belt or chain attached by pulleys or sprockets to a large induction motor. This drive system lowers the ram with great force upon the trash in a container. As the ram bottoms out, a reversing switch is tripped and changes the direction of current through the motor. The motor reverses direction and raises the ram to its original position. At the top of the ram's travel, another reversing switch changes the direction of current to the motor once again (in preparation for the next cycle) and turns the motor off.

The compacting container rests on a pull-out drawer. A paper or plastic bag designed especially for the appliance fits in the container. When filled, the bag removes easily for disposal.

The drawer must be closed in order for the trash compactor to work. A safety interlock switch turns off the motor if the door opens accidentally during a running cycle. In many compactors, an additional safety switch must be closed before the On/Off switch will work.

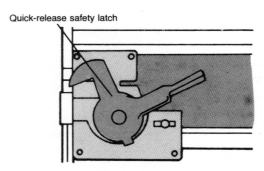

Quick-release safety latch

Trash compactors can be dangerous. Quick-release safety latch is one of many safety switches found on this appliance.

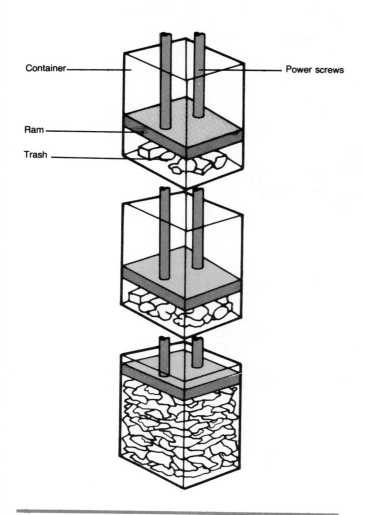

Container — Power screws

Ram

Trash

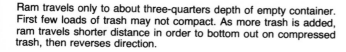

Ram travels only to about three-quarters depth of empty container. First few loads of trash may not compact. As more trash is added, ram travels shorter distance in order to bottom out on compressed trash, then reverses direction.

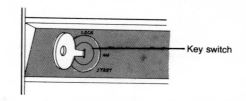

— Key switch

Many models include a key switch. Remove key to prevent accidental operation.

Differences in Trash Compactors

Various deodorizing methods are available on trash compactors. Some models use an aerosol system: As the compactor cycles, it presses the nozzle of an aerosol can. In other models, solid or liquid deodorizer is used.

Within the electrical circuitry, there are minor variations. Some models include a tilt switch to turn the compactor off if the load is uneven, or additional safety switches. The circuitry by which the motor reverses direction may vary from model to model. The motor may be a capacitor-start, split-phase, or repulsion-induction type. The ram and the ram cover may be removable for cleaning, as may the compacting container.

The drive system employs a chain or belt.

Maintenance and Repair

Ram. Remove the ram cover periodically for cleaning; replace it if worn. Follow instructions in owner's manual. If the ram itself becomes bent or damaged, remove it from the power screws and replace it.

Power Screws. In normal use, these should need no attention. If servicing other parts, clean the screws with a cloth and apply a thin film of new lithium grease or a similar lubricant. If the power screws become stripped, bent, or broken, replace them.

How to Reach Interior Components

Compactor Drawer

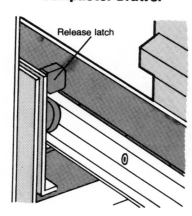

Release latch

To remove the compactor drawer, press the release latches located at the bottom front of the drawer or on the compactor housing, then pull out. The deodorizer holder may be fastened in place with screws or spring clips; remove them to clean or replace this compartment.

The switch console is located on the front of the unit. Remove the retaining screws holding the access panel in place. The switches are held to the chassis with screws. Before removing a switch, disconnect the wires attached to its quick-connect terminals (see page 53). Make a sketch of the colors of wires and the terminals each attaches to.

Control Panel: To reach On/Off switch, other controls

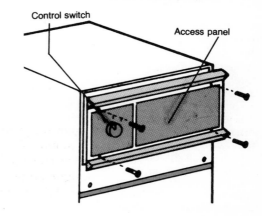

Control switch

Access panel

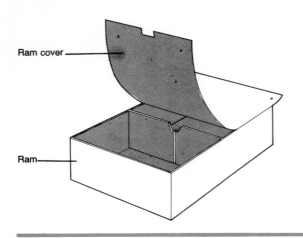

Remove ram cover to clean. Replace it when it works.

Drawer and Container. Clean regularly as instructed in owner's manual. If the container becomes damaged, obtain a replacement from the manufacturer.

Drive Chain. Periodically adjust the tightness of the chain by loosening the motor bolt and shifting the motor. The chain should fit snugly but have about one quarter inch slack between sprockets when pressed with a finger. If the chain will not tighten sufficiently, replace it. When replacing a chain, replace the sprockets as well.

Sprockets. If the appliance is equipped with a chain drive, replace the sprockets at the time the chain is replaced or if they show signs of wear such as bent or curved teeth.

Drive Belt. If the appliance is equipped with a drive belt, tighten it periodically as described under Drive Chain.

With a loose belt, the machine may not complete its cycle, or it may work slowly or sporadically. If the belt breaks, the appliance will not work. Replace the belt.

Pulleys. Pulleys on trash compactors equipped with a drive belt, rarely need service. If they do not turn freely, oil the bearings. If they are loose, tighten the setscrews or other fasteners holding them in place. If they become damaged, replace them.

Motor. See pages 61-65.

Starting Relay. See page 59.

Switches. A trash compactor is equipped with numerous switches (*see pages 55-56*), including the main On/Off, a safety On/Off, a door latch switch, a tilt switch, and possibly other safety switches. Also, direction-reversing switches are mounted in the ram travel area. If the motor stalls without reversing direction, one of the direction-reversing switches may be malfunctioning. If the unit fails to start, and the motor does not hum, suspect one of the other switches.

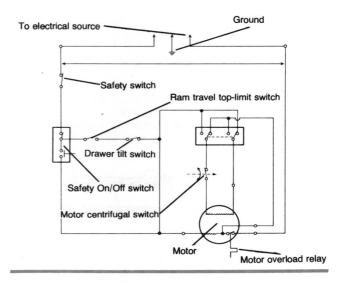

Typical wiring diagram of trash compactor.

Rear Panel: To reach motor, drive system, ram

To get at the motor and drive system, pull the appliance away from the wall. Remove the lower access panel held in place by screws. For increased access, turn the compactor on its side and remove the top cover held in place by spring clips or screws.

To remove the ram, take off the retainers at the top of the two power screws and pull the ram until it is free.

To take off the drive belt, loosen the motor mounting bolt and slide the motor until the belt is at its slackest position. Twist the belt off its pulleys. To remove a chain, loosen in

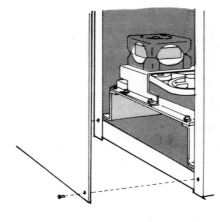

the same manner, then remove the master link. This link, which looks different from all the others, can be pried apart with a screwdriver.

The motor is bolted to the frame pieces; loosen the bolts to remove it. Relays, switches, and other electrical components are also easily removable by unscrewing the retaining screws that attach them to the chassis. Pulleys and chain sprockets may be held in place by setscrews or retaining nuts.

 WARNING: Disconnect power to the trash compactor before disassembly.

A wiring diagram for the appliance may be pasted on the rear access panel. Or obtain one (with a service manual) from the manufacturer. It will help in identifying the switches and their circuitry.

Clean switch contacts and terminals with fine sandpaper or liquid contact cleaner. Then test for continuity (*see pages 26-28*). Replace a defective switch.

Door Latch. If the latch is not closing properly, remove the access plate and lubricate moving parts with lithium grease. The catch mechanism may be mounted on an adjustable plate; loosen the screws and shift the plate so that the latch catches properly. If the latch breaks, replace it with a manufacturer's part.

TRASH COMPACTOR TROUBLESHOOTING

PROBLEM: Trash compactor does not operate or starts and stops before cycle is completed.

Possible Cause	Procedure	Remedy	Rating	Parts	Labor
No power at outlet.	Check fuse or circuit breaker.	Replace fuse or reset circuit breaker.	■		
Plug disconnected.	Check.	Reseat plug in outlet.	■		
Cord defective.	Check for breaks.	Repair or replace.	■ ■	$5	$20
Front door safety lock switch open or faulty.	If faulty, motor will hum when switch is activated.	Relatch door. Replace faulty switch.	■ ■ ■	$6	$20
Other switches faulty (trash compactor has many switches).	Check circuit continuity of all switches.	Replace.	■ ■ ■	$6-12	$25
Drawer more than ¼ inch open.		Push start switch and hold until drawer closes; release immediately.	■		$20
Motor overloaded (ram down).	Let motor cool 10 minutes. Check drive belt and chain for wear. Check circuit continuity.	Repair.	■ ■ ■ ■		$35

PROBLEM: Trash compactor blows fuse or trips circuit breaker.

Possible Cause	Procedure	Remedy	Rating	Parts	Labor
Circuit overloaded.	Reduce number of appliances on circuit. Put compactor on its own circuit.	Replace fuse or reset circuit breaker.	■		
Cord or plug short-circuited.	Inspect for breaks.	Repair or replace.	■ ■	$5	$20
Switch or motor short-circuited.	Test circuit continuity.	Repair or replace.	Switch ■ ■ ■ / Motor ■ ■ ■ ■	$6 / $50-75	$25 / $35

PROBLEM: Trash compactor shocks user.

Possible Cause	Procedure	Remedy	Rating	Parts	Labor
Cord frayed.	Inspect for breaks.	Repair or replace.	■ ■	$5	$20
Case short-circuited.	Test circuit continuity.	Repair and insulate internal wires.	■ ■ ■ ■		$25

PROBLEM: Trash compactor starts but does not compact trash properly.

Possible Cause	Procedure	Remedy	Rating	Parts	Labor
Drive belt loose or broken.	Loosen nuts holding motor mounts to adjust.	Proper deflection is ¼ inch.	■ ■	$8	$25
Drive chain loose or broken.	Visually inspect. Adjust by pulling bolts holding motor mounts.	Proper deflection is ¼ inch.	■ ■	$15	25
Motor pulley or drive pulley loose.	Check.	Tighten.	■ ■		$25
Drive sprocket roll pin broken or bent.	Check.	Replace.	■ ■ ■	$15	$35
Drive shaft faulty.	Check.	Replace.	■ ■ ■	$10	$35
Ram bound.	Check power screws.	Lubricate or replace.	■ ■ ■		$25

PROBLEM: Trash compactor is excessively noisy.

Possible Cause	Procedure	Remedy	Rating	Parts	Labor
Unit needs lubrication.	Consult owner's manual.	Lubricate as required.	■ ■		$20
Drive chain or drive belt needs adjustment.	Check.	Adjust.	■ ■		$20

PROBLEM: Trash compactor has bad odor.

Possible Cause	Procedure	Remedy	Rating	Parts	Labor
Aerosol can empty.	Check.	Replace.	■	$3	$20
Nozzle on aerosol can clogged.	Check.	Clean nozzle with thin wire or replace.	■	$3	$20
Liquid or solid deodorizer exhausted.	Check.	Replace.	■	$15	$25

PROBLEM: Trash compactor leaves mess.

Possible Cause	Procedure	Remedy	Rating	Parts	Labor
Bag placed improperly.	Check.	Proper placement will avoid bag being drawn into machine.	■		$20
Spring holding bag faulty.	Check.	Replace.	■ ■	$3	$20

Washing Machines

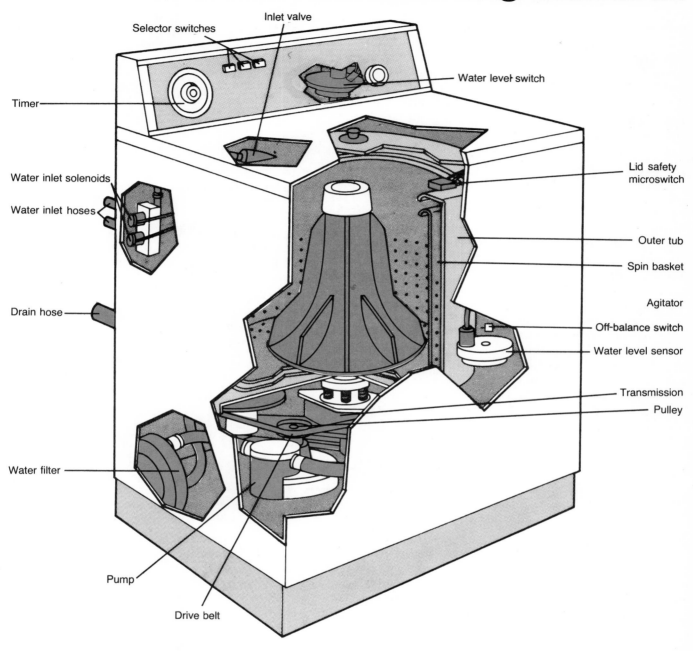

Selector switches
Inlet valve
Timer
Water level switch
Water inlet solenoids
Water inlet hoses
Lid safety microswitch
Outer tub
Spin basket
Agitator
Off-balance switch
Water level sensor
Drain hose
Transmission
Pulley
Water filter
Pump
Drive belt

Principle of Operation

An automatic clothes washer operates in two phases or cycles, wash and rinse. In the wash cycle, the tub fills with water. Soap or detergent is added (either by hand or automatically) and then by oscillation, pulsation, or some other method, the washer churns the clothes in the soap solution. A pump may recirculate the soap solution through a filter during this agitation period. Finally, the tub or an inner spin basket ro-

tates, removing much of the water in the tub by centrifugal force, and the pump forces the soapy water into the drain system outside the machine.

The rinse cycle is the same—fill, agitate, spin, and drain—except that no soap is added to the water. Many washers vary the rinse cycle by adding a high-speed spin phase to extract water from the washed clothing.

A timer (*see page 56*), run by a synchronous motor (*see page 62*), automatically controls the washer as it moves from one phase to another. When the machine is turned on, the timer first activates two intake solenoids (*see page 59*) to allow water to flow through the intake valve. One solenoid controls the hot water valve, and the other controls the cold water valve. The temperature switch can be set for hot, cold, or both (warm).

An air-pressure sensor or other water-level switch signals the timer when the tub is filled. Next, the timer signals a relay (*see page 59*) to engage the clutch so that the motor can drive the agitator transmission. The washer agitates. At the end of the agitation phase, the timer signals the relay to disengage the agitator transmission. Then the timer engages the spin transmission. The spin action may be achieved by a variety of methods, depending on the type of transmission used in the washer. A common method is by reversing the motor: The motor shaft turns in one direction to turn the agitator. When the direction is reversed, the agitator locks in place in the center of the spin basket, causing the spin basket to rotate with it. The pump drive system is also engaged during the spin phase to drain the tub.

This sequence repeats itself when the timer moves the machine into the rinse cycle. Finally, the timer shuts itself off and shuts off the machine.

A clothes washer is the most complicated of all home appliances. Even the chassis and housing are complicated. Various suspension methods are used to protect the washing machine from shaking apart as it works. Springs, shock absorbers, braces, and other devices may all be used. An off-balance switch is mounted on or near the tub to turn the motor off if the shaking becomes too extreme. To guard against the possibility of water spillage, electric shock, and

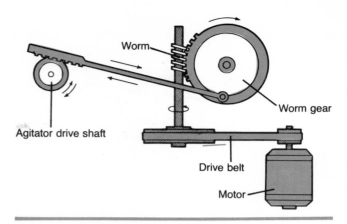

How a washing machine transmission transforms the rotary action of the motor shaft into the oscillating action of the agitator.

damage to the motor, clutch, or transmission, rubber aprons and gaskets insulate the lower part of the machine from the tub area.

The drive system begins with a capacitor-start motor (*see page 62*), which causes the agitator to move, the spin basket or tub to rotate, and the pump to operate. A complex transmission and clutch transform the motor's simple rotation into these various movements. The variety of clutch and transmission

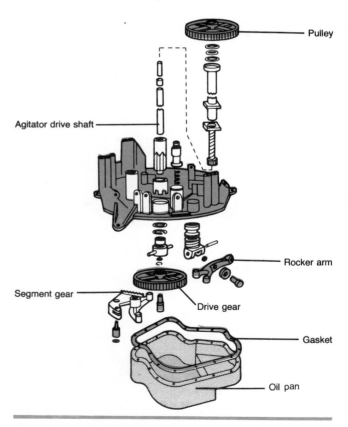

Typical transmission of a washing machine. There are many different designs, all highly complex. If transmission gears break, replace the whole transmission. If gasket leaks, replace gasket and refill transmission with new oil.

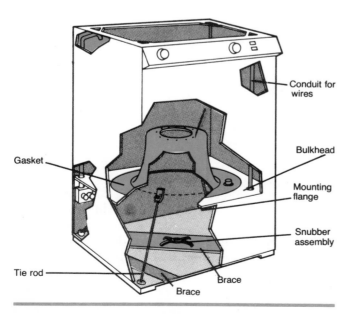

Sturdy construction of washing machine cabinet.

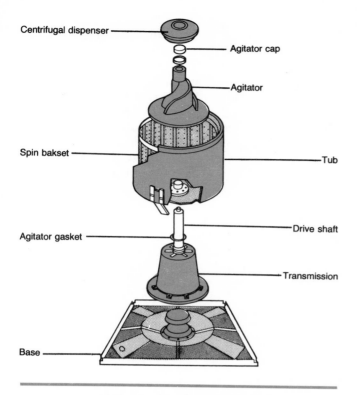

Centrifugal dispenser

Agitator cap

Agitator

Spin bakset

Tub

Agitator gasket

Drive shaft

Transmission

Base

Transmission, basket, agitator assembly

Differences in Washers

There are a number of basic designs for churning the clothes in the tub. The most common is an agitator on a center post in a vertical tub. A different vertical design is the pulsator, where the tub itself slides up and down rapidly on the center post. Vacuum cup models are used in some areas. In still another design, the tub is positioned horizontally and rotates to agitate the clothes. This horizontal design requires a somewhat simpler transmission than the others because there is no moving center post.

Options available on washing machines include more complex controls for a greater range and variety of water temperature, water level, or timer cycles; dual- and multiple-speed motors; automatic dispensers for soap, bleach, and other laundry products; special agitators for fine washables or other fabrics and garments; mini-tubs that fit inside the tub for special wash conditions; and a suds-conserving system in which soapy water is pumped into an exterior tub or sink basin, then pumped back into the machine later.

As mentioned, a wide variety of transmission and clutch designs are in use. In most cases, the transmission gears are enclosed in an oil-filled housing. Variations in transmission design make little difference when doing repairs, as usually the entire transmission is replaced if defective. The clutch, however, is often repairable by replacing worn parts.

The clutch engages the transmission with the motor and absorbs the ensuing shock. Usually, one half of the clutch is mounted on the motor shaft and the other half on the transmission. A relay or solenoid activates the clutch when signaled by the timer. The two halves of the clutch engage slowly, bringing more and more pressure against each other until they are

designs numbers in the hundreds. A brake may be included to slow rotation. A water circulation system consisting of inlet hoses and valves, internal circulation hoses, a filter, a pump, and exhaust hoses adds even more complications. Finally, the electrical system is among the most complex in any appliance; a timer, solenoids, relays, a safety door latch, an off-balance switch, water-temperature and water-level switches, various other switches, an electric motor, and the wiring that connects one component to another.

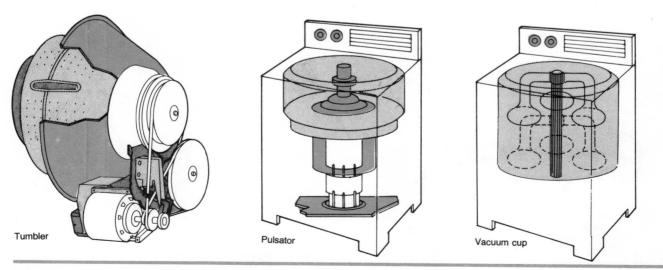

Tumbler

Pulsator

Vacuum cup

Oscillating-agitator washers are the most common type, but several others are manufactured. Shown here are tumbler, vacuum cup, and pulsator types.

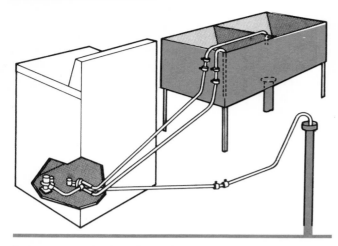

Suds conserver hookup. Suds tub is stoppered, suds are reused. Rinse water drains out. After final wash in cycle, suds are drained through another hose.

fully meshed or synchronized and rotating at the same speed. The following are among the variety of clutches found in washing machines:

A *disk clutch* consists of two metal disks, one mounted on the motor shaft and the other on the transmission shaft. One or both may be faced with brake lining. As the disks come together, there is considerable slippage until they mesh tightly enough to synchronize the motor and transmission.

In a *belt-slip clutch,* a loose drive belt connects the motor pulley and the transmission pulley. When the clutch is not engaged, the drive belt is ineffective. Engaging the clutch causes another pulley to press on the drive belt and tighten it. The motor's force of rotation is then conveyed to the transmission.

A *centrifugal clutch* consists of an inner and outer drum. Attached to the inner drum are clutch shoes (curved plates faced with brake lining), which come into contact with the outer drum when the motor rotates. The inner drum is mounted on the motor shaft, while the outer drum is mounted on the transmission. As the motor turns at full torque, centrifugal force drives the clutch shoe into contact with the outer drum. As the motor slows, return springs cause the clutch to disengage.

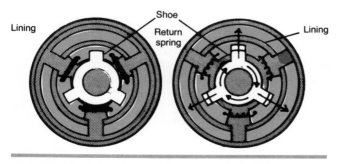

Centrifugal clutch. As shaft rotates, centrifugal force drives shoes into contact with drum, causing drum to rotate.

A *multiple shoe and drum clutch* is a form of centrifugal clutch. Some of the shoes engage a smaller, inner drum, which turns at a high speed. The other shoes engage a larger outer drum, which turns at a slower rate. Consequently, a single-speed motor can be used to run the washer at two different speeds.

An *electrical clutch* consists of an inner and outer drum. One of the drums is wound with wire so that it acts as an electromagnet. As electricity passes through the wire, it creates a magnetic field, causing the other drum to turn. There is no heat from friction in an electrical clutch because the parts never touch, so nothing but the shaft bearings can wear. The windings can, however, burn out.

In a *fluid clutch,* the motor shaft and the transmission shaft are both mounted with impellers and enclosed in a housing filled with oil. As the motor shaft turns, it causes the oil to turn with it. The rotation of the oil drives the transmission impeller, so that the transmission shaft rotates.

Maintenance and Repair

Hoses. Hoses carry water to and from the tub and, in many models, through a recirculation and filtration system. Cracked, obstructed, or kinked hoses may cause poor water delivery, poor drainage, or leaks. Visually inspect hoses for kinks or damage. To remove a kink, reposition the hose. To remove an obstruction, take the hose out of the machine and flush it with water or probe with a long, blunt stick. Replace cracked hoses. If a hose is deteriorated only at the end where it attaches to the machine, cut off the damaged section and refasten the hose.

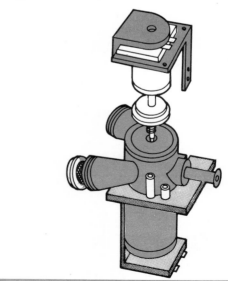

Intake Valve. Mounted in each intake valve is a fine mesh filter. These filters protect the valves and other parts of the machine from sand, grit, and other solid

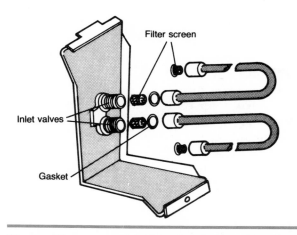

Cleaning filter screens at intake valves is essential maintenance; otherwise, poor water flow results. Replace damaged screens or deteriorated gaskets.

impurities. Periodically, remove the feeder hoses for access to the filters. Remove the filters carefully with fingers or long-nosed pliers and clean them by rinsing in tap water. If the filters are not cleaned periodically, grit and other obstructions may eventually block the water flow.

Other malfunctions of the intake valve may also cause poor water flow or, possibly, leakage. If only one valve fails, water temperature may be inaccurate. Such problems could also be caused by switch or wiring failure. Make sure the timer, water-level, and water-temperature switches all work properly and that there is continuity through all connecting wires.

If either a valve or a solenoid fails, replace the entire valve-solenoid assembly.

Pump. The pump is easily identifiable by its plastic housing, the hoses leading to and from it, and its belt-driven pulley. The pump may have one impeller or two. If two, one is for recirculation, the other for drain. In some one-impeller models, the pump drains when the impeller rotates in one direction, re-

circulates when it rotates in the opposite direction. In others, the single impeller drains the tub.

If the pump becomes obstructed or internal parts break, water in the tub may not drain or recirculate. To clear the pump, drain the water in the tub by siphoning it off or by disconnecting the hoses to the pump

WARNING: To avoid electrical shock, be sure the washing machine is unplugged.

Probe the pump for obstructions with a wooden spoon or other blunt instrument. Sometimes a sock or handkerchief caught in the impeller can be removed in this way. If the pump still does not work properly, remove the pump cover (held in place with screws) for access to the impeller area. Remove any obstructions.

Lint Filter. Most washers have a removable lint filter in the tub area. Clean it after every wash. If it breaks, replace it.

Many washers have an additional filter in the motor area, inaccessible for frequent cleaning. It is in a large housing with a hose connected at either end. When servicing the underside of the machine (motor, pump, clutch, or transmission), remove the filter cover and clean the filter.

Seals, Gaskets, Aprons. Seals, gaskets, and aprons guard against water leakage from the tub. When servicing the tub area, examine these plastic or rubber parts for rotting, cracking, or other deterioration. If any are not in the best condition, replace them.

Drive Belt. Most washing machines have a drive belt between the motor and the pump, and many have other belts from the motor to the transmission. A loose belt causes the motor to run excessively and heat up, and the appliance may also not work effi-

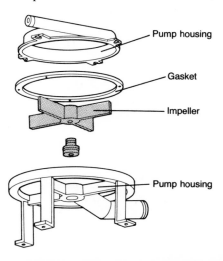

Exploded view of pump

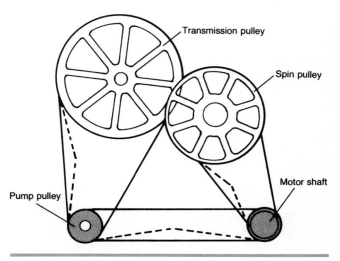

Drive belts should fit snugly but have about half an inch flex. Tighten loose belts by loosening motor or pump mounts, shifting motor or pump, retightening mounts.

ciently. Listen for a squealing noise from a loose belt when the motor or pump is running. Tighten a belt by loosening the pump or motor mounts and shifting the pump or motor slightly. The belt should be snug but flex about one half inch when pressed with a finger in the span between two pulleys.

Replace a broken belt by loosening the motor or pump mounts as described above and twisting the belt over the edges of the pulleys, then tightening the belt.

Transmission. If the transmission fails, the motor will run but the machine will not agitate properly, or it will not spin. A grinding or knocking noise may be heard. Put a pan underneath the transmission case to catch the oil, then remove the cover bolts and the cover. Examine the gears for worn or broken teeth. If any of the gears are damaged, replace the complete transmission. It should unbolt easily from the chassis. If the transmission is undamaged, buy a new gasket and oil from an appliance parts store before reassembling it.

Pry up the old gasket with a putty knife. Be sure all fragments are removed. Then clean the case lip with a cloth dipped in solvent. Let it dry before installing the new gasket.

Transmission oil may leak through a dried or cracked gasket. Replace the oil and gasket as described above.

Clutch. The clutch engages the motor and transmission. If the clutch is not working properly, the motor may labor and the transmission start up slowly. The agitation and spin actions appear slow or sloppy.

For a disk or centrifugal clutch, obtain new linings (similar to brake linings for a car) from an appliance supply store. These linings may have to be riveted in place. Also replace worn bearings, springs, or drums.

A fluid clutch may develop leaks through the gasket. If only a small amount of oil has escaped, tighten the bolts and check the oil level. Fill to the marker or to the edge of the plug hole. If there is a major leak, remove the case and replace the gasket, as on a transmission, then refill with oil.

If an electric clutch fails, replace it. Perform a continuity test on the windings, as on an electric motor (*see page 62*), to tell whether it is defective.

Leveling legs. If a machine is not level, it will vibrate excessively during the spin cycle and cause undue wear to the motor, transmission, or other parts. The off-balance switch may trip; the water-level switch may not work accurately. Adjust the legs as needed.

Motor. See pages 60-65.

Timer. The timer (*see pages 56-57*) controls switches, motor, relays, solenoids, among other parts. Failure of a timer expresses itself in a variety of ways—too fast or too slow movement through a cycle, skipping of part of a cycle, not switching on or off.

In any malfunction that involves the electrical circuitry, suspect the timer.

To work on a timer, unfasten the wires attached to its quick-connect terminals (*see page 53*) and remove it from the machine. Open the cover and look for burned contacts, loose cams, or a frozen shaft. Clean contacts and terminals with fine sandpaper or liquid contact cleaner. If a shaft is frozen, sand and lubricate it. If cams are loose or out of place, tighten them by peening the spacers between them with a punch.

Test a timer for continuity with a continuity tester or multimeter (*see pages 26-28*). Since it is, in effect, a multiple switch, a timer can be tested like any other switch by turning it through its cycle and testing each pair of terminals in turn. Each set of terminals should read approximately zero ohms on the multimeter, show continuity on the continuity tester.

If there are broken parts such as leaf springs or cams inside the timer housing, check to see if there is a timer-rebuilding shop in your area. Obtain replacement parts from this shop or ask the shop to rebuild the timer. Or buy a new timer.

The timer motor is a synchronous type (*see page 62*); if it fails, replace it.

Water-Level Switch. The water-level switch consists of an air-pressure sensor and a capillary tube, the latter fitted into the bottom of the tub. As water rises in the tub, it also rises in the capillary tube. Air pressure increases until it activates the switch. The switch then signals the timer to close the solenoid at the intake valve.

If this switch fails, too much or too little water may come into the tub. First, check the capillary tube for cracks or obstructions that would affect the air pressure in the tube. Clean the capillary tube, and change it if it has deteriorated.

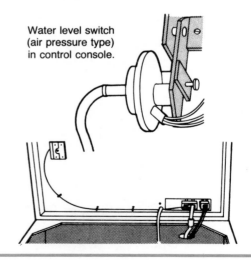

Water level switch (air pressure type) in control console.

Air hose extends from switch in console to bottom of tub. As water rises in tub, it also rises in air hose, increasing air pressure at switch. When switch is tripped, it sends electrical signal to inlet valve solenoids; solenoids shut valves.

How To Reach Interior Components

Control Panel: To reach timer, water level switch, speed selector switch, other controls

Remove the screws that hold the front or rear access panel in place. The controls are attached to the chassis with clamps or screws. Remove the control dial, the clamps or retaining screws, and the wires attached to quick-connect terminals (*see page 53*). Make a sketch of the color of wires and the terminals they attach to for future reference.

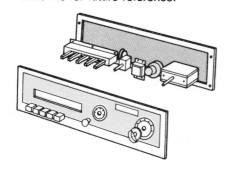

Tub Area: To reach agitator, spin basket, tub, drive post

For access to the tub and agitator assembly, lift up the top of the machine. On many models, it is hinged at the rear and held in place at the front by spring clips (*see page 52*). Or visible screws may secure it. A screw-on cap is located at the top of the agitator. If it does not unscrew by hand, loosen it with gentle taps of a plastic or wooden mallet. The agitator may lift off; or it may itself be screwed down tightly and need to be tapped with the mallet.

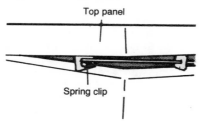

Top panel

Spring clip

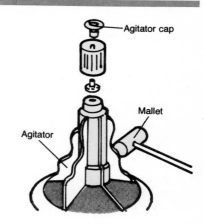

Agitator cap

Mallet

Agitator

The center post on which the agitator is mounted secures the spin basket. Remove this post by unscrewing or unclipping the retainers that hold it in place. Remove the spin basket. The tub may be secured at the bottom and sides as well as at the top. If the tub is suspended with braces, snubbers, springs, or other

(Continued on next page)

Test this switch for continuity (*see pages 26-28*) at its various settings. Pour buckets of water into the tub to check water levels at which the switch trips. (When the switch opens or closes, the multimeter needle should swing to the extreme left or right.) If the switch does not perform as it should, replace it.

Other Switches. The off-balance switch, the safety interlock microswitch in the door, the temperature-selector switch, and other switches that may be found in the machine can all be checked for continuity (*see pages 26-28 and 55-56*). Replace a faulty switch.

Relays. A relay (*see pages 59 and 63*) activates the transmission. In many washers, another relay activates the pump drive system. A starting relay routes the circuitry to the starting and running windings of the motor. Various other relays may be found in a washer; check the wiring diagram pasted to the rear access panel.

If the starting relay fails, the motor may hum but not start up. If one of the other relays malfunctions, the appliance either will not begin or will not end one phase of its cycle—for example, if the relay to the transmission fails, the machine may not agitate, or it may not stop agitating. Test a suspect relay for continuity (*see pages 26-28*). If defective, replace.

Solenoids. Solenoids (*see page 59*) and relays perform similar tasks. In some circumstances, a solenoid may be used in place of a relay. However, to open or close all valves in a washing machine only solenoids are used.

If a solenoid malfunctions, the valve will not operate properly. Too much or too little water will flow through it, or water will flow at the wrong time. Check the plunger action of the solenoid to be certain it is not obstructed or binding. If it moves properly, test it for continuity (*see pages 26-28*). Replace it, together with the valve assembly, if defective.

Agitator. The hollow inside of the agitator eventually wears from the shock of the drive post movement. Or the agitator may split apart.

If the inside of the agitator wears, the agitator will move sloppily during the agitation phase. Grip the agitator firmly. If you can hold it still despite the movement of the drive post, the agitator needs replacement.

If the agitator splits, it may make an irregular knocking sound during the agitation phase, and clothing may be torn by its rough edges. Replace it.

Spin Basket. Under normal circumstances, the spin basket should not need servicing. If, however, it becomes rusted, sand the rusted area thoroughly and paint it with epoxy enamel. If the spin basket becomes damaged, replace it.

Tub. If the tub develops a small leak, stop the leak with a short machine screw that just fits the hole, plus two washers and a nut. If the tub becomes rusted, sand and paint it, as with the spin basket.

Door. The door is an area where rust spots may appear. Sand and paint as suggested for the spin basket.

shock absorbing devices, remove them. If the tub still does not lift out, turn the machine on its side and remove the retaining bolts on the under side of the tub.

The door latch and microswitch assembly is fastened to the door and the underside of the top or front of the machine with retaining screws. Loosen these screws to adjust the position of the switch or to remove it.

To find the off-balance switch, look in the chassis area on or near the top of the tub. Or find it by tracing the wires from the reset button in the control console.

The internal hoses that connect to the inlet valve, the pump, and other parts are usually attached with circular spring clamps. Use a hose pliers to remove them. External hoses may have screw fittings.

The inlet valve assembly, including the solenoid, is accessible from the rear of the machine. Remove the hoses that are attached at both sides

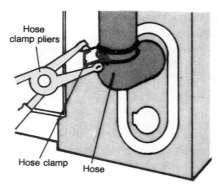

Hose clamp pliers

Hose clamp   Hose

of the valve and take out the screws that hold the valve to the chassis. Remove the wires connected to the solenoid.

Rear Panel: To reach motor, pump, and transmission

Access to the motor, pump, and transmission area is through a removable panel at the rear, held in place with retaining screws. For many service tasks, however, it is necessary to turn the washing

machine on its side. Put an old blanket down on the floor to protect the cabinet surface from scratching. To remove the motor, transmission, pump, or clutch, unbolt them from the frame. The transmission cover can be removed for examination of the gears. Before unbolting the cover, place a pan beneath it to catch the oil that will spill out. The pump cover can also be removed for cleaning the pump. The cover is usually held in place with screws.

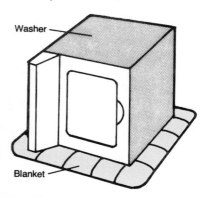

Washer

Blanket

WASHING MACHINE TROUBLESHOOTING

HOW TO DETERMINE LOCATION OF BLOCKAGE IN A WASHING MACHINE THAT DOES NOT DRAIN

Loosen clamp that holds drain hose against side of washing machine. Lower the hose to a point *below* level of pump. Manually release drain valve if there is one. If water flows freely from the hose, the problem is a *mechanical failure in either the valves or pump*.

If water does not flow freely from the drain hose, disconnect it from the pump. If there is no flow, disconnect the pump inlet hose. If there

is a flow from the inlet hose the problem is a *mechanical failure in the pump.*

If there is no water flow from the intake hose, check the drainage valve outtake and intake hoses. If there is no flow from the intake hose, the *valve is malfunctioning.*

If there is no flow from the valve intake hose, remove the spin basket and check the tub drain opening for blockage. If there is no blockage, the problem is a *mechanical failure in either the pump valve or pump.*

If the pump has been disassembled, all seals and washers must be checked for wear and replaced before reassembling in order to avoid leaks.

PROBLEM: Washing machine does not start.

Possible Cause	Procedure	Remedy	Rating	Parts	Labor
No power at outlet.	Check fuse or circuit breaker.	Replace fuse or reset circuit breaker.	■		
Plug disconnected.	Check.	Reseat plug in outlet.	■		
Cord defective.	Check for breaks.	Repair or replace.	■	$5	$20
Connection at terminal block faulty.	Check continuity.	Resplice broken wires. Repair bad connections.	■		$20
Timer set incorrectly.	Check.	Reset.	■ ■		$25
Thermal overload switch shutting off motor.	Turn off motor and cool.	Determine and remove cause of overload.	■		$20
Off-balance or safety switch activated.	Reset off-balance switch.	Check distribution of clothes in tub. Latch securely.	■		$20
Low or incorrect voltage.	Check voltage at appliance with voltmeter.	Replace with heavier size conductors to minimize voltage drop.	■ ■ ■		$25

(Continued on next page)

WASHING MACHINE TROUBLESHOOTING *(Continued from preceding page)*

PROBLEM: Washing machine blows fuse or trips circuit breaker.

Possible Cause	Procedure	Remedy	Rating	Parts	Labor
Circuit overloaded.	Reduce number of appliances on circuit. Put washer on its own circuit.	Replace fuse or reset circuit breaker.	■		
Cord short-circuited.	Inspect for breaks.	Repair or replace.	■ ■	$5	$20
Control switches on wiring short-circuited.	Test for short circuit.	Repair or replace defective part.	■ ■ ■	$5-35	$25
Motor short-circuited.	Test circuit continuity.	Repair or replace.	■ ■ ■ ■	$50-75	$35

PROBLEM: Washing machine shocks user.

Possible Cause	Procedure	Remedy	Rating	Parts	Labor
Cord frayed.	Inspect for breaks.	Repair or replace.	■ ■	$5	$20
Internal wiring short-circuited.	Perform continuity test.	Repair wires.	■ ■ ■ ■		$25

PROBLEM: Washing machine does not fill.

Possible Cause	Procedure	Remedy	Rating	Parts	Labor
Water faucets closed.	Disconnect hose and check house water supply.	Reconnect hose and turn on faucets.	■ ■		$20
Screen clogged.	Disconnect hose and remove filter screen.	Clean. If corroded, replace.	■ ■		$20
Hoses kinked.	Check.	Reposition.	■		$20
Off-balance switch tripped.	Check clothes in tub.	Reset switch according to owner's manual.	■		$20
Solenoid valve faulty.	Check continuity.	Replace.	■ ■ ■	$3-6	$25
Timer defective.	Check machine's wiring diagram. Clean contacts with fine sandpaper.	Repair or replace timer.	■ ■ ■	$35-60	$25
Wires broken.	Check circuit continuity of wires.	Repair.	■ ■ ■ ■		$25
Water temperature selector switch defective.	Check circuit continuity.	Replace.	■ ■ ■	$8	$20

PROBLEM: Washing machine fills but does not start.

Possible Cause	Procedure	Remedy	Rating	Parts	Labor
Overload protector tripped.	Turn off machine. Remove clothes from tub, wait 15 minutes. If protector does not reset, test circuit continuity.	Replace if necessary.	■ ■ ■	$6	$25
Lid safety switch misaligned or defective.	Check.	Adjust or replace.	■ ■ ■	$6	$25
Clutch faulty.	Check for worn springs, bearings, drums and shoes.	Replace worn parts.	■ ■ ■ ■	$25	$30
Wires at motor broken.	Check contacts.	Repair wires.	■ ■ ■		$20
Water level switch defective.	Check circuit continuity.	Replace.	■ ■ ■	$12	$25

(Continued on next page)

PROBLEM: Washing machine fills but does not start.

Possible Cause	Procedure	Remedy	Rating	Parts	Labor
Timer defective.	Check contacts, continuity.	Clean contacts; repair or replace timer.	■ ■ ■	$35-60	$25
Motor faulty.	Repair or replace motor.		■ ■ ■ ■	$50-75	$35
Drive mechanism faulty.	Check for broken or slipped belt, broken slipped pulley or bound pulley bearings.	Adjust or replace.	■ ■ ■	$5-10	$25
Transmission faulty.	Remove.	Replace with rebuilt transmission.	■ ■ ■ ■	$65-75	$45

PROBLEM: Water temperature does not correspond to setting.

Possible Cause	Procedure	Remedy	Rating	Parts	Labor
Faucets improperly adjusted.	Check.	Adjust.	■		$20
Hot water supply inadequate or exhausted.	Check water heater for setting on thermostat (should be 140°F. to 160°F.). Or wait for it to heat again. Reduce use of home water supply while machine is in use.		■		$20
Valve screen clogged.	Check.	Clean or replace.	■ ■		$20
Solenoid defective.	Check.	Repair or replace.	■ ■ ■	$3-6	$25

PROBLEM: Washing machine washes but does not spin.

Possible Cause	Procedure	Remedy	Rating	Parts	Labor
Clutches wedged under spin basket.	Remove top, agitator and basket.	In reassembling unit, replace all seals not in perfect condition.	■	$10	$25
Timer faulty.	Check circuit continuity. Inspect for burned or broken wires.	Clean contacts; repair wires; rebuild or replace entire timer.	■ ■ ■	$35-60	$25
Wires in spin circuit burned or broken.	Test circuit continuity.	Repair or replace.	■ ■ ■		$20
Spin relay or solenoid defective.	Check mechanical action and circuit continuity.	Clean and adjust. If no continuity, replace.	■ ■ ■	$12	$25
Spin selector switch defective.	Check circuit continuity.	Replace.	■ ■ ■	$6	$25
Clutch defective.	Examine for worn or broken parts.	Replace parts.	■ ■ ■ ■	$25	$35
Drive belt loose.	Check.	Tighten or replace.	■ ■ ■	$8	$20
Lid safety switch faulty.	Check for jammed switch, missing tabs or worn gasket.	Clean or replace.	■ ■ ■	$6	$20
Drive pulley broken.	Check bearings and shaft.	Clean and lubricate. Replace broken parts.	■ ■ ■	$10	$25
External brake not releasing.	Check brake linkage.	Replace worn parts.	■ ■ ■	$5	$20
Drain system faulty.	Check hoses.	Repair or replace.	■ ■ ■	$10	$20
Transmission faulty.	Remove.	Replace with rebuilt transmission.	■ ■ ■ ■	$65-75	$45

(Continued on next page)

WASHING MACHINE TROUBLESHOOTING *(Continued from preceding page)* ▬▬

PROBLEM: Washing machine washes but does not rinse.

Possible Cause	Procedure	Remedy	Rating	Parts	Labor
Drain hose too high, will not pump.	Check.	Lower drain pipe.	■ ■		$25
Rinse circuit faulty.	Check circuit continuity.	Replace broken wires.	■ ■ ■		$20
Timer faulty.	Check circuit continuity. Inspect for burned or broken wires.	Clean contacts, repair or replace entire timer.	■ ■ ■	$35-60	$25
Water selector switch faulty.	Check circuit continuity.	Replace.	■ ■ ■	$6	$20
Water inlet valve faulty.	Check circuit continuity in solenoid. Check for clogged valve opening.	Replace solenoid. Clean valve or replace.	■ ■ ■	$6-20	$25

PROBLEM: Washing machine spins but does not wash. ▬▬

Possible Cause	Procedure	Remedy	Rating	Parts	Labor
Clothes wedged under agitator or pulsator.	Remove agitator to free clothes. Check pulsator cups for wear.	Replace worn or split agitator, pulsator cups.	■ ■	$20	$25
Agitator cracked.	Remove.	Replace.	■ ■	$20	$20
Agitator loose.	Remove to check block.	Tighten setscrews on agitator. If block is worn, replace.	■ ■	$4	$20
Transmission jammed.	Remove.	Replace transmission.	■ ■ ■ ■	$55-75	$45

Problem: Washing machine spins but does not drain. ▬▬

Possible Cause	Procedure	Remedy	Rating	Parts	Labor
Drainpipe blocked.	Remove drain hose and inspect.	Clear.	■ ■		$20
Pump not functioning.	Check for loose or broken drive belt.	Tighten or replace.	■ ■ ■	$5-25	$25
	Check for bound bearings.	Clean and lubricate or replace.	■ ■ ■	$5	$25
	Check inside pump for blockage.	Clean. Replace worn seals.	■ ■ ■	$5	$25
Drain valve not functioning.	Check for broken wires.	Repair.	■ ■ ■		$20
	Check circuit continuity in solenoid valve.	Replace solenoid.	■ ■ ■	$12	$20
	Check for blockage inside valve.	Clean. Replace worn seals.	■ ■ ■	$5	$25

PROBLEM: Washing machine vibrates excessively. ▬▬

Possible Cause	Procedure	Remedy	Rating	Parts	Labor
Machine not level.	Check with carpenter's level.	Level machine front to back, side to side.	■ ■		$20
Suspension mechanism broken.	Inspect for broken or worn parts. If a pivot system, check ball and socket and springs.	Replace worn or broken parts.	■ ■ ■	$25	$25
Transmission leaking oil (inspect floor).	Remove.	Replace gaskets or transmission (if damaged).	■ ■ ■ ■	$55-75	$45

(Continued on next page)

PROBLEM: Washing machine leaks or floods.
(Warning: Turn off both faucets and unplug machine.)

Possible Cause	Procedure	Remedy	Rating	Parts	Labor
Hose connections at faucets loose.	Check for worn washers and corrosion on hose fittings.	Replace.	■ ■	$15	$25
Cracked, broken, or disconnected hoses.	Examine all hoses.	Replace.	■ ■	$15	$25
Drain hose kinked.	Check.	Reposition or replace.	■ ■	$10	$25
Too much detergent.	Let machine stand an hour. Check amount and type of detergent used.	Drain machine.	■		$20
Standpipe blocked.	Inspect.	Remove blockage.	■ ■		
Drain valve cracked.	Remove all hoses and mounting screws attached to valve.	Replace valve.	■ ■ ■	$15	$25
Pump leaking.	Remove and inspect.	Replace.	■ ■ ■	$25	$20
Tub gasket seal broken.	Inspect.	Replace.	■ ■ ■	$10	$35
Tub boot torn or punctured.	Inspect.	Replace.	■ ■ ■	$5-15	$35
Water intake valve defective.	Remove.	Clean all foreign objects from inside of valve. Replace filter screens.	■ ■	$5	$25
Timer defective.	Examine mechanical action. Check contacts.	Clean or replace as necessary.	■ ■ ■	$35-60	$25
Water level control switch defective.	Check.	Replace.	■ ■ ■	$12	$25

PROBLEM: Washing machine is too noisy.

Possible Cause	Procedure	Remedy	Rating	Parts	Labor
Washtub oversudsing.	Add cold water and ½ cup white vinegar to reduce suds level.	Check amount and type of detergent used.	■		$20
Load unbalanced.	Rearrange load, or reduce its size.	Consult owner's manual for machine's capacity.	■		$20
Machine not level.	Check with carpenter's level.	Level machine front to back, side to side.	■ ■		$20
Machine unbalanced.	Inspect entire suspension system for worn or broken parts.	Replace if necessary.	■ ■ ■	$25	$30
Timer connections loose.	Check wiring, connections and contacts.	Tighten terminals and contacts or replace.	■ ■ ■	$35-60	$25
Wiring connections loose.	Inspect all wires at connections.	Tighten.	■ ■ ■ ■		
Transmission defective.	Remove	Replace with rebuilt transmission.	■ ■ ■ ■	$55-75	$45
Pump jammed.	Inspect.	See page 00.	■ ■ ■		
Mounting bolts loose.	Inspect moving and stationary parts.	Tighten all bolts and screws.	■ ■ ■		$25

(Continued on next page)

WASHING MACHINE TROUBLESHOOTING *(Continued from preceding page)*

PROBLEM: Washing machine smokes.

Possible Cause	Procedure	Remedy	Rating	Parts	Labor
Belts worn or loose.	Inspect.	Replace or tighten.	■■■	$8	$20
Poor drainage.	Inspect.	Remove blockage.	■■		$20
Timer defective.	Check circuit continuity and contacts.	If possible clean contacts or replace timer.	■■■	$35-60	$25
Solenoid mechanism bound.	Check mechanical movement.	Clean and lubricate.	■■		$20
Clutch slips.	Check for loose or worn parts.	Tighten, replace parts.	■■■■	$25	$25
Foreign objects in pump.	Remove pump cover	Remove object.	■■■		$25
Motor defective.	Inspect.	Clean and lubricate or replace if necessary.	■■■■	$50-75	$35
Motor starting relay or switch defective.	Inspect.	Clean or replace.	■■■	$8	$20
Connections exposed to moisture. Switches loose.	Check for moisture.	Clean all connections. Replace defective switches.	■■■	$5-15	$25

PROBLEM: Washing machine tears clothes.

Possible Cause	Procedure	Remedy	Rating	Parts	Labor
Basket spins during agitation.	Check external tub for worn or broken parts. Inspect transmission.	Replace worn or broken brake parts. Replace with rebuilt transmission.	■■■■	$55-75	$45
Agitator spaced improperly in bottom of basket.	Inspect agitator for cracks. Check shaft block for looseness.	If cracked, replace. Tighten blocks screws.	■■	$20	$20
Foreign objects in tub or basket.	Take out agitator, basket and tub to remove all foreign objects.	Clean parts before reassembling machine.	■■		$25

PROBLEM: Washing machine stains clothes.

Possible Cause	Procedure	Remedy	Rating	Parts	Labor
Chipped porcelain in basket.	Inspect with strong light.	Sand and clean rusted areas and cover with epoxy paint.	■■		$25
Rubber grommets deteriorated.	Check grommets and seals in and around wash basket.	Replace with nylon parts if possible.	■■■	$5	$25
Transmission leaking oil.	Inspect.	Remove and replace with rebuilt transmission.	■■■■	$55-75	$45

PROBLEM: Washing machine does not wash clothes properly.

Possible Cause	Procedure	Remedy	Rating	Parts	Labor
Load too large	Check owner's manual for capacity of of machine.	Use smaller loads.	■		$20

Section Three

YARD AND GARDEN

Introduction to Outdoor Equipment

Outdoor Equipment

Outdoor Equipment

Introduction

The use of various pieces of outdoor equipment for the upkeep of lawns and gardens has grown rapidly in recent years. While some equipment has long been in existence, an improved standard of living, more leisure time, and new technological developments have created the demand for different and more efficient types of machines. Consequently, a wide variety of outdoor equipment is available to the homeowner today.

A majority of the equipment is designed to perform maintenance tasks outdoors. This includes lawn mowers, grass edgers or trimmers, hedge clippers, leaf blowers and vacuums, and snow blowers. Many of these are necessary for the daily upkeep of a yard and garden. A second group of equipment designed to aid the homeowner in completing common nonmaintenance tasks includes chain saws, rototillers, and lawn or garden tractors. These appliances and tools can shorten and make easier countless jobs around the home that may require more than one person's strength. If used and cared for properly, they can save the homeowner dollars as well as labor.

Outdoor equipment is either hand-, electric-, or gasoline-powered. The gasoline engines in outdoor equipment are of two basic types—the four-cycle and two-cycle. Electric-powered outdoor equipment may be classified as cord or cordless.

Cord (AC) and Cordless (DC) Motors

In an electric motor's conversion of electrical energy into mechanical energy (for work), a magnetic field is formed when current flows through a wire. The wrapping of the wire around a shaft to produce a large coil, in turn, produces more magnetism as the current flows. The reverse polarity of the magnetic coil causes the windings and shaft (armature) to rotate. Rotation of the shaft is the conversion of electrical energy to mechanical energy (for work). As with the gasoline engine, various attachments may be connected to the shaft to produce a piece of usable equipment.

Two power sources are available for electric motors. One is the direct electrical supply through a power cord from a 120-volt AC house electrical outlet. The other supply is the rechargeable cordless battery pack. The power output from electric motors is less than that of gasoline engines, so electrically powered outdoor equipment should be selected for jobs requiring lighter workloads.

Cordless (DC) motors are used in appliances such as hedge clippers, shavers, toothbrushes and dental irrigators, power drills, carving knives, and hair dryers. The cordless models have two separate units, a power handle and a battery charger. The charger consists of a transformer and a diode rectifier; the power handle contains a small DC motor, gears, and other working parts of the appliance, plus a power pack made up of one or more batteries.

The direct-current motors closely resemble universal motors, having a wound rotor (armature), carbon brushes, and a commutator. The only difference in a DC motor is the use of permanent magnets instead of field windings, with the result that DC motors can be smaller, more efficient, and can operate on the direct current provided by batteries. They are also somewhat less powerful than universal motors of the same size.

 WARNING: Electric motors start instantly. Disconnect the power source and turn off the starter switch before attempting any maintenance. All electrical outdoor equipment and parts should be Underwriters' Laboratories (UL) approved.

Motor Maintenance and Repair

Electric motors in outdoor equipment, whether powered by direct cord hookup (AC) or battery pack (DC), require very little special care or repair, though some preventive maintenance is necessary. The motors are generally the universal type; refer to Chapter 4 for information about the operation, troubleshooting, testing, and repair of universal motors.

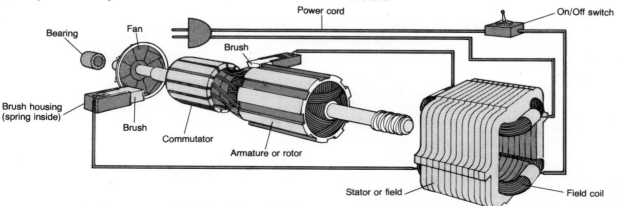

The universal motor, whether powered by direct cord hookup (AC) or battery pack (DC), is the type of electric motor commonly found in outdoor equipment.

Periodic lubrication of the shaft and bearings may be required. Oil ports are located in the motor housing and are normally protected by screws. To lubricate the motor, remove the necessary screws, add a few drops of oil, and replace the screws. Check the manufacturer's specifications for the location of screws, oil ports, and the kind and amount of lubricant to use. Be careful not to drop any lubricant into the motor windings for this may cause the motor to short-circuit and burn. Excessive and insufficient lubrication can be equally harmful, so follow the manufacturer's instructions.

Some electric motors are completely self-contained and require no lubrication. These motors have self-lubricating plastic bearings. If oil is added to the bearings, the result is a thick, gummy mixture which may cause the motor shaft to lock up when stored for a long period of time.

Keeping electric motors clean is essential. Wipe dirt and particles off motors, and use a low-pressure air gun or a vacuum cleaner to remove interior dirt. Some motors require periodic checking and replacement of the armature brushes. Checking the brushes may require removal of the entire motor housing or removal of just the brush assembly. The brush assembly is disassembled by loosening the locking screw on each side of the motor housing. Since the brush is spring-loaded, it will pop out of the motor housing. Check the parts lists for brush specifications and replacement.

The commutator and brushes in DC motors also function like those in universal motors. And, like universal motors, DC motors can develop problems with bound bearings, stripped gears, faulty On/Off switches, or loose connections.

Plug and Cord

In recent years electric motors using a cord and plug have made common use of the three-pronged plug. To accommodate outlets that would only accept old-style, two-pronged plugs, adapters were made available (*See grounding and receptacles in Chapters 1 and 2.*) Adapters include an additional ground wire that can be fastened to the holding screw on the electrical outlet cover plate. Although this is an effective means of grounding a circuit, the method was rarely used because of the inconvenience. Most individuals did not take the time to attach the adapter, unscrew the cover plate screw, attach the ground wire, tighten the screw, and plug in the adaptor prior to using appliances, especially outdoor equipment.

Consequently, a design change in equipment housing called *double insulation* was developed. Double-insulated equipment is housed in a double jacket, each insulated from the other. The outer jacket cannot become part of the electrical circuit even under poor grounding conditions, and thus eliminates the need for the three-pronged (grounded) plug.

Double-insulated equipment also eliminates the three-wire cord (used with three-pronged plugs) and replaces it with heavy-duty two-wire cord, which is lighter in weight and allows for more equipment versatility.

A common problem associated with outdoor cutting equipment is the severing of the power cord. A power cord may be repaired by stripping the insulation, splicing the wires, and wrapping with electrician's tape (*see page 34*). Replace the cord if several splices are necessary. The length of the electric cord may also present a problem. Purchase additional extension cords (after checking manufacturer's specifications for proper wire-gauge requirements) so that equipment can be operated in all areas of the lawn.

Power (Battery) Packs

The power packs attached to cordless equipment may contain a single battery (cell) or several cells connected in series for additional power. The batteries may be standard storage cells or nickel-cadmium cells, each delivering 1.2 volts of direct current. Both kinds may be recharged after partial or full drainage of power. The length of time a fully charged power pack can run an appliance varies according to the amount of power required by the unit and the number of cells in the power pack. If the pack is completely discharged, it will need about fourteen hours of recharging to regain its maximum strength; the charging voltage is normally about 1 volt more than the total output voltage of the power pack. Thus, a unit having five 1.2-volt batteries has a total output of 6 DC volts and requires about 7 volts to be recharged.

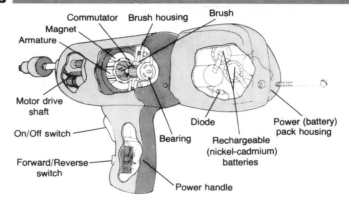

A rechargeable battery pack

Many pieces of cordless equipment have a small charging diode built into their power unit; others have an external charger. The majority of appliances rely on their batteries for power whether the appliance is plugged into an AC outlet or not. Should a unit run when it is connected to a wall outlet but not when it is unplugged, in almost every case it is because the batteries are discharged.

Testing batteries. Usually the cells in a power pack are connected by fixed metal straps which can be used to test the batteries with a multimeter. To test the cells, set the meter to the 25 VDC (DC voltage) scale and touch its probes to the battery contact straps. Turn on the appliance. The voltage should read at least 4 volts if the cells are functional. A reading of below 4 volts indicates that the batteries need recharging. Recharge batteries according to the manufacturer's instructions.

Maintaining batteries. For information about cleaning, protecting, and maintaining batteries, refer to the section on gasoline engines. If battery storage for long periods of time is required, single batteries may be removed from equipment and stored indoors. Multiple batteries should not be removed unless specifically recommended by the manufacturer.

Rechargers (Chargers)

A charger is plugged into a house outlet and draws about 120 volts of AC current. The current enters a transformer that steps it down to about twice the voltage needed to recharge the power pack. It then passes the reduced current through a small solid-state device known as a *diode rectifier*. The rectifier allows electricity to pass through it in one direction only, so it halves the AC current to 6 or 7 volts of pulsating DC current, which flows into the batteries through

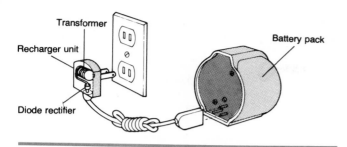

Battery pack and recharger unit

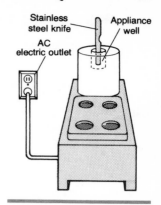

Testing an induction recharger

metal contacts built into both the charger and the power-pack assembly.

A second type of charger is known as an *induction recharger*. This has an induction coil which is energized by direct connection to a 120-volt AC outlet. The coil induces current into a smaller coil inside the power pack without the need for direct contact points. The AC current is smoothed out by a silicon-rectifier-and-filter circuit sealed inside the power pack. With this type of recharger, the appliance must always be stored in the charger and the charger should always be plugged into an AC source. If examination of the well in the charger holding the appliance and the bottom of the power handle reveals no metal contacts, it is safe to assume the unit is charged by an induction recharger. The only way to test this type of charger is to plug it into a wall outlet, turn it on, and then stand a stainless steel knife against the inside of the appliance well. If the knife vibrates, the unit is operational.

Since induction rechargers and their appliances are normally sealed, solid-state components, they cannot be opened for repairs. A disfunctional unit must be returned to its manufacturer for replacement: tampering with the circuitry could void the warranty. On chargers that are accessible, repairs that can be made are replacing the transformer, the rectifier, or the power cord.

Testing chargers

Test for operation. Plug charging unit into AC outlet, and set multimeter to 25 VDC scale. Touch meter probes to charger contacts, then reverse probes. If meter reads 1 volt more than total output of power pack (number of cells × 1.2 V) during either of settings, charger is functioning. If reading is zero volts at both settings, test for AC power.

Test for AC power. Set multimeter to 25 VAC. With charging unit plugged into wall outlet, touch meter probes to

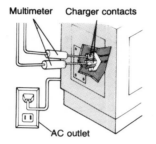

charger contacts. If there is any reading at all, test diode. If reading is zero, test power cord.

Test for power cord. Charging units may plug directly into wall outlet or may have power cord. In either case, set meter to Rx100 scale and clip probes to charger prongs. If meter reads zero, or higher than 500-1000 ohms, either cord or transformer is faulty.

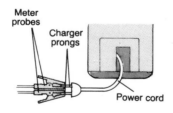

Direct diode test. In appliances where diode is accessible in charger or power handle, either unplug charger or turn off power handle. Set multimeter to Rx1 scale and touch probes to diode leads. Reverse probe setting. The diode is functional if meter reads high at one setting and low at other. If meter reads

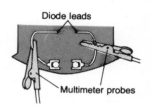

zero, diode has short-circuited and must be replaced.

Indirect diode test. With charging units that cannot be opened, clip jumper cable to one contact in base of charger and to corresponding contact at bottom of power handle. Attach meter probes to two remaining contacts. Set meter to 250 mA (milliampere) scale and plug charger into AC outlet. If meter reads zero, reverse meter probes. Second setting will read approximately 50 mA or higher if diode is functional. A zero reading to-

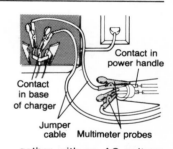

gether with an AC voltage reading means diode has short-circuited.

BATTERY PACK TROUBLESHOOTING

PROBLEM: Battery pack does not run.

Possible Cause	Procedure	Remedy	Rating	Parts	Labor
Batteries not charged.	Test batteries.	Charge or replace batteries.	■ ■		
On/Off switch faulty.	Test switch for continuity.	Repair or replace switch.	■ ■ ■ ■	$5	$10

PROBLEM: Battery charger does not function.

Possible Cause	Procedure	Remedy	Rating	Parts	Labor
No power at outlet.	Test for continuity.	Replace fuse or reset circuit breaker.	■		
Batteries discharging.	Test batteries.	Replace batteries.	■ ■		
Cord set faulty.	Check cord and plug for continuity, loose terminals, and broken or worn wires.	Repair or replace cord set.	■ ■ ■	$10	$10
Charger faulty.	Test for continuity.	Repair or replace.	■ ■ ■	$25	$15

Small Gasoline Engines

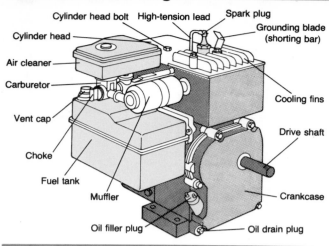

A four-cycle gasoline engine

The primary function of the gasoline engine is to convert chemical energy (gasoline) into mechanical energy for work through a controlled sequence of events. Converting the energy is achieved by the combustion of an air-fuel mixture (within a cylinder) that drives a piston. The movement of the piston forces the crankshaft to turn, producing a rotating power source. A variety of attachments may be connected to this power source to produce a piece of usable equipment. The work cycle of the gasoline engine is comprised of five events: intake, compression, ignition, expansion, and exhaust.

- *Intake*—The air-fuel mixture from the carburetor is fed into the cylinder on the downward stroke of the piston.
- *Compression*—The air-fuel mixture is compressed by the upward movement of the piston in the cylinder.
- *Ignition*—An electric spark ignites the air-fuel mixture.
- *Expansion*—Combustion of the air-fuel mixture creates pressure (through the expanding gas) which forces the piston downward. The power generated by the movement of the piston is transferred to the crankshaft. The revolving crankshaft provides the mechanical energy for the work.
- *Exhaust*—The burned gases are expelled through the exhaust port, which allows the new cycle, the five-event sequence, to begin.

The gasoline engines in outdoor equipment are either four-cycle or two-cycle. The term *four-cycle* actually means four-stroke cycle, referring to the four separate strokes of the piston—intake, compression, expansion, and exhaust. These four strokes comprise the basic operation of a four-cycle small gasoline engine, the most commonly available for outdoor equipment. The *two-cycle* (two-stroke-cycle) engine completes each power cycle with two strokes of the piston. Both engines require periodic cleaning, adjustment, and servicing to perform efficiently.

Operation of a Four-cycle Engine

Intake. The intake valve allows the air-fuel mixture to flow into the combustion chamber at the beginning of the piston's downward stroke. As the piston moves down, a partial vacuum is created in the combustion chamber and atmospheric pressure forces a new fuel-air mixture (through the carburetion system) to flow into the chamber. When the piston reaches the bottom of its stroke, the intake valve closes, trapping the fuel-air mixture above the piston inside the cylinder.

Compression. The crankshaft moves the piston upward, tightly compressing the fuel-air mixture in the combustion chamber. At the top of the upward stroke, the mixture is ignited by an electric spark from the spark plug.

Power. The ignition system transmits voltage to the spark plug, causing a spark to jump between the spark-plug electrodes. The spark causes a controlled explosion (ignition) of the compressed air-fuel mixture in the combustion chamber. The air-fuel mixture becomes an expanding gas that drives the piston downward. The up-and-down motion of the piston is converted to the rotating motion the engine delivers to a load through a connecting rod that joins the piston to the crankshaft. Toward the end of the power stroke, the piston continues downward to the bottom of the stroke and then starts back upward in the exhaust stroke.

Exhaust. As the crankshaft pulls the piston back upward in the exhaust stroke, the burnt gases and fumes are expelled by the exhaust valve through a hole in the engine block.

Operation of a Two-cycle Engine

Compresssion. In the two-cycle engine, every upstroke of the piston is a compression stroke, and every downstroke is a power stroke. Intake and exhaust occur between the two strokes. As the piston moves upward in the compression stroke, the air-fuel mixture above it is compressed, creating

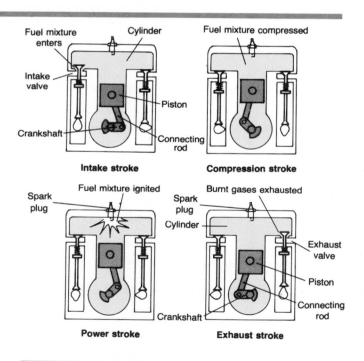

Intake stroke   **Compression stroke**

Power stroke   **Exhaust stroke**

Operation of a four-cycle engine

a slight vacuum in the crankcase. Atmospheric pressure then forces the air-fuel mixture to flow from the carburetor into the crankcase through the reed valve. At the top of the piston's stroke, the spark plug ignites the air-fuel mixture and initiates the power stroke.

Power. After the ignition of the air-fuel mixture starts the piston's downward (power) stroke, the pressure increases in the crankcase and closes the intake (reed) valve. As the piston moves down, the pressure it creates pushes the air-fuel mixture through the intake port into the combustion chamber. The entering air-fuel mixture helps force the exhaust gases out of the exhaust port.

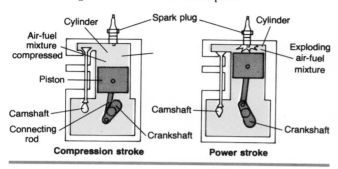

Operation of a two-cycle engine

Engine Tune-up

- Clean and regap or replace spark plug.
- Test compression of engine cylinder.
- Torque all fasteners and bolts in engine according to manufacturer's directions.
- Clean air filter or cleaner of carburetor.
- Clean fuel tank, fuel tank vent caps, fuel line, and fuel filter.
- Adjust carburetor—choke, fuel mixture, and idle speed.
- Adjust governor speed with tachometer.
- Inspect and service valves, including valve seats, springs, and guides.
- Test condenser (capacitor) with ohmmeter and replace if necessary.
- Test primary and secondary windings of ignition coil with multimeter.
- Check and clean breaker points or replace if necessary. Set breaker-point gap.
- Remove carbon buildup from muffler and exhaust ports.

Tools for Engine Tune-up

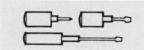

Standard and Phillips-head screwdrivers

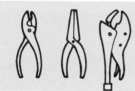

Locking, long-nosed, and adjustable pliers

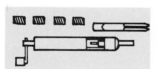

Heli-coil thread repair kit—for repairing stripped bolts and screws

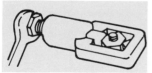

Nut splitter—for destroying frozen nut without harming bolt threads

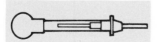

Hydrometer—for checking specific gravity of batteries

Micrometer

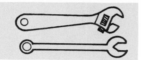

Adjustable and combination wrenches

Grease gun

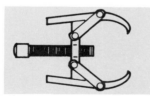

Gear puller—for removing gears from crankshaft

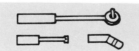

Ratchet wrench and socket set (English and metric sizes)

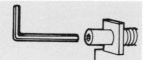

Allen wrenches

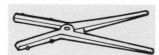

Piston ring expander—for removing and installing piston rings

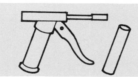

Compression gauge—for measuring engine compression

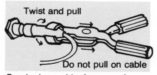

Twist and pull

Do not pull on cable

Spark-plug cable forceps—for removing spark plugs without damaging ceramic casing

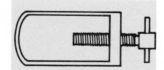

Piston pin extractor—for removing piston pin from connecting rod

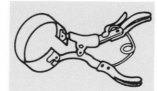

Piston compressor—for squeezing piston rings while replacing piston in cylinder

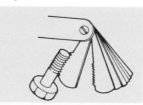

Thread gauge—blade numbers refer to number of threads per inch

Vacuum-and-pressure gauge—for evaluating airtight seals in valves and piston rings

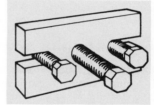

Flywheel puller—for removing flywheels from crankshaft

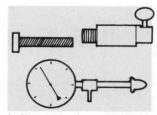

Ignition gauge—for measuring timing in ignition

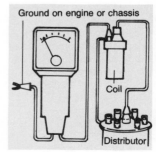

Ground on engine or chassis

Coil

Distributor

Tachometer—for measuring engine speeds (in revolutions per minute)

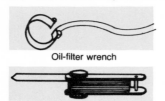

Feeler gauge—blade thickness is marked on each blade

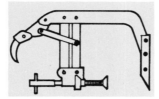

Valve-spring compressor—for removing and installing valve springs

Round wire feeler gauge—hooks are used to bend side electrode

Torque wrench—for measuring torque applied to bolts and screws

Cylinder and Crankcase

Cylinder block

The major component of both two- and four-cycle engines is the cylinder block, which is made from high-quality aluminum or cast iron. The cylinder block has a hole bored through it which forms the inside diameter (bore) of the cylinder, in which the piston moves up and down. The top of the cylinder block is covered by the cylinder head; the bottom of the cylinder block is bolted to the top of the crankcase. Often the two parts are molded together to form a single-piece housing.

Cylinder head

The cylinder head is held to the top of the cylinder block with bolts that must be tightened in a specific order and to specific torque values. A fiber

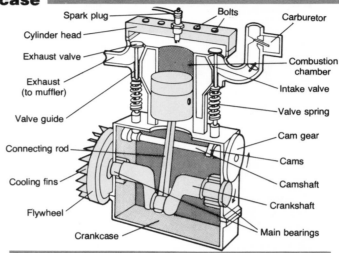

Anatomy of an engine

or cork gasket situated between the cylinder head and cylinder block provides an air-tight seal. The cylinder head forms the top of the combustion chamber in both two- and four-cycle engines. The spark plug, used to ignite the air-fuel mixture, is threaded into the top of the combustion chamber, also to a specific torque value.

Crankcase

The crankcase is a housing designed to hold most of the moving parts in both two- and four-cycle engines. It contains the crankshaft and its bearings, and a connecting rod joined to the bottom of the piston. If the engine is four-cycle, the crankcase also contains a camshaft, cams, cam gears, the lubricating mechanism, an oil reservoir, and a crankcase breather. The bottom of the crankcase may be sealed by either a baseplate or an oil pan.

Maintenance and Repair of Cylinder and Crankcase

Checking Compression

Compression is the pressure buildup in the engine cylinder during the piston's compression stroke; insufficient compression results in a lack of power and operating efficiency. The most common cause of compression loss is a burned or worn valve. A burned valve may be the result of an overheated engine, not enough oil for proper lubrication, or simply too many hours of operation. Compression is lost when the valve does not seat properly and allows the pressure to leak. Other causes for compression loss are a cracked or worn piston ring or a leak in the cylinder-head gasket. Generally, a leaking gasket will cause a high-pitched sound or whistle while the engine is operating.

A simple test for engine compression is to remove the spark plug, place a thumb over the spark-plug hole, and crank the engine. Alternate blowing and sucking action should take place as the piston moves up and down inside the cylinder.

If a compression gauge is available, screw the hose into the spark-plug hole, crank the engine, and read the gauge. Check the manufacturer's specifications for the correct compression reading on the engine.

Engine specifications include the length of the piston stroke, the bore of the engine, piston displacement, and the compression ratio—all of which pertain to the piston. The *length of the piston stroke* is measured in inches from the top dead center of the piston's stroke to the bottom dead center. The *bore of the engine,* also measured in inches, is the internal diameter of the hole in the cylinder block. *Piston displacement* actually describes the relative size of the engine; horsepower is usually in direct proportion to the volume displaced by

the piston during its reciprocating movement. The larger the internal diameter, or bore, of the cylinder and the longer the piston stroke, the greater is the piston displacement. The *compression ratio* is a comparison of the space left in the cylinder when the piston is at bottom dead center *versus* the space remaining above the piston when it is at top dead center. A sample ratio might be 5:1, meaning that there is 5 times more volume left above the piston when it is at the bottom of its stroke than when it is at the top of its upstroke.

Procedure: Removing, Cleaning, and Replacing the Cylinder Head

1. Tag each cylinder-head bolt and mark socket it resides in. Undo bolts with wrench.

2. If cylinder head cannot be pried off by hand, use screwdriver blade to carefully work head loose.

3. Peel off gasket and sealer residue from both cylinder and cylinder-head surfaces. Clean surfaces with lacquer thinner. Be careful not to scratch any metal sealing surface.

4. Remove all carbon from inside of cylinder head, using wire brush attached to electric drill. Then clean head with solvent and inspect carefully for

cracks, scoring, pitting, or wear. When reinstalling, replace old parts with new wherever necessary.

5. Place new gasket between cylinder and cylinder-head surfaces. Never reuse old gasket.

6. Place cylinder-head bolts in correct holes and hand-tighten.

7. Cylinder-head bolts must be tightened in specific order and to specific torque values recommended by manufacturer. Partially tighten each bolt in order; then repeat sequence until all bolts are tightened to proper torque values.

Valves

Valves are the moving engine components that control the exchange of fuel, air, and gases during the internal combustion process. Valves can stick, crack, and develop pits; they can also wear down their stems, seat guides, and lifters. Proper maintenance includes servicing all these components.

Crankcase breather

The breather can be a ball check or a floating disk but most usually is a reed valve. It is found in a small box bolted to the outside of a four-cycle engine, although it may be integrated into the valve access cover. The purpose of the breather is to allow any excessive pressure caused by the expansion of blow-by gases (leaking between the cylinder and piston) to escape from the crankcase.

Whenever the piston begins

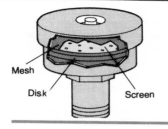
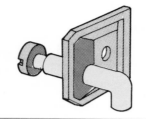

Crankcase breathers

its upward stroke, it creates a vacuum in the crankcase, allowing outside atmospheric pressure to close the valve. If

any gases escape past worn piston rings during the downward stroke of the piston, or if air in the crankcase overheats

and expands too much, excessive pressures will cause the oil seals in the engine to leak. As the piston moves downward, the breather opens to allow either air or gases to escape into the atmosphere. The breather uses a metal mesh, fiber, or polyurethane filter to prevent dirt from being sucked into the crankcase. If oil is detected leaking from the crankcase breather or oil seals, the breather is probably clogged and should be cleaned.

Reed, rotary, and poppet valves

Reed valve. A reed valve is made of thin, flexible steel and is located between the carburetor and crankcase in two-cycle engines. The valve allows the air-fuel mixture to flow from the carburetor into the crankcase whenever the piston rises, creating enough suction to pull the valve open. Otherwise, it remains closed.

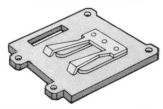

Reed valve

Rotary valve. The rotary valve is used in two-cycle engines as an alternative to the reed valve, but it is attached to

the crankshaft. As the crankshaft turns, a port in the rotary valve comes in line with the crankcase port, allowing the

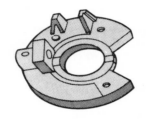

Rotary valve

air-fuel mixture to enter the crankcase as the piston rises to its upper position.

Poppet valve. The poppet valve, occasionally used in two-cycle engines instead of a reed or rotary valve, is almost always used in four-cycle engines. Its function—controlling the flow of the air-fuel mixture into the crankcase—is identi-

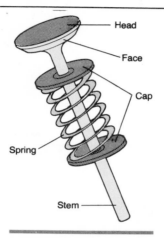

Poppet valves are used on both the intake and exhaust ports.

cal in both types of engine. The poppet valve is kept shut by springs until the upstroke of the piston pushes it open to allow the air-fuel mixture into the crankcase. Two poppet valves are used with each cylinder, one to control the *intake*

port and the other to control the *exhaust* port. While both valves consist of a cap at each end of a spring, the head of the valve seat that opens and closes the port is normally slightly larger on the exhaust port.

Intake and exhaust valves

These valves must be made of special steel that will not corrode from the action of 4500°F. exhaust gases. In four-cycle engines, the valves are used to control the flow of gases in and out of the cylinder; therefore, they must seal the exhaust ports extremely well or there will be a loss of compression. Each valve is held in place in the valve guide by a keeper. The keeper can be in the form of a C-shaped washer, a pin inserted through the valve stem, or a two-piece collar, and is located either in the sides of the cylinder or in the cylinder head.

Valve Maintenance and Repair

Valve springs

Check each valve spring for cracks, bends, breaks, or distortion. The ends of the spring should be square; to check for squareness, place the spring next to a T square. If any distortion in the spring is evident, replace it.

Valve seats

A valve seat may be bored out of the cylinder block, or it may be a separate part inserted into a hole in the block. If the seat is grooved, pitted, or worn to any degree, it should be reconditioned.

Reed valves

The reed valve assembly in two-cycle engines can be cleaned with a solvent. Inspect the assembly for distorted, broken, or cracked parts; any imperfect part should be replaced. The maximum clearance between the reeds and the reed plate is about 0.015 inch (as stated in the engine specifications). Verify the clearance with a feeler gauge; if it is excessive, replace the reeds.

Procedure: Servicing Poppet Valves

1. Remove cylinder head and valve access cover.

2. Lift end of poppet-valve spring with valve spring compressor or screwdriver. Grip keeper (retaining pin, collar, or C-shaped washer) with long-nosed pliers.

3. Pull valve out of cylinder and remove spring from access hole. Tag spring and valve. (Exhaust valves are slightly larger than intake valves and their somewhat heavier springs must be returned to proper access holes.)

4. Use wire brush to clean off carbon from valves and springs. Then rinse them in solvent.

5. Examine valves and springs for burns, cracks, warping, or bent stems. Measure stem diameters with micrometer to be sure they still meet manufacturer's specifications. Resurface valves with reamer to eliminate slight burns or minor pits. Replace valves with major defects.

Procedure: Reconditioning Valve Seats

1. Use reamer to shave off seat surface until solid metal is exposed. Valve must be cut at angles (usually 43° to 45°) and to width (approximately 1/32″ to 3/64″) specified by manufacturer. Use reamer that will produce specified width.

2. Apply fine-grade lapping compound to remove all burrs from reaming and resurfacing.

3. Clean off compound residue with solvent and dry thoroughly.

Procedure: Installing a Valve-Seat Insert

1. If valve seat has been pressed into cylinder block, remove insert with valve-seat puller, or hammer, chisel, and punch.

2. With cutter, drill out block to prescribed depth of new valve-seat insert. Stop to measure hole occasionally to prevent cutting too deeply.

3. Clean all metal chips from bore.

4. Chill valve-seat insert to contract it prior to installation. Install insert with driver; 45° bevel in insert should face driver. When insert is in place, peen top edge to secure in position.

Piston Assembly and Connecting Rod

In both two- and four-cycle engines, the piston is a plunger which moves up and down inside the cylinder. It can be made of cast iron, steel, or, most often, aluminum. The piston is designed to deliver the driving force of the engine via the connecting rod that attaches it to the crankshaft. It is comprised of several parts, including a head (crown), grooves, lands, and a base (skirt). The head can be flat, curved, or almost any shape that will direct the flow of gases in the combustion chamber. The grooves around the outside of the piston hold the piston rings, while the base is attached to the connecting rod with the piston pin.

The piston must fit (with a clearance of 0.003 to 0.004 inch) inside the cylinder so that it can not only move up and down freely but also expand and contract during the heating and cooling of the combustion process. If the piston fits too tightly in the cylinder, it is nonfunctional; if it fits too loosely, it operates inefficiently.

The piston must be checked for cracks, wear, holes, or

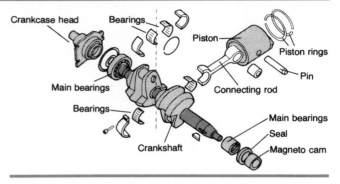

How a piston and connecting rod are attached to the crankshaft

damaged lands and grooves. Replace it when any damage is excessive. Whenever the piston assembly or connecting rod are to be inspected, the cylinder head must be removed.

Piston rings

These rings, made of cast iron or steel, usually fit around the top of the piston to form a solid seal between it and the cylinder wall. There is normally more than one ring on every piston. Some are called *compression rings*, since their task is to maintain compression in the chamber above the valve. Others are known as *oil control rings* and are used only on four-cycle engines. Oil control rings are designed primarily to control the amount of oil that comes up the cylinder wall and flows into the combustion chamber.

Two-cycle engines use two compression rings on the piston to seal the pressure inside the combustion chamber. In four-cycle engines, the piston has two compression rings placed above at least one, and often two, oil control rings. The oil control rings scrape the sides of the cylinder wall to keep any oil from climbing into the combustion chamber, where it would burn and clog the chamber with carbon deposits.

Piston pin

Also known as the *wrist pin*, the piston pin connects the bottom of the piston to the con-

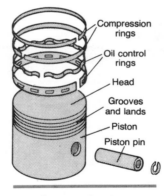

Anatomy of a piston

necting rod. It is made of highly tensile steel or aluminum and can be solid or hollow, depending on how the connection is made. The pin itself may be bolted, clamped, or held between the piston and the connecting rod with retaining rings.

Connecting rod

The connecting rod converts the reciprocating (up-and-down) motion of the piston to the rotary motion of the crankshaft. It is made of forged steel or aluminum in the shape of an I-beam; its big end is bolted to the crankshaft, and its small end is attached to the piston with the piston pin.

Crank and crankshaft

The crank is an offset section of the crankshaft which connects to the big end of the connecting rod and turns the crankshaft. The crankshaft revolves on bearings and has counterweights, either bolted to it or cast as part of it, to balance it as well as reduce vibrations from the engine. One end of the crankshaft is tapered to accept a flywheel while the other end has a power takeoff.

Flywheel

The crankshaft must rotate smoothly through the engine's entire cycle even though it receives its impetus during every other stroke of the piston in a two-cycle engine, and only once in every four strokes of a four-cycle engine. The flywheel is a heavy wheel that attaches to the tapered end of the crankshaft and rotates with it. Because of its relatively extreme weight, the flywheel's momentum forces the rotation of the crankshaft to continue smoothly and evenly. Normally, curved blades, or air vanes, are molded into it to help eliminate heat from the engine or direct air to the cylinder block and head.

Camshaft

The camshaft, which is driven by a *cam gear* attached to the crankshaft that rotates it at exactly half the speed of the crankshaft, opens and closes both the intake and exhaust valves on a four-cycle engine. The camshaft controls valves

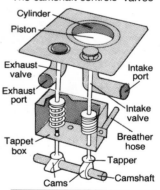

The cam gear and its associated cams for opening and closing the intake and exhaust ports.

with tear-shaped *cams* known as tappets, or lifters, that push against the valve stems to open or close the valves.

Bearings

A bearing is a support for a revolving shaft. There are two types found in small gasoline engines: sleeve and ball bearings. Bearings in their various forms may be sealed in oil or they may be exposed to air and require periodic lubrication. They can be found at the point where the connecting rod and piston unite (as support for the crankshaft in the crankcase) and where the connecting rod and crank come together.

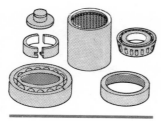

Bearings

Sleeve bearings. These fit around the end of the shaft (like a sleeve). The outside of the bearing is steel or bronze; the inside has a thin layer of soft metal alloy that conforms to any irregularity of the revolving shaft. If this union of metals causes wear, the inner facing of the bearing breaks down before the shaft.

Ball bearings. These consist of a grooved spacer, lodged between inner and outer racers, which holds a series of small steel balls. The ring of balls is slightly larger than whatever shaft it fits over to allow for heat expansion of the shaft and to give the moving surfaces space for lubrication oil.

Procedure: Removing and Servicing the Piston Assembly and Connecting Rod

1. Remove cylinder head and crankcase baseplate. Disassemble connecting rod from crank pin and push piston up through top of cylinder.

2. Remove piston rings with piston-ring expander. Label top and bottom of each ring and its groove.

3. To remove piston pin, pry off retainer ring(s) with screwdriver, and hammer pin out of piston. Be careful not to distort either part.

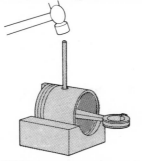

Hammer pin out of piston.

4. Clean carbon residue out of piston-ring grooves and clean grooves with solvent.

5. Measure piston with micrometer at points recommended by manufacturer.

6. Clean piston rings with solvent and inspect for cracks or roughness. Push ring partway down inside of cylinder; measure gap between ends of ring with feeler gauge. If gap is too wide, replace ring; if too narrow, file down ends.

7. Measure side clearance of piston ring. Place outside edge of each ring in its groove; then, using feeler gauge, measure space between it and land above. If distance does not fit specifications, replace ring.

8. Measure diameter of piston pin and inside diameter of bushing with micrometer. If piston pin or bushing does not meet specifications, replace with oversized pin. (A larger pin may necessitate reboring the connecting-rod bushing.)

Procedure: Reinstalling a Piston Assembly and Connecting Rod

1. Reassemble connecting rod, bearing, and retainer ring to piston. Hammer piston pin into place, or heat piston with propane torch and insert pin when metal of piston is warm and has expanded.

2. Replace piston rings in proper order and grooves. Be sure top of each ring faces upward. Ring gaps should be staggered around piston.

3. Oil the piston rings, piston, crankpin, and cylinder wall. In-

sert piston in ring compressor and tighten compressor. Insert piston (while in compressor) into cylinder until compressor touches top of cylinder; then, drive piston out of compressor by hitting with hammer handle.

4. Unite connecting rod and crankpin; put bearing cup into connecting rod. Bolts holding baseplate or oil pan must be tightened to manufacturer's recommended torque values.

Supporting Systems to the Gasoline Engine

Small gasoline engines energize the piston inside their cylinders by using fire, heat, and pressure. The reciprocating action of the piston is converted to the rotary motion of the crankshaft positioned immediately below the cylinder, in the crankcase. The components of the basic engine include the spark plug, cylinder head, cylinder block, piston, piston rod, crank, crankshaft, and crankcase.

Attending the basic engine there are seven distinct supporting systems.

- *Starting system*—activates the engine.

- *Ignition system*—ignites the fuel-air mixture with a spark from the spark plug each time it is required during the two or four cycles of the engine's operation.

- *Carburetion system*—produces the correct mixture of air and fuel at exactly the right moment during the operation cycle of the engine.

- *Lubricating system*—reduces friction between the engine's moving parts by providing them with the proper amount of oil to prevent unnecessary wear.

- *Cooling system*—(technically part of the cylinder design) uses air to remove excess heat caused by the burning of the fuel-air mixture in the combustion chamber.

- *Exhaust system*—utilizes ports bored through the cylinder wall to the combustion chamber and a muffler to discharge exhaust gases from the combustion chamber.

- *Transmission system*—transmits the energy produced by the engine to the piece of equipment it operates.

Starting System

There are a number of systems for starting a two- or four-cycle engine. These range from simple cranks, ropes, and quick-release springs, to the more complex electric starter-motors. Essentially, all starters are designed to use enough of one kind of energy (manual or electric) to activate the mechanical energy produced by the engine.

Manual Starters

The manual starters used to activate small gasoline engines in outdoor equipment are a crank, a simple rope-pull, a retractable (recoil, rewind) rope-pull, and a quick-release (impulse) starter. While none of these are particularly complicated, each requires a certain amount of maintenance to keep it in working order. Periodically disassemble the unit and clean its parts with solvent. All parts should also be inspected for breakage or wear and replaced if they are in poor condition.

Crank starter

The simplest of all starting devices, the crank is used to activate low-speed, multicylinder engines. A crank is inserted in a socket at the end of the crankshaft and then rotated. Manual turning of the crankshaft drives it through one or more cycles until the motor starts. The crank is then removed from the socket.

Regularly check the crank and its socket to be sure there are no burrs on any of the mating surfaces. Burrs can be filed off. If either the base of the crank or its socket becomes overly worn, replace the crank.

Rope-pull starter

A rope-pull starter is a rope with a knot in one end and a handle attached to the other. The knot is inserted into a slot in the rim of a crankshaft pulley and the rope is then wrapped around the pulley. When the handle is pulled, the rope turns the pulley and crankshaft, causing the engine to go through several complete cycles before the rope unwinds and the knot is released from its retaining slot.

Inspect the rope frequently and replace it if either the fibers wear or the handle breaks. Also check the pulley groove that contains the rope knot. File off burrs that might weaken the rope. If the pulley is broken, remove it from its shaft and replace it with an identical-sized unit.

Retractable rope starter

In this rope starter, which functions exactly like the simple rope-pull starter, the rope is permanently connected to the crankshaft pulley or drum. The pulley, in turn, is attached to a flat, heavy-duty spring that winds up tightly as the rope is pulled and immediately unwinds when pressure on the rope decreases. As the spring unwinds, the rotation of the pulley rewinds the rope. There is also a set of pawls, or dogs, attached to the pulley which lock it to the crankshaft as the rope is pulled. The dogs are

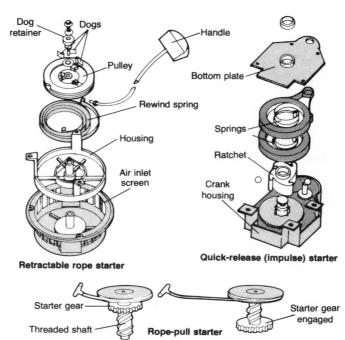

Retractable rope starter

Quick-release (impulse) starter

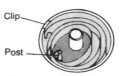

Rope-pull starter

spring-loaded so that, when the rope is released, the pulley disengages from the crankshaft, allowing the flat spring to rewind the rope.

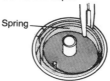

Remove the flat spring in a retractable rope starter with pliers.

When replacing the flat spring, be sure it is clipped to the outside of its housing and firmly seated around the inside post.

Whenever the rope becomes frayed, replace it immediately; it is easier to change the rope when it is still in one piece. Should the rope separate during use, the sudden unwinding of the pulley could break the flat spring. To

replace the spring, unthread the retaining screw in the center of the pulley and lift off its cover. If there is no center bolt, take the entire unit off the engine and turn it over. Free the rope from the pulley to release as much tension as possible from the main spring. The spring can be lifted out of its housing by gripping with long-nosed pliers. Clean and inspect all parts.

Before reassembling the starter, coat the inside of its housing and the coiled spring with lubricating grease. Clip the outer end of the spring to the edge of the housing; then coil the spring, beginning at the outside and working toward the center post. Hook the inner end over its post. Be certain that the spring is coiled in the proper direction and that it hooks into the pulley as the pulley is installed over the spring. Assemble the pawls (dogs) and their washers on the proper shaft. Rotate the pulley by hand to wind up the spring. When the spring is tight, unwind one complete

turn and install the rope. If the spring is wound in the wrong direction or if one full turn is not released, it will not work properly.

Quick-release (impulse) starter

The impulse starter uses a folding crank permanently attached to a heavy, flat spring and ratchet. The crank is rotated until it has completely wound up the spring and is then folded over a release button. When the operator presses down on the folded crank, the button releases the spring, which rotates the ratchet as it rapidly unwinds. The ratchet engages the crankshaft, causing it to turn the engine through several piston cycles.

The power spring inside an impulse starter is extremely forceful, and its removal from the power spring cup can be dangerous. Neither the spring nor its cup usually requires servicing. The main housing of an impulse starter includes the handle assembly, shaft, small gear, pawl, and spring; these should be serviced as a whole assembly. To service an impulse starter, first release the starter spring. Give the handle a few turns and press the release button. Then unbolt the unit from the engine and turn it over, undo the pawl bolt, and lift off the bottom housing. The pawls and their springs can be cleaned with solvent and inspected for wear and damage. If the pawl spring is worn or broken, replace it. Also examine the teeth inside the starter cup positioned on the engine under the starter. If the cup teeth are worn, replace the unit.

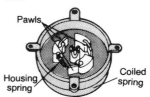

In an impulse starter, the pawls and springs can be reached without touching the coiled spring housed beneath them.

Electric Starters

Larger lawn mowers and small tractors which have high-compression engines and additional features or attachments normally use a starter-motor (which may be called a motor, starter, motor-starter, or motor-generator). The starter-motor requires a battery to become energized with electricity. The battery must also have a generator (if DC) or an alternator (if AC) to recharge it whenever the engine is running.

Before disassembling the entire system when an electric starter fails to work, check the battery cables to be sure they are clean and properly connected to their terminals. Also see whether or not the cut-out switch has broken the connection to the starter because an accessory is not properly attached. Then check the starter-motor for a possible electrical problem.

Starter-motor

Typically, the starter-motor is the universal type. (*See page 61 for the explanation and repair of universal motors.*) The motor draws electricity from a battery connected to it via a starter switch and solenoid. When the starter switch is closed, direct current from the battery flows through the switch into the solenoid relay.

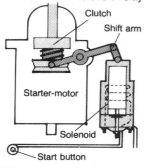

A starter-motor and its components

The solenoid relay contacts close, completing the circuit between the battery and motor. The solenoid is used to draw the starting current from the battery because the high voltage would burn out the starter switch; operation and repair of solenoids is discussed on page 59.

Some small gasoline engines are started by plugging the starter-motor into a 120-volt AC electric outlet. This eliminates the step of recharging the battery.

When inspecting a problematic starter-motor, always check the commutator brushes first. Replace worn brushes. If the starter does not respond or is sluggish, check the battery. Examine all electrical connections for looseness or dirt. Be sure the starter switch is work-

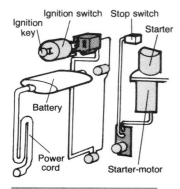

Electric-starter hookup with starter-motor and battery

ing correctly. Replace brushes that show excessive wear. If the battery stops when the pinion engages, the battery may need recharging, the cables may be too long, or the connections may be loose.

Examine the starter solenoid to be sure it is working properly. If the starter-motor starts but the engine does not, check the pinion and crankshaft ring gear for dirt, jamming, worn teeth, or burrs. If the starter keeps running after the engine has started, check the pinion for dirt, jamming, or a broken spring. Examine the gear teeth for wear or damage.

Battery

Batteries used with some small gasoline engines such as those found in lawn mowers may require a battery/key start system. When a battery is used to power the starter-motor to crank the engine, a method of recharging the battery must be included in the starting system. An AC or DC generator is used for this purpose. If an AC generator is used, the AC must be rectified (converted) to direct current and the voltage must be adjusted to meet the battery-charging requirement.

Simple battery maintenance prevents costly replacement and insures more efficient starting of equipment. Clean the surface of the battery oc-

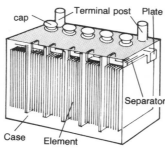

Anatomy of a battery

casionally with a mild solution of baking soda and water to prevent dirt buildup. Dry the top of the battery if any electrolyte is accidentally spilled due to overfilling. Retailers generally service new batteries (add new electrolyte), but some types require the operator of the equipment to add the fresh electrolyte and charge the battery prior to use. Other batteries are manufacturer-sealed and never need servicing.

If necessary, a specific gravity test on the electrolyte can determine the battery's state of charge and whether or not it is being recharged with normal usage. A battery hydrometer may be needed if several pieces of equipment require checking. Battery hydrometers are available at small engine repair shops or local service stations.

Whether installing a new battery or checking an old one, the first step is to secure the battery in place with the hold-down clamp provided on the equipment. Hold-down clamps that have been corroded by electrolyte should be cleaned and coated with grease to prevent further corrosion.

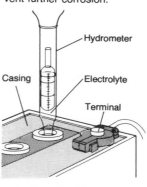

A battery hydrometer

Electrolyte level. Maintain the electrolyte level by adding fresh (distilled or tap) water. Do not add electrolyte because this will change the battery's chemical balance. A visual check of the electrolyte level before and after each use will insure longer battery life. Because electrolyte loss is a major cause of electrolyte loss, check the battery more frequently in extremely hot weather.

Battery caps. Make sure the vent holes of the caps are clear. Dirt, mixed with oil or grease, is a common cause of clogged vent holes.

Battery case. Examine the case frequently for cracks,

leaks, dirt, and corrosion. A battery with a cracked case must be replaced.

Battery cable and connections. Cable connections must be tight for efficient operation. Check the cables, connectors, and battery posts for breaks, dirt, and looseness. After connections have been cleaned with baking-soda solution or a wire brush, tighten all connections and coat with grease to retard corrosion. Do not grease terminals on batteries with permanently sealed terminals. Frayed cables should be repaired or replaced.

Bendix-drive gear

This gear arrangement is used with a starter-motor to engage the flywheel and rotate it through the engine's cycles until the engine starts. Current from the battery causes an armature inside the Bendix-drive gear to turn, forcing a pinion gear to engage and rotate the flywheel ring gear. When the engine has cranked and started, the pinion gear retracts, disengaging the starter-motor from the flywheel ring. While the Bendix-drive gear is a common starting device, several other gear arrangements are also used to unite the starter-motor with the flywheel. Although these vary in outward appearance, all function in exactly the same way.

Periodically check the Bendix-gear's mounting bolts to be sure they are tight. Bolts should not be overtightened for the block may be aluminum (and its threads can be easily stripped). The battery cable is secured to the Bendix-drive gear by means of a threaded post and locking nut. Normal engine vibration may cause the locking nut to loosen, resulting in a poor connection between the power source and starter. A loose nut, indicated by a rapid clicking sound in the Bendix-drive gear while the engine is being started, should be tightened slightly.

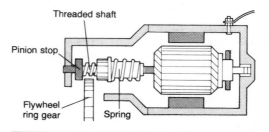

Bendix-drive gear

Ignition System

The ignition system is designed to ignite the air-fuel mixture inside the combustion chamber at the start of each power stroke. To perform its function, the system requires several components: a *battery* or *magneto* to provide the power; a *timer* to cause the ignition spark to occur at the correct moment in the engine cycle; *breaker points* to stop current from entering the ignition coil; a *condenser* to prevent arcing between the points; an *ignition coil* to create the magnetic field; a *spark plug* attached to the top of each cylinder to provide the spark for combustion; and a *high-tension lead* (wire) to carry high voltage to the spark plug.

Solid-state system. In the solid-state system, most of the mechanical parts are replaced with solid-state circuitry. The only moving part is the permanent magnets attached to the flywheel. The other parts of the system are the spark plug and the solid-state module (containing diodes, transistors, rectifiers, and semiconductors), which is hermetically sealed against moisture and dirt.

As the flywheel magnets pass the solid-state package, they induce a low AC voltage into the primary coil. The AC current then passes through a rectifier that converts it to direct current. The DC current flows into the condenser (capacitor), where it is stored. When the rectifier is triggered by the flywheel magnets, it draws about 300 volts from the capacitor and transfers it to the secondary coil, which steps it up to about 30,000 volts before sending it on to the spark plug.

Magneto-ignition system. Most engine-powered outdoor equipment relies on the magneto-ignition system. In this system, permanent magnets attached to the flywheel revolve past the primary and secondary coils, inducing a low voltage into the primary coil. As the breaker cam lobe (high side) on the crankshaft pushes against the pivot arm of the breaker points, the points open, and the magnetic field surrounding the primary coil immediately collapses, inducing voltage into the secondary coil. Voltage builds up in the windings of the secondary coil and is then sent through the high-tension lead to the spark plug.

Battery-ignition system. Oudoor equipment with lights or other electrical accessories may be powered by a battery. Battery ignitions function like magneto-ignition systems except batteries replace the magnets that induce voltage into the primary coil. A 12- or 6-volt battery provides about 100 volts of electricity to the primary coil when the ignition switch is on (the key is turned) and the breaker points are closed. When the breaker cam on the crankshaft opens the breaker points, the voltage delivered from the primary coil to the secondary coil builds up to around 20,000 volts and then passes along the high-tension lead to the spark plug.

Parts of the Ignition System

Spark plug and high-tension lead

The spark plug and high-tension lead (wire) that connects it to the power source provide the electrical spark needed for ignition of the compressed air-fuel mixture. The spark plug, threaded into the cylinder head at the top of the combustion chamber, has a center electrode embedded in an insulated ceramic housing. The high-tension lead from the power source is clipped to the top of the spark plug, usually under a rubber boot. At the bottom of the spark plug, the center electrode protrudes from its ceramic sheath; a side electrode, in the form of an L-shaped piece of metal, extends down from the rim of the plug and over the center electrode. There is a gap between the two electrodes, both of which are exposed to the inside of the combustion chamber.

Current flows from the power source through the high-tension lead to the top of the center electrode, travels down the electrode, and then jumps the gap between the center and side electrodes. During this jump the spark ignites the air-fuel mixture in the combustion chamber. The plug receives intermittent current so that it only fires at the completion of the compression stroke

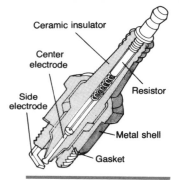

Anatomy of a spark plug

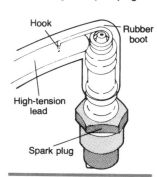

How the high-tension lead is attached to the spark plug

and the start of the ignition stroke.

All parts of an ignition system should be cleaned and inspected periodically. The spark plug, a major source of engine problems, should be checked and maintained reg-

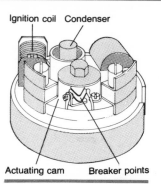

The parts of a magneto-ignition system are positioned near the fixed magnets on the flywheel.

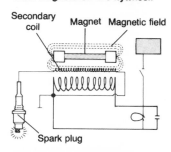

Layout of a battery-powered ignition system

ularly. Spark-plug inspection on the two-cycle engine must be more frequent than on a four-cycle engine because burning the oil with the fuel may foul the plug more quickly. Check the manufacturer's specifications for the type of spark plug to use with a given engine. A spark plug should be changed after every hundred hours of use.

Power source

The power source for the ignition system can be either a battery or a magneto arrangement; both produce electrical bursts of approximately 20,000 volts to create a large enough spark to jump between the electrodes of the spark plug and ignite the air-fuel mixture.

Magneto. The magneto power source is composed of a primary and a secondary circuit. The primary circuit consists of permanent magnets attached to the flywheel, breaker points, a condenser, the primary winding of the ignition coil, and a shorting switch. The secondary circuit includes the secondary winding of the ignition coil, the high-tension lead, and the spark plug. As the powerful permanent magnets rotate, they generate a low voltage in the primary winding of the ignition coil whenever the breaker points are closed. When the breaker points open, the magnetic field around the primary winding collapses and induces current into the secondary winding. The secondary winding has many turns, so that current can build up in series to approximately 20,000 volts before it is re-

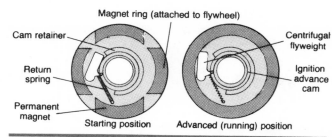

Magnet ring (attached to flywheel)

Cam retainer

Return spring

Permanent magnet

Starting position

Centrifugal flyweight

Ignition advance cam

Advanced (running) position

In a magneto-ignition system, the timing mechanism is inside a magnet ring attached to the flywheel. As the flywheel advances, centrifugal force overcomes the spring holding the flyweight. The flyweight moves into the advanced position and shifts the ignition cam, causing the igniting spark to occur.

leased to the spark plug via the high-tension lead.

Battery. Battery-powered ignitions use a similar arrangement of primary and secondary coils, breaker points, condenser, and spark plug. A 12- or 6-volt battery produces approximately 100 volts of current in the primary coil whenever the ignition key is switched on and the breaker points are closed. When the breaker points open, the voltage induced into the secondary coil builds up to 20,000 volts and is then passed on to the spark plug.

Timer devices

Precise timing of the spark in the combustion chamber is critical to the ignition's operation. If the spark occurs before the piston reaches top dead center, the piston could reverse its direction and make the engine kick back. If the spark occurs after the piston reaches top dead center, there would not be full compression in the combustion chamber and the

engine would run inefficiently. Correct timing of the spark is reckoned in terms of the number of degrees the crankshaft must rotate before it has raised the piston to top dead center. The spark must occur soon enough so that the air-fuel mixture has time to burn and deliver maximum power as the piston begins its downward power stroke.

Solid-state systems control the timing by allowing the flywheel magnets to deliver an electric charge to a rectifier that drains the capacitor of its electricity. Magneto and battery systems rely on a mechanical timer attached to the magnet ring surrounding the permanent magnets on the flywheel. The timer consists of a centrifugal flyweight, return spring, advance cam, and cam retainer. When the engine is just starting, the centrifugal flyweight is held back by the return spring. Once the flywheel is rotating at its running speed, centrifugal force overcomes the return spring and pushes

the flyweight to an advanced position. As the flyweight shifts, it also moves the ignition advance cam, which in turn causes the breaker points to open at the correct instant in the crankshaft's rotation.

While the spark advance is caused automatically with the timer device, the entire timing cycle can be changed by manually rotating the breaker-point assembly and securing it in an advanced or retarded position.

Breaker points

Breaker points are used on magneto- and battery-ignition systems to stop the flow of current to the primary winding of the ignition coil and cause the magnetic field surrounding the coil to collapse.

The breaker point has a stationary arm and a spring-loaded pivoting arm, both of which have tungsten contacts (points) that come together to form a complete circuit in the primary ignition coil. When the points are opened, there is a gap of less than 1/1000 inch.

The points are opened at a specific point in the revolution of the crankshaft by a cam attached to the flywheel. Opening of the points occurs when

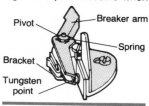

Pivot

Breaker arm

Spring

Bracket

Tungsten point

Anatomy of a breaker point

the cam lobe pushes against the pivotal breaker arm, or against a push rod, plunger, or trip lever that moves against the breaker arm.

Examine breaker points carefully for pitting, proper alignment, good electrical contacts, and wear. Maintenance also includes adjustment of the gap between the points and replacement of the points. If the points are corroded, excessively worn, or pitted, they should be replaced. If they are dirty, dip a piece of clean bond paper in alcohol and pull it between them. Do not touch the contacts; body oil from the skin can act as an insulator and cause them to break down.

If the points do not come together properly, carefully re-bend the stationary arm until correct contact between the points is established.

Condenser and ignition coil

The condenser, also known as a capacitor, is used to store electricity. When used in the ignition system of a small gasoline engine, the capacitor is connected across the breaker points to prevent arcing when they are opened. For the explanation and testing of capacitors, see page 62.

Normally, nothing will happen to either the primary or secondary winding of the ignition coil. Each should be kept clean and maintained securely in its position. The procedure for testing coils with a multimeter is described on page 62.

Ignition-system Maintenance and Repair

Spark Plugs

Removing, inspecting, and replacing spark plugs

When the engine is cool, disconnect the high-tension lead from the top of the plug; then loosen the plug with a wrench and remove it by hand. Inspect the plug to determine whether it is reusable or should be replaced. Prior to installing the spark plug, coat with high-temperature graphite lubricant to eliminate possible seizure and facilitate future removal. The spark plug should be threaded in by hand, hand-tightened, and then secured in place with a half turn of a wrench.

Plugs with evenly colored light tan or gray deposits and

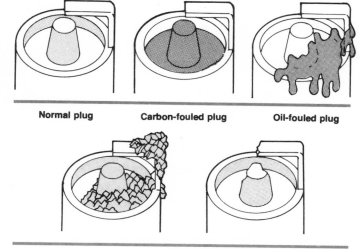

Normal plug

Carbon-fouled plug

Oil-fouled plug

Splash-fouled plug

Mechanically damaged plug

moderate electrode wear (0.005 gap growth since last inspection) can be cleaned, regapped, and reinstalled.

Plugs coated with black, sooty carbon deposits indicate problems. Check for a too rich fuel mixture, a too large spark-plug gap, or low compression (potential mechanical trouble). In addition, check specifications for the plug type and replace with a proper plug if necessary.

Oil-fouled plugs may have been "drowned" with excess fuel during cranking. Check the choke for proper operation, the oil control (piston) rings for leaks, and the plug type for correspondence to engine specifications.

A splash-fouled plug may result after a long delayed

tune-up. Accumulated cylinder deposits are thrown against the plug when the engine is operated at its highest speed. Clean the plug and reinstall.

Mechanical damage, such as a bent electrode or chipped or broken insulation, necessitates replacement of the spark plug. Handle plugs with care. Never attempt to bend the center electrode for the ceramic insulator will crack.

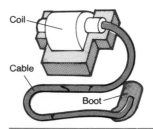

Check the high-tension lead for cracks or breaks; replace if damaged

High-tension lead. Inspect the high-tension lead before it is connected. If the lead is frayed but not badly damaged, electrician's tape may be used for a temporary repair, but the damaged wire ultimately must be replaced. The lead should be connected tightly to both the spark plug and the coil terminals.

Testing sparking

Check the spark plug to see if it is actually sparking. *After*

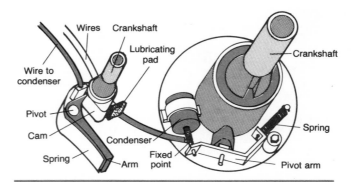

Inspect the mechanical and electrical parts of the ignition system periodically.

removing the spark plug, attach the lead to it. Lay the plug on the surface of the engine so that the metal of the plug is in contact with the engine's metal surface. Crank the engine and watch the spark-plug gap. A visible spark should be seen as the engine is cranked.

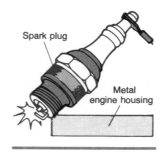

Testing sparking

Cleaning electrodes

If the spark plug and spark are in good condition, use a knife or wire brush to scrape away carbon or dirt around the electrodes. After loosening the particles, blow them away. Do not clean spark plugs with abrasive cleaners such as sandpaper or emery cloth. If the electrodes are rounded, replace the spark plug.

Checking and adjusting the spark-plug gap

The gap between the center and side electrodes should be checked with a wire feeler gauge. Check the manufacturer's specifications for gap size, and place the corresponding wire feeler between the center and side electrodes. If the wire does not fit, the gap must be widened. If the wire fits without

hitting both electrodes, the gap must be narrowed. Use the toothed part of the feeler gauge to adjust the gap. Hook one tooth under or over the front part of the side electrode, depending on the direction in which it must be bent. The other tooth should rest on the back part of the electrode. Bend the side electrode either

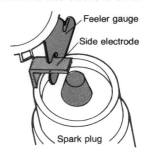

Measure the gap between the side and center electrodes with a feeler gauge.

toward or away from the center electrode to either close or widen the gap. Test again with the correct-size wire feeler. The gap is correctly set if the wire drags slightly when pulled between the electrodes. A wire that is one size smaller should go between the electrodes cleanly; a wire that is one size larger should not go through at all. Check the manufacturer's specifications for the exact width of the gap.

Procedure: Removing the Flywheel to Reach the Breaker Points

1. Lock flywheel to keep it from rotating. Thread piston stop into spark-plug hole to keep piston and assembly immobile. Hold flywheel with chain or strap wrench; place engine with one of flywheel vanes against wood block.

2. Remove flywheel nut with wrench.

3. Remove flywheel with puller (if available). Otherwise, thread a nut on end of flywheel

shaft (do not use flywheel nut) until even with end of shaft. Pull upward on flywheel by gripping underside, and simultaneously tap nut with soft-headed mallet. Flywheel should loosen from tapered portion of crankshaft.

4. Note position of flywheel key; key and flywheel must be replaced in original positions so that flywheel magnets align properly with ignition coils.

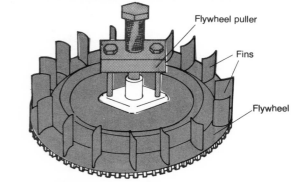

Remove the flywheel with a flywheel puller.

Procedure: Adjusting the Breaker-point Gap

1. Rotate crankshaft until points are wide apart.

2. To set gap, loosen adjustment screw, stationary bracket, or locking screw on station-

ary arm, or move condenser (use applicable procedure), and adjust gap until it meets manufacturer's specifications. Gap must be measured with *clean* (oil-free) feeler gauge.

When points are wide open, there should be slight drag on feeler gauge as it is moved between contacts.

3. Tighten adjusting screw, ro-

tate crankshaft several times, and recheck gap. If gap is not set properly, repeat steps 1 and 2. Gap must be set exactly or ignition timing will be off and engine will operate improperly.

Carburetion System

The carburetion system consists of the fuel-supply system (fuel tank, fuel line, and fuel filter), air cleaner, carburetor, and governor. All these components work together to deliver fuel properly mixed with air to the combustion chamber, to drive the piston. The fuel tank stores gasoline, which is fed to the carburetor through the fuel line. The fuel filter and air cleaner prevent any impurities from entering the air and fuel before they enter the carburetor. The carburetor mixes the gasoline with a proper amount of air and vaporizes the air-fuel mixture prior to its entry into the engine. The governor is used to keep the engine running at a relatively constant speed, no matter what load changes the engine might be subjected to.

Combining air and fuel into a combustible mixture is called *carburetion,* and the component in which it is mixed is known as the *carburetor.* Carburetors are designed to allow a controlled but excessive amount of fuel-air mixture to enter the combustion chamber. The excess is necessary to start a cold engine or an engine not in peak operation condition.

When an engine is running, air enters the carburetor through an *air horn* (passage). The air is actually drawn in because the movement of the piston causes a small vacuum inside the carburetor which has less pressure than the atmospheric pressure outside. The air horn has a restricted passageway known as the *venturi,* which forces the air to speed up. There is a fuel hole at the venturi's connection to the fuel line, so that the increased pressure of air passing through the venturi sucks fuel from the fuel tank, up the fuel line, and into the air horn in the form of a fine spray.

Sometimes—for example, when an engine is being

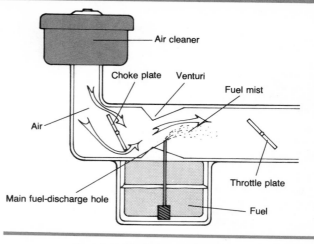

How air and fuel enter a carburetor

started or idling—the mixture of gasoline and air must be richer than normal. A "richer" mixture means that more fuel has been injected in the air-fuel mixture. To provide changes in the mixture there are several jets (fuel holes), a choke; and a throttle located in the air horn. There are also two adjustment screws to establish the main, or operating, speed and the idle speed. The main-speed adjustment screw is located in the venturi, while the idle-speed adjustment screw is positioned downstream in the air horn, just in front of the throttle valve.

Carburetor

Three types of carburetors are used in small gasoline engines: the float carburetor, the diaphragm carburetor, and the suction-feed carburetor.

Float carburetor. The *float carburetor* maintains the fuel level by means of a float and needle valve. As a small reservoir is filled with fuel, the float rises, causing the needle valve to shut off the fuel supply. The float carburetor is designed for operation on nearly level surfaces, requires precise adjustments, and is somewhat expensive to rebuild.

Diaphragm carburetor. The *diaphragm carburetor* utilizes a partial vacuum to operate its diaphragm. As the vacuum increases, the diaphragm is forced against a needle valve which allows more fuel to enter the carburetor.

The diaphragm carburetor is most often used on equipment that must be tilted during use (such as chain saws), because it functions efficiently in a variety of positions. Chain-saw carburetors also use a diaphragm pump.

Suction-feed carburetor. The *suction-feed carburetor* is designed to pull fuel from a shallow tank situated below the carburetor's venturi (narrow part of the air horn). The shallow tank eliminates excessive pressure differences between a full or a nearly empty tank. The suction-feed system should be used on relatively level surfaces and is virtually maintenance free.

Throttle

The throttle regulates the flow of air-fuel mixture through the air horn and therefore controls the speed of the engine. When the throttle is almost closed, it restricts the mixture flow so that the engine can do nothing more than idle. Conversely, when the throttle is wide open, the engine receives more mixture and can run at high speeds.

Choke

The choke is a metal plate used to block off the air entering the carburetor. By reducing

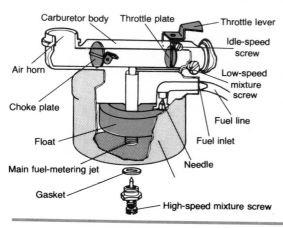

Float carburetor

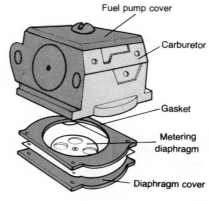

Diaphragm carburetor

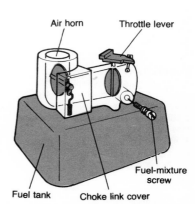

Suction-feed carburetor

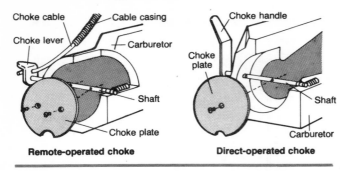

Remote-operated choke   **Direct-operated choke**

Swiveling-plate chokes can be operated either remotely or directly.

the air flow, the choke can change the ratio of air to gasoline and make the mixture richer. A tiny hole in the choke plate allows air to enter the air horn even when the choke is completely closed, as it might be when the engine is started. Two choke designs are used on small gasoline engines: swiveling plate and slide.

Swiveling-plate choke. The *swiveling-plate choke* is a metal disk suspended in the air horn. It is rotated by a choke lever found directly on the carburetor or fastened to a cable linkage attached to the handles on some outdoor equipment. The cable linkage is only

used for convenience and does not change the choke system. Moving the choke lever will either open or close the swiveling plate inside the carburetor.

Slide choke. The *slide choke* has a pair of cylinders which slide into each other. Each cylinder has a hole in it so that when the holes are fully aligned, the choke is open. A slide choke is normally attached to both the throttle and speed-control lever so that whenver the lever is moved, both the choke and throttle adjust their positions automatically.

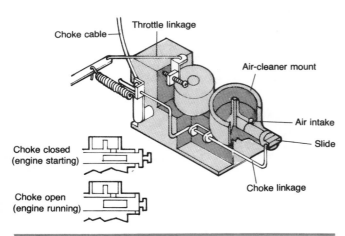

Slide chokes can be operated directly or via a remote cable connection.

Fuel tank

The fuel-supply system consists of a fuel tank and a fuel line. The composition (metal or plastic), shape, and size of the fuel tank can vary. Aside from simply being a vessel to hold gasoline, the tank also has a vented cap, a valve, and a filter.

Vented cap. The vented cap permits air to enter the tank so that atmospheric pressure on the fuel can help to push it to-

ward the carburetor whenever the piston creates a decrease in internal pressure. The vent also prevents a vacuum from building up inside the tank when the fuel is not flowing.

Fuel filter. The fuel filter can be located at various points between the fuel tank and line. Its purpose is to prevent debris that might have fallen into the fuel tank from enterng the fuel line and getting into the carburetor.

Fuel line

The fuel line draws gasoline from the lowest portion of the tank and feeds it to the carburetor. There is often a fuel shut-off valve attached to the tank; the fuel line is connected to the valve nozzle. The fuel line should contain a drain valve. Water or stale fuel may be removed from the tank by opening the drain.

A fuel tank filter is normally positioned in the bottom of the tank. A bowl filter is attached to the outside of the tank.

Air cleaners (filters)

All air enters the carburetor through an air cleaner. Most outdoor equipment is exposed to very dirty working conditions and clean air is a necessity for efficient engine operation.

Air cleaners are available in three types: the dry paper filter, the polyurethane foam filter, and the oil-bath air cleaner. The sole function of the air cleaner is to remove particles and dirt from the air before it enters the carburetor. If the air cleaner becomes clogged, the air flow to the carburetor will be restricted, causing loss of power and carbon buildup on the spark plug.

Governors

Not all small gasoline engines have a *governor,* a device to keep the engine operating at a constant speed despite changes in the load and to keep the engine from running faster than a predetermined maximum speed established by the manufacturer. The governor may be one of two basic designs and is al-

ways connected to the throttle.

The throttle establishes the motor speed, but should the equipment begin to strain, the governor will open the throttle automatically so that the engine can continue running at its preset speed. Similarly, should the load on the equipment ease up, the governor will close the throttle down, to prevent the engine from racing and to maintain a constant speed.

Pneumatic (air-vane) governor. The *pneumatic governor* has a vane positioned near the flywheel so that the flow of air from the flywheel blades can cause it to change positions. A spring connects the vane to a speed-control lever, which in turn is linked to the throttle. As the engine speeds up or slows down, the

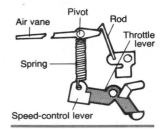

Pneumatic (air-vane) governor

air flow from the flywheel either increases or lessens, causing the air vane to move and adjust the speed-control lever and throttle.

Centrifugal governor. The *centrifugal,* or *mechanical, governor* uses movable flyweights rather than an air vane. The flyweights, most often mounted on the camshaft, move in or out (according to how fast the shaft is rotating) to shift an arm or rod assembly that links them to the throttle. When the engine is idle, the inert weight of the flyweight pulls the throttle open; as the engine is running, the flyweights are thrown outward by centrifugal force to close the throttle.

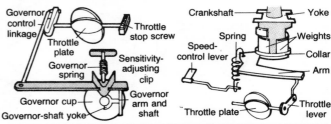

A typical governor-throttle linkage   **Centrifugal governor**

Carburetion-system Maintenance and Repair

Carburetor

Three basic changes that can be made to the carburetor include adjustment of the choke, the fuel mixture, and the idle speed. When making any of these, follow the manufacturer's directions whenever possible. Carburetors vary widely in design and assembly and should not be taken apart without referring to the manufacturer's directions for a specific model. Numerous rubber gaskets in the carburetor can be damaged by solvents containing alcohol, benzol, acetone, or lacquer thinner. Be sure to use a cleaning solvent that will not damage any parts.

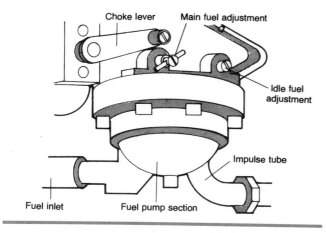

Adjustment points on a carburetor

Procedure: Adjusting the Carburetor

1. Turn off engine. Rotate both main and idle needle-valve adjustment screws clockwise until completely closed. Turn both screws by hand but do not overturn. When completely closed, open by rotating counterclockwise 1 to 1½ turns.

2. Fill fuel tank halfway and start engine. Allow it to reach normal operating temperature before making further adjustments.

3. Pull choke completely open.

4. Set throttle between ⅔ to ¾ maximum speed.

5. All adjustments are made with ⅓ turns of needle-valve adjustment screws. Give engine at least 5 seconds to respond between rotations of screws. Turn screw clockwise ⅛ turn. Wait 5 seconds and turn again. Continue until engine slows. Now turn counterclockwise in ⅛ turns (counting each turn). When engine falters, stop. Divide turns by 2 and go back that number of turns. This sets needle-valve to best setting, where engine is running at fastest and smoothest speed. Main fuel needle is larger of two fuel adjustment screws. If the engine is under a load, this setting should be correct. If the engine is not operating under a load, open the needle ⅛ turn more.

6. To set idle, turn throttle to top speed and then close to slowest speed. Adjust idle needle-valve screw until engine running smoothly, at half of maximum operating speed. Idle speed is located on throttle stop lever and prevents throttle from being completely closed, which would stall engine. If there is governor, throttle must be manually held shut while adjustment is made. Most accurate method of adjusting idle-speed screw is to know manufacturer's specification and use vibrating tachometer.

7. Open throttle from idle position to ¾ engine's maximum speed. Engine should speed up smoothly. If speed transition not smooth, readjust main needle-valve screw to provide richer air-fuel mixture. If engine is sluggish or smokes, adjust screw for leaner mixture.

Fuel tank and filter

Gasoline that has been stored for a season should not be used because it will make the engine hard to start or perform poorly. A sufficient supply of fuel should be maintained in the fuel tank to eliminate the possibility of stirring up dirt and foreign matter from the bottom. Fill the tank after using equipment to prevent condensation from forming inside. Condensation that reaches the carburetor can cause the engine to misfire or run roughly and can rust the interior of the fuel tank.

The surface of the fuel tank should be wiped clean before removing the filler cap, to prevent foreign matter from falling inside. After the cap has been removed, inspect its vent hole. The vent hole should be clear to provide sufficient air to the fuel tank. A visual inspection of the *filler cap gasket* will indi-

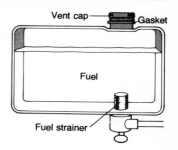

Fuel tank

cate whether the filler cap is sealing properly. A defective *seal* allows fuel to leak out while the engine is running and can create the possibility of explosion. Replace the seal if it is defective.

The fuel filter prevents dirt and foreign matter from entering the fuel line. Periodically remove and clean the filter with a solvent to prevent clogging.

WARNING: Drain the fuel tank only when the engine is cool, to prevent any possibility of fire or explosion.

Air Cleaners

Dry paper filter. Clean the dry paper filter by tapping it lightly on a hard surface to dislodge any dirt particles. The particles may be blown away with a low-pressure air gun or a vacuum cleaner. The paper filter is replaceable.

Polyurethane foam filter. The polyurethane filter may be washed several times with mild soap and water before it must be replaced. Apply a few drops of lightweight oil to the filter before replacing it.

Oil-bath air cleaner. Oil-bath air cleaners are designed for engines that must operate under extremely dirty condi-

tions. The air cleaner, which removes large amounts of dirt from the air, is easily maintained. Regularly clean all parts in kerosene and air-dry; fresh oil should be put in the reservoir (which must be replaced occasionally).

Governors

Use a tachometer to adjust the governor. The operation of most governors is regulated by an adjustment screw, but it may be necessary to slightly bend parts of the linkage assembly or to replace the governor spring. A spring that is too tightly coiled should be replaced, not stretched.

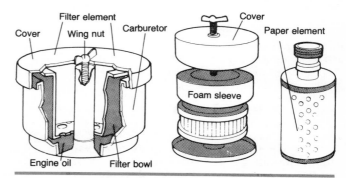

Oil-bath filter   Foam filter   Paper filter

Externally mounted centrifugal governors can be repaired only if the flywheel is removed. To reach internally mounted centrifugal governors, the engine must first be dismantled. All parts in mechanical governors should be closely inspected for wear or damage. Be sure the flyweights or their supports are not bent and that the flyweight collar slides freely on the camshaft or governor gear. The governor shaft should move easily within its bushing. Plastic air vanes that have broken must be replaced. Bent metal vanes can be straightened. Dents or bends in the shroud should be removed so that the air flow from the flywheel blades can move over the governor properly.

Procedure: Disassembling and Repairing the Carburetor

1. Flush carburetor with fuel and blow dry with compressed air. Wipe with lint-free cloth only.

2. Using magnifying glass, check all parts for cracks or breaks, including levers, shafts, swivels, or threads. Replace parts that cannot be repaired.

3. With magnifying glass, inspect valve needles, valve seats, and associated parts. If either valve or seat is damaged, replace both parts.

4. Remove air-filter cover, gasket, and filter screen. Screen is cleaned by flushing with solvent.

5. If fuel pump present, remove cover, diaphragm, and gasket. If diaphragm does not lie flat or has holes, replace.

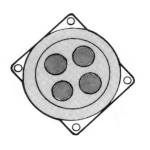

A damaged diaphragm with holes should be replaced.

6. Remove diaphragm cover, diaphragm, and gasket. Check diaphragm for defects. Replace if necessary.

7. Remove fulcrum-pin inlet control lever and spring; inspect for wear or damage. Replace defective parts.

8. Inspect idle bypass holes for clogging; clean with compressed air only.

9. Remove throttle and choke plates and pull shafts out of holes. Examine parts for wear or breaks; replace defective parts.

10. Clean all parts with solvent and reassemble.

Lubricating System

Oil is used in engines to provide lubrication between moving parts, keep all parts and spaces cool and clean, seal in compression, and protect moving parts from wearing down or binding. The oil functions as a cushion between parts that come together with force during combustion of the engine. The connecting rod and crankshaft, for example, must sustain tremendous impact every time they are driven together by the downstroke of the piston; this impact is softened as the oil between their mating surfaces acts like a shock absorber.

The oil eliminates heat from the friction of moving parts by carrying it to the air-cooled walls of the cylinder or crankcase and, in the process, dissipates the heat. As the oil washes over various parts of the engine, it also tends to carry dirt, carbon, and minute particles of metal down to the bottom of the crankcase. And oil helps to seal off the combustion chamber by clinging to the piston rings and filling the grooves in the top of the piston, so that combustion gases cannot escape the chamber and reduce the efficiency of the energy transfer from the piston to the crankshaft.

If the amount of oil in an engine falls below the prescribed level, friction builds up between moving parts, not only wearing them down but also causing excessive heat. The added heat causes the parts to expand more than normal, which increases the amount of friction. With increased friction, microscopic pieces of metal are scraped off mating surfaces and remain there unless there is enough oil to wash them away. Those particles cause even more friction, heat, and wear, until the engine begins to fall apart. Lubrication, therefore, is a most essential process in the performance of any engine.

Access Holes and Slots

The moving parts of an engine are cast with access holes and slots so that oil can flow between the surfaces that touch or interface with the bearings. For example, with a pressurized lubricating system in which the oil is first pumped into the main crankshaft bearings, there are paths inside the crankshaft that lead to the connecting rod bearings.

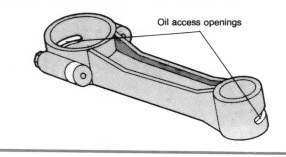

A connecting rod with oil access openings

The oil is then released through holes around the bearing surfaces to splash against the piston and cylinder walls.

Both two- and four-cycle engines have access holes and slots in their moving parts for the transmission of oil to all of the bearing surfaces.

Lubricating Oil

Oils are made with different viscosities and various additives for specific uses. *Viscosity* is the oil's ability to resist flowing; the warmer the oil, the more it flows and the less its viscosity. Manufacturers always specify the type of oil that should be used with their engines, and those specifications should be followed conscientiously.

Oils are designated by the Society of Automotive Engineers (SAE) and the American Petroleum Institute (API) in terms of their weight, which means their thickness or density. The heavier the oil, the thicker it is. The designations indicate different oil weights that can be used to meet different environmental conditions. Oils are also given additives. The additives used include *pour point depressants,* which keep the oil from freezing at low temperatures; *inhibitors* to prevent oxidation, rust, and corrosion that might come from acids, water, or combustion; *detergents* to keep sludge from forming on moving parts of the engine; and *foam inhibitors* to keep the oil in the crankcase from frothing as air is whipped into it by the movement of the crankshaft.

Four-cycle oil

If the manufacturer's recommendations for a four-cycle engine are not available, use any detergent oil having an API classification of SC or SD with the following SAE classifications:

- Over 40°F.—SAE 30, SAE 10W-30, SAE 10W-40

- Below 40°F.—SAE 5W-20, SAE 5W-30, SAE 10W, SAE 10W-30
- Below 0°F.—SAE 10W, SAE 10W-30 with 10% kerosene
- Below 10°F.—SAE 5W

Two-cycle oil

While four-cycle engines generally operate on the same oils as those put in automobiles, two-cycle engines must have only those oils designated particularly for them. Do not use any oil in a two-cycle engine unless its container states that it is a two-cycle oil.

Two-cycle oil must be mixed with the gasoline exactly according to the manufacturer's specifications or carbon deposits will form on the combustion chamber, causing the spark plug to misfire, piston rings to stick, excessive smoking, or poor lubrication of the engine's moving parts. The two-cycle oils are normally nondetergent SAE 30 SB, SC, or SD, and are mixed in a gasoline-to-oil ratio of 20:1 (1 part oil to 20 parts gasoline).

Four-cycle Engine Lubrication

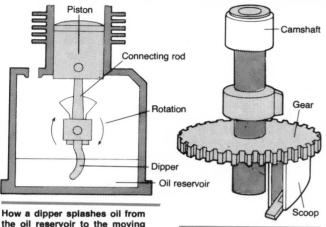

How a dipper splashes oil from the oil reservoir to the moving parts of an engine

Four-cycle engines have an oil reservoir placed under the crankcase. The oil in the reservoir is distributed through the engine by either a splash or a pressure system. If oil in the reservoir is maintained at the specified level, the engine should run evenly at all times.

Splash system

In the splash system, there may be a dipper attached to the connecting-rod bearing cap. As the cap rotates, the dipper throws oil from the reservoir (crankcase) onto the crankshaft bearings, camshaft, and cylinder walls, spreading oil all through the engine.

Instead of a dipper, some splash systems use a scoop attached to the bottom of the camshaft gear; the scoop

A scoop can be used instead of a dipper or slinger to spray oil in the four-cycle engine.

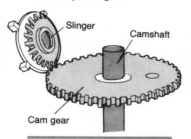

A rotating slinger can distribute lubricating oil in a four-cycle engine.

sprays oil throughout the top of the engine in a circular pattern. Or there can be a rotating slinger driven by the camshaft gear which performs the same function.

Pump system

Some four-cycle engines are lubricated by a pressurized system that relies on a small pump to distribute the oil. The oil pump may be one of several designs, although the three most usual ones are the ejection, rotary dual-gear, and barrel type. The ejection pump is operated by a cam and is aimed at the connecting rod. As oil is ejected at the moving rod, it is splashed in all directions to other engine parts. The rotary dual-gear pump has two gears driven by a pin attached to the hub of the camshaft. As the gears rotate, they force oil from the pump outlet in the gear housing through a hose to the top of the engine. Barrel-type pumps use a plunger to pull oil from an intake port and then squirt it onto the main crankshaft bearings, where it is splashed to other parts of the engine by the movement of the crankshaft and connecting rod.

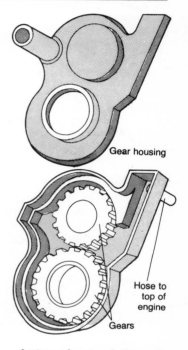

Anatomy of a rotary dual-gear oil pump

Two-cycle Engine Lubrication

Oil and gasoline are always mixed together in the fuel for two-cycle engines. Consequently, no matter what position the engine is operated in, all its parts will still receive their necessary lubrication. As the oil-fuel mixture enters the combustion chamber, the heaviest particles of oil drop out of the mixture and lubricate the engine's moving parts. Some of the oil in the mixture is burned along with the fuel during the combustion stage. The necessary ratio of oil to gasoline is stated by the manufacturer of each engine; mixing procedures should be followed exactly.

Maintenance of the Lubrication Systems

Two-cycle Engine Lubrication

There is no maintenance of the lubrication system in a two-cycle engine, since there is no separate lubrication system per se. The two-cycle engine is internally lubricated by the fuel mixture of oil and gasoline. Check the manufacturer's specifications for the recommended type and weight of oil and the mixing ratio of oil to gasoline. The oil-and-gasoline mixture tends to separate if stored for over two weeks, so it should be re-mixed prior to filling the fuel tank. Two-cycle engines do not have a separate oil reservoir.

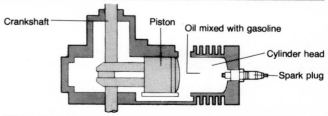

In a two-cycle engine, oil enters the combustion chamber mixed with the gasoline.

Four-cycle Engine Lubrication

The oil reservoir is generally located in the bottom of the engine; the oil level should be checked after approximately every five hours of engine operation. Remove the oil-filler plug and visually check the oil level; add oil if necessary.

Changing the oil at the beginning of the operating season and once during mid-season is recommended. Year-round use of the engine necessitates an oil change approximately every twenty-five hours, under normal operating conditions. Extremely dirty conditions may warrant more frequent changes.

External lubrication of various parts of the engine is also necessary. The rule of thumb is: All moving parts must be lubricated. A drop of lubricant on linkages, springs, control arms, and screw threads extends the life of the parts and provides smoother operation.

Procedure: Changing the Oil in a Four-cycle Engine

1. Start engine and run until warm. Then shut it off. This allows oil to warm, making it easier to drain.

2. Remove oil-drain plug and drain used oil into disposable container. On some engines, drain plug and filler plug are same.

3. Replace drain plug.

4. Check the manufacturer's specifications to determine proper kind and weight of oil.

5. Fill oil reservoir to proper level and replace oil-filler plug. Do not overfill.

Cooling System

Virtually all small gasoline engines used in lawn and garden equipment are air cooled. To prevent the engine's overheating, cool air must constantly flow without obstruction over the outside surfaces of the engine. The engine head is cast with a widely distributed series of metal fins to direct heat away from its operating components. The cooling fins are located at the top of the engine and are covered by the *shroud,* which contains the flywheel and a protective screen. The shroud directs a flow of air across the cooling fins to remove heat from the cylinder block and cylinder head. Operating an engine without the shroud in place usually results in overheating.

The cooling fins on the cylinder and cylinder head, the vanes molded into the flywheel, the screen, and the shroud must be kept free from dirt and other particles, especially on machines such as lawn mowers and rototillers that are used in extremely dirty conditions. If these are kept clean and unobstructed, air can circulate freely around the engine. Use a sharpened, ¼-inch dowel to dig out all foreign matter on the fins and vanes; then clean them with a solvent. Check the parts for cracks or breaks and replace any that cannot be repaired.

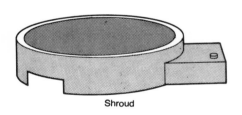

Shroud

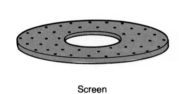

Screen

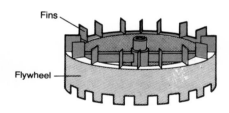

Fins

Flywheel

Keep the flywheel fins, screen, and shroud clean.

Procedure: Cleaning the Shroud

1. Remove any parts covering shroud, such as air cleaner, muffler, spark-plug wire, or governor, and unbolt shroud.

2. Straighten any bent fins, being careful not to break them; replace shroud if it is irreparably damaged.

3. Remove dirt and debris with a wooden or plastic scraper. Brush fins with stiff brush and wipe entire shroud with solvent.

4. Using brush and soft scraper, clean the air-intake screen positioned behind shroud; then wipe with solvent.

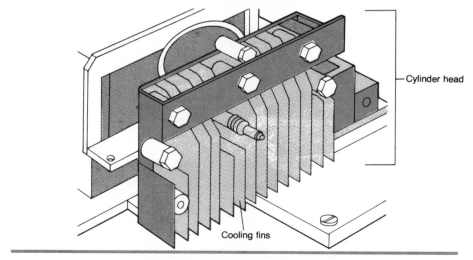

Cylinder head

Cooling fins

Remove foreign matter from the cooling fins on the cylinder and cylinder head.

Exhaust System

The entire exhaust system consists of an exhaust port (hole) bored through the cylinder wall to the combustion chamber and a small canister known as the muffler, which is attached to the outside of the exhaust port. On two-cycle engines, the muffler is normally located at or near the center of the cylinder; on a four-cycle engine, the muffler is near the top of the cylinder head.

Muffler design and size vary considerably. Four-cycle engines usually have a simple metal can threaded into a flange or screwed directly into the exhaust port. Having a can over the exhaust port muffles the sound of the engine and directs exhaust gases away from the machinery. Mufflers used on two-cycle engines not only muffle sound but also help draw exhaust gases out of the combustion chamber so that the new air-fuel mixture can enter more rapidly and burn more completely. To accomplish this, the muffler first amplifies the sound, which helps pull exhaust gases out of the chamber, and then silences the noise with a baffle.

The major problems encountered in the exhaust system are excessive carbon buildup in both the muffler and the exhaust port. Not only does carbon residue cause the motor to become noisy, but it also retards the discharge of exhaust gases from the combustion chamber. When exhaust gases linger inside the chamber, they occupy space that should be taken up by a fresh air-fuel charge. As a result, the engine runs on a partial charge and loses power.

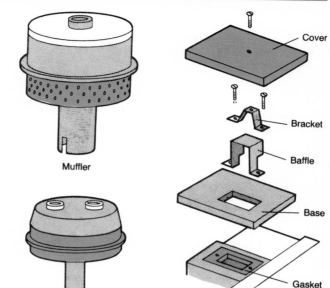

Mufflers come in many designs and sizes.

A two-cycle-engine muffler contains a baffle that allows engine noise to be jaised and then deadened to remove exhaust gases from the combustion chamber more rapidly.

Muffler

Allow the engine to cool before attempting to remove the muffler. Loosen the muffler from its socket with a wrench and then unthread it by hand. Inspect the muffler and muffler gasket. Mufflers frequently rust from the inside out. Tap rust loose and blow it out; replace a muffler with rusted holes. Mufflers on winter equipment (such as the snow blower) rust more quickly than those on other machines due to condensation from exposure to both hot and cold temperatures.

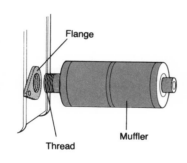

Loosen the muffler with a wrench; then unthread it by hand.

Exhaust Port

Prior to cleaning, pull the rope starter or use the battery/key starter to move the piston so that it covers the exhaust port in the cylinder wall. This will prevent any carbon from accidentally entering the cylinder. The carbon should be removed with a wooden or plastic scraper to eliminate the possibility of scoring the piston or any of the threads in the exhaust port. Blow out all particles scraped from the port before allowing the piston to move away from the hole.

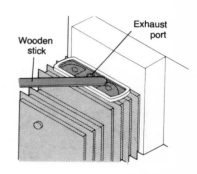

Remove carbon from the muffler and exhaust port with a wooden or plastic scraper.

Transmission System

Energy produced by a small gasoline engine has no value unless it is transmitted to some kind of machinery such as wheels or blades. The transmission system, whatever configuration it takes, forms the link between an engine and the load it operates. In outdoor equipment, the transmission is likely to be a system of belts and pulleys, gears, or merely a rotating shaft.

Most of the problems that arise with transmissions can be avoided by keeping the parts clean and lubricated. The bearings on a drive shaft, pulleys, and chains should be inspected periodically and lubricated every fifty hours of operation. Should any of these parts begin to show signs of excessive wear or damage, replace them.

Belts and Pulleys

Some transmissions are a system of belts and pulleys. Essentially, there is one pulley attached to the engine, a second connected to the driven machinery, and a third pulley known as the *idler pulley*. The idler pulley is arranged somewhere between the two main pulleys so that it can engage the belt(s) to move the equipment forward or backward, or disengage the equipment (and attachments) from the engine without shutting off the power.

Keep each belt properly tensioned and the pulleys aligned with each other so that the belt always travels between them in a straight line. Belt tension, when the belt is engaged, is measured by putting moderate pressure against the belt midway between the main pulleys. Belt deflection should be ¼ to ½ inch. Belt tension can usually be adjusted by moving either a pulley, the machinery, or sometimes the entire engine. Check the equipment manual for specific information concerning belt-tension adjustment.

Belts

Inspect belts for wear. Most of the belts used in outdoor equipment are V-shaped to fit in the grooves of the pulleys they transverse. A new belt should reside entirely within the pulley grooves with the rims of the grooves extending from 1/16 to ⅛ inch beyond the top of the belt. When the belt is more than ¼ inch below the pulley rims, it is considered worn and should be replaced.

Pulleys

Pulleys that contain a belt should be kept aligned; if the belt must move at an angle between them, one side of it will wear down faster than the other. Pulleys are normally held to their shafts with bolts, Allen setscrews or C-clamps and can be moved in or out along their shafts for repositioning.

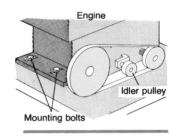

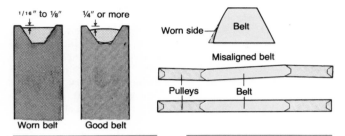

Pulley systems with several pulleys and more than one belt can still be controlled by a single idler pulley.

To increase belt tension, it may be necessary to loosen the engine mounting bolts and shift the entire engine.

Relative positions of a good belt and a worn belt

A misaligned belt wears faster on one side; realign pulleys so the belt path is straight.

Clutches

Some pieces of outdoor equipment use a simple clutch to disengage the engine from its machinery load. (This separation can also be done with gears.) A self-propelled mower, for instance, may have a clutch so that the mower can be driven without turning the cutter blades; a snow blower has a separate clutch for the auger/impeller. An uncomplicated mechanism, the clutch provides a stop-and-go mode and, possibly, a choice of gear ratios (speeds). Two basic types of clutch are used on outdoor equipment: the centrifugal clutch and the spring clutch.

Spring clutch

A spring clutch must be manually engaged by moving a lever. The clutch, a canister with either a pulley or sprocket permanently attached to one end, is held to the crankshaft by a pin or an Allen setscrew. A square spring inside the canister wraps and unwraps around the shaft when the clutch is engaged or disengaged.

Spring clutch repairs. A spring clutch can be removed from the shaft but not disassembled for repair. If the sprocket or pulley on the outside of the clutch can be rotated in both directions by hand, the spring is broken. Free the pin or setscrew, pull off the clutch, and replace the entire unit. If the sprocket is worn or the pulley damaged, again, replace the entire clutch.

Centrifugal clutch

A centrifugal clutch is threaded to the engine camshaft and held in place by a C-shaped keeper or spring clip. The clutch consists of a round drum housing surrounding a two-part hub with two halves held together by springs. The halves are surfaced with a friction material. When the engine is running, centrifugal force throws the hub halves outward so that the friction material on their edges catches the drum, causing it to rotate.

Centrifugal clutch repairs. To remove a centrifugal clutch, first take out the spark plug and then lower the piston to bottom dead center. Stuff a length of clothesline into the cylinder or use a piston stop to keep the piston and camshaft immobile. Remove the clip and housing; then unscrew the hub by turning it clockwise (it has a reverse thread). Examine the inside of the drum for scoring. Rotate the bearings inside the center hole of the drum; they should turn smoothly and evenly. Examine the friction material on the hubs for excessive wear; measure the gap between the material and the hub with a feeler gauge. The gap should be evenly spaced at several points. If the hub movement is irregular, the springs are weak, or the friction material is excessively worn, replace the entire clutch.

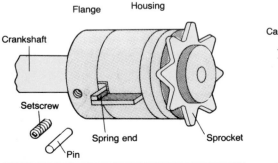

Spring clutch

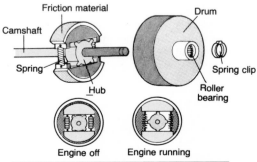

Centrifugal clutch

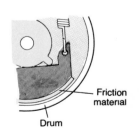

The gap between the drum and friction material should be equal at all points.

GASOLINE ENGINE TROUBLESHOOTING

PROBLEM: Engine does not start or is hard to start.

Possible Cause	Procedure	Remedy	Rating	Parts	Labor
No fuel in tank.	Check fuel tank.	Fill tank with fuel.	■		
No oil (4-cycle engine).	Check oil reservoir.	Add oil.	■		
Fuel line to carburetor blocked.	Check fuel line.	Clean line or remove and replace.	■ ■	$3	$12
Foreign matter or water in fuel.	Drain fuel tank. Clean carburetor and fuel line.	Fill tank with clean, fresh fuel.	■ ■ ■ ■		$12
Stale fuel in tank. tank.	Drain tank. Clean carburetor and fuel line.	Fill tank with clean, new fuel.	■ ■ ■ ■		$12
No spark to jump electrode gap.	Check spark-plug wire.	Reattach wire if loose or disconnected. Repair or replace if damaged.	■ ■ ■	$2	$18-20
Spark plug fouled or faulty.	Remove spark plug.	Replace spark plug.	■	$2	
Internal ignition system malfunctioning.	Test points, condenser, and coil for circuit continuity.	Rework, reset, and replace parts as needed.	■ ■ ■ ■	$10	$24-36
Starting system defective.	Check starting system for damaged or weak parts.	Replace worn or damaged parts as needed.	■ ■ ■ ■	$8-16	$24-36
Engine flooded.	Open choke. Remove air cleaner.	Clean and service air cleaner.	■	$2.50-5	
Carburetor dirty.	Remove carburetor.	Clean carburetor with cleaning solvent.	■ ■ ■ ■		$12
Carburetor choke lever not open far enough.	Check position of lever.	Open choke.	■		
Compression low.	Check rings and valves.	Replace rings and valves.	■ ■ ■ ■ ■	$20	$35
Carbon blocking exhaust ports (2-cycle engine).	Check ports.	Remove carbon buildup from ports.	■ ■		$12-15
Carburetor valve (letting air-fuel mixture into crankcase) defective.	Inspect valve and assembly.	Replace damaged valve or assembly.	■ ■ ■ ■	$8	$12

PROBLEM: Engine runs poorly.

Possible Cause	Procedure	Remedy	Rating	Parts	Labor
Fuel mixture too rich.	Increase air-to-fuel ratio.	Close choke.	■		
Internal ignition faulty.	Check points, condenser, and coil for continuity.	Rework, reset, and replace parts as needed.	■ ■ ■ ■ ■	$10	$24-36
Loss of compression.	Check.	Replace rings and valves.	■ ■ ■ ■ ■	$20	$35
Carburetor malfunctioning.	Check carburetor float level, needle-valve adjustment, linkages, and moving parts.	If float level set too low, reset. Adjust regulator screws.	■ ■ ■		$12
Needle valve clogged.	Check needle valve.	Replace needle valve and float.	■ ■ ■	$4	$12
Governor defective.	Clean.	Repair or replace.	■ ■ ■	$3	$12
Flooding from excess gasoline.	Wait few minutes and check choke.	Release choke.	■		
Fuel tank almost empty.	Check tank. Sediment in bottom may be plugging needle valves.	Fill tank.	■		

PROBLEM: Engine starts but stalls.

Possible Cause	Procedure	Remedy	Rating	Parts	Labor
Fuel-air mixture too lean.	Check carburetor settings and position of choke lever.	Increase fuel-to-air ratio. Open choke until engine warms up.	■		
Stale fuel in fuel tank.	Drain tank. Clean carburetor and fuel line.	Refill tank with clean, new fuel.	■ ■ ■		
Water in fuel.	Since gasoline floats in water, check bottom of tank with straw.	Drain and refill.	■		

GASOLINE ENGINE TROUBLESHOOTING

PROBLEM: Engine starts but stalls.

Possible Cause	Procedure	Remedy	Rating	Parts	Labor
Fuel line blocked.	Remove and inspect.	Remove blockage.	■ ■		
Insufficient air in fuel mixture.	Check air cleaner.	Clean or replace.	■	$2.50-5	
Fuel filter faulty.	Check.	Clean or replace.	■	$3-5	
Fuel not reaching combustion chamber.	Inject fuel manually.	Squirt fuel into cylinder. Replace plug. Crank engine.	■		
Carburetor malfunctioning.	Dismantle.	Replace carburetor.	■ ■	$3	$12
Loss of compression.	Check.	Replace rings and valves.	■ ■ ■ ■ ■	$20	$35
Air cleaner dirty.	Remove from engine.	Clean or replace.	■	$3-5	$12
Choke stuck or defective.	Check.	Clean or replace.	■	$3	$12

PROBLEM: Engine shows lack of power or misses under load.

Possible Cause	Procedure	Remedy	Rating	Parts	Labor
Spark plug fouled or defective.	Remove plug.	Replace spark plug.	■	$2	
Air cleaner dirty.	Remove from engine.	Clean or replace.	■	$3-5	$12
Choke not fully open.	Check position of choke lever.	Open choke.	■		
Carburetor valve assembly faulty (2-cycle engine).	Inspect valve and assembly.	Replace valve assembly.	■ ■	$2	$12
Low oil in crankcase (4-cycle engine).	Drain oil from crankcase.	Refill with proper kind and quantity of oil	■		
Fuel-oil mixture incorrect (2-cycle engine).	Drain tank and carburetor.	Refill with new, correct fuel mix.	■ ■		
Fuel line to carburetor blocked.	Check fuel line.	Clean or replace fuel line. Clean tank.	■ ■	$1.50	$12
Valves and gaskets operating improperly (4-cycle engine).	Check gaskets, seals, and valves.	Clean guides and stems of valves. Replace leaking gaskets or seals. Rework, readjust, or replace valves.	■ ■ ■ ■	$20	$24

PROBLEM: Engine overheats.

Possible Cause	Procedure	Remedy	Rating	Parts	Labor
Fuel-air mixture too lean.	Check carburetor settings.	Adjust.	■ ■		$12
Fuel incorrect.	Empty tank.	Refill with proper, clean fuel.	■		
Dirt in starter.	Check starter.	Clean starter, then check air flow.	■ ■		$12
Low oil in crankcase (4-cycle engine).	Drain oil.	Refill to correct level.	■ ■		$12
Air flow blocked.	Check rotating screen, cooling fins, and head.	Clean out blockage.	■ ■		$12

PROBLEM: Engine is noisy.

Possible Cause	Procedure	Remedy	Rating	Parts	Labor
Piston hitting carbon within cylinder.	Remove head and check cylinder.	Clean carbon from head and top of cylinder.	■ ■ ■		$12
Piston rod worn.	Check piston rod and crankshaft.	Replace if necessary.	■ ■ ■	$5-7	$30
Connecting rod loose or worn.	Check.	Replace.	■ ■ ■	$5-7	$25

PROBLEM: Engine vibrates excessively.

Possible Cause	Procedure	Remedy	Rating	Parts	Labor
Parts off balance.	Disassemble and check.	Rework or replace parts as necessary.	■ ■ ■	$22-26	$24
Engine not securely mounted.	Check mounting bolts and nuts.	Tighten.	■		
Crankshaft bent.	Check.	Replace crankshaft.	■ ■ ■	$26	$24

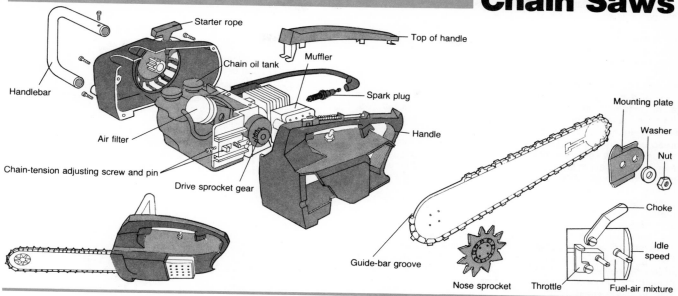

Assembled chain saw

A gasoline-powered chain saw

Principle of Operation

The chain saw is an uncomplicated piece of equipment powered by either a two-stroke-cycle gasoline engine or a double-insulated electric motor. The power from the engine or motor is transferred to a rear sprocket, which in turn drives the chain. This mechanism is very similar to the sprocket and chain system on a bicycle. The "chain" of the chain saw contains many special teeth which are the cutters that work their way into the wood during actual cutting. The chain rotates around a guide bar, which tensions the chain and serves as a stabilizing system for it while cutting is taking place.

Maintenance and Repair

Sawdust and chips from cut wood should be brushed away from the engine housing to prevent clogging around the quick-release (recoil) starter and chain, especially if sawdust

is slightly wet or contains tree sap. Use a small wire to clean oil ports in the guide bar and sprocket teeth. When the guide bar and chain are disassembled, scrape out packed, oily sawdust from the guide-bar groove to prevent the chain from wobbling and wearing.

Chains on electric- and gasoline-powered saws must be lubricated to minimize sawdust buildup and prevent binding. The chain saw has manual or automatic oilers (some with auxiliary manual controls). Oil reservoirs which feed these oilers must be refilled frequently. Manufacturer's specifications should be checked to determine type and grade of oil for lubrication. The saw requires a great amount of oil during cutting; the chain must be oiled constantly; some models may need oil approximately *once each minute* of operation. Oiling as recommended will prevent overheating of the chain and guide bar and consequent damage.

Engine and Housing

Gasoline engine or electric motor. Chain saws are available in either gasoline- or electric-powered models. Gasoline-powered chain saws utilize a two-stroke-cycle engine. The direction of the engine's crankshaft is multi-position so the saw can be used at many angles. Since the two-cycle engine is fueled by a mixture of oil and gasoline, it does not require a separate oil level for lubrication of the engine. Regardless of the angle at which the saw is operated, it is continually lubricated by oil in the fuel mixture. Gasoline-and-oil-in-one fuel also eliminates the problem of oil spilling from the crankcase when

the saw is used in other than level positions. (Oil used to lubricate the chain is a separate solution.) For information on gasoline engines, see Chapter 8; for maintenance and repair of electric motors, see Chapter 4. The following care and repair instructions are applicable to both gasoline and electric chain saws.

Housing. The engine or motor is housed in lightweight plastic to minimize the weight of the chain saw. The housing has a number of openings which must be kept clean so air can circulate freely around the engine. The housing is generally a two-piece unit that is removed by loosening the holding screws; removal is

necessary to gain access to the motor or engine.

Power Drive

In most chain saws the principal part of the drive train is the centrifugal clutch. The clutch mechanism is usually mounted directly on the end of the crankshaft and held in place with a setscrew. When the operator speeds up the engine, the crankshaft spins the center hub of the clutch mechanism. The spinning of the hub forces the two inner shoes of the drum to exert pressure against the outer drum. The outer drum quickly develops the same speed as the inner hub and shoes, and they begin to turn together.

The drum transfers power directly to the cutting chain of the saw. The drum and shoes of the clutch are usually the first parts to wear; when they do, the clutch begins to slip instead of turning the chain. For the repair or replacement of a centrifugal clutch, see Chapter 8, page 302.

Guide Bar

The cutting action of the chain saw is a result of the chain revolving around the guide bar, in the guide-bar groove. The chain contains a series of cutters slightly wider than the guide bar. This allows the guide bar and chain to move through wood without pinching.

Freeing a pinched bar.
Should pinching of the guide bar occur when cutting wood, never attempt to free the saw by twisting the bar or prying open the wood with the saw. This may result in a bent guide bar. The guide bar can rarely be straightened to the accuracy of a new one. Replacement guide bars are available from the manufacturer.

The pinched bar can be freed by inserting a wedge or axe in the saw *kerf,* or cut. It may be necessary to leave the wedge in the kerf while completing most of the cut. Remove the wedge before completing the cut to prevent it from accidentally dropping on the chain saw.

Reversing the guide bar.
During normal cutting operation, the bottom side of the guide bar is under more pressure from the chain than the top side. This pressure height-ens when the operator increases pressure on the saw while cutting. Operators commonly increase the pressure to try to force the cut or to compensate for using a dull chain. Guide bars may be reversible on some models; check the manufacturer's manual for information concerning how often to reverse the bar. Visually inspect the bar every hour of operation. If excess wear is apparent, reverse the bar. After reversing it, make certain that the oil ports in the guide bar line up with the oilers in the housing.

Cleaning the guide bar.
When the guide bar has been removed frm the chain saw, check the edges on either side of the guide-bar groove. If any roughness has developed from cutting, file gently to smoothen. Use a wire or small screwdriver to scrape out packed, oily sawdust from the bar groove.

Procedure: Reversing the Guide Bar

1. Wear gloves to protect hands from sharp cutting edges.

2. Loosen and remove nuts, washers, and plates covering guide bar at base of machine.

3. Lift chain off sprocket and slide guide bar off adjusting pin. Tension on adjusting pin can be eased by turning tension-adjusting screw.

4. Hold bar upright to keep nose sprocket in place.

5. Lift chain off nose sprocket, turn guide bar around (180°), and place chain back on nose sprocket.

6. Slip chain tangs into groove in guide bar.

7. When replacing guide bar on adjusting pin and chain on drive sprocket, be sure cutters on top of bar face away from drive sprocket.

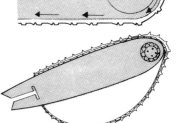
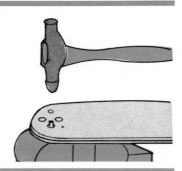

Nose sprocket

More expensive chain saws and those with long guide bars use a nose sprocket in the nose (projecting end) of the guide bar. The nose sprocket is very similar to the rear sprocket except that it is not directly driven by the power of the engine. It runs free and operates around a ball-bearing surface. The purpose of the nose sprocket is to reduce friction from the chain during operation of the saw. Lubricate the ball bearings as recommended by the manufacturer.

Replacing the nose sprocket

If excess wear is apparent, replacement of the nose sprocket may be necessary. To do this, first drive out the rivets holding the sprocket in place. This is called *breaking* the rivets. Break the rivet heads with a small punch and hammer or grind them off with a power drill and attachment.

With a punch, carefully drive out the rivets holding the nose sprocket.

When breaking the heads, be absolutely certain that there is a solid support under the guide bar. Otherwise, the end of the bar may bend. The old sprocket may be removed after the rivets are gone.

The replacement sprocket is usually shipped inside a plastic sleeve contoured to fit the end of the nose of the guide bar.

Keep the nose sprocket in its plastic case while replacing it.

Do not remove the replacement sprocket from this sleeve; it is designed to serve as a jig for holding the new sprocket, with ball bearings, together while sliding the sprocket into the end of the guide bar.

The new sprocket must be fastened to the guide bar. Insert the new rivets one at a

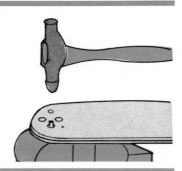

Peen the new rivets with light, firm blows of the hammer.

time. Set the rivets by using the peen (round end) of the ball peen hammer. Continue to tap the rivet heads in order to spread the metal; light tapping is much more effective than hitting very hard. After spreading the heads into the depressions in the bar, the excess metal must be ground off until level with the guide-bar surface.

Chain

The chain of the chain saw is a series of four distinct elements repeatedly connected together to form a flexible, continuous set of cutters. The elements of the chain are the left- and right-hand cutters, the drive links (also called tangs), and the tie straps.

Adjusting chain tension

Chain tension is set by adjusting the chain-tension screw, which is usually found at the base of the guide bar. By loosening the guide-bar locknut and turning the screw, more or less tension is realized. The chain must be adjusted when it is cool. The guide bar should be placed nose (projecting end) upward when adjusting, to prevent the weight of the chain from affecting the setting.

A series of tangs (pointed drive links) run in the guide-bar groove, to hold it on the guide

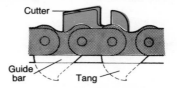

A hot chain and cool chain

bar. Tangs should not be visible on a cool chain that is correctly adjusted. A hot chain should expose approximately half of the tang between the chain and the guide bar.

Replacing the chain

Replacement of the chain

may be necessary, depending on the amount of use, and abuse, the saw receives. Under normal operating conditions, the chain needs periodic sharpening of the cutters to maintain peak cutting efficiency. Repeated sharpenings eventually wear away the saw-teeth (cutting edges) of the individual cutters so that they no longer produce a straight,

clean saw cut. Frequent visual inspections of the chain or the need for excessive pressure during cutting may indicate chain wear and the necessity for chain replacement. Before purchasing replacement parts, consult the manufacturer's specifications. The procedure for chain replacement is similar to that for reversing the guide bar (*see page 306*).

Procedure: Replacing the Chain

1. Loosen guide-bar locknut.

2. Turn guide-bar adjusting screw and move bar as close as possible to *rear* sprocket.

3. Remove old chain.

4. Clean and inspect groove in guide bar, rear sprocket, and nose sprocket (if applicable).

5. Position saw so guide-bar nose is pointing upward (vertical).

6. Lay out new chain. Cutting edges (sawteeth) of cutters

must be facing nose of guide bar along top rim of bar.

7. Drape chain over guide bar, fitting drive links into groove.

8. Start tightening guide-bar adjusting screw while fitting chain onto rear-sprocket teeth.

9. Continue to tighten adjusting screw while simultaneously checking drive links and sprocket holes for alignment.

10. Adjust chain tension as per instructions in operator's manual.

Procedure: Sharpening Cutters

1. Lock chain in bench vise to hold it steady.

2. In field, tighten chain tension to eliminate movement. (Reset tension prior to starting saw.)

3. Position file and holder against face of cutter at a 35° angle. Angle is marked on holder.

4. Keep file level.

5. File only cuts as you push it. File in one direction only.

6. Do not touch cutter on return stroke. This will dull file's teeth.

7. Maintain constant, medium-to-light pressure primarily on rear of cutter tooth.

8. File minimum number of strokes necessary on each cutter. Excess filing will wear down cutter.

9. Rotate file slightly between each stroke to help keep it from clogging.

10. First file all cutters on one side of chain; then, all cutters on other side.

11. Inspect cutting edge of cutter. A sharp edge will not reflect any light. *Do not* touch edge with thumb or finger to test for sharpness.

WARNING: Before making adjustments on the chain saw, be sure the power is off. Wear gloves and handle the chain carefully. Do not test cutter edges for sharpness with fingers.

Cutters

Replacing cutters

Sometimes a single cutter is ruined from hitting a nail or other object in the wood. Individual cutters can and should be replaced if this happens. Use a replacement part recommended by the manufacturer. The rivets holding the old cutter in place will have to be driven out (broken) with a small punch and hammer. While breaking the rivets, support the chain with some type of metal object such as a bench vise. Accessories specifically designed for breaking rivets can be used to hold the chain in place and drive out the rivets on the chain.

Position the chain so that the rivet head is facing up. Using the punch and hammer, drive the rivet down and out of the chain. Driving the rivet will break the head off and allow it to be removed. Remember, the support for the work must have a small hole or groove to allow the rivet to be driven out of the chain. When using a bench vise, open the vise jaws slightly. Most accessories contain several grooves to accommodate various sizes of rivets.

Sharpening cutters

A properly sharpened chain will produce the fastest cut with the least amount of effort from the operator. In addition,

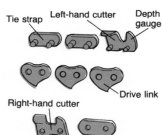

Tie strap Left-hand cutter Depth gauge

Drive link

Right-hand cutter

Parts of a cutting chain

periodic sharpening will result in maximum chain life and reduce the overall cost of operating the equipment. If the saw is producing a powder instead of wood chips, this is a reliable indication of dull cutters.

Sharpening a dull chain is a tedious job but it can be accomplished with appropriate sharpening tools and accessories. Most major manufacturers of chain saws also sell sharpening accessories.

Round file and file holder. Necessary for sharpening cutters is the "fast-cut" round file. Fast-cut is a particular tooth design considered ideal for this work. Check the manu-

facturer's specifications to determine the pitch size of the chain and recommended diameter of a corresponding file. After cutters have been sharpened to half their original size, a second file approximately 1/64 inch smaller in diameter will be needed. Files may be purchased with or without handles.

The *file holder* is a device designed to guide the file while maintaining correct sharpening angles. Filing at the proper angle is *absolutely essential* to insure uniform, exact sharpening of cutters required for the chain to make smooth, straight saw cuts.

Filing gauge and flat file. After a few sharpenings, the cutting edge of each cutter may become shorter than the depth-gauge portion. If this happens, the projecting depth gauge prevents the cutter from biting deeply into the wood when the chain revolves. The depth gauge must therefore be filed down to conform to cutting-edge height. A *filing gauge*, or *gauge jointer*, is an accessory designed to complete this task.

File a cutter's depth gauge by placing the filing gauge on the chain, allowing the depth-gauge portion of the cutter tooth to fit into the gauge slot.

Any portion of the depth gauge above the slot must be filed level with the top of the filing gauge. Use a *flat file* to remove the protruding part of the depth gauge. Since the filing gauge rests on top of several cutters, it automatically corrects the height of the depth gauge.

Finish the filing process by rounding off the front of each depth gauge. Rounding the front helps depth gauges enter the saw kerf and leads to smoother saw cuts. A depth gauge not filed to cutting height will cause the chain saw to grab or cut unevenly.

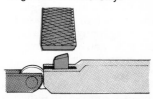

Use file holders to keep the proper angle on sharpened teeth.

Round the front of the depth gauge after filing. This keeps the cutters running smoothly.

CHAIN SAW TROUBLESHOOTING

PROBLEM: Saw does not start.

Possible Cause	Procedure	Remedy	Rating	Parts	Labor
Engine faulty.	SEE GASOLINE ENGINE TROUBLESHOOTING CHART—CHAPTER 8				
Motor faulty.	SEE ELECTRIC MOTOR TROUBLESHOOTING CHARTS—CHAPTER 4				
On/Off switch defective.	Test circuit continuity.	Repair or replace.	■ ■	$3	$7.50

PROBLEM: Engine starts but chain does not turn.

Possible Cause	Procedure	Remedy	Rating	Parts	Labor
Trigger clutch disengaged.	Engage clutch.	Squeeze trigger.	■		
Chain obstructed.	Check chain.	Remove obstruction.	■ ■		$12
Chain dry.	Check chain and oilers.	Lubricate chain. Make sure lubrication system is effective.	■		
Parts loose.	Check nuts and bolts.	Tighten all nuts and bolts.	■ ■		$12
Cutting bar bent.	Check bar.	Replace.	■ ■ ■	$30	$15
Clutch worn or slipping.	Check clutch.	Adjust clutch. If necessary, replace clutch.	■ ■ ■ ■	$15	$12

PROBLEM: Chain turns but does not cut or cuts poorly.

Possible Cause	Procedure	Remedy	Rating	Parts	Labor
Power inadequate.	On gasoline-powered saw, hold saw steady and make adjustment.	Adjust clutch and open throttle.	■		
	On electric-powered saw, check cord and plug.	Repair or replace if damaged.	■ ■	$4	$12
Chain tension incorrect.	Check tension.	Loosen or tighten chain as needed.	■ ■ ■		$12
Cutting edges dull.	Check chain.	Sharpen or replace.	■ ■ ■	$15	$12
Muffler and exhaust ports clogged.	Allow engine to cool. Check for blocked muffler or exhaust ports.	Disassemble muffler; clean parts and scrape off carbon deposits. Replace damaged parts or those that cannot be cleared.	■ ■ ■		$12

Grass Edger/Trimmers

Principle of Operation

The grass *edger* is a widely used piece of lawn-care equipment designed to "edge," or make a vertical cut, along the side of a lawn. The cut allows excess grass to be removed and the resulting straight line of edged grass enhances the appearance of the lawn. Edging also prevents grass from creeping onto sidewalks, driveways, patios, flower beds, gardens, and similar areas bordered by lawns.

A grass edger uses either a gasoline engine or an electric motor to power a set of blades. When the position of the blades is changed from vertical to horizontal, the edger becomes a *trimmer,* designed to cut tall grass and weeds not accessible to the lawn mower. In this position, the machine can reach under bushes and lawn furniture and around permanent fixtures.

Another type of trimmer uses a coil of monofilament line—wound onto a cartridge and inserted into the base of the trimmer—for the "cutter." This line is a heavy, extremely tough, plastic line that has approximately the same diameter as a common wire clothes hanger. This trimmer is powered by electricity and uses either the direct cord hookup or the rechargeable battery pack (*see Chapters 4 and 8*). In operating the trimmer, a portion of the monofilament line is pulled from the cartridge by hand. The trimmer is

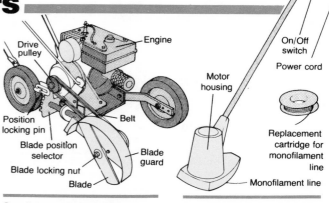

Gasoline-powered grass edger   **Electric-powered grass trimmer**

started and the extremely fast rotation, or whirling action, of the line cuts weeds and grass on contact. The monofilament-type trimmer is very efficient for light-duty tasks and is far more convenient than the blade-type edger/trimmer, but it is not effective on heavy-stemmed weeds. It is lightweight, very portable, and is considered much safer than the blade-type grass trimmer. The monofilament line does not easily damage objects in the path of the cutter and therefore may be used to trim close to any object on the lawn.

Maintenance and Repair

Engine

Grass cutters and edgers are powered by either a gasoline engine or an electric motor. See Chapter 8 for information about the operation, care, and repair of small gasoline engines. See Chapters 4 and 8 for the troubleshooting, maintenance and repair of cord and cordless electric motors.

Blade Housing

The blade housing covers the blades (and wheels, on some models) and is primarily a safety feature. If may also serve as an engine or motor support.

Accumulated dirt, cut grass, and other debris should be removed from the housing after each use. Besides preventing efficient operation of the machine, debris also adds weight, making the equipment more difficult to push.

Scrape the debris from the inside of the housing with a wooden scraper and rinse the housing with a garden hose. Be sure the machine, if electric, is unplugged before rinsing; do not use the hose while the gasoline engine is hot.

Power Drive

Lubricate the pivot point and pin lock used to move the edger/trimmer's blades from a vertical to horizontal position. Lubrication is also required on the linkages from the throttle and clutch controls on the handle. Some models have a "floating" rear wheel which requires lubrication.

V-belt system. Power to the blade is generally transmitted from the engine drive shaft to the blade through a V-belt drive system. The belt must be adjusted to the correct tension to drive the blade. Most models do not have an idler pulley; the best tension is arrived at by increasing the distance between the blade shaft and the drive shaft.

If the belt slips frequently, check the belt for glazing, cracks, and fraying. If necessary, replace the belt. If the belt is wet or some lubricant has dropped onto it, dressing the belt will prevent slipping and may eliminate the need for belt replacement.

Belt dressing may build up on the pulleys after excessive use. If this happens, remove the excess dressing from the pulleys prior to installing a new belt.

Cutting to an excessive depth on a single pass may cause the belt to slip. If the soil is extremely hard or contains gravel, it is recommended that successive passes be made at increasing depths.

Cutters

Adjusting the blade. The edging depth can be changed by adjusting the blade. Check the operator's manual for specific instructions. Lubrication of the adjusting mechanism may be necessary.

Generally, a locking bolt or pin is located near the front wheel mount; the wheel can be adjusted by loosening the bolt or removing the pin. Other models may require adjustment of the rear wheel.

> **WARNING:** The operator should be extremely careful when using the grass edger/trimmer around solid fixtures or objects; the powerful rotation of the blades can mangle objects on contact.

Sharpening the blade. Remove the blade by loosening the blade locking nut with a wrench. Place the blade in a bench vise for sharpening and file the blade *toward* the cutting edges. Remove approximately the same amount of metal from each side of the blade. If the blade is to be used initially as a trimmer, smooth the cutting edge with a whetstone. Edger blades are available in a variety of shapes. These include a beveled point, a two- or three-pronged point, and a blunt point. Check the manufacturer's instructions for suggested sharpening techniques.

Replacing the monofilament line. New line may be purchased from the manufacturer and can be wound onto the cartridge. Winding new line must be done carefully, according to the direction of rotation. Check winding instructions.

Additional cartridges may be purchased with the equipment and are generally available in either 25-foot or 50-foot spools. A new cartridge is snapped onto the drive shaft after the old one is removed.

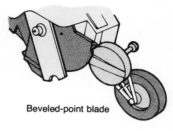
Beveled-point blade

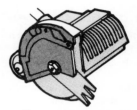
Three-prong-point blade

Blunt-point blade

Grass-edger blades

> **NOTE:** The whirling monofilament line can indeed draw blood if it hits bare skin. The operator should wear long trousers and closed shoes when using the machine.

GRASS EDGER/TRIMMER TROUBLESHOOTING

PROBLEM: Grass edger does not start.

Possible Cause	Procedure	Remedy	Rating	Parts	Labor
No power at outlet.	Examine outlet, fuse, and circuit breaker.	Replace fuse or reset circuit breaker.	■		
Batteries dead.	Test batteries.	Recharge or replace.	■	$40	
Cord set faulty.	Examine plug and cord for breaks.	Repair or replace.	■	$5	$10
On/Off switch faulty.	Test circuit continuity.	Repair or replace.	■ ■ ■	$5	$10

PROBLEM: Grass trimmer starts but does not cut.

Possible Cause	Procedure	Remedy	Rating	Parts	Labor
Filament not in contact with grass.	Check trimming height and filament length.	Lower edge or pull out more filament.	■		
More string required.	Check cartridge.	Replace filament or cartridge. Wind carefully.	■	$5	
Automatic line cutter inoperative.	Check.	Replace trimmer.		$30-50	

Hedge Clippers

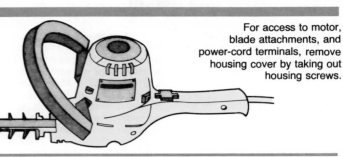

For access to motor, blade attachments, and power-cord terminals, remove housing cover by taking out housing screws.

An electric-powered hedge clipper

Principle of Operation

A hedge clipper operates much like the electric knife. Gears in the housing translate a small motor's rotary motion into the back and forth, reciprocating motion of two cutting blades.

The principal difference among hedge clippers is the method of powering. A hedge clipper's motor may be powered either by 120-volt AC house current or by a rechargeable nickel-cadmium battery. The battery-powered type is cordless.

Blade teeth designs vary. The width between teeth may range from 1 to 2 inches. Generally, blades with widely spaced teeth—though somewhat more dangerous to the user—are more effective than blades with narrowly spaced teeth. In some hedge clippers, only one blade moves and the second is stationary; in others, both blades move. The cutting angles on the blades will vary accordingly. On models having a stationary blade, the teeth of that blade are longer than those of the moving blade—a safety feature, because the longer, stationary teeth make it more difficult to cut fingers or a power cord accidentally.

Maintenance and Repair

Blades

Normal maintenance consists of cleaning the blades after each use (be sure the clipper is unplugged) and light oiling. Run the hedge clipper briefly so the oil spreads to all blade surfaces. Wipe off excess oil. Remove accumulated rust with fine sandpaper or an emery cloth. Then oil the blades as above.

Sharpening blades. Sharpen blades with a smooth-cut flat file. Be sure to maintain the cutting angle on the edge of

NOTE: When using an extension cord with the hedge clipper, make sure its wires are at least 16 gauge. If the power cord has a three-pronged plug, use a three-wire extension cord, plugged into a grounded outlet.

each tooth. (On hedge clippers having one fixed and one moving blade, the angle of the fixed-blade teeth is about 90° and of the moving-blade teeth about 40°.) If the blades still do not cut properly, have them sharpened professionally or buy a new blade set.

Replacing blades. To replace a blade set, remove the screws that hold the housing together and disassemble the housing. Remove the pins or screws that hold the blades in place.

WARNING: To prevent accidents, use both hands to hold the clipper handles, and keep fingers away from the blades. Do not use the clipper in the rain or when the shrubbery or ground is wet.

Power Source

Motor. Oil the electric motor regularly as instructed in the owner's manual. See chapter 4 for information on the troubleshooting, maintenance, and repair of electric motors.

Battery and power pack. Follow recharging directions in the owner's manual. Use the clipper for only about half an hour at a time, then recharge. If the battery will not hold a charge, replace the battery. Or, attempt to restore it by repeatedly running the battery down until the motor stops and then recharging. Do this at least five times.

Power cord. Take care not to cut the power cord or extension cord accidentally. Tie the power cord to the extension cord to prevent them from accidentally separating.

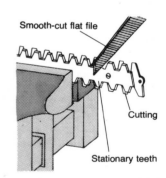

Smooth-cut flat file

Cutting

Stationary teeth

Sharpening the blades of a power hedge clipper

If the power cord becomes frayed or damaged, replace it. Gain access to internal terminals by removing the housing (held together with screws).

HEDGE CLIPPER TROUBLESHOOTING

PROBLEM: Hedge clipper does not run.

Possible Cause	Procedure	Remedy	Rating	Parts	Labor
No power at outlet.	Check fuse or circuit breaker.	Replace fuse or reset circuit breaker.	■	$4	
Batteries dead.	Test batteries.	Recharge or replace.	■	$15-30	
Cord set faulty.	Check plug and cord.	Repair or replace.	■ ■ ■	$3	$12
On/Off switch faulty.	Test switch for continuity.	Repair or replace.	■ ■	$5	$12
Contacts dirty.	Check.	Clean.			

PROBLEM: Hedge clipper starts but does not cut or cuts poorly.

Possible Cause	Procedure	Remedy	Rating	Parts	Labor
Loose nuts.	Check shearing action.	Tighten nuts evenly.	■		
Dull blade.	Unplug. File only cutting teeth.	Sharpen.	■ ■		$4-5
Blades jammed.	Turn off motor. Use stick or other object to loosen object.	Remove obstruction.	■		
Hedges too heavy.	Stronger equipment necessary.	Use for intended purpose.			

Lawn Mowers

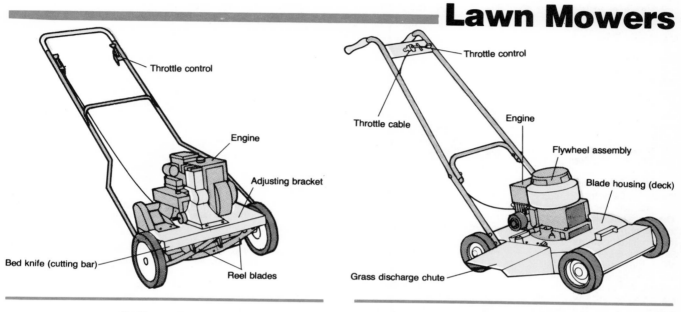

Reel lawn mower

Rotary lawn mower

Principle of Operation

A power mower may be one of two types—a *reel* mower or a *rotary* mower. The cutting action is what designates the type. On the reel mower, curved blades revolve around an axis in a spiral formation. When the mower is in action, these blades move past the surface of a straight, horizontal blade, called the bed knife, creating a shearing motion similar to that of a pair of scissors. The rotary mower cuts grass by means of a chopping action. A sharpened, rotating blade or blades strike the grass. A single blade is attached to the vertical drive shaft of the gasoline engine or electric motor on smaller push-type rotary mowers. Larger mower attachments may use two or three blades to achieve a wider cut.

Maintenance and Repair

Blade Housing

Rotary mowers utilize a blade housing to cover the blade. The housing serves two functions: It is a safety feature to protect the operator from the rotating blade; it is also designed to force the cut grass to be blown out from underneath.

The housing is generally a shell of die-cast aluminum or plastic. The engine or motor is situated on top with the drive shaft projecting down through the housing. The blade is attached to the shaft underneath. The housing is strong, lightweight, and requires very little maintenance.

The aluminum housing (deck) may crack if the lawn mower is dropped, hit with a hard object, or exposed to major vibrations. A cracked housing is usually replaced. It is possible to have a small crack welded (with specialized equipment), but larger cracks should not be welded, since the shape of the repair may cause the blade to become unbalanced.

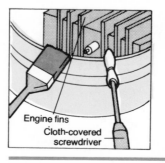
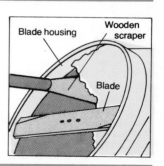

Cleaning the rotary lawn mower. Remove grass and accumulated dirt from the engine's cooling fins with a soft brush and a cloth-covered thin tool, such as a screwdriver or knife. Remove the accumulated grass from beneath the blade housing by tipping the mower on its side and scraping the debris with a wooden scraper. Remove the spark-plug wire before tipping the mower.

Removing grass. The outer and underneath surfaces of the housing collect dirt and grass clippings during use. Caked-on layers of dried dirt and clippings prevent newly cut grass from being blown out and affect the efficiency of the engine. It is therefore recommended that the bottom surface of the blade housing be cleaned after each use. Cleanliness of the housing will also facilitate wheel adjustment.

Disconnect the spark-plug wire, and tip the mower up to allow access to the bottom side of the blade housing. Do not turn the mower upside down because the oil and gasoline will spill out. Scrape off the dirt, grass clippings, and debris with a wooden scraper and flush the surface with a garden hose. Flushing with a hose may be all that is necessary if the mower is cleaned after each use. Clean the fins

sticking out on the engine with a soft brush.

Removing oil. Some oil may be spilled on the surface of the housing, producing sticky areas that collect dirt. Remove oil residue with a household degreasing product or a solution of detergent and water. Do not wash the mower while the engine is hot. Water splashed on a hot engine may cause a cracked block and expensive repair. Furthermore,

some degreasers are flammable and create a fire hazard if used on a hot engine.

Scraping. Metal tools may scratch the painted surface of the blade housing. Use wooden or plastic scrapers to clean the exterior. After scraping and cleaning, apply a protective coating of car wax to the surface to extend the life of the equipment.

Cutting Blades

Reel-mower blades

Adjusting the cutting height. The reel-mower cutting height is changed by loosening the two bolts at either end of the roller, adjusting the roller, and retightening. Maximum height adjustment of the mower will not allow the operator to cut extremely tall grass.

Sharpening. Sharpening of the bed knife or the spiral cutters is not recommended. These are best sharpened with a special machine setup and then backlapped as a unit. Since two blades must be in contact, the machine matches the grinding angles to fit together. A heavy nick in the blade may be removed by filing with a hand file. Subsequent sharpening should only be done by a professional with the appropriate equipment.

Backlapping the bed knife. Backlapping the bedknife can help maintain its cutting edge without the necessity for frequent professional sharpening.

Lubricating. Lubrication of the cutters on the reel mower is necessary. Oil or grease the center shaft of the spiral-blade unit. This shaft may be supported by either bushings or bearings. Check the manufacturer's instructions for lubrication information.

Rotary-mower blades

Adjusting the cutting height. Adjustment of the mower-blade height is accomplished by raising or lowering each wheel. Raising the wheel lowers the cutting blade; lowering the wheel raises the blade. A wire clip, cotter pin, or threaded bolt or nut is usually found inside the blade housing. Remove the fastener and place the wheel shaft in its new location.

Maximum adjustment on many mowers is 2 inches. All wheels should be on the same level to eliminate a twisting

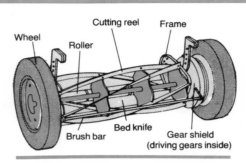

Reel-mower blades. Frequent lubrication of rotating parts with no. 10 oil is recommended. Do not use lightweight, household oil.

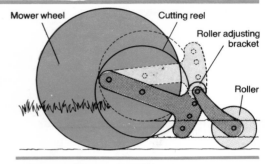

To adjust the cutting height of reel-mower blades, raise or lower the power-drive roller on the adjusting bracket.

pressure on the blade housing and to facilitate even, smooth cutting of the grass.

Removing the blades. On the smaller hand-operated rotary mowers, the angle blade is attached to the vertical drive shaft of the gasoline engine or electric motor. (Larger mower attachments for tractors may use two or three blades.) One or more bolts is threaded through the center of the blade and tightened into the end of the shaft. The direction of the blade rotation is opposite the thread direction of the bolt or bolts, eliminating the possibility of the blade coming loose under normal conditions.

To remove the blade on rotary mowers, tilt the mower up.

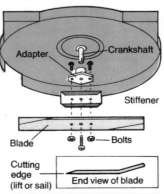

Disassembly of the rotary-mower blade

Block movement of the blade with a piece of wood to keep it from turning with the wrench pressure. Wrap one side in a cloth or wear gloves. Holding the blade firmly, turn the bolts with a box or open-end wrench. If an adjustable wrench is used, push on the stationary jaw, not the movable jaw. When replacing the blade, the lift, or sail, of the blade should point toward the blade housing.

Removal of the blades on the large mower attachments of the lawn tractor is achieved in much the same way. These blades may be attached to a flange on the end of the vertical shaft. Each blade is fastened by two bolts threaded into the flange. This method of fastening is a safety feature, since the equipment requires far more power.

Removing nicks. After removing the blade, examine it for major nicks. Eliminate the nicks with a flat file. The flat file is double cut—it has two series of teeth crossing each other that cut in two directions. This file removes metal faster than a single-cut file. Next, check the blade for balance.

Balancing. The blade must always be balanced before it is sharpened. Check the blade balance by placing a screwdriver through the center hole

and moving the blade to a horizontal position. An unbalanced blade will not remain horizontal. Using an unbalanced blade causes motor vibration and excessive wear on the mower.

To achieve a balanced blade, file the blunt end of the blade to remove the necessary weight. It is not necessary to file the cutting edge. Many times, doing so results in changing the proper cutting angle.

Sharpening. Sharpening the blade (after removal from the mower, filing, and balancing) is accomplished with a file and whetstone. Place the blade securely in a vise and file toward the cutting edge, maintaining the original cutting angle throughout the entire cutting edge. Use a mill file; the mill file is a single-cut file (its teeth cut in only one direction). Filing toward the cutting edge will eliminate a very tiny metal burr from forming on the edge. Finish the sharpening process by whetting the cutting edge to remove any rough edges or burrs.

When sharpening the blade, an equal amount of metal must be removed from each side to maintain balance. Periodic checking of the balance while sharpening will help maintain equal weight on each side.

Procedure: Backlapping the Bed Knife and Reel Blades

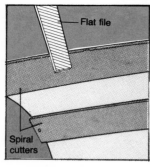

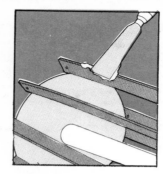

1. Disconnect spark-plug wire. Remove burrs and nicks on bed knife and spiral cuters (blades) with flat file; take care not to file on cutting edges.

2. Adjust bed knife so that revolving spiral blades make contact with it. Apply grinding compound and rotate cutting reel backwards.

3. Clean off all grinding compound. Adjust bed knife and reel blades so that they make firm contact along full length of bed knife.

Power Drive

Some rotary and reel mowers have a power-drive system that propels the mower without its being pushed. Most power-drive systems are single speed and forward direction only. Generally located in conjunction with the wheels on both types of mower, the power drive is engaged by squeezing a drive grip clutch or by pulling the mower handle down to operating position. The rotary mower's power drive is situated on the front wheels; this placement eliminates the possibility of the mower's raising up when the drive is engaged.

A common system found on reel and rotary mowers utilizes rubber rollers at one end of the drive shaft. The power-drive mechanism, positioned above the wheels, receives power from the engine via a drive chain or V-belt. When the drive mechanism is engaged, the rubber rollers are forced into contact with the tires or the wheel rims.

Cleaning and lubricating. All metal parts of the power-drive system should be cleaned and lubricated. Clutch controls, as well as mower-height adjustment devices and locks, require this maintenance. Lubricate the pivot points and linkages. Before making any adjustments, check the owner's manual. Do not allow any lubricant to contact the surface of the rubber gears or wheels. Use a spray lubricant on the throttle and cable.

Mower Attachments

Reel-mower attachments. Lawn and garden tractors use a mower attachment. One style is the combination, or series, of reel mowers that are pulled by the tractor. Maintenance of this system is the same as for the reel mower.

Rotary-mower attachments. The rotary-mower attachment is generally fastened underneath the tractor and positioned between the front and rear tractor wheels. The operator's feet are above the blade housing for safety. This attachment consists of a series of blades fastened to vertical shafts. The shafts project up through the blade housing, and a V-belt pulley is attached to a pulley on each shaft. Power is transmitted from the tractor to the mower attachment via the V-belt. Maintenance on the mower attachment consists of the cleaning and lubrication previously discussed.

In addition to this regular care, certain adjustments are required on the mower attachment due to the use of V-belts. Periodically inspect the V-belts; replace frayed or cracked belts according to the manufacturer's specifications.

To replace the V-belt, loosen the idler pulley locking nut with a wrench and remove the old belt. Inspect the pulleys and clean them if necessary. Place the new V-belt around the necessary pulleys and adjust the idler pulley to the correct V-belt tension.

Loose belts should be tightened by adjusting the idler pulley. If the belt has been slipping, a glaze may have formed on the contact surface of the belt. Applying a small amount of belt dressing should not be used as a substitute for adjusting the belt tension or replacing a belt that is too worn to be tensioned correctly.

Wheels

Cleaning and lubricating. Blowing or hosing should eliminate debris and clean the wheels. For lubrication of the wheels, check the owner's manual for the location of the oil ports and the type of lubricant to use. Some mowers may require grease for wheel lubrication. Do not use a lubricant on wheels with plastic bearings.

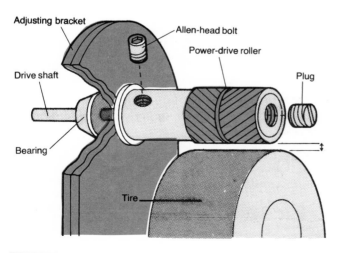

Power-drive mechanism. To lubricate the drive roller, remove the end plug and apply axle grease until it oozes out from under the bearing on the opposite side of the bracket. Keep the Allen-head bolt tight to prevent the power-drive roller from slipping.

WARNING: To avoid accidentally starting the mower while cleaning or repairing, always disconnect the spark-plug wire and tape it back and out of the way.

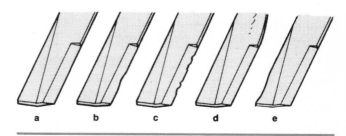

Rotary mower blades: signs of blade wear and the need for sharpening or replacement.
a) A correctly sharpened blade enhances mower efficiency.
b) A dull blade can be sharpened with a file and whetstone.
c) A badly nicked blade can be sharpened after filing nicks away.
d) A twisted blade cannot be straightened; replace it promptly.
e) A blade with no lift (or sail) will not draw grass up for cutting or discharge cut grass properly. It cannot be corrected; replace it.

LAWN MOWER TROUBLESHOOTING

PROBLEM: Mower engine does not start, is hard to start, stalls, or loses power.

Possible Cause	Procedure	Remedy	Rating	Parts	Labor
Engine faulty.	SEE GASOLINE ENGINE TROUBLESHOOTING CHART—CHAPTER 8				
Motor faulty.	SEE ELECTRIC MOTOR TROUBLESHOOTING CHARTS—CHAPTER 4				
Load too heavy.	Check mower (and attachments, if there are any).	Raise cutting blade height. by lowering the wheel, or open throttle.	■		
Additional power equipment engaged when engine is started.	Check to see that power takeoff or self-propulsion equipment is not engaged simultaneously with engine.	Disengage additional power equipment.	■		
Blade loose (rotary mower).	Disconnect spark plug. Check mower for loose blade. If blade can move while flywheel is held in place, blade is attached too loosely.	Tighten blade mounting bolts.	■ ■		$12
Parts worn.	Check bearings, drive wheels, tires, belts, and so on, for wear.	Replace worn parts.	■ ■ ■		$12-15

PROBLEM: Mower vibrates excessively.

Possible Cause	Procedure	Remedy	Rating	Parts	Labor
Bolts loose.	Check mower thoroughly for loose screws and bolts—on engine mounting, blade mounting, wheels, etc.	Tighten all bolts.	■ ■		
Cutting blade imbalanced (rotary mower).	Remove blade from mower and check balance.	Balance blade immediately to avoid damage.	■ ■ ■		$12
Cutting blade dull or nicked (rotary mower).	Remove blade from mower and examine.	File blade to eliminate visible nicks. Sharpen dull blade with a file and whetstone.	■ ■ ■		$12
Cutting blade bent or twisted (rotary mower).	Remove blade from mower and examine.	If blade is bent, twisted, or has no lift, replace.	■ ■	$7	$12
Blade housing split or cracked (rotary mower).	Inspect housing.	Replace cracked or split housing.	■ ■ ■	$18-56	$12-24

PROBLEM: Mower cuts improperly.

Possible Cause	Procedure	Remedy	Rating	Parts	Labor
Cutting height adjustment incorrect (rotary mower).	Check cutting height.	Adjust mower-blade height by raising or lowering wheels.	■		$12
Cutting height adjustment uneven (reel mower).	Check mower roller on each side. Check wheel alignment.	Set roller in parallel slots. Adjust wheels to same level.	■ ■ ■		$12
Bed knife and/or reel improperly aligned (reel mower).	Check alignment.	Align reel and bed knife. If bent badly, take to service center.	■ ■		$12
Blade dull (rotary mower).	Remove blade from housing and inspect.	Sharpen dull blade with file and whetstone.	■ ■ ■		$12
Bed knife or reel blades dull (reel mower).	Check for sharpness.	Have bed knife and reel professionally sharpened if necessary.	■ ■ ■ ■		$1/inch (Blades range from 8"-32")

PROBLEM: Reel on reel mower does not turn.

Possible Cause	Procedure	Remedy	Rating	Parts	Labor
Foreign object blocking reel.	Check reel.	Remove any obstruction.	■ ■		$12
Pinion and pinion gears dry or worn.	Check pinion and pinion gears—first remove left set, then right set.	If dry, clean and lubricate with oil. If worn, replace.	■ ■ ■	$1-5	$12
Bed-knife setting incorrect.	Check setting.	Adjust bed knife.	■ ■		$12

PROBLEM: Wheels on power-drive mower slip, spin, or do not move.

Possible Cause	Procedure	Remedy	Rating	Parts	Labor
Drive not engaged.	Check controls.	Engage drive.	■		
Lubricant on drive wheels.	Visually check.	Clean with degreasing agent.	■ ■		$12
Clutch slipping.	Check clutch system.	Adjust or replace.	■ ■ ■	$15	$12
Tires bald.	Check tires.	Replace tires.	■ ■ ■	$3-6	$12

Lawn and Garden Tractors

Principle of Operation

A lawn and garden tractor is a small vehicle powered by a gasoline engine and equipped with an electrical system, clutch, transmission, brakes, lights, and gauges. The smallest riding tractors are run by single-cylinder, two-cycle engines using a quick-release (impulse) starter. Larger models may use two-cylinder, four-cycle engines with a battery/key starter. Engine size (measured in horsepower, HP), the most essential variable among small riding tractors, ranges from 5 HP to 20 HP, with greater engine power providing increased tractor versatility. See Chapter 8 for the maintenance, troubleshooting, and repair of small gasoline engines.

Tractors can be fitted with rotary or reel mowers, snow blowers, plows, back hoes, electric generators, lawn rollers, carts, and a host of other accessories. Accessories requiring a power drive may be attached to a supplementary belt and pulley system, driven by the engine and usually located on the underside of the tractor.

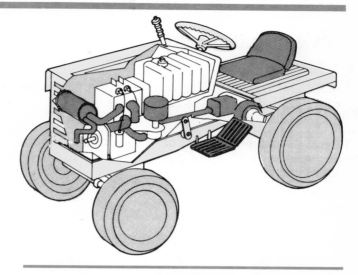

A lawn and garden tractor

Maintenance and Repair

Chassis
This metal covering improves the appearance and protects the internal parts of the tractor. To protect the finish, wash the chassis's painted surfaces regularly. Do not attempt to wash or wax while the engine is hot. Keep the air intake and exhaust ports clear of debris to prevent the engine from overheating.

Power drive
Clutches. The clutch on most lawn and garden tractors is part of a V-belt drive system; disengaging the clutch by releasing the clutch pedal causes an idler pulley to tighten the loose drive belt. (Some larger tractors employ an automotive-type disk drive system.) Lubricate the mechanical linkages periodically with lithium grease or a lubricant specified by the manufacturer.

Belts. Adjust the belt tension and idler-pulley spring tension periodically. Follow the directions in the owner's manual to replace a worn or broken belt. Use caution when replacing a broken clutch V-belt. Hold the idler-pulley arm firmly to avoid injury from the release of the tensioned spring.

Chains. Drive chains closely resemble those used on bicyc-

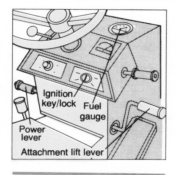

Interior view of tractor controls

les and motorcycles. Adjust chain tension, lubricate chains, and replace chains periodically as instructed in the owner's manual.

Rear view of a tractor with a cultivator attachment

Transmission
Small tractor transmissions are generally two types—manual and automatic. The components are easier to repair and maintain and are more accessible than similar parts on an automobile. Check the oil level regularly, and fill to the specified mark. Refer to the owner's manual for the type of fluid and additional service procedures required.

Linkages. Lubricate steering and attachment linkages regularly as recommended by the owner's manual. Apply a thin coat of new grease prior to attaching accessories. Keep the linkage holes clear by covering them with tape.

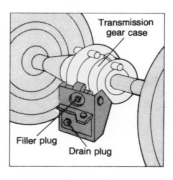

Keep the transmission gear case filled with lubricant to the level of the filler plug.

Pulleys and sprockets.
Lubricate the bearings periodically. Examine each pulley and sprocket for burrs or wear, especially if a drive belt is frayed or if a chain is severely worn. Sand down burrs; replace parts if wear is excessive.

Brakes. Lubricate the brake and parking-brake linkages periodically. Do not allow any lubricant to contact the brake pad because this will bind the brake. Adjust the brakes as described in the owner's manual, and replace worn brake pads with manufacturer's parts.

Wheels and tires
The tires should be inflated to the pressure specified by the manufacturer; check them regularly with an air-pressure gauge. To repair tire punctures or replace tires, the wheel must be removed.

Lights
The front running lights are sealed beams similar to an automobile's headlights. To replace a light that has burned out, first disconnect the battery cables. Then remove the retaining rim around the bulb, held in place with screws. Pull the bulb out of the socket. When replacing the bulb, reverse this procedure.

WARNING: To avoid accidentally starting the engine while cleaning or repairing, always disconnect the spark-plug wire and tape it back .

WARNING: Use caution when replacing a broken clutch V-belt. Hold idler pulley arm firmly to avoid injury from release of tensioned spring.

LAWN AND GARDEN TRACTOR TROUBLESHOOTING

PROBLEM: Tractor engine does not start.

Possible Cause	Procedure	Remedy	Rating	Parts	Labor
Engine faulty.	SEE GASOLINE ENGINE TROUBLESHOOTING CHART—CHAPTER 8				

PROBLEM: Engine starts but tractor does not move.

Possible Cause	Procedure	Remedy	Rating	Parts	Labor
Wheel obstructed.	Check wheels.	Remove obstruction.	■		
Clutch defective.	Check.	Adjust or replace.	■ ■ ■ ■	$25	$20
Belt or chain tension incorrect.	Check belt or chain.	Adjust; replace if worn or damaged.	■ ■	$9	$12

PROBLEM: Tractor drives but attachments cannot be raised or lowered.

Possible Cause	Procedure	Remedy	Rating	Parts	Labor
Hand control bound.	Examine.	Lubricate.	■ ■		$12
Accessories attached incorrectly.	See owner's manual for installation instructions.	Change pulley and attach accessory correctly.	■ ■	$8	$12-30

PROBLEM: Belt slips or wears out too rapidly

Possible Cause	Procedure	Remedy	Rating	Parts	Labor
Belt loose.	Check tension.	Adjust or replace belt.	■ ■	$9	$12
Belt worn.	Examine belt.	Replace worn belt.	■ ■	$9	$12
Pulley damaged.	Check for nicks, holes, or cracks.	Replace damaged pulleys.	■ ■ ■ ■	$8	$20

PROBLEM: Tractor vibrates excessively.

Possible Cause	Procedure	Remedy	Rating	Parts	Labor
Dirt accumulation under housing.	Check for dried grass or other debris.	Scrape away dirt.	■		
Wrong blade or blade adapter used.	Check owner's manual.	Replace with correct blade.	■ ■ ■	$12	$12
Blade damaged or out of balance.	Check.	Replace.	■ ■ ■	$12	$12
Bolts loose.	Check bolts on engine mounts, blade mounts, wheel mounts, and transmission.	Tighten or replace bolts.	■	$.75	$10-45

PROBLEM: Tractor's mowing attachment not cutting properly.

Possible Cause	Procedure	Remedy	Rating	Parts	Labor
Drive belt attached improperly.	Check owner's manual for installation instructions.	Correct.	■		$10
Blade obstructed.	Check housing for obstruction.	Remove obstruction.	■		$10
Drive belt worn.	Examine belt.	Replace if worn.	■ ■	$15	$10-45
V-belt loose.	Check tension.	Tighten if loose.	■ ■		
Belt pulley slipping.	Check pulley for slippage and belt for wear.	Replace pulley.	■ ■ ■ ■	$25-30	$10-15
Blades dull.	Check.	Sharpen.	■ ■ ■		$12
Blade imbalanced.	Check balance.	Grind to balance, or replace.	■ ■ ■	Blade $4	$12
Gears improperly adjusted.	Check gear settings.	Move throttle to ¾- or wide open position. If this does not correct problem, transmission must be adjusted. (On some tractors, this may require engine dismantling.)	■ ■ ■ ■		$50-200

Leaf Blowers and Vacuums

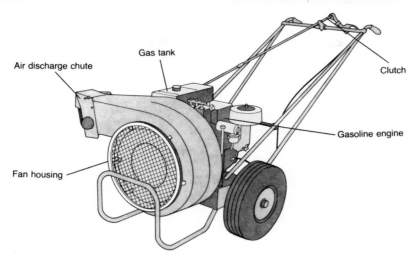

Leaf blower

Principle of Operation

Leaf blower

The basic leaf blower is a large fan powered by a two-cycle gasoline engine with a quick-release (impulse) starter. The fan blades rotate at a high speed to force air out of the fan housing and along the surface of the lawn. Leaves blown away from the blower will form rows on the lawn; if the blower is operated in a circular pattern, the leaves will form a pile in the center of the lawn. Portable gasoline-powered leaf blowers are made in back-pack models. No material is forced through the leaf blower during its operation. Therefore, it is extremely simple to maintain.

Leaf vacuum

The leaf vacuum uses a four-cycle gasoline engine to power the fan in a vacuum-type cleaner. The vacuum contains an intake nozzle that skims the surface of the lawn and sucks in the leaves. The leaves are forced into a bag catcher; the bag must be changed when full. Some leaf vacuums have a hose attachment for reaching into areas not accessible to the machine. Another attachment shreds lawn debris to mulch and collects it in the pickup bag. Material may become clogged in some portion of the vacuum. Do not attempt to clear any obstructions while the equipment is running. The large, powerful fan is rotating at high speed inside the housing.

Maintenance and Repair

General cleaning of the leaf blower and vacuum and lubrication of pivot points and linkages are considered normal maintenance. The leaf blower or vacuum is primarily powered by the gasoline engine. Refer to Chapter 8 for gasoline-engine troubleshooting, operation, maintenance, and repair.

Blower Housing

The leaf-blower fan housing contains the fan which provides air for the blowing action. The housing is designed to bring in air and direct it out through a specifically appointed opening. This design plus the fan creates a powerful blowing action to move leaves along the surface of the lawn.

Leaf vacuum

Although the leaf blower does not move material through the housing, periodic cleaning of the housing interior will help maintain peak operating efficiency.

Removing the housing. The housing cover must be removed to expose the fan. Unfasten a series of small bolts or clips around the housing for access to the inside.

Debris can be blown from the fan and housing with an air hose and may be brushed away with a stiff brush or rinsed off with a garden hose.

 WARNING: Do not attempt to hose the fan housing while the engine is hot, and never start the leaf blower with the housing removed.

Safety lock. Some models may contain a safety lock which will not allow the blower to be started while the housing is off. The housing should be replaced carefully. Check the maintenance instructions for location of the lock. Replace the housing according to the instructions.

Vacuum Housing

The housing of the leaf vacuum should be cleaned regularly. Debris will clog the vacuum, especially if it is used in wet or damp areas. Layers of debris will accumulate inside and should be removed after each use.

Removing the housing. Remove the air intake nozzle and loosen the bolts or clips holding the housing. If debris has dried inside the nozzle or housing, use a wooden scraper for loosening and a garden hose to finish the cleaning job.

Hose. If the hose attachment is used, it should be checked periodically during

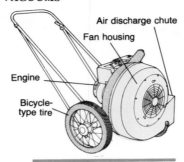

A leaf blower with bicycle-type tire

use and cleaned after each period of operation. Small sticks may become stuck inside and hose obstructions are common. Frequent cleaning is necessary. Do not attempt to

clean the hose or any portion of the vacuum while it is running.

Wheels and Tires

Smaller models of leaf blowers and leaf vacuums have solid tires mounted on wheels with plastic bushings. The plastic bushings are designed to be self-lubricating.

Larger models may use a bicycle-type tire and wheel. The larger wheel is easier to push and not affected by uneven lawn surfaces. Maintenance of the tire consists of checking the air pressure occasionally during the operating season. Low tire pressure will make it difficult to push the vacuum. Check manufacturer's specifi-

cations for recommended tire pressure. Do not operate leaf vacuums on wheel rims with the tires missing because this will damage the rims.

Some models may be equipped with a tube-type bicycle tire. A puncture may be repaired with a tube repair kit, available at hardware stores, service stations, and bicycle shops. The puncture in the tubeless tire will require a repair from a local service station.

Some wheels are ball-bearing mounted. The ball bearings require lubrication to operate efficiently. Oil or grease according to operating instructions.

LEAF BLOWER AND VACUUM TROUBLESHOOTING

PROBLEM: Leaf blower or vacuum does not start.

Possible Cause	Procedure	Remedy	Rating	Parts	Labor
Wheel blocked.	Check.	Remove obstruction.	■		
Wheel bound.	Check.	Lubricate.	■		

PROBLEM: Blower or vacuum does not work.

Possible Cause	Procedure	Remedy	Rating	Parts	Labor
Air intake obstructed.	Check.	Remove obstruction.	■ ■		
Blower clogged.	Check exhaust.	Remove clog.	■ ■		
Hose clogged.	Check.	Remove obstruction.	■ ■		
Fan faulty.	Check fan, bearings, and power connection.	Repair or replace.	■ ■ ■ ■	$20	$15

PROBLEM: Leaf blower or vacuum is excessively noisy.

Possible Cause	Procedure	Remedy	Rating	Parts	Labor
Parts vibrating.	Check all nuts and bolts.	Tighten.	■ ■		
Fan bearings worn.	Check.	Replace.	■ ■ ■ ■	$20	$15
Loose object in fan.	Turn off fan. Check for object.	Remove.	■		

Rototillers

Principle of Operation

The rototiller is designed for tilling, or cultivating, the soil. The blades, called *tines,* are fastened to a shaft, known as the *tine shaft* or *jackshaft,* that is powered by a gasoline engine. The shaft rotates around an axis; the rotation of the shaft causes the tines to cut into the soil at a specific depth (approximately ½ to 2 feet) and break apart any large clods. Breaking up the soil with the rototiller can replace plowing if repeated passes are made to obtain sufficient depth. Removing some of the tines allows the operator to use the rototiller as a cultivator later in the growing season. Tine removal narrows the cutting path of the machine and lessens the likelihood of cutting plants.

The rototiller does not have a power drive. The cutting action of the rotating, fingerlike tines is the force that pulls the tiller forward; the wheels only provide the pivot for lifting the tines. (An exception to tillers conventionally pro-

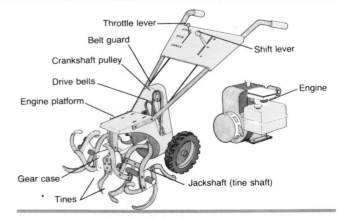

A gasoline-powered rototiller uses a one-cylinder engine to power the jackshaft and tines.

pelled by tines is the new rear-tine rototiller in which the engine powers the wheels. Large front wheels are powered to propel the tiller forward while the rear tines till the soil.) A *stabilizer bar,* an adjustable depth control bar, extends down from the back side of the tiller into the soil to prevent it from digging too deeply into the ground. The bar controls the depth of cut and amount of forward pull exerted on the tiller. If the tiller seems difficult to control, the stabilizer bar can be adjusted to slow its movement and make operation easier.

The rototiller uses a one-cylinder gasoline engine to power the rotation of the tines. Power is transferred to the tine shaft through a chain drive, V-belt drive, or gear drive system. The rototiller handles have both clutch and throttle controls, which vary on different models. Some may have a deadman-type clutch that stops the tiller the instant the operator's grip on the handle is released.

Maintenance and Repair

The working conditions of the soil greatly influence the rototiller's efficiency. Compacted, very wet soil tends to prevent the tiller from cutting; hard soil necessitates several passes to obtain depth. The equipment should not be blamed for inefficient operation if soil conditions are questionable.

Rototiller maintenance includes general cleaning and lubrication of moving parts such as cables and controls. (A lubricant recommended by the manufacturer should be used.) Afterward, controls and linkages may need adjustment. Lubricate the wheels as per the manufacturer's instructions.

The rototiller is powered by a gasoline engine. See Chapter 8 for troubleshooting, maintenance, and repair of small gasoline engines.

Power Drive

Chain drive
The tine shaft is mounted below the engine and housing. Power is transferred from the engine to a drive chain, causing the chain sprocket on the tine shaft to turn. This forces the shaft and tines to rotate.

Clean chain and chain sprockets by scraping off dirt with a stiff wire brush. Lubricate these parts as well. The tiller is used in the worst of conditions, directly in the soil.

The abrasive action of the soil will cause parts to wear out quickly if lubrication is inadequate.

Chains are made with a coupler, or breakaway, link. If excess pressure is exerted on the chain, the breakaway link is designed to break. Repairing the chain requires correct repair parts; a new coupler link must be inserted while the chain is *on* the tiller. If the tines contact large objects such as

rocks or tree roots, the chain will break and must be repaired.

V-Belt drive
Some tillers are equipped with a V-belt drive system that includes both forward and reverse. Typical belts stretch in use, so check them periodically for wear and proper adjustment. Replace as necessary. Adjustment of the idler pulley is necessary for belt

replacement. To use the correct replacement parts, check the manufacturer's specifications for belt length, width, and material.

Use of a belt dressing may be helpful but is not a substitute for proper maintenance and belt replacement. Excessive use of dressing causes the pulleys to clog and stick to the belts when the tiller is stored.

Procedure: Repairing Chains

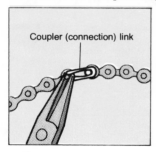 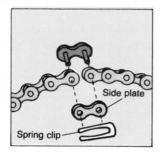  

1. To remove chain, find spring clip on coupler link. Pry off clip with screwdriver (and possibly the aid of pliers).

2. Remove side plate by sliding it off posts of coupler link. Remove coupler link by sliding it out of holes in adjacent links.

3. To remove broken link, force rivet out of hole with punch. Place rivet over hard surface that will allow it to drop through, such as a nut.

4. Replace coupler link in reverse order of disassembly. Slide posts through adjacent-link holes, slide side plate over posts, force spring clip on posts with pliers. The open end should be opposite the direction of travel (for safety).

Procedure: Replacing or Adjusting Drive Belts

1. To remove worn belt, put transmission in Neutral and loosen nut holding idler pulley. Move pulley as far away from belt as possible. Pull belt off drive shaft and jackshaft pulleys. Place new belt on drive shaft and jackshaft pulleys; then move idler pulley to point where it puts some tension on belt. To adjust loose belt, follow same procedure except for removing belt.

2. Shift into gear and test belt

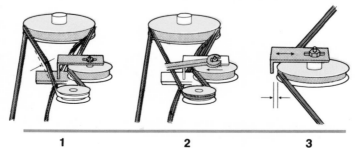

on side opposite idler pulley; see if belt can be deflected ½

inch. If it can move more than ½ inch, adjust idler pulley to-

ward belt to tighten tension. If belt can move less than ½ inch, adjust idler pulley away from belt to loosen tension. test again for ½-inch deflection.

3. When belt is correctly tensioned, move guide to within 1/16 inch of belt. Start engine and operate tiller to check belt. Minor adjustments may still have to be made. Idler pulley should not rub on belt while transmission is in Neutral.

Tines and Shaft

The tine shaft is positioned in a thrust bearing or gear case. The bearing allows side pressure to be applied to the shaft without its binding or breaking. Usually the bearing has an oil port with a spring-loaded cap. Wipe the cap before opening to prevent dirt from falling into the port. Lubricate as required by the manufacturer. If the tiller has a gear case, check the oil level periodically and refill as needed. Should the gear case leak oil, tighten the bolts or replace the gasket.

Adjusting tines. Each tine is locked on the tine shaft by a locking bolt. The bolt must be loosened with a wrench to remove or adjust the tines. Blowing or wiping away excess dirt on the shaft facilitates move-

ment of the tines. Consult the manufacturer's booklet for specific tine positions on the shaft.

Sharpening tines. Sharpen tines occasionally but do not balance them. Sharpen especially when the tiller is to be used in new soil that has not been turned. Sharp tines require less power from the engine and are safer to use; dull tines may cause the tiller to jump around on hard soil.

To sharpen tines, remove them from the shaft and lock them in a bench vise. File in the direction of the cutting edge, and reassemble the tines in their proper positions on the shaft. It is not necessary to whet the tines. Replace severely bent, worn, or damaged tines.

Procedure: Replacing Tines

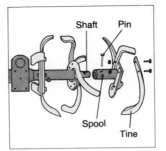

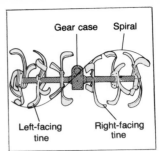

1. Remove dirt from tines and shaft. Take out retaining pin to gain access to tine spool. Loosen tine locking bolt and remove tine. Replace each tine before going on to another; this guarantees correct placement of right- or left-facing tines on shaft. Right- and left-facing tines are not interchangeable.

2. Consult instruction booklet for proper tine position on shaft. If no booklet is available, check to be sure that leading, sharp edges of tines form spiral when assembled on shaft.

ROTOTILLER TROUBLESHOOTING

PROBLEM: Rototiller does not start.

Possible Cause	Procedure	Remedy	Rating	Parts	Labor
Engine faulty.	SEE GASOLINE ENGINE TROUBLESHOOTING CHART—CHAPTER 8				

PROBLEM: Engine starts but tines do not rotate.

Possible Cause	Procedure	Remedy	Rating	Parts	Labor
Rototiller not in gear.	Check gear chart.	Engage drive clutch and put in gear.	■		
Object obstructing tines or wheels.	Check tines and tires.	Remove obstruction.	■		
Gear-shift linkage not connected to gear box.	Check linkage, nuts, and pins.	Readjust.	■		
Load too heavy.	Check load.	Raise tiller depth to reduce load.	■		
Tine clutch not engaged.	Check tine clutch.	Engage tine clutch.	■		
Depth control set too deep.	Check depth setting.	Raise stabilizer bar.	■ ■		
Drive chain dry.	Check chain.	Lubricate.	■	$10-12	$12-36
Drive chain broken.	Check chain.	Repair or replace chain.	■ ■	$10-12	$12-36
Tine clutch worn or loose.	Check clutch.	Tighten or replace.	■ ■ ■ ■	$6-12	$12-36
Gears in gear case obstructed or worn.	Check gears in gear case.	Replace entire gear case.	■ ■ ■ ■ ■	$40-80	$25

PROBLEM: Rototiller is difficult to control or handle.

Possible Cause	Procedure	Remedy	Rating	Parts	Labor
Handlebars too high.	Check height for operator.	Lower handlebars.	■		
Tines bent.	Check tines for damage.	Correct or replace tines.	■ ■ ■ ■ ■	$25-50	$12-36
Depth control set too deep.	Check depth setting.	Raise stabilizer bar.	■		
Soil too wet.	Check ground.	Wait for soil to dry out.			

PROBLEM: Rototiller is excessively noisy.

Possible Cause	Procedure	Remedy	Rating	Parts	Labor
Muffler faulty.	Check muffler for leaves.	Replace muffler.	■ ■	$5	$12
Tines bent.	Check tines for damage.	Correct or replace tines.	■ ■ ■ ■ ■	$25	$12

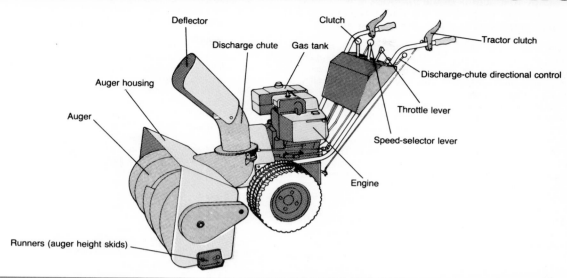

Deflector · Clutch · Tractor clutch · Discharge chute · Gas tank · Discharge-chute directional control · Auger housing · Throttle lever · Auger · Speed-selector lever · Engine · Runners (auger height skids)

A gasoline-powered snow blower

Principle of Operation

Snow blowers are powered by either electric motors or gasoline engines. The electric models are used for light-duty work only, while the larger, gasoline-powered blowers can work faster and handle heavier snowfalls. The snow blower uses an *auger,* a series of spiral blades attached to a rotating horizontal shaft, to collect and feed the snow into the machine. Turned by the engine or motor, the auger in front of the snow blower cuts the snow into large pieces, moves the pieces toward the center of the housing, and

forces them upward for the next stage of discharge. The forward motion of the drive wheels plus the pressure from the auger blades feeds the snow into an internal chute. The snow is then pushed upward through the chute and blown out and away from the machine. Some blowers have a fan-like *impeller* (with two to four blades) revolving at a high velocity inside the chute to hurl the snow upward and blast it out of the top at great speed. A deflector at the end of the discharge chute then directs the stream of snow to one side.

Maintenance and Repair

An assortment of peculiar problems are associated with the snow blower. The equipment is always used in cold climates and frequently the worst of conditions. In addition, the operator cannot see underneath the snow, which increases the possibility of his or her accidentally hitting a foreign object and damaging the machine. Because of these problems, the snow blower must be maintained conscientiously and repaired promptly. Otherwise, the equipment will not function when needed.

Engine Controls

Speed selector, found on handle, should be used to set speed of forward drive, not of auger's rotation. The depth of snow determines speed selection—snow blower should move at the fastest speed that does not cause the auger or impeller to clog.

Throttle controls engine speed and functions like a normal throttle. Move control to Fast (wide-open) position when storing snow blower so that it can be started even if throttle cable freezes.

Hand crank, located on handle, controls direction of discharge chute.

Primer button, generally found on larger snow blowers only, is depressed to inject gasoline directly into carburetor; use it in addition to choke for cold-weather starts.

Attachment clutch activates auger and impeller. Separate clutches for drive and auger/impeller allow operator to stop forward motion of snow blower and let clogged snow be blown out. Before using snow blower at start of season, make sure drive and auger/impeller clutches are in working order.

Interlock lever (switch) is a safety device to keep operator

away from auger (and impeller). The switch must be depressed while attachment clutch is activated. If switch is released, engine shuts down instantly. This prevents operators from taking both hands off handles and keeps them from attempting to clear auger path while engine is running.

Starter switch (on models with battery/key start system) must be plugged into 120-volt AC electrical outlet to start engine in very cold weather. Starter cord must be plugged into outlet and switch flipped to start engine. Once engine has caught, cord is disconnected from starter and from electric outlet. This system reduces initial load put on battery. After engine is warm, battery can be used for subsequent starts.

Starting system

Maintenance of the starting system is crucial for the snow blower. Lubricate all control linkages and bearings with the lubricant recommended by the manufacturer. Extremely cold weather conditions will not enhance the possibility of the snow blower starting. If possible, store it in a heated facility.

Power Drive
V-Belt drive system

Power is usually transmitted to the wheels through a V-belt drive system. Snow blower repair literature may refer to the V-belt pulleys as *sheaves.* The belt runs from the pulley on the engine to the drive pulley on the wheel axle. The belt is tensioned with an adjustable idler pulley. Drive belts can stretch through use and cause the

WARNING: Never leave the driver position behind the snow blower unless the auger and drive (propulsion) clutches are disengaged and the engine is turned off.

WARNING: Absolutely no attempt should be made to disconnect the interlock lever. Clearing the auger path while the auger is rotating will almost always result in the loss of a limb.

snow blower's wheels to slip. Loose belts should be tightened promptly; those that are damaged or too worn to be tensioned should be replaced. To gain access to the drive belts, it may be necessary to remove the auger housing.

Replacing drive belts. Put wheel drive in Neutral. Remove belt guard and bolts at top of auger housing. Loosen nuts on idler pulley and slide pulley away from belt. There should now be sufficient space to slide belt off both engine and drive pulleys. Slip new belt over both pulleys and move idler pulley toward belt into its original position. To adjust belt tension, use following procedure.

Adjusting drive belts. Put wheel drive in gear and check belt on side opposite idler pulley. By pushing on belt with thumb, it should be possible to deflect belt ½ inch. If belt moves more than ½ inch, return wheel drive to Neutral and move idler pulley a bit more toward belt. If belt deflects less than ½ inch, move idler pulley slightly away from belt. Adjust until belt deflection is ½ inch. Always put wheel drive in gear to test the belt.

Aligning pulleys. Some snow blowers require that the engine pulley be aligned with the drive pulley on the wheel. This system prevents the engine mounting from bending or cracking if the snow blower hits

a solid object. To align the pulleys, loosen the engine locking nuts and place the two pulleys in the aligned position.

Disk drive system

Some snow blowers have a disk drive rather than a belt drive system. A vertical (drive) disk is raised or lowered to put the machine in Neutral or in Drive. When lowered to a horizontal (speed) disk for Drive, the vertical disk is a specific distance away from the center of the horizontal disk. This distance determines the particular forward gear (speed)—the farther away from the center, the slower the speed. Regular use of the snow blower may lessen the pressure contact between the two disks, causing slippage of the wheels and a resultant loss of power. When this happens, the vertical (drive) disk should be adjusted to restore the original pressure and power.

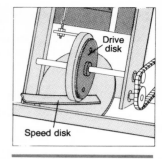

Checking the drive-disk clearance

Adjusting drive-disk clearance. Put machine into Neutral. Remove plate from back of unit to gain access to disks. There should be ⅛-inch clearance between drive disk and horizontal (speed) disk when shift lever is in Neutral. Use a ⅛-inch-thick piece of cardboard or wood to check clearance. If it is more than ⅛ inch, lower drive disk.

On the control panel, find end of shifting rod. Rod is held to a metal strap by a nut; strap is attached to shift lever. Loosen nut and lower rod until drive disk just touches ⅛-inch-thick test piece. Tighten nut. Move test piece under drive disk to see if it slides without dragging. If it drags, loosen nut above and raise shifting rod slightly. Tighten nut and test again. When drive-disk clearance is set correctly, snow blower should move over snow with full power.

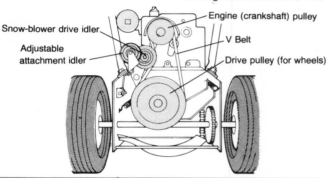

A snow-blower V-belt drive system

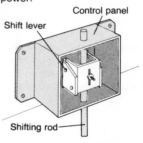

Adjusting the drive-disk clearance

Wheels and Tires

Wide, inflatable tires mounted on wheels are typical of the snow blower. These are special tires designed for better traction on slippery surfaces. Maintenance consists of checking tire pressure periodically and occasional repair.

Disengaging wheels. Axles on most snow blowers are straight—both wheels drive equally. Turning the snow blower is consequently awkward unless the drive clutch is disengaged. Some models have drive pins or axle pins on the wheels that permit the operator to disengage a wheel so that maneuvering on rough terrain or around turns is easier. By removing the pin or inserting it into a different slot, the wheel becomes freewheeling. When an operator

wants to restore drive, the pin is replaced in the drive position.

Other models may have a differential which allows the snow blower to be turned around without disengaging the drive clutch. If one wheel spins on slippery ice, an operator can temporarily engage the differential with a lock so that both wheels turn.

Checking tire pressure. Tire pressure should be checked regularly. Tires should have equal pressure; uneven pressure will cause blower to pull to one side when power drive is engaged.

Repairing tire punctures. To repair a puncture, the tire must be removed by taking off the lug nuts or hub nut on the wheel. Generally, the snow-

blower tire is tubeless and will require repair at a local service station. Be extremely careful to hold on to lugs after removing them from wheels. Lugs can be left with the snow blower only if they are partially threaded back onto studs. Larger snow blowers may have four lugs per wheel. If a set of lugs is lost, remove one lug from each of the remaining wheels for temporary repair. Replace missing lugs promptly.

Using tire chains. Accessory chains add traction to tires and facilitate snow removal. Chains are recommended if there is a layer of ice underneath the snow. Purchase chains to fit particular size of tire on the snow blower. Manufacturer's specifications will

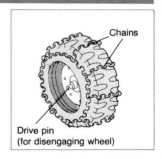

A snow-blower tire with chains

contain the necessary information. Chains must be unhooked, straightened, and wrapped around the tire. The hook is attached to the end of the chain to lock it on the tire.

Snow Discharge Unit

WARNING: Do not attempt maintenance on the auger and impeller while they are rotating.

Auger

Auger. The auger is a helix of spiraling blades attached to a horizontal shaft called an auger shaft. Power to auger is transmitted from V-belt pulley system to drive shaft. Drive shaft drives auger shaft via a worm gear. Two sets of spiral blades are attached to auger shaft. Each blade is attached by a shear bolt which is designed to shear, or break, if the auger hits a solid object.

Replacing a shear bolt. Drive old shear bolt out of hole with pin punch. Occasionally, shear bolt or pin may be tapered; determine the correct direction for driving it out. Line up auger-blade hole with hole in shaft and insert a new shear bolt. Check manufacturer's specification for correct shear-bolt size.

Auger gear case. This is a small housing surrounding worm-gear assembly on auger shaft. This assembly must be lubricated. Normally, an oil-fill port is used for adding oil to gear case. Check oil level periodically. Grease may tend to become too hard in cold weather. Use lubricant recommended by manufacturer to maintain snow-blower warranty.

Auger blades. Keep blades clean. Before snow season begins, check blades for bends and nicks. Straighten bent blades or replace. Badly nicked blades may be filed, although they do not have to be extremely sharp for efficient operation. If blade is damaged, repair it immediately before use of snow blower continues.

Auger housing

Auger housing. This deck contains runners and scraper blade and houses auger assembly. It is designed to direct snow particles toward central discharge chute. A clean surface will lessen friction and help remove snow. Coat surface with a (non-oily) silicone spray lubricant. Do not use any type of oily lubricant for this purpose.

housing base. Uneven terrain will require a thicker layer of snow to be left. Do not attempt to clear snow down to ground level. This will cause blower to pick up gravel and other foreign objects and discharge them. Adjust runners to hold main auger at least an inch above gravel surfaces; less space is needed above even surfaces.

Scraper blade. The scraper blade should not rub on the surface. If scraper wears, adjust it to extend past housing. Usually, loosening mounting bolts on each side of scraper will allow adjustment. Excessive wear of scraper blade may

The auger and auger housing

Shear bolts · Zerk fittings · Auger housing · Oil-drain post · Oil-fill port · Auger shaft · Runner (auger height skid) · Auger gear case · Auger

Runners (auger height skids or depth gauges). Located on lower, outside portion of auger housing, determine amount of snow left after snow blower has been moved over surface. To adjust them for snow-removal height, loosen locking bolts with wrench.

Both runners must be adjusted to same height from

allow auger housing to scrape surface. If this happens, replace scraper promptly before permanent damage to auger housing has resulted.

Impeller (discharge fan)

Before snow season begins, examine impeller blades for bends or nicks and repair or replace them as necessary. Before starting engine, check to make sure blades can rotate freely.

Discharge chute

Direction of chute can be controlled with equipment handle. To change direction of chute, crank hand crank or pull lever attached to discharge chute. High-speed rotation of impeller discharges snow with great force from chute. Always direct chute away from people, houses, and vehicles. A small particle of gravel or piece of ice thrown from snow blower with snow could injure someone or damage surfaces.

Using snow blower in wet snow may cause chute to clog and ice up. Stop blower and clean discharge chute periodically. Prior to using snow blower, coat chute with a silicone spray lubricant to help keep snow from sticking to inner surface.

Deflector. Some blowers have deflector mounted on top of discharge chute. Deflector forces snow to change directions upon discharge. Some deflectors can force snow to be exhausted at nearly right angles to original discharge direction. A sudden change in direction of snow can cause clogging and subsequent icing of chute. Every attempt should be made to discharge snow with minimal direction change and minimal contact with snow-blower parts.

WARNING: Never attempt to clean the discharge chute while the snow blower is running. Turn the engine off and be absolutely certain the impeller blade has stopped rotating completely (if applicable) before looking or reaching inside.

SNOW BLOWER TROUBLESHOOTING

PROBLEM: Snow blower does not start.

Possible Cause	Procedure	Remedy	Rating	Parts	Labor
Engine faulty.	SEE GASOLINE ENGINE TROUBLESHOOTING CHART—CHAPTER 8				
Motor faulty.	SEE ELECTRIC MOTOR TROUBLESHOOTING CHARTS—CHAPTER 4				

PROBLEM: Engine runs but wheels slip or do not turn.

Possible Cause	Procedure	Remedy	Rating	Parts	Labor
Oil insufficient.	Check oil level in transmission gear case.	Refill if necessary.	■		
Throttle cable frozen.	Check.	Thaw in garage or warm room.	■		

(Continued on next page)

SNOW BLOWER TROUBLESHOOTING (Continued from preceding page)

PROBLEM: Engine runs but wheels slip or do not turn. (Continued from preceding page)

Possible Cause	Procedure	Remedy	Rating	Parts	Labor
Drive belt worn or incorrectly adjusted.	Examine belt. Check tension on belt.	Replace if worn. Readjust if necessary.	■ ■	$12	$12-15
Attachment idler slipping.	Check idler belt tension and idler pulley.	Tighten idler belt or replace pulley.	■ ■	$8	$12-30
Speed-selector control frozen.	Check.	Thaw in garage or heated room.	■		
Drive pins missing, broken, or set incorrectly.	Check drive pins on wheels.	Replace if broken or missing. Reposition pins to engage wheels.	■ ■	$1	$12
Drive-disk clearance incorrect.	Check for proper clearance.	Correct drive-disk clearance.	■ ■ ■		$15

PROBLEM: Discharge chute does not turn.

Possible Cause	Procedure	Remedy	Rating	Parts	Labor
Chute control frozen.	Check.	Thaw in garage or warm room.	■		
Pin or bolt broken.	Check chute controls.	Tighten or replace bolts.	■ ■	$5	$12

PROBLEM: Wheels drive but snow blower does not discharge snow or discharges poorly.

Possible Cause	Procedure	Remedy	Rating	Parts	Labor
Clutch cable loose.	Examine nuts and pins.	Replace.	■ ■	$10	$12
Overload of snow.	Reduce load.	Slow engine speed.	■		
Oil low.	Check oil level in auger gear case.	Refill.	■		
Snow sticks to auger or impeller.	Examine for clogging. Check for ice in auger or impeller housing.	Thaw in garage or warm room. Chip out ice and snow. Coat auger housing and chute with silicone lubricant.	■		
Discharge chute clogged with snow or ice.	Shut off engine. Check for snow being blown out.	Remove snow or ice.	■ ■		
Friction wheel worn.	Check friction wheel.	Correct drive-disk clearance or replace friction wheel.	■ ■ ■	$10	$15
Auger or impeller drive belts loose or worn.	Examine belts. Check tension on belts.	Tighten or replace.	■ ■ ■	$12	$12-15
Auger shear bolts broken.	Check shear bolts.	Replace if broken.	■ ■ ■	$5	$12
Worm gear in auger shaft dry or worn.	Check gear.	If dry, lubricate. If worn, replace.	■ ■ ■		$12
Auger blades bent or dirty.	Inspect.	Clean if dirty. Replace if bent.	■ ■ ■ ■		

PROBLEM: Snow blower is excessively noisy or vibrates too much.

Possible Cause	Procedure	Remedy	Rating	Parts	Labor
Parts loose.	Check all nuts and bolts.	Tighten nuts and bolts.	■ ■		$12

PROBLEM: Snow blower is difficult to steer.

Possible Cause	Procedure	Remedy	Rating	Parts	Labor
Tire inflation incorrect.	Check tire pressure.	Inflate or deflate tires.	■		
Oil insufficient.	Check oil level in transmission gear case.	Refill if necessary.	■		
Differential lock not engaged.	Check clutch mechanism.	Rotate differential lock.	■		

Index